Multidisciplinary Perspectives in Cryptology and Information Security

Sattar B. Sadkhan Al Maliky
University of Babylon, Iraq

Nidaa A. Abbas
University of Babylon, Iraq

A volume in the Advances in Information Security, Privacy, and Ethics (AISPE) Book Series

Information Science
REFERENCE
An Imprint of IGI Global

Managing Director:	Lindsay Johnston
Production Editor:	Jennifer Yoder
Development Editor:	Erin O'Dea
Acquisitions Editor:	Kayla Wolfe
Typesetter:	John Crodian
Cover Design:	Jason Mull

Published in the United States of America by
Information Science Reference (an imprint of IGI Global)
701 E. Chocolate Avenue
Hershey PA 17033
Tel: 717-533-8845
Fax: 717-533-8661
E-mail: cust@igi-global.com
Web site: http://www.igi-global.com

Library of Congress Cataloging-in-Publication Data

Multidisciplinary perspectives in cryptology and information security / Sattar B. Sadkhan Al Maliky and Nidaa A. Abbas, editors.
     pages cm
  Includes bibliographical references and index.
  ISBN 978-1-4666-5808-0 (hardcover) -- ISBN 978-1-4666-5809-7 (ebook) -- ISBN 978-1-4666-5811-0 (print & perpetual access) 1. Data encryption (Computer science) 2. Wireless communication systems--Security measures. 3. Computer networks--Security measures. I. Al Maliky, Sattar B. Sadkhan, 1954- editor of compilation. II. Abbas, Nidaa A. editor of compilation.
  QA76.9.A25M846 2014
  005.8'2--dc23
                                    2014011686

This book is published in the IGI Global book series Advances in Information Security, Privacy, and Ethics (AISPE) (ISSN: 1948-9730; eISSN: 1948-9749)

British Cataloguing in Publication Data
A Cataloguing in Publication record for this book is available from the British Library.

All work contributed to this book is new, previously-unpublished material. The views expressed in this book are those of the authors, but not necessarily of the publisher.

For electronic access to this publication, please contact: eresources@igi-global.com.

Advances in Information Security, Privacy, and Ethics (AISPE) Book Series

ISSN: 1948-9730
EISSN: 1948-9749

MISSION

As digital technologies become more pervasive in everyday life and the Internet is utilized in ever increasing ways by both private and public entities, concern over digital threats becomes more prevalent.

The **Advances in Information Security, Privacy, & Ethics (AISPE) Book Series** provides cutting-edge research on the protection and misuse of information and technology across various industries and settings. Comprised of scholarly research on topics such as identity management, cryptography, system security, authentication, and data protection, this book series is ideal for reference by IT professionals, academicians, and upper-level students.

COVERAGE

- Access Control
- Device Fingerprinting
- Global Privacy Concerns
- Information Security Standards
- Network Security Services
- Privacy-Enhancing Technologies
- Risk Management
- Security Information Management
- Technoethics
- Tracking Cookies

IGI Global is currently accepting manuscripts for publication within this series. To submit a proposal for a volume in this series, please contact our Acquisition Editors at Acquisitions@igi-global.com or visit: http://www.igi-global.com/publish/.

Titles in this Series

For a list of additional titles in this series, please visit: www.igi-global.com

Cases on Research and Knowledge Discovery Homeland Security Centers of Excellence
Cecelia Wright Brown (University of Baltimore, USA) Kevin A. Peters (Morgan State University, USA) and Kofi
Adofo Nyarko (Morgan State University, USA)
Information Science Reference • copyright 2014 • 357pp • H/C (ISBN: 9781466659469) • US $215.00 (our price)

Multidisciplinary Perspectives in Cryptology and Information Security
Sattar B. Sadkhan Al Maliky (University of Babylon, Iraq) and Nidaa A. Abbas (University of Babylon, Iraq)
Information Science Reference • copyright 2014 • 334pp • H/C (ISBN: 9781466658080) • US $245.00 (our price)

Analyzing Security, Trust, and Crime in the Digital World
Hamid R. Nemati (The University of North Carolina at Greensboro, USA)
Information Science Reference • copyright 2014 • 281pp • H/C (ISBN: 9781466648562) • US $195.00 (our price)

Research Developments in Biometrics and Video Processing Techniques
Rajeev Srivastava (Indian Institute of Technology (BHU), India) S.K. Singh (Indian Institute of Technology (BHU),
India) and K.K. Shukla (Indian Institute of Technology (BHU), India)
Information Science Reference • copyright 2014 • 279pp • H/C (ISBN: 9781466648685) • US $195.00 (our price)

Advances in Secure Computing, Internet Services, and Applications
B.K. Tripathy (VIT University, India) and D.P. Acharjya (VIT University, India)
Information Science Reference • copyright 2014 • 405pp • H/C (ISBN: 9781466649408) • US $195.00 (our price)

Security Engineering Techniques and Solutions for Information Systems Management and Implementation
Noureddine Boudriga (Engineering School of Communications, Tunisia) and Mohamed Hamdi (Engineering
School of Communications, Tunisia)
Information Science Reference • copyright 2014 • 359pp • H/C (ISBN: 9781615208036) • US $195.00 (our price)

Trust Management in Mobile Environments Autonomic and Usable Models
Zheng Yan (Xidian University, China and Aalto University, Finland)
Information Science Reference • copyright 2014 • 288pp • H/C (ISBN: 9781466647657) • US $195.00 (our price)

Network Security Technologies Design and Applications
Abdelmalek Amine (Tahar Moulay University, Algeria) Otmane Ait Mohamed (Concordia University, USA) and
Boualem Benatallah (University of New South Wales, Australia)
Information Science Reference • copyright 2014 • 330pp • H/C (ISBN: 9781466647893) • US $195.00 (our price)

www.igi-global.com

701 E. Chocolate Ave., Hershey, PA 17033
Order online at www.igi-global.com or call 717-533-8845 x100
To place a standing order for titles released in this series, contact: cust@igi-global.com
Mon-Fri 8:00 am - 5:00 pm (est) or fax 24 hours a day 717-533-8661

Editorial Advisory Board

Table of Contents

Detailed Table of Contents

Chapter 1

Sattar B. Sadkhan Al Maliky, University of Babylon, Iraq

Nidaa A. Abbas, University of Babylon, Iraq

To reach the high depths of knowledge and expertise that are required nowadays, scientists focus their attention on minute areas of study. However, the most complex problems faced by scientists still need the application of different disciplines to tackle them, which creates a necessity for multi-disciplinary collaboration. Cryptology is naturally a multidisciplinary field, drawing techniques from a wide range of disciplines and connections to many different subject areas. In recent years, the connection between algebra and cryptography has tightened, and established computational problems and techniques have been supplemented by interesting new approaches and ideas. Cryptographic engineering is a complicated, multidisciplinary field. It encompasses mathematics (algebra, finite groups, rings, and fields), probability and statistics, computer engineering (hardware design, ASIC, embedded systems, FPGAs), and computer science (algorithms, complexity theory, software design), control engineering, digital signal processing, physics, chemistry, and others. This chapter provides an introduction to the disciplinary, multidisciplinary, and their general structure (interdisciplinary, trans-disciplinary, and cross-disciplinary). And it also gives an introduction to the applications of the multidisciplinary approaches to some of the cryptology fields. In addition, the chapter provides some facts about the importance of the suitability and of the multidisciplinary approaches in different scientific, academic, and technical applications.

Chapter 2

Eva Volna, University of Ostrava, Czech Republic

Tomas Sochor, University of Ostrava, Czech Republic

Clyde Meli, University of Malta, Malta

Zuzana Kominkova Oplatkova, Tomas Bata University in Zlin, Czech Republic

This chapter deals with using soft computing methods in information security. It is engaged in two big areas: (1) information security and spam detection and (2) cryptography. The latter field is covered by a proposal of an artificial neural network application, which represents a way of further development in this area. Such a neural network can be practically used in the area of cryptography. It is a new approach, which presents a development of automatic neural networks design. The approach is based on evolutionary algorithms, which allow evolution of architecture and weights simultaneously. A spam filter is an automated tool to recognize spam so as to prevent its delivery. The chapter contains a survey of current and proposed spam filtering techniques with particular emphasis on how well they work. The primary focus is spam filtering in email, but the role of the spam filter is only one component of a large and complex information universe. The chapter also includes experimental demonstrations.

The aim of this chapter is to emphasize the multidisciplinary nature of the research in the field of Quantum Key Distribution Networks (QKDNs). Such networks consist of a number of nodes that can perform security protocols protected by some basic laws of physics. The operation of QKDNs mainly requires the integration of Quantum Key Distribution (QKD) protocols with the already-existing network security infrastructures. The authors report on the current state-of-the-art in the field and give some recommendations for future research. As computer simulation can be very useful in dealing with advanced technology subjects like QKDNs, they outline a simple and efficient modeling and simulation approach for various QKDN configurations. Then, the issue of unconditionally secure authentication of the public channel in QKD is considered. This issue is of crucial importance from both theoretical and practical sides. In this context, the proposed hybrid authentication strategy is reviewed and an authenticated version of the Bennett-Brassard-84 (BB84) QKD protocol based on this strategy is described. Next, a novel extension of the SSL protocol for QKDN settings, which the authors call Quantum SSL (QSSL), is explained. Finally, the chapter is concluded.

Chapter 4

Chaos theory was originally developed by mathematicians and physicists. The theory deals with the behaviors of nonlinear dynamic systems. Chaos theory has desirable features, such as deterministic, nonlinear, irregular, long-term prediction, and sensitivity to initial conditions. Therefore, and based on chaos theory features, the security research community adopts chaos theory in modern cryptography. However, there are challenges of using chaos theory with cryptography, and this chapter highlights some of those challenges. The voice information is very important compared with the information of image and text. This chapter reviews most of the encryption techniques that adopt chaos-based cryptography, and illustrates the uses of chaos-based voice encryption techniques in wireless communication as well. This chapter summarizes the traditional and modern techniques of voice/speech encryption and demonstrates the feasibility of adopting chaos-based cryptography in wireless communications.

Chapter 5

Breaking contemporary cryptographic algorithms using any binary computer has at least sub-exponential complexity. However, if a quantum computer was used effectively, then our asymmetric cryptography would not be secure anymore. Since the code-based cryptography (cryptography based on error-correcting codes) relies on different problems, it is not as threatened as, for example, RSA or ECC. Recent years have been crucial in the progress of cryptography based on error-correcting codes. In contrast to the number-theoretic problems typically used in cryptography nowadays, certain instances of the underlying problems of code-based cryptography remain unbroken even employing quantum cryptanalysis. Thus, some code-based cryptography constructions belong to the post-quantum cryptography, especially cryptosystems based on binary irreducible Goppa codes. Many attempts to replace this underlying code in order to reduce the key size already have been proposed. Unfortunately, almost all of them have been broken. For instance, just a while ago, Reed Muller, Generalized Reed-Solomon Codes, and Convolutional codes were broken. Against some rank metric codes, a new attack was introduced. On the other hand, two prospective countermeasures in order to hide the exploitable code structure of the broken codes were fashioned. However, only the choice of binary irreducible Goppa codes remains secure in the post-quantum sense. This chapter surveys the more recent developments in code-based cryptography as well as implementations and side channel attacks. This work also recalls briefly the basic ideas, and provides a roadmap to readers.

Chapter 6

Sattar B. Sadkhan Al Maliky, University of Babylon, Iraq

Sabiha F. Jawad, Al-Mustansyria University, Iraq

The main aim of this chapter is to provide a security evaluation method based on fuzzy logic "for a pseudo-random sequences used (mainly) in stream cipher systems. The designed Fuzzy rules consider two main parameters, which are the length of the maximum period of the key sequence obtained from Linear Feedback Shift Register (LFSR) and the entropy of the result in sequences obtained from different lengths of the shift registers. The security (complexity) evaluation method is applied to the summation generator (a type of non-linear feedback shift register) in this chapter. First it is applied to its original well-known form (with one bit memory); then the evaluation method is applied to the developed summation generator (by varying the number of the delayed bits by two and by three bits). The acceptability of the results of developed evaluation method indicates a goodness of such developed approach in the security evaluation.

Chapter 7

W. K. Hamoudi, University of Technology, Iraq

Nadia M. G. Al-Saidi, University of Technology, Iraq

Information security can provide confidentiality, integrity, and availability for society to benefit efficiently from data storage and open networks. Free space communication networks suffer from adversaries who interfere with data on networked computers. Inventing new protection techniques has arisen to ensure integrity and authenticity of digital information. This chapter introduces Nano and Bio techniques in cryptography to enhance the information security systems. Tasks unfeasible on a classical computer can now be performed by quantum computers, yielding a big impact on online security. Threats of exponentially fast quantum algorithms on business transactions could be overcome by this new technology. Based on biological observations, the exploration of biometric cryptography and authentication to determine individuals' authenticity can be done through numeric measurements. This provides very reliable automated verification and strong protection against biometric system attacks.

Chapter 8

Blind Source Separation (BSS) represented by Independent Component Analysis (ICA) has been used in many fields such as communications and biomedical engineering. Its application to image and speech encryption, however, has been rare. In this chapter, the authors present ICA and Principal Component Analysis (PCA) as a category of BSS-based method for encrypting images and speech by using Blind Source Separation (BSS) since the security encryption technologies depend on many intractable mathematical problems. Using key signals, they build a suitable BSS underdetermined problem in the encryption and then circumvent this problem with key signals for decoding. The chapter shows that the method based on the BSS can achieve a high level of safety right through building, mixing matrix, and generating key signals.

Chapter 9

This chapter presents a new area-efficient composite field inverter of the form $GF(q1)$ with $q=2n.m$ suitable for the hardware realization of an elliptic curve (EC) cryptosystem. Considering both the security aspect and the hardware cost required, the authors propose the utilization of the composite field $GF(((22)2)41)$ for EC cryptosystem. For efficient implementation, they have derived a compact inversion circuit over $GF(2164)=GF(((22)2)41)$ to achieve an optimal saving in the hardware cost required. Furthermore, the authors have also developed a composite field digit serial Sunar-Koc multiplier for the multiplication in the extension field. All of the arithmetic operations in the subfield $GF(24)$ are performed in its isomorphic composite field, $GF((22)2)$, leading to a full combinatorial implementation without resorting to the conventional look-up table approach. To summarize the work, the final hardware implementation and the complexity analysis of the inversion is reported towards the end of this chapter.

Chapter 10

The importance of Public Key Cryptosystems (PKCs) in the cryptography field is well known. They represent a great revolution in this field. The PKCs depend mainly on mathematical problems, like factorization problem, and a trapdoor one-way function problem. Rivest, Shamir, and Adleman (RSA) PKC systems are based on factorization mathematical problems. There are many types of RSA cryptosystems. Rabin's Cryptosystem is considered one example of this type, which is based on using the square order (quadratic equation) in encryption function. Many cryptosystems (since 1978) were implemented under such a mathematical approach. This chapter provides an illustration of the variants of RSA-Public Key Cryptosystems based on quadratic equations in Finite Field, describing their key generation, encryption, and decryption processes. In addition, the chapter illustrates a proposed general formula for the equation describing these different types and a proposed generalization for the Chinese Remainder Theorem.

Cryptographic key distribution and management is one of the most important steps in the process of securing data by utilizing encryption. Problems related to cryptographic key distribution and management are hard to solve and easy to exploit, and therefore, they are appealing to the attacker. The purpose of this chapter is to introduce the topics of cryptographic key distribution and management, especially with regards to asymmetric keys. The chapter describes how these topics are handled today, what the real-world problems related to cryptographic key distribution and management are, and presents existing solutions as well as future directions in their solving. The authors present the cryptographic key management and distribution problems from a multidisciplinary point of view by looking at its economic, psychological, usability, and technological aspects.

This chapter offers an overview of new developments in quasigroup-based cryptography, especially of new defined quasigroup-based block ciphers and stream ciphers, hash functions and message authentication codes, PRNGs, public key cryptosystems, etc. Special attention is given to Multivariate Quadratic Quasigroups (MQQs) and MQQ public key schemes, because of their potential to become one of the most efficient pubic key algorithms today. There are also directions of using MQQs for building Zero knowledge ID-based identification schemes. Recent research activities show that some existing non-quasigroup block ciphers or their building blocks can be represented by quasigroup string transformations. There is a method for generating optimal 4x4 S-boxes by quasigroups of order 4, by which a more optimized hardware implementation of the given S-box can be obtained. Even some block ciphers' modes of operations can be represented by quasigroup string transformations, which leads to finding weaknesses in the interchanged use of these modes.

Chapter 13

This chapter presents a comprehensive study on the influence of the intra-modal facial information for an identification approach. It was developed and implemented a biometric identification system by merging different intra-multimodal facial features: mouth, eyes, and nose. The Principal Component Analysis, Independent Component Analysis, and Discrete Cosine Transform were used as feature extractors. Support Vector Machines were implemented as classifier systems. The recognition rates obtained by multimodal fusion of three facial features has reached values above 97% in each of the databases used, confirming that the system is adaptive to images from different sources, sizes, lighting conditions, etc. Even though a good response has been shown when the three facial traits were merged, an acceptable performance has been shown when merging only two facial features. Therefore, the system is robust against problems in one isolate sensor or occlusion in any biometric trait. In this case, the success rate achieved was over 92%.

Chapter 14

It is important to know that absolute security does not exist, and the main goal of the security system is to reach an optimal approach that satisfies the customer requirements. Biometrics is a small part of the security system that aims to replace a traditional password or a key. Biometrics offer higher security levels by simply ensuring that only the authorized people have access to sensitive data. It is easy to copy or get a traditional password using different methods (legal or illegal), but it is difficult to copy a key of biometric pattern such as iris or fingerprint or other patterns. Recent years have seen a boom in the use of biometric techniques in the design of modern equipment to maintain the information and personal identification. This chapter focuses on biometrics (types and technologies), personal identification, and specifications, and then how to implement these performances in security. Finally, a future aspect of merging technologies and disciplines is a good issue to treat via a specific concentration of information technology. In this chapter, two approached are proposed: a novel thinning algorithm for fingerprint recognition and a novel e-passport based on personal identification.

Chapter 15

Even though it is an essential requirement of any computer system, there is not yet a standard method to measure data security, especially when sending information over a network. However, the most common technique used to achieve the three goals of security is encryption. Three security metrics are derived from important issues of network security in this chapter. Each metric demonstrates the level of achievement in preserving one of the security goals. Routing algorithms based on these metrics are implemented to test the proposed solution. Computational effort and blocking probability are used to assess the behavior and the performance of these routing algorithms. Results show that the algorithms are able to find feasible paths between communicating parties and make reasonable savings in the computational effort needed to find an acceptable path. Consequently, higher blocking probabilities are encountered, which is the price to be paid for such savings.

Chapter 16

The increasing portability of computing devices combined with frequent reports of privacy breaches and identity theft has thrust data encryption into the public attention. While encryption can help mitigate the threat of unintentional data exposure, it is equally capable of hiding evidence of criminal malfeasance. The increasing accessibility and usability of strong encryption solutions present new challenges for digital forensic investigators. Understanding forensic analysis as a multidisciplinary field that searches evidence of crime, the authors focus their topic on particularity of cross-disciplinary issues arising in this area: Forensic analysis uses cryptology, information technology and mathematics in extracting encryption keys from memory. The chapter highlights the virtues of volatile memory analysis by demonstrating how key material and passphrases can be extracted from memory and reconstructed to facilitate the analysis of encrypted data. The authors show current methods for identifying encryption keys in memory and discuss possible defeating techniques and cryptosystem implementation strategies that could be used to avoid the key extraction.

Preface

It is well known that information is a driver of society and its integrity, confidentiality, and authenticity must be insured. Security methods and techniques are critical elements of requested infrastructure for secure communication and processing of the flow of information in different applications. Security methods and techniques are not the only components needed to ensure such security features. With most services and products now offered through digital communications, new challenges have emerged for cryptology specialists. *Multidisciplinary Perspectives in Cryptology and Communication Security* presents a range of topics on the Cryptology methods and safety of information and communication technology. It brings together methods in applied mathematics, computer science, engineering, telecommunication sciences, physics, chemistry, digital signal processing, error correcting codes, information theory, electrical engineering, and hardware realization aspects.

The book provides:

- Knowledge of the principals involved in multidisciplinary fields (interdisciplinary, cross-disciplinary, trans-disciplinary) and their importance in the cryptology and communication security.
- Covers main topics currently found in the new types of cryptology (cryptography, cryptanalysis, and complexity evaluation) that are based on multidisciplinary, like code-based cryptography, nano-based cryptography, bio-based cryptography, quantum-based cryptography, chaos-based cryptography, ICA-based cryptography, and fuzzy logic-based cryptography.
- Comprehensive coverage along with the latest developments in cryptography.
- Discusses many widely used cryptographic and cryptanalysis algorithms that are based on multidisciplinary disciplines.

The potential contexts in which the book will be utilized are:

- As a reference for graduate courses in cryptology
- As a guide reference for researchers in scientific research centers and institutes.
- As a knowledge base for researchers in many disciplines (who are) far from cryptology to understand the importance of joining many disciplines to create a new discipline.

The target audience of this book is composed of professionals and researchers working in the field of information and knowledge management in various disciplines (e.g. cryptology, information and communication sciences, computer science and engineering, physics, chemistry, education, information technology, digital signal processing, soft computing techniques, bioinformatics, and wireless communication systems).

Chapter 1 provides an introduction to the disciplinary, multidisciplinary, and their general structure (interdisciplinary, trans-disciplinary, and cross-disciplinary). It also gives an introduction to the applications of the multidisciplinary approaches to some of the cryptology and information security fields.

Chapter 2 contains a survey of current and proposed spam-filtering techniques with particular emphasis on how well they work. The primary focus is spam-filtering in email, but the role of the spam filter is only one component of a large and complex information universe.

Chapter 3 aims to emphasize the multidisciplinary nature of the research in the field of Quantum Key Distribution Networks (QKDNs). Such networks consist of a number of nodes that can perform security protocols protected by some basic laws of physics. The operation of QKDNs requires the integration of Quantum Key Distribution (QKD) protocols with the already-existing network security infrastructures.

Chapter 4 reviews most of the encryption techniques that adopt chaos-based cryptography and illustrates the use of chaos-based voice encryption techniques in wireless communication as well. The review in this chapter summarizes the traditional and modern techniques of voice/speech encryption and demonstrates the feasibility of adopting chaos-based cryptography for wireless communications.

Chapter 5 shows the progress of cryptography based on error-correcting codes. In contrast to the number-theoretic problems typically used in cryptography nowadays, certain instances of the underlying problems (the code-based cryptography problem) remain unbroken, even when employing quantum cryptanalysis. The chapter surveys the more recent developments in code-based cryptography as well as implementations and side channel attacks. This work also recalls briefly the basic ideas and provides a roadmap to readers.

Chapter 6 provides a "security evaluation method based on fuzzy logic" for pseudo-random sequences used (mainly) in stream cipher systems. The designed Fuzzy rules consider two main parameters, which are the length of the maximum period of the key sequence obtained from Linear Feedback Shift Register (LFSR) and the entropy of the result in sequences obtained from different lengths of the shift registers.

Chapter 7 introduces nano and bio techniques in cryptography to enhance the information security systems. Tasks unfeasible on a classical computer can now be performed by quantum computers and could have a big impact on online security. Threats of exponentially fast quantum algorithms on business transactions could be overcome by this new technology. Based on biological observations, the exploration of biometric cryptography and authentication to determine individuals' authenticity can be done through numeric measurements.

Chapter 8 provides Independent Component Analysis (ICA) and Principal Component Analysis (PCA) as categories of the Blind Source Separation (BSS)-based method for encrypting images and speech, since the encryption technologies depend on many intractable mathematical problems. Using key signals, the authors build a suitable BSS underdetermined problem in the encryption and then circumvent this problem with key signals for decoding.

Chapter 9 presents a new area-efficient composite field inverter of the form $GF(q^l)$ with $q = 2^{n.m}$ suitable for the hardware realization of an Elliptic Curve (EC) cryptosystem. Considering both the security aspect and the hardware cost required, the authors propose the utilization of the composite field $GF(((2^2)^2)^{41})$ for EC cryptosystem.

Chapter 10 provides illustration of the variants of RSA-Public Key Cryptosystems based on quadratic equations in finite field, describing their key generation, encryption, and decryption processes. In addition, the chapter illustrates a proposed general formula for the equation describing these different types and a proposed generalization for the Chinese Remainder Theorem.

Chapter 11 describes the real-world problems related to cryptographic key distribution and management and presents existing solutions as well as future directions in their solving. The chapter presents the cryptographic key management and distribution problems from a multidisciplinary point of view by looking at its economic, psychological, usability, and technological aspects.

Chapter 12 offers an overview of new developments in quasigroup-based cryptography, especially of new defined quasigroup-based block ciphers and stream ciphers, hash functions and message-authentication codes, PRNGs, public key cryptosystems, etc. Special attention is given to Multivariate Quadratic Quasigroups (MQQs) and MQQ public key schemes, because of their potential to become one of the most efficient pubic key algorithms today.

Chapter 13 presents a comprehensive study on the influence of the intra-modal facial information for an identification approach. A biometric identification system was developed and implemented by merging different intra-multimodal facial features: mouth, eyes, and nose. The principal component analysis, independent component analysis, and discrete cosine transform were used as feature extractors.

Chapter 14 focuses on biometrics (types and technologies), personal identification, and specifications, and then how to implement these performances in security. Two approached are proposed: a novel thinning algorithm for fingerprint recognition and a novel e-passport based on personal identification.

Chapter 15 shows the three security metrics that have been derived from important issues of network security. Each metric demonstrates the level of achievement in preserving one of the security goals. Routing algorithms based on these metrics have been implemented to test the proposed solution. Computational effort and blocking probability were used to assess the behavior and the performance of these routing algorithms.

Chapter 16 highlights the virtues of volatile memory analysis by demonstrating how key material and passphrases can be extracted from memory and reconstructed to facilitate the analysis of encrypted data. The chapter also shows current methods for identifying encryption keys in memory and discusses possible defeating techniques and cryptosystem implementation strategies that could be used to avoid the key extraction.

The book can be considered as an introduction on multidisciplinary aspects and their importance in implementation of the new methods and algorithms designed for cryptography, cryptanalysis, and complexity evaluation of the designed algorithms. It improves the ability to process and manage information and knowledge-related processes in order to create new knowledge. In the fields of information security, information transmission, knowledge security management, cryptology, etc., there exists a need for an edited collection of articles in this area.

Sattar B. Sadkhan Al Maliky
University of Babylon, Iraq

Nidaa A. Abbas
University of Babylon, Iraq

Acknowledgment

The editors of the book *Multidisciplinary Prospective in Cryptology and Information Security* would like to thank to all authors for their ideas and the excellent work in their chapters. We appreciate the originality of their works. Moreover, we would like to express our deep appreciation to the editorial advisory board for their excellent review of the book chapter. The editors acknowledge the remarkable collaboration and the efforts of all the reviewers to ensure the technical quality of this book.

Finally, this book is the result of great teamwork. For this reason, we would like to thank all the efforts of IGI Global.

Sattar B. Sadkhan Al Maliky
University of Babylon, Iraq

Nidaa A. Abbas
University of Babylon, Iraq

Chapter 1
Multidisciplinary in Cryptology

Sattar B. Sadkhan Al Maliky
University of Babylon, Iraq

Nidaa A. Abbas
University of Babylon, Iraq

ABSTRACT

To reach the high depths of knowledge and expertise that are required nowadays, scientists focus their attention on minute areas of study. However, the most complex problems faced by scientists still need the application of different disciplines to tackle them, which creates a necessity for multi-disciplinary collaboration. Cryptology is naturally a multidisciplinary field, drawing techniques from a wide range of disciplines and connections to many different subject areas. In recent years, the connection between algebra and cryptography has tightened, and established computational problems and techniques have been supplemented by interesting new approaches and ideas. Cryptographic engineering is a complicated, multidisciplinary field. It encompasses mathematics (algebra, finite groups, rings, and fields), probability and statistics, computer engineering (hardware design, ASIC, embedded systems, FPGAs), and computer science (algorithms, complexity theory, software design), control engineering, digital signal processing, physics, chemistry, and others. This chapter provides an introduction to the disciplinary, multidisciplinary, and their general structure (interdisciplinary, trans-disciplinary, and cross-disciplinary). And it also gives an introduction to the applications of the multidisciplinary approaches to some of the cryptology fields. In addition, the chapter provides some facts about the importance of the suitability and of the multidisciplinary approaches in different scientific, academic, and technical applications.

INTRODUCTION

It is not enough to be within the field of specialty to gather various cognitive issues related to this field. Scientist, today, cannot claim that she/ he is alone capable of owning the "Science flag" undisputed. Today, the tributaries of knowledge overlapping the various types of science, scientific and humanitarian. And there is great importance of the consequences of sciences overlap each other: agricultural, historical, geological, mathemat-

ics, computer science, communication, control, economics, medicine..... etc. Therefore, human knowledge would not be able to evolve without such wonderful overlap of scientific and humanitarian fields. There is a fact that the expert in any field of knowledge (whatever this field) can't alone answer all the questions, she/ he must be assisted by other scientists with different scientific disciplines, to test and study "her/ his area" from different scientific and humane perspectives (Wyn, 2010).

DOI: 10.4018/978-1-4666-5808-0.ch001

Over long periods of time, an approach prevailed callings for disciplinary segregation in subjects in schools and universities and led to a distortion of perception of holistic context of knowledge, and thus to an impaired ability to see relations and ideas and the broad framework. It has established 'separatist' and specialized knowledge deepened since the seventh century and increased in the twentieth century, where complete separation has occurred between different branches of knowledge, there have been independent disciplines and which are far apart from each other, such as mathematics, sociology, astronomy, physics, chemistry, biology, psychology and the humanities, and others. And this is reflected on the curriculums, which have become an island spaced and do not reflect the integrated aspects of life.

Science develops within moments, and the added values result from the applications of result in increase of devised. Every day showing us science and new disciplines previously unknown. The future direction is focusing on multi-disciplinary research. While the Informatics is characterized by control, interaction and time communication, which increase their use in the teaching and learning process. The future directions are focusing on intelligent systems and what is known as (collective intelligence) (Simon et al, 2011).

This approach was used extensively prepared in the light of the programs and decisions of integrated various branches of knowledge have been adopted in many universities in the world, including: biomechanics, health sciences and sports medicine (Lee, 2005).

Computer scientists and engineers are no exception to this rule – fields such as bioinformatics, cybernetics, information science and quantum computing reside in the intersection between computer science and other disciplines. Researchers in computer science and engineering will therefore benefit greatly from developing such collaborative skills during the course of their studies. For if he or she wishes to participate in multidisciplinary ventures in the future, he or she must become able to appreciate differing perspectives and methods. Computer scientists and engineers apply their skills to many multidisciplinary fields. Different specialized profiles have a place in modern research and industry (Vacca, 2013).

Quantum computation is a field which will be acquiring more and more importance in the next years. Computer scientists with a good understanding of the physical foundations involved will participate in the development of the new technologies that will become more of a practical reality in the medium (Schneider & Gresting, 2012; Sergienko, 2005)

Grid computing has emerged as a fast evolving and important field which has gained substantial attention from multidisciplinary researchers worldwide due to its broad applicability. It is seen as the next generation computing technology, offering virtually "unlimited" resource sharing for computationally intensive advanced science and engineering problems (Michael & Isaac, 2010)

The Network System Security specialization area focuses on researching information security technologies for networked systems and applications of the communication-intensive future. The technological topics covered include system and network security, security of communication systems and applications, and security in system design (Earle, 2005). The goal of this specialization area is to give its students profound and substantial education and expertise in the networked systems security field. The topic is approached in a multi-disciplinary fashion with obligatory studies also on cryptographic and management aspects of information security. Optional studies selected personally for each student build a special individual information security expertise profile. The graduates of this specialization area will benefit from the strong technological, theoretical and practical understanding and skills they have obtained in the program in building a successful career in securing the information and communication technology industry (Katarina et al, 2009).

DISCIPLINE

A discipline refers to types of knowledge, expertise, skills, people, projects, communities, problems, challenges, studies, inquiry, approaches, and research areas that are strongly associated with academic areas of study (academic disciplines) or areas of professional practice (profession). As an example, phenomenon of gravitation is strongly associated with academic discipline of physics. So "gravitation" is considered as a part of the disciplinary knowledge of physics. A discipline can be defined as; the study, or practice, of a subject using a specific set of methods, terms and approaches. History is a discipline, as is archaeology, chemistry and biology. Disciplinary knowledge is associated with academic disciplines and professions and results in people who are known as experts or specialists, as opposed to generalist who may have studied liberal arts or systems theory (Clinton, 2009). . Academic disciplines tend to coevolve with systems of professions. The academic disciplines and professions may be said to 'own' knowledge and the privilege / responsibility for validating / authorizing new knowledge extensions in particular disciplinary areas. For example, astronomers define what is and is not a planet, and so the knowledge about the status of Pluto as a planet can change. Within the framework of Scientific Knowledge, the "discipline", is considered as fundamental organizational concept, since it establishes the principle of Knowledge Distribution to a variety of scientific fields or disciplines. A discipline usually tends to have independency through the drawing of its own boundaries, and putting linguistic terminology, and identifying technologies, and perhaps the theories - which it employs (Krishnan, 2009). Disciplines have certain advantages:

- Focus the limited mental capacity of a person (individual) on the specific knowledge domain.

- Remove of Science from the uncertainty and the danger of exterior.
- Help scientists to deepen their researches and attention in the molecules and atoms
- Avoid acting rashly and on impulse.
- Fulfill promises you make to yourself and to others.
- Overcome laziness and procrastination.
- Continue working on a project, even after the initial rush of enthusiasm has faded away (David, 2011).

On the other hand disciplines have, also, certain disadvantages:

- Closing (some scientists) within a very narrow scientific sphere
- Forgetting that the "thing" they use, are not a truncated portion of a total.
- Leaving the search for a relationship of a part to other parts of the whole.
- Isolation from other disciplines that overlap and intersect with it.
- The "spirit of specialization" produces unjustified exaggerations in the division of some fields to "classes" firstly, and then to the new independent disciplines.
- Development of science and technology has led to the emergence of new disciplines. And whenever there is a new scientific branch, it soon turns into a new specialty. Out of the distribution of work and the nature of the higher qualification most experts (scientist) seek to become the "king" within their specialty, and do not hesitate to engage in competition and conflict with opponents at home and abroad to defend their specialty (David, 2011).

MULTIDISCIPLINARY

The approach to collective understanding of the group associated with particular subject (or specialty), is moving this specialty forward. It is not necessary that one brain be familiar with all results of other brains related to the same discipline (subject under consideration). It is a difficult issue of verification. Today there are hundreds of disciplines, then how a specialist in theoretical physics (particles), can treat with a specialist in neurophysiology, and a specialist in mathematics work with the poet, and Biologist with economist, and Politian with Information specialist? . This means that the specialization language is considered as an obstacle that can not be overcome easily by the beginners in the knowledge understanding (Cecilia, 2011)

The wise man like "Pico Della Mirandola" can be imagined in our time like "supercomputer". Such computer can receive all the knowledge of different specializations and accept anything, but without understanding the meanings of what it received !. And even the users of the "supercomputer" are not in a better situation. Since they will have the results of any requested discipline, the user can not understand many concepts hidden within the boundaries of that discipline. Even the users can not be able to find the relations among the different disciplines. The group of different specialists facing a certain problem can not be considered as equal to sum of the different specializations of each member in the group. Technically, the intersection of different disciplines is an empty set. Hence the problem is: in such case who will be able to take decision in such case?.

The urgent needs for relations among disciplines is translated into the appearance of "Multidisciplinary", "Interdisciplinary", "trans-disciplinary", and " cross-disciplinary" in the middle of the last centaury. Multidisciplinary is related to study different disciplines (simultaneously) for certain topic related to a specific discipline. For example (Choi & Pak, 2008):

- We can study the painting of " Giotto" from the view point of "Art history" crossed with perspectives of physics, chemistry,

history of religions, History of Europe, and engineering.

- We can study the "Marxist Philosophy" from the point of philosophy crossed with Physics, Economics, psychoanalysis, and literatures.

Hence the result of the study will be more valuable within such cross activation of the different disciplines. Then the subject knowledge in that discipline (under consideration) will be deeper as a result of using the approach of treatment to the (problem) using different approaches. Hence "multidisciplinary perspective" approach offers "more" benefits for the cases under study, but this "more" is related to serve the problem itself. The "Multidisciplinary" approach overcomes the efforts of individual disciplines, but its main output results will be included in the main predicted research results. Figure 1 shows the concept of treatment of the problem under consideration with the multidisciplinary prospective, whatever the nature of this problem. Mainly it will need a participation of more than one discipline to treat together to help in finding solution. Note that Disciplines (1, 2, … n) are different disciplines.

Hence Multidisciplinary refers to knowledge associated with more than one existing academic discipline or profession. A multidisciplinary community or project is made up of people from different disciplines and professions who are engaged in working together as equal stakeholders in addressing a common challenge (Valerie & Anne, 2000).

The most important question is how well can the challenge be divided into nearly separable subparts, and then addressed via the distributed knowledge in the community or project team. The communication overhead and the lack of shared vocabulary between people are considered as an additional challenge in these communities and the project under consideration.

A multidisciplinary person is a person with degrees from two or more academic disciplines.

Figure 1. Multidisciplinary concept to treat a problem under consideration by applying different disciplines together simultaneously

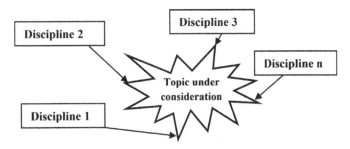

Hence such a person can take the place of two or more people in a multidisciplinary community or project team. For experts there is a key challenge related to the question: How is it possible that the "problem under consideration" can be decomposed into nearly separable subparts, and then addressed via the distributed knowledge in the Community or project team. This aspect related to another challenge which is represented by a fact that there is a lack of shared vocabulary among experts, and there is a communication overhead in these communities and teams (Mokiy, 2013).

It is well known that multidisciplinary approaches encourages the shaping of innovation of the future. For example, political dimensions of forming a new partnerships based on multidisciplinary collaboration to solve the "Social Grand Challenges" is presented in the "Innovation Union", and In the "European Frame work Program". The Horzin 2020 operational overlay, the Innovation with multi- disciplines, is considered as a pivotal foresight of the creation of new products, systems and processes to the benefits for society's growth. According to (Masaru, 2008), participation in cross disciplinary can occur at three levels: multidisciplinary, interdisciplinary, and trans-disciplinary (Mjolsnes, 2012), as shown in Figure 2.

Through the multidisciplinary the researchers from different fields work independently or sequentially, each from his or her own disciplinary perspective, to address a particular research topic. While the umbrella of Interdisciplinary requires greater sharing of information and closer coordination among researchers from different disciplines and fields than occurs in multidisciplinary projects, and the participants remain related to their respective disciplinary models and methodologies as do

Figure 2. Relations among disciplinary and others approaches of multidisciplinary

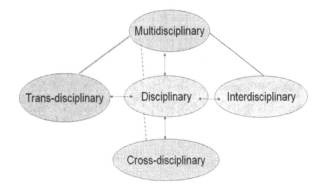

the members of multidisciplinary teams (Valerie & Anne, 2000).

The Openness in the "fields of scientific research" remains necessary and vital and it is vital also that view on the area of specialization is received from outside the specialty, even though they look innocent and naive. For example, a graduate student in chemical engineering at Princeton University developed a technique for high-speed, low-cost printing of ultra-small lines for possible use in electronics (Dharmapalan, 2012).

The definition of a "discipline" and discussions of the interdisciplinary, cross-disciplinary, multidisciplinary, and trans-disciplinary researches have occupied much scholarly controversy. It is clear that areas of research are dynamic - continually emerging, melding, and transforming, although there is not always agreement on these definitions. What is considered interdisciplinary today might be considered disciplinary tomorrow.

Examples (1): Data Science is Multidisciplinary: The reality is that the skill set of a Data Scientist will be much larger. The diagram in Figure 3 includes most of the skills with an out circle of more fundamental skills. It is this outer ring of skills that are fundamental to becoming a data scientist. The skills in the inner part of the diagram are skills that most people will have some experience in one or more of them. The other skills can be developed and learned over time, all depending on the type of person you are (Jolita, 2011).

This center aims to develop a new framework consisting of the multidisciplinary science solving such interdisciplinary problems and of the design science applying the multidisciplinary science to creation artifacts (Keio University). Three methodologies are used here, i.e., multi-scale, multi-physics and multi-aspect, integrate science and design that can be common bases for multiple discipline, as shown in Figure 4.

Figure 3. Center for multidisciplinary and data science

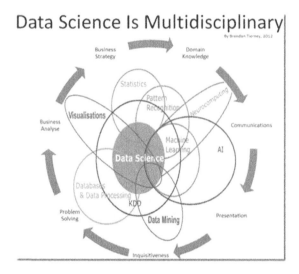

TRANS-DISCIPLINARY

"Trans-disciplinary" is specialized in what existing within the different disciplines, through different approaches, and what is cross over different disciplines. The *trans-disciplinary* is approach for allowing members of an educational team to integrate their knowledge and skills, collaborate with other members, and collectively determine the services that most would a benefit. This approach can be described in more detail as: "approach which requires share roles and systematically (of the team members) cross discipline boundaries".

The primary purpose of this approach is integrating the expertise of team members so that more efficient and comprehensive assessment and intervention services may be provided. The communication aspect in such a team involves continuous give-and-take among all members on a regular, planned basis. This will lead to the fact that professionals from different disciplines will teach, learn, and work together to accomplish a common set of intervention goals for problem under consideration. The role differentiation between disciplines is defined by the needs of the situation rather than by discipline-specific characteristics.

Figure 4. Integration of science and design to get multiple disciplines

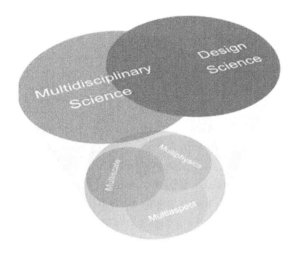

Assessment, intervention, and evaluation are carried out jointly by designated members of the team. This teamwork usually results in a decrease in the number of professionals who interact with the child on a daily basis." (Nicolescu, 2002).

Other literatures describe the "trans-disciplinary" as: An area of research and education that addresses contemporary issues that cannot be solved by one or even a few points-of-view. It brings together academic experts, field practitioners, community members, research scientists, political leaders, and business owners among others to solve some of the pressing problems facing the world, from the local to the global. Trans- disciplinary studies are related to a set of ideas such as interdisciplinary, multidisciplinary, and integrative studies. What sets trans- disciplinary studies apart from the others is a particular emphasis on engagement, investigation, and participation in addressing present-day issues and problems in a manner that explicitly destabilizes disciplinary boundaries while respecting disciplinary expertise (Nicolescu, 2008). They are built around three key concepts:

- Transformative praxis
- Constructive problem-solving
- Real-world engagement

An advantage of trans-disciplinary collaborations is that they often lead to fundamentally new conceptualizations of scientific and societal phenomena and transcend traditional disciplinary boundaries that frame multi- and interdisciplinary analyses.

Example (2): In 1987, the International Center for *Trans-disciplinary Research* (CIRET) adopted the Charter of *Trans-disciplinary* at the 1st World Congress of Trans-disciplinarily. The primary places to find continuing trans-disciplinary work are mostly European, although one can find American and Australian groups as well. CIRET is based in Paris, is a central force in the propagation of trans-disciplinary studies (Mokiy, 2013).

Td-net: network for trans-disciplinarily in sciences and humanities, at the Swiss Academy of Sciences, acts as a resource for writing and work on trans-disciplinary topics.

Russian School of Trans-disciplinarily is focused on creating a unified methodology for trans-disciplinary studies on teaching it in institutions of higher education as an independent scientific discipline (Mittelstrass, 2000).

United States program in *Trans-disciplinary Studies* have been created at the University of North Carolina, Woodbury University, New York University, Claremont Graduate University, and Parsons the New School for Design, among others.

In Portugal there is the Centre of Trans-disciplinary Studies for Development at University of Trás-os-Montes and Alto Douro (Margaret & David, 2000).

INTERDISCIPLINARY

The "Interdisciplinary" aims to achieve different results from that of "Multidiscipline". It relates to transfer the "methods" from one discipline to another. Three steps of interdisciplinary can be identified:

1. **Applicability Degree:** It leads the methods of nuclear physics translated to medicine, such as: new treatment of cancer
2. **Epistemology Degree:** It generates transfer of methods from "Formal Logic" to "Law field", as for example: important analysis in Law of Epistemology.
3. Production of new discipline degree.

Example (3): The transfer of mathematical methods into physics to produce "mathematical physics", and from 'particular physics", Quantum Cosmology, and from mathematics into meteorological, or financial markets, and to chaos theory. And from information to art for producing the "information art".

Hence Interdisciplinary refers to new knowledge extensions that exist between or beyond existing academic disciplines or professions. The new knowledge may be claimed by members of none, or one, both, or an emerging new academic discipline or profession. An interdisciplinary community or project is made up of people from multiple disciplines and professions who are engaged in creating and applying new knowledge as they work together as equal stakeholders in addressing a common challenge. The key question is what new knowledge (of an academic discipline nature), which is outside the existing disciplines, is required to address the challenge. Aspects of the challenge cannot be addressed easily with existing distributed knowledge, and new knowledge becomes a primary sub goal of addressing the common challenge. The nature of the challenge, either its scale or complexity, requires that many people have interactional expertise to improve their efficiency working across multiple disciplines as well as within the new interdisciplinary area. An interdisciplinary person is a person in degrees from

one or more academic disciplines with additional interactional expertise in one or more additional academic disciplines, and new knowledge that is claimed by more than one discipline. Over time, interdisciplinary work can lead to an increase or a decrease in the number of academic disciplines (Koichiro, 2009).

1. Combining or involving two or more academic disciplines or fields of study: The economics and history departments are offering an interdisciplinary seminar on Asia.
2. Combining or involving two or more professions, technologies, departments, or the like, as in business or industry.

Interdisciplinary research is a mode of research by teams or individuals that integrates information, data, techniques, tools, perspectives, concepts, and/or theories from two or more disciplines or bodies of specialized knowledge to advance fundamental understanding or to solve problems whose solutions are beyond the scope of a single discipline or area of research practice (Clinton, 2009).

Interdisciplinary work is that which integrates concepts across different disciplines. New disciplines have arisen as a result of such syntheses. For instance, quantum information processes elements of quantum physics and computer science. Bioinformatics combines molecular biology with computer science. And Interdisciplinary research is important because.

- Creativity often requires interdisciplinary knowledge.
- Immigrants often make important contributions to their new field.
- Disciplinarians often commit errors which can be best detected by people familiar with two or more disciplines.
- Some worthwhile topics of research fall in the interstices among the traditional disciplines.

- Interdisciplinary knowledge and research serve to remind us of the unity - of – knowledge ideal.
- With bridging fragmented disciplines, interdisciplinary might play a role in the defense of academic freedom.

Example (4): From 1999 to 2002 the institute (Institute for Information, Telecommunications and Media law (ITM)) has been part of the Research Alliance on Data Security North Rhine – Westphalia, an *interdisciplinary project* which has united mathematicians, sociologists, electrical engineers, computer scientists and law experts to research and develop applications in the field of cryptography (Institute for Information, Telecommunication and Media Law).

Example (5): "Cyber Security" has transformed into an everyday reality for all users of Internet connected devices. Joining wireless networks, shopping or paying bills online, logging into password-protected Web accounts, and toting always-connected mobile devices present a constant security challenge. Cisco estimates that 1 trillion unique devices will be connected to the Internet by the year 2013, amplifying issues of information security and reliability. Researchers at Stevens Institute of Technology are planning for an even bigger challenge to cryptography and cyber security. While scientists and engineers worldwide are working intently to make the dream of quantum computing a reality, information security managers are watching the horizon with some apprehension (Sergienko, 2005).

Example (6): In biology, bioinformatics is an interdisciplinary field that develops and improves upon methods for storing, retrieving, organizing and analyzing biological data. A major activity in bioinformatics is to develop software tools to generate useful biological knowledge. Bioinformatics has become an important part of many areas of biology. In experimental molecular biology, bioinformatics techniques such as image and signal processing allow extraction of useful results from large amounts of raw data. In the field of genetics and genomics, it aids in sequencing and annotating genomes and their observed mutations. It plays a role in the textual mining of biological literature and the development of biological and gene ontologies to organize and query biological data. It plays a role in the analysis of gene and protein expressions and regulation. Bioinformatics tools aid in the comparison of genetic and genomic data and more generally in the understanding of evolutionary aspects of molecular biology. At a more integrative level, it helps analyze and catalogue the biological pathways and networks that are an important part of systems biology. In structural biology, it aids in the simulation and modeling of DNA, RNA, and protein structures as well as molecular interactions. Bioinformatics uses many areas of computer science, mathematics and engineering to process biological data. Complex machines are used to read in biological data at a much faster rate than before. Databases and information systems are used to store and organize biological data. Analyzing biological data may involve algorithms in artificial intelligence, soft computing, data mining, image processing, and simulation. The algorithms in turn depend on theoretical foundations such as discrete mathematics, control theory, system theory, information theory, and statistics. Commonly used software tools and technologies in the field include Java, C#, XML, Perl, C, C++, Python, R, SQL, CUDA, MATLAB, and spreadsheet applications (Bal, 2005).

Example (7): University of Regina - CANADA offers the only: *Fine Arts-based Interdisciplinary Studies program.* It offer exciting opportunities for undergraduate and graduate students interested in developing unique programs of study that *integrate knowledge from a variety of traditional disciplines* within and outside of Fine Arts (Interdisciplinary Studies).

CROSS-DISCIPLINARY

It refers to knowledge that explains aspects of one discipline in terms of another. Common examples of cross-disciplinary approaches are studies of the physics of music or the politics of literature. Or it can be described as (education) linking two or more fields of study.

Example (8): "Computer Forensics", concentrations on cross-disciplinary undergraduate studies (Kelich et al, 2009). In this project, two academic departments, Computer and Information Sciences (CIS), and Sociology and Criminal Justice (SCJ), will develop a cross-disciplinary computer concentration in digital forensics that positions students for professional certification. Such concentration is suitable for undergraduate students and law enforcement professionals.

Example (9): The international, multi-ethnic, and cross-disciplinary group of scholars investigates the meaningful ways in which fantasy and Native America intersect, examining classics by American Indian authors such as Louise Erdrich, Gerald Vizenor, and Leslie Marmon Silko, as well as non-Native fantasists such as H.P. Lovecraft, J.R.R. Tolkien, and J.K. Rowling (Graduate Program)

Example (10): DNA Cryptography is a new branch of cryptography which utilizes DNA as an informational and computational car-

rier with the aid of molecular techniques. It is relatively a new field which emerged after the disclosure of computational ability of DNA. The DNA Cryptography gains attention due to the vast storage capacity of DNA, which is the basic computational tool of this field. One gram of DNA is known to store about 108 Ttera-Bytes. This surpasses the storage capacity of any electrical, optical or magnetic storage medium]. By utilizing DNA cryptography, several methods have been designed to break many modern algorithms like Data Encryption Standard (DES), RSA and Number Theory Research Unit (NTRU). The research into DNA cryptosystem is still in its early stage. Thus, the scope of doing research on this new field is multi-dimensional (The emerging science of DNA cryptography) .Work needs to be done from theory to realization, as both of the dimensions yet to be matured. Recent developments have showed that some key technologies in DNA research, such as Polymerase Chain Reaction (PCR), DNA synthesis, and DNA digital coding, have only been developed. Traditional cryptographic systems have long legacy and are built on a strong mathematical and theoretical bases. Traditional security systems like RSA, DES or NTRU are also found in real time operations. So, an important perception needs to be developed that the DNA cryptography is not to negate the tradition, but to create a bridge between existing and new technology. The power of DNA computing will strengthen the existing security system by opening up a new possibility of a hybrid cryptographic system (Tornea & Borda, 2009)

Example (11): Security Engineering: The system building process remains dependable in the face of malice, error, or mischance. As a discipline, it focuses on the tools, processes, and methods needed to design, implement, and test complete systems, and to adapt existing systems as their environment evolves. Security engineering requires cross-disciplinary expertise, ranging from cryptography and computer security through hardware tamper-resistance and formal methods to knowledge of economics, applied psychology, organizations and the law. Figure 5 shows a block diagram of the structure for the security engineering from point of view of cross-disciplinary (Ross, 2001).

SOME FACTS RELATED TO MULTIDISCIPLINARY

1. There are a lot of difficulties facing some disciplines, which have not found *a solution* from outside the Discipline.
2. History proves the existence of concepts, methods and theories (*cross disciplines*) that could be employed in more than one

specialty, that a particular discipline is produced.

3. There are "Areas *of Researches*" imposed by their natures on the specialists to be open to other disciplines and search for finding integration or sharing knowledge with them. Such "Areas *of Researches*" necessarily call interaction and cooperation of more than one discipline.
4. It is certainly the scientist who specializes in prehistoric times also must master geology and mythology and science of genes and environment.
5. Some of the important discoveries that the world has seen in the last fifty years, especially in the field of mathematics, computer, physics, chemistry and biology (genes) and anthropology, are the result of *overlapping* of a number of disciplines.
6. The "*Convergence*" that has arisen between engineers and mathematicians since the Second World War has led to the emergence of the so-called "Cybernetics" on which the

Figure 5. Security engineering as cross-disciplinary approach

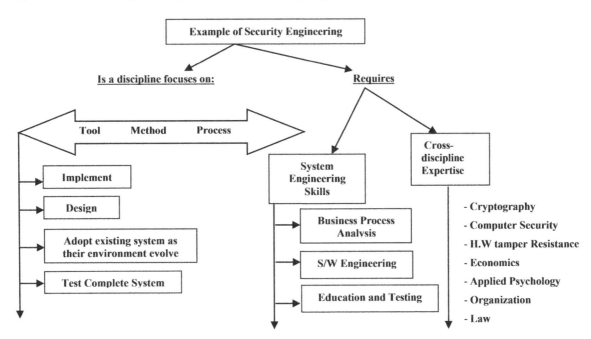

computer science and artificial intelligence science are founded.

7. In the last three decades, a great convergence has been done in three different types of industries (Computer, communication, and Multimedia) to produce what is called (IT Industry), or (InfoTech). This convergence process is a kind of multidisciplinary prospective among different disciplines, as shown in Figure 6.

The emergence and development of "computer science" since the mid-twentieth century has forced most disciplines to restructure themselves.

8. There are many factors which lead to break down barriers among disciplines and help the movement of researchers and curriculum and theoretical concepts of "*specialization*" to "another" , and from "*field of research*" to another, to the point that: "*the operation on the principle of specialty*" will not be justified today and acceptable only if each "*discipline*" tries to be open up to all that is going on outside, and believe in "*membership*" and "*logics*" relations between it and the other disciplines.

9. The history and development of sciences (not only have the subsidiary and dominant but they also establish new specialties), also include the emergence of intersection and overlapping of several areas of different disciplines

Figure 6. Convergence of computer, communication, and multimedia

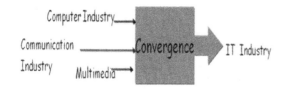

10. During the past five decades, a number of hybrids scientific disciplines have been established.

11. In the second half of the twentieth century, a large number of " knowledge and new sciences and social developments and professionals" that worked on reducing (or removing) borders between disciplines (in cognitive and scientifically and professionally), have emerged to the degree that overlap and cooperation among the "various disciplines" have become the latest trend that most universities and research centers in developed countries try to attain.

12. The scientific knowledge and professional developments forced the responsible specialists in scientific research and higher education in developed countries to "*reconsider*" the organization of academic and affiliated research institutions to accommodate the requirements of "*overlapping disciplines*" and disciplines in rehabilitation programs, education and scientific research.

13. Many institutions of higher education in the world have embarked on the establishment of related disciplines of dual purpose for training future scientists who will be completely faithful to and interacting with the "*overlapping disciplines*".

14. Some universities developed pilot programs to accommodate in suitable form the concept of "*interdisciplinary* " or " *trans-disciplinary*" in more than one scientific department and sometimes in more than one college, for example: "Program of health information: the overlap of Computer Science, Community Health, and biomechanics, participate in the program prepared by sections of Physical Education and mechanical engineering and physical therapy.

15. Some universities proceeded to create "Special Graduate Colleges" which combine Applied Sciences and the Humanities, as is the case of the "Montreal University

in Canada". That grants degrees in double scientific disciplines and does not relate to traditional scientific specializations of the undergraduate study of university education, such as a "Ph.D." in "Applied Humanities" or "Vital Computer Science", or "Social Statistics Science".

16. Health Management Department and the Department of Community Services at the "University of Aden" is a pioneering experiment in Yemeni universities for applying multidisciplinary prospective in postgraduate education.

17. Interdisciplinary of science does not mean "interference rooted aversion" of specialization but openness to other sciences, to cope with the concept that: One of the tasks of the university is; not to produce knowledge for knowledge, But the "production of knowledge" to solve problems encountered in improving the conditions of communities.

18. Today, there is no one who claims that he is alone capable of owning the corner flag unchallenged.

19. There is a great importance in the consequences of the overlap of science types among them: agriculture, history, geology ...etc.

20. 20- The human knowledge cannot developed without such "Scientific and humanitarian wonderful Interaction".

21. Scientist (specialist researcher) alone, whatever his specialty, cannot answer all the questions that he faced during his research. He must be assisted by others from different scientific disciplines, to test and study "his area" with different scientific and humane approach.

22. The real work today, is under the management of "an *integrated scientific team*" of different scientific and humanitarian disciplines. Successful action today is a collective work (Team work) which depends on the exchange of scientific expertise and human knowledge whatsoever, between its members.

23. Informatics is characterized by control, and time interaction and communication, which increase employment in the teaching and learning process, and lead to the *emergence* of patterns and new educational institutions. And the future direction is stationed in intelligent systems, and the development of what is known as the (*Collective Intelligence*).

24. Global variables produce many effects and challenges "opportunities and risks" to the objectives and functions of educational institutions and programs, and the roles and functions of a members of the educational staff and the basic skills required.

25. In the third world countries environment, generally, a school or university is an entity separate from the reality of life. Teachers of mathematics don't like science, and science teachers do not understand history, all teach using the separatist specialist approach. Here, students continue to have the inability to connect knowledge with other subjects, making them unable to see knowledge in the context of the total.

26. Current academic frameworks cannot handle simultaneously optimizing problems related to multiple disciplines because they are significantly specialized and subdivided in each field in accordance with remarkable growth of scale and complexity in this particular field and with sophistications of science and technology.

COMMUNICATION AND INFORMATION SECURITY

Information and Communication Technologies (ICT) which were introduced in the second half of the last century have shaped substantially the way we interact with each other, do business, and learn.

ICT are encouraging globalization, exchange of information and the proliferation of cyber space. The benefits of using these technologies are immense. We are living in an era of digital revolution when every day we become more dependent on such technologies and their by-products (Epsten, 2011). One of the main issues with ICT today is security. In the last thirty years we have witnessed the flourishing of a myriad of electronic attacks, malware, vulnerabilities and intrusions in the domain of information and communication technologies. There are at least five distinct problem areas where security related issues are currently impacting in a negative way ICT. These areas are:

- Lack of security awareness and training,
- Operating system design and security,
- Open source issues,
- Design complexity and
- Multiple layer approach (Morsund, 2005), as shown in Figure 7.

Communication Security includes means by which people can share information with varying degrees of certainty that third parties cannot inter-

cept what was said. With many communications taking place over long distance and mediated by technology, and increasing awareness of the importance of interception issues, and technologies are at the heart of this debate. Communications Security (COMSEC) is the *discipline* of preventing unauthorized interceptors from accessing telecommunications in an intelligible form, while still delivering content to the intended recipients. The field includes *crypto security*, *emission security*, *traffic-flow security*, *physical security of equipment*, and transmission *security* (Earle, 2005). COMSEC is used to protect both classified and unclassified traffic on military communications networks, including voice, video, and data. It is used for both analog and digital applications, and both wired and wireless links, as shown in Figure 8.

- **Crypto Security:** Is the component of communications security that results from the provision of technically sound cryptosystems and their proper use. This includes ensuring message confidentiality and authenticity.

Figure 7. Block diagram of secure communication systems

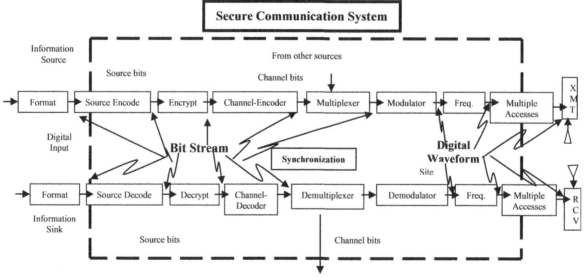

Figure 8. Block diagram of different techniques used for communication security

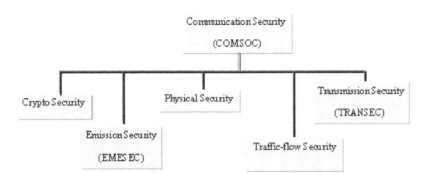

- **Emission Security (EMSEC):** Is protection resulting from all measures taken to deny unauthorized persons information of value which might be derived from intercept and analysis of compromising emanations from crypto equipment, automated information systems, and telecommunications systems.

- **Physical Security (PHSEC):** Is the component of communications security that results from all physical measures necessary to safeguard classified equipment, material, and documents from access thereto or observation thereof by unauthorized persons.

- **Traffic-Flow Security:** Is measures that conceal the presence and properties of valid messages on a network. They include the protection resulting from features, inherent to some crypto equipment, that conceal the presence of valid messages on a communications circuit, normally achieved by causing the circuit to appear busy at all times.

- **Transmission Security (TRANSEC):** Is the component of communications security that results from the application of measures designed to protect transmissions from interception and exploitation by means other than cryptanalysis (e.g. frequency hopping and spread spectrum).

- **Information Security (InfoSec):** Is the practice of defending information from unauthorized access, use, disclosure, disruption, modification, perusal, inspection, recording or destruction. It is a general term that can be used regardless of the form the data may take (electronic, physical, etc...). Two major aspects of information security are:

- **IT Security:** Sometimes referred to as computer security. Information Technology Security is information security applied to technology. IT security specialists are almost always found in any major enterprise/establishment due to the nature and value of the data within larger businesses.

- **Information Assurance:** The act of ensuring that data is not lost when critical issues arise. These issues include but are not limited to; natural disasters, computer/server malfunction, and physical theft. The information assurance is typically dealt with by IT security specialists. One of the most common methods of providing information assurance is to have an off-site backup of the data in case one of the mentioned issues arises (Gavrilovska, et al, 2011).

SECURITY TYPES

Security can be broadly classified under the following headings as shown in Figure 9, with examples:

- Hiding the content or nature of a communication.
- **Encoding:** A rule to convert a piece of information (for example, a letter, word, phrase, or gesture) into another form or representation (one sign into another sign), not necessarily of the same type.
- Encryption
- Steganography
- **Hiding the parties to a communication:** Preventing identification, promoting anonymity.
- Hiding the fact that a communication takes place.
- **Random Traffic:** Creating random data flow to make the presence of genuine communication harder to detect and traffic analysis less reliable (Keith, 2012).

Encryption is where data is rendered hard to read by an unauthorized party. Since encryption can be made extremely hard to break, many communication methods either use deliberately weaker encryption than possible, or have backdoors inserted to permit rapid decryption. Many methods of encryption are also subject to "man in the middle" attack whereby a third party who can 'see' the establishment of the secure communication. The encryption can be implemented in a way to require the use of encryption, i.e. if encrypted communication is impossible then no traffic is sent, or opportunistically. Opportunistic encryption is a lower security method to generally increase the percentage of generic traffic which is encrypted. This method does not generally provide authentication or anonymity but it does protect the content of the conversation from eavesdropping. An Information-theoretic security technique known as physical layer encryption ensures that a wireless communication link is provably secure with communications and coding techniques (Keith, 2012).

Information Hiding (hidden writing): Is the means by which data can be hidden within other more innocuous data. Thus a watermark proving ownership is embedded in the data of a picture, in such a way that it is hard to find or remove unless you know how to find it. Or for communication, the hiding of important data (such as a telephone

Figure 9. Classification of information security techniques

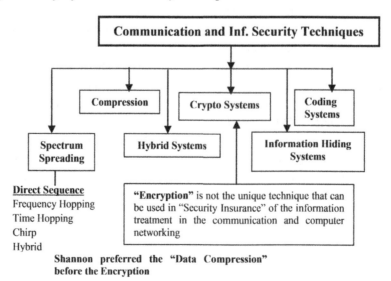

number) is in apparently innocuous data (an MP3 music file) (Lijuan & Wang, 2010).

Spectrum Spreading Technologies: In telecommunication and radio communication, *spread-spectrum* techniques are methods by which a signal (e.g. an electrical, electromagnetic, or acoustic signal) generated with a particular bandwidth is deliberately spread in the frequency domain, resulting in a signal with a wider bandwidth. These techniques are used for a variety of reasons, including the establishment of secure communications, increasing resistance to natural interference, noise and jamming, to prevent detection, and to limit power flux density (e.g. in satellite downlinks) .

Compression Techniques: In computer science and information theory, data compression, source coding, or bit-rate reduction involves encoding information using fewer bits than the original representation. Compression can be either lossy or lossless. Lossless compression reduces bits by identifying and eliminating statistical redundancy. No information is lost in lossless compression. Lossy compression reduces bits by identifying unnecessary information and removing it. The process of reducing the size of a data file is popularly referred to as data compression, although its formal name is source coding (coding is done at the source of the data before it is stored or transmitted) (Mark & Gaily, 1995). Compression is useful because it helps reduce resources usage, such as data storage space or transmission capacity. Because compressed data must be decompressed to use, this extra processing imposes computational or other costs through decompression; this situation is far from being a free lunch. The design of data compression schemes involves trade-offs among various factors, including the degree of compression, the amount of distortion introduced (e.g., when using lossy data compression), and the computational resources required to compress and decompressed the data (Thomas, 1985).

Hybrid Techniques: Such technique can collect two or more from the well-known security techniques simultaneously in one system. For example, a security system can integrate the spread spectrum with the cryptography, or integrate Information Hiding with Cryptography, and so on. The main aims behind such approach are to get more security through the transmission of the information within the channel (Marvin et al, 2004).

OVERVIEW OF CRYPTOLOGY

Cryptology is a science which is used from thousands of years. It concerns the encryption as well as decryption of secret data in such a way that valuable information will remain safe from unauthorized users. Earlier the cryptology was used in military and government. Due to advent of internet technology over the past few years, people are now using internet to share information and for communication purpose. For this reason, secure communication is main requirement for online trading because internet is an unsafe channel. Cryptology techniques are used to protect individual privacy as well as commercial secrets. Nowadays security, integrity, non-repudiation, confidentiality, and authentication services are the most important factors in the field of the Cryptology (Stinson, 2005). The main objective of the cryptography is to ensure secure communication over insecure channel (like Internet), as shown in Figure 10.

The message which is normally a plaintext is encrypted using the encryption key. The encrypted data (Cipher Text) is sent over the communication channel to the receiver. On the receiver side the cipher text is decrypted using decryption key. The cipher text can be generated in the stream or block form.

Figure 10. Basic structure of cryptology

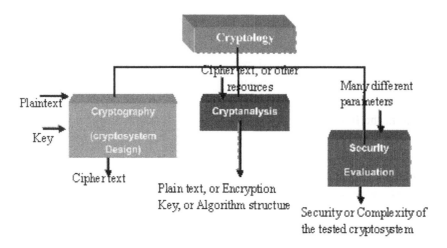

Goals of Cryptography

1. Confidentiality means to keep secret the content of information from all unauthorized users.
2. Data integrity deals with the unauthorized modification of data. In order to assure data integrity, one must have the ability to detect data manipulation (i.e. insertion, deletion and substitution) by unauthorized parties.
3. Authentication means identification. It is applicable to both users and information itself. When two users start communication then they should identify each other. Information delivered over a channel should be authenticated as to origin, date of origin, data content, time sent, etc.
4. Non-repudiation is a service which prevents an entity from denying previous commitments or actions (Katz & Lindell, 2007)

Nowadays the cryptography is classified into two categories, symmetric key cryptography and a symmetric key cryptography. In private-key cryptography, the encryption and the decryption are same.

SYMMETRIC KEY CRYPTOGRAPHY

The encryption and decryption are performed using the same key. The key should be kept secret between sender and receiver. There are various types of the encryption algorithms. Block ciphers are now widely used in industry. Data Encryption Standard (DES) was adopted in 1977 by National Institute of Standards and Technology. The architecture of DES is based on Feistel cipher (developed by IBM), with 16 rounds of identical operations. In each round of DES, substitution and permutation are performed by S-Boxes and P-Boxes. It is to provide confusion and diffusion in the encrypted data. Now DES is no longer a secure encryption standard because of the short key and various types of attacks. Advanced Encryption Standard (AES) was issued by National Institute of Standards and Technology in 2001 to overcome the problem of the DES. It is intended to replace DES. It supports key lengths of 128, 192, and 256 bits and a block size of 128 bits. It does not use Feistel Cipher structure. Here, each round uses byte substitution, permutation, arithmetic operations over a finite field, and XOR technique (Matt & Curtin, 2005).

A SYMMETRIC KEY CRYPTOGRAPHY

This concept was introduced by Diffie and Hellman in 1976. This technique is referred to as a public key cryptosystem in which encryption and decryption are done using two different keys (Public and Private Key). The private is secret and public key is open which anyone can use. The pair is selected in such a way that private key determination on the basis of public key is infeasible.

The main advantage of the public-key cryptosystem is that there is no need for transmission of secret key because private key is never transmitted hence there is no chance of interception because secret key is not transmitted.

The main disadvantage is that the speed of encryption is very slow compared to that of private key cryptography. Second the Certification of Authentication is required from those who are using Public key. No public-key encryption has been proven to be secure. Integer Factorization Problem (IFD), Discrete Logarithm Problem (DLP) and Elliptic Curve Discrete Logarithm Problem (ECDLP) are the mathematical tools which are used in public-key cryptography system (Hankerson, et al, 2005).

Rivest, Shamir and Adleman (RSA) used the IFD concept for public-key cryptography as equivalent to find the prime factors p and q given a very large number n. Diffie and Hellman used the concept of DLP. Digital Signature Algorithm (DSA) issued by the NIST to provide the authentication mechanism that provides communication parties with proving and verifications.

ECDLP concepts used in Elliptic Curve Cryptography (ECC). It is an emerging technique alternative of RSA and DSA. Solving of the elliptic curve discrete logarithm problem is infeasible (Neal, 2011).

Cryptography is an interdisciplinary subject, drawn from several fields. Before the time of computers, it was closely related to linguistics. Nowadays the emphasis has shifted, and cryptography makes extensive use of technical areas of mathematics, especially those areas collectively known as discrete mathematics. This includes topics from number theory, information theory, computational complexity, statistics and combinatory. It is also a branch of engineering, but an unusual one as it must deal with active, intelligent and malevolent opposition (Shier & Wallenius, 2000)

Cryptography science today enjoys great prestige among the other sciences, such that its practical applications diversified to include multiple areas, including: the diplomatic, military, and security, trade, economic, media, banking and medical informatics. It depends on multiple sciences: mathematics and computer science, and science of communication, and science of statistics, and others. Recent trends in computation technology, and what could lead to him in the subject of very modern encryption systems, such as (Quantum, Nano, Chaos, Neural Network, Fuzzy, Genetic, Cloud Networking, Mobile Agent, Ad hoc.. etc., raise a question: Why are these trends?, and are there any logical reasons?.

CRYPTANALYSIS

It is the study of methods for obtaining the meaning of encrypted information, without access to the secret information that is normally required to do so. Typically, this involves knowing the way the system works and finding a secret key. A very important fact is that the development of the cryptanalysis is based entirely on the development of the cryptography (Hankerson, et al, 2000), beginning with pen and paper, to computer-based systems, through electro – mechanical devices. It is noted that the results of cryptanalysis techniques have changed - which no longer possess unlimited capabilities to break the code, or their success is limited in this scientific aspect, which offers a major challenge for the creative potential of its users, and their knowledge and experience in the science of several overlapping fields. For

Table 1. Gives the structure of cryptography components

No	Cryptosystem Types	Different Types of Knapsack Based Cryptosystem
1	**Knapsack based cryptography**	• Conventional Markle Hellman • Modified Markle Hellman • LU- Lee Cryptosystem • Goodman- Maculey • Conventional Adna De Parto • Modified Adna De Parto • Piperzyk • Shor Rivest • Jange
2	Pairing based cryptography	
3	RSA based cryptography	
4	Curve based cryptography	
5	Elliptic based cryptography	
6	Stream cipher based cryptography	
7	Block cipher cryptography	
8	Quasi Group based cryptography	
9	Polynomial Reconstruction Problem based cryptography	
10	Fuzzy Logic based cryptography	**Knapsack Problems with different Mathematical and Computer Methods** • Modular multiplication with different methods • Factorization problem to prime factors • Polynomials with elements of equal powers. • Knapsack problem • Linear programming problem • Ideal finite field • Discrete logarithm problem.
11	Genetic algorithm cryptography	
12	Multivariate cryptography (Isomorphism of polynomial Problem)	
13	Lattice based cryptography	
14	Quantum based cryptography	
15	Chaotic based cryptography	
16	Number Theory based cryptography	
17	Biometric based cryptography	
18	Algebraic cryptography	
19	**Artificial Neural Network Cryptography**	**ANN in Cryptology and its branches** • Analysis of NN based crypto. • ANN approach to RSA. • Public key exchange based on ANN. • Secure Inf. exchange based on ANN. • Determination Number of roots of polynomials.
20	Identity Based Cryptography	
21	Homomorphic cryptography	
22	Combinatorial cryptography	
23	Probabilistic cryptography	
24	Group Based cryptography	

example in 1976 a revolution occurred in the crypto science, through the discovery of asymmetric crypto systems. Therefore, methods required to break these systems are radically different from methods used with analogue encryption systems. They depend on purely mathematical matters, the most famous question is: Integer Factorization. It is well known "Computation" is used to generate a significant impact on the field of cryptanalysis during World War II, but at the same time it provides an opportunity to find "Modern types of encryption systems with high-complexity" relative to previous systems (Helen, 1989). Figure 11 shows

a brief comparison the requested knowledge by each specialist in cryptography and cryptanalysis.

On the other hand Figure 12 shows the general classification of cryptanalysis methods and techniques well known in literature.

Scientific Important Problems Facing Workers in this Specialized Area

1. Mathematics related to modern methods of designing Crypto algorithms, or the development of content and the used ones. And such knowledge is used to find appropriate

Figure 11. Comparison between requirements of cryptographer and cryptanalyst

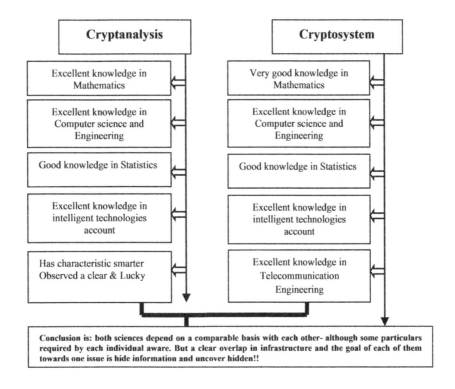

Figure 12. Different cryptanalysis methods and techniques

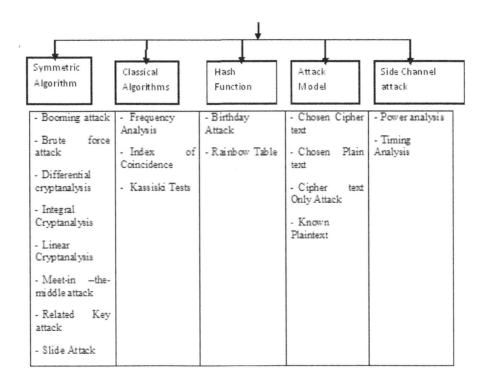

ways to be able to analyze modern encryption systems. The main mathematical problems are:

a. Quadratic Residue Problem
b. High Residue Problem
c. Discrete Logarithm Problem (DLP) and Elliptic Curve DLP
d. Subset Problem
e. One Way Function Problem
f. Tensor based Problem
g. Inverse Identity Problem
h. Integer Factorization Problem
i. Probabilistic Signature Problem
j. Birthday Problem

2. The Computer side, and includes three aspects of science Cryptology, especially in the area of analysis and evaluation of the computational complexity for encryption algorithms (security degree).
3. Smart Computational Techniques, include neural networks, and Fuzzy logic, and genetic algorithm. Cloud Computing, Grid Computing, and Mobile Computing.
4. Statistical Side offers many techniques and it is reflected on the design and analytical aspects, such as technical: ICA
5. Linguistic Aspect, and its reflection on the analysis of encryption systems.

6. Modern Communications and modern standards in mobile wireless communication systems and systems requirements of the code.

MULTIDISCIPLINARY COLLABORATION IN CRYPTOLOGY

According to the information mentioned in the previous section of this chapter, we can propose a structure that describes the role of the multidisciplinary collaboration in Cryptology and information security. As shown in Figure 13. One can imagine the multidisciplinary as an integrating machine, that collects (interactively) the different disciplines in order to produces a specific item in cryptology (considering the three different classes of the cryptology shown in Figure 10).

EVOLUTIONARY ALGORITHMS IN CRYPTANALYSIS

The cryptanalysis of various cipher problems can be formulated as NP-Hard combinatorial problem. The solution of these problems requires time and/or memory, which are related directly to the size

Figure 13. The cryptology view as a multidisciplinary prospective of different disciplines

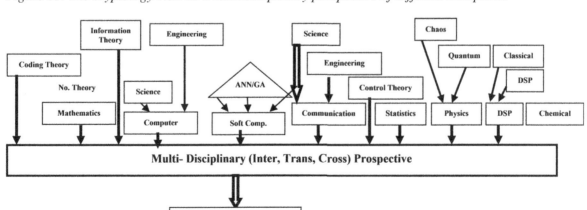

of the specific problem. The used techniques for solving combinatorial problems fall into two broad groups:

- The exact algorithms, which guarantee the foundation of the optimal solution to the problem such as simplex method, branch and bound, brute force etc.
- The evolutionary computation algorithms, which are used to find an adequate solution to the problem under consideration.

The evolutionary computation algorithms provide a robust and suitable methods for crypt-analysis. The main aim of such techniques is to find sufficient "good" solution efficiently into consideration the characteristics of the cryptosystem under consideration (Hardik & Nidhi, 2011). For example, the cryptanalysis of simplified data encryption standard problem (SDES) was implemented using several evolutionary computation techniques like memetic algorithm, genetic algorithm and simulated annealing. The comparison among genetic algorithm, simulated annealing, and memetic algorithm was implemented to investigate the performance of the SDES cryptanalysis. The methods were tested and the computational results show that memetic algorithm performs better than simulated annealing and the genetic algorithms for such type combinatorial problem (Poonam, 2009). The cryptanalytic attacks using GA are sequential. A hybrid cryptanalysis technique uses both Genetic Algorithm and Hill climbing in attacking different cipher systems.

FUZZY LOGIC IN SECURITY EVALUATION

In designing Fuzzy based cryptosystem, the designer will make use of one of the techniques of soft computing, which is the Fuzzy Logic Technique, and with the main features of this new technique, the designer will elaborate and integrate many features from other disciplines like mathematics (Number Theory), and statistics, and computer science, and communication engineering in order to produce the requested system with good (or acceptable) security characteristics (Lijuan & Wang, 2010). Two examples will be considered under these applications, which are:

1. Network Security Evaluation

It is important to apply fuzzy evaluation method to "network security" evaluation because the "network security" has close relationships with the followings:

a. Physical environment of information carriers,
b. Information transmission,
c. Information storage,
d. Information management and so on,

These relations have much ambiguity. The core of "network security" fuzzy evaluation is the calculation of membership degree transformation.

e. Data mining technology based on entropy can be used to:
f. Mine knowledge information about object classification hidden in every index,
g. Affirm the relationship of object classification and index membership, and
h. Eliminate the redundant data in index membership for object classification by defining distinguishable weight and extracting valid values to compute object membership (Lijuan &Wang, 2010).

2. Knapsack Cryptosystem Security Evaluation

The knapsack cryptosystem is based on the well-known mathematical concept, i.e., the choosing of one way function. All the attacking methods against the knapsack cryptosystem aim towards breaking the security of the system under consideration. Sometimes, the users need to know the level of security (complexity) of the used knapsack cryptosystem, or she / he needs to know what the advantage given by any development performed on any knapsack cryptosystem. Hence she / he must look for evaluation criteria that can be used as an evaluation method or (procedure). Till now the "security evaluation" is considered as a new field. Most of interested experts consider it as a part of cryptanalysis. In 2006 Fuzzy logic based evaluator was used for the first time as a complexity evaluator for stream cipher system. And then the Fuzzy logic evaluation method was applied to another type of cryptosystems, that is knapsack cryptosystems. Two input variables are taken into consideration, and according to them the complexity evaluator based on Fuzzy logic was designed and simulated. Many knapsack cryptosystems were tested by this security evaluator like: Lu-li, Chor Rivest, Traditional and Advance Adina Diparto Systems. The results are promising (Sattar, et al, 2011).

NEURAL CRYPTOGRAPHY

Different scaling properties of the complexity of bidirectional synchronization and unidirectional learning are essential for the security of neural cryptography. Incrementing the synaptic depth of the networks increases the synchronization time only polynomially, but the success of the geometric attack is reduced exponentially and it clearly fails in the limit of infinite synaptic depth. This method is improved by adding a genetic algorithm, which selects the fittest neural networks. The probability of a successful genetic attack is calculated for different model parameters using numerical simulations. The results show that scaling laws observed in the case of other attacks hold for the improved algorithm, too. The number of networks needed for an effective attack grows exponentially with increasing synaptic depth. In addition, finite-size effects caused by Hebbian

and anti- Hebbian learning are analyzed. These learning rules converge to the random walk rule if the synaptic depth is small compared to the square root of the system size (Nakun & Xiaofeng, 2013).

Good cryptography gets its security by using incredibly long keys and using encryption algorithms that are resistant to other forms of attack. The neural network application represents a way for the next development in good cryptography (Nankun, et al, 2011).

Neural cryptography is based on a competition between attractive and repulsive stochastic forces. A feedback mechanism is added to neural cryptography which increases the repulsive forces. Using numerical simulations and an analytic approach, the probability of a successful attack is calculated for different model parameters. Scaling laws are derived which show that feedback improves the security of the system. In addition, a network with feedback generates a pseudorandom bit sequence which can be used to encrypt and decrypt a secret message (Wright & Manic, 2010)

REFERENCES

Bal, H. (2005). *Bioinformatics: Principles and Applications*. New Delhi: Tata McGraw-Hill.

Cecilia, B. (Ed.). (2009). Security: A Multidisciplinary Normative Approach. BrillOnline.com Publishers.

Choi, B., & Pak, A. (2008). Multidisciplinarity, interdisciplinarity and transdisciplinarity in health research, services, education and policy: Discipline, inter-discipline distance, and selection of discipline. *Clinical and Investigative Medicine. Medecine Clinique et Experimentale*, (31): 41–48. PMID:18312747

Clinton, G. (2009). *Integrating the disciplines: Successful interdisciplinary subjects*. Austria Centre for the Study of Higher Education publication.

David, A. (2011). Multidisciplinarity, Interdisciplinarity, Transdisciplinarity, and the Sciences. *International Studies in the Philosophy of Science, 25*(4), 387–403.

Dharmapalan, B. (2012). *Scientific Research Methodology*. Amazon.com Publisher.

Earle, A. (2005). *Wireless Security Handbook*. CRC Press.

Epstein, J. (2011). *Onward to the Digital Revolution: Merchants of Culture*. New York: Scribner Books Publisher.

Gavrilovska, L., Krco, S., Milutinovic, V., Stojmenovic, I., & Trobec, R. (Eds.). (2011). *Application and Multidisciplinary Aspects of Wireless Sensor Networks: Concepts, Integration, and Case Studies*. Springer-Verlag.

Hankerson, D., Hoffman, G., Leonard, D., Lindner, C., Phelps, K., Rodger, C., & Wall, J. (2000). *Coding Theory and Cryptography: The Essentials* (2nd ed.). CRC Press.

Hankerson, D., Menezes, A., & Vanstone, S. (2005). *Guide to Elliptic Curve Cryptography*. New York: Springer-Verlag.

Hardik, S., & Nidhi, A. (2011). Solving Crypt-Arithmetic problems via genetic algorithm. *International Journal of IT & Management, 1*(1), 12–17.

Helen, F. (1989). *Cryptanalysis: A Study of Ciphers and Their Solution*. Amazon.com.

Jolita, R. (2011). Applying Transdisciplinarity Principles in the Information Services Co-creation Process. In *Proceedings of 2012 Sixth International Conference on Research Challenges in Information Science* (RCIS), (pp. 1 – 11). IEEExplore – Digital Library.

Katarina, S., Thomas, W., & Santi, R. (2010). *Grid and Cloud Computing: A Business Perspective on Technology and Applications*. Berlin, Germany: Springer-Verlag.

Katz, J., & Lindell, Y. (2007). *Introduction to Modern Cryptography: Principles and Protocols*. Chapman and Hall/CRC.

Keith, J., Richard, B., & Curtis, W. (2009). *Real Digital Forensics: Computer Security and Incident Response*. Amazon.com.

Keith, M. (2012). *Everyday Cryptography: Fundamental Principles and Applications*. Amazon.com.

Koichiro, D. (2009). Strategy and Methodology of Science Integration in Transdisciplinarity. In *Proceedings of ICROS-SICE International Joint Conference 2009* (pp. 5107 – 5110). IEEExplore Digital Library.

Krishan, A. (2009). *What are Academic Disciplines? Some observation on the Disciplinarty vs. Interdisciplinarity debate*. University of Southampton, National Centre for Research Methods.

Lee, K. (2005). *The Information Revolution and Ireland: Prospects and Challenges*. Amazon.com.

Lijuan, Z., & Wang, Q. (2010). A network security evaluation method based on fuzzy and RST. In *Proceedings of 2nd International Conference on Education Technology and Computer* (ICETC) (vol. 2, pp. 40-44). IEEExplore Digital Library.

Margaret, A., & David, A. (2002). *Transdisciplinarity: recreating Integrated Knowledge*. Amazon.com.

Mark, N., & Gailly, J. (1995). *The Data Compression Book*. IDG Books Worldwide, Inc.

Marvin, S., Jim, O., Robert, S., & Barry, L. (2004). *Spread Spectrum Communications Handbook*. New York: The McGraw-Hill, Inc.

Masaru, Y., Yoshiyuki, T., & Yuya, K. (2008). Patterns of Collaboration in Emerging Fields of Trans-Disciplinary Science: The Case of Sustainability Science. In *Proceedings of Portland International Conference on Management of Engineering & Technology* (PICMET 2008) (pp. 174–180). Cape Town, South Africa: IEEEExplore Digital Library.

Matt, C., & Curtin, M. (2005). *Brute Force: Cracking the Data Encryption Standard*. New York: Springer.

Michael, A., & Isaac, L. (2010). Quantum Computation and Quantum Information (10th Anniversary Ed.). Cambridge, UK: Cambridge University Press.

Mittelstrass, J. (2000). *Transdisciplinarity - New Structures in Science*. Retrieved from http://xserve02.mpiwg-berlin.mpg.de/ringberg/Talks/mittels%20-%20CHECKOUT/Mittelstrass.html

Mjolsnes, F. (2012). *A Multidisciplinary Introduction to Information Security*. Chapman and Hall/CRC.

Mokiy, V. (2013). *Methodology of transdisciplinarity-4, (solution of complicated multi-factor problems of nature and society)*. Amazon.com.

Moursund, D. (2005). *Introduction to Information and Communication Technology in Education*. Retrieved from http://pages.uoregon.edu/moursund/Books/ICT/ICTBook.html

Nankun, M., & Xiaofeng, L. (2013). An Approach for Designing Neural Cryptography. *Lecture Notes in Computer Science, 7951*, 99–108.

Nankun, M., Xiaofeng, L., & Tingwen, H. (2011). Approach to design neural cryptography: A generalized architecture and a heuristic rule. *Physical Review E: Statistical, Nonlinear, and Soft Matter Physics, 87*(6), 99–108.

Neal, K. (2011). The Uneasy Relationship Between Mathematics and Cryptography. *Notices of the AMS, 54*(8), 972–979.

Nicolescu, B. (2002). Manifesto of Transdisciplinarity. New York: Amazon.com Publisher.

Nicolescu, B. (Ed.). (2008). Transdisciplinarity – Theory and Practice. New York: Amazon.com Publisher.

Poonam, G. (2009). Cryptanalysis of SDES via evolutionary computation techniques. [IJCSIS]. *International Journal of Computer Science and Information Security, 1*(1), 1–7.

Ross, G. (2001). *Security Engineering: A Guide to Building Dependable Distributed Systems*. Wiley Publisher.

Sattar, B., Azhar, H., & Sabiha, F. (2011). Complexity Evaluation of Knapsack Crypto System using Fuzzy Set. *Journal of Basrah Researches (Sciences), 37*(4), 473–480.

Schneider, G., & Gersting, J. (2012). *Invitation to Computer Science*. Amazon.com.

Sergienko, A. (2005). *Quantum Communications and Cryptography*. CRC Press.

Shier, D., & Wallenius, K. (2000). *Applied Mathematical Modeling: Multidisciplinary Approach*. Chapman and Hall/CRC.

Simon, M., Eimear, B., McDowell, J., & Aideen, R. (2011). *Disciplinary Procedures in the statutory Professions*. Amazon.com.

Stinson, D. (2005). *Cryptography: Theory and Practice* (3rd ed.). Chapman and Hall/CRC.

Thomas, J. (1985). *Data Compression: Techniques and Applications*. Lifetime Learning Publications.

Tornea, O., & Borda, M. (2009). DNA Cryptographic Algorithms. *IFMBE Proceedings, 26*, 223–226.

Vacca, J. (Ed.). (2013). *Network and System Security*. Elsevier Inc.

Valerie, W., & Anne, P. (2000). Multidisciplinary Teamworking: Indicators of Good Practice. *Spotlight 77*. Retrieved from http://www.modern-timesworkplace.com/good_reading/GRWhole/Multi-Disciplinary.Teamwork.pdf

Wright, J., & Manic, M. (2010). Neural Network Architecture Selection Analysis with Application to Cryptography Location. In *Proceedings of IEEE World Congress on Computational Intelligence* (WCCI 2010). Barcelona, Spain: IEEExplore Digital Library:Publisher.

Wyn, G. (2010). *The Development of a Discipline: The History of the Political Studies Association*. Wiley Publisher.

ADDITIONAL READING

Dennis, V. (2000), Secure Introduction of One-way Functions. In Proceeding of 13th IEEE Computer Security Foundations Workshop. (pp: 246 – 254), Mordano, Italy. IEEExplore – Digital Library: Publisher.

Gonçal, G. (2010). Computer Science in a Multidisciplinary Environment. Quantum Cryptography and Econophysics. Kochi University of Technology. Available at: http://riunet.upv.es/bitstream/handle/10251/14792/Memoria.pdf?sequence=1

International Atomic Energy Agency (IAEA) (2010), Educational Programme in Nuclear Security. Austria, VIENNA. Published by IAEA.

Jim, V. (2010). Cutting Across the Disciplines, IEEE Computer magazine 43(4), 87-89.

Juan, Z., et al. (2010). A Cross-disciplinary Collaborative Research Platform - Study on Qinghai Lake Joint Research Environment, 2010 Sixth International Conference on Signal-Image Technology and Internet Based Systems (SITIS), (pp: 211 – 216). IEEExplore – Digital Library: Publisher.

Kang, N. (2009). A Pseudo DNA Cryptography Method. Available at: http://arxiv.org/abs/0903.2693

Mazumdar, D., & Raha, S. (2008). Evolution to Revolution: A review on Bioinformatics. *Advanced Modeling and Optimization*, *10*(1), 51–62.

Motohisa, F. (2010). Towards Trasdisciplinary Science and Technology as Emerging Systems Thinking for Service Oriented Society. In Proceeding of 7th International Conference on Service Systems and Service Management (ICSSSM) (pp. 1-5). United State: IEEExplore.

Motohisa, F., & Koichi, H. (2009), Transdisciplinary Approach for Industrial Innovation Management, ICROS-SICE International Joint Conference 2009, (pp: 5117 – 5120), Fukuoka International Congress Center, Japan. IEEExplore Digital Library: Publisher.

Nketiah, E. (2011). Distance Forum: A Multi-disciplinary Book of Scholarly Articles. United State, Author House Publisher.

Renato, V. et al. (2013). Preparing Undergraduate Computer Science Students to Face Intercultural and Multidisciplinary Scenarios. *IEEE Transactions on Professional Communication*, *56*(1).

Shier, D., & Wallenius, K. (1999). *Applied Mathematical Modeling: A Multidisciplinary Approach. United State*. Chapman & Hall /CRC.

Stavroulakis, P., & Stamp, M. (Eds.). (2010). *Handbook of Information and Communication Security*. Germany: Springer-Verlag.

Sumit, G., & Elliot, T. (Eds.). (2010). *Cybercrimes: A Multidisciplinary Analysis*. Berlin, Germany: Springer-Verlag.

Tom, K., & Les, O. (2002). *Wireless Network Security 802.11, Bluetooth and Handheld Devices*. United State. NIST Special Publication.

UNESCO. (2006). *Positive discipline in the inclusive, learning-friendly classroom: a guide for teachers and teacher educators*. Bangkok, Thailand: UNESCO Asia and Pacific Regional Bureau for Educatio.

Wil, P. (2014). Data Scientist: The Engineer of the Future. In K. Mertins et al. (Eds.), *Enterprise Interoperability VI*. Switzerland: Springer International Publishing.

KEY TERMS AND DEFINITIONS

Communication Security: Includes means by which people can share information with varying degrees of certainty that third parties cannot intercept what was said. With many communications taking place over long distance and mediated by technology, and increasing awareness of the importance of interception issues, and technologies are at the heart of this debate.

Cross-Disciplinary: It refers to knowledge that explains aspects of one discipline in terms of another. Common examples of cross-disciplinary approaches are studies of the physics of music or the politics of literature. Or it can be described as (education) linking two or more fields of study.

Disciplinary: A discipline refers to types of knowledge, expertise, skills, people, projects, communities, problems, challenges, studies, inquiry, approaches, and research areas that are strongly associated with academic areas of study (academic disciplines) or areas of professional practice (profession).

Emission Security (EMSEC): Is protection resulting from all measures taken to deny un-

authorized persons information of value which might be derived from intercept and analysis of compromising emanations from crypto equipment, automated information systems, and telecommunications systems.

Information Security (InfoSec): Is the practice of defending information from unauthorized access, use, disclosure, disruption, modification, perusal, inspection, recording or destruction.

Interdisciplinary: Refers to new knowledge extensions that exist between or beyond existing academic disciplines or professions. The new knowledge may be claimed by members of none, or one, both, or an emerging new academic discipline or profession.

Multidisciplinary: Refers to knowledge associated with more than one existing academic discipline or profession. A multidisciplinary community or project is made up of people from different disciplines and professions who are engaged in working together as equal stakeholders in addressing a common challenge.

Traffic-Flow Security: Is measures that conceal the presence and properties of valid messages on a network. They include the protection resulting from features, inherent to some crypto equipment, that conceal the presence of valid messages on a communications circuit, normally achieved by causing the circuit to appear busy at all times.

Transc-Disciplinary: Is approach for allowing members of an educational team to integrate their knowledge and skills, collaborate with other members, and collectively determine the services that most would a benefit. This approach can be described in more detail as: "approach which requires share roles and systematically (of the team members) cross discipline boundaries".

Transmission Security (TRANSEC): Is the component of communications security that results from the application of measures designed to protect transmissions from interception and exploitation by means other than cryptanalysis (e.g. frequency hopping and spread spectrum).

Chapter 2
Soft Computing–Based Information Security

Eva Volna
University of Ostrava, Czech Republic

Tomas Sochor
University of Ostrava, Czech Republic

Clyde Meli
University of Malta, Malta

Zuzana Kominkova Oplatkova
Tomas Bata University in Zlin, Czech Republic

ABSTRACT

This chapter deals with using soft computing methods in information security. It is engaged in two big areas: (1) information security and spam detection and (2) cryptography. The latter field is covered by a proposal of an artificial neural network application, which represents a way of further development in this area. Such a neural network can be practically used in the area of cryptography. It is a new approach, which presents a development of automatic neural networks design. The approach is based on evolutionary algorithms, which allow evolution of architecture and weights simultaneously. A spam filter is an automated tool to recognize spam so as to prevent its delivery. The chapter contains a survey of current and proposed spam filtering techniques with particular emphasis on how well they work. The primary focus is spam filtering in email, but the role of the spam filter is only one component of a large and complex information universe. The chapter also includes experimental demonstrations.

INTRODUCTION TO INFORMATION SECURITY AND SPAM DETECTION

As defined in (Siripanwattana & Srinoy, 2008), intrusion detection is "the process of monitoring the events occurring in a computer system or network and analyzing them for signs of intrusions. It is also defined as attempts to compromise the confidentiality, integrity, availability, or to bypass the security mechanisms of a computer or network."

Intrusion detection is a critical component of secure information systems. Many approaches have been proposed which include statistical, machine learning (Lane, 2000), data mining (Lee, Stolfo & Mok 2000) and immunological

DOI: 10.4018/978-1-4666-5808-0.ch002

inspired techniques (Dagupta & Gonzalez 2002). Identification of suspicious activities is important before they have an impact; to perform situational assessment and to respond in a more timely and effective manner. Events that may not be actual security violations but those that do not fit in the normal usage profile of a user may be termed as suspicious events. Monitoring of suspicious activities may help in finding a possible intrusion. There are two main intrusion detection systems. The first one, anomaly intrusion detection system, is based on the profiles of normal behaviors of users or applications and checks whether the system is being used in a different manner (Lee, Stolfo & Mok, 2000). The second one is called misuse intrusion detection system that collects attack signatures, compares a behavior with these attack signatures, and signals intrusion when there is a match.

Generally, there are four categories of attacks (Alves at al., 2004): 1) DoS (denial-of-service), for example ping-of-death, teardrop, smurf, SYN flood, and the similar, 2) R2L: unauthorized access from a remote machine, for example guessing password, 3) U2R: unauthorized access to local super user (root) privileges, for example, various "buffer overflow" attacks, 4) PROBING: surveillance and other probing, for example, port-scan, ping-sweep, etc. Some of the attacks (such as DoS, and PROBING) may use hundreds of network packets or connections, while on the other hand attacks like U2R and R2L typically use only one or a few connections.

The email spam was defined at the Text Retrieval Conference (Cormack & Lynam, 2005) as "Unsolicited, unwanted email that was sent indiscriminately, directly or indirectly, by a sender having no current relationship with the recipient." We generalize the definition of spam to capture the essential adversarial nature of spam and spam abatement (Cormack, 2007).

Spam: Unwanted communication intended to be delivered to an indiscriminate target, directly or indirectly, notwithstanding measures to prevent its delivery.

Spam filter: An automated technique to identify spam for the purpose of preventing its delivery.

While this article confines itself to email spam, we note that the definitions above apply to any number of communication media, including text and voice messages (Dantu & Kolan, 2005), social networks (Zinman & Donath, 2007), and blog comments (Cormack, Gómez Hidalgo, & Sanz, 2007). It applies also to web spam, which uses a search engine as its delivery mechanism (Webb, Caverloo, & Pu, 2006).

INTRODUCTION TO CRYPTOGRAPHY

The cryptography deals with building such systems of security of news that secure any from reading of trespasser. Systems of data privacy are called the cipher systems. The files of rules are made for encryption of every news is called the cipher key. Encryption is a process, in which the open text is transformed, e.g. message to cipher text according to rules. Cryptanalysis of the news is the inverse process, in which the receiver of the cipher transforms it to the original text. The cipher key must have several heavy attributes. The best one is the singularity of encryption and cryptanalysis. The open text is usually composed of international alphabet characters, digits and punctuation marks. The cipher text has the same composition as the open text. Very often we find only characters of international alphabet or only digits. The reason for it is the easier transport per media. The next cipher systems are the matter of the historical sequence: transposition ciphers, substitution ciphers, cipher tables and codes.

Simultaneously with secrecy of information the tendency for reading the cipher news without knowing the cipher key was evolved. Cipher keys were watched very closely. The main goal of cryptology is to guess the cipher news and to reconstruct the used keys with the help of good analysis of cipher news. It makes use of mathematical statistics, algebra, mathematical linguistics, etc., as well as known mistakes made by ciphers too. The legality of the open text and the applied cipher key are reflected in every cipher system. Improving the cipher key helps to decrease this legality. The safety of the cipher system lies in its immunity against deciphering.

The goal of cryptanalysis is to make it possible to take a cipher text and reproduce the original plain text without the corresponding key. Two major techniques used in encryption are symmetric and asymmetric encryption. In symmetric encryption, two parties share a single encryption-decryption key (Khaled, Noaman, & Jalab, 2005). The sender encrypts the original message (P), which is referred to as plain text, using a key (K) to generate apparently random nonsense, referred to as cipher text (C), i.e.:

$$C = \text{Encrypt}\ (K, P) \tag{1}$$

Once the cipher text is produced, it may be transmitted. Upon receipt, the cipher text can be transformed back to the original plain text by using a decryption algorithm and the same key that was used for encryption, which can be expressed as follows:

$$P = \text{Dencrypt}\ (K, C) \tag{2}$$

In asymmetric encryption, two keys are used, one key for encryption and another key for decryption. The length of cryptographic key is almost always measured in bits. The more bits that a particular cryptographic algorithm allows in the key, the more keys are possible and the more secure the algorithm becomes. The following key size recommendations should be considered when reviewing protection (Ferguson, Schneier, & Kohno, 2012):

How to Protect Yourself

Assuming you have chosen an open, standard algorithm, the following recommendations should be considered when reviewing algorithms (adapted from https://www.owasp.org/index.php/Guide_to_Cryptography):

Symmetric key:

- Key sizes of 128 bits (standard for SSL) are sufficient for most applications.
- Consider 168 or 256 bits for secure systems such as large financial transactions.

Asymmetric key:

- Key sizes of 1280 bits are sufficient for most personal applications.
- 1536 bits should be acceptable today for most secure applications.
- 2048 bits should be considered for highly protected applications.

Hashes:

- Hash sizes of 128 bits (standard for SSL) are sufficient for most applications.
- Consider 168 or 256 bits for secure systems, as many hash functions are currently being revised (see above).

NIST and other standards bodies will provide up to date guidance on suggested key sizes.

SOFT COMPUTING METHODS

Prior to 1994 prof. Lotfi. A. Zadeh (1994) first defined soft computing as follows:

Basically, soft computing is not a homogeneous body of concepts and techniques. Rather, it is a partnership of distinct methods that in one way or another conform to its guiding principle. At this juncture, the dominant aim of soft computing is to exploit the tolerance for imprecision and uncertainty to achieve tractability, robustness and low solutions cost. The principal constituents of soft computing are fuzzy logic, neurocomputing, and probabilistic reasoning, with the latter subsuming genetic algorithms, belief networks, chaotic systems, and parts of learning theory. In the partnership of fuzzy logic, neurocomputing, and probabilistic reasoning, fuzzy logic is mainly concerned with imprecision and approximate reasoning; neurocomputing with learning and curve-fitting; and probabilistic reasoning with uncertainty and belief propagation.

Soft computing could therefore be seen as a series of techniques and methods so that real practical situations could be dealt with in the same way as humans deal with them, i.e. on the basis of intelligence, common sense, consideration of analogies, approaches, etc. In this sense, soft computing is a family of problem-resolution methods headed by approximate reasoning and functional and optimization approximation methods, including search methods. Soft computing is therefore the theoretical basis for the area of intelligent systems and it is evident that the difference between the area of artificial intelligence and that of intelligent systems is that the first is based on hard computing and the second on soft computing. Soft computing is still growing and developing.

From this other viewpoint on a second level, soft computing can be then expanded into other components, which contribute to a definition by extension, such as the one first given. From the beginning (Bonissone, 2002), the components considered to be the most important in this second level are probabilistic reasoning, fuzzy logic and fuzzy sets, neural networks, and genetic algorithms, which because of their interdisciplinary, applications and results immediately stood out over other methodologies such as the previously mentioned chaos theory, evidence theory, etc. The popularity of genetic algorithms, together with their proven efficiency in a wide variety of areas and applications, their attempt to imitate natural creatures (e.g. plants, animals, humans) which are clearly soft (i.e. flexible, adaptable, creative, intelligent, etc.), and especially the extensions and different versions, transform this fourth second-

level ingredient into the well-known evolutionary algorithms which consequently comprise the fourth fundamental component of soft computing, as shown in the following diagram, see Figure 1.

Fuzzy Logic

Fuzzy Logic, the core of the Fuzzy Computing, can handle qualitative values instead of quantitative values. It can define the so called linguistic variables, instead of the classical numeric variables, and can perform computing with theses variables, using fuzzy rules, simulating in a certain way the human reasoning processes. Incomplete or uncertain information can be used for computing, like:

- "This man is tall."
- "That object is heavy."
- "Warm this food a little."
- "Increase the speed a lot."

In all those cases, the meaning of tall, heavy, a little and a lot are relevant to solve the problem, and not the precise numerical value. To represent and compute with that kind of statements, daily used in human communication, we can use Fuzzy Sets.

The classical logic defines the classical sets. A set is a collection of objects of any kind. In a classical set, a given object belongs or not to a set. There are operations that can be applied to

Figure 1. What does soft computing mean? (adapted from http://modo.ugr.es)

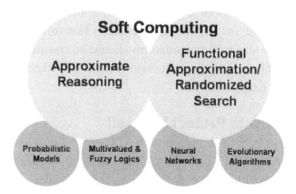

sets: union, intersection and complementation. Defining a set is defining a membership function F(x), which returns {0,1} for a x meaning that x belongs (1) or do not belongs (0) to the set. Fuzzy approach extends the classical sets by letting the F(x) function returns a value in the [0,1] range. A given x value can belong to the set in some certain degree. Fuzzy sets are represented by their membership function. The Figure 2 shows a fuzzy set A with its membership function. In this example, we can say that 10 does not belong to the set A, 20 belongs with a membership degree 0.5, 25 belongs with a membership degree of 0.75 and 40 belongs with a membership degree 1. Fuzzy operators on fuzzy sets are defined to perform union, intersection and complementation. Those operators match the linguistic meaning of AND, OR and NOT, respectively.

In particular, fuzzy logic allows us to use linguistic variables to model dynamic systems by a set of fuzzy rules. Each rule consists of a set of linguistic variables. These variables take fuzzy values, which are characterized by fuzzy membership functions. In addition, there is a reasoning mechanism, fuzzy inference engine, which operates on the fuzzy rules based on the

Figure 2. Fuzzy set A with its membership function. (Adapted from http://www.aforgenet.com/articles/fuzzy_computing_basics/)

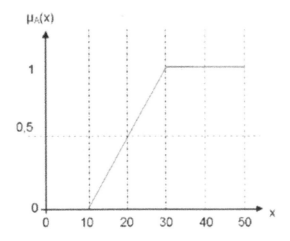

generalized modus-ponens. A comprehensive review of fuzzy logic and fuzzy computing can be found in (Ruspini, Bonissone, & Pedycz, 1998).

Artificial Neural Network

An Artificial Neural Network (ANN) is the information-processing paradigm that is inspired by the way biological nervous systems, such as the brain, process information. The key element of this paradigm is the structure of the information processing system. It is composed of a large number of highly interconnected processing elements (neurones) working in unison to solve specific problems. ANNs, like people, learn by example. An ANN is configured for a specific application, such as pattern recognition or data classification, through a learning process. Learning in biological systems involves adjustments to the synaptic connections that exist between the neurones. This is true of ANNs as well.

A neural network with backpropagation training algorithm is one of the most complex neural networks for supervised learning. Regarding topology, the network belongs to a multilayer feedforward neural network. See Figure 3 left side (Volna, 2000), usually a fully connected variant is used, so that each neuron from the *n-th* layer is connected to all neurons in the (*n+1*)-*th* layer, but it is not necessary and in general some connections may be missing – see dashed lines, however, there are no connections between neurons of the same layer. A subset of input units has no input connections from other units; their states are fixed by the problem. Another subset of units is designated as output units; their states are considered the result of the computation. Units that are neither input nor output are known as hidden units.

A basic computational element is often called a neuron (Figure 3 right), node or unit (Fausett, 1994). It receives input from some other units, or perhaps from an external source. Each input has an associated weight *w*, which can be modified so as to model synaptic learning. The unit

Figure 3. A general three layer neural network (left), A simple artificial neuron (right, adapted from http://encefalus.com/neurology-biology/neural-networks-real-neurons)

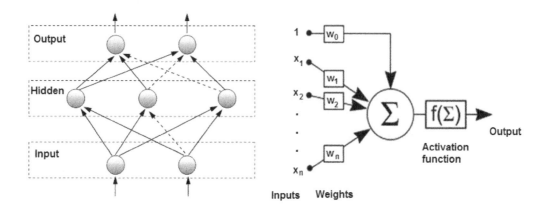

computes some function f of the weighted sum of its inputs (3):

$$\text{Output} = f\left(\sum_{i=0}^{n} x_i w_i\right) \qquad (3)$$

Its output, in turn, can serve as input to other units. The weighted sum is called the net input to unit i. Note that w_{ij} refers to the weight from unit j to unit i (not the other way around). The function f is the unit's activation function. Backpropagation algorithm usually uses a logistic sigmoid activation function (4) for values of t in the range of real numbers from $-\infty$ to $+\infty$.

$$f(t) = \frac{1}{1+e^{-t}} \qquad (3)$$

Backpropagation algorithm belongs to a group called "gradient descent methods". An intuitive definition is that such an algorithm searches for the global minimum of the weight landscape by descending downhill in the most precipitous direction. The initial position is set at random selecting the weights of the network from some range (typically from -1 to 1 or from 0 to 1).

Considering the different points, it is clear, that backpropagation using a fully connected neural network is not a deterministic algorithm. The basic backpropagation algorithm can be summed up in the following equation (the *delta rule*) for the change to the weight w_{ji} from node i to node j (5):where the local gradient δ_j is defined as follows (Seung, 2002):

1. If node j is an output node, then δ_j is the product of $\varphi'(v_j)$ and the error signal e_j, where $\varphi(\_)$ is the logistic function and v_j is the total input to node j (i.e. $\Sigma_i w_{ji} y_i$), and e_j is the error signal for node j (i.e. the difference between the desired output and the actual output);

2. If node j is a hidden node, then δ_j is the product of $\varphi'(v_j)$ and the weighted sum of the δ's computed for the nodes in the next hidden or output layer that are connected to node j.

The actual formula is $\delta_j = \varphi'(v_j)$ & $\text{Sigma}_k \delta_k w_{kj}$ where k ranges over those nodes for which w_{kj} is non-zero (i.e. nodes k that actually have connections from node j. The δ_k values have already

Table 1. Equation 5

Weight Change		Learning Rate		Local Gradient		Input Signal to Node j
Δw_{ji}	$=$	η	x	δ_j	x	y_i

been computed as they are in the output layer (or a layer closer to the output layer than node j).

Evolutionary Algorithms

In artificial intelligence, an evolutionary algorithm is a subset of evolutionary computation, a generic population-based metaheuristic optimization algorithm. An evolutionary algorithm uses mechanisms inspired by biological evolution, such as reproduction, mutation, recombination, and selection. Candidate solutions to the optimization problem play the role of individuals in a population, and the fitness function determines the environment within which the solutions exist. Evolution of the population then takes place after the repeated application of operators (mutation, recombination etc.). Artificial evolution describes a process involving individual evolutionary algorithms.

Evolutionary algorithms implement the following biological processes (Bäck, Fogel, & Michalewicz, 1997):

- Generate the initial population of individuals randomly - first generation.
- Evaluate the fitness of each individual in that population.
- Repeat on this generation until termination (time limit, sufficient fitness achieved, etc.):
  ◦ Select the best-fit individuals for reproduction – parents.

  ◦ Breed new individuals through cross-over and mutation operations to give birth to offspring.
  ◦ Evaluate the individual fitness of new individuals.
  ◦ Replace least-fit population with new individuals.

Evolutionary algorithm techniques differ in the implementation details and the nature of the particular applied problem. Some of them are the following (Ashlock, 2006):

- **Genetic Algorithm:** GA seeks the solution of a problem in the form of strings of numbers (traditionally binary, although the best representations are usually those that reflect something about the problem being solved), by applying operators such as recombination and mutation (sometimes one, sometimes both). This type of EA is often used in optimization problems.
- **Evolutionary Programming:** Similar to genetic programming, but the structure of the program is fixed and its numerical parameters are allowed to evolve.
- **Gene Expression Programming:** Like genetic programming, GEP also evolves computer programs but it explores a genotype-phenotype system, where computer programs of different sizes are encoded in linear chromosomes of fixed length.
- **Evolution Strategy:** Works with vectors of real numbers as representations of solu-

tions, and typically uses self-adaptive mutation rates.

- **Differential Evolution:** Based on vector differences and is therefore primarily suited for numerical optimization problems etc.

CRYPTOGRAPHY BASED ON NEURAL NETWORK

Neural cryptography (Kinzel & Kanter, 2002), (Kinzel, 2006) is based on the effect that two neural networks are able to synchronize by mutual learning (Ruttor, Kanter, & Kinzel, 2006). In each step of this online procedure they receive a common input pattern and calculate their output. Then, both neural networks use those outputs present by their partner to adjust their own weights. This process leads to fully synchronized weight vectors.

Synchronization of neural networks is, in fact, a complex dynamical process. The weights of the networks perform random walks, which are driven by a competition of attractive and repulsive stochastic forces. Two neural networks can increase the attractive effect of their moves by cooperating with each other. However, a third network, which is only trained by the other two, clearly has a disadvantage because it cannot skip some repulsive steps. Therefore, bidirectional synchronization is much faster than unidirectional learning (Ruttor, Reents, & Kinzel, 2004).

Two partners A and B want to exchange a secret message over a public channel. In order to protect the content against an attacker T, who is listening to the communication, A encrypts the message, but B needs A's secret key over the public channel (Kinzel & Kanter, 2002). This can be achieved by synchronizing two TPMs (Three Parity Machines), one for A and one for B, respectively. After synchronization, the system generates a pseudorandom bit sequence which passes test on random numbers. When another network is trained on this bit sequence it is not possible to extract some information on the statistical properties of the sequence. The TPMs generate a secret key and also encrypt and decrypt a secret message (Prabakaran, Loganathan, & Vivekanandan, 2008).

In this chapter, we present an encryption system based on an Artificial Neural Network (ANN). ANN is used to construct an efficient encryption system by using a permanently changing key. The ANN topology is an important issue, as it depends on the application the system is designed for. Consequently, since our application is a computation problem, we have used a multi-layer topology. In the present chapter, Backpropagation network is proposed for the encryption-and-decryption process. Neural networks offer a very powerful and general framework for representing non-linear mapping from several input variables to several output variables. The process to determining the values of these parameters on the basis of a data set is referred to as learning or training, and so the data set is generally referred to as a training set. A neural network can be viewed as suitable choice for the functional forms used for encryption and decryption operations.

Design on the Proposed ANN-Based Encryption System

Every practical encryption system consists of four fundamental parts (Garfinger, 1995), see Figure 4:

- The message that you wish to encrypt (called the *plain text*).

Figure 4. A simple example of the encryption system

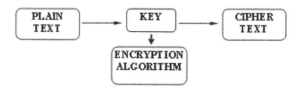

- The message after it is encrypted (called the *cipher text*).
- The encryption algorithm.
- The *key* (or keys), which is used by encryption algorithm.

In this chapter, we conducted an experimental study with using neural network in cryptography. Thus, it means:

- To design the topology of the neural network.
- To design the method of training algorithm of the neural network.
- To design the training set for training.

We successfully used neural networks as an encryption and decryption algorithm in cryptography. Parameters of both adapted neural networks were then included into cryptography keys. Multilayer neural networks were used, which were adapted by backpropagation. Both networks were trained on binary representations of symbols. In each training set, chains of numbers of the plain text are equivalent to binary values of their ASCII code, chains of letters of the plain text are equivalent to their binary value, which are 96 less than their ASCII code, each chain of some punctuation symbol of the plain text is equivalent to a binary value of ASCII code of space (e.g. 32), and chains of others chars of the plain text are equivalent to zero. Then, the cipher text is a random chain of 6 bits.

Application of Evolutionary Algorithm to Neural Network Topology

The neural network topology should correspond to the complexity of task, e.g. the number of training pattern, its inputs and outputs and the structure of relations that are described. By the adaptation of a small net (this adaptation) is stopped in local minimum and the network must be enlarged by other units. Conversely, the big network allows finding the global minimum of error function, however, the computing absorption is increased. The found configuration of network usually generalises the training pattern including its inaccuracies to a great extent and for untaught patterns, which gives false results. Topology of each neural network is based on their training sets (see Table 2). In the encryption process, the input message is divided into 6-bit data sets and also 6-bit sets are produced after the encryption process. Thus, both systems were designed as follows: 6 units on the input layer and 6 output units. There is no predetermined number of units in the hidden layer.

Among the stochastic evolutionary algorithms the genetic algorithms are used for optimisation of the designed neural network topology. One of the main conditions for representation of variables is the appropriate representation of variables with chain of characters (e.g. bit chain with 0 and 1) and the speed of calculation of fitness function in the given point. We proposed the following method appropriate to neural network topology optimisation (Volna, 2000):

At first, we must propose maximal architecture of neural network (e.g. maximum number of hidden units) before the main calculation. Every individual in the population is characterised by its representation scheme. To optimise the population is it necessary to solve the defined problems. Thereafter the process of genetic algorithms is applied. The algorithm ended, when the population achieves the maximal generation.

Three digits are generated for every connection coming out from each input and hidden unit. In case the connection does not exist, three zeros are attached to the given place. To every non zero weight value numerated in the following way is thus assigned (6):

$$w_{i,j,k,l} = \alpha \times [e_2 \, (e_1 \times 2^1 + e_0 \times 2^0)] \tag{6}$$

Table 2. The training set

The Plain Text			The Cipher Text	The Plain Text			The Cipher Text
Char	Ascii Code (Dec)	The Chain of Bits	The Chain of Bits	Char	Ascii Code (Dec)	The Chain of Bits	The Chain of Bits
0	48	110000	111111	h	104	001000	010010
1	49	110001	110010	i	105	001001	001000
2	50	110010	101100	j	106	001010	011110
3	51	110011	111010	k	107	001011	001001
4	52	110100	101010	l	108	001100	010110
5	53	110101	100011	m	109	001101	011000
6	54	110110	111000	n	110	001110	011100
7	55	110111	000111	o	111	001111	101000
8	56	111000	010101	p	112	010000	001010
9	57	111001	110011	q	113	010001	010011
punct.	32	100000	101111	r	114	010010	010111
others	0	000000	011101	s	115	010011	100111
a	97	000001	000010	t	116	010100	001111
b	98	000010	100110	u	117	010101	010100
c	99	000011	001011	v	118	010110	001100
d	100	000100	011010	w	119	010111	100100
e	101	000101	100000	x	120	011000	011011
f	102	000110	001110	y	121	011001	010001
g	103	000111	100101	z	122	011010	001101

where

$$w_{i,j,k,l} = w(x_{i,j}, x_{k,l})$$

is the weight value between the j-th unit in the i-th layer and the l-th unit in the k-th layer,

α is a parameter of learning

e_i $i = 0, 1)$ is a randomly generated digit

e_2 is a sign bit: if $e_2=0$ resp. $e_2=1$ the expression is positive resp. negative

Every population is then described by chromosomes of an individual, ordered descending according of the value to its fitness function. See Figure 5.

For every scheme the number of connections between units, and number of hidden units are calculated. Error (E) between the desired and the real output is calculated in a procedure which implements the forward distribution of signals in multi layer neural network (Fausett,1994) . On the basis of it, these entries for every topology of the appropriate individual its fitness function is calculated as follows (Equation 7):

$$Fitness_i = (E_i + k \times hidden\_units_i) \qquad (7)$$

for $i = 1, ...,N$, where

Figure 5. Population of chromosomes

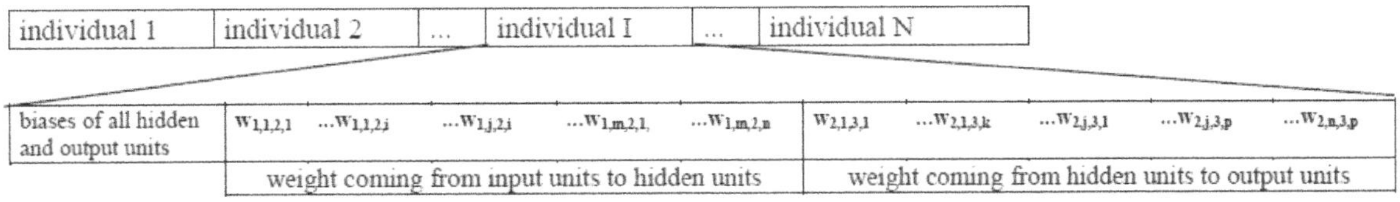

individual 1	individual 2	...	individual I	...	individual N

biases of all hidden and output units	$w_{1,1,2,1}$ ...$w_{1,1,2,j}$	...$w_{1,j,2,i}$	...$w_{1,m,2,1}$	...$w_{1,m,2,n}$	$w_{2,1,3,1}$ ...$w_{2,1,3,k}$	...$w_{2,j,3,1}$	...$w_{2,j,3,p}$	...$w_{2,n,3,p}$
	weight coming from input units to hidden units				weight coming from hidden units to output units			

E is error for the i-th network;

hidden_units$_i$ are the number of hidden units for the i-th network;

k is a constant;

N is the number of individuals in the population.

Value of a constant k is assigned with the dependency of solution tasks. All calculated fitness function values of the two consecutive generations are sorted descending and the neural network representation attached to the first half creates the new generation. For each fitness function is calculated the probability of reproduction its existing individual by standard method (Bäck, Fogel, & Michalewicz, 1997). The main *crossover* runs in two following steps: we choose two suitable parents to crossover randomly. Next we generate two numbers randomly. The first of them is from the above limitation of number of biases (e.g. coded biases values). The other is from the above limitation of number of weight connections (e.g. coded weight values). The chosen individuals exchange their substrings of bias and weight connections from the places defined in substrings. If the input condition of *mutation* is fulfilled, one of the individual is randomly chosen and in its genetic representation is randomly chosen in one place. The main mutation has one of the two forms and runs in two following steps: if a weight connection in this place does not exist, it is added and at the same time its weight value is randomly generated. If a connection in this place exists, its weight value contains only zeros and this connection is not defined anymore. After application of genetic operators (crossover and mutation), we have to check whether the new neural network representation has the following problems: (1) the unit from an input layer does not transfer its input signal; (2) the unit from an output layer does not accept the input signal. If it has some given problem, its fitness function value equals zero. Provided that during maximal number of generations no optimal solution is found (primarily with adaptation), the best found network architecture is adapted with backpropagation rule (eq. 5).

Cryptographic Key

The security for all encryption and decryption systems is based on a cryptographic key. The simple systems use a single key for both encryption and decryption. The good systems use two keys. A message encrypted with one key can be decrypted only with the other key. If the neural network is used as an encryption and also a decryption algorithm, their keys have been adapted by neural networks´ parameters; which are their topologies (architecture) and their configurations (weight values on connections in the given order). We can successfully use the backpropagation neural network. Topology of this neural network is based on the training set (see Table 2). Thus, both neural network topology as encryption and decryption system were the following: 6 - ? - 6, where symbol „? " is a unknown number of hidden units. The number of units in the hidden layer is suggested using the above described method. Generally, each key is written as follow (Volna at al., 2012):

```
[Input, Hidden, Output, Weights com-
ing from the input units, Weights
coming from the hidden units] where

Input is the number of input units;

Hidden is the number of hidden units;

Output is the number of output units;

Weights coming from the input units
are weight values coming from the in-
put units to hidden units in a pre-
defined order;

Weights coming from the hidden units
are weight values coming from the
hidden units to output units in a
predefined order.
```

Parameter values in our experimental study are the following:

- Maximum number of generation: 5000;
- Probability of mutation: 0.04;

- α from (6): 0.1;
- k from (7): 0.3;
- Number of individuals in the population (N): 100.
- Number of input units: 6;
- Number of input units: 6;
- A sigmoid activate function;
- η from (5): 0.3;
- Desired accuracy of adaptation is 0.01;
- Maximum number of training cycles of backpropagation is 5000.

In the cases of encryption and also for decryption tasks, the best individual in population represents neural network architecture 6 - 4 - 6 (e.g 6 input, 4 hidden, and 6 output units). After termination of evolutionary algorithm, the best individual in population was adapted by backpropagation rule (5). History of both Error functions (E) is shown in Figure 6. There are shown average values of error function, because adaptation with backpropagation algorithm was applied 10 times in each calculation. Other numerical simulations give very similar results.

Figure 6. The history of error functions

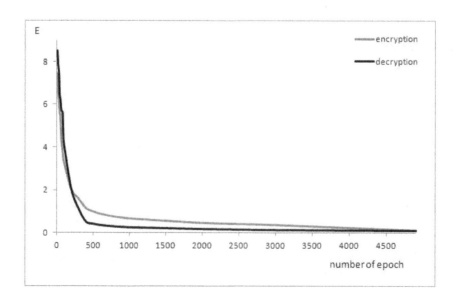

Configuration of the adapted network, which is part of the encryption cryptographic key, is evident from the graphs in the upper part of Figure 7.

Configuration of the adapted network, which is part of the decryption cryptographic key is evident from the graphs in the lower part of Figure 7.

Sending and Receiving Messages

In this model, a 6-bit plain text is entered ($N = 6$) and a 6-bit cipher text is the output (2^N).

Imagine that we want to send the following message: "The university is the highest educational institution."

The first steps of our encryption process are to convert all uppercase letters to lowercase and to replace all punctuation symbols by a space. After this process, our message is the following: "the university is the highest educational institution "

Then we replace all two spaces by one space, we get the following plain text: "the university is the highest educational institution "

The plain text is coded into the chain:

01010000100000010110000001010011100
0100101011000010101001001001100100101
0100011001100000001001010011100000010
100001000000101100000001000001001000
111001000000101010011010100100000000010
1000100010101010001100000101010000010010
0111110011100000010011001000000100100
11100100110101000010010101010001010101010
100001001001111001110100000

Now, we break it down into blocks ($N = 6$), thus:

010100 001000 000101 100000 010101 001110
001001 010110 000101 010010 010011 001001
010100 011001 100000 001001 010011 100000
010100 001000 000101 100000 001000 001001
000111 001000 000101 010011 010100 100000

Figure 7. Network configuration of the encryption (upper part) and decryption system (lower part)

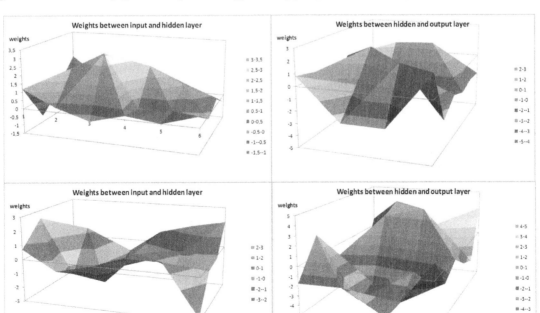

000101 000100 010101 000011 000001 010100
001001 001111 001110 000001 001100 100000
001001 001110 010011 010100 001001 010100
010101 010100 001001 001111 001110 100000

The corresponding cipher text is the following:

001111010010100001011110101000111000
010000011001000000101111001110010000
111101000110111100100010011110111001
111010010100000101111010010001000100
101010010100000100111001111101111110000
001101001010000101100001000111100010001
010000111000000100101101011110010001
110010011100111100100000111010100001
11100100010100001110010111

The encrypted data will then be transmitted
to the recipient.

Encryption Discussion and Remarks

We have tested the behaviour of the neural network described in the previous section so that we have generated messages (plain text) that were encrypted via the first adapted neural network. Then we have received some cipher text, which represented some input into the decryption process carried out via the second adapted neural network. Each obtained cipher text was compared with the original message after its pre-processing. The whole procedure is demonstrated in Figure 8. We found that:

- The neural network works reliably and absolutely no errors are found in the outputs during encryption;
- The neural network also works reliably during the decryption process, which is the reverse of the encryption process.

Figure 8. Tested process of a behaviour of neural networks

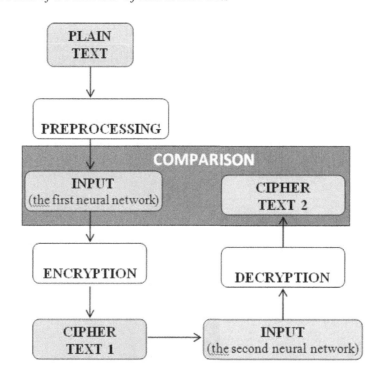

This model presents an attempt to design an encryption system based on artificial neural networks of the backpropagation type. The proposed ANN has been tested for various numbers of plain text. The simulation results have shown very good results.

MODERN APPROACH TO SPAM DETECTION

Not only the security of the transmitted data that can be addressed by the above described encryption is an issue in respect to information security. An important part of security issues are those associated to service security and availability. Among them the protection against unsolicited messages is one of key challenges.

Spam in the sense described in the Introduction (i.e. only email spam) is a phenomenon well known to the majority of electronic mail users in the Internet. spam itself does not represent direct security threat but due to the fact that it is closely associated with other threats (virus and malware attacks, phishing, cross-scripting of www pages etc.) it is considered to be a part of security issues and its elimination to be a part of security measures.

SPAM Detection Principles

Fighting against spam is a complex task performed by numerous e-mail server owners as well as by e-mail end users with various level of success. Its complexity is due to the changing nature of spam messages and permanently developing ways of spam delivery. Spam suppression is usually based on spam detection and subsequent removal or putting-aside of spam messages. Direct removal of spam messages is used rather seldom because it could cause undesired and potentially irreversible removing of a legal message in case of erroneous (so-called "false-positive") spam detection. On the other hand this approach results in subsequent increase of message-handling overhead.

Conventional approaches to the spam detection can be classified into two major categories:

- Detection based on searching the message contents and subsequent filtering including formal conditions (HTML structures, colour combination etc.),
- Detection based on message handling and behaviour during message transport usually applied before message delivery (e.g. greylisting and blacklisting).

The nature of spam detection problem always requires certain level of self-adaptation to be reliable in long run as mentioned further. There are several reasons why it is so difficult to find any satisfactory and persistent solution of spam elimination. The dominant role is played by the vague definition of "unsolicitedness" and its (user-) relativity (Lueg, 2005). Also the fact that both contents and form of unsolicited e-mail messages change continuously makes the problem difficult. The continuous change does not apply only to the message contents and form (and the source of course) of unsolicited messages but the way of message delivery can vary, too.

There are some recent data showing that the total number of spam starts decreasing (Symantec, 2009 - 2012). Despite this fact and bearing in mind that such trend is not necessarily permanent and usually is reflected by the similar tendency in individual SMTP servers) the spam detection remains to be an important part of the security of email services.

Contents-Searching Methods of SPAM Detection

The oldest approach to spam detection is based on searching form certain patterns (e.g. character strings) in the message body (or contents). Therefore such methods are known as "content-based" ones. The obvious weakness of such approach consists in the fact that the patterns should be kept up-to-date to keep reasonable efficiency of search. The detection of a specific string can be misled by replacing certain characters by similar ones (e.g. "A" with two opposite slashes "/\") too.

The efficiency of the content-based spam detection varies much and it is strongly dependent on regular updates of search patterns that become more and more complex. Therefore the detection also becomes more and more resource demanding. Due to the fact it is often combined with other protection mechanisms, either spam detection before delivery, as described in the following part, or more general protecting measures like IPS. The main purpose of such combination is that the costly content-based search is applied only to certain (usually significantly smaller) subset of all incoming messages after rough filtering by IPS and/or other less resource-demanding spam detection methods like greylisting. The common layout of the spam protection is illustrated in Figure 9 where components of the SMTP reception at the SMTP server of the University of Ostrava are shown.

The efficiency of the main components of spam detection in Figure 9 (i.e. Postgrey where greylisting is used, and spam scanner where content-based search using Amavis and VirusBuster are used) has been studied for several years. The impact of implementation of both main components of the spam detection illustrated above is shown in Figure 9. It can be seen that the majority of spam is detected (and immediately refused) by Postgrey. But the smaller part of spam detected by Amavis and VirusBuster is not less significant because the content-based search processes only those messages that are not detected as spam by Postgrey.

BRIEF SPAM FIGHTING HISTORY OVERVIEW

Early Email Spam Detection with Primitive Filters

Initial spam detection software in the era of first spam blockers focused to simple searching through files for a text pattern such as 'Call now'. Most of these tools were typically home-brewed. Some tools used the mail processing software procmail. A few commercial solutions were sold at that time with a subscription service. Some email clients like Microsoft Outlook detected well-known

Figure 9. Spam detection components (University of Ostrava)

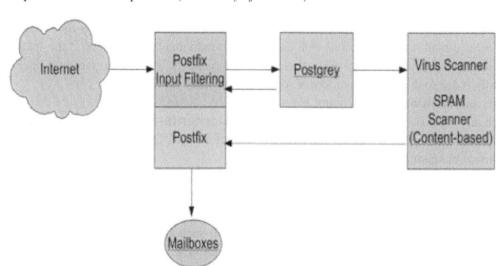

spammer sender email addresses using a simple list. But this was not a scalable solution, around 1997 spammers escalated their war using new ways to obfuscate their messages and most filters resulted ineffective, and this marked the end of primitive filters.

BLACKLISTING

Blacklisting (Levine, 2010) was the next step ahead in spam blocking. A blacklist is a database containing information about blacklisted entries. Back in 1997 Paul Vixie developed the first free subscription-based Real-time Blackhole List (RBL) called the MAPS RBL. It blocked any traffic from a certain known spammer network. This can be thought of an Internet "death sentence". Blacklisted networks can ask for removal, but this depends upon the maintainer, who might ignore the removal request at times. The blacklist causes traffic sourced from the spammer network to be dropped by any system utilising the blacklist, creating what was called an *"intentional network outage"*. Around 2001 other anti-spam RBL's started being created. These had different definitions of what makes a network a spammer network. Some blocked open mail relays (mailservers which anyone could use to send email) while others blocked mail servers after they had been used to send spam whether they were open relays or not. Others blocked spamware providers. Most RBL's work using DNS lookups (which is the most efficient way to distribute the blacklist), where the client checks the source of an email message and looks up this ip within the RBL's DNS, thus they are sometimes called DNS blacklists (DNSBLs). Some of these include MAPS RBL, Spamhaus RBL, SORBS, SPEWS and Spamcop. Spamcop and Spamhaus target spam sources. Users can use Spamcop.Net to report spam emails, and their website will find the source IP of the email spam. Some have closed down, e.g. ORBS. Nowadays MAPS RBL is called an IP Reputation Service

("Trend Micro Email Reputation Services," n.d.) and it is run by Trend Micro. It lists spam rates for different countries. As at October 2012, the UK's rate is 35%, the USA's rate is 33%, Italy's one is 58% while Malta's is 34%, very similar to the rates reported for the UK and USA.

The biggest disadvantage of the RBL is that it is a reactive approach that works only after a network has begun spamming and it cannot stop that initial flood of spam. The second one is that address spaces can and do change. Companies are bankrupted and their address space can be taken over by other organisations. All these changes can be a headache for an RBL maintainer. Some RBL maintainers might ignore these changes. Using an RBL may be risky for these reasons alone. To be more proactive some maintainers began blocking all dialup and ISDN user ip addresses, since these would change quite a bit. All of these issues may make reliability of an RBL quite doubtful and it is clear that as an anti-spam approach it cannot be relied on 100% by itself since it can block legitimate emails. eTesting Labs did a study ("eTesting Labs Conducts Performance Test of Anti-Spam Software," 2001) on various spam filters and found that the MAPS RBL blocked 12.49% of spam and 5.71% of legitimate spam. (The actual study was not found, only press releases) They did other tests ("Could We Be Winning the Spam Wars?," 2003) on various RBLs. One should choose RBLs which are professionally run and which have prompt delisting procedures. It is important to note that quite innocently an IP address can get listed because of viruses, worms, spyware and other malware that can send out spam emails from your machine. Another reason to get listed is if one has an open relay, by mistake (misconfiguration).

The report by Haselton (2012) (this author is known in anti-spam circles, he testified in the US Congress against COPA) has been made about some domains ending up incorrectly on the Spamhaus RBL blacklist, and the domain registrars disabled these domains, so they disappeared from the web. It seems that Spamhaus allows anyone to remove any blacklisted domain, it gives an advantage to spammers who would know how to do this, while other regular non-spamming domain owners would take much more time to find out that their domains had been deactivated, and to get them re-enabled. Unfortunately, there is no way to contact Spamhaus if you have been wrongly blacklisted. Spamhaus claims to be a "zero false positive" list but the Slashdot website showed that this is in doubt. In fact, some posters on the site called Spamhaus an abusive site. The author recommends NOT using Spamhaus' aggregate blacklist (Zen) and instead one can use any of the other three lists offered by Spamhaus (XBL, SBL and PBL, used to list exploited machines, human-detected spam sources and service-policy-denied relays respectively). Also one should ideally use a blacklist to contribute to scoring systems such as SpamAssassin.

Other RBL's have problems too. Some of them have ended up listing gmail's ip addresses at some time or another, for instance NJABL ("Gmail listed in the RBL dnsbl.njabl.org," 2009) and spamcop ("Exempt IP ranges from RBL lookup," 2011). Spamtips.org publishes a DNSBL reliability report ("Spamassassin Tips: DNSBL Safety Report 5/14/2011," 2011), this is worth checking to decide whether to use a DNSBL or not.

Levine (2012) in his blog writes that in the practical day to day usage, large systems use RBL's by special arrangement where they download their own copies of the RBL data, typically via rsync or some other protocol, whereas small systems send ordinary DNS queries to the RBL servers, probably using a local DNS cache. Levine claims that caches do not help the small systems much, because there is little repeat traffic from the same IP to reuse cache results. Also large systems are not likely to use or need a cache, because their RBL server process runs locally on their own systems. A new problem arises from the use of IPv6. It has such a large address space that spammers can easily send every message from a different and unique IP address. This may swap out DNS caches used by the small systems mentioned earlier. Another method used is whitelisting. Disadvantage of this is a high false positive rate, though no spam will reach the user. Also, bulk mailers increasingly match the From: header to the recipient's own domain, fooling simple whitelister software.

HEURISTIC FILTERING

The usage of Heuristic Rules was the next step for spam detection back in the 1990's. Using custom manually built rules to detect both spam and ham (legitimate email), heuristic filters could avoid labeling legitimate emails with spammy characteristics as spam if they had a number of matching ham rules. Brightmail is believed to have been the first commercial anti-spam product in 1999, with free versions offered as well. In 2004 it was acquired by Symantec ("Symantec to Acquire Brightmail," 2004). The early Brightmail used "spam experts" or "spam masters" that picked out characteristics from spam and ham and listed them in a database.

The second and probably the most popular heuristic solution still in use today is SpamAssassin. While it uses blacklist lookups, basic pattern matching and heuristic rules, it requires frequent updating to keep current. It uses a GA to determine appropriate weights for its heuristic rules, plus users can modify weights accordingly.

Heuristic rules suffer from the weakness that spammers can simply run their spam through the tool and modify their message until they evade detection. Subsequently filter authors keep improving their rules and the cycle goes on. Heuristic rules (Salib, 2002) may include RBL lookups, DNS checks, malformed message ID checks, etc. A large number of heuristics (Salib, 2002) may need, which will slow down the filter. Heuristics may improve accuracy, however it looks like it can be improved by combining with Bayes rather than just heuristics or Bayes on their own.

WHITELISTING

The opposite of blacklisting, whitelisting, utilizes a list of those senders you completely trust never to send you spam. Whitelisting, while some claim it is 100% accurate, suffers from "overzealousness". For instance, mail from a newsgroup or mailing list, or mail from legitimate people who want to contact you, will all be rejected. To workaround this problem, some systems issue a challenge to the sender, expecting them to respond to it to be allowed to send you an email. This is the so-called "Challenge-Response" (see next section) that suffers from the same problems as whitelisting as well as the fact that it can annoy some recipients due to the fact that it pushes the burden of maintaining the whitelist onto the recipients. Some other systems just throttle the sender to limit the speed and number of emails that the unknown sender may send.

The main problem of whitelisting turns out to be forgeries. Email addresses like support@ microsoft.com might have been added to the whitelist, and some spammers use well-known support addresses and then can send as much spam as they want, bypassing all protection.

Sun (Eric Sun 2002) says that a good whitelist will accept all your email coming in from family, clients and other people you communicate with, while rejecting most spam emails. SpamAssassin's automatic whitelist attempts to improve on the usual disadvantage of whitelists, by combining the incoming email's score with the average of all previous emails from that person. Over time it learns which emails are from regular correspondents, begins to filter them less aggressively and as a result the number of false positives drops. Of course, it also possible to use Greylisting (Harris, 2003) with SpamAssassin.

Challenge-Response and Make Sender Pay

Challenge-Response is just one particular type of the "Make Sender Pay" concept. A good overview can be found in Dwork (2002). The concept behind Challenge-Response is putting an onus on the sender, though it must be said, this is not a perfect solution, since may be seen as telling the sender "my time is much more important than yours", as Orloff (2011) writes. This makes the sender "pay" by having to do a moderately hard computation (Back, 1997), (Dwork & Naor, 1993), by human intervention or Challenge-Response (Naor, 1996) (since 2000 commonly called a CAPTCHA - Completely Automated Public Turing test to tell Computers and Humans Apart) or by having to pay real world money (called email postage). The latter was proposed by Microsoft's Bill Gates (Hansell, 2004) himself at the World Economic Forum a few years ago. This would make sending spam prohibitive in price (while known senders would be able to send email to you for free), however a system for issuing these "stamps" would be bigger than the credit card system, as shown by Taughannock ("Taughannock Networks," 2004). Such a system would also be a target for a DOS (Denial of Service) attack, as found by Abadi (Abadi at al. 2003).

Laurie and Clayton (2004) researched the computation approach and after examining the computation power available to spammers using zombies as opposed to legitimate senders, determined that any proof of work system which is sufficiently demanding to be a spammer deterrent, would also prevent legitimate individuals from being able to send their emails. In an attempt to address this, Camp and Liu (2006) added a reputation system, showing that it would allow mostly all the legitimate emails to get through while keeping spam hosts from sending more than a few messages.

Examples of the computation approach include Hashcash (Back, 1997) and Camram ("Camram antispam system," 2009). An example of the e-postage model was Jim McCoy's now defunct p2p file sharing network MojoNation ("Mnet," 2009) and ("Mojo Nation," 2009). MojoNation was the e-currency that aimed in a distributed way to provide load balancing as well as secure resistance from attacks.

More recently, Facebook is intending to monetize spam messages sent to people who are not your facebook friends (Walsh, 2012).

Another disadvantage of the Challenge-Response method is that spam sender emails are usually forged, thus the challenges get sent to innocent third parties. This annoys these people, who generally do not understand the reason why they received this challenge email. Furthermore, a false negative can happen if these people actually answer the challenge correctly, and thus the original spam email will get through. The Challenge-Response method fails to work correctly when ham email is received from a mailing list. Typically the challenge will be sent to the whole mailing list, which can be annoying. Also registration emails from websites will also fail to get through, since they are received from automated mailers and will not answer a challenge request. The person running the Challenge-Response software will have to whitelist any such emails. Finally Challenge-Response slows down emails received from new senders. Nowadays spammers are forging even Challenge-Response messages. If one answers one of these emails, you are guaranteed to receive even more spam since the spammer will know that you read your emails and are likely to take action on receiving an email.

COLLABORATIVE FILTERING

The concept of collaborative filtering implies combining spam reports from different people in a community and using that information to build better "intelligence" for future spam detection. There is a high risk of false positives, when this is automated. Moreover as (Mehta, Hofmann, & Fankhauser, 2007) comment, it is all too easy for this crowd-sourcing or collaborative recommender system to be manipulated by a malicious element. Mehta et al. use multivariate analysis techniques to perform outlier detection, where spam users are the outliers, making it possible for a system to filter out malicious users. Also, a smaller network may be more reliable and more real-time yet it will not be able to cover all fresh inbound spam as much a larger network would. Mehta and Hoffman (2008) give a good survey of attack-resistant collaborative filtering algorithms. Mehta and Nejdl (2008) introduced an SVD-based algorithm for this purpose.

AUTHENTICATED SMTP

The concept of adding on to the SMTP (Simple Mail Transfer Protocol) protocol (Authenticated SMTP or SMTP AUTH) has been proposed for a number of years, for instance Sciberras (2007) extended it to authenticate local senders of a system before allowing users to send an email. Sciberras' implemented system required IIS to work. The majority of ISP's still do not use this technique, though some use it to allow mobile users to send emails from a remote location, as well as to track users. However, its popularity started increasing again, thanks to the introduction of SPF (Sender Policy Framework, see below). Most implementations of Authenticated SMTP require the sender to authenticate himself/herself before being able to send emails. Nowadays even mail packages such as Postfix (Koetter, 2004) allow this. Spammers however, tend to compile and build their own mail servers and host them on a network that is unaware of their presence. Thus they can easily bypass any security restrictions on the network's main mail server. Also it has been reported (Blank, 2008) that some spammers have been using brute-force techniques on mail servers running Authenticated SMTP, guessing the right user/password combination and bypassing the "lock" which would have prevented them from using that mail server. Mail queues should be regularly monitored so that high volumes will be noticed, especially since this may indicate spam being sent. Also enabling diagnostics, checking for *auth* requests arising from outside of the organization will usually find this type of attack.

SENDER POLICY FRAMEWORK

Sender Policy Framework (SPF) was a proposal to fight spam using a computationally light add-on to the SMTP protocol that checks DNS records for text entries that indicate which domains are allowed to send email using our domain name as a sender. Text entries in DNS records exist to allow comments, in this case it is used to allow which domains can send email using our domain name, and prohibit forged email from being sent without being recognized. For SPF to work, the recipient's mail system has to check the SPF entry. SPF is being used by a number of large providers. The US Financial Services Industry Group has now endorsed SPF ("The SPF Project," 2007). While SPF has changed SMTP network etiquette, this may not be a bad thing. Previously one would send email using any SMTP server that was available. For instance when abroad one would use one's foreign ISP to send email. Now this is not permitted with SPF, unless the DNS record is amended to allow this ISP to send email for one's domain.

Microsoft's Sender ID is not the same as SPF. Sender ID was an independent experiment that is now obsolete. Both use the same syntax in DNS records and validate email sender addresses. It is controversial because Sender ID is incompatible with existing email specifications, and thus should

not be used. Regarding this, Microsoft has stated it has no plans to fix this ("The SPF Project," n.d.).

SPAM FILTERING AT THE TRANSPORT LEVEL

A recent new development involves inspecting the TCP session that happens during email delivery. It has been observed that typical bots utilize cable or ADSL connections with slow congested upstream. Kakavelakis et al (2011) show that machine learning analysis of this traffic can be used to accurately distinguish between legitimate and illegitimate sources (spam, botnet, etc). They presented a system achieving better than 95% accuracy and recall after reception of approximately 1000 emails."

LANGUAGE CLASSIFICATION

Language Classification attempts to classify a given text into some category. It could involve the determination of a genre of a book, categorizing a document, or even deciding whether an email is spam or not. Since this approach utilizes concept learning, *training* of the filter is necessary. This could be implemented in any combination of these two ways:

- Training with a corpus of spam and ham.
- Learning on-the-go with email as it arrives.

A human can tell the filter whether an email is really spam or not. In the case of a corpus human intervention will not be needed during training. According to Yerazunis (2002), the average human is actually approximately 99.84% accurate and a modern filter is typically five to ten times more accurate than a human. This was retested and confirmed by Graham-Cumming (2005) who found human accuracy to be of 99.46% after manually classifying more than 3000 of his own personal emails. This was similar for both men and women, and all age groups.

A language classifier is made up of a historical dataset (learnt characteristics; also known as wordlist, database, lexicon or dictionary), tokenizer (breaks down email to tokens) and analysis engine (reasoning mechanism, chooses key characteristics in an email and analyses them to decide whether it is spam or ham).

Statistical filtering is a way most spam filters implement language classification. Using machine learning concepts, statistics and probability, the spam can filter can calculate how much a message is likely to be spam.

One popular way to perform this is *Bayesian analysis*, also called *Bayesian Content Filtering* (BCF). This method was proposed by Paul Graham in his seminal research paper "A Plan For Spam" (Graham, 2002) and further developed in his paper "Better Bayesian Filtering" (Graham, 2003). Bayesian filters do not have a fixed set of rules but have to be *trained* with known ham and spam messages before they can be used to classify emails or messages.

Bayesian spam filters include SpamProbe (Burton Computer Corporation, n.d.) by Burton Computer Corporation, SpamBayes by Peters et al. (n.d.), POPFile by Graham-Cumming, DS-PAM by Zdziarski et al (n.d.) and Classifier4J (Lothian, 2005).

Generic attacks against these filters would include Tokenization (splitting up of words with spaces), adding of html tokens and css layouts, as well as Obfuscation (using html entity encoding, letter substitution, Base64/UUencode/Quoted Printable encoding) (Wittel & Wu, 2004).

Other well-known attacks specifically used against Bayesian spam filters include Random Word Attacks, Common Word Attacks, Frequency Ratio Attacks and Random Text Attacks. In the Random Word Attack or Word Salad Attack, a number of words are added to compensate for the original high spam probabilities of the original spam message. The words themselves are taken

from a large set of words, typically called a dictionary, also html tags are typically added, or random text excepts, and these are all chosen in such a way to skew the new message into having a lower overall spam probability. This weak statistical attack is controversial since several authors have found this attack to be ineffective.

In the Common Word attack, the spammers add words that are often found in ham messages, thus these words will tend to have lower spam probabilities. While this type of attack typically works, as has been shown, the number of words which have to be added to make the message fail to be detected by a Bayesian filter will vary. Wittel & Wu (2004) showed that 50 extra words were enough to mask a spam message (without headers) from detection. Lowd and Meek (2005) estimated that approximately 1000 words were enough to hide a spam email with an average spam probability (this included headers).

The Frequency Ratio attack was demonstrated by Lowd and Meek (2005). This involves adding words common in the language but not common in spam messages. They used a spam corpus and representative English text corpora. They calculated that adding around 150 words with a high frequency ratio to a spam message would be enough to bypass a Bayesian filter.

In the Random Text Attack, also known as "Bayesian Poisoning" or a "Hash Breaking Attack", words are added to the spam messages that are taken from randomly chosen alphabet letters. There are various variants of this attack, two of which are given by Bayler (2008).

Other attacks include Strong Statistical Attacks that involve feedback from spam recipients using web bugs (Graham-Cumming, 2004), (Wittel & Wu 2004).

Besides these attacks, Bayler et al. (2008), Karlberger at al. (2007) proposed a Word Substitution attack. This attack involved selecting spam messages such that the words in them have similar spam probabilities in different Bayesian spam filters run by receivers. Messages with this precondition were then processed as follows: words with a high spam probability are substituted automatically with words with a lower spam probability. This was more effective on SpamAssassin with local tests only and on the DSPAM filter. SpamAssassin with network tests and Gmail were the least effected. Problems with this kind of attack are that the disguised messages offer poor readability and there is a low effectiveness in disguising spam emails for most spam filters. Bayler (2008) suggests spammers could replace individual words by their synonyms, e.g. from WordNet (Princeton University, n.d.) and rewrite passages to use words with a reduced spam probability. Defending from these attacks will require that spammers receive no feedback and the retraining of spam filters.

Not all statistical filters use Bayesian filtering. For instance according to Zdziarski (2005) the initial versions of Bogofilter written by Eric S. Raymond did not use Baye's Theorem at all, but was somewhat similar to "A Plan For Spam". More recently from its own website, it claims to be a Bayesian filter. Also Bayler (2008) lists it as a Bayesian spam filter in his book.

Methods of Detection SPAM Before Message Delivery

The most important method of spam detection before the message delivery is greylisting relying on the form of the message delivery. Greylisting basic idea comes from the fact that spam sources usually are not able to attempt the message delivery again after being rejected for the first time. Just such temporary failure is artificially applied to all new incoming messages when greylisting is used. New message here means the new message sender for the specific recipient.

Greylisting method (sometimes spelled "graylisting") was proposed in Harris (2003) almost ten years ago. Greylisting is often used as a complementary method of anti-spam protection

thus forming a front line of anti-spam defence as it is illustrated in Figure 9.

The operation of greylisting method (as implemented in Postgrey) consists of the following three steps:

1. The SMTP server receives the request to deliver an e-mail message into one of its inboxes from certain sending SMTP server (hereinafter indicated as an "SMTP client" or "client"). This request is the first part of the process usually called "SMTP dialog". But unlike normal operation of SMTP server, i.e. instead of immediate delivery of the message, the SMTP server refuses the delivery of the message temporarily and the corresponding error message (with the error code 450 and the text where the reason is announced as "greylisted for ... seconds") is sent to the SMTP client. An example of the SMTP dialog both in case of normal delivery and in case greylisting is applied is shown in Table 2.

2. The sending SMTP client should repeat the attempt to send the message again after certain period. The length of this period depends on the sending server decision but its optimum length is the time for which the message is greylisted as advertised in the error message describer in the Step 1. The shortest possible period for accepting the repeated delivery (called "minimum delay") is set at the receiving SMTP server and it is usually recommended to be 5 minutes. The receiving server usually advertises this period in its temporary error message as described above. If the SMTP client repeats the attempt during the minimum delay period since first attempt, the message delivery is refused again.

3. If the SMTP client repeats the delivery of its message after the minimum delay period elapsed the message is delivered in ordinary

Figure 10. Efficiency comparison of spam detection components. Lower part of each column expresses the percentage of spam messages detected by Postgrey while the upper darker part of each column represents the percentage of spam messages detected by content-based scanners. Both ratios are calculated using the total number of attempts to deliver a message

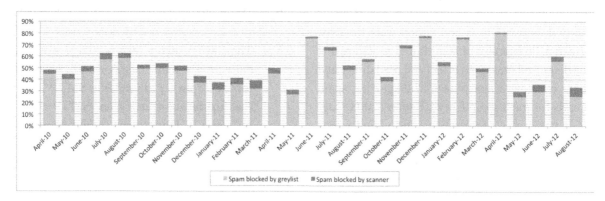

way. In such case the identification of the sender and the recipient in the form of a new triplet (see below) is stored.

In order to decide whether the sender of an e-mail message is "new" so called identification triplet is formed. The identification triplet consists of:

1. Sender IP address taken from the IP packet header when TCP connection is established,
2. Sender e-mail address transmitted by the sender during an initial SMTP dialog, and
3. E-mail address of the recipient also taken from initial SMTP dialog.

If all three components of the triplet of the message attempting to be delivered has the same values as existing triplet in the underlying database then the message is not subject to

It should be noted that the procedure described above is applied only to messages from unknown sources (i.e. sources not yet listed in the *Automatic White List* or in other white lists). The SMTP server with greylisting keeps the lists of triplets

for all successfully delivered messages. If several messages (in the implementation of greylisting in the network being analyzed several means five) are successfully delivered through greylisting from the same source to the same recipient (i.e. with identical data in the triplet, see below), the IP address of the sender is automatically stored in so-called Automatic White List (AWL) listing "legal" senders. Then the procedure described above is not applied to subsequent messages sent by senders from AWL and their messages are delivered without any additional delay. The IP address inserted into AWL is kept there until no messages are sent from the source for longer period (defined by the parameter "verified tripled lifetime").

Greylisting Efficiency

The authors have been performing certain monitoring of greylisting since it was introduced at the studied SMTP server, i.e. since the beginning of 2007. Summary results for the period of almost 5 years are shown in Figure 11.

Table 3. Example of SMTP dialog in case of normal delivery and changed part in the case of greylisting is applied and active

Normal SMTP Delivery	Differences in the Case Greylisting is Applied
S: 220 .com.com ESMTP Postfix	
C: EHLO client.com	
S: 250-our.server.com Hello client.com	
C: MAIL FROM: sender@client.com	
S: 250 2.1.0 OK	
C: RCPT TO: addressee@our.server.com	
S: 250 2.1.5 OK	S: 450 Greylisted for 300 seconds (delivery refused, nothing more is sent)
C: DATA	C: QUIT
S: 354 Enter mail	S: 221 2.0.0 Bye
C: message …	
C: (dot ends the message)	
S: 250 2.0.0 Message accepted for delivery	
C: QUIT	
S: 221 2.0.0 Bye	

Greylisting has proven to be successful by immediate dramatic lowering the amount of spam in mailboxes as demonstrated by the diagram in figure 14 as well as (Sochor, 2010). While before greylisting implementation almost 70% of all incoming e-mail messages were identified as spam by the contents-filter (by Virus/spam scanner, see figure 12), after greylisting implementation the ratio dropped to approx. 10%. Such dramatic decrease looks very well but due to the nature of greylisting method the long-term stability of achieved results is an important issue. Therefore one of the main goals of the study of greylisting efficiency was to investigate longer-term results.

The idea of greylisting as a method for protecting against receiving spam messages is based on the assumption that regular sources of SMTP messages are able to cope with irregularities in message delivery without troubles. This is usually not the case of spamming programs that are usually very simple pieces of software optimized for fast automatic operation so that most of them is unable to perform more complex behaviour in message delivery process. The greylisted server therefore inserts such irregularity consisting in temporary refusal of the message delivery. When regular SMTP client is sending the message and it gets such an answer the server is able to repeat the request after certain time. Most spam producing SMTP clients do not do so.

There is one risk in the application of greylisting however. It is easy to expect that when spamming SMTP clients are going to be more sophisticated and potentially able to pass through an obstacle

Figure 11. Monthly percentage of accepted deliveries obtained from postgrey

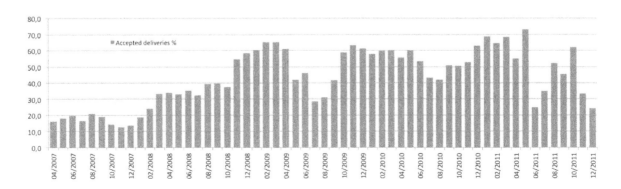

represented by greylisting and as a result the efficiency of the greylisting method could go down. Therefore probably the most important question associated with greylisting is whether the efficiency of the method is stable throughout long-term periods or not. This issue was the primary matter of interest in our study too.

Based of the long-term study and experience with greylisting and content-based spam detection efficiency some general recommendation can be formulated for spam detection implementation and use. The recommendations are as follows:

- Do not rely on greylisting alone.
- Consider applying longer initial delay with sophisticated second tier spam scanner, preferably connected with greylisting's AWL.
- D not put greylisting away, it is still very good tool, especially combined with other filtering tools (e.g. in Postfix ingress filtering).

The combination of contents-based spam detection with greylisting as isolated elements as illustrated in Figure 11 is not efficient enough. Therefore their feedback linkage has been proposed recently. So far the experiments with such link have been limited to the one-time AWL cleaning repeated on regular basis. The simulation of the efficiency increase from such link showed however that it could increase the spam detection success ration significantly so the implementation of the link will start in the near future.

NEW WAYS OF SPAM DETECTION

Also some introductory experiments oriented to the application of ANN in the spam detection has been done recently and results seemed to be promising. The adverse aspect of this approach is that the results could depend strongly on the architecture of the specific ANN. Therefore we

suggest another new approach to the spam detection using the application of Linguistic Fuzzy Logic Controller (Dvorak et al., 2003). The new approach is based on the re-evaluation of each heuristic criterion including its weight as evaluated by the content-based spam detection system and subsequent new independent classification of each received message. So far only preliminary feasibility tests have been performed. The pilot results will be available soon however.

GENETIC PROGRAMMING WITH FEATURE DETECTION

A new promising approach is described in (Meli, 2013a). The author implemented a Genetic Programming System (based on a Genetic Algorithm) that evolves the better RPN (Reverse Polish Notation) that can then be used to distinguish between spam and ham. The RPN utilises expressions with operators such as addition, subtraction, multiplication, division, sine and cosine, plus operands that can be constant values or evaluated features. Evaluated features include average words per sentence, Yule's Measure, Hapax Legomena and other similar features. It is planned to extend this system to use the author's own Millipede extended genetic algorithm representation (Meli, 2013b) in future.

CONCLUSION

The neural net application represents a way of the further development in cryptography, but we can ask a question. What are the limitations of the system? The limitations of this system type are a few, but potentially significant. This is effectively a secret-key system where the key consists of the weights and architecture of the network. With the weights and the architecture, breaking the encryption becomes trivial. However, both the weights and the architecture are needed for encryption and decryption. Knowing only one or the other is not enough to break it. What are the advantages to this system? The advantages of this system are that it appears to be exceedingly difficult to break it without knowledge of the methodology behind, as shown above. In addition, it is tolerant to noise. Most messages cannot be altered by even one bit in a standard encryption scheme. The system based on neural networks allows the encoded message to fluctuate and still be accurate.

The spam blocking is described here in details as a complex task suitable for application of neural net into filtering. Results on efficiency of greylisting and content-based searching are shown. At the end, promising ways of fuzzy control and genetic programming application into spam detection and removal are proposed.

ACKNOWLEDGMENT

The research described here has been financially supported by the University of Ostrava grant SGS16/PrF/2014 and by the European Regional Development Fund under the project CEBIA-Tech No. CZ.1.05/2.1.00/03.0089. Any opinions, findings and conclusions or recommendations expressed in this material are those of the authors and do not necessarily reflect the views of the sponsors.

REFERENCES

Abadi, M., Birrell, A., Burrows, M., Dabek, F., & Wobber, T. (2003). Bankable Postage for Network Services. In V. A. Saraswat (Ed.), *Advances in Computing Science – ASIAN 2003: Progamming Languages and Distributed Computation Programming Languages and Distributed Computation* (pp. 72–90). Springer. Retrieved from February 11, 2013, http://link.springer.com/chapter/10.1007/978-3-540-40965-6_6

Alves, R. T., Delgado, M., Lopes, H. S., & Freitas, A. A. (2004). An artificial immune system for fuzzy-rule induction in data mining. *Lecture Notes in Computer Science, 3242,* 1011–1020. doi:10.1007/978-3-540-30217-9_102

Ashlock, D. (2006). *Evolutionary Computation for Modeling and Optimization.* Berlin: Springer-Verlag.

Back, A. (1997). *Hashcash postage implementation announcement.* Retrieved February 14, 2013, from http://www.hashcash.org/papers/announce.txt

Bäck, T., Fogel, D., & Michalewicz, Z. (Eds.). (1997). *Handbook of Evolutionary Computation.* Oxford, UK: Oxford Univ. Press. doi:10.1887/0750308958

Bayler, G. (2008). *Penetrating Bayesian Spam Filters.* Saarbrucken: VDM Verlag.

Blank, N. (2008). *Fighting SPAM: SMTP auth attacks from spammers on the rise.* Retrieved October 10, 2012, from http://www.allspammedup.com/2008/05/fighting-spam-smtp-auth-attacks-from-spammers-on-the-rise/

Burton Computer Corporation. (n.d.). *SpamProbe - A Fast Bayesian Spam Filter.* Retrieved February 14, 2013, from http://spamprobe.sourceforge.net/

Bonissone, P. P. (2002). Hybrid Soft Computing for Classification and Prediction Applications. In *Proceedings of the First International Conference on Computing in an Imperfect World* (pp. 352-353). Berlin: Springer-Verlag.

Camp, L. J., & Liu, D. (2006). *Proof of Work (Cannot, Can, Does Currently) Work.* Retrieved February 11, 2013, from http://papers.ssrn.com/abstract=2118235

Camram Antispam System. (2009). *SourceForge.* Retrieved February 14, 2013, from http://sourceforge.net/projects/camram/

Cormack, G. V., & Lynam, T. R. (2005). *TREC 2005 Spam Track Overview*. Retrieved January, 10, 2013, from http://plg.uwaterloo.ca/~gvcormac/trecspmtrack05

Cormack, G. V. (2007). Email spam filtering: A systematic review. *Foundations and Trends in Information Retrieval*, *1*(4), 335–455. doi:10.1561/1500000006

Cormack, G. V., María, J., Sánz, E. P., & Hidalgo, G. (2007). Spam filtering for short messages. In *Proceedings of the 16th ACM conference on Conference on Information and Knowledge Management* (pp. 313-320). New York: ACM.

Dantu, R., & Kolan, P. (2005). Detecting spam in VoIP networks. In *Proceedings of the Steps to Reducing Unwanted Traffic on the Internet on Steps to Reducing Unwanted Traffic on the Internet*. Berkeley, CA: USENIX Association.

Dvorak, A., Habiballa, H., Novak, V., & Pavliska, V. (2003). The concept of LFLC 2000 - Its specificity, realization and power of applications. *Computers in Industry*, *51*(3), 269–280. doi:10.1016/S0166-3615(03)00060-5

Dwork, C. (2002). Fighting spam may be easier than you think. *Microsoft Research SVC*. Retrieved February 14, 2013, from www.cis.upenn.edu/spyce/presentations/Cynthia-Sep-02.pdf

Dwork, C., & Naor, M. (1993). Pricing via processing or combatting junk mail. In *Proceedings of Advances in Cryptology—CRYPTO'92* (pp. 139–147). Berlin: Springer-Verlag. doi:10.1007/3-540-48071-4_10

eTesting Labs Conducts Performance Test of Anti-Spam Software. (2001). *PRNewswire*. Retrieved October 6, 2012, from http://www.prnewswire.com/news-releases/etesting-labs-conducts-performance-test-of-anti-spam-software-82337887.html

Exempt IP ranges from RBL lookup? (SpamCop and GMAIL issue). (2011). *SmarterTools*. Retrieved Mar 28, 2014, from http://forums.smartertools.com/threads/exempt-ip-ranges-from-rbl-lookup-spamcop-and-gmail-issue.24180/

Fausett, L. V. (1994). *Fundamentals of Neural Networks*. Prentice-Hall, Inc.

Ferguson, N., Schneier, B., & Kohno, T. (2012). *Cryptography engineering: design principles and practical applications*. Oxford, UK: John Wiley & Sons.

Garfinger, S. (1995). *PGP: Pretty Good Privacy*. O'Reilly &Associates.

Gmail Listed in the RBL dnsbl.njabl.org. (2009). *Google*. Retrieved Mar 6, 2014, from http://productforums.google.com/forum/#!topic/gmail/fXdzg9vfzO4

Graham, P. (2002). A Plan for Spam. *Paul Graham*. Retrieved August 26, 2013, from http://www.paulgraham.com/spam.html

Graham, P. (2003). Better Bayesian Filtering. *Paul Graham*. Retrieved March 26, 2014, from http://www.paulgraham.com/better.html

Graham-Cumming, J. (2004), How to beat an adaptive spam filter. In *Proc. of MIT Spam Conference*. Retrieved February 11, 2013, from http://jgc.org/pdf/spamconf2004.pdf

Graham-Cumming, J. (2005). People and Spam. In *Proceedings of MIT Spam Conference 2005*. Retrieved February 14, 2013, from http://jgc.org/pdf/spamconf2005.pdf

Hansell, S. (2004). *TECHNOLOGY, speech by GatesLends visibility to e-mail stamp in war on spam*. Retrieved February 14, 2013, from http://www.nytimes.com/2004/02/02/business/technology-speech-by-gateslends-visibility-to-e-mail-stamp-in-war-on-spam.html

Haselton, B. (2012). *Zero Errors? Spamhaus Flubs Causing Domain Deletions*. Retrieved October 18, 2012, http://yro-beta.slashdot.org/story/12/10/16/175248/zero-errors-spamhaus-flubs-causing-domain-deletions

Harris, E. (2003). *The next step in the spam control war: Greylisting*. Retrieved February 14, 2013, from http://projects.puremagic.com/greylisting/

Kakavelakis, G., Beverly, R., & Young, J. (2011). Auto-learning of SMTP TCP transport-layer features for spam and abusive message detection. In *Proceedings of USENIX Large Installation System Administration Conference*. Retrieved February 14, 2013, from http://rbeverly.net/research/papers/autolearn-lisa11.pdf

Karlberger, C., Bayler, G., Kruegel, C., & Kirda, E. (2007). Exploiting redundancy in natural language to penetrate Bayesian spam filters. In *Proceedings of the first USENIX Workshop on Offensive Technologies*. Retrieved February 11, 2013 from http://dl.acm.org/citation.cfm?id=1323276.1323285

Khaled, M., Noaman, G., & Jalab, H. A. (2005). Data security based on neural networks. *Task Quarterly*, *9*(4), 409–414.

Kinzel, W. (2006). Theory of interacting neural networks. In Handbook of Graphs and Networks: From the Genome to the Internet. Weinheim, Germany: Wiley-VCH Verlag GmbH & Co. KGaA.

Kinzel, W., & Kanter, I. (2002). *Neural cryptography*. arXiv preprint cond-mat/0208453

Koetter, P. B. (2004). *Postfix SMTP AUTH (and TLS) HOWTO*. Retrieved October 10, 2012, from http://postfix.state-of-mind.de/patrick.koetter/smtpauth/

Lane, T. (2000). *Machine learning techniques for the computer security*. (Doctoral dissertation). Purdue University.

Laurie, B., & Clayton, R. (2004). Proof-of-Work proves not to work, version 0.2. In *Proceedings of Workshop on Economics and Information Security*. Cambridge, UK: University of Cambridge.

Lee, W., Stolfo, S. J., & Mok, K. W. (2000). Adaptive intrusion detection: A data mining approach. *Artificial Intelligence Review*, *14*(6), 533–567. doi:10.1023/A:1006624031083

Levine, J. (2010). *RFC 5782: DNS blacklists and whitelists*. Retrieved February 15, 2013 from http://tools.ietf.org/html/rfc5782

Levine, J. (2012). *IPv6 DNS blacklists reconsidered*. Retrieved February 15, 2013, from http://www.circleid.com/posts/ipv6_dns_blacklists_reconsidered/

Lothian, N. (2005). *Classifier4J*. Retrieved February 14, 2013, from http://classifier4j.sourceforge.net/

Lowd, D., & Meek, C. (2005). Good word attacks on statistical spam filters. In *Proceedings of the Second Conference on Email and Anti-Spam (CEAS)*. Redmond, WA: Microsoft.

Lueg, C. (2005). From spam filtering to information retrieval and back: Seeking Conceptual Foundations for Spam Filtering. *Proceedings of the American Society for Information Science and Technology*, *42*(1).

Mehta, B., Hofmann, T., & Fankhauser, P. (2007). Lies and propaganda: detecting spam users in collaborative filtering. In *Proceedings of the 12th international conference on Intelligent user interfaces* (pp. 14-21). ACM.

Mehta, B., & Hofmann, T. (2008). A Survey of Attack-Resistant Collaborative Filtering Algorithms. *IEEE Data Eng. Bull.*, *31*(2), 14–22.

Mehta, B., & Nejdl, W. (2008). Attack resistant collaborative filtering. In *Proceedings of the 31st annual international ACM SIGIR conference on Research and development in information retrieval* (pp. 75–82). New York, NY: ACM. doi:10.1145/1390334.1390350

Meli, C. (2013a). *Application and improvement of genetic algorithms and genetic programming towards the fight against spam and other internet malware.* (Doctoral dissertation). University of Malta.

Meli, C. (2013). Millipede, an Extended Representation for Genetic Algorithms. *International Journal of Computer Theory & Engineering, 5*(4).

Mnet. (2009). *SourceForge.* Retrieved February 15, 2013, from http://sourceforge.net/projects/mnet/

Mojo Nation. (2009). *SourceForge.* Retrieved February 15, 2013, from http://sourceforge.net/projects/mojonation/

Naor, M. (1996). *Verification of a human in the loop or Identification via the Turing Test.* Unpublished draft. Retrieved October 5, 2012, from http://www.wisdom.weizmann.ac.il/~naor/PAPERS/humanabs.html

Orloff, J. (2011). *5 Criticisms of the challenge-response solution.* Retrieved February 15, 2013, from http://www.allspammedup.com/2011/05/5-criticisms-of-the-challenge-response-solution/

Peters, T., et al. (n.d.). *SpamBayes.* Retrieved February 14, 2013, from http://spambayes.sourceforge.net/

Prabakaran, N., Loganathan, P., & Vivekanandan, P. (2008). Neural Cryptography with Multiple Transfers Functions and Multiple Learning Rule. *International Journal of Soft Computing, 3*(3), 177–181.

Princeton University. (n.d.). *WordNet.* Retrieved February 14, 2013, from http://wordnet.princeton.edu/

Ruspini, E. H., Bonissone, P. P., & Pedycz, W. (1998). *Handbook of Fuzzy Computation.* Bristol, UK: Institute of Physics Pub. doi:10.1887/0750304278

Ruttor, A., Reents, G., & Kinzel, W. (2004). Synchronization of random walks with reflecting boundaries. *Journal of Physics. A, Mathematical and General, 37*(36), 8609. doi:10.1088/0305-4470/37/36/003

Ruttor, A., Kanter, I., & Kinzel, W. (2006). Dynamics of neural cryptography. *Physical Review E: Statistical, Nonlinear, and Soft Matter Physics, 75*(5), 056104. doi:10.1103/PhysRevE.75.056104

Salib, M. (2002). Heuristics in the Blender. In *Proceedings of the 2003 Spam Conference.* Boston: MIT.

Sciberras, N. (2007). *Extending the SMTP protocol's security by allowing authenticated users to use only their email address when sending emails.* (Doctoral dissertation). University of Greenwich.

Seung, S. (2002). *Multilayer perceptrons and backpropagation learning.* Received February 14, 2013, from http://hebb.mit.edu/courses/9.641/2002/lectures/lecture04.pdf

Siripanwattana, W., & Srinoy, S. (2008). Information Security based on Soft Computing Techniques. In *Proceedings of the International MultiConference of Engineers and Computer Scientists* (Vol. 1). Hong Kong: International Association of Engineers.

Sochor, T. (2010). Greylisting method analysis in real SMTP server environment: Case-study. In *Innovations and Advances in Computer Sciences and Engineering* (pp. 423–427). Springer Netherlands. doi:10.1007/978-90-481-3658-2_74

Spamassassin Tips. DNSBL Safety Report 5/14/2011. (2011). *Spamassassin Tips.* Retrieved March 6, 2014, from http://www.spamtips.org/2011/05/dnsbl-safety-report-5142011.html

Symantec. (2012). *Symantec Intelligence Report.* Retrieved December 6, 2012, from http://www.symantec.com/theme.jsp?themeid=state_of_spam

Symantec to Acquire Brightmail. (2004). *Symantec.* Retrieved October 7, 2012, from http://www.symantec.com/press/2004/n040519.html

Taughannock Networks. (2004). *An Overview of E-Postage.* Retrieved October 7, 2012, from http://taugh.com/epostage.pdf

Project, S. P. F. (2007). US Financial Services Industry Group Endorses SPF. *SPF.* Retrieved Mar 10, 2014, from http://www.openspf.org/Press_Release/2007-04-21

Project, S. P. F. (n.d.). SPF vs Sender ID. *SPF.* Retrieved Mar 10, 2014, from http://www.openspf.org/SPF_vs_Sender_ID

Trend Micro Email Reputation Services. (n.d.). *Trend Micro.* Retrieved October 6, 2012, from https://ers.trendmicro.com/

Volna, E. (2000). Using Neural network in cryptography. In *The State of the Art in Computational Intelligence* (pp. 262–267). New York: Physica-Verlag HD. doi:10.1007/978-3-7908-1844-4_42

Volna, E., Kotyrba, M., Kocian, V., & Janosek, M. (2012). Cryptography based on neural 1network. In *Proc. 26th European Conference on Modelling and Simulation* (pp. 386-391). Koblenz, Germany: Univ. of Koblenz-Landau.

Walsh, S. (2012). *Facebook to Monetize Spam.* Retrieved February 15, 2013, from http://www.allspammedup.com/2012/12/facebook-to-monetize-spam/

Webb, S., Caverloo, J., & Pu, C. (2006). Introducing the webb spam corpus: Using email spam to identify web spam automatically. In *Proceedings of CEAS 2006 — 3rd Conference on Email and Anti-Spam* (CEAS). Redmond, WA: Microsoft.

Wittel, G. L., & Wu, S. F. (2004). On Attacking Statistical Spam Filters. In *Proceedings of CEAS 2006 — third conference on email and anti-spam.* Retrieved October 7, 2012, from http://130.203.133.150/viewdoc/summary,jsessionid=D95619A23260FC405817FD63A207B68E?doi=10.1.1.59.8759

Yerazunis, B. (2002). Better that human. *Paul Graham.* Retrieved Mar 7, 2014, from http://www.paulgraham.com/wsy.html

Zadeh, L. A. (1994). Soft Computing and Fuzzy Logic. *IEEE Software, 11*(6), 48–56. doi:10.1109/52.329401

Zdziarski., et al. (n.d.). *DSPAM Project Homepage.* Retrieved February 14, 2013, Retrieved October 7, 2012, from http://dspam.nuclearelephant.com/

Zdziarski, J. (2005). *Ending Spam: Bayesian Content Filtering and the Art of Statistical Language Classification.* Sebastopol, CA: No Starch Press.

Zinman, A., & Donath, J. (2007). Is Britney Spears spam&quest. In *Proceedings of the 4th International Conference on Email and Anti-Spam* (CEAS). Redmond, WA: Microsoft.

KEY TERMS AND DEFINITIONS

Artificial Neural Networks: An Artificial Neural Network (ANN) is the information-processing paradigm that is inspired by the way biological nervous systems. Its key element is the structure of the information processing system. It is composed of a large number of highly interconnected processing elements (neurones) working in unison to solve specific problems.

Backpropagation: Backpropagation algorithm belongs to a group called gradient descent methods. The algorithm searches for the global minimum of the weight landscape by descending downhill in the most precipitous direction.

Blacklisting: The method of blocking of an incoming e-mail message (or other contents) based on the existence of the message sender on the list of sources of non-desirable contents.

Evolutionary Algorithms: An evolutionary algorithm uses mechanisms inspired by biological evolution, such as reproduction, mutation, recombination, and selection. Candidate solutions to the optimization problem play the role of individuals in a population, and the fitness function determines the environment within which the solutions exist.

Greylisting: The method of temporary refusing of an incoming e-mail message from an unknown sender as a tool of SPAM elimination.

Soft Computing: Soft computing is a partnership of distinct methods. The dominant aim of soft computing is to exploit the tolerance for imprecision and uncertainty to achieve tractability, robustness and low solutions cost.

SPAM: Unsolicited electronic mail message, often sent to multiple addresses and with malicious intent (virus, malware or phishing spread).

Chapter 3
Quantum Key Distribution Networks

Sufyan T. Faraj Al-Janabi
University of Anbar, Iraq

ABSTRACT

The aim of this chapter is to emphasize the multidisciplinary nature of the research in the field of Quantum Key Distribution Networks (QKDNs). Such networks consist of a number of nodes that can perform security protocols protected by some basic laws of physics. The operation of QKDNs mainly requires the integration of Quantum Key Distribution (QKD) protocols with the already-existing network security infrastructures. The authors report on the current state-of-the-art in the field and give some recommendations for future research. As computer simulation can be very useful in dealing with advanced technology subjects like QKDNs, they outline a simple and efficient modeling and simulation approach for various QKDN configurations. Then, the issue of unconditionally secure authentication of the public channel in QKD is considered. This issue is of crucial importance from both theoretical and practical sides. In this context, the proposed hybrid authentication strategy is reviewed and an authenticated version of the Bennett-Brassard-84 (BB84) QKD protocol based on this strategy is described. Next, a novel extension of the SSL protocol for QKDN settings, which the authors call Quantum SSL (QSSL), is explained. Finally, the chapter is concluded.

INTRODUCTION

Data transmission has always been vulnerable to eavesdropping. Conventional cryptography has provided many security services in data communication; however, it has serious limitations when dealing with passive eavesdropping. Indeed, security with today's cryptography can usually be achieved on the basis of computational complexity. Thus, almost all cryptosystems can be broken with enormous amounts of calculations.

The recent application of the principles of quantum mechanics to cryptography has led to remarkable new dimension in secret communication. The most important contribution of Quantum Cryptography (QC) or, more precisely, quantum key distribution (QKD) is a mechanism for detecting eavesdropping. This is totally new contribution to the field of cryptography. Neither symmetrical cryptographic systems nor public–key systems have such a capability. QKD delivers cryptographic keys whose secrecy is guaranteed

DOI: 10.4018/978-1-4666-5808-0.ch003

by the laws of physics. QKD offers new methods of secure communications that are not threatened even by the power of quantum computers.

The only cipher system known to have guaranteed (unconditional) security is the Vernam cipher (the one-time pad). This system is a symmetric cryptosystem that requires a key as long as the message; the key is used only once and then carefully destroyed. Furthermore, it requires the correspondents to share initial secret key information. Hence, the key management and distribution problems become terrifying with this kind of cipher systems. In QC, physically secure quantum key distribution is usually combined with the mathematical security of the Vernam cipher to produce a significantly secure system.

In order to facilitate the evolution of QC towards a practical "quantum information security era" in which QC becomes more closely integrated with conventional information security systems and communication networks infrastructures, a more collaborated scientific research among specialists from several fields is required. In particular, this research activity has to bring together theoretical and experimental physicists, computer scientists and electrical engineers, and communications and information security specialists.

QKD basically enables two parties (traditionally referred to as Alice and Bob) to produce the shared secret keys required for secure communications, through a combination of quantum and conventional communication steps. Today QKD systems can be operated over metro-area distances on optical fibers and across line-of-sight "free-space" paths. Thus, in addition to standalone point-to-point (PTP) systems, QKD can be integrated within optical communication networks at the physical layer, and with key-management infrastructures. This significantly facilitates applications in the environments of "QKD networks" (QKDNs). In general, it is possible to define a QKDN as an infrastructure composed of quantum links connecting multiple distant nodes that have the capability of performing QKD.

The main goal of this chapter is to bring the attention of people working in both QC and traditional network security fields so as to reach a better understanding of all theoretical and practical issues related to the integration of QKD with the already-existent information security infrastructure. We will report on theoretical, simulation, and practical work in the field of QKDNs. Modeling and simulation can be used efficiently to study and analyze QKDN various possible settings. Various secure communication network models can be studied. The security of these network models is solely achieved using QKD. Both point-to-point and multiple-access broadcast networks might be considered. To reach this goal, some basic configurations for communication nodes and communications channels in QKD networks have to be developed at first. Details of the required modeling and simulation approach will be described in this chapter.

Furthermore, it is well known that QKD requires a classical public channel with trusted integrity as otherwise a potential eavesdropper (Eve) can easily amount a man-in-the-middle attack. In case that Eve can manipulate messages on the public channel, it is clear that she could sit between Alice and Bob impersonating each of them to the other. As a result, Eve would thus share two independent keys with the two the legitimate parties and gain full control of all the subsequent communication, without being noticed (Peev et al., 2005; Bennett, Bessette, Brassard, Salvail, and Smolin, 1992). It was suggested that this crucial property of the public channel can be implemented using either of the followings (Bennett et al., 1992):

- An inherently unjammable public channel.
- An information–theoretically (i.e., unconditionally) secure authentication scheme to certify that the public messages have not been altered in transit.

It is obvious that the first case above is not feasible for most practical situations. Hence, we are left with the second case in which Alice and Bob need to initially share secret information to serve as an authentication key. Subsequently in each QKD session they repeatedly renew the mutual secret by reserving part of the newly generated key. This is used to authenticate communication in the next session. Hence in this case the protocol implements key expansion or key growing rather than key distribution (Cederlof, 2005). However, it was noted by some researches that authentication in QKD is "a vital but often neglected part of the method" (Paterson, Piper, and Schack, 2005). Thus, it is crucial to present an accurate treatment for this problem that considers its practical consequences as a real-life communication protocol. In this chapter, some important theoretical and practical aspects of unconditionally secure authentication in QKD are explained and a fully authenticated QKD protocol, which is based on using a hybrid unconditionally secure authentication strategy for protecting public channel transmissions, is presented.

Later on in the chapter and after surveying some important aspects of practical realizations of QKDNs that have been addressed in the literature, especially the US DARPA QKD network and the European SECOQC project, we will outline our extension of SSL/TLS (Secure Socket Layer/ Transport Layer Security) that we have called QSSL (Quantum SSL). QSSL allows the integration of QKD capabilities within the Internet (or intranet) security architecture. This significantly facilitates applications in the environments of QKDNs.

BACKGROUND

Quantum information technology can support entirely new modes of information processing based on quantum principles. Indeed, there are many useful tasks in the field, such as QC, which involve only a few consecutive quantum computational steps. In such cases, the unwelcome effects of decoherence can be adequately diminished by improving technology and communication protocols. QC delivers cryptographic keys whose secrecy is guaranteed by the laws of physics. QC offers new methods of secure communications that are not threatened even by the power of quantum computers. QKD has already made its first steps outside labs both for fiber optic networks and also for satellite-based communications. It is expected that within a decade, it will be possible to place sources of entangled photons on satellites. This would allow global quantum communication, teleportation, and perfectly secure cryptography (Zoller, 2005). While conventional methods continue to meet the more-demanding information security needs of our increasingly networked world, they face increasing technological challenges, such as (Hughes, 2004):

- Unanticipated advances in mathematics, high-performance computing, and the possibility of large-scale quantum computations.
- Increasing complex future requirements for secure network communications to support dynamically reconfigurable groups of users with multi-level security.
- Projections for the ever growing bandwidth demands for secure communications.

It is well believed now that QC has the potential to counter these threats and help to meet these future requirements. However, this implies reaching a practical "quantum information security era" in which QC would be integrated with conventional information security infrastructures. This definitely requires collaboration among researchers and specialists from multidisciplinary fields including physicists, computer scientists, electrical engineers, and cryptographers. Throughout this chapter, a focus is maintained on the subfield of QKD. Away from stand-alone PTP systems,

QKD can be integrated within optical communication networks (mainly at the physical layer). However, there are several issues to be explored by research in this direction. Among these issues that are addressed in this chapter are the following (Hughes, 2004):

- Investigation of network support concerns beyond PTP connectivity.
- Integration of QKD with conventional cryptographic and secure communications infrastructures.
- Exploration of system-level security attributes of QKD (including unconditionally-secure authentication).

The fundamental building block of any quantum cryptography protocol is the qubit which is the quantum analogue of the classical bit. Thus, a qubit is simply a two-level quantum system that carries quantum information by its state. According to quantum mechanics, if we let $\{|0, |1\}$ denote an orthonormal basis, the general state of a qubit can be written as:

$$\left| \o = \cos\frac{\e}{2} \right| 0 + \sin\frac{\e}{2} e^{i\phi} \left| 1 \right. \tag{1}$$

where $\phi \in [0: 2\pi]$, and $\theta \in [0: \pi]$. This type of parameterization allows us to represent all (pure) qubit states on the surface of a sphere. This is the so-called Poincare sphere (see Figure 1). In this sphere, any couple of antipodal points corresponds to an orthonormal basis. There are many physical systems (such as quantum dots and electronic levels of atoms in cavities) whose degrees of freedom can be used to implement a qubit. However, polarization is often used to encode photonic qubits because they are relatively immune to decoherence when compared to other implementations (Gisin, Iblisdir, Tittel, and Zbinden, 2006).

The first QKD protocol, called BB84, was invented in 1984 by Bennett and Brassard (1984). Here, the authorized parties (Alice and Bob who rely on the Heisenberg uncertainty principle) have access to two channels: a one-way quantum channel for sending quantum signals and a two-way classical public channel for verification and reconciliation. This is depicted in Figure 2, where

Figure 1. The poincare sphere representation of qubit states

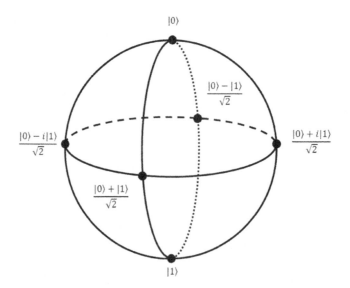

eavesdropping actions by Eve (an eavesdropper) are also shown. There are QKD protocols other than BB84 (The scheme based on photon entanglement proposed by Ekert (1991) is an important alternative). However, there are three main reasons for choosing to emphasize BB84 in this chapter. First, it is the first of QKD protocols. Secondly, it is the most widely studied and implemented one. And finally, given that the known laws of quantum physics hold, there is more than one proof on the unconditional security of BB84 (Mayers, 2001; Gottesman, Lo, Lutkenhaus, and Preskill, 2002; Gottesman & Lo, 2005).

We can give a brief description of the BB84 protocol steps, as it is usually described in the literature (for example, see (Khan & Sher, 2003; Lomonaco, 1998)). Conventionally, the BB84 QKD protocol when extended to a noisy environment, Alice and Bob usually adopt the assumption that all errors in raw key are caused by Eve. This is simply because they cannot distinguish between errors caused by noise and errors caused by eavesdropping. Now this protocol can be described in terms of polarization states of a single photon (in fact as just mentioned previously, it can be described in terms of any other two-state quantum system). Let H be the two dimensional Hilbert space whose elements represent the polarization

state of a single photon. The BB84 uses two different orthogonal bases of H. Let them be the linear polarization basis which consists of the vertical and horizontal polarization states; and the circular polarization basis consisting of the right and left circular polarization states. It is now possible to compose the required two alphabets. First, the linear polarization quantum alphabet is constructed by interpreting the vertical polarization state as binary "1" and the horizontal polarization state as binary "0". Then, the circular polarization quantum alphabet is constructed by interpreting the right-circular polarization state as binary "1" and the left-circular polarization state as binary "0". Keeping in mind that Alice and Bob have access to a one-way quantum channel and two-way public channel (as illustrated in Figure 2), the protocol proceeds as follows:

1. Using the quantum channel, Alice sends a random string of bits. For each bit, she uses randomly with equal probability one of the orthogonal quantum alphabets. For each photon sent by Alice, Bob randomly and independently uses one of the orthogonal polarization bases to perform his measurement (detection). He records his sequence of

Figure 2. A schematic for the basic BB84 QKD setting

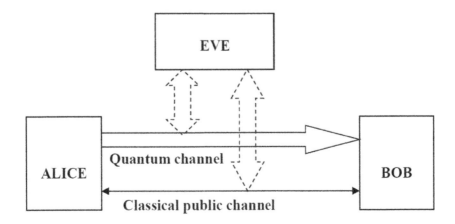

used bases and measurement results. This is the so-called quantum transmission phase.

2. Using the public channel, Bob announces the measurement operators he used for each of the received pulses. Alice then publicly tells Bob which of his measurements operators were correct. This step is the so-called "sifting" or raw key extraction.

3. Alice and Bob use the public channel to estimate the error rate in raw key. They can select a random sample of raw key, and then publicly they compare these sample bits to obtain an estimate of the so-called quantum bit error rate (QBER).

4. Using the public channel, Alice and Bob apply a reconciliation (i.e. error elimination) procedure to produce an error free common key, called reconciled key. There are many possible procedures for reconciliation, for example, see (Lutkenhaus, 1999; Maurer, 1993; Brassard & Salvail, 1994; Buttler et al., 2005).

5. Alice and Bob now have a common reconciled key which is only partially secret from Eve. They now begin the process of "privacy amplification", which is the extraction of the common final secret key from a partially secret one (Bennett, Brassard, and Roberts, 1998; Bennett, Brassard, Crepeau, and Maurer, 1995).

In securing a PTP link, QKD can be used to achieve unconditional security over that link. In this case, keys established by QKD are used for one-time pad (OTP) encryption and for information-theoretically secure authentication (based on universal hashing). This unconditional security over the PTP link can be proven because of the fact that the security of QKD can be expressed in the framework of universal composability (Alleaume, 2007; Canetti, 2001). This definitely is one of the most important applications of QKD. Alternatively, it is possible to compose keys obtained from QKD with a classical computationally

secure encryption scheme (such as AES). In this case, it would be possible to encrypt large rates of classical data over the PTP link. However, the final security of the data exchanged over such a link cannot be stronger than the security of the encryption scheme. Nevertheless, it is still possible to show that QKD has important advantages over other key distribution techniques in terms of key security and key renewal rate (Hughes, 2004; Alleaume, 2007).

In spite of these advantages obtained from applying QKD over PTP links, such an application also has important weaknesses. These include vulnerability to denial of service attacks, vulnerability to traffic analysis, distance- and location-dependence, and the insufficient key delivery in certain situations (Elliott, 2002). The recent work in building practical QKD networks is aiming to strengthen the performance of QKD in these weaker areas. Also, its goal is to overcome all limitations inherited by PTP links and to obtain the full advantages of networking environments.

Some aspects of QKDNs have been recently addressed in the literature. The "world's first" QKD network that is composed of trusted relays and/or untrusted photonic switches had been continuously running since June 2004 under the sponsorship of the US DARPA (Elliott, 2002; Elliott, Pearson, and Troxel, 2003; Elliott, 2004; Elliott et al., 2005). This network uses a modification of IPSec to integrate it with QKD. In Europe, the SECOQC project culminated in demonstrating information-theoretically secure QKD over a fiber-based MAN in 2008. In this project, a dedicated key distribution network infrastructure had been adopted. It is the so-called "network of secrets" (Dianati & Alleaume, 2006). In (Sfaxi, Ghernaouti-Helie, and Ribordy, 2005), a performance analysis for a proposal that integrates QKD into IPSec was presented. Also, a scheme integrating QC in 802.11i security mechanisms for the distribution of encryption keys was outlined in (Nguyen, Sfaxi, and Ghernaouti-Helie, 2006). Some issues of authentication and routing in simple

QKDNs were addressed in (Pasquinucci, 2005; Bechman-Pasquinucci & Pasquinucci, 2005). Similar efforts in QKDNs are underway in other countries such as Japan (Nambu, Yoshino, and Tomita, 2006) and China (Xu et al., 2009).

Our research in the field of QC in Iraq was started about fifteen years ago by modeling and simulation of various QKDN configurations (Faraj, 1999a; Faraj, 1999b). In that work, several QKDN models based on the BB84 protocol were presented. Both PTP and multiple access configurations were considered. These models were used for software simulation purposes. Error elimination and privacy amplification protocols were also investigated (Faraj, Al-Naima, and Ameen, 2000; Faraj, Al-Naima, and Ameen, 2002). Then, we considered the issue of unconditionally-secure authentication in QKD settings in deeper research (Faraj, 2007). In a more recent research, we dealt with the issue of integrating QC protocols with the classical information security infrastructure. More specifically, we presented an extension of SSL that allows QKD to be integrated with the current Internet infrastructure. We called that extension Quantum SSL (Faraj, 2008). Other colleagues had also participated in QC research. For example, some of them used software simulation to study a quantum cryptography systems based on polarization entangled pairs of photons using Ekert protocol (Maki, 2004). Others presented lab-scale experimental realization of quantum cryptography system based on the BB84 protocol (Tawfeeq, 2006) and a physical random number generator based on the dark pulses thermally generated in single photon avalanche photodiodes (Tawfeeq, 2009). More examples of QC work in Iraq can also found in (Faraj, 2005; Abbas, Khaleel, and Tawfeeq, 2011; Abdulhussein, 2012).

Regarding the hardware of QKDNs, it is convenient to characterize different QKDN models by the functionality that is implemented within the nodes. Thus, beyond stand-alone QKD PTP links, it is possible from this perspective to differentiate three main categories of QKDNs (Alleaume, 2007; Elliott, 2002):

a. **Optically Switched QKD Networks:** In this category, some classical optical functions like beam splitting, switching, multiplexing, etc., can be applied at the network nodes on the quantum signals sent over quantum channels. These optical functions can be used to achieve multi-user QKD. One-to-many connectivity between QKD devices has already been demonstrated at gigahertz clock-rate over passive optical access networks (Fernandez et al., 2007). Active optical switching can also be used to enable selective connection of any QKD nodes, as in DARPA network (Elliott et al., 2005). One important advantage of this category is that the corresponding nodes (which perform classical optical functions) need not to be trusted. However, due to the extra mount of optical losses introduced, this network model cannot be used to increase the distance of QKD.

b. **Trusted Relays QKD Networks:** In this category, local keys are generated over QKD links and then stored in nodes that are placed on both ends of each link. Global key distribution is performed over a QKD path, i.e. a one-dimensional chain of trusted relays connected by QKD links, establishing a connection between two end nodes. Hence, secret keys are forwarded in a hop-by-hop fashion along the QKD path. This concept of classical trusted relays can be used to significantly increase the distance of QKD, provided that the intermediate nodes can be trusted. Thus, this network model has been exploited by the DARPA QKD network and also adopted by the SECOQC network.

c. **"Full" Quantum Networks:** These are networks that aim to extend the distance of QKD by using "quantum repeaters", which can be used to an effective perfect quantum channel by overcoming propagation losses. In this scheme, it is not necessary to trust the intermediate network nodes. However, quantum repeaters are still difficult to be realized with current technologies. In addition, it was shown in (Collins, Gisin, and de Riedmatten, 2003) that another form of quantum nodes called "quantum relays" can be used to extend the distance of QKD. Quantum relays are simpler to implement than quantum repeaters; however, they remain technologically difficult to build.

As far as the QKDN software is concerned, we can notice that there are two main strategies that are globally considered in building practical QKDNs. It is possible to differentiate between them on the basis of the degree of dependence of the developed QKDN software on the pre-existing conventional network security infrastructure. We shall name these two strategies as: tightly-coupled protocol stack strategy and loosely-coupled protocol stack strategy. They are explained as follows:

- **Tightly-Coupled Protocol Stack Strategy:** In this strategy, secret random bits obtained from QKD (which is mainly a physical layer technology) are merged directly somehow into a conventional higher-layer security protocol suite. Thus, the consumer security protocol has to be modified to enable the integration of QKD within it. The work of DARPA QKD network is a good representative of such an approach where IPSec is used as the consumer protocol. Indeed, the work presented in this paper can also be considered under this category with SSL/TLS being used as the consumer higher-layer protocol. The advantage of this strategy is that it greatly facilitates direct implementation of QKD on private intranets (with an open possibility of a practical Internet implementation at some later mid-term stage). This is mainly

because that we make use of already existing capabilities of networking and security protocols with some modifications.

- **Loosely-Coupled Protocol Stack Strategy:** The focus here is to develop original multi-layer protocol infrastructures that are dedicated to QKDNs. In such a case, the QKDN infrastructure can be viewed as a "new cryptographic primitive" that is completely independent of the way by which random secret bits obtained from QKD would be used. This is the approach adopted by the SECOQC project. Of course, this approach may get the more of network environments by developing original routing and network management techniques. Hence, this strategy can be considered as a rather longer-term version of QKDNs.

STATE-OF-THE-ART IN QKDNS

It is not easy to report on the state-of-the-art in a highly multidisciplinary subject like QKDNs in a single chapter, especially if we are willing to maintain an acceptable level of rigorous treatment and deep discussion. Thus, we have chosen to focus on some important aspects of this issue that we believe they can make the reader better appreciate the required level of collaboration between researchers and specialist in multi-disciplines in order to facilitate design, deployment, and standardization of QKDNs. As, computer simulation is usually one of the first phases to track such technologically advanced issues, we will dedicate the following subsection to review our modeling and simulation approach which has been started about fifteen years ago and continued to develop with time (Faraj, 1999a; Faraj, 1999b). Then, the issue of using authentication codes for achieving unconditionally secure authentication in QKD is considered in some detail. This issue is crucial for QKDN from both theoretical and practical sides.

To emphasize this further, our developed fully authenticated version of the BB84 QKD protocol is described next. Finally, in this section and in order to show a detailed example of integrating QKD with the classical network security infrastructure, our extension of SSL (QSSL) is discussed.

Modeling and Simulation of QKDNs

In computer simulation, it is possible to consider various QKDN models. The security of these network models is achieved using QKD. Both PTP and multiple-access broadcast networks can considered. In developing these models, it is important to maintain simplicity, generality, and flexibility. This enables the efficient use of these models for software simulation purposes. Each network model is assumed to be composed of N communication nodes that are connected by links. Both fiber optic channels and free-air links can be considered in the simulation. Quantum transmission differs from classical information transmission in many aspects. Hence, many parameters have to be accurately set in the simulation. Some of the most important of these parameters and considerations are:

1. For fiber-optic links, we should decide the fiber type (Using polarization-preserving single-mode fiber is the most suitable choice for the construction of quantum channels).
2. Choosing the appropriate communication window (band) for fiber-optic links.
3. Choosing the parameters of the free-air (or free-space) links.
4. Setting the inter-node distance.
5. The number of nodes in the network and the network topology.
6. The type of transmission on the quantum channel (e.g. single photons, faint laser pulses, etc.).
7. The type and parameters of laser (photon) sources and detectors.

8. Type of encoding of the quantum channel signals.
9. Synchronization using ordinarily single-mode optical fiber as timing channel, for carrying time pulses from a global clock.
10. The parameters of other QKDN components (such as the passive optical network elements).
11. Compensation for environmental changes in fiber polarization (for polarization bases encoding).

In addition, the user can choose among several techniques for each of the basic phases of the BB84 QKD protocol, especially the error elimination (or key reconciliation) and privacy amplification phases. The user can also decide the type of authentication scheme used for achieving unconditional authenticity. Concerning the communication node types, it can be shown that assuming three basic configurations for communication nodes in QKDNs is sufficient. These configurations are *quantum transmission (QT)*, *quantum reception (QR)*, and *quantum transmission/reception (QTR)* nodes. Figure 3 shows simplified diagrams representing these configurations. These node models are classified according to their ability for transmitting and/or receiving quantum signals. Each node configuration is assumed to contain a controller that comprises a microprocessor, memory, and controller interface. The control commands of the controller are synchronized by clock pulses from a global clock, which is connected to each communication node via the timing channel. The controller of each node is also connected to the authenticated public channel.

As illustrated in Figure 3, and to keep generality and simplicity of presentation, the node configurations shown use polarization-based single photon systems for the quantum channel transmission (Only single photon systems were assumed in our first version of simulation software. Other more practical choices were then added later). The QT node configuration contains an apparatus

Figure 3. Basic configurations for communications nodes: (a) QT node configuration, (b) QR node configuration, and (c) QTR node configuration

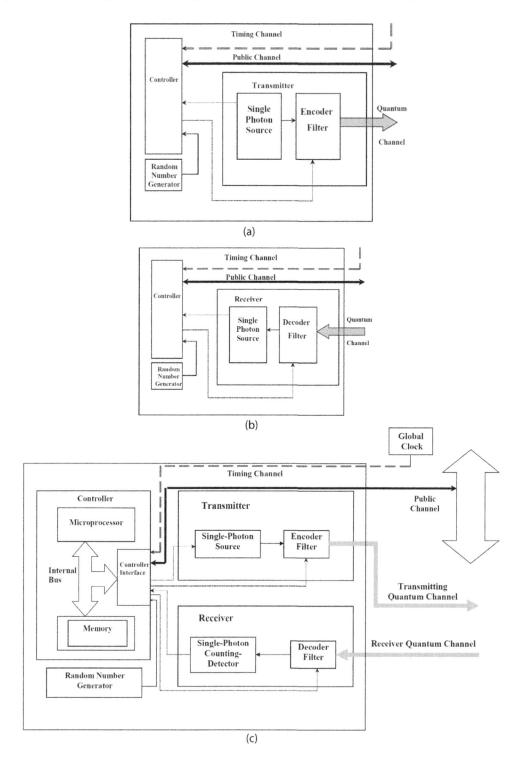

Figure 4. Examples of point-to-point QKDN models: (a) Decentralized fully-connected point-to-point network, and (b) Centralized point-to-point network with star topology

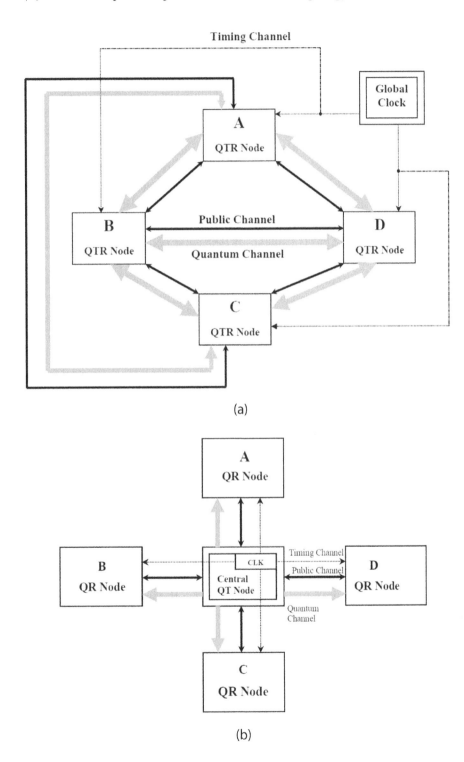

(a)

(b)

for transmitting individual quantum systems. Thus, a single photon source is incorporated in the transmission apparatus. The output of the single photon source is sent to an encoder filter. The encoder filter preferably uses an electro-optic polarization modulator to alter the states of polarization of single photons. The QR node configuration incorporates an apparatus for receiving encoded single-photons from the quantum channel. The receiver employs a complementary architecture with the incoming optical signal being received via the decoder filter at a photon detector. The decoder filter may be formed from an electro optic polarization modulator, similar to that used in the transmitter. For the case of single photon signals, the photon detector is preferably be an APD based on Germanium technology.

The QTR node configuration contains an apparatus for both transmission and reception of single photons. In fact, such a node configuration may contain more than one transmitter and/or more than one receiver of single photons, according to the type of application. The choice of encoding (polarization) states at the transmitter, and choice of reading basis at the receiver, have to be made randomly (not pseudorandomly). Thus, a random number generator (RNG) is incorporated in each node configuration. In all node configurations, the encoder and decoder filters are managed by their respective controllers to encode or decode photons in different encoding (rectilinear or diagonal polarization) states. Each photon can be identified by the clock period in which it is transmitted (or measured). This information is exchanged via the public channel. It is obvious that all node configurations must contain additional transmission and receiving equipment, which are required for exchanging "classical" messages on the public channel.

In the simulation of PTP QKDN models, both centralized and decentralized design concepts can be followed. In our simulation of such QKDN models, we have not allowed the possibility of including intermediate switching systems (rout-ers). So, store-and-forward routing algorithms cannot be used. This is because that, at present, such technology is not mature. However, including such systems into our simulation tool is planned to be done in the near future. In decentralized PTP QKDNs, all communication nodes have almost the same capabilities. The most important network topology to be considered may be the fully-connected PTP network, as shown in Figure 4(a). In this network, there are two bidirectional connections between each pair of nodes, one for quantum transmission and another for exchanging authenticated public messages. Each node has a QTR node configuration. The connection of each node to quantum channels is achieved using electro-optic switches. One or more of lithium-niobate Y-junction devices can be used for implementing the required electro-optic switch. Two electro-optic switches are used for each communication node, one for the transmission quantum channel and the other for the reception quantum channel. Control signals from each node are used to set the required configuration for the transmission and reception electro-optic switches, and hence choosing the appropriate quantum channel for transmitting and receiving single photons, respectively.

Centralized PTP QKDNs incorporate one or more central nodes and many terminal nodes. Central nodes act as secure interpreters for handling communication between different terminal stations. In this context, two basic network configurations can be considered: star and tree networks. In the star network topology, one central node is used with many terminal nodes are connected to it, as shown in Figure 4(b). In this network, one central QT node performs quantum cryptography protocols with four terminal QR nodes. It is obvious that the number of terminal nodes can be in the order of several tens of nodes or even more. The central node controls an electro-optic switch so that only the required output branch can be enabled to send quantum signals. Assuming equal priority terminal nodes, if the central node is busy in doing quantum cryptography protocol with some terminal node, all other terminal nodes have to wait until the central node becomes idle. Since terminal nodes have no ability for transmitting quantum signals, they must request (on the public channel) from the central node to start a quantum cryptography protocol.

The PTP tree QKDN may comprise one main central node connected to two or more (lower level) central nodes. Each of these in turn can be connected with several terminal nodes in the hierarchy. The main central node is a QT node, while other central nodes are QTR nodes. All terminal nodes are QR nodes. Quantum signals always are sent from a higher level node to a lower level node.

Broadcast (multiple access) QKDN models can be also considered in simulation. For example, we can consider a multiple access protocol that uses a centralized design concept so that the network contains a central node (which is a QT node) and many terminal nodes (which are QR nodes). It is possible to consider different network topologies that are suitable for the application of this protocol, such as star, tree, and bus topologies. In the multiple access star QKDN, the star connection of the quantum channel is implemented using the "passive star" configuration, which is a 1-to-N fiber coupler, where N is the number of the terminal nodes in the network. While, in the multiple access tree topology, several 1-to-M couplers (where M<N) can be used for achieving quantum channel connections.

This is actually a type of probabilistic multiple-access protocol. The reason for calling this protocol as a probabilistic multiple-access protocol is the probabilistic arrival of quantum signals (photons) at receivers. When the central node transmits quantum (single photon) pulses to the quantum channel, the quantum mechanical properties of such quantum systems ensure that a given photon will either be detected by one of the terminal nodes or will be lost from the system. Indeed, this process occurs in a totally random and unpredictable way. Thus, all terminals make photon measurements, with appropriate detecting gate width, at the clock rate. For each successful detection of a photon, they record the basis used for measurement, the actual result of measurement, and the time slot in which the photon arrived. When this probabilistic random access protocol is completely implemented the central node is in possession of N secret keys, each one is shared with a specific terminal node on the network. Also, each terminal has no knowledge of any other key apart from its own. Hence, this protocol is suitable for use in static channel allocation multiple access networks.

Indeed, other more sophisticated QKDN multiple-access models can be considered. Here we present two such configurations, which are the controlled multiple-access bus and the distributed access ring QKDNs. The controlled multiple-access bus can achieve dynamic channel allocation and hence multicasting operation. A centralized design concept is used in this network. It comprises a central node and N terminal nodes. The central node (which is a QT node) sends single-photon pulses onto the "quantum bus" channel to which terminal nodes (which are QR nodes) are connected, as shown in Figure 5(a). Each terminal station is connected into the quantum bus via an electro-optic interface, which can be in one of three states, depending on a switch control signal from terminal station. These states are:

- Open-Bus Open-Terminal (OBOT) State.
- Open-Bus Close-Terminal (OBCT) State.
- Close-Bus Open-Terminal (CBOT) State.

When the central node is broadcasting single-photons to all N terminal nodes, all electro-optic interfaces will act as simple passive 1-to-2 splitters (OBOT State). In this case, the system will be very similar to the probabilistic multiple-access network. When the central node performs a multicasting process, only some of terminal stations are incorporated in the quantum key distribution

Figure 5. Quantum channel configurations for: (a) The controlled multiple-access bus QKDN, and (b) The distributed access ring QKDN

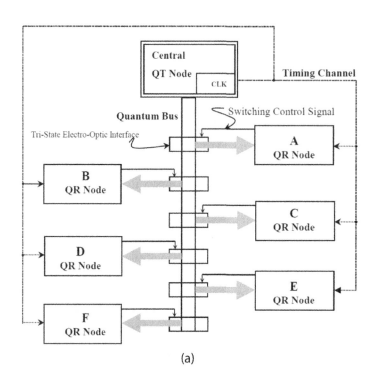

(a)

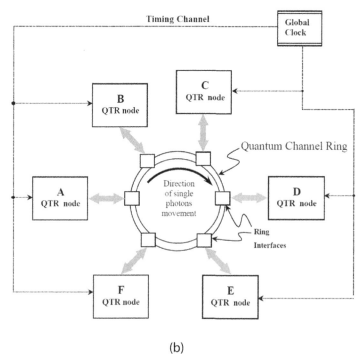

(b)

protocol. In this case, the tri-state electro-optic interfaces have to be reconfigured in such a way that only the required nodes receive quantum signals. It is interesting to note that if any terminal node on the network, which is not incorporated in multicasting, has tried to eavesdrop on the quantum key distribution between central nodes and some other terminal nodes, it will be in no better situation than an outside eavesdropper (Bennett, 1994).

The distributed access ring QKDN protocol can be developed in such a way that a decentralized dynamic channel allocation is achieved. The distributed access ring can be used for quantum key distribution in both broadcasting and multicasting modes with no need for using a central node in the network, as shown in Figure 5(b). Communication nodes on this network need to be QTR nodes. Quantum (single-photon) pulses can move only in one direction down the ring. Each station is connected to the quantum channel ring via a "ring interface". This interface is used for transmitting and/or receiving single photons from that quantum channel ring. The station reception quantum channel is connected to the ring via an electro-optic switch (which is a tri-state electro-optic switch similar to that used in the controlled multiple-access bus). This switch is controlled by station commands. The transmission quantum channel of the station is connected to the ring via a passive fiber coupler. The reception electro-optic switch can be in either one of three states, which are:

- Open-Ring Open-Station (OROS) State.
- Open-Ring Close-Station (ORCS) State.
- Close-Ring Open-Station (CROS) State.

When one station is transmitting single photons to some other station(s), all stations that are not incorporated in this multicasting process will turn their reception switches to be in the ORCS State. Thus, they are blocked. Stations that are required to receive single photons will turn their tri-state reception switches to be in OROS State. While, the node that is transmitting single photons will turn its switch to be in CROS State. Hence, photons that are not received by other stations are directed back to the original node, and they are prevented from recycling around the ring again. In fact these photons that are received at the same node which they are transmitted from, can be measured to check for the presence of an eavesdropper.

Unconditionally Secure Authentication

In spite of the fact that Eve is unable to gain any non-negligible information about the final key material from passively monitoring public channel communications, it is essential that these messages are authenticated. Thus, Alice and Bob can verify that they are communicating with each other, and that their public messages have not been altered in transit. This is essential to prevent Eve performing a "man-in-the-middle" attack. Although using public–key authentication techniques (e.g. digital signatures) for authentication the public channel messages in QKD may still offer some security advantages over traditional (i.e. non QKD-based) approaches (Paterson, Piper, and Schack, 2005), we are more interested in using unconditionally secure authentication method. It is important to notice that all currently existing unconditionally secure authentication schemes requires an initially shared secret key. The first unconditionally secure authentication scheme was invented by Carter and Wegman who published their discoveries in (Carter & Wegman, 1979; Wegman & Carter, 1981). It is commonly referred to as Wegman-Carter authentication.

One important difference between unconditionally secure encryption (the one-time-pad) and unconditionally secure authentication is that with unconditionally secure encryption, the required key needs to be at least as long as the message to be encrypted. This is the main problem with the one-time-pad (Bennett et al., 1992). Fortunately, Wegman-Carter authentication does not share this problem. The shared key required is only logarithmic in the size of the message being authenticated. The fact that required keys can be much shorter than the message to be authenticated is crucial for any QKD protocol. Each round of QKD generates a certain amount of newly shared secret key bits and requires far more communication which needs to be authenticated. If the key consumed by the authentication process is larger than the generated key, then the process would not be "quantum key expansion" but "quantum key shrinking" which is quite pointless (Cederlof, 2005).

In the usual model for authentication (without secrecy) (Stinson, 1992; Atici & Stinson, 1996), there are three participants: a transmitter, a receiver, and an opponent. The transmitter wants to send information using a public communication channel. The source state (i.e. a plaintext message) in concatenated with an authenticator (i.e. a tag) to obtain a message (i.e. an encoded message or an authenticated message), which is sent through the channel. An authentication rule (or key) e defines the authenticator e(s) to be appended to the source state s. It is assumed that the transmitter has a key source from which a key is obtained. Before any (authenticated) message is sent, this key is transmitted to the receiver by means of a secure channel. If we compare this model with that of QKD, we may notice two things. First, in general any of Alice and Bob can be a transmitter or a receiver. This depends on the direction of communication required on the two–way public channel. The second is that the quantum channel is used subsequently for the establishment of the required secret key.

Let us assume that the same key (authentication rule) is used to authenticate up to w consecutive source states, where w is some fixed positive integer. Also assume that an opponent observes $i \leq w$ distinct message which are sent using the same key. Suppose the opponent has the ability to introduce messages into the channel and/or to modify existing messages. Assume the opponent places a message $m' = (s', a')$ into the channel by either of these methods, where m' is distinct from the i messages already sent. If e is the key being used, then the opponent is hoping that $a' = e(s')$. This is sometimes called a spoofing attack of order i. The specific case i = 0 and i = 1 have received the most attention. The case i = 0 is called *impersonation*, and the case i = 1 is called *substitution*.

Let ξ be a set of authentication rules. It can be assumed that there is some probability distribution on the source states, which is known to all participants. Given this, the transmitter and receiver choose a probability distribution for ξ, called and "authentication strategy". This strategy is also assumed to be known to the opponent. Then, for each $i \geq 0$, it is possible to calculate P_{di}, which is the probability that the opponent can deceive the transmitter/receiver with a spoofing attack of order i. The following theorem gives a lower bound on P_{di} (Atici & Stinson, 1996; Massey, 1986).

Theorem 1. Suppose we have an authentication code (without secrecy) with n authenticators. Then $P_{di} \geq 1/n$ for all $i \geq 0$.

Cryptographically secure hash functions are widely used today in cryptography. However, they are only computationally secure, i.e. they can be broken with enough computation power or good enough algorithms (if they exist). Despite that hash functions cannot be unbreakable, message authentication can. It is important to note that although the fundamental block of unconditionally secure authentication (such as Wegman–Carter scheme) is called universal families (also classes or sets) of hash functions, those hash functions are quite different from the cryptographically secure hash functions just mentioned above. They have similarities, but the individual hash functions of Wegman–Carter (and other similar schemes) are not, and need not be, cryptographically secure in the classical sense (Cederlof, 2005).

In order to understand the requirements of (unconditionally secure) authentication codes obtained from universal hash families, some relevant definitions of various types of hash families are recalled from (Stinson, 1992; Atici & Stinson, 1996; Stinson, 1996) as follows:

- An (N; m, n) "hash family" is a set $\Im$ of N functions such that $f: A \to B$ for each $f \in \Im$, where $|A| = m$, $|B| = n$. There will be no loss in generality in assuming m $\geq$ n.

- An (N; m, n) hash family is "ε-universal" (ε-U) provided that for any two distinct elements x_1, $x_2 \in A$, there exist at most εN functions $f \in \Im$ such that $f(x_1) = f(x_2)$.

- An (N; m, n) hash family is "ε–almost–strongly–universal" (ε–ASU) provided that the following two conditions are satisfied:
  - For any $x \in A$ and $y \in B$, there exit exactly N/n functions $f \in \Im$ such that $f(x) = y$.
  - For any two distinct element x_1, $x_2 \in$ A, and for any two (not necessarily distinct) elements y_1, $y_2 \in B$, there exist at most ε N/n functions $f \in \Im$ such that $f(x_i) = y_i$, i = 1, 2.

- An (N; m, n) hash family $\Im$ of functions from A to B is "strongly-universal" (SU) provided that, for any two distinct elements x_1, $x_2 \in A$, and for any two (not necessarily distinct) elements y_1, $y_2 \in B$, we have

$$\left| \left\{ f \in \Im : f(x_i) = y_i \, , \, i = 1, 2 \right\} \right| = \frac{N}{n^2}$$

(2)

An SU hash family is also called "pairwise independent random variables". It is obvious that a hash family is SU if and only if it is 1/n–ASU. For authentication a definition of ε–ASU is sufficient, where each function in the family corresponds to

a key. In this case, elements of A are considered as source states, elements of B are considered as authenticators, each hash function gives rise to an authentication rule, and the authentication rules are used with equal probability. The proof of the following theorem is straightforward (Stinson, 1992; Atici & Stinson, 1996).

Theorem 2. If there exists an ε–ASU (N; m, n) hash family, $\Im$, then there exists an authentication code without secrecy for m source states, having n authenticators and N authentication rules, such that $P_{do} = 1/n$ and $P_{d1} \leq \varepsilon$.

From Theorem 1, it can be noted that SU families achieve the minimum possible deception probability P_{d1}. Wegman and Cater began with this stronger requirement in (Carter & Wegman, 1979) but the keys needed to be for too big for authentication to be practical. In (Wegman & Carter, 1981) they showed that is possible to construct ε–ASU hash families, having ε a bit larger than 1/n, that are much smaller than SU hash families. This means that by allowing a slightly larger deception probability P_{d1}, the length of the key required for authentication can be reduced significantly. Since then other papers have used this approach either explicitly or implicitly (Atici & Stinson, 1996).

Authentication codes have a level of security that does not depend on any unproven assumptions. In our simulation, three examples of unconditionally secure authentication schemes are offered. The first is the original Wegman–Cater scheme. While the second, due to Peev et al. (2005), uses a two-step procedure to achieve an efficient authentication for small messages. Finally, a scheme due to Taylor (1995) uses a similar approach to the first; however, it achieves improved characteristics in terms of both the required key material and authentication computations.

Another important issue to be considered here is the issue of multiple authentication. It is the situation where we would like to authenticate a sequence of messages with the same key. The authentication schemes basically do not allow us to tag more than one (plaintext) message using the same function (authentication rule), since once Eve knows two message–tag pairs she may be able to determine more such pairs. The definition of ϵ-ASU families makes no guarantees about the hardness of such a guess. Therefore the keys must never be reused (Cederlof, 2005; Wegman & Carter, 1981). To get around this problem, Wegman and Carter suggested in (Wegman & Carter, 1981) an approach so as to authenticate multiple messages using any ϵ-ASU class of hash functions. To apply this technique, the i th message in the sequence must be labeled with a counter (message number) having the value i, $1 \leq i \leq w$. This is the so-called counter-based multiple authentication.

This counter–based scheme is much more efficient than simply using w independent keys, since we need only add $\log_2 n$ new key bits for each extra message to be authenticated. However, this scheme has some drawbacks. For example, when a message is lost in transmission, then subsequent messages will not authenticate properly. Thus there in an interest in achieving multiple authentication without counters. Atici and Stinson (1996) had generalized the theory of universal hashing to construct authentication codes that allow the authentication of a sequence of plaintext messages without the use of counters. However, their construction requires considerably more key bits than the counter–based scheme described above.

The counter–based authentication method makes authentication of a constant stream of messages works fine and requires a minimal amount of previously shared data on condition that completely secret one–time pads are available. However, when the one–time pads are not guaranteed to be totally secret, Eve will learn something about the hash function for each massage/tag pair she sees (Cederlof, 2005). In QKD, information leakage in the quantum transmission phase is unavoidable. Thus, privacy amplification is used to significantly reduce Eve's knowledge

of the key, but not to exactly zero. However, in subsequent QKD sessions, Alice and Bob will start using some of the data obtained from some previous QKD sessions as initial shared information for further authentication. This situation represents counter–based authentication with (not completely) secret key. A possible attack for Eve in this case is to passively eavesdrop the messages and the encrypted tags and combine that information with whatever she knows about the one–time pads until she feels that her information on the used hash function enables her adjust an active attack that succeeds with acceptable probability. This off course does not work in the normal situation when a new hash function is used for authenticating each message.

In (Faraj, 2007), a fundamental solution was proposed to counter feat the above attack scenario on QKD systems that use counter–based authentication. This solution deals with the problem of using (not completely) secret one–time pads in counter– based authentication, as well as some other possible drawbacks of QKD systems. The solution is based on using a hybrid authentication strategy of normal authentication (where a new hash function is used for each message) and counter–based authentication. The system starts with the counter–based authentication mode. In this mode, a new one–time pad is used for each authenticated message. However, this does not continue indefinitely. Instead, we define a new parameter, γ, which represents the number of successive times that the value of the counter, in the counter-based mode, has been changed (i.e. the number of the new one-time pads used). When γ reaches a certain pre-defined maximum value, i.e. $\gamma = \gamma_{max}$, the system changes its state from the counter-based authentication mode to the second mode, which is the normal authentication mode.

Now, the system starts using a new hash function for authentication. As soon as this happens, the system automatically returns back to the counter–based authentication mode and the value of γ resets to zero. The value of γ is increased by one for each a new one–time pad used in this mode until it reaches γ_{max}, whereby the systems goes to normal authentication mode, and so on. This is illustrated in Figure 6. It is obvious that the parameter γ in this case is a security parameter. Alice and Bob need to agree on a certain value of γ depending on system details (particularly the privacy amplification protocol) and the required level of security. Another important point is that the value of γ_{max} need not to be a constant for all QKD sessions. Its value can be made variable according to a predefined formula. The proposed hybrid authentication strategy, defeats possible attacks on QKD systems that use counter–based authentication (with "not completely" secret one–time pads) by suitably adjusting γ_{max} such that Eve never reaches to a situation that she can launch an active attack on authentication tags with any promising probability of success.

The Authenticated BB84 QKD Protocol

This sub-section describes a specific implementation of the BB84 protocol with all the required unconditionally secure authentication steps. It is obvious that quantum channel transition need not to be authenticated because its security is protected by deep physical laws. Instead, the messages exchanged between Alice and Bob on the public channel have to be considered for authentication. Certainly authenticating all public channel messages is an inefficient extreme possibility. In fact, it is not necessary to authenticate all individual messages sent along the public channel. It is sufficient to authenticate some essential steps. Recalling back the basic BB84 protocol steps described previously, the following remarks can be made on the essential steps that are necessary and sufficient to authenticate them:

- The quantum transmission phase needs not to be authenticated since it is done using the quantum channel.
- All sifting phase messages have to be authenticated. This is crucial since otherwise Eve can exchange separate shifted keys with Alice and Bob and then choose only the bits where their all three choice of bases coincide. This is a serious man-in-the-middle-attack situation. In our implementation of the sifting phase, the following two messages have to be authenticated:

Figure 6. A state diagram for the proposed hybrid authentication strategy

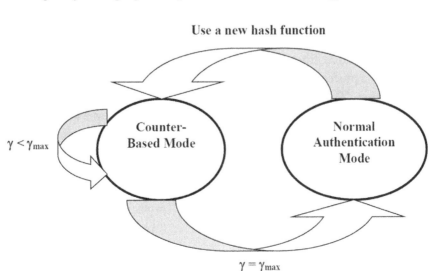

○ Bob's message indicating the indices of photon pulses detected by him and his choice of basis for each one of them.

○ Alice's message indicating her choice of basis for pulses detected by Bob.

Let N_i be the total number of photon pulses that are initially sent by Alice in quantum transmission phase of a QKD protocol session and let N_s be the length (in bits) of the obtained sifted key (the string obtained after the sifting phase). Thus, usually $N_i \gg N_s$. Then, the first message requires N_i bits for indicating whether a photon pulse was detected or not for each pulse index in addition to $2N_s$ bits for indicating the choice of basis for each detected pulse (this is because that there is on average a probability of 50% that Bob's choice of basis coincides with Alice's). This gives a total of $N_i + 2N_s$ bits of message length. The second message requires Alice sending $2N_s$ bits. In order to reduce these messages length, and hence reducing the authentication requirements or cost (i.e., number of exhausted initially shared secret bits), a form of run-length encoding is used. This also reduces the communication overhead in the system.

1. The steps used for the estimation of the QBER (and hence the estimation of Eve's knowledge on the raw quantum transmission) have to be authenticated. Both of the selection of the random subset from the sifted (or raw) key and the process of comparison need authentication. This is particularly important in order not to underestimate Eve's knowledge. This approach (of doing authenticated estimation of the QBER after the authenticated sifting) is more efficient in terms of the authentication cost since we deal with the sifted key rather than the initially transmitted block of photon pulses (remembering that $N_s \ll N_i$).

2. There are many techniques for key reconciliation. Despite the details of implementation of the reconciliation phase, Eve's interaction with system during this phase would not give her additional information about the secret bits; however she could fool Alice and Bob into correcting the wrong set of bits. Thus the reconciliation procedure could actually fail while they think it works. This is can be crucial since it is well understood that the privacy amplification technique cannot work if there is even a one bit error in the reconciled strings. Accordingly, there are at least two possible solutions for the problem of Eve interaction with the system in the reconciliation phase. The first is for Alice and Bob to verify the equivalence of their strings at the end of the reconciliation phase. The second is verifying equivalence of the final keys (i.e. after privacy amplification). As a result, both solutions effectively authenticate the prior communications between Alice and Bob (namely the reconciliation phase communications). This authentication can either be made asymmetric or symmetric. One good technique for accomplishing the equivalence check is using the set equality tester proposed by Wegman and Carter (1981). An asymmetric scenario for implementing this equality tester is proposed in (Gilbert & Hamrick, 2000). While a symmetric authentication of final key had been proposed in (Lutkenhaus, 1999). In our simulation work, a scenario similar to that of (Gilbert & Hamrick, 2000) is used since symmetric authentication would almost duplicate the authentication cost of this step without an obvious benefit for the application. Also, the equivalence check is done before privacy amplification in order that we can adjust the privacy amplification phase to deal with any (even small) additional information leakage to Eve during the equivalence check step.

3. It was noted previously in (Gilbert & Hamrick, 2000) that the privacy amplification phase needs no authentication. This is because that there is no need to exchange public messages for privacy amplification. The trick is that the sifting phase supplies random strings of sufficient length to define the hash index required to implement privacy amplification.

Based on these remarks, we can describe the fully authenticated version of the BB84 protocol to be consisting of the following steps:

- The quantum transmission phase is done as in the basic protocol.
- The messages of the sifting phase have to be authenticated as follows:
  - Bob sends one authenticated message indicating the indices of the pulses detected by him and his choice of basis for each one of them.
  - Alice responds with an authenticated message indicating her choice of basis for those pulses.
- In order to estimate the QBER, Alice and Bob use authenticated messages for the selection of the required random subset and for performing the comparison process. If the estimated QBER is below a defined maximum value (this value practically is highly dependent on the system implementation details), they continue the procedure. Otherwise, they abort the protocol.
- The key reconciliation (or error–elimination) procedure is done as usually done in the basic protocol.
- Alice and Bob use an asymmetric authentication technique to apply the Wegman–Carter set equality tester for checking the equivalence of their strings after reconciliation. If they find that their strings are equal, they proceed to the privacy amplification stage. Otherwise, the abort the protocol.

- The privacy amplification technique is applied as usual without need for public discussion, and hence no need for further authentication. Thus the final key is obtained.

Quantum SSL

SSL was originally developed by Netscape. SSLv3 was designed with public review and input from industry (Stallings, 2011). Then, the TLS working group was formed within IETF (Internet Engineering Task Force) and published TLSv1.0 (Dierks & Allen, 1999) that is very close to SSLv3 and can be viewed as SSLv3.1. Later, TLSv1.1 (Dierks & Rescorla, 2006), which is a minor modification of TLSv1.0, had been proposed. The "socket layer" lives between the application layer and the transport layer in the TCP/IP protocol stack. SSL/TLS (or just simply SSL) contains two layers of protocols. The SSL Record Protocol provides basic security services to various higher-layer protocols and defines the format used to transmit data. Also, SSL defines three higher-layer protocols that use the SSL Record Protocol. These three protocols are used in the management of SSL exchanges. The first is the Change Cipher Spec Protocol, which updates the cipher suite (list of a combination of cryptographic algorithms) to be used on SSL connection. The second is the Alert Protocol that is used to convey SSL-related alerts to the peer entity. The third is the Handshake Protocol, which is the most complex part of SSL.

In this section, we describe our extension of SSL for QKDNs which we called Quantum SSL (QSSL) (Faraj, 2010). This is mainly done by describing the most important modifications and extensions introduced to the "conventional" SSL/TLS. In the beginning, some important design issues of QSSL are presented as follows:

- **The Choice of SSL/TLS:** SSL has been chosen as the basic protocol for this work because it is a very widely used, relatively simple, and well-designed security protocol.

- **Simplicity and Efficiency:** During the development of QSSL, we have tried to introduce the minimum possible modifications and extensions to SSL that result in an efficient integration of QC within SSL. This approach also has enabled the avoidance of designing a completely new protocol, which may contain unexpected security flaws

- **Traditional vs. Unconditionally Secure Encryption:** Each of the unconditionally secure encryption using the one-time pad (OTP) and traditional encryption (such as 3DES, AES, etc.) has its own advantages and requirements. Hence, QSSL supports both types of encryption (Note that "conventional" SSL/TLS does not support OTP).

- **Message Authentication:** Traditionally used MACs can only offer computationally-secure data integrity. But authentication codes based on universal hashing may offer unconditionally-secure data integrity. However, these authentication codes need secret bits to be initially shared by authorized parties. As QKD can be used as a source for these bits, QSSL supports both types of message authentication for the data traffic.

- **Network Initialization:** To achieve unconditional security (which is the main reason for the deployment of QKDNs), QKDNs need initially pre-distributed secret keys. These keys are required to perform the first rounds of unconditionally-secure authentication for the QKD public channel. However, there is another possibility of using public-key cryptography for the initialization of the network by authenticating only the first rounds of QKD. Then, unconditionally-secure authentication can be used for subsequent QKD sessions.

Despite the fact that such kind of hybrid authentication and network initialization technique does not offer unconditional security in a strict sense, they still present a security advantage over any other conventional key distribution technique, as argued in (Alleaume, 2007). Thus, both of these QKD network initialization modes are supported by QSSL.

- **Applicability:** In a contrast with classical open networks (such as the Internet), QKDNs can be considered as "closed" networks, especially at this early development stage. This is mainly due to the physical limitations they have. Thus, QSSL is more suitable (at least for the time being) for application in private intranets rather than the public Internet. However, as such private networks are already used by many organizations; the deployment of QSSL would bring a considerable security advantage for these intranets.

Various aspects of QSSL are described below. Note that for a reason of clarity, QSSL handshake is described as two modes. Mode-1 is based on the traditional public-key initialization of SSL/TLS. Mode-2 is based on PSK cipher suites. Otherwise, it is straight forward to only describe a single QSSL handshake mode by just labeling some messages as situation dependent and specifying the use of suitable cipher suites. The protocol version to be initially used for QSSL is 3.5 (remember that SSLv3 uses 3.0, TLSv1.0 uses 3.1, and TLSv1.1 uses 3.2).

1. **Introducing a New SSL/TLS Content Type:** A fifth content type is introduced for the SSL Record Protocol (which originally contains four types only). This new type is to be called "quantum-cryptography" and it is related to any QC protocol to be integrated within SSL/TLS. By defining this content type, the QC protocol (e.g. QKD) is to be

considered as an additional higher-layer SSL/TLS protocol just like the Handshake, the Change Cipher Spec, and the Alert protocols. The message format of the QSSL Quantum Cryptography Protocol is shown in Figure 7. Each message of the Quantum Cryptography Protocol has the following fields:

a. **Type (2 bytes):** Indicates one of the messages used in the public exchange phase of the QC protocol. Some of the messages defined for QKD are listed in Table 1.

b. **Protocol (1 byte):** The QC protocol used (e.g. the BB84 QKD protocol).

c. **Version (1 byte):** Enables the use of more than one version of a certain QC protocol. Thus, components of different characteristics can be used to implement any phase of that protocol. For example, different techniques for sifting, reconciliation, estimating eavesdropper's (Eve) information, and/or privacy amplification may be used for implementing the BB84 protocol.

d. **Length (4 bytes):** The length of the message in bytes.

e. **Job no. (2 bytes):** Enables the operation of multiple QC protocol jobs (or instances), all belonging to a one QSSL session.

f. **Authentication (1 byte):** Indicates whether this message is authenticated. It may also contain some additional information about this authentication (if any).

g. **Encoding (1 byte):** Indicates if a certain encoding technique is used for the content field of the message. It may also contain some additional information about this encoding (if any). For example, a form of run-length encoding is used for the (sparse) messages of the QKD sifting phase.

h. **Content (≥ 0 bytes):** The parameters and data associated with this message.

i. **Tag:** If the message is authenticated, this field would contain the corresponding authentication tag. Its size depends on the authentication code used.

2. **Defining New Cipher Suites:** Two new sets of cipher suites are defined to be used for QSSL. The first of these sets uses public-key cryptography to initialize the QKD process. This set is to be applied whenever there is no possibility for authorized users to initially have the pre-shared secret keys (PSKs) required for universal hashing. This set may also be used when users believe that the security offered by such cipher suites is adequate for them. This situation represents what we call QSSL Mode-1. The second set of cipher suites uses PSKs to facilitate the use of unconditionally-secure authentication for protecting the QKD public channel. This set can offer provable security and it corresponds to the second mode of QSSL handshaking (QSSL Mode-2). Table 1 lists some representative examples of these two sets of cipher suites. In this table, the first three cipher suites belong to the first set just described above, while the last three cipher suites belong to the second set. To increase the flexibility of using different software components in implementing QKD, two distinct implementations of BB84 (BB84 version 1 and BB84 version 2) have been assumed to be available to each user. Indeed, in this table, UHASH1, UHASH2, and UHASH3 represent three different unconditionally-secure authentication codes (such as Wegman-Carter scheme [49], Taylor scheme [54], etc.). As far as the first set of cipher suites is concerned, network initialization can be done using any of following "conventional" SSL/TLS key exchange methods, which are: RSA, fixed DH, or

Figure 7. Message format of the QSSL quantum cryptography protocol

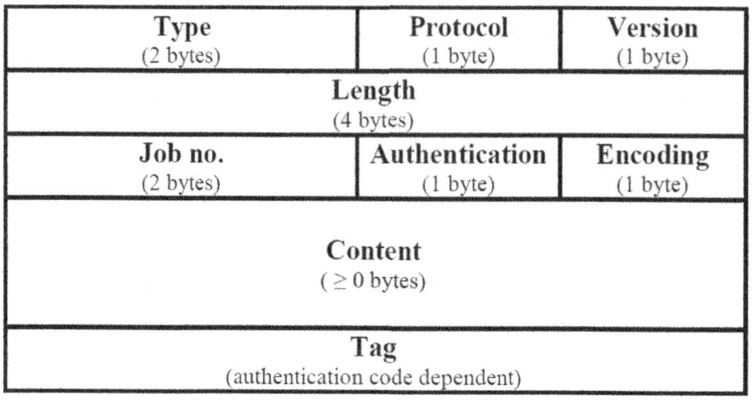

Type (2 bytes)	Protocol (1 byte)	Version (1 byte)
Length (4 bytes)		
Job no. (2 bytes)	Authentication (1 byte)	Encoding (1 byte)
Content (≥ 0 bytes)		
Tag (authentication code dependent)		

Table 1. Some QSSL ciphersuites

	Ciphersuite	Key Exchange	QKD Public Channel	Initialization	Cipher	Hash
1-	QSSL-BB84-1-SHA-RSA-WITH-OTP-MD5	BB84v1	SHA	RSA	OTP	MD5
2-	QSSL-BB84-2-SHA-DHE-DSS-WITH-DES-CBC-UHASH1	BB84v2	SHA	DHE with DSS signature	DES in CBC mode	UHASH1
3-	QSSL-BB84-1-MD5-DH-RSA-WITH-AES-128-CBC-SHA	BB84v1	MD5	fixed DH with RSA signature	128-bit key AES in CBC mode	SHA
4-	QSSL-BB84-1-UHASH1-PSK-WITH-OPT-UHASH2	BB84v1	UHASH1	PSK	OTP	UHASH2
5-	QSSL-BB84-2-UHASH2-PSK-WITH-AES-256-CBC-UHASH3	BB84v2	UHASH2	PSK	256-bit key AES in CBC mode	UHASH3
6-	QSSL-BB84-1-UHASH3-PSK-WITH-OTP-SHA	BB84v1	UHASH3	PSK	OTP	SHA

ephemeral DH (DHE). However, the use of anonymous DH key exchange is not supported by QSSL because it makes the system vulnerable to man-in-the-middle attacks. Furthermore, this set can only use traditional MACs (such as SHA and MD5) for protect-ing the QKD public channel. This is obviously due to the assumption unavailability of PSKs required for unconditionally-secure authentication. In contrast, the second set of cipher suites always use unconditionally-secure authentication for protecting QKD public channel discussions. This is implied by using PSKs for system initialization in this latter mode. It is very important to notice that both sets of cipher suites support the use of traditional encryption algorithms and OTP. Also, they both support either traditional MACs or unconditionally-secure authentication codes to offer data integrity for QSSL application traffic.

3. **Cryptographic Computations:** QSSL uses QKD to directly generate the following cryptographic parameters: client write MAC secret, server write MAC secret, client write key, server write key, client write IV, server write IV, and pre-master-secret. Note that we have used the same terminology of SSL/TLS. However, the write MAC secrets are used in the generation of both of traditional and unconditionally-secure message digests. Similarly, the write keys are used for both traditional and unconditionally-secure encryption. The write IVs are only generated when traditional block ciphers are used for encrypting application traffic. Whenever unconditionally-secure encryption and/or authentication are to be used, the size of the required write keys and/or the size of the required write MAC secrets have to be negotiated during QSSL handshake. The pre-master-secret generated from QKD is divided into two parts. The first 48 bytes of it compose the first part, which we call pre-master-secret-1. The remaining bits of the pre-master-secret compose the second part that is to be called pre-master-secret-2. Then, the master-secret is calculated from pre-master-secret-1. The function used for calculating the master-secret in QSSL is similar to that used by SSL/TLS. Next, the master-secret can be used for authenticating the finished handshake messages and for resuming QSSL sessions (when it is allowed). QSSL sessions can be resumed if and only if both of encryption and message digest

algorithms used for application traffic are not unconditionally-secure. The pre-master-secret-2 is to be used as a PSK for initiating future QSSL sessions. Hence, its size has to be negotiated by users during handshaking such that its size is adequate to enable the use of unconditionally-secure authentication for protecting the QKD public channel. Note that this separation of the pre-master-secret into two independent parts is necessary from the respective of unconditional security.

4. **QSSL Mode-1:** This mode represents QSSL handshaking based on using public-key cryptography for initialization. Any of the traditional SSL/TLS key exchange techniques (except for the anonymous DH) can be used. The sequence of message exchange of QSSL Mode-1 is very similar to that of the traditional SSL/TLS. However, there are some required modifications to be noted. The most important of these are:

a. At least three new parameters should be added for negotiation in the client-hello and server-hello messages. These parameters are the size of write MAC secrets, the size of write keys, and the size of the pre-master-secret. The first of these is to be added whenever unconditionally-secure authentication is required for QSSL application traffic. The second parameter is included when it is intended to use OTP encryption. Finally, the third parameter is added whenever users have the intention to generate PSKs for future Mode-2 initialization (The size of this parameter should be ≥ 48 bytes). Note that this point also applies to QSSL Mode-2.

b. QKD (or generally any QC protocol) can only be started after both sides mutually authenticate each other. Also, QKD has to be finished before exchanging any change-cipher-spec message. Hence, the whole QKD message exchange is inserted between Phase 3 and Phase 4 of SSL Handshake described previously.

c. QKD continues until the complete generation of the negotiated key sizes. After this point only, change-cipher-spec and finished messages (Phase 4) can be exchanged (This issue also applies to QSSL Mode-2).

5. **QSSL Mode-2:** This handshaking mode uses PSK based initialization. This offers a very high speed session initialization compared with the relatively slow public-key cryptography based Mode-1 initialization. Figure 8 shows the basic Mode-2 message exchange. QKD message exchange is completely inserted just before the transmission of change-cipher-spec and finished messages. Besides the three security parameters added to the negotiation by the client-hello and server-hello messages mentioned previously, there is an important modification to server-key-exchange and client-key-exchange messages in this mode. In QSSL Mode-2, these two messages are used for identification and synchronization of PSK pads. At first, the server-key-exchange message is used to carry a "PSK identity hint". One possibility for this "PSK identity hint" is to be a hash value of some bits from the beginning of the PSK pad. This may also be accompanied by some sort of a sliding-window technique to discard some (unsynchronized) bits from the beginning of pads. The client-key-exchange message, when received, is to be interpreted as a positive acknowledgement of the "PSK identity hint". Otherwise, an unknown-psk-identity alert message has to be sent by the client.

6. **Key Pads Management:** Basically, QSSL can be considered to be a protocol that uses QKD to supply users with on-the-fly cryptographic keys. This is accepted as far as the

Figure 8. QSSL mode-2 handshake

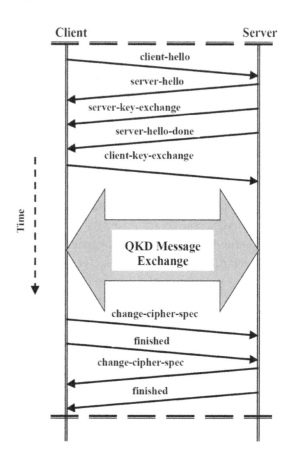

write keys and write MAC secrets are used directly after their generation for protecting application data traffic. In this case, only PSK pads (when generated) need somewhat a loner-term management. However, it is also possible to use QSSL in a key-store operation mode, wherein all keys are generated in much larger sizes and stored for future usage. This requires the development of management and synchronization mechanisms for five key pads per user (one pad for each of the five keys generated from QKD). This number would be duplicated considering any additional security relation with a new user.

The system architecture of a typical QSSL application is shown in Figure 9. As the figure indicates, QSSL is located between application layer protocols and TCP. On transmission, QSSL accepts data traffic from the application layer and adds the required security protection before sending it down to lower layers. The BB84 is used as the QC protocol in this architecture. QSSL uses the network to send two types of traffic. The first is application data traffic, which is encrypted and authenticated according to user's requirement. The second is the traffic corresponding to the classical public channel exchanges required for implementing BB84. This latter traffic type is transmitted during QSSL handshake and it has

to be authenticated in order to defeat man-in-the-middle attack on the QKD protocol.

The quantum transmission phase of BB84 is done using the quantum channel. This is mainly a physical layer technology. Hence, management and control of this phase is performed at the lower layers of the architecture. Other phases of BB84 (namely sifting, reconciliation, estimating Eve's information, and privacy amplification) uses the classical public channel for the required discussions. These phases are implemented using a specific user-mode application module that we call BB84 QKD protocol engine. The input of this engine is raw quantum bits resultant from quantum transmission, while its output is secret bits that

Figure 9. System architecture for a typical QSSL application

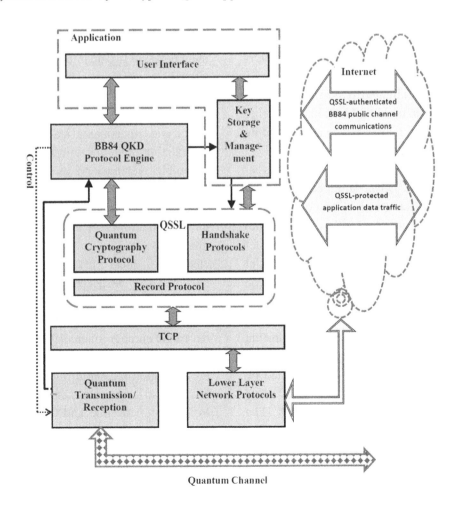

are (temporarily) stored in the key storage and management module. These bits are used by QSSL as cryptographic keys in accordance to the specified cipher suites.

FUTURE RESEARCH DIRECTIONS

QKD has already been achieved on metropolitan distances (of the order of 100 km). However, due to the unavoidable photon loss in the transmission, it is technically not possible to directly extend the quantum transmission beyond this distance scale. It is not possible to receive quantum transmission when the probability of a dark count in the photon detectors becomes comparable to the probability that a photon is correctly detected (Yuan et al., 2008). Therefore, to further increase the distance coverage of QKDNs, the usage of specialized devices called quantum repeaters is required. Building efficient and practical quantum repeaters is very hot research topic at the present and future. Its importance is not limited to its role in QKDNs. In fact, it is a basic building block in many other quantum information processing areas including distributed quantum computing.

A quantum repeater is different from a classical signal amplifier. Quantum repeater does not copy a quantum state (as this is a contradiction with the no-cloning theorem). In fact, quantum repeaters use teleportation in order to transfer quantum data. Teleportation allows the transfer of a quantum state via classical communication via the concept of entanglement. Two entangled quantum systems can share a non-local correlation even if they are physically separated. Despite that QKD does not directly require entangled states, entangled (or distributed Bell) pairs created by repeaters can enable long-distance QKD (Van Meter, Ladd, Munro, and Nemoto, 2009). The concept of quantum repeaters was introduced by Briegel, Dur, Cirac and Zoller (BDCZ) (1998) based on combining entanglement swapping and quantum memory. However, the difficulty

of constructing of quantum memory is still the main obstacle of using the BDCZ protocol for implementing quantum repeaters. In their seminal paper, Duan, Lukin, Cirac and Zoller (DLCZ) (2001) proposed an alternative quantum repeater protocol that is based on linear optics and atomic ensembles (This can incorporate the required entanglement action and quantum memory into a single unit). Furthermore, a novel solution for realizing a quantum repeater might be combining the atomic quantum memory in DLCZ and the strategy of BDCZ (Yuan et al., 2008).

In general, a quantum memory can be demonstrated as a stationary quantum system that can store information encoded in a photon. Constructing such a quantum memory would significantly facilitate the realization of a quantum repeater. In this case, a quantum repeater can be thought to be a small quantum computer. It can be shown that a set of quantum repeaters can produce an entanglement between two quantum systems separated by a very large distance (Shahriar, 2011). Indeed, Sangouard, Simon, de Riedmatten, and Gisin (2011) presented a good survey paper on the theoretical and experimental status of the active field of realizing quantum repeaters based on atomic ensembles and linear optics (the DLCZ protocol). Indeed, the potentials of different approaches are compared quantitatively. They concluded that the first quantum repeater that beats direct transmission is expected to be realized using atomic ensembles, linear optics, and photon counting. However, they suspected that approach might be overtaken by other alternatives with increased capabilities, in the longer run. The new capabilities might come from modifying ensemble-based schemes. Despite the significant progress toward the realization of quantum repeaters reported in the literature so far (See for example (De Greve, 2012; Vollbrecht, Muschik, and Cirac, 2011; Clausen et al., 2011)), it is expected that this direction of research will continue to still be very hot in the coming years.

Away from the quantum technology, another research field that needs further investigation can be the classical aspects of conventional cryptography that would be integrated with QC techniques. Such issues might need revisions from both theoretical side and from practical side projections and consequences. One such issue is the authentication cost of the QKD protocol. In order to maintain the flavor of unconditional security of QKD, an unconditionally secure authentication primitive has to be used for authenticating public channel communications. However, developing an authenticated QKD protocol with a practical level of efficiency is not a trivial task. In addition, there are some proposed applications of QKDNs (e.g. via satellites) that impose critical limitations on hardware (and software) resources. Thus, building authenticated QKD protocol with low or moderate computational requirements is of high benefit. We believe that our proposed hybrid authentication strategy is very beneficial in this direction. This is mainly related to the number of successive times the hybrid authentication primitive stays in counter-based mode before making a transition to normal authentication mode, i.e. the value of γ_{max}. As this value increases, the authentication cost decreases and vice versa. However, a higher value of γ_{max} may increase the chances of Eve for launching a successful active attack. Thus, by adjusting such parameters into suitable values, it would be possible to make a fine trade-off between a higher level of security and efficiency. However, further research is required to build more efficient constructions and more reliable protocols.

From practical point of view, the most apparent real world applications of QSSL can be these where unconditionally-secure services are required. However, there are other real world scenarios that still need more exploration. Such scenarios are mainly related to various possibilities offered by QSSL for combining unconditionally secure authentication (based on pre-shared secrets) with some public-key systems (especially those public key systems that are not directly threatened

by quantum computers). More investigation of the practical challenges of implementing QKD in real world can be very useful. Finally, near future work in the field should consider the issue of standardization of some aspects of QKDNs. Such effort requires a worldwide coordination among organizations and specialists involving in the field from multi-disciplinary areas. This is an important step towards internationalization and spreading of QKDNs. Scientific societies, industrial corporations, and international expert groups can be involved in this work.

CONCLUSION

It is obvious now that developing commercial QKDN services is a broad interdisciplinary area, which calls for cooperation between experts from a variety of research, industrial, and infrastructure-provision disciplines. Thus, in order to move quantum cryptosystems from laboratory into real life applications, strategies in which many correspondents are exchanging individual quantum systems to build many identical pairs of secret keys, have to be considered. Software simulation can be an important tool for developing and studying such systems. However, to achieve an efficient and constructive simulation, certain models with accurate specifications have to be developed first. Modeling simplicity, generality, and flexibility must be considered in any applied procedure.

It has been also shown that it is well justified and prudent for the time being to obtain unconditionally-secure services based on combining QKD with OTP and/or unconditionally-secure authentication codes. However, investigating the full flavor of such services requires multi-disciplinary research efforts. We believe that proposed QSSL protocol is a useful step towards a better understanding of the requirements of integrating QKD into the already existent and well-tested information security infrastructure. This can also lead us to deeper insights on the various aspects of integrating QC protocols within different layers and locations of the classical information infrastructures.

The development of industrial QKDN prototype that can be interoperated with the existing IT-infrastructure requires many jobs to be done. The technological development in the framework of such projects should focus on the following issues:

- Quantum signals (single photons) generation, transmission, and detection.
- Development of adequate electronic components for real-time processing of data and exact time synchronization. Indeed, these components should guarantee security against unauthorized intrusion.
- Concepts for adequate infrastructure and new networking protocols have to be developed.
- Development of suitable methods for authentication, error elimination, and privacy amplification.
- Dedicated software has to be developed, which, on the one hand, marshals the information flow and manages automatic tasks and, on the other, interoperates with existing IT-infrastructure thus integrating QC applications with existing services.
- All equipment components must be scaled down to fit into a compact system that is adequate for real-life use.

Finally, and in order to give more emphasis on the importance of interdisciplinary cooperation in the field of QKDNs, we add on more comment on related research in Iraq as an example. As we have mentioned previously, this research was started since late 1990s. During this period, a number of researchers and postgraduate students have worked in several QC projects. However, it can be noticed that most of QC work in Iraq has been related to theoretical analysis, mathematical modeling and software simulation, and lab-based realizations of some basic quantum cryptosystems. We claim that the main reason for our inability to build more practical and large-scale realizations of QKDNs is the lack of a coordination entity or organization that can activate and manage multidisciplinary scientific collaboration between researchers from related fields in Iraq. Some other countries that started QC research several years later after Iraq are currently in much better situation due to the better cooperation between people and organizations working in relevant specializations.

REFERENCES

Abbas, A., Khaleel, A., & Tawfeeq, S. (2011). Detection of the photon number splitting attack by using decoy states QKD system. *International Journal of Research and Reviews in Computer Science*, *2*(4), 1010–1013.

Abdulhussein, A. (2012). *Design and implementation of an active quenching driving circuit for single-photon detection*. (M.Sc. Thesis). Institute of Laser for Postgraduate Studies, University of Baghdad, Baghdad, Iraq.

Alleaume, R. (Ed.). (2007). SECOQC white paper on quantum key distribution and cryptography. Secoqc-WP-v5, Version 5.1.

Atici, M., & Stinson, D. (1996). Universal hashing and multiple authentication. *Lecture Notes in Computer Science*, *1109*, 16–30. doi:10.1007/3-540-68697-5_2

Bechman-Pasquinucci, H., & Pasquinucci, A. (2005). Quantum key distribution with trusted quantum relay. *arXiv:* quant-ph/0505089v1.

Bennett, C. H. (1994), Interferometric quantum cryptographic key distribution system. *US Patent* No. 5, 307, 410.

Bennett, C. H., Bessette, F., Brassard, G., Salvail, L., & Smolin, J. (1992). Experimental quantum cryptography. *Journal of Cryptology*, *5*(3), 3–28.

Bennett, C. H., & Brassard, G. (1984). Quantum cryptography: public key distribution and coin tossing. In *Proceedings of International Conference on Computers, Systems and Signal Processing*. Academic Press.

Bennett, C. H., Brassard, G., Crepeau, C., & Maurer, U. (1995). Generalized privacy amplification. *IEEE Transactions on Information Theory, 41*, 1915–1923. doi:10.1109/18.476316

Bennett, C. H., Brassard, G., & Roberts, J.-M. (1988). Privacy amplification by public discussion. *SIAM Journal on Computing, 17*(2), 210–229. doi:10.1137/0217014

Brassard, G., & Salvail, L. (1994). Secret-key reconciliation by public discussion. *Lecture Notes in Computer Science, 765*, 410–423. doi:10.1007/3-540-48285-7_35

Briegel, H.-J., Dur, W., Cirac, J. I., & Zoller, P. (1998). Quantum repeaters: The role of imperfect local operations in quantum communication. *Physical Review Letters, 81*, 5932–5935. doi:10.1103/PhysRevLett.81.5932

Buttler, W., Lamoreaux, S., Torgerson, J., Nickel, G., Donahue, C., & Peterson, C. (2005). *Fast, efficient error reconciliation for quantum cryptography*. Univ. of California, Los Alamos National Lab., *arXiv:* quant-ph/0203096.

Canetti, R. (2001). Universally composable security: A new paradigm for cryptography protocols. In *Proceeding of FOCS'01*, (pp. 136-145). FOCS.

Carter, J., & Wegman, M. (1979). Universal classes of hash functions. *Journal of Computer and System Sciences, 18*, 143–154. doi:10.1016/0022-0000(79)90044-8

Cederlof, J. (2005). *Authentication in quantum key growing*. (M. Sc. Thesis). Department of Applied Mathematics, Linkopings University, Sweden.

Clausen, C., Usmani, I., Bussieres, F., Sangouard, N., Afzelius, M., & de Riedmatten, H. et al. (2011). Quantum storage of photonic entanglement in a crystal. *Nature, 496*, 508–512. doi:10.1038/nature09662 PMID:21228774

Collins, D., Gisin, N., & de Riedmatten, H. (2003). Quantum relays for long distance quantum cryptography. *arXiv:* quant-ph/0311101.

De Greve, K., Yu, L., McMahon, P., Pelc, J., Natarajan, C., & Kim, N. et al. (2012). Quantum-dot spin–photon entanglement via frequency downconversion to telecom wavelength. *Nature, 491*, 421–426. doi:10.1038/nature11577 PMID:23151585

Dianati, M., & Alleaume, R. (2006). *Architecture of the Secoqc quantum key distribution network*. GET-ENST, France, *arXiv:* quant-ph/0610202v2.

Dierks, T., & Allen, C. (1999). The TLS protocol version 1.0. *RFC 2246*.

Dierks, T., & Rescorla, E. (2006). The TLS protocol version 1.1. *RFC 4346*.

Duan, L.-M., Lukin, M. D., Cirac, J. I., & Zoller, P. (2001). Long-distance quantum communication with atomic ensembles and linear optics. *Nature, 414*, 413–418. doi:10.1038/35106500 PMID:11719796

Ekert, A. (1991). Quantum cryptography based on Bell's theorem. *Physical Review Letters, 67*, 661–663. doi:10.1103/PhysRevLett.67.661 PMID:10044956

Elliott, C. (2002). Building the quantum network. *New Journal of Physics, 4*, 46.1-46.12.

Elliott, C. (2004). *The DARPA quantum network*. BBN Technologies, *arXiv:* quant-ph/0412029.

Elliott, C., et al. (2005). *Current status of the DARPA quantum network*. BBN Technologies, *arXiv:* quant-ph/0503058.

Elliott, C., Pearson, D., & Troxel, G. (2003). Quantum cryptography in practice. In *Proceedings of ACM SIGCOMM'03 Conference*. ACM.

Faraj (Al-Janabi). S. T. (1999a). Development of new secure optical network models based on quantum cryptography. In *Proceedings of the Federation of Arab Scientific Research Councils Conference on Super-Highway Networks*. Academic Press.

Faraj (Al-Janabi). S. T. (1999b). *Quantum cryptographic key distribution in optical communication networks*. (Ph.D. Thesis). College of Engineering, Al-Nahrain University, Iraq.

Faraj (Al-Janabi). S. T., Al-Naima, F., & Ameen, S. (2000). Quantum cryptographic key distribution in multiple-access networks. In *Proceeding of 16th IFIP World Computer Congress*, (pp. 42-49). IFIP.

Faraj (Al-Janabi). S. T., Al-Naima, F., & Ameen, S. (2002). Optical network models for quantum cryptography. In *Proceeding of 17th IFIP/Sec2002 Conference*. IFIP.

Faraj (Al-Janabi). S. T. (2005). A novel quantum cryptographic error elimination technique using simple hamming codes. In *Proceedings of the International Conference on Advanced Remote Sensing for Earth Observation Systems*. KACST and ISPRS.

Faraj (Al-Janabi), S. T. (2007). Unconditionally secure authentication in quantum key distribution. *i-Manager's Journal on Software Engineering, 1*(3), 31-42.

Faraj (Al-Janabi). S. T. (2008). A novel extension of SSL/TLS based on quantum key distribution. In *Proceedings of the International Conference on Computer and Communication Engineering (ICCCE08)*, (Vol. 1, pp. 919-922). ICCCE.

Faraj (Al-Janabi), S. T. (2010). Integrating quantum cryptography into SSL. *Ubiquitous Computing and Communication Journal, 5*, 1778–1788.

Fernandez, V. et al. (2007). Passive optical network approach to gigahertz-clocked multiuser quantum key distribution. *IEEE Journal of Quantum Electronics, 43*(2). doi:10.1109/JQE.2006.887175

Gilbert, G., & Hamrick, M. (2000). *Practical quantum cryptography: a comprehensive analysis (part one)*. MITRE Technical Report.

Gisin, N., Iblisdir, S., Tittel, W., & Zbinden, H. (2006). Quantum communications with optical fibers. In A. V. Sergienko (Ed.), *Quantum communications and cryptography* (pp. 17–43). Taylor & Francis Group.

Gottesman, D., & Lo, H.-K. (2005). Proof of security of quantum key distribution with two-way classical communications. *arXiv:* quant-ph/0105121.

Gottesman, D., Lo, H.-K., Lutkenhaus, N., & Preskill, J. (2002). Security of quantum key distribution with imperfect devices. *arXiv:* quant-ph/0212066.

Hughes, R. (Ed.). (2004). A quantum information science and technology roadmap, part 2: Quantum cryptography. Report of the quantum cryptography technology expert panel, ARDA, LA-UR-04-4085, Version 1.0.

Khan, M. I., & Sher, M. (2003). Protocols for secure quantum transmission: a review of recent developments. *Pakistan J. of Information and Technology, 2*(3), 265–276. doi:10.3923/itj.2003.265.276

Lomonaco, S. J. (1998). *A quick glance at quantum cryptography*. Dept. of Computer Science and Elect. Engineering, Univ. of Maryland Baltimore County. *arXiv:* quant-ph/9811056.

Lutkenhaus, N. (1999). Estimates for practical quantum cryptography. *Physical Review A., 59*, 3301–3319. doi:10.1103/PhysRevA.59.3301

Maki, A. (2004). *Simulation of quantum key distribution based on polarization entangled pairs of photons using the basic Ekert protocol*. (M.Sc. Thesis). Institute of Laser for postgraduate studies, University of Baghdad, Baghdad, Iraq.

Massey, J. (1986). Cryptography- a selective survey. In E. Biglieri, & G. Prati (Eds.), *Digital communications* (pp. 3–21). North-Holland.

Maurer, U. M. (1993). Secret key agreement by public discussion from common information. *IEEE Transactions on Information Theory, 39*, 733–742. doi:10.1109/18.256484

Mayers, D. (2001). Unconditional security in quantum cryptography. *Journal of the ACM, 48*(3), 351–406. doi:10.1145/382780.382781

Nambu, Y., Yoshino, K., & Tomita, A. (2006). One-way quantum key distribution system based on planar lightwave circuits. *Japanese Journal of Applied Physics, 45*, 5344. doi:10.1143/JJAP.45.5344

Nguyen, T., Sfaxi, M., & Ghernaouti-Helie, S. (2006). 802.11i encryption key distribution using quantum cryptography. *Journal of Networks, 1*(5), 9–20. doi:10.4304/jnw.1.5.9-20

Pasquinucci, A. (2005). Authentication and routing in simple quantum key distribution networks. UCCI.IT, Italy, *arXiv:* cs.NI/0506003v1.

Paterson, K. G., Piper, F., & Schack, R. (2005). *Why quantum cryptography*. Department of Mathematics, University of London. *arXiv:* quant-ph/0406147.

Peev, M., Nolle, M., Maurhardt, O., Lorunser, T., Suda, M., Poppe, A., et al. (2005). A novel protocol-authentication algorithm ruling out a man-in-the-middle attack in quantum cryptography. *arXiv:* quant-ph/0407131.

Sangouard, N., Simon, C., de Riedmatten, H., & Gisin, N. (2011). Quantum repeaters based on atomic ensembles and linear optics. *Reviews of Modern Physics, 83*, 33–79. doi:10.1103/RevModPhys.83.33

Sfaxi, M., Ghernaouti-Helie, S., & Ribordy, G. (2005). Using quantum key distribution within IPSec to secure MAN communications. In *Proceedings of the IFIP-MAN 2005 Conference on Metropolitan Area Networks*. IFIP.

Shahriar, S. (2011). A long-distance quantum repeater gets one step closer. *Physics, 4*, 58. doi:10.1103/Physics.4.58

Stallings, W. (2011). *Cryptography and network security* (5th ed.). Pearson Education International.

Stinson, D. (1992). Universal hashing and authentication codes. *Lecture Notes in Computer Science, 576*, 74–85. doi:10.1007/3-540-46766-1_5

Stinson, D. (1996). On the connections between universal hashing, combinatorial designs and error-correcting codes. *Congressus Numerantium, 114*.

Tawfeeq, S. (2006). *Experimental realization of quantum cryptography system based on the BB84 protocol*. (Ph.D. Thesis). Institute of Laser for Postgraduate Studies, University of Baghdad, Baghdad, Iraq.

Tawfeeq, S. (2009). A random number generator based on SPAD dark counts. *Journal of Lightwave Technology, 27*(24), 5665–5667. doi:10.1109/JLT.2009.2034119

Taylor, R. (1995). Near optimal unconditionally secure authentication. *Lecture Notes in Computer Science, 950*, 244–253. doi:10.1007/BFb0053440

Van Meter, R., Ladd, T., Munro, W., & Nemoto, K. (2009). System design for a long-line quantum repeater. *IEEE/ACM Transactions on Networking, 17*(3), 1002–1013. doi:10.1109/TNET.2008.927260

Vollbrecht, K., Muschik, C., & Cirac, J. (2011). Entanglement distillation by dissipation and continuous quantum repeaters. *Physical Review Letters, 107*(120502), 1–5. PMID:22026761

Wegman, M., & Carter, J. (1981). New hash functions and their use in authentication and set equality. *Journal of Computer and System Sciences, 22*, 256–279. doi:10.1016/0022-0000(81)90033-7

Xu, F. X., Chen, W., & Wang, S. et al. (2009). Field experiment on a robust hierarchical metropolitan quantum cryptography network. *Chinese Science Bulletin, 54*(17), 2991–2997. doi:10.1007/s11434-009-0526-3

Yuan, Z., Chen, Y., Zhao, B., Chen, S., Schmiedmayer, J., & Pan, J. (2008). Experimental demonstration of a BDCZ quantum repeater node. *Nature, 454*(28). PMID:18756253

Zoller, P. (Ed.). (2005). Quantum information processing and communication: Strategic report on the current status, visions, and goals for research in Europe. QIST ERA-Pilot Project, Version 1.1.

ADDITIONAL READING

Alleaume, R., Roueff, F., Diamanti, E., & Lutkenhaus, N. (2009). Topological optimization of quantum key distribution networks. *New Journal of Physics*, 11, 075002 (*arXiv:*0903.0839v1 [quant-ph], 2009).

Blumenthal, U., & Goel, P. (2007). Pre-shared key ciphersuites with NULL encryption for TLS. *RFC* 4785.

Capmany, J., & Fernandez-Pousa, C. (2010). Optimum design for BB84 quantum key distribution in tree-type passive optical networks. *Journal of the Optical Society of America*, B, 27, A146-A151 (*arXiv:*0911.0745v2 [quant-ph], 2011).

Chen, T., Wang, J., Liang, H., Liu, W., Liu, Y., Jiang, X., et al. (2010). Metropolitan all-pass and inter-city quantum communication network. *Optics Express*, 18, 27217-27225 (*arXiv:*1008.1508v2 [quant-ph], 2010).

Chou, C., Laurat, J., Deng, H., Choi, K., de Riedmatten, H., & Felinto, D. et al. (2007). Functional quantum nodes for entanglement distribution over scalable quantum networks. *Science, 316*, 1316–1320. doi:10.1126/science.1140300 PMID:17412919

De, A., & Sen, U. (2010). Quantum advantage in communication networks. *Physics News, 40*(4), 17-32 (*arXiv:*1105.2412v1 [quant-ph], 2011).

Eronen, P., & Tschofeing, H. (Eds.). (2005). Pre-shared key ciphersuites for TLS. RFC 4279.

Faraj (Al-Janabi). S. T. (2006). Towards arab scientific collaboration in the field of quantum cryptography. *Proceedings of the 4th Symposium on Scientific Research and Technological Development Outlook in the Arab World*, Damascus, Syria.

Faraj (Al-Janabi). S. T., & Sagheer, A. (2011). Enhancement of e-government security based on quantum cryptography. *Proceedings of the International Arab Conference on Information Technology (ACIT'2011)*, Naif Arab University for Security Science (NAUSS), Riyadh, KSA.

Faraj (Al-Janabi). S. T., & Rabee, R. (2011). Key reconciliation techniques in quantum key distribution. *Proceedings of the First Engineering Conference of the College of Engineering*, University of Anbar, Ramadi, Iraq.

Garcia-Escartin, J., & Chamorro-Posada, P. (2012). Quantum computer networks with the orbital angular momentum of light. *Physical Review* A 86, 032334 (*arXiv:*1207.0585v1 [quant-ph], 2012).

Gyongyosi, L., & Imre, S. (2012). Private quantum coding for quantum relay networks. *Lecture Notes in Computer Science*, 7479, 239-250 (*arXiv:*1208.0661v1 [quant-ph], 2012).

Jain, R. (2010). Resource requirements of private quantum channels and consequences for oblivious remote state preparation. *Journal of Cryptology*, International Association for Cryptologic Research (published online: 02 October 2010).

Kar, G., & Rahaman, R. (2012). Local cloning of multipartite entangled states. [Springer Science+Business Media, LLC.]. *Quantum Information Processing, 11,* 711–727. doi:10.1007/s11128-011-0281-7

Khan, M., et al. (2006). A quantum key distribution network through single mode optical fiber. *Proceedings of the International Symposium on Collaborative Technologies and Systems,* 386-391 (*arXiv:*0901.4646v1 [cs.CR], 2009).

Mendonça, F., de Brito, D., & Ramos, R. (2011). An optical scheme for quantum multi-service network. *arXiv:*1105.2289v2 [quant-ph].

Peev, M., Pacher, C., Alléaume, R., Barreiro, C., Bouda, J., & Boxleitner, W. et al. (2009). The SECOQC quantum key distribution network in Vienna. *New Journal of Physics, 11*(075001), 1–37.

Phoenix, S., & Barnett, S. (1994). Quantum cryptography using discarded data. British Telecommunications PLC., *International Patent Publication* No. 94/08409.

Phoenix, S., & Townsend, P. (1993). Quantum cryptography and secure optical communications. *BT Technology Journal, 11*(2), 65–75.

Qi, B., Zhu, W., Qian, L., & Lo, H. (2010). Feasibility of quantum key distribution through dense wavelength division multiplexing network. *New Journal of Physics, 12,* 103042 (*arXiv:*1006.0726v2 [quant-ph], 2010).

Razavi, M. (2012). Multiple-access quantum key distribution networks. *IEEE Trans. Communications,* 60, 3071 (*arXiv:*1112.3218v1 [quant-ph], 2011).

Rieffel, E., & Polak, W. (2000). An Introduction to quantum computing for non-physicists. [CSUR]. *ACM Computing Surveys, 32*(3), 300–335. doi:10.1145/367701.367709

Sasaki, M., Fujiwara, M., Ishizuka, H., Klaus, W., Wakui, K., Takeoka, M., et al. (2011). Field test of quantum key distribution in the Tokyo QKD network. *Optics Express, 19*(11), 10387-10409 (*arXiv:*1103.3566v1 [quant-ph], 2011).

Spiller, T. (1996). Quantum information processing: Cryptography, computation, and teleportation. *IEEE Proceedings, 84*(12), 1717-1746.

Stucki, D., Legre, M., Buntschu, F., Clausen, B., Felber, N., Gisin, N., et al. (2011). Long term performance of the SwissQuantum quantum key distribution network in a field environment. *New Journal of Physics,* 13, 123001 (*arXiv:*1203.4940v1 [quant-ph], 2012).

Treiber, A., Poppe, A., Hentschel, M., Ferrini, D., Lorünser, T., Querasser, E., et al. (2009). Fully automated entanglement-based quantum cryptography system for telecom fiber networks. *New Journal of Physics,* 11, 045013 (*arXiv:* 0901.2725v2 [quant-ph], 2009).

Van Meter, R., Touch, J., & Horsman, C. (2011). Recursive quantum repeater networks. *Progress in Informatics,* 8, 65-79 (*arXiv:*1105.1238v1 [quant-ph], 2011).

Wang, S., Chen, W., Yin, Z., Zhang, Y., Zhang, T., Li, H., et al. (2010). Field test of the wavelength-saving quantum key distribution network. *Optics Letters,* 35, 2454-2456 (*arXiv:*1203.4321v1 [quant-ph], 2012).

KEY TERMS AND DEFINITIONS

Authentication Codes: They are mathematical constructions that can achieve unconditionally-secure authentication. Usually, the fundamental block of unconditionally secure authentication is called universal families of hash functions. However, those hash functions are quite different from the cryptographically secure hash functions used in conventional cryptography.

Quantum Cryptography (QC): QC is one of the major sub-fields of the quantum information processing field which offers new methods of secure communications that are not threatened even by the power of quantum computers. As QKD is the most crucial task of QC, the terms QC and QKD usually are used interchangeably.

Quantum Information Technology (QIT): It is a technology that can support entirely new modes of information processing based on quantum principles.

Quantum Key Distribution (QKD): QKD basically enables two parties (traditionally referred to as Alice and Bob) to produce the shared secret keys required for secure communications, through a combination of quantum and conventional communication steps.

Quantum Key Distribution Network (QKDN): It is an infrastructure composed of quantum links connecting multiple distant nodes that have the capability of performing QKD.

Secure Socket Layer (SSL): An SSL connection is a transport (in the OSI layering model definition) that provides a peer-to-peer type of service. SSL connections are transient and each connection is associated with one SSL session. An SSL session is an association that defines a set of cryptographic security parameters that can be shared among multiple connections.

Unconditional Security: In contradiction with computational security, unconditional security refers to cryptographic systems that remain secure even when the adversary has unlimited computing power. Thus, we are using this term interchangeably with Information-theoretic security.

Vernam Cipher (the One-Time Pad or OTP): This is the only known cipher that can achieve perfect secrecy if used correctly. It requires that the key is truly random, as large as or greater than the plaintext, never reused in whole or part, and kept secret.

Chapter 4
Chaos–Based Cryptography for Voice Secure Wireless Communication

Sattar B. Sadkhan Al Maliky
University of Babylon, Iraq

Rana Saad
University of Babylon, Iraq

ABSTRACT

Chaos theory was originally developed by mathematicians and physicists. The theory deals with the behaviors of nonlinear dynamic systems. Chaos theory has desirable features, such as deterministic, nonlinear, irregular, long-term prediction, and sensitivity to initial conditions. Therefore, and based on chaos theory features, the security research community adopts chaos theory in modern cryptography. However, there are challenges of using chaos theory with cryptography, and this chapter highlights some of those challenges. The voice information is very important compared with the information of image and text. This chapter reviews most of the encryption techniques that adopt chaos-based cryptography, and illustrates the uses of chaos-based voice encryption techniques in wireless communication as well. This chapter summarizes the traditional and modern techniques of voice/speech encryption and demonstrates the feasibility of adopting chaos-based cryptography in wireless communications.

INTRODUCTION

Due to the increased demand for wireless communications by military and civilian applications, there are studies oriented towards the protection of information from eavesdroppers and attackers. This information is transmitted through communication channels between users. It can be text, image or voice signal (Lawande et al., 2005). The voice signal information is commonly used in the applications of wireless communications. It needs protection more than text / image information against eavesdroppers through wireless channel. The reason for such need arises from the fact that voice encryption process must encrypt all parts of signal information to get on indistinguishable voice (Mosa et al., 2009) (S. Sridhan et al., 1993). Cryptography algorithms must evolve with the development of wireless communication technologies. The reason for this development is to give

DOI: 10.4018/978-1-4666-5808-0.ch004

higher security. Cryptographic techniques can utilize number theory and Chaos theory. One of the new multidisciplinary approaches for designing and implementing a new cryptosystem is based on Chaos Theory (Jian et al,. 2010) . It is found that the ideas of chaos have been very fruitful in such diverse disciplines as biology, economics, chemistry, engineering, fluid mechanics, physics, just to name a few. Chaos is a multidisciplinary science, and this is reflected in the fact that the members of the group are affiliated with diverse disciplines such as: Physics, Mathematics, Electrical Engineering, Physical Sciences and Technology (IPST), Electronics and Applied Physics (IREAP), Systems Research (SR), Applied Math and Scientific Computation (AMSC).

The deterministic property means that every next state of chaos function depends on the previous state. The irregular property shows the behavior of chaotic system has irregular continuity. Nonlinear property means that chaos function has nonlinear transformation. The sensitivity to initial conditions property means that some small changes in the initial state of chaotic systems could result dramatically in various behaviors at the final state. The long term prediction means that when achieving irregular and sensitive to initial conditions properties, then the prediction of the system's behavior will have obstacles (Munakata, 2008).

The aim is to show the techniques of three main objectives of this chapter. The objectives are chaos based cryptography, secure wireless communication and voice encryption. Also this aim makes the reader know how to use chaos in cryptography, what the generations of secure wireless communication, which use the chaos based cryptography.

MULTIDISCIPLINARY IN CHAOS BASED CRYPTOGRAPHY

Multidisciplinary is composed of several separate branches of learning or fields of expertise. These different disciplines (fields) can use chaos theory in their applications as illustrated in Figure 1 (David et al., 2012) .

Figure 2 gives the schematic presentation of the chaos behavior. It shows the detail of these applications that exploit the chaos behavior. The behavior of chaos can be seen in the labs, in the nature, in an economics (Kyrtsou & Labys, 2006), in finance (Hristu-Varsakelis & Kyrtsou, 2008), in different other studies such as medical studies (White, 1999), quantum chaos theory study (Berry, 2003), electrical engineering and computer science chaotic systems as well as numerical analysis (Strang, 1991).

Chaos theory is an area of study in the competence of mathematics. It is formulated in 1961 (Berry. and Mainieri, 1996). Chaos is short of the term "chaotic system". It is a dynamic system because each outcome depends on one or more of its previous outcomes (Kellert, 1993) (Chesnes, 2001).

Figure 1. Different disciplines (fields) used within the chaos applications

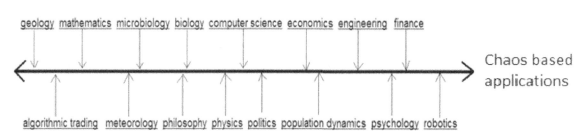

Figure 2. The different applications use chaos

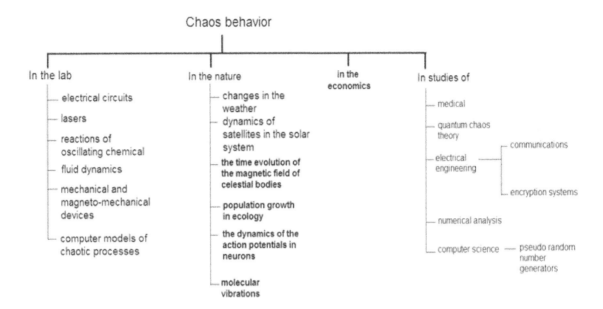

The following two examples show the behavior of chaos. The purpose of these two examples is to exhibit that chaos is a dynamic system, and also has high sensitivity feature.

Example 1: Pseudo Random Number Generator (PRNG)

Pseudo random number generator (PRNG) shows the chaos behavior in the computer science. The following simple generator is used to show chaotic behavior. This generator has the form: $x_{n+1} = cx_n \mod m$, where (c) is initial condition, (x_n) is initial state when n = 0, (x_{n+1}) is the next state and n = 1,2,3,... N. If (mod m) function is removed, this equation becomes linear equation and no chaotic behavior in it. On the other hand, if (mod m) function is not removed, this generator has nonlinear behavior and also has chaotic behavior (Munakata, 2008). Any change in the initial condition (c) or in the initial state (x_0), will give various sequences of random irregular numbers. For example, an equation has (c = 29) and (m=

997), $x_{n+1} = 29x_n \mod 997$. If we apply $x_0 = 117$ and $x_0 = 118$ (Note that there is a little difference between them), The result of this equation will give two different sequences as presented in Figure 3 (Munakata, 2008). Figure 3 illustrates that this PRNG has chaotic behavior. Also it has high sensitivity feature. Since any changes of the initial state x_0 will give different sequences, this PRNG is a dynamic system.

Example 2: Logistic map

The another example of chaotic behavior is logistic map, $x_n + 1 = rx_n(1-x_n.)$ Any change in the initial parameter (r) or in the initial state (x_0), will give various sequences of random numbers and irregular.

1.   Change of parameter r

The map has (r = 2.5, r=3.2, r=3.5, and r=3.8). If we apply x_0=0.6, the result of this equation will give four different sequences as presented in Fig-

Figure 3. Chaotic behavior of PRNG example with a small changes in intial state values (x_0 and a)

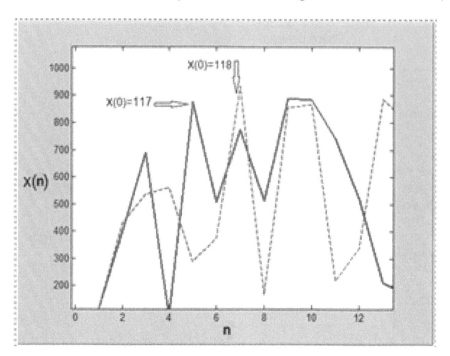

ure 4, which illustrates the application of 4 initial parameters (r) with one initial state x_0=0.6, the randomness can occurr from this equation when r is increased to 3.8. Figure 4.a shows r =2.5 then the values of x_n are equal to 0.6. Figure 4.b gives r = 3.2 then the values of x_n are increased in the range [0.5, 0.8]. Figure 4.c illustrates r = 3.5 then the values of x_n are increased in the range of [0.4, 0.9] with few randomness. Figure 4.d shows r = 3.8 then the values of x_n are increased in the range of [0.2, 1] with more randomness. (Chesnes, 2001). .

2.   Change of initial state x_0

The map has (r = 3.8) . If we apply x_0=0.7 and x_0=0.8 (Note that there is a little difference between them), the result of this map will give two different sequences as presented in Figure 5.

These sub-examples show that logistic map has chaotic behavior. Also thry have high sensitivity if there is any change of initial states or parameters. This map is a dynamic system. Since each outcome

state ($x_{(n+1)}$) depends on previous input (x_n). The result of x_n sequence is random and irregular.

From the above two sub-examples (a and b), it is clear that chaos has high sensitivity to its initial state x_n, to its initial condition (c) or to its parameter (r). They can be considered as secret key and must be kept secret between two shared parties of communications (Kanso, & Smaoui, 2007).

DIFFERENT CHAOS MAPS

In early 1950s, Shannon mentioned that the mechanism of stretch and fold can be exploited in cryptography. Hence it is clear that Shannon actually discussed a typical route to chaos via stretching and folding, which is well-known in today's chaos theory (Alvarez & Li, 2006). There was a silent period about this fact until the late 1980, chaos theory becomes popular and cryptography becomes more important (Blackledge,

Figure 4. Chaotic behavior for logistic map when changing the parameter r

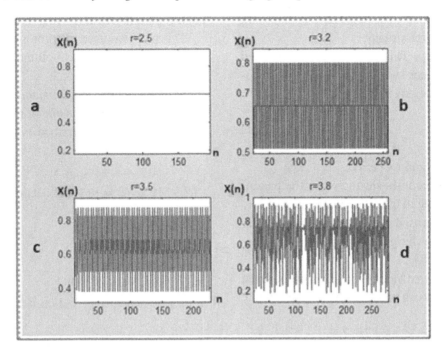

Figure 5. Chaotic behavior for logistic map when change the initial state (x_0)

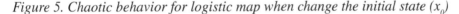

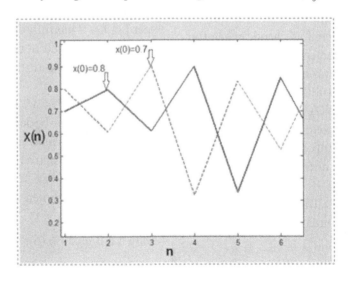

2010). From 1990, the publications started to suggest various cipher methods, used chaos in synchronization and in cryptography to provide secure communication (Yang, 2003). This section will list the types of chaos map used with cryptography. Also it will illustrate the literature review of chaos based cryptography. And finally it gives the advantages and disadvantages of using chaos theory with cryptography.

Chaos map: The desirable features of chaos are Deterministic, nonlinear, irregular, long term prediction, and sensitivity to initial conditions. These features attracte many researchers to use the chaos in cryptography and synchronization to provide secure communication. This section shows some types of chaos maps used in researches into chaos based cryptography.

Logistic map: This map is famous and used more in nonlinear system. This map can be described in Equation (1):

$$X_{n+1} = rx_n(1-x_n) \tag{1}$$

where: $x_n (0,1)$ and $r \in (1, 4)$.

This map becomes chaotic when the parameter (r) has value in the following range ($3.57 < r \leq 4$). And it is used in cryptography by (Patidar et al., 2008) to design pseudo random number generator (PRNG).

Standard map: One of standard map types used in cryptography can be as shown in Equations (2):

$$X_{n+1} = X_n + k \sin y_n \bmod 2\pi \quad (2.a)$$

$$y_{n+1} = y_n + X_{n+1} \bmod 2\pi \quad (2.b)$$

where: X_n and $y_n \in [0,2\pi]$

This map is considered as chaotic when the parameter k has value larger than or equal to 18.9 ($k \geq 18.9$). This map was used in cryptography by (Patidar &, Sud, 2009) to design pseudo random number generator (PRNG).

Picewise linear chaotic map (PLCM): This map has a different style of equations. These types of equations are used in different researches. And they expressed as:

The type 1 of PLCM : This type of PLCM can be described in Equation (3):

$$x\left(t+1\right) = F\left(x\left(t\right), p\right) =$$
$$\begin{cases} x(t)/p, 0 \leq x(t) \leq p, \\ (x(t)\text{-}p)/(1/2\text{-}p), p < x(t) < 1/2, \\ F(1\text{-}x(t), p), 1/2 < x(t) \leq 1, \end{cases} \tag{3}$$

where: $0 < p < \frac{1}{2}$

x serves as an initial condition, and p is the control parameter for the map F.

This map was used in cryptography by (Asim & Jeoti, 2008) to design a Subtituation box (S-box) (Xingyuan et al., 2011).

The type 2 of PLCM (Tent map): This map can be one dimensional. It is one of piecewise linear map types. It can be described as in Equation (4):

$$x_{i+1} = \begin{cases} f(x_i,\mu) = \mu x_i, \text{if } x_i < 0.5 \\ f(x_i,\mu) = \mu(1 - x_i), \text{otherwise} \end{cases} \tag{4}$$

where: $f:[0,1] \rightarrow [0,1]$

$x_i \in [0,1]$, for i ≥ 0, and
ì can be a positive real constant $\in [0,2]$

The initial value x_0 and ì considered as initial condition and control parameters of the map.

This map becomes chaotic when the parameter $1 < i < 2$ has fully chaotic behavior at $i = 2$. This map was used in cryptography by (Kanso, 2010) to design pseudo random number generator (PRNG).

The type 3 of PLCM: This type of PLCM is one dimensional. It can be described as in Equation (5)

This map was used in cryptography by (Zaibi et al., 2010) to design a Subtituation box (S-box).

The type 4 of PLCM (affine map): This type of PLCM is three dimensional. This map is defined on the unit cube $[0; 1] \times [0;1] \times [0;1]$. It can be as shown in Equation (6):

$$x\left(n\right) = \left|1 - \left|(2.x\left(n-1\right) + y\left(n-1\right) + z\left(n-1\right)/2 - 1\right|\right| \tag{6.a}$$

$$y\left(n\right) = \left|1 - \left|(2.y\left(n-1\right) + x\left(n-1\right) + z\left(n-1\right)/2 - 1\right|\right| \tag{6.b}$$

$$z(n) = \left| 1 - \left| (2.z(n-1) + y(n-1) + x(n-1) / 2 - 1 \right| \right|$$
$$(6.c)$$

where the initial conditions are x_0, y_0, z_0 $\in [0, 1]$

This map was used in cryptography by (Zaibi et al., 2010) to design a Subtituation box (S-box).

Lorenz map: This map can be described as three dimensional as shown in Equations (7):

$$\dot{x}_1 = \sigma (x_2 - x_1) \qquad (7.a)$$

$$\dot{x}_2 = rx_1 - x_1 x_3 - x_2 \qquad (7.b)$$

$$\dot{x}_3 = x_1 x_2 - px_3 \qquad (7.c)$$

where: $x_1(0), x_2(0), x_3(0)$ are initial conditions, and $\acute{o}, r, \tilde{n}$ are positive constants

This map can be chaotic when ($r > 24.74$), ($\sigma = 10$) and ($\tilde{n} = 8 / 3$). This map was used in cryptography by (Ahmad et al., 2012) to design keystream generator for voice encryption.

Chen map: This map can be described as three dimensional as shown in Equations (8):

$$\dot{x}_1 = a (x_2 - x_1) \qquad (8.a)$$

$$\dot{x}_2 = (c - a) x_1 - x_1 x_3 + cx_2 \qquad (8.b)$$

$$\dot{x}_3 = x_1 x_2 - bx_3 \qquad (8.c)$$

where: $x_1(0), x_2(0), x_3(0)$ are initial conditions, and a, b, c are parameters

This map can be chaotic when (a=35), (b=3) and ($20 \le c \le 28.4$). This map was used in cryptography also by (Ahmad et al., 2012) with a Lorenz map to design keystream generator for voice encryption.

Henon map: This map can be two dimensional map to generate two chaos signals as in Equations (9):

$$x_{n+1} = 1 + by_n - ax_n^2 \qquad (9.a)$$

$$y_{n+1} = x_n \qquad (9b)$$

This map can be chaotic when a=1.4 and b=0.3. This map was used in cryptography by (Liu et al., 2008) with logistic map to create database of chaotic model for voice encryption .

Cat map (Arnold map): This map can be two dimensional map and is also called Arnold cat map which can be described as shown in Equation (10.a) (Chen et al., 2004).

$$\begin{bmatrix} x_{n+1} \\ y_{n+1} \end{bmatrix} = \begin{bmatrix} 1 & a \\ b & ab+1 \end{bmatrix} \begin{bmatrix} x_n \\ y_n \end{bmatrix} \mod (1) \qquad (10.a)$$

where a and b are control parameters.

This map can be reformulated as in Equation (10.b), which was used by (Ashtiyani et al., 2012) to encrypt the voice signal.

$$\begin{bmatrix} x_{n+1} \\ y_{n+1} \end{bmatrix} = \begin{bmatrix} 1 & a \\ b & ab+1 \end{bmatrix} \begin{bmatrix} x_n \\ y_n \end{bmatrix} \mod (N) \qquad (10.b)$$

Furthermore, this two dimensional map is extended to be three-dimensional as in Equation (10.c) (Chen et al., 2004)):

Also it can be extended to higher dimensional ($N^{th}D$) cat map as in Equation (10.d). It was used by (Gnanajeyaraman et al., 2009) to generate look-up tables to perform voice encryption.

$$\begin{bmatrix} A_{n+1} \\ B_{n+1} \\ . \\ . \\ . \\ H_{n+1} \end{bmatrix} = x \begin{bmatrix} A_n \\ B_n \\ . \\ . \\ . \\ H_n \end{bmatrix} \mod \left(1\right) \quad (10.d)$$

where: a_{ij}, b_{ij} are integers in $[0,2^L-1]$, L is number of bits (e.g. L=16)m is the number of tables that are used for encryption of (e.g. m=8)

Baker map: This two dimensional map can be expressed as in Equation (11):

$$F\left(x,y\right) = \begin{cases} \left(2x, \dfrac{y}{2}\right) if\, 0 \leq x < \dfrac{1}{2} \\ \left(2x-1, \dfrac{y+1}{2}\right) if\, \dfrac{1}{2} \leq x < 1 \end{cases} \quad (11)$$

This chaotic map converts two dimensional (2D) square into itself chaotic square by dividing it into two halves and each half is stretched and compressed to obtain an interval of horizontal width 1 and vertical height 1/2 and then put on top of each other as shown in Figure 6 . This map was used by (Mosa et al., 2009) for permutation to encrypt the voice signal.

Chebyshev map: Chebyshev map is a chaotic map. It is defined as in Equation (12.a)

$$T_{n+1}(x)=2xT_n(x)\text{-}T_{n-1}(x) \quad (12a)$$

where: $n \geq 2$

$T_0(x)=1$ and $T_1(x)= x$

This equation was used by (Kocarev et al., 2004) and by (Prasadh et al., 2009)) to design Public Key Cryptosystem. In (Kocarev et al. 2004) rewrote this equation to be Equations (12.b) and (12.c).

$$\begin{bmatrix} x_{n+1} \\ y_{n+1} \end{bmatrix} = \begin{bmatrix} 0 & 1 \\ -1 & 2k \end{bmatrix}\begin{bmatrix} x_n \\ y_n \end{bmatrix}\left(\mod 1\right) \quad (12.b)$$

$$\begin{bmatrix} X_{n+1} \\ Y_{n+1} \end{bmatrix} = \begin{bmatrix} 0 & 1 \\ -1 & 2k \end{bmatrix}\begin{bmatrix} X_n \\ Y_n \end{bmatrix}\left(\mod N\right) \quad (12.c)$$

where X, Y and N are integers.

Beta-transformation map.($AA_{\hat{a}}\left(X\left(m\right)\right)$: This function can be defined in Equation (13). This equation used by (Ariffin & Abu, 2009) to design public key cryptosysetm.

$$X\left(m+1\right) = AA_{\beta}\left(X\left(m\right)\right) = \begin{cases} \left[X\left(m\right)+aX\left(m-1\right)\right]\left(\mod 1\right), b_i = 0 \\ \left[\beta X\left(m\right)+X\left(m-1\right)\right]\left(\mod 1\right), b_i = 1 \end{cases} \quad (13)$$

where: , $\beta > 0$ and a $\neq \beta$, and b_i is binary bit

Figure 6. Baker map

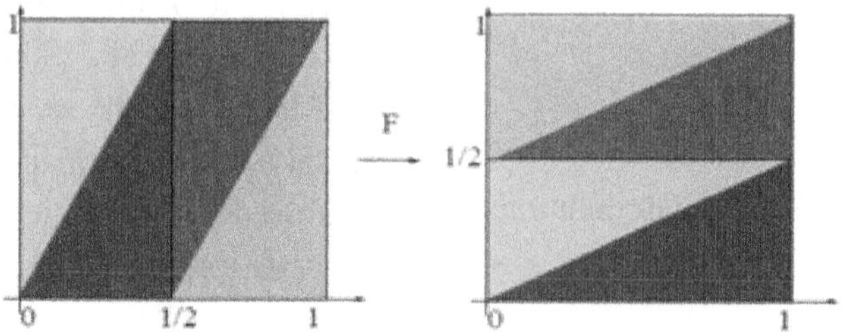

CHAOS BASED CRYPTOGRAPHY

The well-known techniques of cryptography are symmetric key algorithms (stream cipher and block cipher), and asymmetric key algorithms (public key cryptography) and cryptographic hash function.

Chaos based Stream cipher: There are researches which use one chaotic map as random generator. And the other researches use two chaotic maps. Figure 7 illustrates the researches that use chaos- based random number generator for stream cipher applications.

(Li et al, 2001), presente a pseudo-random bit generator. This generator is based on a couple of chaotic systems called CCS-PRBG. This generator can be used in stream ciphers. (Kanso & Smaoui, 2007)) presente two generators to generate pseudorandom binary sequence. These generators are based on the logistic map. This map is shown in Equation (1). The first generator depends on a single one-dimensional logistic map while the second generator depends on a combination of two logistic maps. Both generators use threshold (0.5) to generate a binary sequence. On the other hand, (Kanso, 2010) presente another keystream generator by applying the technique of self shrinking to the chaotic tent map. This map is shown in Equation (4). (Patidar et al., 2008), presents a pseudo random number generator (PRNG) to generate a binary sequence. This generator based on compariison between the outputs of two chaotic logistic maps. On the other hand, (Patidar, & Sud, 2009) presente another pseudo random

number generator (PRBG). It gave good results of (National Institute of Standard Statistical Tests) NIST statistical tests. This generator is based on comparison between two chaotic standard maps. These maps are shown in Equations (2). (Xingyuan et al., 2011)) presente an encryption algorithm. This algorithm uses Picewise linear map (PLCM) to design two pseudo-random number generators. This map is shown in Equation (3). The designe of this generator is based on the research by (Li et al., 2001)). The generated pseudo-random number is applied to choose which encryption mode is to be used. Encryption mode is either stream cipher mode or block cipher mode. This algorithm is used to encrypt/decrypt files (such as TXT, DOC, WMA, and JPEG). (Ahmad et al., 2012) have designed keystream generator to protect voice bitstreams over insecure transmission channel. This generator utilizes the features of high dimensional chaos like Lorenz and Chen systems. The equations of Lorenz map are shown in Equation (7). The equations of Chen map are shown in Equation (8).

Chaos based block cipher: There are research which used chaotic map to improve the design of S-box for block cipher applications. Figure. 8 illustrates the researches that use chaos-based S-box.

(Asim & Jeoti, 2008) present a method to design S-boxes by using a mixing property of piecewise linear chaotic maps. This map is shown in Equation (3). The main idea of this research is to construct S-box based on the property of chaotic nonlinear dynamic system. (Wang & Zhang, 2009) present two methods to encrypt the image. These two

Figure 7. Chaos in stream cipher systems

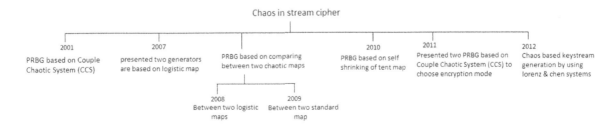

Figure 8. Different chaos used in block cipher for design of s-boxes

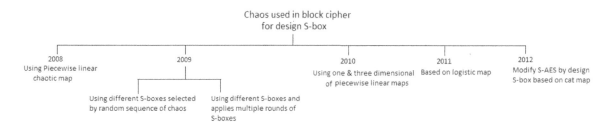

methods are based on the theory of S-box in AES and on the chaotic logistic map. This map is shown in Equation (1). The first method uses different S-boxes which are selected by using a random sequence of chaos to do substitution for each byte. The second method uses different chosen S-boxes and applies multiple rounds of S-boxes to do substitution for encryption. The S-boxes are chosen by using achaos random sequence.

(Zaibi et al., 2010)) present the S-box that is based on one and three dimensional piecewise linear maps. These maps are shown in equation. (5) and Equation (6) in sequentially. This research uses NIST statistical test to study the statistical properties of these two maps. The result of this test verifies that these two maps have random like behavior. (Jeyamala et al., 2011) use chaos theory to generate new elements of P-arrays and S-boxes for blowfish block cipher. This research depends on logistic map. It is shown in equatin (1). This design of S-box can be tested with blowfish block cipher algorithm for text and image encryption. The result shows that a high quality of encryption, minimal memory requirement and low computational time.

(Ashtiyani et al., 2012) propose voice signal encryption using chaotic symmetric cryptography. This research uses chaos cat map to scramble the signal. This map is shown in Equation (10.b). And also it uses Lorenz map for design the S-box to do diffusion. This map is shown in Equations (7). The designed chaotic S-box is applied with a Simplified version of Advance Encryption Standard (S-AES).

Chaos based public key: There are researches which use chaotic map with public key for asymmetric encryption applications. Figure 9 illustrates the researches that use chaos based public key.

(Kocarev et al., 2004) presente a public-key encryption algorithm. It uses the property of semi-group in Chebyshev maps. This map is shown in Equation (12.a) and rewritten to (12.c). Also (Prasadh et al., 2009), presente a public key encryption based on chebyshev polynomials as shown in Equation (12.a). The (Ariffin & Abu, 2009) presente a public key cryptosystem. This cryptosystem is built by using chaotic beta-transformation mapping. Beta-transformation is shown in Equation (13).

Figure 9. Chaos based public key cryptosystems

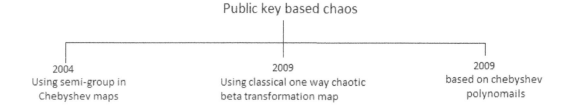

Advantages and Disadvantages of Using Chaos Theory in Cryptography

Chaos theory can be implemented in cryptography. Table 1 explains how to use each of these features in cryptography. Chaotic system can be implemented in cryptography as pseudo-chaotic system. Pseudo-Chaos has a *finite* number of states. It involves approximation of continuous chaos with floating- or fixed-point arithmetic. This leads to discrete chaos-like system with low cycle lengths. The initial condition(s) and/or parameter(s) of chaos can be used as key in cryptography. The sensitivity to the initial condition and parameters of chaos can be used as diffusion in cryptography . The initial state of chaos can be used as plaintext in cryptography. Final state can be used as ciphertext in cryptography. An asymptotic independence of initial and final states in chaos can be used as confusion in cryptography (Blackledge, 2008),(Blackledge, 2010).

Chaos based cryptography has other advantage. It is the encryption of the continuous waveforms of signal without sampling and quantization. Since the algorithms of chaos based cryptography can be defined over continuous number field compared with traditional cryptography algorithms, it can be defined over integer number fields (Tenn, 2003). Table 2 shows the comparision between cryptography and chaos. There are some disadvantages compared with the conventional cryptography such as slow, used floating point numbers, cycle length is low, and data are redundant.

Although chaos based cryptography has these disadvantages, researches found solutions to overcome these problems. One of these researches is presented by (Blackledge, 2010). This research describes multialgorithmic cryptography using deterministic chaos. Thus the essential advantage of chaos is that provides the potential for developing an unlimited number of algorithms that can be used to produce a *multi-algorithmic solution*. The use of different algorithms for encrypting different blocks of data provides an approach called 'multi-algorithmic'. This also leads to overcome low cycle lengths which are associated with chaotic iterates. The other researches use algorithm that depends on perturbance to make the cycle length high. This research is presented by (Tao et al., 1998). While the research presented by (Li et al., 2003) discusse some of the problems faced by the chaos based cryptography, it gives solutions and recommendations to overcome these problems. And also it encourages the researchers to take these solutions and recommendations as future trends to improve the conventional cryptography.

Table 1. Chaos theory and cryptography

Chaos Theory	Cryptography
Chaotic System	Pseudo-Chaotic System
Nonlinear Transform	Non-Linear Transform
Infinite number of states	Finite State
Infinite Number of Iterations	Finite Iterations
Initial state	Plaintext
Final stste	Ciphertext
Initial condition(s) and/or parameter (s)	Key
Asymptotic independence of initial and final states	Confusion
Sensitivity to initial condition(s) and parameter(s) mixing	Diffusion

Table 2. Comparison between two techniques

Chaos Based Cryptography	Conventional Cryptography
Floating point arithmetic	Integer arithmetic
Computationaly slow	Computationally fast
Based on any nonlinear function	Usually based on the "Mod" function
Coesnt require prime numbers	Usually based on prime number
Low cycle lenths	High Cycle Lenth
Statistical Bais	No Statistical bais
Data Redundant	Data compatible

SECURE WIRELESS COMMUNICATION BASED ON CHAOS THEORY

Communication security that depends on chaos can be considered as a new approach which provides protection and security of communications and maintains confidentiality. Communication security that relies on chaos started 1992 and so far through four generations. (Yang, 2003) describes the evolution of chaos based secure communication. The first and second generations use chaos in synchronization only while the third and fourth generations use chaos in both synchronization and cryptography as shown in Figure 10.

The first generation of secure communication system: There are two methods of this generation: they are additive chaos masking and chaotic shift keying.

Additive chaos masking method: This method is shown in Figure 11. The transmitter uses chaotic system to generate sequence of states c(t). This sequence is added to signal of original message m(t) to give new signal s(t). This new signal can be transmitted through channel to the receiver. The receiver gets the received signal r(t), and tries to get sequence of chaotic states c̄(t) by applying chaotic synchronization and using the same chaotic system at transmitter. After that subtraction process is applied between r(t) and c̄(t) to get the recovered message signal m̄(t).

Chaotic shift keying method: This method is shown in Figure 12. The message signal is digital. The transmitter uses two chaotic systems to generate two attractors which are switched by depending on message signal m(t). These two systems have an identical structure and various parameters. These attractors are used to encode the bits of the message signal (0 and 1), and try to get the received signal r(t). The reciever tries to get sequence of chaotic states c̄(t) by applying chaotic synchronization and using the same chaotic system at transmitter. The subtraction process is applied between r(t) and c̄(t) to get the error signal of synchronization e(t). After that the low pass filtering (LPF) and threshold are applied to get the recovered message signal m̄(t). This generation was proposed in 1993 and has some weak security points.

The second generation of secure communication system: This generation is called chaotic modulation. Two modulation metods are *chaotic parameter* and *non-autonomous* modulations. In the first method, the message signals modulate the parameters of the chaotic system. This method is illustrated in Figure 13. In the second method, the message signals modulate the attractor of the chaotic system directly in the phase space as illustrated in Figure 14. To compare between these two modulations types, the transmitter in the first modulation can switch between different trajectories of the different chaotic attractors. In the second modulation, the transmitter can switch between different trajectories of the same chaotic attractor. The receiver in the first modulation uses adaptive controller. And also to get free synchronization error and recover message signal. While in the second modulation, because it is free of error, there is no use to adaptive controller at receiver. Note that this generation created since 1993 to 1995 to overcome some weak points of the first generation. It still needs improvement of some security points.

The third generation of secure communication system: This generation can be called chaotic cryptosystem. It uses the classical techniques of cryptography with chaos to improve the security of the second generation. This generation was proposed in 1997 as shown in Figure 15. The transmitter uses chaotic system to generate key signal c(t). The input message signal m(t) can be encrypted by this key signal c(t) with using encryption rule e(.) to give the encrypted signal y(t). This encrypted signal y(t) can be used to drive

Figure 10. Generation of chaos based communication system

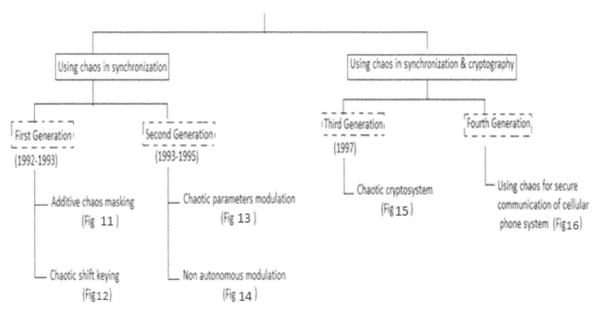

Figure 11. First generation additive chaos masking

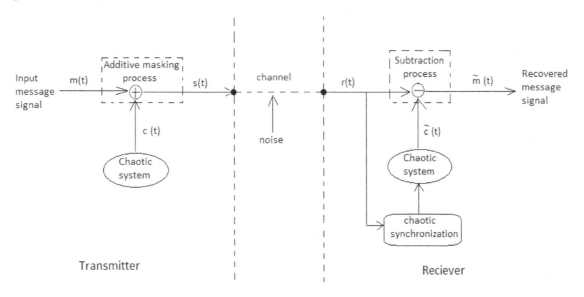

the chaos. The output states s(t) are transmitted through channel. The receiver gets these states s(t) with the addition of noise n(t). The chaotic system used in the reveiver is the same as the transmitter. From this system we will get the key signal c (t) and the decrypted signal y (t). These two signals will be used with the decryption rule

d(.) to recover the message signal m (t).

Figure 12. First generation: Chaotic shift keying

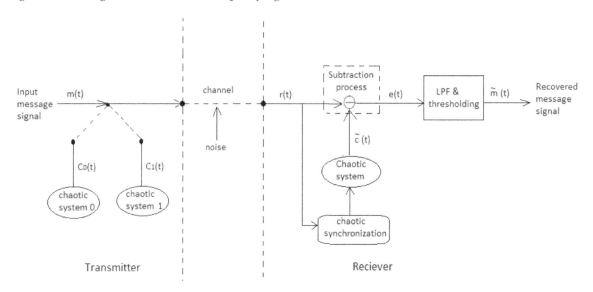

Figure 13. Second generation: Chaotic parameters modulation

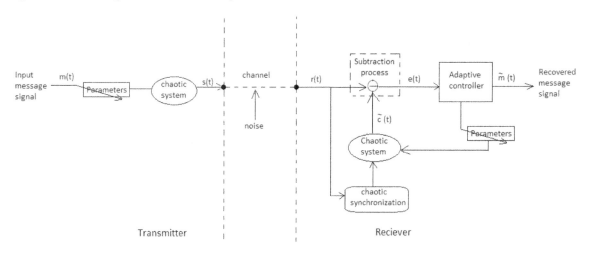

The fourth generation of secure communication system: This generation shown in Figure 16 to provide secure communication for cellular phone system. The transmitter uses chaos to generate the sequence of keys c(t) to do stream encryption, and also to generate the sequence of synchronization x(t) for the synchronization purpose. This generation uses synchronization impulse method. The encryption stream s(i) is generated. The composition and coding processes will be applied

to this encryption stream s(i) with the existing of digitized synchronization impulse to give new stream d(i). The modulation process will be applied to this result stream d(i) and transmitted through channel. On the other hand, the receiver uses demodulation, decoding and decomposition to get synchronization sequence x (t). The sequence will be needed by chaos to generate sequence of keys c (t). These keys will be used to

Figure 14. Second generation: Non-autonomous chaotic modulation

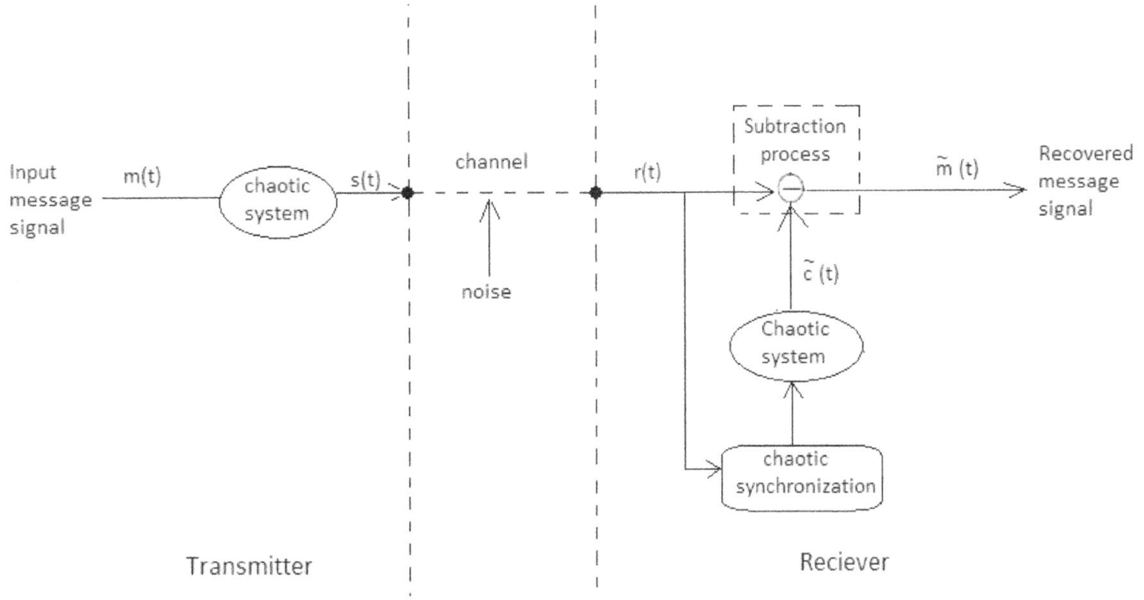

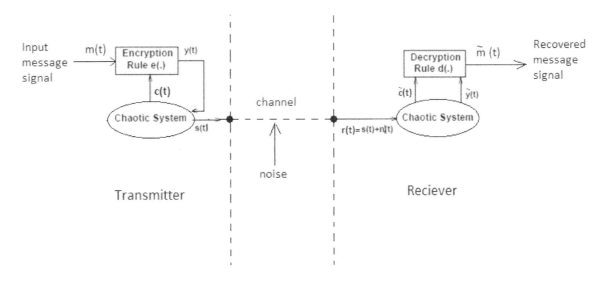

Figure 15. Third generation of chaos used for secure communication

decrypt stream and recover the voice signal. Many researches use chaos based cryptography which are described in section 3 of this chapter. The other researches uses chaos based synchronization such as (Abid et al., 2009). This research presents a method of a synchronization by using chaos

based Pseudo-True Random Bit Generator (PTRBG). Also there are other researches which present chaos based cryptography without using synchronization such as (Jian et al, 2010).

This research presents a secure wireless communication illustrated in Figure 17. This secure

Figure 16. Fourth generation of chaos used for secure communication

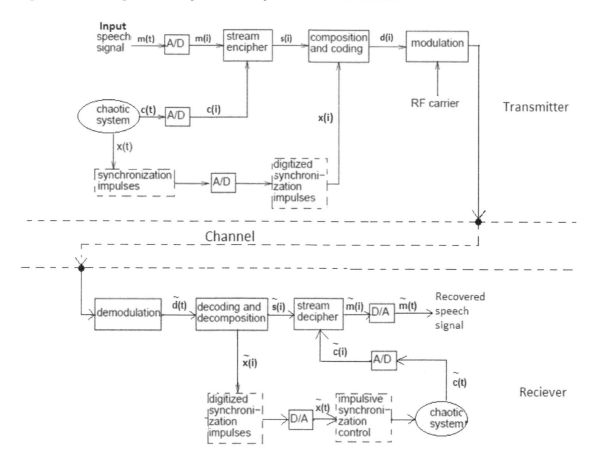

communication use three types of encryption algorithms which are AES, RSA and Chaos Pseudo Random sequence (CPRs), where AES is used for terminal protection and to provide confidential communications, RSA is used for identity authentication, and CPR is used for encryption. To provide secure communication between two parties there must be encryption card for each one. This encryption card contains startup password such as (AES cipher key) and user's identity such as (RSA cipher key). Each one uses AES cipher key to decrypt the source program of system. This program is encrypted by AES algorithm. After successful decryption process. Each one uses RSA cipher key to get the authentication

from each other to establish the communication. After they get the validation of authentication then they use the CPRs to encrypt the data flow (Jian et al., 2010).

VOICE SECURE WIRELESS COMMUNICATION

Voice encryption system in wireless communication became very important. The advancement of modern wireless telecommunication and multimedia technologies makes a huge amount of sensitivity voice information travel over the open and shared networks. Voice-based communication

Figure 17. Secure communication system

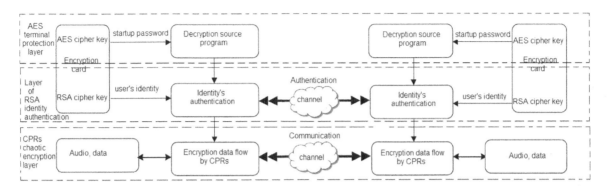

becomes prominent in the application areas of military, voice over IP, e-learning, voice-conferencing, telephone banking, telephone services of market securities, etc. These applications are critical broadcast regarding the protection of data integrity and authorized user privacy (Ahmad et al., 2012).

There are two ways to encrypt the voice signal: digital and analogue encryptions. In case of digital encryption, at first the analog signal must be digitized. The resulting signal is compressed to produce stream of bits at an adequate bit rate. Then this stream is encrypted and transferred by channel (Sridharan et al., 1990). The analogue encryption, is also known as "voice scrambling" or "speech scrambling". This way operates on the samples of voice themselves without the need for digitization and compression. The purpose of voice encryption is to convert the voice signal from the original form into unintelligible voice signal, making it difficult to decrypt this signal when the key is unknown (Sridharan et al., 1990) (Sadkhan .& Abbas, 2011). Note that this chapter will use " Voice" and "Speech" interchangeably.

The voice encryption can be used in wireless communications which include high frequency (H.F), satellite communications and mobile communications to protect the contents and privacy from the eavesdroppers and attackers (Sadkhan & Abbas, 2012) (Su et al., 2012). Figure 18 illustrates the main secure voice communication between two humans.

Secure communication means that two authorized parties (transmitter and receiver parties) are communicating and do not want a third (unauthorized) party to listen (Agrawal & Zeng, 2005) (Kurose & Ross, 2003). Encryption is a process which is done by authorized party (Transmitter) to encrypt the information with using secret key and encryption algorithm. Decryption is a process done by authorized party (Receiver) to decrypt the information with using secret key and decryption algorithm (Goldreich, 2004).

Figure 18 illustrates the parameters are the voice, the Encryption system with using secret key at transmitter part, the Decryption system with using secret key at receiver part, and the public channel. For the voice parameters, the voice is simply a sound signal generated by a human. Every human has different anatomy from another, so that the sound signal is never the same from one to another. Then there are different frequencies of three classes of humans: men, women and children (Brandau, 2008). The key parameter is a security measure. It can be considered as a piece of information that determines the output of encryption/decryption algorithm. The encryption system uses the key to turn data into unreadable cipher (Yuksel et al., 2011). The length of key must be long enough that an attacker cannot try all possible keys. For a symmetric algorithms, which use the same secret key at encryption and decryption processes, a key length can be 80 bits

Figure 18. Secure voice communication

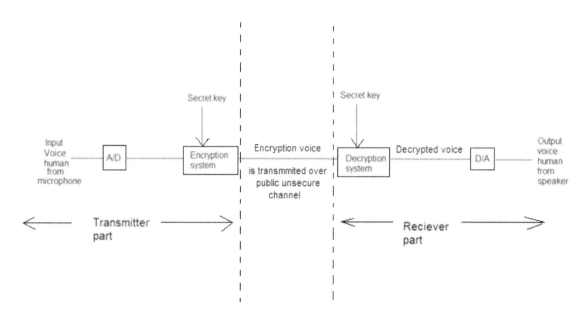

at minimum for strong security and also can be 128 bits for very strong. The choice of key is important to prevent an attacker guesse that keys which need to be generated truly randomly and contain sufficient entropy (Barker et al. 2007).

The encryption algorithm is a process where data is hard to read by an unauthorized party over public channel. Secure communication is obtained by providing an encryption algorithm correctly programmed, and sufficiently powerful. The keys cannot be intercepted. The encryption process protects the content of the conversation from eavesdropping (Stallings, 2011).

Different Evaluation Parameters for Voice Encryption

In the previous sections it is mentioned that there are two ways of voice encryption: analoge and digital encryption. The encryption algorithm must have the efficiency to give an ambiguous voice signal when hearing it. The effectiveness of voice encryption algorithm is evaluated by the following evaluation parameters:

Residual Intelligibility (R.I.): R.I. is an amount of redundant information in the encrypted voice signal. The R.I. of encrypted voice and the quality of recovered voice can be evaluated by using subjective tests. These tests require a large number of trained and untrained human listeners to listen to the encrypted voice. These tests have three levels of intelligibility which are word, sentence and digit. Intelligibility scores can be between (0-100) percent. When (R.I=0%) this represenrs the ideal intelligibility, when (R.I=(1-10)%) this is lower intelligibility, when (R.I=(11-30)%) it is medium intelligibility, and when (R.I=(31-50)%) it is higher intelligibility (Sridharan et al., 1993) (Srinivasan & Selvan, 2012). Disadvantages of these tests are: they take much time and they require a large number of listeners (Sridharan et al., 1993). The other tests are called objective tests as indicator for R.I. of the encrypted voice and the corresponding quality of recovered voice. The commonly used tests are Linear Predictive Coding (LPC) distance, Cepstral Distance (CD), and Segmental Spectral Signal to Noise Ratio (SSNR) (Sridharan et al., 1990). The greater value of distances (LPC and CD) with small value of

SSNR is that give the low R.I. The greater value of distances (LPC and CD) is considered as the more spectral distortion in the original voice signal. The cause of small value of SSNR, is that the human ears are in sensitive to phase errors. That SSNR is defined in the frequency domain as a useful indicator of voice quality or loss of intelligibility (Sridharan et al., 1993).

Key space: The security of encryption algorithm depends on the number of keys used in the algorithm. That is when the key space is large then the level of security is increased. This space must have properties such as uniform distribution of keys, appropriate length of key and key sensitivity (Srinivasan & Selvan, 2012).

Encoding delay: Encoding delay is the number of times that requires encrypting one segment. When the number of segments, length of each segment and the number of samples in each segment increase then the number of permutation samples increase. This causes the increase of encoding delay. That is the appropriate length of segment is 256 samples per frame (Srinivasan & Selvan, 2012).

Voice Encryption Techniques

This section classifies the Voice encryption techniques into four categories which are *conventional methods, orthogonal transformation, blind source separation, and chaotic system* as illustrated in Figure 19.

Conventional methods technique: This category can be a single dimension or two dimensions as illustrated in Figure 20.

Single dimension method: The single dimension is a traditional analog encryption that manipulates voice signal in the time domain, frequency domain and amplitude domain.

Amplitude domain techniques: There are four techniques to do encryption of voice in the amplitude domain. Figure 21 illustrates these four methods with their evaluation (Srinivasan & Selvan, 2012).

The first technique is *sample interchange* was proposed in 1971 which includes interchange or permutation of voice samples. This technique can be implemented by three methods. The first method is "reordering of individual samples by using delay networks". This method has medium

Figure 19. The classification of voice encryption techniques

Figure 20. The conventional voice encryption techniques

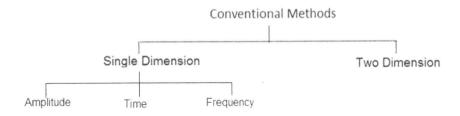

Figure 21. Amplitude voice encryption techniques

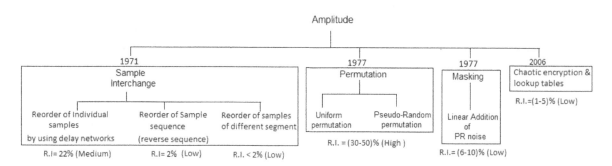

R.I. (22%). The second method is "reordering of sample sequence by reverse sequence". This method has low R.I. (2%). The third method is reordering of samples of different segments". This method has lower R.I (R.I. < 2%) compared with first two methods (Phillips et al., 1971) (Srinivasan & Selvan, 2012).

The second technique is permutation proposed in 1977. This technique can be done by two methods, they are "Uniform permutations" or "Pseudo-Random Permutations". Both of these two methods have high R.I. (30-50)% (Kak & Jayant, 1977) (Srinivasan & Selvan, 2012).

The third technique is masking also proposed in 1977. This technique can be realized by "linear addition of PR noise". This method has low R.I. (6-10)% (Kak & Jayant, 1977) (Srinivasan and Selvan, 2012).

The forth technique is "chaotic encryption with using lookup tables" proposed in 2006. This technique is based on chaotic encryption in conjunction with lookup tables. The lookup tables are created by using Arnold map is shown in Equation (10.b). This table contains index number and iterated decimal value.

In this method, the input quantized audio data varies between 0 and 19512. These data are converted to the amplitude values by depending on lookup table . These resulting amplitude values vary between 0 and 65284. This method has lower R.I. (1-5)% since there is higher dynamic

range and randomized amplitude values (Ganesan et al., 2006)

Time domain techniques: There are two methods to perform the voice encryption in the time domain as illustrated in Figure 22 with their evaluation .

- The first method is *permutation of samples in each block* proposed in 1981. This method has low and high R.I. (99-100)% since it gives poor quality of descramble signal (Beker & Piper, 1985) (Jayant et al., 1981) (Bopardikar,1995)

- The second method is *permuted of segments of one sample in each block*. This method has six techniques:

The first technique "time inversion" proposed in 1981. In this technique, the order of samples in each block is inverted. The R.I. of this technique depends on segment size. To have the lower R.I., the segment size is made larger (Jayant, 1982) .

The second technique "Time Segment Permutation (TSP)" proposed in 1982. It is implemented by two types. One type is (block TSP also called hopping window), and the other type is (sequential TSP also called sliding window). In the Block TSP type, all the Segments in each block are scrambled and transmitted before the segments of the next block are brought into the scrambler memory. But in a sequential TSP, individual segments are

Figure 22. Time domain voice encryption techniques

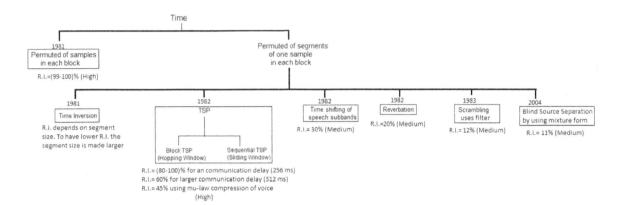

transmitted instead of waiting for the block. This technique has high R.I. (45-100)% (Jayant, 1982).

The third method "time shifting of voice subbands" was proposed in 1982. The time segment corresponds to the lower frequency signal and is delayed by time interval τ. The result of this delay is added to the time segment corresponding to the higher frequency signal for transmission. This method has medium R.I. (30%)(Jayant, 1982).

The fourth method " reverberation" proposed in 1982. It can be implement by mixing multiple numbers of fixed interval discrete time echoes with the current voice amplitude to give the encrypted output. This method has medium R.I. (20%)(Jayant, 1982).

The fifth method "scrambling uses filter" was proposed in 1993. This method uses a time vary-

ing transversal filter. The incoming time-samples are selected randomly by this filter and multiplied by constant values. This method has medium R.I. (12%) [Huang & Stansfield, 1993].

The six method "blind source separation by using mixture form" proposed in 2004. This method uses unknown and mutually independent source signals. These signals are in the mixture form as pseudorandom key signals. It also uses masking method to do scrambling of each segment. This method has medium R.I. (11%) (Lin et al., 2004) .

Frequency domain techniques: There are four methods to do voice encryption in frequency domain as illustrated by this chapter in Figure 23 with their evaluation (Srinivasan & Selvan, 2012).

The first method "frequency inversion" proposed in 1977. it involves flipping the sign of

Figure 23. Frequency domain techniques

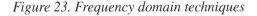

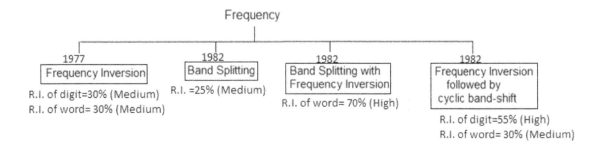

samples. It has medium R.I. (30% for digit and word levels) since the experienced eavesdroppers can recognize the parts of voice (Cox et al. 1987) (Bopardikar, 1995) (Srinivasan & Selvan, 2012).

The second method "band splitting" proposed in 1982. This method splits the block into M-bands of frequency. These bands are shuffled between themselves and re-synthesized to get the scrambled signal. This method has medium R.I. (25%) (Beker & Piper, 1985) .

The third method "band splitting with frequency inversion" proposed in 1982. This method realizes frequency inversion on a particular frequency sub-bands. This method has high R.I (70% for word level) (Srinivasan & Selvan, 2012).

The fourth method "frequency inversion followed by cyclic band-shift" proposed in 1982. It shifts each sub-band by the factor (n modulo k). It has high R.I. (55% for digit level) and medium R.I. (30% for word level) (Jayant et al., 1983) .

Two dimension method: The previous traditional analog encryptions do not provide adequate security against cryptanalysis. The number of permutable elements by these encryptions is not large enough. The two dimension category is in-troduced to strengthen the security. This category which is analog encryption manipulates voice signal in both time and frequency domains (Jayant et al. 1983), (Sadkhan.& Abbas, 2012). There are three methods of this category as illustrated by this chapter in figure. 24 with their evaluation by (Srinivasan & Selvan, 2012).

The first method " frequency inversion with block TSP" proposed in 1982 and it has low R.I. (20% for digit level). The second method " *frequency inversion followed by one of cyclic band shift type with time manipulation*". The types of cyclic band shift are: "dynamic time reverberation" which has low R.I. (18-28% for digit level) and (0-1% for word level), and "time shifting between two frequency sub-bands" which has medium R.I. (25-38% for digit level) and low R.I. (2-3% for word level). The third method "Time –Frequency segment permutation (TFSP)" proposed in 1982. It has low R.I. (25% for digit level) and (0-1% for word level) (Jayant, 1982),(Srinivasan & Selvan, 2012).

Orthogonal Transformation Technique: To more enhance the security of the voice encryption, the second technique (orthogonal transformation)

Figure 24. Two dimensional voice encryption techniques

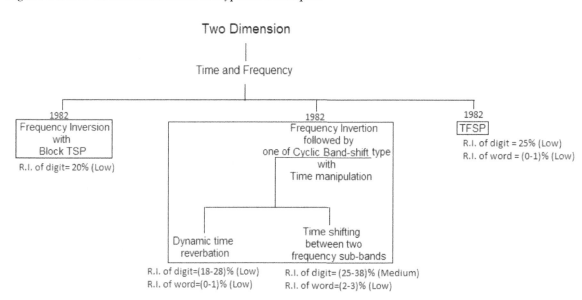

was proposed (Sridharan et al., 1990) (Bopardikar, 1995) (Sadkhan .& Abbas, 2012), (Srinivasan & Selvan, 2012). This technique can be *"single transformation"* or *"many transformations"* as illustrated in Figure 25. That means in case of single transformation, one of orthogonal transformations is used, and in case of many transformation, two orthogonal transformations are used. Orthogonal transformations are Discrete Prolate Spheroidal Transform (DPST), Fast Fourier Transform (FFT), Discrete Cosine Transform (DCT), Modified discrete cosine Transform (MDCT), Walsh Hadamard Transform (WHT), Karhonen loeve (KLT), Circulant Transformation (CT), and Wavelet Transform (WT) (Sadkhan.& Abbas, 2012) .

Single Transformation

1. **Using of Prolate Spheroidal Transform (PST):** PST was used in 1979 to perform a simple encryption scheme. This encryption can be done by the permutation of the coefficients of the transform sequence. Becuase the input sequence of band-limited is encrypted, the output is the encrypted sequence of band-limited (Wyner, 1979)) (Srinivasan & Selvan, 2012).
2. **Using of Fast Fourier Transform (FFT):** (Sakurai et al, 1984)), propose a voice encryption using Fast Fourier Transform (FFT)

techniques. Fast Fourier algorithm is well known Discrete Fourier Transform (DFT). The selected FFT coefficients are encrypted using a permutation matrix which is either stored in the ROM memory or generated instantaneously from a key value. (Tseng & Chiu, 2007), presented a technique based on the combination of Quadrature Amplitude Modulation (QAM) mapping method and an orthogonal frequency division multiplexing (OFDM). An OFDM needs only two FFT operations instead of the four as required by the FFT-based voice encryption technique in the system structure. The signal of voice in Pulse-Code Modulation (PCM) format is converted by using QAM mapping to complex value of frequency components. These components are permuted and then inverse transformed to get the encrypted signal (Srinivasan & Selvan, 2012).

3. **The comparsion among KLT, PST, WHT, DCT and DFT:** (Sridharan et al., 1990) made a comparison among five discrete orthogonal transforms (KLT, PST, WHT, DCT and DFT). This comparison shown in Figure 26. By using four objective measures (LPC distance (d_{LPC})), the cepstral distance (CD), the segmental spectral signal to noise ratio (SSNR), and the frequency variant spectral distance (FVSD)). The result shows that DCT

Figure 25. Orthogonal transformation techniques for voice encryption

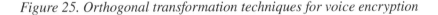

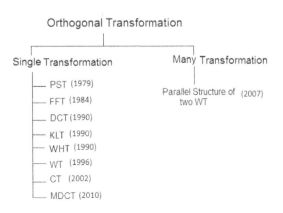

is the best transform and has better residual intelligibility of the encrypted voice and the recovered voice quality. Although DFT has inferior results with DCT, DCT offers speed in implementation compared with DFT.

On the other hand, (Theberge, M. (1996)) made a coparison as illustrated in Figure 26 between DCT and DFT. The DCT gives encrypted voice with lowest residual intelligibility and a closely followed by DFT (Sridharan et al, 1993). This comparison uses: 1) subjective tests (Jayant Number test (JN), and Modified Caplan Sentence test (MCS)), and: 2) objective tests (Log Spectral distance (Logs), LPC distance, Cepstral distance, segmental spectral signal to noise ratio (SSNR), and frequency weighted log spectral distance (FWLogs)). Also cryptanalytic attacks (Known plaintext attacks and ciphertext attacks) are applied to the encrypted voice. These tests would be performed between 1) the original voice signal and the encrypted voice signal, 2) the original voice signal and the decrypted voice signal, and 3) the original voice signal and the cryptanalyzed voice signal. The results of these tests show that transform domain based voice encryption techniques are all vulnerable to cryptanalytic attacks. And they also show that the DCT based voice encryption technique was found to be more secure than DFT based voice encryption technique. But both of DCT and DFT based voice encryption techniques are equally susceptibile to cryptanalytic attacks (Theberge, 1996).

In contrast with (Sridharan et al, 1993) claimed that DCT based voice encryption techniques have more strength against cryptanalysis than the DFT based voice encryption techniques. Since (Sridharan et al, 1993) used the same length of both DCT and DFT then that means DCT has double coefficients to permutation. Therefore (Theberge, 1996) compares between DCT and DFT based voice encryption techniques based on the same number of coefficients to permutation (Theberge, 1996). While (Theberge, 1996) proposed using the noise addition modulo with transform domain voice encryption technique to defeat the cryptanalytic attacks. This modulo will be applied to a certain constant to quantized the spectrum of voice signal. This method encrypts voice in such a way that it resembles white Gaussian noise, and thus traditional cryptanalysis techniques cannot be used to attack it. As it is, this encryption is relatively prone to failure in very noisy channels, since additive white Gaussian noise increases the quantization errors. It was also found that very tight channel equalization is needed in order to obtain decrypted voice of acceptable quality (Theberge, 1996).

Figure 26. Comparison of orthogonal transformations based voice encryption

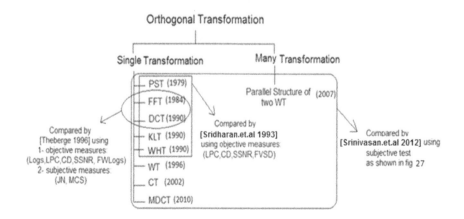

4. **Using of wavelet transform (WT):** (Ma et al., 1996)) presented an analog voice encryption based on Wavelet Transform (WT) to do encryption of the voice signal for both time and frequency domains. In this method the voice signal is converted into wavelet-analyzed signal by means of the filter banks which are based on wavelet basis. These wavelet signals are multiplexed and collected as frames with constant length. The encryption involves permutation of these frames. Then the spectrum of signal becomes irregular.

(Sadkhan et al., 2011) presented another system of voice encryption based on wavelet transform and permutation. This system uses four types of wavelets, they are (Haar, Daubechies 3 (db3), Symlets 2 (sym2) and Symlets 4 (sym4)). And each one is used with decomposition levels 1, 2 and 3. This system is examined against the actual Arabic speech signals. This system is evaluated by using distance measures with different assumed channel noise.

5. **Using of circulant transformation (CT):** (Manjunath & Anand, 2002) presented an encryption of voice by using circulant transformations. In this method the voice signal is submitted to Circulant Transformation (CT). Then the phase distortion is used. The signal energy redistributed by this phase distortion to the entire frame. The order of circulant matrix depends on the frame lengths. Such that the order of circulant matrix increases when the frame length becomes high.

6. **Using of Modified discrete cosine Transform (MDCT):** (Wang et al., 2010) presented a technique that depends on MDCT to provide a method of audio encryption to be applied to wireless sensor networks. In this technique, the sampled audio signal is transformed by MDCT. The results of transformed samples are sorted and packetized according to their importance by an index. A subset of the important packets is selectively encrypted and the rest of the packets is either discarded or left in its original form.

Many transformation: (Sadkhan et al, 2007). presented a technique that uses two wavelet transforms and are combined as parallel structure. These two transforms must be different in types with the same levels of decomposition. They used the following combinations of two different wavelets which are Daubechies 1 (Db1) with Haar wavelets, Daubechies 2 (Db2) with Symlets 2 (Sym2) wavelets and Daubechies 4 (Db4) with Symlets 4 (Sym4) wavelets.

The comparisons of using all orthogonal transformation techniques: (Srinivasan & Selvan, 2012)) made residual intelligibility comparison of all orthogonal transformation techniques as shown in figure 27. The R.I. of voice encryption that uses PST and FFT is low (9-10) %. The R.I. of voice encryption that uses DCT is low (7-8) %. The R.I. of voice encryption that used WT is low, (4-6) %. The R.I. of voice encryption that uses CT is low, (7-10) % and dependent on the order of the circulant matrix and frame length. The R.I. of voice encryption that uses QAM based FFT plus OFDM is low, (5-7) % . The R.I. of voice encryption that uses two parallel wavelet transforms is low, (1-3) %. The results show that using wavelet transform as a single dimension or many dimensions is preferred. The rest of techniques will be arranged in order of preference of using transforms which are QAM by FFT plus OFDM, DCT, CT, FFT, PST and MDCT in sequentially.

Blind source separation technique: The third category of voice encryption techniques is blind source separation. The term "*blind*" means that the source signals are not observed and no information is available about the mixture used in encryption process. This statistical strength of this approach is often physically plausible assumption of independence between the source signals (Amari

Figure 27. The comparison between all orthogonal transformations based voice encryption techniques

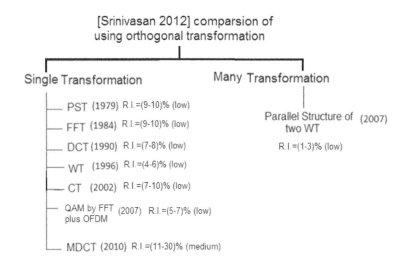

& Cichocki, 1998) (Cardoso, 1998) (Hyvarinen, 1999). This is shown in Figure 28.

- **Using of mixtural form for time element and masking method:** (Lin et al., 2004) presented an algorithm of voice encryption based on blind source separation. In this algorithm, unknown and mutually independent source signals which are in the form of mixtures are used. The algorithm proposes combining the time element for encryption and masking methods, wherein segments of voice signal are mixed with equal number of pseudorandom key signals. (Srinivasan & Selvan, 2012) compared the R.I. of this algorithm with time domain techniques as illustrated in figure 22. This figure shows that the time domain techniques have lower residual when using blind source separation method.

- **Using of Independent Component Analysis (ICA):** (Sadkhan & Abbas, 2006) present a technique called the Independent Component Analysis (ICA) technique. This encryption technique is based on

techniques of adaptive signal processing. Decryption algorithm uses JADE algorithm. The objective test uses LPC and SNR which are applied to evaluate the proposed system.

- **Using of Principal Component Analysis (PCA):** (Abbas, 2009) proposes the application of analog voice encryption using statistical method called Principal Component Analysis (PCA). Decryption algorithm uses traditional PCA algorithm. The objective test uses LPC and SNR which are applied to evaluate the proposed system. It was shown via simulation that the proposed technique is more robust in the case of 8KH frequency samples.

The comparison of using ICA and PCA: (Sadkhan & Abbas, 2011) made a comparison as illustrated in Figure 28 between ICA and PCA based voice encryption techniques by using objective tests (LPC and SNR). These tests applied to the original, scrambled and descrambled forms of the tested signals. The results showed that the PCA algorithm is better than ICA (JADE).

Figure 28. Blind source separation voice encryption techniques

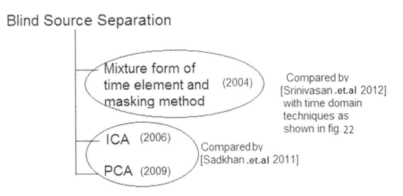

Chaotic based Voice Encryption Technique

The fourth category of voice encryption techniques useschaotic system as illustrated by this chapter in Figure 29. There are three methods for chaos based encryption. These methods are chaos encryption in amplitude domain, chaos encryption in transform domain and chaos symmetric encryption.

1. **Chaos in amplitude domain:** (Ganesan et al., 2006) presented a technique based on amplitude domain technique. This technique

used chaotic encryption in conjunction with lookup tables. The lookup tables are created by using Arnold map is shown in Equation (10.b). This table contains index number and iterated decimal value. In this method, the input quantized audio data varies between 0 and 19512. This data is converted to the amplitude values depending on lookup table . The resulting amplitude values vary between 0 and 65284. Thus the randomized amplitude value is generated with a higher dynamic range. (Srinivasan & Selvan, 2012) compared the R.I. of this technique with

Figure 29. The fourth category using chaos based voice encryption techniques

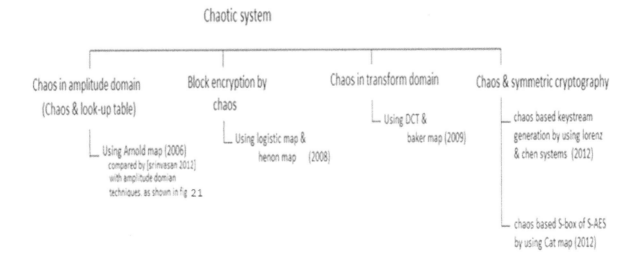

amplitude domain techniques as illustrated in Figure 21. The result shows that this technique has lower R.I. (Gnanajeyaraman et al., 2009) presented audio encryption based on a look-up table. This table generated by using chaotic cat map . This cat map can has high dimension (N^{th} D) as shown in Equation (13). The variables of this table can be treated as keys of encryption to protect the audio signal through transmission.

2. **Block encryption by chaos:** (Liu, J., Gao, F. and Ma, H. (2008)) present an algorithm to encrypt the digital voice. This algorithm depends on block encryption with chaotic sequences. These sequences can come from database of chaotic model by using logistic map and henon map as shown in Equations (1) and (9) sequentially. This algorithm solves the problem of loss of some data packages at receiver when it is decrypted during real time transmission. (Su et al., 2012).

3. **Chaos in transform domain:** (Mosa et al., 2009) presented an encryption of voice signals in transform domain by chaos. This algorithm, divides the segments of voice into two blocks each with fixed size. The elements of these blocks are permuted by using baker map as shown in Equation (11). The DCT used to substitute these permuted elements to different values. Then the resulting values are permuted again. (Mosa et al. 2010) presented another cryptosystem. This cryptosystem uses DCT or DST, AES and baker map. It uses permutation and mask. This mask works by circular shift which is calculated from key bits.

4. **Chaos and symmetric cryptography:** (Ahmad et al., 2012) designed a keystream generator. This generator utilized the features of high dimensional chaos like Lorenz (as in Equation 7) and Chen (as in Equation 8) systems to generate highly unpredictable and random-like sequences. These sequences considered as encryption keystream and created from the pre-processed chaotic mixed sequences. This keystream applied to encrypt the voice bitstream for the integrity protection of voice data. (Ashtiyani et al, 2012) presented the encryption of voice signal by using chaotic symmetric cryptography. The encryption based on chaotic cat map (as shown in equation. (10.b) to perform the encryption of voice signal. And also it is based on a modified form of simplified version of Advanced Encryption Standard (S-AES) to provide a security of voice. This modification is made on the design of S-box by using cat map.

CONCLUSION

The development aspect of cryptographic algorithms is considers as an mportant and necessary aspect, since there are various developments of wireless communication techniques and multimedia technologies (Su et al., 2012). The voice signal encryption (scrambling) is very important discipline compared with the image and text encryption. The design of voice encryption (scrambling) algorithm is requested to investigate the fast, low bandwidth expansion, very lower Residual Intelligibility (R.I.) and large key space. Chaos theory has desirable features. It attracts the researchers to use it with cryptography. Although there are problems in using chaos theory with cryptography, there are researches who tried to solve these problems and encourage the researchers to use chaos based cryptography as current future directions. Such trend in cryptography (Chaos based Cryptography) considered as one of the important approached in multidisciplinary application with the cryptography field.

REFERENCES

Abbas, N. (2009). Speech Scrambling Based on Principal Component Analysis. *MASAUM Journal of Computing*, *1*(3), 452–456.

Abid, A., Nasir, Q., & Elwakil, A. (2009). Implementation of a Chaotically Encrypted Wireless Communication System. In *Proceedings of IEEE international conference on Communications*. IEEExplore-Digital Library. doi: 10.1109/ICC.2009.5199069

Agrawal, D., & Zeng, Q. (2005). Introduction to Wireless and Mobile Systems (2nd Ed.). Amazon.com.

Ahmad, M., Alam, B., & Farooq, O. (2012). Chaos based mixed keystream generation for speech data encryption. [IJCIS]. *International Journal on Cryptography and Information Security*, *2*(1), 36–45. doi:10.5121/ijcis.2012.2104

Alvarez, G., & Li, S. (2006). Some Basic Cryptographic Requirements for Chaos-Based Cryptosystems. *Bifurcation and Chaos*, *16*(8), 2129–2151. doi:10.1142/S0218127406015970

Amari, S., & Cichocki, A. (1998). Adaptive Blind Signal Processing- Neural Network Approaches. *IEEE*, *86*(10), 2026-2048.

Ariffin, M., & Abu, N. (2009). Cryptosystem: A Chaos Based Public Key Cryptosystem. *International Journal of Cryptology Research*, *1*(2), 149–163.

Ashtiyani, M., Birgani, P., & Madahi, S. (2012). Speech Signal Encryption Using Chaotic Symmetric Cryptography. *J. Basic. Appl. Sci. Res.*, *2*(2), 1678–1684.

Asim, M., & Jeoti, V. (2008). Efficient and Simple Method for Designing Chaotic S-Boxes. *ETRI Journal*, *30*(1), 170–172. doi:10.4218/etrij.08.0207.0188

Barker, E., Barker, W., Burr, W., Polk, W., & Smid, M. (2007). *Recommendation for Key Management-Part 1: General (Revised) (Special Publication 800-57 Part 1 Rev. 3)*. National Institute of Standards and Technology. NIST.

Beker, H., & Piper, F. (1985). *Secure Speech Communications*. Elsevier Science & Technology Books.

Berry, M., & Mainieri, R. (1996). A brief history of chaos. Chaos with us. *cns*. physics.gatech.edu. Retrieved from http://www.cns.gatech.edu/~predrag/courses/PHYS-7224-07/appendHist.pdf

Blackledge, J. (2008). Multi-algorithmic Cryptography using Deterministic Chaos with Applications to Mobile Communications. *ISAST Transactions on Electronics and Signal Processing*, *2*(1), 23–64.

Blackledge, J. (2010). *Cryptography using chaos*. Warson University. Retrieved from http://www.konwersatorium.pw.edu.pl/wyklady/2010_VLZ7_02_wyklad.pdf

Bopardikar, A. (1995). *Speech Encryption Using Wavelet Packets*. (Master thesis). department of electrical communication engineering, Indian Institute of Science, India.

Brandau, M. (2008). *Implementation of a real-time voice encryption system*. (Master Thesis). University of Applied Sciences Cologne.

Cardoso, J. (1998). Blind Signal Separation: Statistical Principles. *Proceedings of the IEEE*, *86*(10), 2009–2025. doi:10.1109/5.720250

Chen, G., Mao, Y., & Chui, C. (2004). A symmetric image encryption scheme based on 3D chaotic cat maps. *Chaos, Solitons, and Fractals*, *21*, 749–761. doi:10.1016/j.chaos.2003.12.022

Chesnes, M. (2011). *Dynamical Systems and Chaos: Mathematics and Economic Applications*. *Mathematics Senior Exercise*. Kenyon College.

Cox, R., Bock, D., Bauer, K., Johnston, J., & Snyder, J. (1987). The analog speech privacy system. *AT & T Tech. Journal, 66*, 119–131.

David, K., Qi, O., & Sudeshna, S. (2012). Chaos an interdisplinary. *Journal of nonlinear sciences.* Retrieved from http://chaos.aip.org/about/about-the-journal

Ganesan, K., Muthukumar, R., & Murali, K. (2006). Look-up table based chaotic encryption of audio files. In *Proceedings of IEEE Asia Pacific Conference on Circuits and Systems* (APCCAS), (pp. 1951 – 1954). IEEE.

Gnanajeyaraman, R., Prasadh, K., & Ramar, D. (2009). Audio encryption using higher dimensional chaotic map. *International Journal of Recent Trends in Engineering, 1*(2).

Goldreich, O. (2004). *Foundations of Cryptography: Basic Applications.* Cambridge, UK: Cambridge University Press. doi:10.1017/CBO9780511721656

Huang, F., & Stansfield, E. (1993). Time sample speech scrambler which does not require synchronization. *IEEE Transactions on Communications, 41*, 1715–1722. doi:10.1109/26.241752

Hyvarinen, A. (1999). Survey on Independent Component Analysis. *Neural Computing Surveys, 2*(1), 94–128.

Jayant, N. (1982). Analog scramblers for speech privacy. In *Computers and Security.* North-Holland Publishing Company.

Jayant, N., Cox, R., McDermott, B., & Quinn, A. (1983). Analog scramblers Based on sequential permutations in time and frequency. *The Bell System Technical Journal, 62*(1), 25–46. doi:10.1002/j.1538-7305.1983.tb04377.x

Jayant, N., McDermott, B., Christensen, S., & Quinn, A. (1981). A comparison of four methods for analog speech scrambling. *IEEE Transactions on Communications, 29*(1), 38–23. doi:10.1109/TCOM.1981.1094870

Jeyamala, C., Subramanyan, B., & Raman, G. (2011). Ensembles of blowfish with chaos based S-box design for text and image encryption. [IJNSA]. *International Journal of Network Security & Its Applications, 3*(4), 165. doi:10.5121/ijnsa.2011.3415

Jian, W., Xu, L., & Xiaoyong, J. (2010). A Secure Communication System with Multiple Encryption Algorithms. In *Proceeding of The International Conference on E-Business and E-Government.* Guangzhou, China: IEEExplore- Digital Library.

Kak, S., & Jayant, N. (1977). On speech encryption using waveform scrambling. *The Bell System Technical Journal, 56*(5), 781–808. doi:10.1002/j.1538-7305.1977.tb00539.x

Kanso, A. (2010). Self-shrinking chaotic stream ciphers. *Communications in Nonlinear Science and Numerical Simulation, 16*(2), 822–836. doi:10.1016/j.cnsns.2010.04.039

Kanso, A., & Smaoui, N. (2007). Logistic chaotic maps for binary numbers generations. *Chaos, Solitons, and Fractals, 40*(5), 2557–2568. doi:10.1016/j.chaos.2007.10.049

Kellert, S. (1993). *In the Wake of Chaos: Unpredictable Order in Dynamical Systems.* University of Chicago Press Book. doi:10.7208/chicago/9780226429823.001.0001

Kocarev, L., Sterjev, M., Fekete, A., & Vattay, G. (2004). Public-key encryption with chaos. *American Institute of Physics, 14*(3), 1078–1081. PMID:15568922

Kurose, J., & Ross, K. (2003). *Computer Networking. A Top-Down Approach Featuring the Internet* (2nd ed.). Addison Wesley.

Kyrtsou, C., & Labys, W. (2006). Evidence for chaotic dependence between US inflation and commodity prices. *Journal of Macroeconomics, 28*(1), 256–266. doi:10.1016/j.jmacro.2005.10.019

Lawande, Q., Ivan, B., & Dhodapkar, S. (2005). Chaos based Cryptography: A New approach to Secure Communication. *BARC Newsletter, 258*(7), 1–11.

Li, S., Mou, X., & Cai, Y. (2001). Pseudo-Random Bit Generator Based on Couple Chaotic Systems and its Applications in Stream-Cipher Cryptography. *Lecture Notes in Computer Science, 2247*, 316–329. doi:10.1007/3-540-45311-3_30

Li, S., Mou, X., & Cai, Y. (2003). *Chaotic Cryptography in Digital World: State-of-the-Art, Problems and Solutions*. Retrived Feb. 16, 2014 from citeseerx.ist.psu.edu/viewdoc/download?doi=10.1.1.5.9967

Lin, Q., Yin, F., Mei, T., & Liang, H. (2004). A speech encryption algorithm based on blind source separation. In *Proceedings of ICCCAS 2004, International Conference on Communications, Circuits and Systems*, (pp. 1013-1017). IEEExplore Digital Library.

Liu, J., Gao, F., & Ma, H. (2008). A speech chaotic encryption algorithm based on network. [Harbin, China: IEEExplore Digital Librarey.]. *Proceedings of IIHMSP, 08*, 283–286.

Ma, F., Cheng, J., & Wang, Y. (1996). Wavelet transform-based analogue speech scrambling scheme. *Electronics Letters, 32*(8), 719–720. doi:10.1049/el:19960471

Manjunath, G., & Anand, G. (2002). Speech encryption using circulant transformations. In *Proceedings of IEEE International Conference on Multimedia and Expo* (pp. 553-556). IEEExplore Digital Library. doi: 10.1109/ICME.2002.1035841

Mosa, E., Messiha, N., & Zahran, O. (2009). Chaotic encryption of speech signals in transform domains. In *Proceedings of ICCES*. Cairo: IEEE Press.

Mosa, E., Messiha, N., Zahran, O., & Abd El-Samie, F. (2010). Encryption of speech signal with multiple secret keys in time and transform domains. *Springer, 13*(4), 231-242.

Munakata, T. (2008). *Fundamentals of the New Artificial Intelligence, Neural, Evolutionary, Fuzzy and More* (2nd ed.). Springer-Verlag London Limited.

Patidar, V., & Sud, K. (2009). A Novel Pseudo Random Bit Generator Based on Chaotic Standard Map and its Testing. [EJTP]. *Electronic Journal of Theoretical Physics, 6*(20), 327–344.

Patidar, V., Sud, K., & Pareek, N. (2008). A Pseudo Random Bit Generator Based on Chaotic Logistic Map and its Statistical Testing. *Informatica, 33*, 441–452.

Phillips, V., Lee, M., & Thomas, J. (1971). Speech scrambling by the re-ordering of amplitude samples. *Radio and Electronic Engineer, 41*(3).

Prasadh, K., Ramar, K., & Gnanajeyaraman, R. (2009). Public key cryptosystems based on chaotic chebyshev polynomials. In *Proceedings of International Conference on Advances in Recent Technologies in Communication and Computing, ARTCom '09*. IEEExplore-Digital Library. doi: 10.1109/ARTCom.2009.64

Sadkhan, S., & Abbas, N. (2006). A Proposed Speech Scrambler Based on Independent Component Analysis. *MJC010368, 1*(1), 1- 6. Retrieved Feb. 16, 2014 from https://uobabylon.academia.edu/CscUob/Posts/311799/list_of_some_published_E_Papers_and_Pre_Prints_on_University_of_Babylon_Website

Sadkhan, S., & Abbas, N. (2011). Performance evaluation of speech scrambling methods based on statistical approach. *Atti della Fondazione Giorgio Ronchi, 66*(5), 601–614.

Sadkhan, S., & Abbas, N. (2012). Speech scrambling based on wavelet transform. In *Advances in wavelet theory and their applications in engineering physics and technology* (pp. 41–58). InTech. doi:10.5772/37350

Sadkhan, S., Abdulmuhsen, N., & Al-Tahan, N. (2007). A proposed analog speech scrambler based on parallel structure of wavelet transforms. In *Proceedings of National Radio Science Conference.* IEEExplore - Digital Library.

Sakurai, K., Koga, K., & Muratan, T. (1984). A speech scrambler using the fast Fourier transform technique. *IEEE Journal on Selected Areas in Communications, 2*(3), 434–442. doi:10.1109/JSAC.1984.1146074

Sridharan, S., Dawson, E., & Goldburg, B. (1990). Speech Encryption using discrete orthogonal transforms. In *Proceedings of 1990 International Conference on Acoustics, Speech, and Signal Processing,* (pp.1647 – 1650). Albuquerque, NM: ICASSP.

Sridharan, S., Dawson, E., & Goldburg, B. (1993). Design and Cryptanalysis of transform based analog speech scramblers. *IEEE Journal on Selected Areas in Communications, 11*(5), 735–744. doi:10.1109/49.223875

Srinivasan, A., & Selvan, P. (2012). A Review of Analog Audio Scrambling Methods for Residual Intelligibility. *Innovative Systems Design and Engineering, 3*(7), 22–38.

Stallings, W. (2010). Cryptography and network security (5th ed.). Amazon.com.

Strang, G. (1991). A chaotic search for i. *The College Mathematics Journal, 22*(1), 3–12. doi:10.2307/2686733

Su, Z., Zhang, G., & Jiang, J. (2012). Multimedia security: a survey of chaos based encryption technology. In *Multimedia – A multicplinary Approach to Complex Issues* (pp. 99–124). InTech. doi:10.5772/36036

Tao, S., Ruli, W., & Yixun, Y. (1998). Perturbance-based algorithm to expand cycle length of chaotic key stream. *IEEE Electronics Letters, 34*(9), 873–874. doi:10.1049/el:19980680

Tenn, R. (2003). *Symmetric and Asymmetric Secure Communication Schemes using Nonlinear Dynamics.* (PhD Thesis). University of California, San Diego, CA.

Theberge, M. (1996). *Security Evaluation of transform domain speech scramblers.* (M. Sc. Thesis). Columbia University.

Tseng, D., & Chiu, J. (2007). An OFDM speech scrambler without residual intelligibility. In *Proceedings of IEEE Region 10 Conference TENCON.* Taipei, Taiwan: IEEExplore-Digital Library.

Wang, D., & Zhang, Y. (2009). Image Encryption Algorithm Based on S-boxes Substitution and Chaos Random Sequence. In *Proceedings of International Conference on Computer Modeling and Simulation ICCMS,* (pp. 110–113). IEEExplore-Digital Library. doi: 10.1109/ICCMS.2009.26

Wang, H., Hempel, M., Peng, D., Wang, W., Sharif, H., & Chen, H. (2010). Index-based selective audio encryption for wireless multimedia sensor networks. *IEEE Transactions on Multimedia*, *12*, 215–223. doi:10.1109/TMM.2010.2041102

White, V. (1999). *Chaos Theory Helps To Predict Epileptic Seizures*. Office Of Public Information, University Of Florida Health Science Cente. Retieved Feb. 16, 2014 from http://news.bio-medicine.org/medicine-news-2/Chaos-theory-empowers-researchers-to-predict-epileptic-seizures-10007-1/.

Wyner, A. (1979). An analog scrambling scheme which does not expand bandwidth, part 1: Discrete time. *IEEE Transactions on Information Theory*, *25*, 261–274. doi:10.1109/TIT.1979.1056050

Xingyuan, W., Xiaojuan, W., Jianfeng, Z., & Zhenfeng, Z. (2011). Chaotic encryption algorithm based on alternant of stream cipher and block cipher. *Nonlinear Dynamics*, *63*(4), 587–597. doi:10.1007/s11071-010-9821-4

Yang, T. (2003). A survey of chaotic secure communication systems. *Int. J. Comp. Cognition*, *2*, 81–130.

Yuksel, E., Nielson, H., & Nielson, F. (2010). Characteristics of Key Update Strategies for Wireless Sensor Networks. In *Proceedings of the International Conference on Network Communication and Computer* (ICNCC), (pp. 132-136). Technical University Denmark.

Zaibi, G., Peyrard, F., Kachouri, A., Fournier-Prunaret, D., & Samet, M. (2010). *A new design of dynamic S-Box based on two chaotic maps*. Academic Press. doi:10.1109/AICCSA.2010.5586946

ADDITIONAL READING

Amiri, I., Nikoukar, A., Ali, J., New System of Chaotic Signal Generation based on Coupling Coefficients Applied to an ADD/DROP System, International Journal of Advances in Engineering & Technology (IJEAT), 6(1), 78-87.

Anghelescu, P. (2013). Programmable Cellular Automata Encryption Algorithm Implemented in Reconfigurable Hardware, International Journal of Advances in Telecommunications, Electrotechnics. *Signals and Systems*, *2*(2), 73–78.

Arroyo, D., Alvarez, G., & Fernandez, V. (2008), On the inadequacy of the logistic map for cryptographic applications, In Her- nandez, L., Martin, A. (Eds.), X Reunio'n Espan~ola sobre Criptolog'ıa y Seguridad de la Informacio'n (X RECSI), Universidad de Salamanca, Salamanca, Spain, 77–82

Banerjee, S., & Ariffin, M. (2013). Noise induced synchronization of time-delayed semiconductor lasers and authentication based asymmetric encryption. *Optics & Laser Technology*, *45*, 435–442. doi:10.1016/j.optlastec.2012.06.012

Blackledge, J., & Ptitsyn, N. (2011), On the applications of deterministic chaos for encrypting data on the cloud. *CYBERLAWS 2011: The Second International Conference on Technical and Legal Aspects of the e-Society.*

Das, D., & Misra, R. (2011). Programmable Cellular Automata Based Efficient Parallel AES Encryption Algorithm [IJNSA]. *International Journal of Network Security & Its Applications*, *3*(6), 197–211. doi:10.5121/ijnsa.2011.3615

Donati, S., & Mirasso, C. (2002). Introduction to the Feature Section on Optical Chaos and Applications to Cryptography. *IEEE Journal of Quantum Electronics*, *38*(9), 1138–1140. doi:10.1109/JQE.2002.801951

Faraoun, K. (2010). Chaos-Based Key Stream Generator Based on Multiple Maps Combinations and its Application to Images Encryption, The International Arab. *Journal of Information Technology*, *7*(3), 231–240.

Jakimoski, G., & Kocarev, L. (2001), Chaos and Cryptography: Block Encryption Ciphers Based on Chaotic Maps, IEEE Transactions on Circuits and Systems-I: Fundamental Theory and Applications, 48(2).163-169.

Lin, C., & Wang, B. (2011). A 2D CHAOS-BASED VISUAL ENCRYPTION SCHEME FOR CLINICAL EEG SIGNALS. *Journal of Marine Science and Technology*, *19*(6), 666–672.

Menon, S., & Sarila, S. (2013). Image encryption based on chaotic algorithms: An overview, International Journal of Science [IJSETR]. *Engineering and Technology Research*, *2*(6), 1328–1332.

Misra, A., Gupta, A., & Rai, D. (2011). Analysing the Parameters of Chaos Based Image Encryption Schemes. *World Applied Programming*, *1*(5), 294–299.

Özkaynak, F., Özer, A., & Yavuz, S. (2012). Cryptanalysis of Bigdeli Algorithm using Çokal and Solak Attack. *International Journal of Information Security Science*, *1*(3), 79–81.

Reddell, N., Bollt, E., & Welch, T. (2005). A Dual-Synchrony Chaotic Communication Scheme. *Circuits Systems Signal Processing*, *24*(5), 557–570. doi:10.1007/s00034-005-2407-6

KEY TERMS AND DEFINITIONS

Advanced Encryption Standards (AES): Is a specification for the encryption of electronic data established by the U.S. National Institute of Standards and Technology (NIST) in 2001. It is based on the Rijndael cipher[5] developed by two Belgian cryptographers, Joan Daemen and Vincent Rijmen, who submitted a proposal to NIST during the AES selection process. Rijndael is a family of ciphers with different key and block sizes. For AES, NIST selected three members of the Rijndael family, each with a block size of 128 bits, but three different key lengths: 128, 192 and 256 bits. AES has been adopted by the U.S. government and is now used worldwide. It supersedes the Data Encryption Standard (DES), which was published in 1977. The algorithm described by AES is a symmetric-key algorithm, meaning the same key is used for both encrypting and decrypting the data.

Block Cipher: In cryptography, a block cipher is a deterministic algorithm operating on fixed-length groups of bits, called blocks, with an unvarying transformation that is specified by a symmetric key. Block ciphers are important elementary components in the design of many cryptographic protocols, and are widely used to implement encryption of bulk data.

Chaos: Chaos theory is a field of study in mathematics, with applications in several disciplines including meteorology, physics, engineering, economics, biology, and philosophy. Chaos theory studies the behavior of dynamical systems that are highly sensitive to initial conditions—an effect which is popularly referred to as the butterfly effect. Small differences in initial conditions (such as those due to rounding errors in numerical computation) yield widely diverging outcomes for such dynamical systems, rendering long-term prediction impossible in general.

Chaos Maps: In mathematics, a chaotic map is a map (= evolution function) that exhibits some sort of chaotic behavior. Maps may be parameterized by a discrete-time or a continuous-time parameter. Discrete maps usually take the form of iterated functions. Chaotic maps often occur in the study of dynamical systems. Chaotic maps often generate fractals. Although a fractal may be constructed by an iterative procedure, some fractals are studied in and of themselves, as sets rather than in terms of the map that generates them. This is often because there are several different iterative procedures to generate the same fractal.

Chaotic Shift Keying: Uses fluctuations in wavelength to encode and hide a communications signal. In an optoelectronic implementation, a laser is configured so that its output fluctuates chaotically—that is, in a deterministic way that nevertheless looks random. To change from one bit value to another (1 to 0 or vice versa) the chaotic mechanism is altered slightly. Because the output is still chaotic, an eavesdropper should not see any change in the transmission. However, the receiver detects that the chaos is sometimes synchronized, sometimes not, allowing the signal to be extracted.

National Institute of Statistacal Standards (NIST): The NIST Statistical Test Suite is the result of collaborations between the Computer Security Division and the Statistical Engineering Division at NIST. Statistical tests in the package include the: frequency, block frequency, cumulative sums, runs, long runs, Marsaglia's rank, spectral (based on the Discrete Fourier Transform), nonoverlapping template matchings, overlapping template matchings, Maurer's universal statistical, approximate entropy (based on the work of Pincus, Singer and Kalman), random excursions (due to Baron and Rukhin), Lempel-Ziv complexity, linear complexity, and serial. Additional information may be found at http://www.itl.nist.gov/div893/staff/soto/jshome.html.

Pseudorandom Number Generator (PRNG): Also known as a deterministic random bit generator (DRBG), is an algorithm for generating a sequence of numbers that approximates the properties of random numbers. The sequence is not truly random in that it is completely determined by a relatively small set of initial values, called the PRNG's state, which includes a truly random seed. Although sequences that are closer to truly random can be generated using hardware random number generators, pseudorandom numbers are important in practice for their speed in number generation and their reproducibility. PRNGs are central in applications such as simulations (e.g. of physical systems via the Monte Carlo method), in procedural generation, and in cryptography. Cryptographic applications require the output to also be unpredictable, and more elaborate algorithms, which do not inherit the linearity of simpler solutions, are needed.

Secure Wireless Communicatin: The National Institute of Standards and Technology, Information Technology Laboratory, has published recommendations to improve the security of wireless networks in NIST Special Publication (SP) 800-48, Wireless Network Security, 802.11, Bluetooth, and Handheld Devices. Written by Tom Karygiannis and Les Owens, NIST SP 800-48 discusses three aspects of wireless security: security issues associated with wireless local area networks (WLANs) that are based on Institute of Electrical and Electronics Engineers (IEEE) standards 802.11; security issues related to wireless personal area networks based on the Bluetooth specifications, which were developed by an industry consortium; and security of wireless handheld devices.

Speech Scrambling: In telecommunications, a scrambler is a device that transposes or inverts signals or otherwise encodes a message at the transmitter to make the message unintelligible at a receiver not equipped with an appropriately set descrambling device. Whereas encryption usually refers to operations carried out in the digital domain, scrambling usually refers to operations carried out in the analog domain. Scrambling is accomplished by the addition of components to the original signal or the changing of some important component of the original signal in order to make extraction of the original signal difficult.

Stream Cipher: Is a symmetric key cipher where plaintext digits are combined with a pseudorandom cipher digit stream (keystream). In a stream cipher each plaintext digit is encrypted one at a time with the corresponding digit of the keystream, to give a digit of the ciphertext stream. An alternative name is a state cipher, as the encryption of each digit is dependent on the current state. In practice, a digit is typically a bit and the combining operation an exclusive-or (xor).

Voice Encryption: Secure voice (alternatively secure speech or ciphony) is a term in cryptography for the encryption of voice communication over a range of communication types such as radio, telephone or IP.

Wireless Communication: Wireless communication is the transfer of information between two or more points that are not connected by an electrical conductor. The most common wireless technologies use radio. With radio waves distances can be short, such as a few meters for television or as far as thousands or even millions of kilometers for deep-space radio communications. It encompasses various types of fixed, mobile, and portable applications, including two-way radios, cellular telephones, personal digital assistants (PDAs), and wireless networking.

Chapter 5
Cryptography Based on Error Correcting Codes:
A Survey

Marek Repka
Slovak University of Technology, Slovak Republic

Pierre-Louis Cayrel
Université de Saint-Etienne, France

ABSTRACT

Breaking contemporary cryptographic algorithms using any binary computer has at least sub-exponential complexity. However, if a quantum computer was used effectively, then our asymmetric cryptography would not be secure anymore. Since the code-based cryptography (cryptography based on error-correcting codes) relies on different problems, it is not as threatened as, for example, RSA or ECC. Recent years have been crucial in the progress of cryptography based on error-correcting codes. In contrast to the number-theoretic problems typically used in cryptography nowadays, certain instances of the underlying problems of code-based cryptography remain unbroken even employing quantum cryptanalysis. Thus, some code-based cryptography constructions belong to the post-quantum cryptography, especially cryptosystems based on binary irreducible Goppa codes. Many attempts to replace this underlying code in order to reduce the key size already have been proposed. Unfortunately, almost all of them have been broken. For instance, just a while ago, Reed Muller, Generalized Reed-Solomon Codes, and Convolutional codes were broken. Against some rank metric codes, a new attack was introduced. On the other hand, two prospective countermeasures in order to hide the exploitable code structure of the broken codes were fashioned. However, only the choice of binary irreducible Goppa codes remains secure in the post-quantum sense. This chapter surveys the more recent developments in code-based cryptography as well as implementations and side channel attacks. This work also recalls briefly the basic ideas, and provides a roadmap to readers.

DOI: 10.4018/978-1-4666-5808-0.ch005

INTRODUCTION

Present asymmetric cryptography is mainly based on discrete logarithm problem, such as cryptosystems like Diffie-Hellman key exchange protocol, DSA, or ElGamal. Elliptic Curve Cryptography (ECC) relies on the hardness of discrete logarithm defined over elliptic curves (ECDLP). Another problem is the integer factorization problem that RSA is based on. Note that the first purpose, the elliptic curves were used in cryptography, was integer factorization. In solving the discrete logarithm or factorization problem, fast progress has been made. For integer factorization, the general number field sieves are used, and for solving the discrete logarithm, the index calculus algorithm can be employed. Even the binary computation power has grown as Moore's law states. We have new integrated circuit technologies, and special devices for cryptanalysis. We have clusters, grids and clouds today. But we still believe that the complexity of present asymmetric cryptography is at least sub-exponential. Since cryptography based on error-correcting codes relies on different problems as the discrete logarithm or integer factorization, it is not threaten by breaking those problems. Furthermore, a more serious problem is that the threat of an effective use of quantum computer has arisen significantly. Clearly, if an adversary is able to use a quantum computer effectively, almost all the asymmetric cryptography algorithms are threatened (Shor, 1997). The Shor's quantum algorithm (Shor, 1997) complexity is analyzed and improved in (Zalka, 1998). Regarding this quantum algorithm, the discrete logarithm problem as well as the integer factorization problem has polynomial complexity, even on a quantum computer. The case of ECDLP quantum cryptanalysis is investigated more deeply in (Proos, & Zalka, 2003). In certain cases of the error-correcting code-based cryptography, there

is no better than a sub-exponential quantum attack (Bernstein, 2010).

As mentioned above, the code-based cryptography is based on different problems as usually used today. This, in certain cases, gives the code-based cryptography a feature that is called quantum attack resistance. Quantum attack resistance means that the problem a cryptographic primitive is based on is NP-complete, thus at least sub-exponential, to solve on binary and quantum computer. Such cryptography is called post-quantum cryptography. Note that another possibility how post-quantum cryptography can be constructed is to use lattices, multivariate quadratic equations, or hash functions. More about post-quantum cryptography can be found in the book of Bernstein, Buchmann, and Dahmen (2008).

Yes, post-quantum cryptography is unbreakable today. But, despite the post-quantum cryptography being very resistant to known attacks, problems can arise when such strong cryptographic algorithms, like McEliece PKC (McEliece, 1978) or Niederreiter PKC (Niederreiter, 1986), are implemented in real devices, and post-quantum cryptography is not an exception. By this, we are pointing out the Side-Channel Attacks, which we summarize in the Section Cryptanalysis.

In this work, we are focused on the progress in the last three years particularly, thus we refer a reader that is interested in the earlier work in this field to the (Overbeck, & Sendrier, 2008) or Cayrel et al. (2011) surveys.

This chapter is sectioned as follows. Construction of the code-based cryptography is surveyed in Section Code-based cryptography survey. In this section we mention the underlying problems used in this kind of cryptography and their variants, we list cryptographic primitives and attempts to replace the fundamental error-correcting code, the binary irreducible Goppa code, in order to reduce key size. Many of the attempts to replace the code in order to reduce the key size have not been successful as we will see, and thus the key size still remains as an issue. In Section Post-quantum cryptography based on error-correcting codes, we list cryptosystems and their constructions that have not been broken yet, and thus belong to the post-quantum cryptography. The following section, the Section Implementations, provides an overview of implementations published. In this section, we will see that post-quantum cryptography can be better performing than RSA, or even ECC. The Section Cryptanalysis consists of a survey of recent progress in side channel attacks, structural attacks, and generic attacks like information set decoding, collision decoding, or general birthday attacks. Thus, it summarizes the recent work in cryptanalysis of cryptography based on error-correcting codes. Finally, we conclude this chapter in Section Conclusions.

CODE-BASED CRYPTOGRAPHY SURVEY

In the code-based cryptography, there exist several promising candidates to public-key cryptosystem (PKC). Without a doubt, the most inspiring code-based cryptosystem is the McEliece PKC (McEliece, 1978). The McEliece PKC has never been the subject of as much attention as RSA (1977), mostly because of the relatively large size of its private and public-keys. Everything changed when it was observed that these schemes have been untouched by quantum cryptanalysis. The original McEliece PKC has been resistant to all known attacks (even using quantum cryptanalysis) for more than 35 years. Its resistance roots from the general decoding problem (Berlekamp, McEliece, & van Tilborg, 1978). Note that it is resistant to all known attacks except for the side channel attacks (Section Cryptanalysis), but what cryptographic scheme is not. Many contributions have been made in the last few years in this field. Significant part of them dealt with the key size reduction by alter-

ing the underlying error-correcting code. Almost all these attempts failed.

Inspired by the McEliece PKC, another very promising possibility for a public-key cryptosystem is the Niederreiter PKC proposed by Niederreiter (1986). This design is based on equivalent problem as the one that McEliece PKC is based on, namely the syndrome decoding problem. Also the Niederreiter PKC has not escaped the key size issue. But, now it is experimentally verified that while McEliece PKC and Niederreiter PKC require bigger keys, an implementation of McEliece and Niederreiter PKC can perform better than a RSA or even ECC implementation (Biswas, & Sendrier, 2008; Heyse, & Güneysu, 2013). Moreover, regarding the key size issue, in these times, a McEliece PKC implementation on a smart card is not a problem (Strenzke, 2010). We list more details in Section Implementations.

As we will see below, using code-based cryptography, one can construct cryptographic primitives like public-key encryption, signatures, identification, hash functions, stream ciphers, or pseudo-randomness. Their construction is based on special instances of the two crucial NP-complete decision problems in coding theory we list in the following subsection. The following two instances are used in particular. They are equivalent in terms of complexity:

1. General decoding problem that is used in two variants, namely general decoding problem over binary and q-ary finite fields.
2. Syndrome decoding problem used in three variants, namely syndrome decoding problem over binary and q-ary finite fields, and syndrome decoding problem in rank metric.

The general decoding problem relies on the difficulty of correcting and decoding a word given the code generator matrix, or given the parity check matrix equivalently. And the syndrome decoding problem relies on the hardness of finding the error vector that corresponds to a given parity check matrix and a given syndrome.

The Two Crucial NP-Complete Problems Used in Code-Based Cryptography

In the following text, we recall the two well-known decision NP-complete problems that error-correcting code-based cryptography is based on. All other problems used in code-based cryptography are derived from them, and thus they can be reduced to them (Berlekamp, McEliece, & Tilborg, 1978). A definition list of the derived problems can be found, for example, in (Overbeck, & Sendrier, 2008).

We state the two NP-complete problems here as problems stated in NP-completeness theory. There is an input that is encoded into binary string and then fed into deterministic Touring machine. The machine outputs 1 if the input has the desired property, and it outputs 0 if otherwise. In certain cases of linear error-correcting codes, there is no such a machine that would produce the correct answer in polynomial time even it was a quantum computer. The following two decision problems are NP-complete (Berlekamp, McEliece, & van Tilborg, 1978).

- **The Coset Weights Decision NP-complete Problem:**
  - **Input:** A binary matrix H, a binary vector s, and a nonnegative integer w.
  - **Property:** There exists a vector e of hamming weight less then w such that $s = eH$.
- **The Subspace Weights Decision NP-complete Problem:**
  - **Input:** A binary matrix H, and a non-negative integer w.
  - **Property:** There exists a vector x of hamming weight w such that $xH = 0$.

The first decision NP-complete problem listed here can be viewed as following minimization problem. Let us have a linear code of length n and dimension k. We received word y. Its syndrome s is computed as $s = yH$, where H is the $n \times (n - k)$ parity check matrix of the code. There is a solution e of the minimum weight that gives the same syndrome, i.e. $s = eH$. The solution e is the best approximation of the error vector that has been added to the transmitted code word x trough a binary symmetric channel.

The second NP-complete decision problem stated here can be viewed as decision problem whether a linear code contains a code word of the given weight.

List of Cryptographic Primitives

A brief list of the last proposals or improvements of cryptographic primitives based on error-correcting codes follows. For a more detailed list, we refer a reader to the survey published by Cayrel (2011).

Encryption: For the encryption purpose, we have the McEliece PKC, or Niederreiter PKC (Section Post-quantum cryptography based on error-correcting codes). An appropriate choice of parameters for them is listed in the paper (Bernstein, Lange, & Peters, 2008). We should also not forget about the Indistinguishability under Adaptive Chosen Ciphertext Attack (IND-CCA2) conversions necessity (see below). Note, encryption cryptosystem presented in (Lu et al., 2011) is IND-CCA2-secure naturally.

Since the key size issue, several attempts to replace the underlying code have been designed. Unfortunately, many attempts to change the code the cryptosystems are based on were not successful. So we have to be very careful in modifications of the McEliece/Niederreiter PKC. Also in the Niederreiter PKC the Goppa codes designed for the McEliece PKC should be used. In order to hide the exploitable structure of a code, one can try to use one of the countermeasures listed below.

Identification: Recently, Cayrel, Véron, and Alaoui (2011) presented an identification scheme using q-ary codes instead of binary codes. Based on maximum-rank-distance codes, a new proposal has been introduced (Gaborit, Schrek, & Zémor, 2011).

Signature: Barreto, Misoczki, and Simplício (2011) developed the syndrome-based one-time signature scheme (BMS-OTS). An improved version of a threshold ring signature can be found in (Cayrel et al., 2012), a one-time signature scheme is presented in (Gaborit, & Schrek, 2012), and a signcryption scheme is proposed in (Mathew, Vasant, & Rangan, 2012).

Pseudo-randomness: Fischer, and Stern (1996) presented the first pseudo-random generator based on error-correcting codes. Security of the generator is conditioned by the hardness of the syndrome decoding problem for random binary linear codes. Hence, the generator is based on the fact that the greater the weight of error vectors, the exponentially greater the number of words having the same syndrome. Regarding the code length and the dimension of a linear error-correcting code, the weight of error vectors is chosen close to the Gilbert-Varshamov bound (Gilbert, 1952; Varshamov, 1957). The sampling algorithm originally proposed for this generator can be found in the (Fischer, & Stern, 1996). Another very good choices are mentioned in (Biswas, & Sendrier, 2008; Heyse, 2010).

Digest: Bernstein et al. (2011) proposed RFSB (which stands for Really Fast Syndrome-Based Hashing). RFSB is based on random functions, and uses the AES algorithm.

Stream ciphers: Using the ideas from RFSB, Meziani, Hoffmann, and Cayrel (2012) improved the code-based stream cipher SYND.

On the Underlying Error-Correcting Code

Since the key size of the original McEliece PKC is large in comparison with RSA or ECC, there has been proposed many attempt to replace the irreducible binary Goppa codes. Unfortunately, almost all of them were not successful. In this subsection, only unbroken error-correcting codes are listed. The full list of codes proposed to be used in code-based cryptography, and whether the proposed code was broken or not, can be found in the Table 1.

Binary irreducible Goppa codes with maximal length: The concept to use binary irreducible Goppa codes with maximal length routes from McEliece (1978). This choice of error-correcting code still remains unbroken even using quantum

Table 1. State of error-correcting codes survival in code-based cryptography

Underlying Error-Correcting Code	Attack
Binary irreducible Goppa codes	No attack
Goppa codes over q-ary finite fields (q ≥ 31)	No attack
Moderate density parity-check codes	No attack
Convolutional codes	(Landais, & Tillich, 2013)
Generalized Reed-Solomon Codes and sub-codes	(Couvreur et al., 2013; Gauthier, Otmani, & Tillich 2012)
Goppa codes over q-ary finite fields (2 < q < 31)	(Peters, 2010)
Maximum-rank-distance codes	(Gaborit, Ruatta, & Schrek, 2013)
Reed-Muller codes	(Chizhov, & Borodin, 2013)
Quasi-Cyclic Alternant, Quasic-Dyadic Goppa, BCH, Low density parity-check codes	(Faugère et al., 2010)
Algebraic geometric codes in case of low genus hyperelliptic curves	(Faure, & Minder, 2008)
Generalized Srivastava codes	(Sidelnikov, Shestakov, 1992)

cryptanalysis. Thus, in construction of post-quantum error-correcting code-based cryptography, random instances of this error-correcting code are used. We define this codes in Section Post-quantum cryptography based on error-correcting codes.

Goppa Codes over q-ary finite fields: Bernstein, Lange, and Peters (2010) demonstrated usage of Goppa codes defined over fields that are characteristic of power of an odd prime (q-ary finite fields). This cryptosystem is called Wild McEliece. Bernstein, Lange, and Peters (2010) claimed that, using smaller keys, they achieve the same security level as the original McEliece PKC. Their proposal had just one weakness. The pool of Goppa polynomials is not as big as in the original McEliece PKC case. This vulnerability can be misused by the support splitting algorithm (Sendrier, 2000). In order to eliminate this vulnerability, Bernstein, Lange, and Peters (2011) introduced the Wild McEliece Incognito. In this PKC, the Goppa polynomial is multiplied by a co-prime polynomial. In these codes it is possible to correct more errors than in the case of binary irreducible Goppa codes.

Moderate density parity-check codes: Since (Faugère et al., 2010), the Low-Density Parity-Check (LDPC) codes (and their Quasi-Cyclic variant) were replaced by Moderate Density Parity-Check Codes (MDPC) that has been suggested to use by Misoczki et al. (2013).

Promising Countermeasures for the Weak Error-Correcting Code Choices

Baldi, Bodrato, and Chiaraluce, (2008) showed that if the secret permutation matrix is changed to a dense transformation matrix increasing the density of the public parity check matrix, the attacks against cryptosystems using QC, QD, Generalized Srivastava and its sub-codes, and also LDPC codes become significantly more complex. This idea has been improved and generalized into a non-binary case in the work (Baldi et al., 2011).

Another very promising modification of the McEliece PKC seems to be the work (Gueye, & Mboup, 2013). They modified the key generation algorithm in a way that a random matrix is connected to the private-code generator matrix from the right. Then the new matrix is hidden multiplying it by a secret random dense scramble matrix, and by a secret random permutation matrix, as was originally proposed (McEliece, 1978). The decoding algorithm is also modified. After the secret permutation is removed from the cipher-text, only the first number of bits (equal to the code length) are considered in the following process, which is as originally proposed in (McEliece, 1978). This modification is presented on Reed-Muller codes that were broken (Chizhov, & Borodin, 2013).

IND-CCA2-Secure Conversions

Clearly, the original McEliece/ Niederreiter PKC proposal is vulnerable to the adaptive chosen-ciphertext attack (CCA2). Possible CCA2-secure conversions can be found, for instance, in (Kobara & Imai, 2001; Dowsley, Müller-Quade, & Nascimento, 2009; Dottling et al., 2012). An efficient CCA2-secure variant of the McEliece PKC in the standard model can be found in (Rastaghi, 2013). The indistinguishability under adaptive chosen cipher-text attack (IND-CCA2) is addressed by Persichetti (2012). Mathew et al. (2012) proposed a new and efficient IND-CCA2-secure conversion of the Niederreiter PKC.

POST-QUANTUM CRYPTOGRAPHY BASED ON ERROR-CORRECTING CODES

Many attempts to change the underling error-correcting code, or to modify the original McEliece (1978) or Niederreiter (1986) proposal, were not successful, and those proposals that have not been broken yet can be broken in the close future. Only the original McEliece proposal (to use the binary irreducible Goppa codes with the maximal length) is credible. This original proposal has not been broken since 1978. The next credible post-quantum code-based public-key cryptosystem is the Niederreiter PKC, but only when the binary irreducible Goppa codes with maximal length are used. For better understanding, let us recall those two cryptosystems, and the underlying error-correcting code as well as the Patterson's algebraic decoding algorithm (Patterson, 1975).

Binary Irreducible Goppa Codes with Maximal Length

Goppa codes were introduced by Goppa (1970). In the original McEliece PKC proposal (McEliece, 1978), random binary irreducible Goppa codes are used. However, in PKCs like McEliece and Niederreiter, not only binary irreducible Goppa codes can be used. Unfortunately, cryptanalytic community identified most of them to be less secure or less efficient than the binary irreducible Goppa codes, as we mentioned in Section Code-based cryptography survey. Thus, Goppa codes (Goppa, 1970) play a special role in the code-based cryptography, especially in construction of the post-quantum cryptography based on error-correcting codes. Let us sketch out definition of binary irreducible Goppa codes designed for McEliece PKC.

Let us have a finite field characteristic of two. Irreducible Goppa polynomial $g(X)$ is a monic polynomial that is irreducible over the finite field. Code support Λ is an ordered set of λ_i, or a vector of all the elements of the finite field, that are not zeros of the Goppa polynomial. Since the Goppa polynomial is irreducible, we have all the field elements in the code support. The code support elements are distinct of course. A binary irreducible Goppa code is a linear code represented by the code support and the irreducible Goppa polynomial. Obviously, a binary vector c length of n, the code length, is in the code if its

syndrome polynomial $S(X)$ is congruent to zero modulo the irreducible Goppa polynomial.

$$\Gamma\left(\Lambda, g\right) = \left\{ c \in F_{2^n} \mid S_c\left(X\right) \equiv 0 \bmod g\left(X\right) \right\},$$
(1)

$$S_c\left(X\right) = \sum_{i=0}^{n-1} \frac{c_i}{X - l_i}.$$
(2)

This binary irreducible Goppa code has length equal to the number of the code support elements, i.e. the number of the field elements in this case. The dimension of this code is equal to the number of the field elements minus the degree of the irreducible Goppa polynomial multiplied by the degree of the irreducible polynomial used to create the finite field. Finally, the minimum distance of the code is at least two times the degree of the irreducible Goppa polynomial plus one.

Goppa codes are a subclass of Alternant codes (Helgert, 1974). This knowledge can be used in order to reduce required key size. But nobody has been successful yet (Section Code-based cryptography survey). On the other hand, the same knowledge can be misused in order to design a code distinguisher (Faugère et al., 2013). Such a Goppa code distinguisher, which is able to distinguish a Goppa code generator matrix from a random matrix, can threat McEliece PKCs.

Patterson's Algebraic Decoding Algorithm

In the Patterson's algebraic decoding algorithm (Patterson, 1975), the syndrome of an error vector has to be determined first. It can be determined using the secret parity check matrix, or simply by evaluating the syndrome polynomial $S(X)$ modulo the irreducible Goppa polynomial $g(X)$.

$$S_e\left(X\right) \equiv \sum_{i=0}^{n-1} \frac{y_i}{X - \lambda_i} \bmod g\left(X\right).$$
(3)

In the syndrome polynomial, y_i is the i-th bit of a being corrected word, λ_i is the i-th element of the code support, and n is the code length as well as the number of code support elements. When the error syndrome is determined, the next main step is to compute the corresponding error-locator polynomial.

An error-locator polynomial $\sigma(X)$ is a polynomial over the finite field the code is defined. Positions of zeroes of the error-locator polynomial in the code support gives error bit positions in the word that is being corrected.

$$\sigma_e(X) = \prod_{i=0}^{n-1}(X - \lambda_i)^{e_i}. \tag{4}$$

The syndrome polynomial is congruent to the fraction of the error-locator polynomial's first derivative and the error-locator polynomial, modulo the irreducible Goppa polynomial.

$$S(X) \equiv \frac{\sigma'(X)}{\sigma(X)} \bmod g(X). \tag{5}$$

Since a binary irreducible Goppa code is being corrected, the first derivative of the error-locator polynomial consists only of all the even terms, i.e. the error-locator polynomial can be split into squares and non-squares, see below where

$$\beta^2(X) = \sigma'(X). \tag{6}$$

$$\sigma(X) = \alpha^2(X) + X\beta^2(X). \tag{7}$$

Therefore, the error-locator polynomial multiplied by the syndrome polynomial is congruent to the first derivative of the error-locator polynomial, modulo the irreducible Goppa polynomial. This equation can be rewritten as the square root of the first derivative of the error-locator polynomial times the square root of (X plus the inversion of the syndrome) congruent to the square root of non-square terms in the error-locator polynomial, modulo the irreducible Goppa polynomial. This equation is called Key equation.

$$T(X) \equiv X + S^{-1}(X) \bmod g(X). \tag{8}$$

$$b(X)\sqrt{T(X)} \equiv a(X) \bmod g(X) \tag{9}$$

The key equation is solved by applying the Extended Euclidean Algorithm that stops when the

$$\deg(a_k(X)) \le \left\lceil \frac{\deg(g(X)) + 1}{2} - 1 \right\rceil, \tag{10}$$

where k is iteration number of the Extended Euclidean Algorithm. Once the square root of the error-locator polynomial's first derivative and the square root of non-square terms of the error-locator polynomial are revealed, the error-locator polynomial is computed by squaring them, and after the multiplication of the error-locator polynomial's first derivative by X, by adding them.

In this case, the case of McEliece/Niederreiter PKC, the resulting error-locator polynomial has degree equal to the degree of the irreducible Goppa polynomial. This is the maximum number of errors the Patterson's algebraic decoding algorithm is capable to correct, and also the maximum number of errors that can be corrected in any binary irreducible Goppa code.

Finally, in order to determine the error vector, the roots of the error-locator polynomial have to be found. For this purpose, one can simply evaluate the obtained error-locator polynomial over the code support or use a factorization method like the Berlekamp trace algorithm (Berlekamp, 1971), or Chien method (Chien, 1964), or any other. Efficiency of some factorization methods that can be used here is discussed in (Strenzke,

2011). Finally, indexes of the code support elements that are zeros of the error-locator polynomial give indexes of error bits in the received word.

As an alternative to the Patterson's algebraic decoding algorithm (Patterson, 1975), one can use decoding algorithm described in (Sugiyama et al., 1976) which is very similar to the Patterson's one, or recently published List decoding for binary Goppa codes that was presented by Bernstein (2011).

The McEliece PKC

The McEliece PKC (McEliece, 1978) is based on the general decoding problem. More precisely, it is based on the problem how to find the secret code which is permutation equivalent to the public one. It still remains unbroken in this original design where the binary irreducible Goppa codes with maximal length are used.

A private key K_{priv} consists of a secret random binary irreducible Goppa code (Goppa, 1970) with maximal length n, and dimension k, as we defined above. The corresponding public-key K_{pub} is derived from the private one so that the generator $k \times n$ matrix G_{priv} of the secret code is multiplied by a random dense invertible scramble $k \times k$ matrix S and a random permutation $n \times n$ matrix P respectively, which are also secret. Those random matrices are then the next part of the private key.

$$G_{pub} = SG_{priv}P. \qquad (11)$$

The Generator matrix G_{pub} of the public binary irreducible Goppa code together with t that is the degree of the irreducible Goppa polynomial form the corresponding public-key. It is clear that the public generator matrix generates a permutation equivalent code to the private one. Therefore,

$$K_{priv} = \left(\Gamma\left(\Lambda, g \right), S, P \right), \qquad (12)$$

where the code support is randomly ordered, and g is a random irreducible Goppa polynomial, and

$$K_{pub} = \left(G_{pub}, t \right). \qquad (13)$$

The encryption algorithm is very simple. Given a public-key, one message block m is encoded to the corresponding code word. Then a random error e hamming weight of the degree of the irreducible Goppa polynomial is added to the code word. The result of these several bitwise exclusive OR (XOR) additions and binary multiplications produces a cipher-text y.

$$y = mG_{pub} + e. \qquad (14)$$

At start of the decryption algorithm, the secret permutation matrix is removed— the public generator matrix generates a permutation code equivalent to the secret one. Subsequently, the Patterson's algebraic decoding algorithm (Patterson, 1975) is applied in order to remove the error. In the time the error vector is removed, only the information coordinates are read from the code word, and finally the secret invertible scrambling matrix is removed. As a result the plain-text is obtained.

$$m' = \text{Patterson}(yP^{-1}), \qquad (15)$$

$$m = \text{getInformationCoords}(m')S^{-1}. \qquad (16)$$

Note, the IND-CCA2 conversions are mentioned in the Section Code-based cryptography survey.

Niederreiter PKC Using Binary Irreducible Goppa Codes with Maximal Length

From a security point of view, this cryptosystem is equivalent to the McEliece PKC. It is based on the syndrome decoding problem. From the performance perspective this scheme should be better performing than the McEliece PKC.

The main difference is that instead of a generator matrix, the Niederreiter PKC uses a party check matrix only. A block of a plaintext is mapped to an error vector of desired weight. The corresponding cipher-text is then the syndrome of the error vector. It is clear that the mapping φ has to be a bijective function that is easy to compute, invert, and implement. Here are several proposals for the mapping function (Fischer, & Stern, 1996; Biswas, & Sendrier, 2008; Heyse, 2010).

In the original Niederreiter PKC proposal (Niederreiter, 1986), any linear error-correcting code can be used. However, due to the fact that most of them were turned out to be less secure or less efficient (Section Code-based cryptography survey), it is suggested to use binary irreducible Goppa codes with maximal length. Thus, we restrict the interpretation in the following paragraph in to such a case only.

A private key K_{priv} consists of a $\left(n \times mt\right)$ parity check matrix H_{priv} of a secret random binary irreducible Goppa code $\Gamma\left(\Lambda, g\right)$ with maximal length. The corresponding public-key K_{pub} is generated as the product of a $\left(n \times n\right)$ random binary permutation matrix P, the secret parity check matrix, and a $\left(mt \times mt\right)$ random dense non-singular binary matrix S, respectively, resulting in a public parity check matrix H_{pub}.

$$H_{pub} = PH_{priv}S. \tag{17}$$

The corresponding public-key K_{pub}, thus, consists of the public parity check matrix and *t* that is the degree of the irreducible Goppa polynomial.

$$K_{priv} = \left(\Gamma\left(\Lambda, g\right), S, P\right). \tag{18}$$

$$K_{pub} = \left(H_{pub}, \, t\right). \tag{19}$$

Once a public-key is given, in order to encrypt one message block m, one has to map the message block onto an error vector of the code length and hamming weight equal to the degree of the irreducible Goppa polynomial. For the mapping the bijective function φ is used. Consequently, the product of the public parity check matrix and the error vector obtained results in the cipher-text that is basically the syndrome.

$$y = \varphi\left(m\right)H_{pub}. \tag{20}$$

The cipher-text can be decrypted using the corresponding private key only. First the random dense non-singular binary matrix is removed. Then, the Patterson's algebraic decoding algorithm (Patterson, 1975) is applied. Now the random binary permutation matrix is removed. And finally, the inverse mapping is performed in order to reveal the message. For an IND-CCA2 conversion consult the Section Code-based cryptography survey.

$$\mathrm{m} = \varphi^{-1}\left(\mathrm{Patterson}(yS^{-1})P^{-1}\right). \tag{21}$$

IMPLEMENTATIONS

For more than 25 years there has not been published any paper devoted to a McEliece PKC implementation because of its large public-key size.

Encryption

McEliece: Although the key size in McEllie PKC is rather large, it is not such a problem nowadays, as can be seen, for instance, in the implementation of McEliece PKC on a smart card with an Infineon SLE 76 chip (Strenzke, 2010). Strenzke (2010) implemented two instances of McEliece PKC. One instance has the length of the code equal to 1024 with 40 errors (62 security bits), and the second instance has the code length 2048 with 50 errors (102 security bits). In order to reduce the key size of the McEliece PKC, the public-key is generated from a private one in such a way that the public generator matrix is in the systematic form. The McEliece PKC vulnerability to the adaptive chosen-ciphertext attack (CCA2) is thwarted using CCA2-secure conversion. For interest, encryption took 970ms and decryption took 690ms for the first instance, and the encryption and decryption for the second instance took 1390ms and 1060ms respectively. The QC-MDPC McEliece variant (key size 4.8KB only) was implemented by (Heyse, von Maurich & Güneysu, 2013) (Table 2, Table 3).

For embedded devices, the first McEliece PKC implementation was published by Eisenbarth et al. (2009). They implemented an instance of McEliece PKC with code length 2048 with 27 errors what corresponds to an 80 security bits, which they named MicroEliece, on an 8-bit AVR microprocessor, and on a Xilinx Spartan-3AN FPGA. They used several clever ideas –like the public code generator matrix in the systematic form, special generation method and representation of permutation and scrambling matrices and appropriate representation of the code support– in order for keys to save the memory size required. Despite the clever ideas, the FPGA was too small to implement the whole McEliece. Thus, they implemented encryption first and decryption afterwards. They achieved following results. In the case of the microcontroller, encryption process and decryption process took 450ms and 618ms respectively. For a comparison, they mentioned computation time

Table 2. Performance of McEliece PKC implemented on Microcontroller platform

Cryptosystem Implementation /Code length, Number of Errors Correcting, Security Bits/	Device	Computation Time for Encryption, and Decryption Respectively	Reference
McEliece PKC /1024, 40, 62/	Infineon SLE76CF5120P controller, 16-bit CPU @ 33 MHz	970ms, 690ms	(Strenzke, 2010)
McEliece PKC /2048, 50, 102/	Infineon SLE76CF5120P controller, 16-bit CPU @ 33 MHz	1390ms 1060ms	(Strenzke, 2010)
McEliece PKC /2048, 27, 80/	AVR ATxMega192, 8-bit CPU @ 32MHz	450ms, 618ms	(Eisenbarth et al., 2009).
QC-MDPC McEliece PKC /9600, 84, 80/	AVR ATxMega256A3, 8-bit CPU @ 32MHz	800ms, 2700ms	(Heyse, von Maurich & Güneysu, 2013).

Table 3. Performances of ECC and RSA implementations on Microcontroller platform

Cryptosystem Implementation	Device	Computation time	Reference
ECC-P160 (SECG)	ATMega128@8MHz	203ms (scaled for 32MHz)	(Eisenbarth et al., 2009).
RSA-1024	ATMega128@8MHz	20748ms (scaled for 32MHz)	(Eisenbarth et al., 2009).

for ECC-P160 (SECG) and random instances of RSA-1024 on the same platform. The computation time for the ECC-P160 (SECG) was 203ms, and the computation time for the RSA-1024 was 2748ms. On the FPGA platform, the encryption took 1.07ms and the decryption took 10.82ms while the running time for the ECC-P160 (SECG) and RSA-1024 was 5.1ms and 51ms respectively. Note that ECC is better performing here, but in the McEliece PKC, there still exist opportunities for optimization. Indeed, ECC has been studied more notoriously than McEliece PKC due to the disadvantage of the key size.

The whole McEliece PKC processor architecture for a Virtex-5 FPGA and its implementation results were published by Shoufan et al. (2009). The published architecture involves key generator, encryptor, and decryptor. Their implementation of McEliece PKC with 2048 code length correcting 50 errors spent 84% of slices and 50% of BRAMs (2700 Kb).

Finally, The QC-MDPC McEliece variant, with 4.8KB key size, was implemented on Xilinx Virtex-6 FPGA by (Heyse, von Maurich & Güneysu,

2013). The achieved results are very promising (Table 4. Table 5).

Moreover, not only hardware implementations or implementations for embedded devices have been published. The HyMES implementation in C language running under Linux was published by (Biswas & Sendrier, 2008).

Niederreiter PKC: The Niederreiter PKC was also implemented on an embedded platform (Heyse, 2010). Heyse (2010) implemented Niederreiter PKC on an 8-bit AVR ATxMega256A1 microcontroller. He used log and antilog tables for multiplication computation purpose. Niederreiter PKC with a code length of 2048 and 27 errors corresponding to an 80 security bits was implemented. The performance the implemented Niederreiter PKC achieved is comparable to the performance of ECC-P160 (SECG) and a random RSA-1024 instance. The encryption took 1.6ms and the decryption took 180ms. For ECC-P160 (SECG) the running time was 203ms, and for the random RSA-1024 instance the running time was 2748ms (Table 6).

Table 4. Performance of McEliece PKC implementations on FPGA platform

Cryptosystem Implementation /Code length, Number of Errors Correcting, Security Bits/	Device	Computation Time for Encryption, and Decryption Respectively	Reference
McEliece PKC /2048, 27, 80/	Spartan-3AN 1400 FPGA, Enc@150MHz, Dec@85Mhz	1.07ms, 10.82ms	(Eisenbarth, Güneysu, Heyse, & Paar, 2009).
McEliece PKC /2048, 50, 102/	Xilinx Virtex-5, 163MHz	0.5ms, 1.4ms	(Shoufan et al., 2009).
QC-MDPC McEliece PKC /9600, 84, 80/	Xilinx Virtex-6 Enc@351.3MHz, Dec@190.6MHz.	0.14ms, 0.86ms	(Heyse, von Maurich & Güneysu, 2013).

Table 5. Performance of ECC and RSA implementations on FPGA platform

Cryptosystem Implementation	Device	Computation time for Encryption, and Decryption Respectively	Reference
ECC-P160 (SECG)	Spartan-3 1000-4	5.1ms	(Eisenbarth et al., 2009).
ECC-K163	Virtex-II	0,0358ms	(Heyse, & Güneysu, 2012)
RSA-1024	Spartan-3E 1500-5	51ms	(Eisenbarth et al., 2009).

Table 6. Performances of Niederreiter PKC implementations

Cryptosystem Implementation / Code length, Number of Errors Correcting, Security Bits /	Platform, Device	Computation Time for Encryption, and Decryption Respectively	References
Niederreiter PKC /2048, 27, 80/	Microcontroller AVR ATxMega256A1, 8 bit CPU, 32MHz	1.6ms, 180ms	(Heyse, 2010)
Niederreiter PKC /2048, 27, 80/	FPGA, Xilinx Virtex6LX240, Enc@300MHz, Dec@250MHz	0.00066ms, 0.05878ms	(Heyse, & Güneysu, 2012)

The very promising implementation of the Niederreiter PKC was published by Heyse, and Güneysu (2012). Their implementation on Xilinx Virtex-6 FPGAs providing 80-bit security was able to run 1.5 million encryption and 17000 decryption operations per second, respectively. This result is in dimension of ECC performance. Afterwards, they optimized the implementation in (Heyse, & Güneysu, 2013).

Derived cryptosystems: On embedded platform, there have been implemented also variants considering the key size issue that is addressed by code structure. Inspirited by LDPC and MDPC codes, on embedded platform, Barreto, Misoczki, and Ruggiero (2012) implemented a variant of McEliece based on QC-LDPC and cyclosymmetric MDPC codes. Subsequently, Cayrel, Hoffmann, and Persichetti (2012) implemented a CCA2-secure McEliece variant based on QD generalized Srivastava codes.

Signature

In order to save space required for keys storing, Strenzke (2012) proposed an approach how to compute digital signature on memory-constrained devices like smart cards. The public-key is not stored on the device, but rather it is send to the device part after part. The device then computes intermediate results using the parts of the public-key it receives. In order to shrink the size of private keys, the syndrome is computed evaluating the syndrome polynomial instead of using the secret parity check matrix.

On hardware platform, Beuchat et al. (2004) published a McEliece like signature scheme implementation on Xilinx Virtex XCV300E FPGA.

Identification

Using QC codes instead of random codes, Cayrel, Gaborit, and Prouff (2008) proposed an efficient implementation of Stern's protocol on a smartcard. For the security level of 80 bits, they obtained an authentication in 6 seconds and a signature in 24 seconds without cryptographic co-processor. This is a promising result when compared to an RSA implementation which would take more than 30 seconds in a similar context.

Other Cryptographic Primitives

Further cryptographic primitives, like identification, hash function, stream ciphers, and also encryption and signature implemented in C and Java languages can be found on the web page of Cayrel (2012).

Cryptanalysis

The two main types of attacks in code-based cryptography are structural and information set decoding attacks. The structural attacks rely on the specific structure of an error-correcting code. The information set decoding attacks are generic attacks. Further, there are code distinguishers and quantum attacks. This section starts with side channel attacks. Indeed, side channel attacks are very dangerous implementation attacks.

Side Channel Attacks

The first side channel analysis of the McEliece PKC was published by Strenzke et al. (2008). They presented a timing attack realized in the Patterson's algebraic decoding algorithm in the decryption process, a power attack on the construction of the parity check matrix during key generation, and a CACHE timing attack on the permutation of code words during decryption. The timing attack against the Patterson's algebraic decoding algorithm misuses the fact that the error-locator polynomial degree equals exactly to the number of errors in the received word (cipher-text). Thus, in order to determine the message (plain-text), one can try to request decryption of a fake cipher-text which was created XORing the true cipher-text with a vector with hamming weight one. If the flipped bit in the fake cipher-text is an error bit, then its error-locator polynomial has one less degree than the error-locator polynomial of the true cipher-text. Strenzke et al. (2008) misused this fact and they measured running time of the error-locator polynomial evaluation in the Patterson's algebraic decoding algorithm, which is linearly dependent to the degree of the error-locator polynomial. By this method, one can reveal the whole error vector. They stated that it is possible to mount this attack also against the CCA2-secure conversion like one published in (Kobara & Imai, 2001) as an example. In the following part of their work, they discuss a possibility to reveal coefficients of the irreducible Goppa polynomial assuming that the code support is known. If the code support is known, the irreducible Goppa polynomial can be revealed by analyzing the power consumption caused by the evaluation of the irreducible Goppa polynomial in the parity check matrix construction in the key generation phase. In the remaining part

of the Strenzke et al. (2008) work, the CACHE timing attack against the first step of decryption is mentioned. In this attack scenario, it is assumed that the permutation matrix is stored as a look-up table in memory, and that an adversary is able to run a spy process in parallel to the decryption process. The spy process role is to prepare the CAHCE for the attack and to measure the running time of the decryption process. If it is so, it is possible to determine which part of the cipher-text was accessed. This attack works well only if the CACHE size is small enough.

The work of Strenzke et al. (2008) was worked out into a deeper timing analysis of the Patterson's algebraic decoding algorithm in (Shoufan et al., 2009). They presented that not only the error-locator polynomial evaluation leaks, but furthermore that the construction of the error-locator polynomial leaks in the same manner. The construction of the error-locator polynomial follows after the Extended Euclidean Algorithm step (used for key equation solving in the Patterson's algebraic decoding algorithm). Since the number of iterations of the Extended Euclidean Algorithm depends on the error vector hamming weight, also the Extended Euclidean Algorithm step can be misused in the same manner. These timing attacks in combination with fault injection attacks reveal just a message, and not the private key. Sensitivity of McEliece and Niederreiter like PKCs to fault injection attacks is investigated by Cayrel, and Dusart (2010).

Strenzke in the work (Strenzke, 2010) presented a different approach to the timing attack against the Patterson's algebraic decoding algorithm in the decryption process. The presented attack exploits fundamental behavior of Extended Euclidean Algorithm in the Patterson's algebraic decoding algorithm, namely the fact that if the number of errors in a received word (i.e. cipher-text) is exactly four, the number of Extended Euclidean Algorithm iterations, when solving the key equation, can be either zero or one. This obviously leads to different computation time, what allows the adversary to determine the number of the iterations. He found that the third coefficient of the irreducible Goppa polynomial can be rewritten as a function of error positions. Therefore, if the attacker is allowed to make a number of cipher-texts with four errors (the attacker knows the error vectors), by misusing the information about the number of the iterations, the adversary can construct a list of linear equations describing the secret permutation. Afterwards, Gaussian elimination can be applied on to the equation system. In the case of code length 1024 with 27 errors, the adversary needed to generate 2,163,499 messages in average, and in the case of code length 2048 with 50 errors, 7,848,229 messages were needed to be generated. The rank of the matrix of the linear equations was 1013, and 20136 respectively.

Strenzke (2013) presented a timing attack against the syndrome inversion step in decryption process. The paper describes a timing attack revealing the secret key. It is based on his previous work (Strenzke, 2010) mentioned above. In this paper, not only cipher-text with four errors is generated, but also with one and six errors. These numbers of errors are chosen especially in order to reveal certain coefficients of the error-locator polynomial, and these coefficients reveal some information about the secret code support. Cipher-texts with one error are generated in order to reveal position of the zero element in the code support. Cipher-texts with four errors results in the list of linear equations, and cipher-texts with six errors are used to make a cubic equation system, which have to be solved respectively.

The first practical evaluation of a power analysis attack revealing the secret permutation, and the scrambling matrix, during the decryption process can be found in (Heyse, Moradi, & Paar, 2010). Heyse, Moradi, and Paar (2010) conducted and evaluated the attack against the McEliece PKC decryption algorithm implemented on the embedded device proposed by Eisenbarth et al. (2009). They assumed two main scenarios. In the first scenario, the secret permutation is removed before

the Patterson's algebraic decoding algorithm. By observing a power trace of syndrome computation, an adversary can determine when additions of the parity check matrix rows are performed. In their implementation, those additions are performed sequential. Thus, a column rows are summed only if the corresponding coordinate of the cipher-text after the secret permutation removal is one. Thanks to the knowledge which columns of the parity check matrix was summed up, the secret permutation is not secret anymore. In the second scenario, in respect to the secret permutation, the parity check matrix in the syndrome computation is permuted. Next their observation is that if the Goppa polynomial is loaded, for example, at the start of the syndrome polynomial inversion, using a simple power analysis, one can predict hamming weight of all the Goppa polynomial elements. So, given the secret permutation that was revealed by the simple power analysis above, the secret scrambling matrix and the secret Goppa polynomial can be revealed. If the private generation matrix is in the systematic form, the secret scrambling matrix is revealed using public-key. The Goppa polynomial is revealed afterwards by computing the great common divisor of a two different syndromes, with high probability. In the case of the scenario two, the attack is not working. Thus, another approach is to use a simple power analysis in order to find the secret parity check matrix and reveal the secret code support from that. Each row of the parity check matrix is totally defined by a code support element, Goppa polynomial evaluated at that support element, and the Goppa polynomial coefficients. Regarding the hamming weight derived from a measured power trace, a list of candidates for parity check matrix cell is created. For each column of the parity check matrix, a code support element and its value of Goppa polynomial is chosen randomly over all the possible elements. Now, they go recursively into the rows of the actual column. At each recursion level, the corresponding coefficient of the Goppa polynomial has to be chosen randomly, and actual cell candidate is computed. Only if this value is in the candidate list, recursion continues. If the recursion processed the last row of the parity check matrix, a code support element, its Goppa polynomial evaluation, and all the Goppa polynomial coefficients are selected. Now whether the selected Goppa polynomial evaluates in the evaluation candidate at the selected support elements has to be checked. If yes, a final candidate of the Goppa polynomial and the code support element is chosen. While the algorithm continues to search another candidates, the actual candidate is validated by the next column of the parity check matrix and next code support element. As a result of this procedure, several pairs of code support and Goppa polynomial are obtained. The correct pair decodes all the cipher-texts. The attack running time for Xeon E5345CPUs and 16GB RAM took 69 min, wherein the subject of the attack was a cryptosystem instance with code length 2048 and 27 errors.

The timing attack in combination with fault injection attack (Strenzke, 2010), which is focused on the Extended Euclidean Algorithm for solving the key equation in the Patterson's algebraic decoding algorithm, was modified by Molter et al. (2011). In order to determine whether less iterations of the Extended Euclidean Algorithm was performed, they used information about the number of peaks in a measured power trace instead of timing information.

Avanzi et al. (2011) used idea of template or profiling attacks. They extended the attack of Strenzke et al. (2008) by including a profiling phase, wherein the adversary builds a simple statistical profile of decryption computation time regarding all the possible correctable error vectors of the desired hamming weight. Thanks to this profiling phase of attack, the success of the attack has been improved significantly. Furthermore, Avanzi et al. (2011) introduced vulnerability of computation of square roots modulo the Goppa polynomial in the decryption process. For the computation, the suggestion of Huber (1996) is used. The leakage is presented in a polynomial multiplication in the algorithm of Huber (1996). By misusing this vulnerability, one can reveal the Goppa polynomial. Finally, they discuss next possibility how to reveal the Goppa polynomial, namely several leakage pints of the Extended Euclidean Algorithm used to solve the key equation in the Patterson's algebraic decoding algorithm.

Structural Attacks

Structural attacks, as one can deduce from the expression, are focused on the specific structure of error-correcting codes. The idea of using some codes with specific structure comes from the key size issue. There have been many proposals attempting to reduce the key size by altering the underlying error-correcting code. Often, the authors used highly structured codes which can be stored more efficiently (Section Code-based cryptography survey). And for detailed survey of the structural attacks before year 2011, consult Cayrel et al. (2011). As can be observed from the mentioned sources, and from the recent works, only the binary irreducible Goppa codes with maximal length (Section Post-quantum cryptography based on error-correcting codes) remain untouched. From the recent works, we note out that Landais, and Tillich (2013) proposed a structural attack against cryptosystems using convolutional codes. Next new structural attack is proposed by Gaborit, Ruatta, and Schrek (2013); it is aimed against cryptosystems based on rank metric codes, and thus aimed against cryptosystems based on generic rank syndrome decoding problem.

Information Set Decoding Attacks

Again, we refer a reader to the survey of Cayrel et al. (2011) for seeing what had been done before year 2011. From the very recent works we point out that Hamdaoui, and Sendrier (2013) proposed a non-asymptotic analysis of the Stern-Dumer variant, the May-Meurer-Thomae variant (May,

Meurer, & Thomae, 2011), and the Becker-Joux-May-Meurer variant (Becker et al., 2012) of the generic information set decoding attack. They stated that if the error weight is less or approximately equal to the Gilbert-Varshamov distance, the best attack is information set decoding attack. But when it is vice versa then it cannot be predicted whether the information set decoding attack, or generalized birthday algorithm is better.

Distinguisher Based Attacks

Faugère et al. (2013) presented a Goppa code distinguisher. Provided that the code rate (code dimension divided by code length) is very high, the distinguisher algorithm allows distinguishing Goppa codes from random codes. Next, Gauthier, Otmani, and Tillich (2012), and Couvreur et al. (2013) showed that even the choice of Generalized Reed-Solomon codes proposed in (Baldi et al., 2011) is not secure, as we mentioned in Section Code-based cryptography survey.

Quantum Attacks

The fastest quantum cryptanalytic attack against code-based cryptography can be found in (Bernstein, 2010). It is a quantum structural attack. Its complexity is still at least sub-exponential in case of the post-quantum cryptosystems.

CONCLUSION

We saw that many contributions have been made in the past three years. Construction of cryptographic primitives has been improved. Unfortunately, the key size issue has not been resolved yet. Almost all the attempts to change the underlying error-correcting code (a cryptographic primitive is based on) have failed regarding the recent cryptanalysis. On the other hand, two prospective countermeasures that can hide the structure of a secret error-correcting code have been proposed.

But the only credible post-quantum constructions are those using the binary irreducible Goppa codes as the principal building block. We showed that implementations of post-quantum error-correcting code-based cryptography (namely McEliece and Niederreiter PKC) can be even better performing than the ECC. But still, there are many opportunities for optimization and standardization. Although the post-quantum cryptography is very resistant to attacks even employing post-quantum cryptanalysis, from the view of side channel attacks it is still equally vulnerable.

REFERENCES

Avanzi, R., Hoerder, S., Page, D., & Tunstall, M. (2011). Side-channel attacks on the McEliece and Niederreiter public-key cryptosystems. *Journal of Cryptographic Engineering*, *1*(4), 271–281. doi:10.1007/s13389-011-0024-9

Baldi, M., Bianchi, M., Chiaraluce, F., Rosenthal, J., & Schipani, D. (2011). A variant of the McEliece cryptosystem with increased public key security. In *Proceedings of WCC 2011 - Workshop on coding and cryptography* (pp. 173-182). Paris, France: Inria.

Baldi, M., Bianchi, M., Chiaraluce, F., Rosenthal, J., & Schipani, D. (2011). Enhanced public key security for the McEliece cryptosystem. *CoRR*. Retrieved August 11, 2011, from http://arxiv.org/abs/1108.2462

Baldi, M., Bodrato, M., & Chiaraluce, F. (2008). A New Analysis of the McEliece Cryptosystem Based on QC-LDPC Codes. In *Proceedings of 6th International Conference, SCN 2008* (LNCS), (pp. 246-262). Amalfi, Italy: Springer.

Barreto, P. S. L. M., Misoczki, R., & Simplício, M. A. Jr. (2011). One-Time Signature Scheme from Syndrome Decoding over Generic Error-Correcting Codes. *Journal of Systems and Software*, *84*(2), 198–204. doi:10.1016/j.jss.2010.09.016

Becker, A., Joux, A., May, A., & Meurer, A. (2012). Decoding random binary linear codes in 2n/20: How 1+1=0 improves information set decoding. In *Proceedings of Advances in Cryptology - EUROCRYPT (LNCS)* (Vol. 7237, pp. 520–536). Cambridge, UK: Springer.

Berlekamp, E., McEliece, R., & van Tilborg, H. (1978). On the inherent intractability of certain coding problems. *IEEE Transactions on Information Theory*, 24(3), 384–386. doi:10.1109/TIT.1978.1055873

Berlekamp, E. R. (1971). Factoring polynomials over large finite fields. In *Proceedings of the second ACM symposium on Symbolic and algebraic manipulation (SYMSAC '71)*. New York: ACM.

Bernstein, D. J. (2010). Grover vs. McEliece. In *Proceedings of Post-Quantum Cryptography, Third International Workshop, PQCrypto 2010,* (pp. 73-80). Darmstadt, Germany: Springer.

Bernstein, D. J. (2011a). List decoding for binary Goppa codes. In *Proceedings of Coding and cryptology-third international workshop, IWCC 2011,* (LNCS), (vol. 6639, pp. 62-80). Qingdao, China: Springer.

Bernstein, D. J. (2011b). Simplified high-speed high-distance list decoding for alternant codes. In *Proceedings of the 4th international conference on Post-Quantum Cryptography. PQCrypto'11* (pp. 200-216). Taipei, Taiwan: Springer.

Bernstein, D. J., Buchmann, J., & Dahmen, E. (Eds.). (2008). *Post-Quantum Cryptography*. Springer.

Bernstein, D. J., Lange, T., & Peters, C. (2008). Attacking and Defending the McEliece Cryptosystem. In *Proceedings of the 2nd International Workshop on Post-Quantum Cryptography PQCrypto '08* (pp. 31-46). Cincinnati, OH: Springer Berlin Heidelberg.

Bernstein, D. J., Lange, T., & Peters, C. (2010). Wild McEliece. *Cryptology ePrint Archive: Report 2010/410*. Retrieved Jul 22, 2010, from http://eprint.iacr.org/2010/410

Bernstein, D. J., Lange, T., & Peters, C. (2011a). Wild McEliece Incognito. In *Proceedings of Post-Quantum Cryptography - 4th International Workshop, PQCrypto 2011* (pp. 244-254). Taipei, Taiwan: Springer.

Bernstein, D. J., Lange, T., & Peters, C. (2011b). Smaller decoding exponents: ball-collision decoding. In *Proceedings of 31st Annual Cryptology Conference,* (pp. 743-760). Santa Barbara, CA: Springer.

Bernstein, D. J., Lange, T., Peters, C., & Schwabe, P. (2011). Faster 2-regular Information-Set Decoding. In *Proceedings of the Third international conference on Coding and cryptology (IWCC'11)* (pp. 81-98). Qingdao, China: Springer.

Bernstein, D. J., Lange, T., Peters, C., & Schwabe, P. (2011). Really Fast Syndrome-Based Hashing. *Cryptology ePrint Archive: Report 2011/074*. Retrieved February 14, 2011, from http://eprint.iacr.org/2011/074

Beuchat, J.-L., Sendrier, N., Tisserand, A., & Villard, G. (2004). FPGA Implementation of a Recently Published Signature Scheme. *Research Report INRIA*. Retrieved 2004, from http://hal.inria.fr/docs/00/07/70/45/PDF/RR-5158.pdf

Biasi, F. P., Barreto, P. S. L. M., Misoczki, R., & Ruggiero, W. V. (2012). Scaling efficient code-based for embedded platforms. *CoRR*. Retrieved December 18, 2012, from http://arxiv.org/abs/1212.4317

Biswas, B., & Sendrier, N. (2008). McEliece Cryptosystem Implementation: Theory and Practice. In *Proceedings of Post-Quantum Cryptography Second International Workshop, PQCrypto 2008* (pp. 47-62). Cincinnati, OH: Springer.

Carlos, A., Gaborit, P., & Schrek, J. (2011). A new zero-knowledge code based identification scheme with reduced communication. *CoRR*. Retrieved November 7, 2011, from http://arxiv.org/abs/1111.1644

Cayrel, P.-L. (2012). Code-based cryptosystems: implementations. *cayrel.net: Code based cryptography*. Retrieved 2012, from http://cayrel.net/research/code-based-cryptography/code-based-cryptosystems/

Cayrel, P.-L., Alaoui, S. M. E. Y., Hoffmann, G., & Véron, P. (2012). An improved threshold ring signature scheme based on error correcting codes. In *Proceedings of Arithmetic of Finite Fields - 4th International Workshop, WAIFI 2012,* (pp. 45-63). Bochum, Germany: Springer.

Cayrel, P.-L., & Dusart, P. (2010). McEliece/Niederreiter PKC: Sensitivity to Fault Injection. In *Proceedings of FEAS, 2010 5th International Conference on Future Information Technology* (pp. 1-6). Busan, Korea: IEEE.

Cayrel, P.-L., ElYousfi, M., Hoffmann, G., Meziani, M., & Niebuhr, R. (2011). Recent progress in code-based cryptography. In *Proceedings of Information Security and Assurance - International Conference,* (pp. 21-32). Brno, Czech Republic: Springer.

Cayrel, P.-L., Gaborit, P., & Prouff, E. (2008). Secure Implementation of the Stern Authentication and Signature Schemes for Low-Resource Devices. In *Proceedings of 8th IFIP WG 8.8/11.2 International Conference, CARDIS 2008,* (pp. 191-205). London, UK: Springer.

Cayrel, P.-L., Hoffmann, G., & Persichetti, E. (2012). Efficient Implementation of a CCA2-Secure Variant of McEliece Using Generalized Srivastava Codes. In *Proceedings of 15th International Conference on Practice and Theory in Public Key Cryptography,* (pp. 138-155). Darmstadt, Germany: Springer.

Cayrel, P.-L., Véron, P., & Alaoui, S. M. E. Y. (2011). A zero-knowledge identification scheme based on the q-ary syndrome decoding problem. In *Proceedings of the 17th international conference on Selected areas in cryptography SAC'10* (171-186). Waterloo, Canada: Springer.

Chien, R. (1964). Cyclic decoding procedures for Bose-Chaudhuri-Hocquenghem codes. *IEEE Transactions on Information Theory*, 10(4), 357–363. doi:10.1109/TIT.1964.1053699

Chizhov, I. V., & Borodin, M. A. (2013). The failure of McEliece PKC based on Reed-Muller codes. *Cryptology ePrint Archive: Report 2013/287*. Retrieved May 15, 2013, from http://eprint.iacr.org/2013/287

Couvreur, A., Gaborit, P., Gauthier, V., Otmani, A., & Tillich, J. P. (2013). Distinguisher-based attacks on public-key cryptosystems using Reed-Solomon codes. *CoRR*. Retrieved Jul 24, 2013, from http://arxiv.org/abs/1307.6458

Dottling, N., Dowsley, R., Muller-Quade, J., & Nascimento, A. C. A. (2012). A CCA2 Secure Variant of the McEliece Cryptosystem. *IEEE Transactions on Information Theory*, 58(10), 6672–6680. doi:10.1109/TIT.2012.2203582

Dowsley, R., Müller-Quade, J., & Nascimento, A. C. A. (2009). A CCA2 Secure Public Key Encryption Scheme Based on the McEliece Assumptions in the Standard Model. *Lecture Notes in Computer Science*, 5473, 240–251. doi:10.1007/978-3-642-00862-7_16

Eisenbarth, T., Güneysu, T., Heyse, S., & Paar, C. (2009). MicroEliece: McEliece for Embedded Devices. In *Proceedings of Cryptographic Hardware and Embedded Systems - CHES 2009, 11th International Workshop,* (pp. 49-64). Lausanne, Switzerland: Springer.

Faugère, J.-C., Gauthier-Umaña, V., Otmani, A., Perret, L., & Tillich, J.-P. (2013). A Distinguisher for High Rate McEliece Cryptosystems. *IEEE Transactions on Information Theory*, *59*(10), 6830–6844. doi:10.1109/TIT.2013.2272036

Faugère, J.-C., Otmani, A., Perret, L., & Tillich, J.-P. (2010). Algebraic Cryptanalysis of McEliece Variants with Compact Keys. In *Proceedings of the 29th Annual international conference on Theory and Applications of Cryptographic Techniques EUROCRYPT'10* (pp. 279-298). Springer.

Faure, C., & Minder, L. (2008). Cryptanalysis of the McEliece cryptosystem over hyperelliptic curves. In *Proceedings of the eleventh International Workshop on Algebraic and Combinatorial Coding Theory* (pp. 99-107). Pamporovo, Bulgaria: ACCT.

Finiasz, M. (2010). Parallel-CFS: Strengthening the CFS Mc-Eliece-Based Signature Scheme. In *Proceedings of Selected Areas in Cryptography - 17th International Workshop,* (pp. 159-170). Waterloo, Canada: Springer Berlin Heidelberg.

Finiasz, M., & Sendrier, N. (2009). Security Bounds for the Design of Code-based Cryptosystems. In *Proceedings of Advances in Cryptology - ASIACRYPT 2009, 15th International Conference on the Theory and Application of Cryptology and Information Security,* (pp. 88-105). Tokyo, Japan: Springer.

Fischer, J.-B., & Stern, J. (1996). An efficient pseudo-random generator provably as secure as syndrome decoding. In *Proceedings of the 15th annual international conference on Theory and application of cryptographic techniques EUROCRYPT'96* (pp. 245-255). Saragossa, Spain: Springer.

Gaborit, P., Ruatta, O., & Schrek, J. (2013). On the complexity of the Rank Syndrome Decoding problem. *CoRR*. Retrieved January 6, 2013, from http://arxiv.org/abs/1301.1026

Gaborit, P., & Schrek, J. (2012). Efficient code-based one-time signature from automorphism groups with syndrome compatibility. In *Proceedings of IEEE International Symposium on Information Theory, ISIT 2012* (pp. 1982-1986). Cambridge, MA: IEEE.

Gauthier, V., & Leander, G. (2009). Practical Key Recovery Attacks on Two McEliece Variants. *Cryptology ePrint Archive: Report 2009/509.* Retrieved October 21, 2009, from eprint.iacr.org/2009/509.pdf

Gauthier, V., Otmani, A., & Tillich, J.-P. (2012). A distinguisher-based attack on a variant of McEliece's cryptosystem based on Reed-Solomon codes. *CoRR*. Retrieved April 29, 2012, from http://arxiv.org/abs/1204.6459

Gauthier, V., Otmani, A., & Tillich, J.-P. (2012). A Distinguisher-Based Attack of a Homomorphic Encryption Scheme Relying on Reed-Solomon Codes. *Cryptology ePrint Archive: Report 2012/168.* Retrieved March 29, 2012, from http://eprint.iacr.org/2012/168

Gilbert, E. N. (1952). A comparison of signaling alphabets. *The Bell System Technical Journal*, *31*(3), 504–522. doi:10.1002/j.1538-7305.1952.tb01393.x

Goppa, V. D. (1970). A new class of linear error-correcting codes. *Probl. Peredach. Inform.*, *6*(3), 24–30.

Gueye, C. T., & Mboup, E. H. M. (2013). Secure Cryptographic Scheme based on Modified Reed Muller Codes. *International Journal of Security and Its Applications*, *7*(3), 5.

Helgert, H. J. (1974). Alternant Codes. *Information and Control*, *26*(4), 369–380. doi:10.1016/S0019-9958(74)80005-7

Heyse, S. (2010). Low-Reiter: Niederreiter Encryption Scheme for Embedded Microcontrollers. In *Proceedings of Post-Quantum Cryptography, Third International Workshop, PQCrypto 2010,* (pp. 165-181). Darmstadt, Germany: Springer.

Heyse, S., & Güneysu, T. (2012). Towards One Cycle per Bit Asymmetric Encryption: Code-Based Cryptography on Reconfigurable Hardware. In *Proceedings of Cryptographic Hardware and Embedded Systems - CHES 2012 - 14th International Workshop,* (pp. 340-355). Leuven, Belgium: Springer.

Heyse, S., & Güneysu, T. (2013). Code-based cryptography on reconfigurable hardware: tweaking Niederreiter encryption for performance. *Journal of Cryptographic Engineering*, *3*(1), 29–43. doi:10.1007/s13389-013-0056-4

Heyse, S., Moradi, A., & Paar, C. (2010). Practical Power Analysis Attacks on Software Implementations of McEliece. In *Proceedings of Post-Quantum Cryptography, Third International Workshop, PQCrypto 2010,* (pp. 108-125). Darmstadt, Germany: Springer.

Heyse, S., von Maurich, I., & Güneysu, T. (2013). Smaller Keys for Code-Based Cryptography: QC-MDPC McEliece Implementations on Embedded Devices. In *Proceedings of Cryptographic Hardware and Embedded Systems - CHES 2013 - 15th International Workshop,* (pp. 273-292). Santa Barbara, CA: Springer.

Huber, K. (1996). Note on decoding binary Goppa codes. *Electronics Letters*, *32*(2), 102–103. doi:10.1049/el:19960072

Kobara, K., & Imai, H. (2001). Semantically Secure McEliece Public-Key Cryptosystems-Conversions for McEliece PKC. In *Proceedings of the 4th International Workshop on Practice and Theory in Public Key Cryptography: Public Key Cryptography (PKC '01)*. London, UK: Springer.

Landais, G., & Tillich, J.-P. (2013). An Efficient Attack of a McEliece Cryptosystem Variant Based on Convolutional Codes. In *Proceedings of 5th International Workshop, PQCrypto 2013,* (pp. 102-117). Limoges, France: Springer.

Lee, P. J., & Brickell, E. F. (1988). An observation on the security of McEliece's public-key cryptosystem. *Lecture Notes in Computer Science*, 275–280. doi:10.1007/3-540-45961-8_25

Lu, R., Lin, X., Liang, X., & Shen, X. S. (2011). An efficient and provably secure public-key encryption scheme based on coding theory. *Security and Communication Networks*, *4*(12), 1440–1447. doi:10.1002/sec.274

Mathew, K. P., Vasant, S., & Rangan, C. P. (2012). On Provably Secure Code-based Signature and Signcryption Scheme. *Cryptology ePrint Archive, Report 2012/585.* Retrieved October 15, 2012, from http://eprint.iacr.org/2012/585

Mathew, K. P., Vasant, S., Venkatesan, S., & Rangan, C. (2012). An Efficient IND-CCA2 Secure Variant of the Niederreiter Encryption Scheme in the Standard Model. In *Proceedings of 17th Australasian Conference, ACISP 2012,* (pp. 166-179). Wollongong, Australia: Springer.

May, A., Meurer, A., & Thomae, E. (2011). Decoding random linear codes in O(2^0.054n). In *Proceedings of Advances in Cryptology - ASIACRYPT 2011 - 17th International Conference on the Theory and Application of Cryptology and Information Security,* (pp. 107–124). Seoul, South Korea: Springer.

McEliece, R. (1978). A Public-Key Cryptosystem Based on Algebraic Coding Theory. *Deep Space Network Progress Report, DSN PR 42–44,* NASA Code 310-10-67-11. Retrieved April 15, 1978, from http://ipnpr.jpl.nasa.gov/progress_report2/42-44/44title.htm

Meziani, M., Hoffmann, G., & Cayrel, P.-L. (2012). Improving the Performance of the SYND Stream Cipher. In *Proceedings of Progress in Cryptology - AFRICACRYPT 2012 - 5th International Conference on Cryptology in Africa,* (pp. 99-116). Ifrane, Morocco: Springer.

Misoczki, R., Tillich, J.-P., Sendrier, N., & Barreto, P. S. L. M. (2013). MDPC-McEliece: New McEliece Variants from Moderate Density Parity-Check Codes. In *Proceedings of the 2013 IEEE International Symposium on Information Theory,* (pp. 2069-2073). Istanbul, Turkey: IEEE.

Molter, H. G., Stöttinger, M., Shoufan, A., & Strenzke, F. (2011). A simple power analysis attack on a McEliece cryptoprocessor. *Journal of Cryptographic Engineering*, *1*(1), 29–36. doi:10.1007/s13389-011-0001-3

Niederreiter, H. (1986). Knapsack-type Cryptosystems and Algebraic Coding Theory. *Problems of Control and Information Theory*, *15*(2), 159–166.

Overbeck, R. (2008). Structural Attacks for Public Key Cryptosystems Based on Gabidulin Codes. *J. Cryptology*, *21*(2), 280–301. doi:10.1007/s00145-007-9003-9

Overbeck, R. (2008). An Analysis of Side Channels in the McEliece PKC. *Enhancing Crypto-Primitives with Techniques from Coding Theory. NATO OTAN*. Retrieved 2008, from https://www.cosic.esat.kuleuven.be/nato arw/slides participants/Overbeck slides nato08.pdf

Overbeck, R., & Sendrier, N. (2008). Code-Based Cryptography. In *Post-Quantum Cryptography* (pp. 95–145). Springer.

Patterson, N. (1975). The algebraic decoding of Goppa codes. *IEEE Transactions on Information Theory*, *21*(2), 203–207. doi:10.1109/TIT.1975.1055350

Persichetti, E. (2012). On a CCA2-secure variant of McEliece in the standard model. *IACR Cryptology ePrint Archive*. Retrieved May 11, 2012, from http://eprint.iacr.org/2012/268

Peters, C. (2010). Information-Set Decoding for Linear Codes over F_q. In *Proceedings of Post-Quantum Cryptography, Third International Workshop, PQCrypto 2010,* (pp. 81-94). Darmstadt, Germany: Springer.

Proos, J., & Zalka, C. (2003). Shor's discrete logarithm quantum algorithm for elliptic curves. *Quantum Info. Comput.*, *3*(4), 317–344.

Rastaghi, R. (2013). An Efficient CCA2-Secure Variant of the McEliece Cryptosystem n the Standard Model. *CoRR*. Retrieved February 2, 2013, from http://arxiv.org/abs/1302.0347

Sendrier, N. (2000). Finding the permutation between equivalent linear codes: the support splitting algorithm. *IEEE Transactions on Information Theory*, *46*(4), 1193–1203. doi:10.1109/18.850662

Shor, P. W. (1997). Polynomial-Time Algorithms for Prime Factorization and Discrete Logarithms on a Quantum Computer. *SIAM Journal on Computing*, *26*(5), 1484–1509. doi:10.1137/S0097539795293172

Shoufan, A., Strenzke, F., Molter, H. G., & Stöttinger, M. (2009). A Timing Attack against Patterson Algorithm in the McEliece PKC. In *Proceedings of Information, Security and Cryptology - ICISC 2009, 12th International Conference,* (pp. 161-175). Seoul, Korea: Springer.

Shoufan, A., Wink, T., Molter, G., Huss, S., & Strenzke, F. A. (2009). Novel Processor Architecture for McEliece Cryptosystem and FPGA Platforms. In *Proceedings of Application-specific Systems, Architectures and Processors* (pp. 98–105). Boston, MA: IEEE. doi:10.1109/ASAP.2009.29

Sidelnikov, V. M., & Shestakov, S. (1992). On Cryptosystems based on Generalized Reed-Solomon Codes. *Discrete Mathematics*, *4*(3), 57–63.

Sidelnikov, V. M., & Shestakov, S. O. (1992). On insecurity of cryptosystems based on generalized Reed-Solomon codes. *Discrete Mathematics*, 2(4), 439–444.

Stern, J. (1994a). A New Identification Scheme Based on Syndrome Decoding. In *Proceedings of the 13th Annual International Cryptology Conference on Advances in Cryptology* (pp. 13-21). Santa Barbara, CA: Springer.

Stern, J. (1994b). Designing Identification Schemes with Keys of Short Size. In *Proceedings of Advances in Cryptology – Proceedings of CRYPTO '94,* (vol. 839, pp. 164-173). Santa Barbara, CA: Springer Berlin Heidelberg.

Strenzke, F. (2010). A Smart Card Implementation of the McEliece PKC. In *Proceedings of 4th IFIP WG 11.2 International Workshop, WISTP 2010,* (pp. 47-59). Passau, Germany: Springer.

Strenzke, F. (2010). A Timing Attack against the Secret Permutation in the McEliece PKC. In *Proceedings of Third International Workshop, PQCrypto 2010,* (pp. 95-107). Darmstadt, Germany: Springer.

Strenzke, F. (2011). Fast and Secure Root-Finding for Code-based Cryptosystems. *IACR Cryptology ePrint Archive.* Retrieved December 11, 2011, from http://eprint.iacr.org/2011/672

Strenzke, F. (2012). Solutions for the Storage Problem of McEliece Public and Private Keys on Memory-Constrained Platforms. In *Proceedings of 15th International Conference, ISC 2012,* (pp. 120-135). Passau, Germany: Springer.

Strenzke, F. (2013). Timing Attacks against the Syndrome Inversion in Code-Based Cryptosystems. In *Proceedings of 5th International Workshop, PQCrypto 2013,* (pp. 217-230). Limoges, France: Springer.

Strenzke, F., Tews, E., Molter, H. G., Overbeck, R., & Shoufan, A. (2008). Side Channels in the McEliece PKC. In *Proceedings of the Second international Workshop on Post-Quantum Cryptography PQCRYPTO 2008,* (LNCS), (pp. 216-229). Cincinnati, OH: Springer.

Sugiyama, Y., Kasahara, M., Hirasawa, S., & Namekawa, T. (1976). An erasures-and-errors decoding algorithm for Goppa codes. *IEEE Transactions on Information Theory*, 22(2), 238–241. doi:10.1109/TIT.1976.1055517

von Maurich, I., & Güneysu, T. (2012). Embedded Syndrome-Based Hashing. In *Proceedings of Progress in Cryptology - INDOCRYPT 2012, 13th International Conference on Cryptology in India,* (pp. 339-357). Kolkata, India: Springer.

Yang, B.-Y. (Ed.). (2011). *Proceedings of 4th International Workshop.* Taipei, Taiwan: Springer.

Zalka, C. (1998). Fast versions of Shor's quantum factoring algorithm. *Coronell University Library arXiv.org.* Retrieved 24 June 1998, from http://arxiv.org/abs/quant-ph/9806084

KEY TERMS AND DEFINITIONS

Code-Based Cryptography: Cryptography that is based on an NP-complete problem in coding theory, namely General decoding problem, or Syndrome decoding problem.

General Decoding Problem: Given a code generator matrix (or parity check matrix equivalently) and a vector that is not from the code, try to correct and decode the vector.

Identification: Or also Authentication is technique (real-time-) verifying identity of one entity asking for a secret that is able to answer correctly only the entity of identity that is claimed.

NP-Complete Problem: It is a decision problem that is as hard as any nondeterministic polynomial time problem, i.e. the decision running time for a NP-complete problem is at least sub-exponential.

Post-Quantum Cryptography: Cryptography for which the best know attack has at least a sub-exponential complexity even using quantum cryptanalysis. Post-quantum Cryptography can be Code-based, Hash-based, Lattice-based, or Multivariate-quadratic-equation based.

Public Key Cryptosystem: An asymmetric cryptosystem that uses a key pair, namely private key and corresponding public key.

Side Channel Attacks: Attacks that exploits information obtained from any source, not only cipher-text or plaintext.

Signature: Stands for digital signature process applied onto a message resulting in a data string that is afterwards used in order to verify integrity, authenticity, and signatory non-repudiation.

Syndrome Based Cryptography: Code-based cryptography based on syndrome decoding problem.

Syndrome Decoding Problem: Given a parity check matrix, and a syndrome find the corresponding error vector.

Chapter 6
Fuzzy Logic–Based Security Evaluation of Stream Cipher

Sattar B. Sadkhan Al Maliky
University of Babylon, Iraq

Sabiha F. Jawad
Al-Mustansyria University, Iraq

ABSTRACT

The main aim of this chapter is to provide a security evaluation method based on fuzzy logic "for a pseudo-random sequences used (mainly) in stream cipher systems. The designed Fuzzy rules consider two main parameters, which are the length of the maximum period of the key sequence obtained from Linear Feedback Shift Register (LFSR) and the entropy of the result in sequences obtained from different lengths of the shift registers. The security (complexity) evaluation method is applied to the summation generator (a type of non-linear feedback shift register) in this chapter. First it is applied to its original well-known form (with one bit memory); then the evaluation method is applied to the developed summation generator (by varying the number of the delayed bits by two and by three bits). The acceptability of the results of developed evaluation method indicates a goodness of such developed approach in the security evaluation.

INTRODUCTION

Stream cipher systems have a great role in data encryption field. The security of these systems is a direct function of the complexity of the used key sequence generators. Many scientific efforts has been made to develop a complex structure of these generators that ensures the nonlinearity and complexity of the generated pseudorandom sequences. Fuzzy logic is one of the technologies that allow realistic complex models of the real world to be defined with some simple and understandable fuzzy variables and fuzzy rules.

The pseudorandom sequences generators (used in stream ciphers) can be described by a fuzzy set and degree of membership to a certain parameters of the key sequence generators. (Muna, 1999), (Elmer, 2012), (Marc & Lars, 2005).

Fuzzy sets are a further development of the mathematical concept of a set. Sets were first studied formally by the German mathematician Geory Cantor (1845-1918). His theory of sets met much resistance during his lifetime, but nowadays most mathematicians believe it is possible to express most, if not all, of the mathematics in the language of set theory. Many researchers are

DOI: 10.4018/978-1-4666-5808-0.ch006

considering the consequences of 'fuzzifying' set theory, and much mathematical literature is the result (Peter, 1995). The notion of fuzzy set was introduced by Lotfi Zadeh in 1965. He developed many of the methods of fuzzy logic based on this single notion. It took a couple of decades for the rationale of fuzzy sets to be understood and applied by other scientists. Fuzzy Logic, as a robust soft computing method has demonstrated its ability in many different applications. Moreover, fuzzy systems have several important features which make them suitable for many requested applications. Various methods have been suggested for automatic generation and adjustment of fuzzy rules without the aid of human experts.

The key technology of the trusted computing is the trust platform. In theory to verify if a model is trusted is an important research task. Hence there was an approach to apply the trust level evaluation method and trusted computing model based on Fuzzy logic (Li & Dan, 2010). The Fuzzy logic was applied for classifying the decision magnitude in multiple group combined interference cancelation (MGCIC) used in the intermediate stage of collusion resilient spread spectrum watermarking in M-band Wavelet using GA-Fuzzy hybridization (Sant et al, 2013). The Fuzzy logic was applied for foundation of uncertain evidence in the information system security risk assessment. The used model provided a way to define the basic belief assignment in fuzzy measure. The model offers a method of testing the evidential consistency, which reduces the uncertainty derived from the conflict of evidence (Nan & Minqiang, 2011). An approach was proposed based on using fuzzy logic and expert system for network forensics that can analyze computer crime in network environment and make digital evidences automatically. The experimental results show that the proposed system can classify most kinds of attack types (91.5% correct classification rate on average) and provided analyzable and comprehensible for forensic experts (Niandong, Shengfeng, & Tinghua, 2009). A fuzzy logic used instead of crisp value to improve the accuracy level of event detection was proposed by (Krasmira, et al, 2012). Their proposal shows that the fuzzy logic approach provides higher event detection accuracy than other well-known classification algorithms. They developed a number of techniques that help to reduce the size of the rule based by more than 70% while preserving the accuracy of event detection for fuzzy logic to deals with trust evaluation, business-interaction review and credibility adjustment. A paper of (Stefan, et al, 2007) proposes a customizable trust evaluation model based on fuzzy logic and demonstrates the integration of post interaction process like business interaction reviews and credibility adjustment. Since the design of secure routing protocol is a critical task in Ad Hoc network, the (Jing, et al., 2006) propose a fuzzy logic based security level routing protocol (FLSL). It is based on using the local multicast mechanism and security level to select the highest security level route (which is an adaptive fuzzy logic based algorithm that can adapt itself with the dynamic conditions of mobile hosts). The proposed system results in improving the security of mobile ad hoc network. The authors claim that the FSLS routing protocol is feasible to the weak security character of MANET (Mobile ad hoc Network). The evaluation of management of Urban Ecological Security (UES) has become a hotspot in concerned sciences due to the fact that the (UES) is the basis and the core of regional and National Ecological Security. (Xiao, 2011) introduced fuzzy mathematics into (UES) evaluation and established an evaluation model. An improved multilevel fuzzy evaluation algorithm based on fuzzy sets and entropy parameters is presented in the (Li, & Shen, 2006). The authors designed the multilevel fuzzy comprehensive evaluation model of P2P network security performance, and the proposed algorithm used to make an instant computation based on the proposed model. (Angel, et al, 2010) propose development of a tool which accurately prioritizes the Information Security Control (ISC) in organizations. The proposed tool used fuzzy set theory to allow for more accurate assessment of imprecise parameters than traditional methods. An approach based on fuzzy logic for threat evaluation in distributed computing systems was proposed in (Essam, & Tarek, 2004). The fuzzy logic is explored as a threat evaluation engine for anomaly – based threat detection system by presenting a novel anomaly threat detection architecture using Fuzzy Logic to overcome the anomaly detection systems drawbacks and to present an accurate and flexible threat evaluation system.

FUZZY LOGIC APPLICATIONS

Fuzzy Logic is applied in a number of scientific areas that were suffering from certain limitations when applying other techniques to resolve the non-technical Fuzzy logic. Most current applications of Fuzzy Logic use software as an intermediary for the implementation of these logic algorithms (William & Bilal, 2012).

- **Fuzzy Logic based random sequences generator are used for Spread Spectrum Communication Systems**: The systematic random number generator of the Laboratory of Mathematics and Statistics World (IMSL) gives samples used for training, where that type of adaptive learning relationship (Associations) is between previous samples, the current sample symbolizes this relationship as fuzzy bases. The fuzzy group for output, each rule operates as a conditional probability density function (Sattar et al, 2013).
- **Fuzzy Bit Generator:** A method for generating pseudo-random (PN) binary sequence based on fuzzy logic is applied to copy the behavior of real random source. The system generates pseudorandom binary sequences. The generated fuzzy binary sequences successfully pass all standard randomness tests and their length can be made arbitrary long. Such sequences are suitable for data encryption, and secure Direct Sequence- Spread-Spectrum (DS-SS). The use of the developed fuzzy binary generator to generate code families with good auto and cross correlation properties is also developed in (Said et al, 2005). Although the generated codes appear to be random and enjoy most of the properties of random codes, they are deterministic. In other words, they can be exactly regenerated by fixing the parameters of the fuzzy random number generator. On the other hand, by changing the initial condition for this system we obtain a new binary sequence. The fuzzy system rules are constructed using numerical data pairs during the training stage then combined with linguistic information to form the working of " if-then rules".

- **Delete the overlap in multiple access systems with the symbolic division of Code Division Multiple Access (CDMA) systems:** It is known that load spread spectrum systems (SSS) are systems with more flexible scalability in deleting the overlap of loading systems is based on the principle of symbolic access. However, the increase in telecommunications services caused an increase in the ability of interlaced signals. In particular, the unauthorized frequency ranges, such as the frequency range for industry applications and uses medicine may saturate seriously portability interference rejection of spread-spectrum systems. The Condition Mean (CM) and Maximum-A posteriori (MAP) can be considered a perfect method for digital and analogue interference deleting. Also the communication process can be exposed to distortion by noise Kausih which leads to increased complexity of the installation of the ideal detector. The research presents a proposal for interference deleting overlap based on the use of fuzzy logic and fuzzy set which allows deleting either overlaps analogue or digital interactions and reduces the required computational challenge when using assessor type CM and detector type MAP (Poor & Wang, 1997).

- **Signal detection for air sensing system:** The human and the machine in the air control, and analytical considerations was analyzed. Search displays techniques fuzzy signal detection theory, that involves fuzzy logic and traditional signal detection theory of the default data. (E. Dawson, 1996) presentation of two studies related to the air control. First study uses data from the primary calendar field for voluntary air sensing system. The second study uses data from a controlled laboratory simulation in a free flight conditions. A "response" depends on the likelihood of critical event or the cruelty of changing symbols – colored (Peter et al, 2000).

- **Assigning the data in Simulation of Command, Control, Communications, Computers and Intelligence systems (C⁴I):** There are a number of models to build a knowledge base system for the scrutiny process data using artificial intelligence techniques. The main aim of such models is to solve the problem of uncertainty in the information systems scrutinized data with multiple sources. The process of scrutiny of information is critical to the process systems C⁴I. Since it must deal with a huge amount of information available through a large number of sources of information (sensors), these sources differ widely in reliability, complexity and imprecision to translate tactical to complete picture of the location field. The method used consists of a mixture of factors and fuzzy logic to blend information. The results show the possibility of using such model for blending different sensors data types, and fuzzy logic to classify different types of goals (Muna, 1999), (Arindam & Mandal, 2012).

- **Movement prediction in mobile communication systems:** Formerly many efforts were made to implement the scientific movement prediction using the statistical method or clustering silhouettes. The research presents a way to address this issue by using the statistical method and system web-based reasoning - Adaptive fuzzy (Adaptive Neuro-Fuzzy Inference System ANFIS). Both the statistical model and the model of ANFIS can be implemented, which show comparable merit and disadvantages (Peter, 1995), (Maria et al, 2009). In the paper presented by (Mohammed & Aisha, 2009) a linear regression model is suggested based on fuzzy c-means algorithm for prediction and estimation of handover times in Mobile WiMAX. Mobility in WiMAX suffers high handover latency at layer-3. This prediction may help layer-3 handover to trigger prior to layer-2, and to meet the WiMAX Forum recommendation at even higher mobility speeds. The time reduction factor at which to speed up the handover process in layer-3 is left open for future research.

- **Data communications based fuzzy system:** This system includes the use of the first fuzzy calculator to store fuzzy functions and rules, and transmitter collects functions and rules of fuzzy stored in the calculator and turn them into a viable message to send. You receive the message sent and analyze fuzzy functions and rules, the second fuzzy calculator makes completion of inference based fuzzy functions and fuzzy rules (Khan, 2009), (Simon, 2001).

FUZZY LOGIC

Fuzzy Logic is a powerful tool for decision making to handle imprecise and uncertain data. In contrast to classical set. Fuzzy set is a set without crisp boundaries; the transition from (belonging to a set) to (not belonging to a set) is gradual. Membership function is utilized to reflect a degree of membership and is indicated by a value in the range [0.0, 1.0]. The traditional way of representing elements u of a set A is through the characteristics function:

$\mu_A(u) = 1$, if u is an element of the set A, and

$\mu_A(u) = 0$, if u is not an element of the set A,

That is an object either belongs or does not belong to a given set.

In fuzzy sets an object can belong to a set partially. The degree of membership is defined through a generalized characteristic function called membership function:

$\mu_A(u): U [0,1]$

where U is called the universe, and A is a fuzzy subset of U. The general observations about fuzzy logic are:

- Conceptually easy to understand.
- Flexible.
- Tolerant of imprecise.
- Model nonlinear function of arbitrary complexity.
- Built on top of the experience of experts.
- Blended with conventional control techniques.
- based on natural language (Poor & Wang, 1997).

There are two main components in fuzzy logic systems:

- Fuzzy variable and fuzzy rules. The fuzzy variables take a range of numeric values. The value of a fuzzy variable is referred to as a "crisp value". The range can be divided into several sub-ranges by defining qualifiers for the fuzzy variable (Wang & Yao, 1993). Fuzzy variable qualifiers consist of a name, known as a linguistic qualifier, and membership function which shows for each possible "crisp value" of the fuzzy variable, its degree of membership of the fuzzy set. The function that ties number to each element χ of the universe is called the membership function $\mu(x)$. The membership function is defined by its overall shape, its curvature and some relevant points. This could be represented by a graph where the (vertical Y- axis) shows the degree of membership of the set, and the (Horizontal X- axis) the "crisp value" of the fuzzy variable as shown Figure 1.

The degree of membership is a value somewhere between [0, 1]. Fuzzy sets have gradations of set membership which is represented by a function referred to as a membership function, and so they resemble the kinds of categories ordinary people use in natural thought or communication.

- **Fuzzy Rules:** Another major aspect of a fuzzy logic system is the set of rules. Rules consist of a set of ' IF ' condition and one 'THEN' conclusion and an optional 'ELSE' conclusion. The condition of fuzzy rule refers to fuzzy variable and their qualifiers. Multiple conditions are joined together using the connectivees 'AND ','OR ' and 'NOT'. Depending on the type of connection applied to the condition, the conclusion of the rule is calculated in different ways (Jerry, 2010).

Figure 1. The fuzzy logic terminology

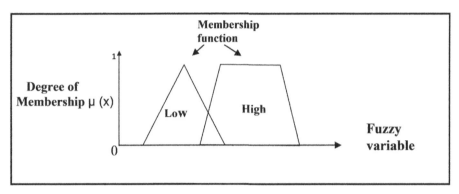

Fuzzy Logic (FL) offers several unique features that make it a particularly good choice for many control problems. Linguistic variables are used, making it similar to the way humans think. Simplicity allows the solution of previously unsolved problems, because they do away with complex analytical equations used to model traditional control systems. Rapid prototyping is possible because a system designer doesn't have to know everything about the system before starting work. They are cheaper to make than conventional systems because they're easier to design (Paul & Daniel, 1993).

Fuzzy Logic is not limited to a few feedback inputs and one or two control outputs, nor is it necessary to measure or compute rate-of-change parameters in order for it to be implemented. Any sensor data that provides some indication of a system's actions and reactions is sufficient. This makes the sensors inexpensive and imprecise thus keeping the overall system cost and complexity low (George & Maria, 1995).

Because of the rule-based operation, any reasonable number of inputs can be processed (1 up to 8 or more) and numerous outputs (1 up to 4 or more) generated. Although defining the rule base quickly becomes complex if too many inputs and outputs are chosen for a single implementation. Since rules defining their interrelations must also be defined. It would be better to break the control system into smaller chunks and use several smaller FL controllers distributed over the system, each

with more limited responsibilities. FL can control nonlinear systems that would be difficult or impossible to model mathematically.

SECURITY EVALUATION OF CRYPTOSYSTEM

In order to compare the security level and the algorithm complexity of different encryption systems, we need to evaluate the security level of the designed encryption system (John & Dominic, 2006), (Charles & Shari 2003). This aspect depends on using a number of measures, as follows:

- Synthesis parameters of the equivalent shift register (Berlkamp Massey Method).
- Mathematical Complexity theoretic parameters.
- Using orthogonal transformations such as (Discrete Fourier Transform (DFT), Walsh Transform (WT), Wavelet Transform (WT), Z- transform)
- Information Theory parameters (Jun & Ryutaroh, 2012).
- Computational complexity parameters (Davies & Pira, 1984), (Feng et al, 2009).
- Various statistical parameters (Lotfi, 1999).
- Artificial Neural Network parameters
- Genetic Algorithm parameters (Clark, 1998).

Because of the small number of publications in the field of security evaluation of cryptosystem, the scientific academic efforts are guided to age the process of evolution. In other words, there are some efforts to use artificial intelligence in executing activates of evolution. The presence of Artificial Intelligence and its techniques made a promising and modern entry in encryption system security evaluation (Beker & Piper, 1982), (Sabiha, 2004). The main goal of complexity theory is to provide mechanisms for classifying computational problems according to the resources needed to solve them. The classification should not depend on a particular computational model, but rather should measure the intrinsic difficulty of the problem. The resources measured may include time period, storage space, random bits, number of processors, etc., but typically the main focus is time period, and sometimes space (Sanjeev & Boaz, 2009).

Definition (1): An algorithm is a well-defined computational procedure that takes a variable input and halts with an output (Lane & Mitsunori, 2002).

Definition (2): A polynomial-time algorithm is an algorithm whose worst- case running time function is of the form $O(n^k)$, where n is the input size and k is a constant. Any algorithm whose running time cannot be so bounded is called an exponential-time algorithm (Wang & Wu, 2001). Polynomial-time algorithms can be equated with good or efficient algorithms, while exponential-time algorithms are considered inefficient. There are, however, some practical situations when this distinction is not appropriate. When considering polynomial-time complexity, the degree of the polynomial is significant.

Definition (3): A sub exponential-time algorithm is an algorithm whose worst-case running time function is of the form $e^{O(n)}$, where n is the input size. A sub exponential-time algorithm is asymptotically faster than an algorithm whose running time is fully exponential in the input size, while it is asymptotically slower than a polynomial-time algorithm.

Definition (4): The complexity class P is the set of all decision problems that are solvable in polynomial time (Eric et al,1998)

Definition (5): The complexity class NP is the set of all decision problems for which a YES answer can be verified in polynomial time given some extra information, called *a certificate.*

Definition (6): The complexity class co-NP is the set of all decision problems for which a NO answer can be verified in polynomial time using an appropriate certificate.

Definition (7): A decision problem L is said to be NP-complete if:

◦ $L \in$ NP, and
◦ $L_1 \leq p\ L$ for every $L_1 \in$ NP.

The class of all NP-complete problems is denoted by NPC.

NP-complete problems are the hardest problems in NP in the sense that they are at least as difficult as every other problem in NP (William, 2003).

Example (1): (Subset Sum Problem)

The subset sum problem is as follows: Given a set of positive integers $\{a_1, a_2, ..., a_n\}$ and a positive integer s, determine whether or not there is a subset of the a_i that sums to s . The subset sum problem is NP-complete (Beker & Piper,1982).

Berlkamp-Massay Method: The main purpose of the Berlekamp-Massey (or as abbreviated, BM) Algorithm is to evaluate Binary Bose–Chaudhuri–Hocquenghem (BCH) codes. Berlekamp published his algorithm in 1968 and it was followed shortly by Massey's publication of a variation on the algorithm in 1969. The algorithm is most widely used as a fast way to invert matrices with constant diagonals. It works over any field. But the finite fields that occurs most in coding theory are the most often used. The algorithm is specifically helpful for decoding various algebraic codes. Berlekamp's algorithm uses a "Key equation" to input a known number of coefficients of the generating functions and then determines the remaining coefficients of the polynomial. This process is equivalent to finding the linear complexity of the system. The BM algorithm is an algorithm that will find the shortest linear feedback shift register (LFSR) for a given binary output sequence. The algorithm will also find the minimal polynomial of a linearly recurrent sequence in an arbitrary field. Elwyn Berlekamp invented an algorithm for decoding (BCH) codes. James Massey recognized its application to LFSR and simplified the algorithm. Massey termed the algorithm the LFSR Synthesis Algorithm (Berlekamp Iterative Algorithm), but it has been known as the BM algorithm since 1985 (Reeds & Sloane, 1985). The applications and implementation of this algorithm were advanced and extended by Massey who used the physical interpretation of a (LFSR) as a tool to better understand the algorithm. What the variation does is to synthesize LFSR's that have a specified output sequence. This physical interpretation of LFSR's provides a physical explanation of the length of the encoded message needed to decode it using the algorithm. The length of message needed is only twice the length of the LFSR used or 2n. Now that we have a handle on what the algorithm is trying to do, we can see where it is useful. BM can be considered as a method to calculate the equivalent linear generator (shorter registered offset with a linear feedback) that generates the same sequence of bilateral subjects to testing, and access to multiple transactions within feedback to the registrar of displacement by giving section of the successive bilateral lengths (2L). If the length of the resulting L achieves relationship $2L \leq n-1$, the recorder displacement of this technique records offset single smallest length which generates these successive and, if $2L \geq n$,

this condition is not achieved and there are more than registered displacement which generates these successive,(Rueppel, 1985). The BM algorithm, solves the following problem:

Given a sequence $s = s_1, s_2, \ldots\ldots, s_l$ of length l, find a shortest LFSR, such that it produces the sequence s in the first l symbols.

For instance, assume a binary sequence, $s_8 = 10011101$ (the 8 denotes the length of the sequence) is produced by an LFSR with connection polynomial $C(D) = 1 + D + D^3$ over $F_2[D]$. This is shortest length of an LFSR that reproduces that sequence. It should be noted here that we totally ignore what it produces after the 8th symbol (it is not important), we only care about the first 8 symbols.

The main idea of the BM algorithm is that we "make a guess" about what LFSR we are having. Then the LFSR is simulated up to symbol i and we see if symbol i is correct, if it is not, we alter the LFSR connection polynomial so that it produces a correct symbol. A very important remark is that our correction cannot cause previous symbols to be incorrect, because then we would have to start all over again. This makes the BM algorithm a so-called exact greedy algorithm (it produces an optimal solution that, however, needs not to be unique unless the length of the solution is less than or equal to half the length of the sequence).

BM Algorithm is an alternate method to solve the set of linear equations described in Reed–Solomon Peterson decoder which can be summarized as:

$$S_{i+v} + \Lambda_1 S_{i+v-1} + \ldots\ldots\ldots + \Lambda_1 S_{i+v-1} + \Lambda_1 S_{i+v-1} = 0 \tag{1}$$

In the code examples below, $C(x)$ is a potential instance of $\Lambda(x)$. The error locator polynomial $C(x)$ for L errors is defined as:

$$C(x) = C_L X^L + C_{L-1} X^{L-1} + \ldots\ldots$$

$$+ C_2 X^2 + C_1 X + 1 \tag{2}$$

or reversed:

$$C(x) = 1 + C_1 X + C_2 X^2 + \dots\dots + C_{L-1} X^{L-1} + C_L X^L \qquad (3)$$

The goal of the algorithm is to determine the minimal degree L and $C(x)$ which results in:

$$S_n + C_1 S_{n-1} + \dots\dots + C_L S_{n-L} = 0 \qquad (4)$$

for all syndromes, $n = L$ to $(N-1)$.

Algorithm: $C(x)$ is initialized to 1. L is the current number of assumed errors, and initialized to zero. N is the total number of syndromes. n is used as the main iterator and to index the syndromes from 0 to $(N-1)$. $B(x)$ is a copy of the last $C(x)$ since L was updated and initialized to 1. b is a copy of the last discrepancy d (explained below) since L was updated and initialized to 1. m is the number of iterations since L, $B(x)$, and b were updated and initialized to 1.

Each iteration of the algorithm calculates a discrepancy d. At iteration k this would be:

$$d = S_k + C_1 S_{k-1} + \dots\dots + C_L S_{k-L} = 0 \qquad (5)$$

If d is zero, the algorithm assumes that $C(x)$ and L are correct for the moment, increments m, and continues.

If d is not zero, the algorithm adjusts $C(x)$ so that a recalculation of d would be zero:

$$C(x) = C(x) - (d/b)\, x^m\, B(x) \qquad (6)$$

The x^m term *shifts* $B(x)$ so it follows the syndromes corresponding to 'b'. If the previous update of L occurred on iteration j, then $m = k - j$, and the recalculated discrepancy would be:

$$d = S_k + C_1 S_{k-1} + \dots\dots - (d/b)(S_j + B_1 S_{j-1} + \dots\dots) \qquad (7)$$

This would change a recalculated discrepancy to:

$$d = d - (d/b)\, b = d - d = 0 \qquad (8)$$

The algorithm also needs to increase L (number of errors) as needed. If L equals the actual number of errors, then during the iteration process, the discrepancies will become zero before n becomes greater than or equal to $(2 L)$. Otherwise L is updated and algorithm will update $B(x)$, b, increase L, and reset m = 1. The $L = (n + 1 - L)$ formula limits L to the number of available syndromes used to calculate discrepancies, and also handles the case where L increases by more than 1. The flow chart of this algorithm is shown in Figure 2 (Norton, 2010).

Example (2): Find complex linear (the length of the shortest recorded offset with a linear feedback) for bilateral sequential linear generated from binary sequences generator written as unknown composition.

$$S_n = 1\ 0\ 1\ 0\ 1\ 1\ 0\ 0\ 1\ 0\ 0$$

Solution: Table 1 shows the steps using the "Berlkamp–Massey" method to calculate the complexity of the of the tested sequence (Sabiha, 2004).where a and b are constant numbers, T(x) a temporary tank, D variable average. Thus the length of the shortest recorded successive displacement generates this (4) and multiple border feedback registered for this is: $C(x) = 1 + x + x^4$ as shown Figure 3.

Entropy: Let X be a random variable which takes on a finite set of values $x_1, x_2, \dots x_n$ with probability $P(X = x_i) = p_i$, where $0 \leq p_i \leq 1$ for each i, $1 \leq i \leq n$, and where $\sum_{i=1}^{n} p_i = 1$ .and, let Y and Z be random variables which take on finite sets of values. The entropy of X is a mathematical measure of the amount of information provided by an observation of X. Equivalently, it is the uncertainty about the outcome before an observa-

Figure 2. The flow chart of the Berlkamp–Massy algorithm

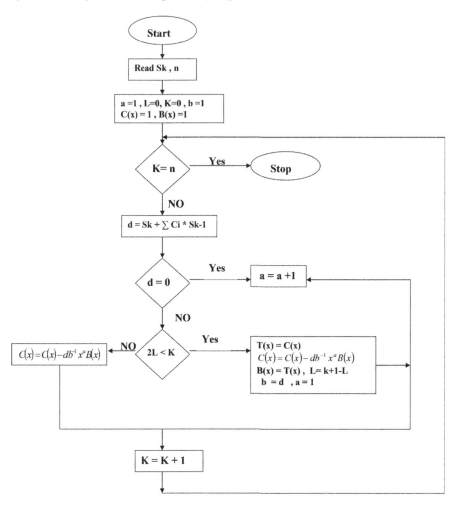

Table 1. Berllkamp-Massy method

n	Sn	D	T(x)	C(x)	L	b	a
				1	0	1	1
0	1	1	1	$1+x$	1	1	1
1	0	1	1	1	1	1	2
2	1	1	1	$1+x^2$	2	1	1
3	0	0	1	$1+x^2$	2	1	2
4	1	0	1	$1+x^2$	2	1	3
5	1	1	$1+x^2$	$1+x^2+x^3$	4	1	1
6	0	1	$1+x^2$	$1+x+x^2$	4	1	2
7	0	1	$1+x^2$	$1+x+x^4$	4	1	3
8	1	0	$1+x^2$	$1+x+x^4$	4	1	4
9	0	0	$1+x^2$	$1+x+x^4$	4	1	5
10	0	0		$1+x+x^4$	4	1	6

Figure 3. Structure of linear feedback shift register of 4- bits

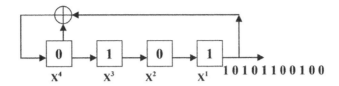

tion of *X*. Entropy is also useful for approximating the average number of bits required to encode the elements of *X* (Robert, 2013), (James, 2011). Entropy or uncertainty *of X* is expressed as:

$$H(X) = -\sum_i^n p_i \log p_i = \sum_i^n p_i \log\left(\frac{1}{p_i}\right)$$
(9)

where, convention yields

$$p_i . \log\left(\frac{1}{p_i}\right) = 0 \text{ if } p_i = 0$$
(10)

where *p(x)* is the probability of the outcome *x* occurring for event *X*, and when *p(x) =0, p(x)log₂* *p(x)* is defined as 0. As one can see, the lower the probability of an event *x* is occurring, the higher its entropy. The evaluation of encryption system depends on the measurement of the designed encryption system security, because of the relation of security with the complexity of this system, so we can consider this complexity as a corner stone of evaluation process of the designed encryption system. We can also consider the evaluator as a processor that depends on the entries (like cipher text sequence or key generator sequence) to determine the security level (security of complexity (of generator part of evaluator input (Thomas & Joy, 1991).

SECURITY EVALUATION OF STREAM CIPHER

The stream cipher has mixed function for key sequence and plaintext sequence. The security of stream cipher depends on the degree of complexity of the generated key sequence. Hence the complexity can be considered as an evaluation parameter of the designed key generator. The key generator may combine one or more Linear Feed Back Shift Registers (LFSR), generally of different linear lengths and with different feedback primitive polynomials. Since the security is related to the complexity of the algorithm of key generator, hence the complexity can be considered as an evaluation parameter of the designed key generator (Menezes et al, 1996). The linear stream cipher system contains a (LFSR) with specified lengths and (XOR) Boolean functions for mixing the key sequence with the plaintext sequence.

The nonlinear cipher algorithms provide an increase in the complexity of generated sequence. There are many techniques for using nonlinear algorithm with stream cipher system such as (Key, 1976), (Gong, 1990)

- Non-linear Combination techniques.
- Non-linear Filtration techniques.
- Non-linear Hybrid techniques.

Non Linear Binary Sequence Generator: One of the used practical examples of nonlinear binary sequence generator is summation generator; it

Figure 4. Summation generator

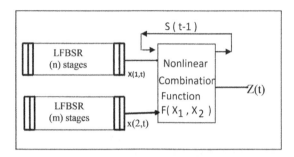

consists of two or more Linear Feed Back Shift Registers (LFSR) of different lengths, combined by nonlinear function that has one bit memory. (Amparo, 2003). That means the presence of (k) of pseudo random sequences, represented by a(i,t) for the values i= 1,2,…,k that result from a LFSR, as shown in Figure 4 (Berndt & Rainer, 1986).

This generator has output key sequence z(t) and memory sequence s(t), as given by equations:

$$s(t) = \sum_{i=1}^{k-1} x(i,t) \oplus s(t-1)$$

$$s(t) = x\ (1,t) * x(2,t) \oplus (x\ (1,t) \oplus x(2,t) * s(t-1))$$

$$z(t) = \sum_{i=1}^{k} (x(i,t) \oplus s(t-1))$$

$$z(t) = x(1,t) \oplus x(2,t) \oplus s(t-1)$$

$$(12)$$

The nonlinear sequence z(t) has the following properties (Bardis et al, 2004):

- The maximum period length of the generated is: $(2^n-1)(2^m-1)$.
- The linear complexity equals the length of the maximum period.
- A first order correlation immunity of the resulting sequence.

Example (3): Suppose that two LFSR's are used to form summation generator, where the first LFSR has three stages with initial value of (111), and primitive polynomial function of $(S_0 + S_3)$, second LFSR has four stages

with initial value of (0101), and primitive polynomial function is $(S_0 + S_4)$, and we take s(t-1) bit memory. Table 2 shows the sequence generation steps of this generator.

Another practical example of nonlinear binary sequence generator is (J-K) Flip Flop generator. It consists of two linear feed-back shift registers of different lengths and the output sequence based on using truth table for (J-K) Flip Flop, as shown in Figure 5, which shows the (J-K) Flip Flop generator, and it is expressed as:

$$q_n = (a_n\ b_n\ 1) * q_{n-1}\ a_n \qquad (13)$$

Example (4): Suppose that two LFSR's are used to form J-K Flip Flop key sequence generator, where the first LFSR has three stages with initial value of (111), and primitive polynomial function of $(S_0 + S_3)$, second LFSR has four stages with initial value of (0101), and primitive polynomial function of $(S_0 + S_3)$. Table 3 shows the sequence generation steps of this generator (Sattar & Sabiha, 2005).

Table 2. The work of summation generator

t	x(1,t)	x(2,t)	S(t)	S(t-1)	Z(t)
0	1	1	0	0	0
1	1	0	1	0	1
2	1	1	1	1	1
3	0	0	0	1	1
4	1	1	0	0	0
5	0	1	0	0	1
6	0	0	0	0	0
7	1	0	0	0	1
8	1	1	1	1	1
9	1	0	1	1	0
10	0	0	1	1	1

Table 3. The work of J-K Flip Flop generator

n	a_n		qn-1	qn
0	0	0	0	0
1	1	1	0	1
2	1	0	1	1
3	1	1	1	0
4	0	0	0	0
5	1	1	0	1
6	0	1	1	0
7	0	0	0	0
8	1	0	0	1
9	1	1	1	0
10	1	0	0	1

Implementation of Security Evaluator

Summation Generator Case Study

The important properties that must be considered for the linear feedback shift registers are:

- The length of the maximum period of the generated sequence,
- The number of stages of LFSRs, and
- The statistical properties of the binary sequence that is generated from LFSR.

These properties are processed using fuzzy sets with two input parameters and one output parameter which can be considered as an evaluation of the proposed method, as shown in Figure 6, which represents the case study for the security

Figure 5. J-K flip flop

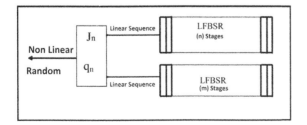

evaluation of the key sequence generated by summation generator (Sabiha, 2004).

- The first input variable is length of period of the generated key sequence, it has the values varing between the (0 and 2097151), since it is calculated according to the formula:

$$L = 2^n - 1 \qquad (14)$$

where: L is the length of maximum period of the generated key sequence and n is the number of stages used in LFSRs. (We tried in our design to change (n) from 5 stages up to 25 stages). This variable (L) can be divided into five sets, as follows:

First set: L_1: Represents as triangle [0,31,31] .
Second set: L_2: Represents as triangle [15, 511, 511] .
Third set: L_3: Represents as triangle [255, 8191, 8191] .
Fourth set: L_4: Represents as triangle [4095, 131071, 131071] .
Fifth set: L_5: Represents as trap [65535, 2097151, 33266417, 33266417] .

- The second input variable is the Entropy H(x). This variable is expressed mathematically in Equation (9) as:

$$H(x) = -\sum_{i=1}^{N} X_i \log_2 X_i$$

where N is the number of property function, and X_i is the probability of each property.

The universality of discourse of this variable is varied between the values (0 and 25), this variable can be divided into five sets as follows:

First set: $H(x)_1$: Represents as Triangle [0,5,5] .
Second set: $H(x)_2$: Represents as triangle [4, 9, 9] .
Third set: $H(x)_3$: Represents as triangle [8,13,13] .

Figure 6. The proposed fuzzy logic based evaluator of key sequences

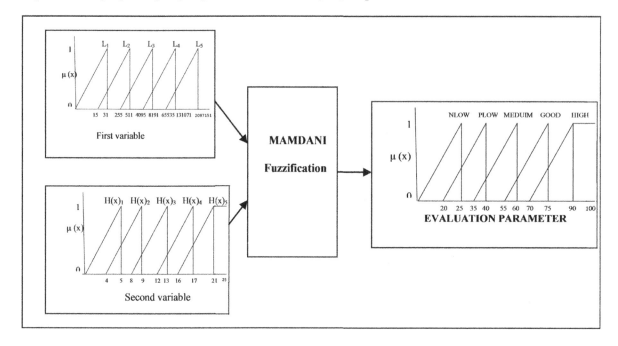

Fourth set: H (x)$_4$: Represents as triangle [12,17,17] .

Fifth set: H (x)$_5$: Represents as trap [16, 21, 25, 25] .

  ○ The output variable:is Security Evaluation parameter variables, it can be calculated by the following equation:

$$Y= L_i * 100/L_{max} \qquad (15)$$

where:

L_i: The maximum length for (ith) LFSR .

L_{max}: The maximum length of period in first input variable and it is taken to be equal to (2097151).

The range of output variable is between the values (0 and 100), and it can be divided into five sets which are:

First set: Negative low: Nlow: triangle [0, 25, 25] .

Second set: Positive low: Plow: triangle [20, 40, 40] .

Third set: Medium : triangle [35, 60, 60] .

Fourth set: Good : triangle [55, 75, 75] .

Fifth set: High : trap [70, 90, 100, 100] .

Table 4, shows the result of output variable, and table (6) shows the fuzzy rules of the proposed evaluator.

Other Case Studies of Security Evaluation of Summation Generator

We consider case study for summation generator as follows:

1. **S(t-1) Bit Memory:** We take the lengths of first LFSR and second LFSR to be different with different initial values, as shown in Table 4 .

2. **The lengths of two LFSRs are equal:** The length of first LFSR and second LFSR are taken equal with different initial values, as shown in Table 4.

Table 4. The different cases of summation generator

Linear Equivalence after input in Massey	Length of sequence	Initial value	Feedback function	No. of LFSR
25	50	111	$1+x+x^3$	2
30	60	0101	$1+x+x^4$	
35	70		with s(t-1)	
41	80			
45	90			
49	100			
27	50	0101	$1+x+x^4$	2
32	60	111	$1+x+x^3$	
36	70		with s(t-1)	
40	80			
45	90			
50	100			
25	50	111	$1+x+x^3$	2
31	60	101	$1+x^2+x^3$	
34	70		with s(t-1)	
41	80			
43	90			
50	100			
25	50	111	$1+x+x^3$	2
30	60	0101	$1+x+x^4$	
36	70		with	
39	80		S(t-2)	
45	90			
50	100			
26	50	111	$1+x+x^3$	2
30	60	0101	$1+x+x^4$	
36	70		With	
40	80		S(t-3)	
45	90			
50	100			

3. **S(t-2) & S(t-3) bit memory:** We take S(t-2) and S(t-3) bit memory instead of S(t-1) bit memory, based on the equations:

$$s(t) = a(1,t)*a(2,t) \oplus ((a(1,t) \oplus a(2,t)) *s(t-2)) \tag{16}$$

$$s(t) = a(1,t)* a(2,t) \oplus ((a(1,t) \oplus a(2,t)) *s(t-3)) \tag{17}$$

First Case Study

We take step (1) and step (2) from Table (4). That means we can take two LFBRs, the first one with feedback function of $f(x_1)= 1+ x + x^3$, and the second LFBR with feed back function of $f(x_2) = 1+ x + x^4$. The initial value are given in column (3) of Table 4.

•   The used logic operation, is (AND) relation.
•   Create the rules: using the two rules:

Rules Creation

1. **First rule**

IF length of period is L_2 and Entropy is $H(x)_2$ then evaluation parameter is high.

By applying the equation:

$$Y= (x- a) / (b-a) \tag{18}$$

where

Y: degree of membership $\mu(x)$.

x: maximum length of period for output linear equivalent after applying Berlkamp-Massey to sequence.

    a.   First value of fuzzy set.

    b.   Second value of fuzzy set.

Then we get degree of membership of antecedent **1** and antecedent **2** as:

$$\mu(x) = 1.0$$

$$\mu(H(x)_5) = 1.0$$

then determine the implication of rules by using logic relation:

min (1.0,1.0) = 1.0 high

2. Second rule

IF length of period is L_5 and Entropy $H(x)_5$ then evaluation parameter is high .

Then we apply the steps as first rule to determine the degree of membership of antecedent1 and antecedent 2 and implication of rules as:

$\mu(x) = 1.0$

$\mu(H(x)_5) = 1.0$

min (1.0,1.0) = 1.0 high

a. **Aggregation method:** We use Mamdani method to get fuzzy output as follows:

Max (1.0,1.0) = 1.0 high

b. **Deffuzification method:** The centroid method is used to get the crisp output as:

Defuzz (1.0) = 89 high

Second Case Study

We take step (1) and step(2) and step(5) from Table 5 for (J.K Flip Flop) generator. That means we can take two LFBRs, the first one with feedback function of $f(x_1) = 1 + x + x^3$, and the second LFBR with feed back function of $f(x_2) = 1 + x + x^4$, and in the fifth step we choose the second LFBR with

feed back function is $f(x_3) = 1 + x^2 + x^5$ The initial values are given in Table 5.

- Logic operation used is (AND) relation.
- Create rules, using the two rules as:

Table 5. The cases of J-K Flip Flop Generator

Linear Equivalence after input of Massey	Length of sequence	Initial Value	Feedback function	No. of LFSR
25	50	111	$1+x+x^3$	2
30	60	0101	$1+x+x^4$	
35	70			
41	80			
45	90			
49	100			
27	50	0101	$1+x+x^4$	2
32	60	111	$1+x+x^3$	
36	70			
40	80			
45	90			
50	100			
25	50	111	$1+x^2+x^3$	2
31	60	0101	$1+x^3+x^4$	
34	70			
41	80			
43	90			
50	100			
25	50	0101	$1+x^3+x^4$	2
30	60	111	$1+x^2+x^3$	
36	70			
41	80			
45	90			
49	100			
25	50	1101	$1+x+x^4$	2
30	60	11111	$1+x^2+x^5$	
36	70			
39	80			
45	90			
50	100			

Table 6. The fuzzy rules of the proposed evaluator

	L_1	L_2	L_3	L_4	L_5
$H_1(x)$	Nlow	Nlow	Nlow	Nlow	Nlow
$H_2(x)$	Nlow	Plow	Plow	Nlow	Nlow
$H_3(x)$	Nlow	Plow	Plow	Medium	Nlow
$H_4(x)$	Nlow	Nlow	Medium	good	good
$H_5(x)$	Nlow	Nlow	Nlow	good	high

Rules Creation

1. **First Rule:**

   IF length of period is L_5 and Entropy is $H(x)_5$ then evaluation parameter is high .

   By applying the equation:

   $$Y = (x-a) / (b-a) \qquad (19)$$

   where:

   Y: Degree of membership $\mu(x)$.

   x: Maximum length of period for output linear equivalent after applying Berlkamp-Massey to sequence .

      a. First value of fuzzy set .

      b. Second value of fuzzy set .

   Then we get degree of membership of antecedent1 and antecedent 2 as:

   $$\mu(x) = 1.0$$

   $$\mu(H(x)_5) = 1.0$$

   Then determination of the implication of rules is achieved by using logic relation:

   $$\min(1.0, 1.0) = 1.0 \text{ high}$$

2. **Second Rule:**

   IF length of period is L_5 and Entropy is $H(x)_5$ then evolution parameter is high .

   Then we apply the steps as in first rule to determine the degree of membership of antecedent1 and antecedent 2 and implication of rules as:

   $$\mu(x) = 1.0$$

   $$\mu(H(x)_5) = 1.0$$

   $$\min(1.0, 1.0) = 1.0 \text{ high}$$

c. **Aggregation method:** "Mamdani method" is used to get fuzzy output as shown below:

$$\text{Max } (1.0, 1.0) = 1.0 \text{ high}$$

d. **Deffuzification method:** Centroid method is used to get the crisp output as:

$$\text{Defuzz } (1.0) = 89 \text{ high}$$

As a result of the above mentioned case studies these results can be formulated as shown in Table 6.

CONCLUSION AND SUGGESTIONS FOR FUTURE WORKS

The FL based evaluation method was applied to the summation generator firstly to its original well known form (with one bit memory) and then we developed the summation generator itself by varying the number of the delayed bits by two and by three bits. All the results of the complexity measures are compared to the complexity results obtained from the well-known "Berlkamp-Massey" method. Promising results were obtained, that gave a good and acceptable indication of the performance of the proposed method.

One can recognize the following essential points as being prominent points overcoming the security evaluation of stream cipher based on FL aspect:

- It is well known that continuously the designer of the new cryptosystem is searching for an evaluation system that helps in a decision about the security of the designed system. Hence the search for new methods (like Fuzzy Logic based Evaluator) is an important field of research in this direction.
- It is considered that the length of the maximum period obtained from LFSR, and the second parameter is the Entropy. These are not the only parameters that can be consid-

ered as key parameters for security evaluation process. The research is open in this topic, and the choice of the parameters be depend on many approaches, like for example statistical parameters. Especially if we take into consideration another type of cryptosystems like Public Key cryptosystem (Knapsack type).

- It needs to be emphasized that security evaluation is a complex evaluation process. It is not cryptanalysis process. This process helps in identifying the efforts needed to treat stream cipher cryptosystems with different realization approaches, like linear or nonlinear realization in producing the key sequence (which is considered the main part in the security evaluation approaches)..

- The evaluation of Information security using Fuzzy Set theory leads to a more detailed and precise assessment and therefore an effective selection of the information security control in an organization.

- Multilevel Fuzzy Comprehensive Evaluation can be tested on the Security Evaluation of Stream Cipher to find out and overcome unexpected problems and provide new results.

REFERENCES

Amparo, F. (2003). Aspects of Pseudorandomness in Nonlinear Generators of Binary Sequences. *Lecture Notes in Computer Science, 2841*, 329–341. doi:10.1007/978-3-540-45208-9_26

Angel, R., et al. (2010). A Fuzzy Logic-based Information Security Control Assessment for Organization. In *Proceedings of 2012 IEEE Conference on Open Systems* (ICOS). IEEExplore Digital Library.

Arindam, S., & Mandal, J. (2012). Secured Wireless Communication Using Fuzzy Logic based High speed Public Key cryptography (FL-HSPKC). [IJACSA]. *International Journal of Advanced Computer Science and Applications, 3*(10), 137–145.

Bardis, N., Markovsky, A., & Andrikou, D. (2004). *Method for designing pseudorandom binary sequences generators on Nonlinear Feedback Shift Register (NFSR)*. Retrieved August 8, 2013 from http://www.wseas.us/e-library/conferences/athens2004/papers/487-804.pdf

Beker, H., & Piper, F. (1982). *Cipher System: The Protection of Communications*. Northwood Publication.

Berndt, M., & Rainer, G. (1986). *Linear Filtering of Nonlinear Shift-Register Sequences*. Retrieved August 8, 2013 from http://citeseerx.ist.psu.edu/viewdoc/download?doi=10.1.1.86.7961&rep=rep1&type=pdf

Charles, P., & Shari, L. (2003). *Security in Computing*. Prentice Hall Professional.

Clark, A. (1998). *Optimization Heuristics for Cryptology*. (PhD thesis). Queensland University of Technology.

Davies, D., & Pria, W. (1984). *Security for Computer Network, An Introduction to Data Security in teleprocessing and Electronic funds transfer*. Wiley and Sons.

Dawson, E. (1996). Cryptanalysis of Summation Generator. In *Proceeding of Auscrypt*. Auscrypt.

Eric, A., Michael, C., & Kenneth, W. (1998). Complexity Classes. In *Handbook on Algorithms and Theory of Computation*. CRC Press, Inc.

Erin, C. (2000). *Berlekamp-Massey Algorithm*. University of Minnesota REU. Retrieved July 5, 2013 from www.math.umn.edu/~garrett/students/reu/MB_algorithm.pdf

Essam, M., & Tarek, S. (2004). A Flexible Fuzzy Threat Evaluation Computer System. In *Proceedings of 2004 International Conference on Electrical, Electronic and Computer Engineering*. Cairo, Egypt: IEEExplore Digital Library.

Feng, Y., et al. (2009). On the Computational Complexity of Parameter Estimation in Adaptive Testing Strategies. In *Proceedings of 15th IEEE Pacific Rim International symposium on Dependable Computing*. IEEExplore Digital Library.

George, B., & Maria, B. (1995). *Fuzzy Sets, Fuzzy Logic, Applications*. World Scientific.

Gong, G. (1990). *Nonlinear Generators of Binary Sequences with Controllable Complexity and Double Key*. In *Proceedings of the International Conference on Cryptology: Advances in Cryptology*. London, UK: Springer-Verlag.

James, P. (2011). *Statistical Mechanics: Entropy, Order parameters, and Complexity*. Oxford, UK: Oxford University Press.

Jerry, M. (2010). *Uncertain Rule-Based Fuzzy Logic Systems: Introduction and New Directions*. University of Southern California, Los Angeles. Retrieved August 8, 2013 from http://sipi.usc.edu/~mendel/book/

Jing, N. et al. (2006). An Adaptive fuzzy logic based secure routing protocol in mobile ad hoc networks. *Science Direct –. Fuzzy Sets and Systems*, *157*(12), 1704–1712. doi:10.1016/j.fss.2005.12.007

John, T., & Dominic, W. (2006). *Complexity and Cryptography- an Introduction*. Cambridge University Press.

Jun, K., Tomohiko, U., & Ryutaroh, M. (2012). *New Parameters of Linear Codes Expressing Security Performance of Universal Secure Network Coding*. Retrieved August 8, 2013 from http://arxiv.org/abs/1207.1936

Key, E. (1976). An analysis of the structure and complexity of nonlinear binary sequence generators. *IEEE Transactions on Information Theory*, *22*(6), 732–736. doi:10.1109/TIT.1976.1055626

Khan, M. (2009). Anomaly Detection in data streams using fuzzy logic. In *Proceedings of International Conference on Information and Communication Technologies* (pp. 167 – 174). IEEExplore Digital Library.

Krasimira, K., Sang, H., & Kyoung, D. (2012). Using Fuzzy Logic for robust event detection in wireless sensor networks. *Ad Hoc Networks*, *10*(4), 709–722. doi:10.1016/j.adhoc.2011.06.008

Lane, A., & Mitsunori, O. (2002). *The Complexity Theory Companion*. Springer-Verlag.

Li, J., & Shen, L. (2006). An Improved multi-level fuzzy comprehensive evaluation algorithm for security performance. *The Journal of China Universities of posts and Telecommunication*, *13*(4), 48-53.

Lotfi, A. (1999). Fuzzy Systems Handbook (2nd ed.). Amazon.com.

Maria, E., Abbas, M., & Elisabeth, R. (2009). Fuzzy Logic Applications in Wireless Communications. [IFSA.]. *Proceedings of IFSA-EUSFLAT*, *2009*, 763–767.

Massy, J. (1969). Shift-register synthesis and BCH decoding. *IEEE Transactions on Information Theory*, *15*(1), 122–127. doi:10.1109/TIT.1969.1054260

Muna, M. (1999). *Design of A Prototype for A Fuzzy Data Fusion System for C^4I System*. (Unpublished doctoral dissertation). University of Technology, Baghdad, Iraq.

Norton, G. (2010). *The Berlekamp-Massey Algorithm via Minimal Polynomials*. Retrieved on July 16, 2013 from http://arxiv.org/pdf/1001.1597.pdf

Paul, F. & Daniel, M. (1993). *Fuzzy Logic*. Amazon.com.

Peter, A., Anthony, J., & Raja, P. (2000). On the Theory of Fuzzy Signal Detection: Theoretical and Practical Considerations. *Theoretical Issues in Ergonomics Science*, *1*(3), 207–230. doi:10.1080/14639220110038640

Peter, J. (1995). Adaptive Fuzzy Frequency Hopper. *IEEE Transactions on Communications*, *43*(6), 8111–2117.

Poor, V., & Wang, X. (1997). Code-Aide Interference suppression for DS/CDMA communications: Parallel Blind Adaptive Implementation. *IEEE Transactions on Communications*, *45*(9), 1101–1111. doi:10.1109/26.623075

Reeds, J., & Sloane, J. (1985). Shift-Register Sequences (Modulo m). *SIAM Journal on Computing*, *14*(3), 505–513. doi:10.1137/0214038

Robert, M. (2013). *Entropy and Information Theory*. Springer-Verlag.

Sabiha, F. (2004). *Complexity Evaluation of Binary Pseudo random sequences, using Fuzzy Logic*. (Unpublished Master Thesis). Al-Mustanseryah University, Iraq.

Said, E., Mona, L., & Adel, H. (2005). *A New Fuzzy Logic Based Pseudo-Random Bit Generator for Secure DS-CDMA System*. IEEExplore Digital Library.

Sanjeev, A., & Boaz, B. (2009). *Computational Complexity: A Modern Approach*. Cambridge University Press.

Sattar, B., & Sabiha, F. (2005). A proposed Method to Evaluate pseudo random of Hadmard generator using Fuzzy Logic. *AL-Mustanseryah University Journal*, *20*(3), 17-24.

Sattar, B., Sawsan, K., & Najwan, A. (2013). Fuzzy Based Pseudo Random Number Generator used for Wireless Networks. *Journal of Al-Nahrain University*, *16*(2), 210–216.

Stefan, S. et al. (2007). Fuzzy trust Evaluation and credibility development in multi-agent systems. *Science Direct: Applied Soft Computing*, *7*(2), 492–505.

Thomas, M., & Joy, A. (1991). *Entropy, Relative Entropy and Mutual Information*. John Wiley & Sons, Inc.

Wang, C., & Wu, M. (2001). A New Narrowband Interference Suppression Scheme for Spread-spectrum CDMA Communications. *IEEE Transactions on Signal Processing*, *49*(11), 2832–2838. doi:10.1109/78.960430

William, L., & Bilal, M. (2012). *Multicriteria Security System Performance Assessment Using Fuzzy Logic*. Retrieved August 8, 2013 from http://www.scs.org/pubs/jdms/vol4num4/McGill.pdf

William, S. (2003). *Cryptography and Network Security Principles and practices*. Prentice- Hall.

Xiao, J. (2011). Urban Ecological Security Evaluation and analysis based on Fuzzy Mathematics. *Procedia Engineering*, *15*, 4451–4455. doi:10.1016/j.proeng.2011.08.836

ADDITIONAL READING

Elmer, P. (Ed.). (2012). *Fuzzy Logic – Emerging Technologies and Applications*. United State, InTech.

George, J., & Bo, Y. (2009). *Fuzzy Sets and Fuzzy Logic: Theory and Applications* (1st ed.). PHI Learning.

Li, F., & Dan, W. (2010). Research on Trust Evaluation of Secure Bootstrap in Trusted Computing Based on Fuzzy Set Theory, Proceeding of the Ninth Int. conf. on Machine Learning and Cybernetics (ICMLC). (pp. 592-595). United State. IEEExplore Digital Library.

Marc, B., & Lars, W. (2005). Fuzzy Logic Based Handoffs in Vehicular Communication Environments, Retrieved August 8, 2013 from: http://www.ibr.cs.tu- s.de/users/bechler/myPublications/marc_BeWo05.pdf

Menezes, A., Van, O., & Vanstone, S. (1996). *Handbook of Applied Cryptography*. CRC Press. doi:10.1201/9781439821916

Mohammed, K. & Aisha. (2009). A Fuzzy-based Mobility Prediction [IJCNIS]. *International Journal of Communication Networks and Information Security*, *1*(1), 14–19.

Nan, F., & Minqiang, L. (2011). An Information system Security risk assessment model under uncertain environment. *Applied Soft Computing*, *11*(7), 4332–4340. doi:10.1016/j.asoc.2010.06.005

Niandong, L., Shengfeng, T., & Tinghua, W. (2009). Network Forensics based on fuzzy Logic and expert system. *Computer and Communication Journal*, *32*(17), 1881–1892. doi:10.1016/j.comcom.2009.07.013

Nikola, K. (1996). *Foundations of Neural Networks, Fuzzy system, and Knowledge Engineering*. MIT Press.

Rajjan, S. (2013). *Introduction to Fuzzy Logic*. PHI Learning.

Rueppel, A. (1986). *Analysis and Design of Stream Cipher*. Springer Verlag. doi:10.1007/978-3-642-82865-2

Rueppel, R. A. (1985). *Correlation Immunity and the summation generator, Advances in Cryptology – Crypto'85, LNCS 219* (pp. 260–272). Springer-Verlag.

Santi, P. et al. (2013). Collusion resilient spread spectrum watermarking in M-band wavelets using GA-fuzzy hybridization. *Journal of Systems and Software*, *86*(1), 47–59. doi:10.1016/j.jss.2012.06.057

Sattar, B., & Sabiha, F. (2004). A proposed Method to Evaluate pseudo random of (J-K) Flip Flop generator using Fuzzy Logic, Applied Science University, 2004.

Simon, J. (2001). Network Application Security Using the Domain Name System., thesis, Retrieved August 8, 2013 from: http://josefsson.org/exjobb/josefsson_simon_master_thesis.pdf.

Timothy, J. (2004). *Fuzzy Logic with Engineering Applications*. Wiley.

Wang. K., & Yao Y. (1993). New Nonlinear Algorithms for Narrowband Interference Suppression in CDMA Spread-Spectrum Systems, IEEE J. Selected Areas in communication., *17*(12), 2148-2153.

KEY TERMS AND DEFINITIONS

Adaptive Neuro-Fuzzy Inference System (ANFIS): Is a kind of neural network that is based on Takagi–Sugeno fuzzy inference system. Since it integrates both neural networks and fuzzy logic principles, it has potential to capture the benefits of both in a single framework. Its inference system corresponds to a set of fuzzy IF–THEN rules that have learning capability to approximate nonlinear functions.[1] Hence, ANFIS is considered to be a universal estimator.

Code Division Multiple Access (CDMA): Is a channel access method used by various radio communication technologies. CDMA is an example of multiple access, which is where several transmitters can send information simultaneously over a single communication channel. This allows several users to share a band of frequencies (see bandwidth). To permit this to be achieved without undue interference between the users CDMA employs spread-spectrum technology and a special coding scheme (where each transmitter is assigned a code). CDMA is used as the access method in many mobile phone standards such as cdmaOne, CDMA2000 (the 3G evolution of cdmaOne), and WCDMA (the 3G standard used by GSM carriers), which are often referred to as simply CDMA.

Condition Expectation (CE): In probability theory, a conditional expectation (also known as conditional expected value or conditional mean) is the expected value of a real random variable with respect to a conditional probability distribution. The concept of conditional expectation is extremely important in Kolmogorov's measure-theoretic definition of probability theory. In fact, the concept of conditional probability itself is actually defined in terms of conditional expectation.

Fuzzy C-Means Clustering: Clustering of numerical data forms the basis of many classification and system modeling algorithms. The purpose of clustering is to identify natural groupings of data from a large data set to produce a concise representation of a system's behavior. Fuzzy c-means (FCM) is a data clustering technique in which a dataset is grouped into n clusters with every datapoint in the dataset belonging to every cluster to a certain degree. For example, a certain datapoint that lies close to the center of a cluster will have a high degree of belonging or membership to that cluster and another datapoint that lies far away from the center of a cluster will have a low degree of belonging or membership to that cluster.

Fuzzy Control System: Is a control system based on fuzzy logic—a mathematical system that analyzes analog input values in terms of logical variables that take on continuous values between 0 and 1, in contrast to classical or digital logic, which operates on discrete values of either 1 or 0 (true or false, respectively).

Maximum A Posteriori Estimation: In Bayesian statistics, a maximum a posteriori probability (MAP) estimate is a mode of the posterior distribution. The MAP can be used to obtain a point estimate of an unobserved quantity on the basis of empirical data. It is closely related to Fisher's method of maximum likelihood (ML), but employs an augmented optimization objective which incorporates a prior distribution over the quantity one wants to estimate. MAP estimation can therefore be seen as a regularization of ML estimation.

Maximum Likelihood (ML): In statistics, maximum-likelihood estimation (MLE) is a method of estimating the parameters of a statistical model. When applied to a data set and given a statistical model, maximum-likelihood estimation provides estimates for the model's parameters. The method of maximum likelihood corresponds to many well-known estimation methods in statistics. For example, one may be interested in the heights of adult female penguins, but be unable to measure the height of every single penguin in a population due to cost or time constraints. Assuming that the heights are normally (Gaussian) distributed with some unknown mean and variance, the mean and variance can be estimated with MLE while only knowing the heights of some sample of the overall population. MLE would accomplish this by taking the mean and variance as parameters and finding particular parametric values that make the observed results the most probable (given the model).

Chapter 7
Information Security–Based Nano– and Bio–Cryptography

W. K. Hamoudi
University of Technology, Iraq

Nadia M. G. Al-Saidi
University of Technology, Iraq

ABSTRACT

Information security can provide confidentiality, integrity, and availability for society to benefit efficiently from data storage and open networks. Free space communication networks suffer from adversaries who interfere with data on networked computers. Inventing new protection techniques has arisen to ensure integrity and authenticity of digital information. This chapter introduces Nano and Bio techniques in cryptography to enhance the information security systems. Tasks unfeasible on a classical computer can now be performed by quantum computers, yielding a big impact on online security. Threats of exponentially fast quantum algorithms on business transactions could be overcome by this new technology. Based on biological observations, the exploration of biometric cryptography and authentication to determine individuals' authenticity can be done through numeric measurements. This provides very reliable automated verification and strong protection against biometric system attacks.

INTRODUCTION

There is an increasing need for a multidisciplinary, the system-oriented approach to manufacturing Micro/Nano-devices that function reliably (Bharat, 2007). This can be achieved through the intermixing of ideas from different disciplines and the systematic flow of information (Ahmad, Amri, Zuriati & Elissa, 2009). Cryptography is the science of protecting the privacy of information during communication under hostile conditions.

With this information era that is full of various information and knowledge, and the increasing use of digital devices, many applications such as, electronic mail, electronic fund transfer, classified files, etc., are easily transmitted and suitable for communicating over the insecure communication channels. However, the security and authentication is still a challenging problem, and there is always a growing demand of cryptographic techniques, which has spurred a great deal of intensive research

DOI: 10.4018/978-1-4666-5808-0.ch007

activities in the study of cryptography (Ganesan, Ishan, & Mansi 2008).

Quantum key distribution (QKD) is a very advanced encryption method of Quantum Cryptography (QC) for distributing a secret key. It allows the exchange of a cryptographic key between two remote parties with absolute security, guaranteed by the laws of quantum physics. QKD can be used in conjunction with existing network services for businesses communication services when a higher degree of confidentiality and protection are needed. Practical realization of QKD technology relies on availability of systems providing production, propagation, and detection of single photons. Single photon sources based on; Nano quantum dots, carbon nanotubes and diamond nanowires have enabled the development and recent demonstration of a number of commercial products.

Bio-cryptography is an emerging multidiscipline technology which combines biometrics with cryptography. It inherits the advantages of both and provides strong means to protect against biometric system attacks. Biometric is the science or technology which analyzes and measure the biological data. It is first used for recognition and identification, while it is used now for automatic identification and authentication. The characteristic features of the individual's is stored in a database using input devices, which then compared with the features extracted from the traits of the individual need to be identified. This type of schemes provides an essential security requirement. The biometric data have many advantages over traditional systems, they cannot be guessed, forgotten, stolen or lost. There is nothing to remember or carry, and are more users friendly, where their efficiency makes it easily to be applied alone or hybrid with other security and authentication methods (Al-Saidi, Said & Othman, 2012). Authentication is the first step of information security. It refers to the process used to identify and confirm the validity of the user. It is a mechanism used to authenticate user identity over insecure communication network.

Traditional alphanumeric passwords are widely used for authentication. They have memorability problem for secure passwords and their security is based on the password only. It is always threatened due to the availability of simple, rapid and perfect duplication and distribution means using simple dictionary attacks.

The material of this chapter is arranged into 6 sections, and as follows:

1. Introduction
2. Nano and bio-assemblies.
3. Cryptography and Information security.
4. Nano-technology applications in information systems.
5. Quantum dots in cryptography.
6. Authentication based on Nano and Biometric techniques.
7. Nano and Bio in cryptanalysis (from Bio to Nano: how to defeat attacks).
8. Conclusion.

NANO AND BIO-ASSEMBLIES

Nanotechnology is a multidisciplinary use of materials and processes that refer to the control, manipulation, and applications of Nano-scale devices. Materials in a scale below 100 nm have different characteristics from their bulk counterpart; then new size and shape properties appear; see Figure 1. Nanotechnology has proved its success in consumer products, chemistry, environmental science, security, mathematics, medicine, physics, and many other fields. Manipulating molecules and atoms directly was suggested by Feynman (Feynman, 1960). According to Norio Taniguchi, Nanotechnology consists of the processing of separation, consolidation, and deformation of materials by one atom or one molecule (Taniguchi, 1974). The real historic and pivotal reference for Nanotechnology is Drexler's book "Engines of Creation: The Coming Era of Nanotechnology" (Drexler, 1986). A quantum dot (few to tens of

Figure 1. Nanotechnology dimensions of some assemblies

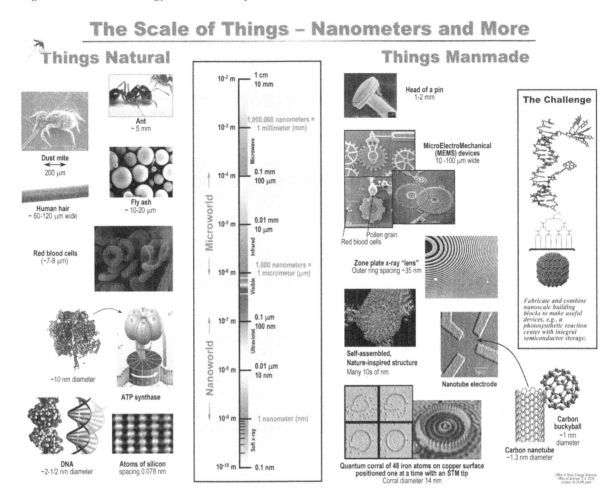

nm) is fabricated from semiconducting core and shell materials such as CdSe surrounded by ZnS.

The shell works as a cage for electron and behaves like a big atom having one to thousands of electrons (Ehud, 2007). The confinement of these electrons will quantize the energy levels of a quantum dot; see Figure 2.

The band gap between two energy levels of a big atom determines the energy and wavelength of quanta emitted as a result of electronic transition between energy levels. Metal, semiconductors, and magnetic based conductive Nano structures have attracted great interest to manufacturing high-density data storage, contrast agents in MRI, and in making Nano-scale reading heads. Fuller-

ene is a 0.7 nm diameter, 60 carbon atom cage of very high electrical and heat conductivity can serve as a Nano-container for drug delivery and anti-viral agent. Carbon nanotubes, the strongest known material for their weight, have unique electrical and mechanical properties with a tensile strength, 10 times the steel, and about 25% the weight. DNA, a singled stranded structure of 2 nm diameter and few to thousands nm in length, is an attractive material for nanotechnology due to its relative thermal stability. DNA, as well as its transcription mediates the duplication of the biological information media into the ribosome input. In complex multicellular organisms, transcription factors (cellular proteins) serve as on

Figure 2. The organization of fluorescence quantum dots (Ehud, 2007)

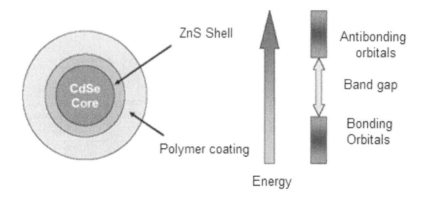

and off switches for the expression of this data in accordance with the correct external conditions of the cell. Other cellular entities maintain the correct DNA composition by error-correction mechanism. Quantum cryptography is based on the secret quantum encryption (entanglement) key and on the probability of eavesdropping. Quantum entanglement refers to quantum dots that emit two photons travelling in opposite directions with their polarization entangled (connected); i.e. if one is observed "up", the other is observed "down" and vice versa.

CRYPTOGRAPHY AND INFORMATION SECURITY

For thousands of years, people have tried to communicate secretly and securely. Cryptography satisfies this purpose by converting information to a completely gibberish message, or performing the inverse process by decoding an encrypted message). Cryptography is a key technology for achieving information security in computer systems, communications, electronic commerce, ATM cards, computer passwords, and has long been of interest to intelligence agencies. There are two basic forms of cryptographic processes,

- Symmetric key cryptography, in which the same key is used to encrypt and decrypt a message. The key, with some sort of protection, is transmitted securely between parties that wish to employ the process.
- Asymmetric key cryptography, in which the key employed to encrypt a message, is different from the key employed to decrypt the message.

Information age has brought some unique challenges to society; internet changed our thinking method, life style, communication means and others. With these rapid developments, there has been an increasing need for cryptographic methods which prompted many fields such as nanotechnology, biotechnology, chaos fractals and others to provide a contribution toward this goal. Information security, the protection of information in hostile environments, is a crucial factor in industry, business, and administration which ensures a balance between reasonable assessment of information risks, and a proper selection of information controls (James, 2003). It is concerned with the study of mathematical techniques related to aspects that support the requirements for strong security. Cryptography can provide the goals required by information security; these are: confidentiality, integrity, authentication, and availability.

Confidentiality (Privacy): Means the protection of all personally identifiable data by maintaining some authorized restrictions on information access and disclosure. It is main objective of cryptography and the most common factor of information security. It retains the individual's right to hold his personal information from the others.

Authentication: It is the mechanism that allows the receiver to know the exact identity of the sender, i.e. to authenticate the identity of a device, a user, or a process, over an insecure communication channel. The sender and the receiver share the same secret key to exchange information in an authenticated manner and they can detect eavesdropping.

Integrity: Data integrity, achieved using a digital signature, enables knowing the true validity of data as being sent from the master source and guarding against improper information modification or destruction. This means that the data must be received exactly as they were sent. If a message is altered, the decoded message is unreadable.

Availability: It is the capability of receiving/ sending data and providing these data when needed. Availability is a quality-of-service (QoS) feature rather than a security issue and the attacks against it are known as denial of service (DoS) attacks.

The main mechanisms of cryptography are: encryption, digital signature, message authentication code, and security certificate (Moreau, 2004). In the case of a Public Key Infrastructure (PKI), the initial key distribution is a two-fold process for each end-user and the issuing of security certificate must be protected from attacks. For inadequate controls of initial cryptographic key establishment, the protection of privacy and integrity are easy to establish when confidentiality and non-repudiation are necessary. The frequent use of a key strengthens the authentication assurance (key history) and allows an adequate key authentication. Secret Authentication Key Establishment Method

(SAKEM) can authenticate secret cryptographic keys by service provider procedures (Drexler, 1986). Those, however, are affected partly by a credentials service provider (CSP) and partly by a registration authority (RA). To establish an initial key, the new subscriber should request an enrollment from the RA and present the expected identity proof. Based on human attention and judgment, the registration authority may verify the identity of the new subscriber. Once enrollment is granted, the CSP or RA grants the access permission, and sends the secret key to the subscriber's computing environment, (William et al., 2004).

The SAKEM procedure is suitable for use against some attack on the mobile user registration process. Besides, it is used in high risk applications and in field initialization of network devices where the new subscriber's and the identity verifier roles are met by a field technician or a security officer providing.

NANO-TECHNOLOGY APPLICATIONS IN INFORMATION SYSTEMS

The big advancement in computers industry is linked to the ultra-miniaturization of the electronic components which is getting very close to atomic scale after the implementation of Nanotechnology. With the use of quantum dots, one bit of information could be stored in the energy states of a single electron. This may however, face some problems such as "tunneling" which arises at atomic Nano scales; see Figure 3.

In quantum cryptography, the wave function of the small scale system "quantum dot" is used to process and manipulate the information using the concepts of quantum physics which offers a secure route of transmission. Quantum computers are capable of doing tasks which are impossible to perform by a classical computer. For its unique properties of superposition and entanglement, a quantum Computer is favored over the classical

Figure 3. Tunneling phenomenon particle can be found at the other side of a barrier

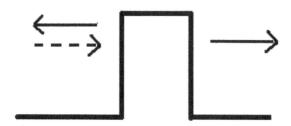

type. Superposition permits simultaneous mathematical operations while entanglement allows much better correlations in answers than what the classical type can offer. The difficulty of amplifying a quantum signal (cloning) is considered as an advantage for the establishment of secure communication channels (Calixto, 2009).

Cryptography is concerned with the building and analyzing of information to overcome the negative interference of eavesdroppers. In this context, information is transformed from readable to gibberish states using mathematical models and computer. Quantum cryptography is the field that can break encrypted messages, securely exchange a key (quantum key distribution, QKD) and perform cryptographic tasks. QKD is a unidirectional security mechanism in which a key is established and shared strictly between two parties; a sender and a receiver. The sender encodes the key bits as quantum data and sends them to the receiver. When entanglement is considered, the receiver and the sender will notice any interference with these bits by eavesdroppers; see Figure 4.

In a cryptographic security, the commitment allows the sender to fix a certain value that the receiver cannot change or know about until the sender decides to do so. Oblivious transfer protocol (OT) is a type of protocol in which a sender can transfer one of many pieces of information to a receiver by using an oblivious protocol, but remains oblivious as to what piece was sent. The bounded quantum storage model (BQSM) can be used to build unconditional secure quantum commitment and quantum oblivious transfer (OT) protocols. In BQSM, the amount of quantum data to be stored is limited by Q quantum bits. A random sequence of zeros and ones is called a key, which is used to exchange information between two users. After mapping this key on a known alphabet, the secret data can be sent through a public channel. Optimum security is obtained when the key length is equal to the length of the message. There are two mechanisms used for key distribution in quantum cryptography: One is based on single non-splitting photon (key) quantum states and the other is based on a source of correlated photon pairs. These two mechanisms make simultaneous measurements of the single photon at two distance point of an interferometer; see Figure 5. A photon from a quantum dot can be emitted after exciting a single electron in a semiconductor a circularly polarized light (Moloktov & Nazin 1996).

In quantum communication systems, a laser light is used to excite a single quantum dot and generate a train of single-photon pulses with no probability for detecting two photons (Michler, et al., 2000). Quantum Information Processing (QIP) is based on the concept of entanglement (connection) and superposition (Bouwmeester, Ekert, & Zeilinger, 2000). Feynman suggested that quantum mechanical systems can simulate and compute other quantum mechanical systems. This has ignited the idea of the theoretical quantum computer by Deutsch (Deutsch, 1985).

Figure 4. Quantum key distribution

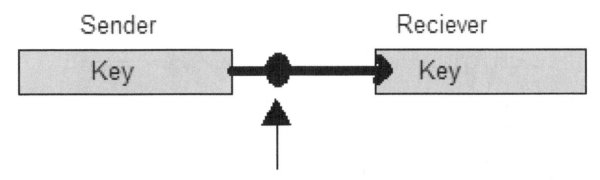

The applications in QIP began to arise when experimental quantum teleportation (Sudbury, 1993) and quantum cryptography (Charles et al., 1993) were born.

In cryptography, the original text is encrypted to produce a ciphertext which is then taken to a receiver who should decrypt it into the original text again to read it. The message secrecy depends on the encryption and decryption procedures (Calixto, 2009). For ciphering, encryption and decryption algorithm are known, but requires a key for the original text to be ciphered. Secrecy requires a random key, known only by the sender and the receiver of the message. Key distribution means sharing the secrecy between two people who initially share nothing. To do this, mathematical public key cryptography and quantum cryptography schemes are used. In the first scheme (not very secure), some mathematical operations are easier to perform in one direction but not in the other. In the second scheme, a complete secure key distribution is established by utilizing a quantum channel to send single quanta from the sender to the receiver. Eavesdropping of these quanta changes their state and this can be detected by the sender and the receiver (perfect security). In addition to the quantum channel, there is a public channel which gives an access to the communication by

anybody but without the ability to forge identities or messages. To make quantum key distribution, single or entangled particles are used; see Figure 6.

In the first case, the sender uses a single photon and a fast switching polarizer. The '0' and '1' bits are encoded into the horizontal-vertical polarization basis while rotating the second basis by 45 degrees. Two sensors are used to detect horizontal and vertical beams to discriminate between the $\oplus$ polarization bases at 0 degrees rotation or between the $\otimes$ polarization bases at 45 degrees rotation; see Figure 7.

Sending a bit and measuring it by a receiver in the $\oplus\otimes$ basis will let the detector to have a probability of ½ of measuring '0' and another ½ probability of measuring '1'. The receiver detects the polarization of each bit in a random binary code transmitted by the sender. After sending sufficient bits, the sender and receiver will use a public channel to choose the basis for each separate bit. They will omit all bits that have not been detected at the receiver. For any bit in the protocol, if the receiver and sender have unintentionally selected the correct basis, then an intruder, not knowing their basis, will detect the bit in each of the two bases and sends it again in the same basis. If the intruder sends the bit in the wrong basis with respect to the sender and receiver, he

Figure 5. Single photon carrying information

Polarization for 0 & 1

A polarizing beam splitter is employed to re-establish 0 or 1

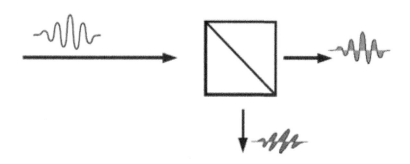

will have a 50% chance of reading either bit and after resending it, the receiver will also have a 50% chance of reading the wrong bit. If the intruder does this to all data string, bits of the sender and receiver will then have a 25% average error rate. If there is no intruder, the unused testing bits can be considered now as the key and a perfectly secure key is then generated.

Charles H. Bennett and Gilles Brassard have suggested the first protocol (the BB84) for quantum communications (Charles & Gilles, 1984). In this protocol, Alice and Bob, the two users, want to make secret random key on their communication channel. This protocol employs four polarization states which make two different bases; rectilinear (+) and diagonal (×). Alice transmits single photons to Bob in random states (→, ↑, ↗ and ↘) which represent four linearly polarization states (0°, 90°, +45° and -45°). In this step Alice is also allowed to transmit the binary 0 to {↑, ↗} and the binary 1 to {→, ↘}. The photons are received and measured by Bob in one of the randomly chosen two bases, and then he informs Alice the basis he

used for measuring each photon. Finally, Alice lets Bob know the correct basis so that only the data from correctly measured photons are kept. Alice and Bob will then use this secret key (binary string) to share secret information. It is possible to test eavesdropping if Alice and Bob use subsets of the photons on which they publicly disclose the polarization of the photons sent by Alice and measured by Bob. When an eavesdropper (Eve) makes a measurement, he changes the quantum state of the photon sent by Alice. This will be discovered by Bob when receiving an error bit. Comparing the photon polarization sent by Alice and measured by Bob will lead to a discovery of an eavesdropping in the communication channel.

Instead using single photons, Artur Ekert proposed in 1991 that QKD can be implemented using quantum entangled states (Artur, 1991). Entanglement exists between two quantum systems that interact at some point. The idea replaces the quantum channel used by Alice and Bob by another one having a common source that emits pairs of entangled particles, such as polarized

Figure 6. Single photon based quantum system

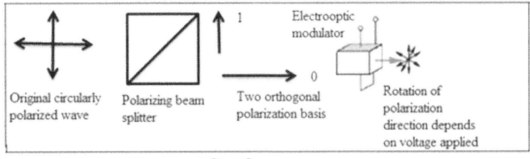

Sender

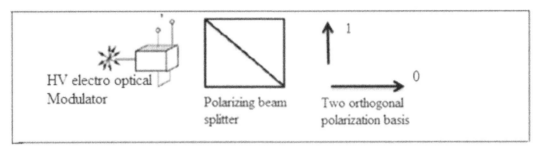

Receiver

photons. Alice and Bob receive a single photon from each entangled photon pairs. They measure their separated particle and in one of the two bases, chosen randomly and independently. The source then announces the bases, and Alice and Bob keep the data only when they make their measurements in the compatible basis.

In 1992, Charles Bennett proposed a simplified version of the BB84; the B92 quantum protocol in which only two non-orthogonal states are em-

Figure 7. Horizontal, vertical and 45 degree rotation polarizations

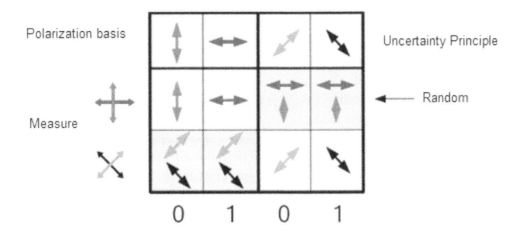

ployed (Charles, 1992). The security of the B92 depends on the lack of means of an eavesdropper to distinguish clearly without changing the polarization states sent by Alice to Bob. In this protocol $0°$ is the binary level 0 and $45°$ is the binary level 1. In this protocol, however, Alice chooses which bases she must use while Bob randomly chooses either rectilinear or diagonal basis. Wrong basis chosen by Bob will not allow him to measure anything. In the public discussion, Bob will tell Alice after each bit she sends whether or not his measurements are correct. Despite its simplicity, B92 suffers from security problems. Although two non-orthogonal states can-not be treated as different without perturbation, Eve can distinguish them with some losses in the quantum channel. Therefore, to ensure a high security, both Alice and Bob should monitor the attenuation of the quantum channel, but this can be overcome by Eve if he replaces part of the quantum channel by a low loss medium. This will necessitate the use of a bright pulse in the quantum channel in addition to the single photon so that Bob can monitor the pulses brightness to discover any removal of any part of the quantum channel by Eve.

The polarization encoded QKD, employed by Bennett et al and many others suffers from random fluctuation of polarization in a long-distance fiber (Charles, Francois, Louis & John, 1992). This will necessitate some control on the polarization of the photons in the fiber. A major limitation for all quantum communication is the fiber loss. This requires the use of very low attenuation pure silica core fibers if long distance secured communication link is to be established. In single photon communication, very low percentage of photons can get through and that amount drops as the transmission distance increases. Besides; the random polarization inside these fibers is another problem in all optical communication systems (Gordon, & Kogelnik, 2000). All fiber-based schemes of QKD including the phase-based systems suffer from this problem (Nicolas, Gregoire, Wolfgang, & Hugo, 2002). As compared with phase encod-ing, polarization encoding needs no precise active modulation to overcome the instability and error rate caused by the phase shift in fibers. It can be easily implemented in a one -way fiber system with the decoy-state QKD protocol to enhance its security in the high loss transmission channels (Chen, Gwu, Xu, Gu, Ewu, & Zeng, 2009). The polarization encoded QKD, however, suffers from random fluctuation of polarization in a long-distance fiber. This will require an efficient control on the polarization of the signal photons in the fiber.

QUANTUM DOTS IN CRYPTOGRAPHY

A quantum dot is a nanometers size semiconductor containing few free quantum confined electrons, holes, and excitons (electron-hole pairs). This confinement is explained in terms of the average distance (Bohr radius, a) separating the electron from the hole; which is different for different materials. The density of states in bulk semiconductor is continuous and the bandgap is fixed. In a quantum dot, the electronic states are discrete and determined by the shape and size of the quantum dot itself. Tuning the band gap is possible when altering the dimensions of the quantum dot. This tuning facility in quantum dots is advantageous over bulk semiconductors for the fabrication of tunable lasers. Decreasing the size of the quantum dots will shift the emitted spectrum towards the blue (higher energy photons) while increasing the size will shift the spectrum towards red (lower energy photons). In quantum dots, the absorption and emission wavelengths are stable when varying the temperature; a feature that is of great importance in optical communications. In quantum entanglement, it is possible to have 2 entangled particles or photons with their states are superposed with one another. The electronic states of the quantized electromagnetic field are defined by their photon number n and having an electric field $E_o = \sqrt{(n+1/2)}$ (Loudon, 2000). The values of n define fundamental modes which are superposition with the excitations of this field. As a result, the electric field magnitude becomes unknown, while the phase becomes more defined. States of light are confined to a wave-packet, and for a single photon emitter, the non-classical single photon state 1 needs to be created. Quantum cryptography can be realized by the superposition between 0 and 1 photon states but with a probability of no photon (0 state) if this superposition is transmitted. The probability of detecting one photon in a weak pulse is small and is even smaller for detecting two photons per pulse. However, a very low emission rate would lead to a high probability of detecting no photon (0) state. The confined levels in the upper and lower states of a quantum dot are similar to levels in the finite potential cubic or spherical wells (Fox, 2001). In a quantum dot the electronic states are localized and interact weakly with their surroundings. This creates narrow transition lines with an emission frequency of a single exciton level within this quantum dot depending on the total number of holes and electrons in the valence and conduction bands separately. This eliminates the possibility of emitting a single photon at the same frequency if the quantum dot has two exciton states. When a laser pulse is used to excite a quantum dot, then, with the aid of a monochromator, a single transition frequency is selected and single photon pulses are produced. To facilitate the emission of single photons by a quantum dot, the carriers' lifetime in the host semiconductor must be shorter than that of the carriers in the quantum dot Cryptography is a technique used to securely transmit information in the presence of adversaries so that only the intended people have access to the information. Classically, a message is ciphered using a mathematical algorithm and a key. The receiver deciphers the message y using the same key in addition to a mathematical algorithm. Cryptosys-

tems can be either symmetric or asymmetric. The first scheme uses only one key for encryption and decryption, and this the key must be transmitted securely. In the second scheme which also called "public-key cryptosystem", the receiver chooses a private key to compute a public key in order to distribute it to anyone. Using the public key, the encrypted information can be sent but can only be opened with the private key. In cryptosystems, the security of Public key depends on one-way mathematical functions; it is easy to work out a function of a variable but difficult to find the variable from the function. An integer number key is used to decrypt and encrypt. The larger the integer number the key has the more difficult and longer it takes to decrypt it. In quantum cryptography, computational techniques can handle operations that are difficult to perform by classical methods (David, 1985). The negative aspect of the uncertainty principle "any measurement does not allow complete accurate measurements" is considered as an advantage in quantum cryptography to send a key (photons). Qubits (information) are stored in the photons by the photon horizontal, vertical, and diagonal polarizations. The sender selects randomly a sequence of photon polarization and sends them to the receiver, who measures the photons in one of the polarization basis (Nicolas, Gregoire, Wolfgang & Hugo, 2002). The sender and the receiver then compare the results. If they find the same photon correlations as predicted unperturbed probability, this means no eavesdropper measurements were made on the system, i.e. the system is secured. If their photons measurement gives higher perturbation than average, third party interference is assumed i.e. insecure communication channel and the key sent could be ignored. Total security in information transfer can be achieved with quantum cryptography and this can made to give even better results if quantum entanglement is employed to ensure security in storage and transmission of information.

AUTHENTICATION BASED ON NANO AND BIOMETRIC TECHNIQUES

Authentication based on Nano and Biometric techniques

Authentication is the assertion of user identification who wants to make an access to:

1. Systems that the user knows, such as PIN, password, etc.
2. Systems that the user possesses, such as key, smart cards, etc.
3. Systems that the user has, such as biometric features.

Modern communications are classified into: digital type which employ different sorts of transmitters and media, and novel one that uses quantum and biological systems for sending information using Nano quantum dot-single photon emitters and complex proteins as information carrier.

Biometrics is a scientific discipline which utilizes biological traits (DNA, speech, face fingerprint, iris signature, ear, etc.) to verify and identify an individual through the analysis and measurement of his biological data; see Figure 8.

It is used to improve the authentication process by realizing the genuineness of the user presence. In biometric authentication, each person has his own biometric features which are different from person to person. The fast growing information technology necessitates security of the transmitted information to those needing it, while maintaining integrity and confidentiality. Bio-communications are based on the release of inorganic calcium signaling or on complex proteins; whereas Nano-communications are materialized using carbon nanotubes RF radio transmitters as antenna. In calcium based bio-signaling, data is encoded in proteins to permit a very high information density. Fluids, Nano-motors, or bacteria can be employed to transfer molecules to a distant target. Depending on the binding receptors at the Nano target and the molecules structure, diffusion

process may be adopted to achieve signaling. From simple undirected to targeted unicast, all communication schemes are possible to achieve; relying on quantum and biological means of addressing. Security goals (confidentiality, integrity, data consistency and availability) are not altered when replacing the classical communications by Nano communication. To prevent intruders' disturbances to Nano communication, a high level of authenticity is required. Attackers should be denied access of knowing the content of a message (confidentiality), modifying (integrity), or disrupting it (availability). Authenticity is achieved from confidentiality and integrity, where a receiver can verify the identity of the sender to prevent message spoiling. To introduce cryptographic schemes and algorithms in Nano communication, the existing cryptographic security solutions and protocols must be transferred to Nano networks and this will depend on the communication form and the Nano machines. When used for authentication, Conventional cryptography uses keys, passwords or cards, but these are vulnerable to theft, misplacement and guess leading to inefficient authentication. Biometrics are therefore, employed to overcome these problems through the provision of more reliable and secure authentication. Biometric systems are, however, vulnerable to many attacks, so an integration of conventional cryptography with biometrics in a new system called bio-cryptography is needed. This system therefore emerges to present stable cryptographic keys from uncertain biometrics. In molecular communication, information encoding is introduced as molecule's presence, concentration. To transmit information, an enzyme-like key lock is used and the molecules can be embedded in vesicles (one for every communication pair) to release its information to a matching molecule. The vesicle's configuration represents a key in the classical symmetric crypto-system (Falko & Frank, 2012). In biometric password based authentication, smart cards are employed as remote user authentication/verification. Fingerprint, the

Figure 8. Biological classification traits

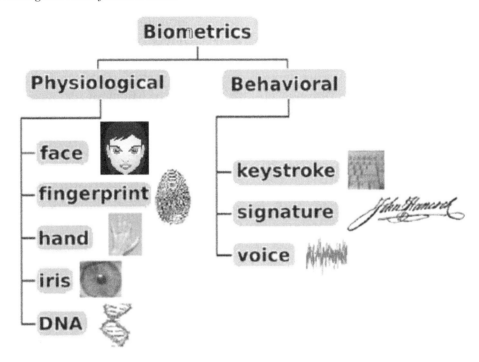

most successful biometric system, is used for on-card matching and as a key binding algorithm to protect the key retrieval process. Accepting the output of the biometric model means a release of the cryptographic key while its denial means no key release. Denial-of-service attack is hard to address by cryptography as attackers could jam Nano-based transmission or to flood the communication channel with molecules and impair the communication. To solve this problem, the system should go to fail-safe state. Injecting incorrect data into the system is another challenge that necessitates checking the data consistency to verify plausibility against known rules or information from multiple sources. Individuals' recognition by biometric features, such as photographs, voices, irises, finger prints, sound, or handwriting style is very desirable to identify people in many applications. The identity verification of travellers, for instance, requires detailed descriptive information in their passports and sometimes interrogation or third party testimonials. Individuals' recognition

by biometric features is very desirable to identify travellers which normally require detailed descriptive passport information and interrogation or third party testimonials. Biometric user authentication requires and error free means in additional access control to buildings or computers over multimedia authentication of authors, copyright holders and consumers of digital media. They offer automatic recognition of operating systems with embedded computer technology or individuals wondering in permeated environments, to ensure safe and forensic inspection. Single authentication schemes employing biometrics can provide one specific security aspect to computerized verification of individual authenticity. Security provisions of reference data from all users enrolled to authentication are required by biometric systems to using them for comparison in the authentication scheme. Fingerprint images authentication, for example needs the blocking of reference images from attackers who could use them to produce physical or digital forgeries of fingerprints. Cryptographic means can be utilized to solve the problem associated with password and possession based authentications. In multimedia service, to authorize using a specific service or to protect copyrights in digital media, logical binding of multimedia content to human identities is needed. The present Automated Fingerprint Identification Systems (AFIS) can automatically perform the fingerprint traces matching against stored specimens to serve individuals proving their authenticity (Vielhauer, 2006).

Human-to-Computer Interaction (HCI) is used to enhance the accuracy and performance by identifying biometric traits of users. In speech recognition, if the user's voice is identified, then a speech recognition system could be endorsed to a specific speaker, and thus enhancing the recognition accuracy, especially in multiple speaker environments. Biometric authentication can confirm the identity of a user in access control applications; ranging from logical access to fingerprint protected -small memory stick drives to access control to buildings.

The automated bio-authentication of individuals is important for many applications such as human-to-human interaction (face image, voice, handwriting analysis, etc. ....), electronic access to computers, electronic signatures, and immigration check points. Biometrics can be used to implement handwriting schemes or voice recognition to optimize automatic verification rates or individual's personal belongings, like cars. In applications where hand-written signatures of persons are stored electronically, information about the writing process can be used for an automated writer authentication. Biometric authentication methods are referred to by IT security with goals based on the three components of security; these are (Falko & Frank, 2012):

- **Confidentiality:** Is the concealment of information which requires keeping the information secret and obscuring the identity of communication partners exchanging information; preserving anonymity.

- **Integrity:** Refers to the trustworthiness of data or resources and includes aspects of integrity of data and sources of information. Both of the above authentication means can be combined to ensure Non-Repudiation.

- **Availability:** Is the ability of using the information needed. Besides reliability, protection against Denial-of-Service Attacks is important to ensure this goal.

Symmetric and asymmetric encryption schemes provide confidentiality, cryptographic hash functions and are utilized to verify data integrity. Additional objectives arise, when data and user authentication needs to be combined as in in signed documents, where the agreement text as well as the identities of signers and their declarations of intent needs to be authenticated (Vielhauer, 2006). For the last few years, authenticated electronic signatures have been promoted as methods to transform legal signatures to ensure integrity and reliable proofs of the identity of subjects. Any biometric authentication system has two levels: in the first one, all users enrolled should register with the system. Each individual will have his identity together with reference features stored in the system. After pre-processing, features are extracted and stored (reference storage) to a location in the authentication system. In the second level, the identity verification is found by the authentication system. To obtain an authentication result, a comparison of the data should be performed from the presented features to stored references. Classification will be made according to comparison of results. Copies of samples' recognition can be stored after using analog-to-digital converter for further use by an evaluation system. Enrollment and recognition samples are recorded only for evaluation reasons. References can be ensured by repeating the enrollment from samples stored in the evaluation database. User verification and identification are two alternative modes to achieve biometric authentication. In user verification, if the person's biometric features match those of the reference templates, then the claimed identity is confirmed. This biometric verification of an individual always results a binary yes or no decision. User identification is a process that determines his identity by making use of his biometric features. Verification is a one-to-one comparison in which one biometric sample is compared to stored reference data of one single registered individual. This means that identification is achieved by a comparison between actual biometric samples and references of all registered individuals in the biometric system (Vielhauer, 2006). The comparison will give the identity related to those references revealing the highest similarity. The biometric authentication accuracy is a function of an algorithm (τ): a low value of τ gives low matching whereas a higher (τ) value causes the opposite effect. To achieve a desired security level, a trade-off threshold between the security level required and the acceptance level of the user should be made. Signal processing is used to achieve analog-digital conversion of the biometric features and preprocessing steps whereas pattern recognition schemes are needed to extract adequate features for comparisons to references and finally to classify the incoming features.

NANO AND BIO IN CRYPTANALYSIS

Cryptanalysis is the retrieval of plain text from cipher text by finding a fault in the design without knowing the algorithm or the key. Although quantum cryptography, QC, solves the problem of secret key distribution, still, there is the eavesdropping problem that takes place when exchanging the information via a classical channel. In QC this problem is solved since the only information exchanged is the measurements type they made,

which does not give a clue about the key. In QC, a random key is generated without any transmitting information bits; therefore, an eavesdropper has no access to the precise measurement.

With the growth of confidential information and computer based business transactions, encryption is badly needed to guarantee the secrecy of information (Hughes et al., 1995). Quantum Key Distribution (QKD) strengthens the Public Key Cryptography (PKC) by preventing key sharing from being compromised. It is achieved when linking two communicators with a quantum and a classical channel. The realization of QKD is connected to the existence of quantum dot based-single photon sources. To check security, the communicators exchange data via a classical communication channel, and eavesdropping is confirmed when imperfect correlation between the exchanged bits are received. A fully automated quantum key distribution protocol prototype running at 625 MHz clock rate employs very low loss fibers and low noise superconducting detectors was presented. It is capable of distributing 6000 secret bits s^{-1} over 100 Km and 15 bits s^{-1} over 250 Km (Stucki et al., 2009). A high-dimensional quantum key distribution (QKD) protocol that employs temporal correlations of entangled photons was employed. The security of the protocol relies on measurements by Alice and Bob in one of two conjugate bases, implemented using dispersive optics. This dispersion-based approach is secure against collective attacks. The protocol, which represents a QKD analog of pulse position modulation, is compatible with standard fiber telecommunications channels and wavelength division multiplexers. Enhancing the transmission rate is suggested across 200 km of fiber (Jacob et al., 2013). High correlation means high security low value reflects a poor security; see Figure 9. To assemble a QKD system, quantum dot based-single photons are produced and random/difficult to guess cryptographic key is used to ensure confidentiality and integrity of information.

Figure 9. The discovery of an eavesdropping is materialized by testing the entanglement and by the noise associating the signal

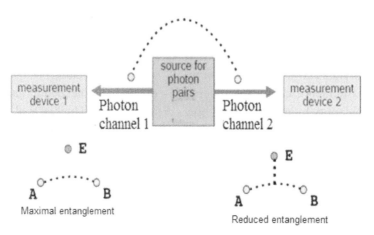

In QC security all transmitted quantum states are manipulated as a whole and pairs of quantum photon polarization states are used to securely encode the transmitted bits. These quantum states were first proposed by Wiesner in 1984 and taken forward by Bennett-Brassard in 1984; see Figure 10.

The strategy of eavesdropping relies on a loophole in the communicators' set-up when testing the transmitted states. One possibility of this kind of eavesdropping depends on eliminating any immediate interaction with transmitted quantum states to avoid inducing transmitted errors that discloses his presence. Intercept and resend is another type of attacks on QC in which eavesdroppers generate detectable light pulses the communicators, while, the original state is not setting off. The receiver will not discriminate his detection results from normal, and this gives the communicators the basis and bit chosen by eavesdroppers.

Biometric-based authentication depends on the unchangeable, distinct personal traits. Biometric template is however, not very secure and can be stolen or replaced in the system database. Traits left unintentionally by a person, can be recorded by cameras. The secrecy level of these traits varies; e.g. stealing a voice sample is easier than retina

sample. Protection passwords could be employed in biometric cryptosystems to enhance security against attacks. Biometrics cryptosystems are in three types. In key release type, the cryptographic key and the biometric data are stored separately. The key is released when the client is biometrically authenticated but biometric matcher can be overridden. The key generation type suffers from high false rejection rate because the cryptographic key is derived from the biometric data and not stored anywhere. The last is the key binding type in which the biometric template and the key are coupled to form an irretrievable biometric lock. Security evaluation of (BCK) is not strong due to the existence of error correction codes, and redundancy in the biometric key (Al-Assam & Jassim, 2012). A cryptographic key is randomly generated during the enrolment of biometric templates and a predefined error correcting code is generated to bind a binary key in the Fuzzy Commitment scheme. Biometric templates, extracted from samples, are transformed into a secure domain then a binary form of the biometric sample is made to bind to the cryptographic key. Error correcting scheme is required to eliminate noise from variation between traits and the key retrieval stages. In the binary representation of the

Figure 10. Principle of the BB84 protocol

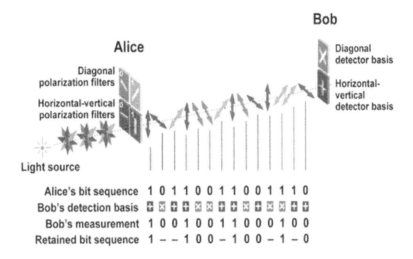

biometric data, the encoded cryptographic key is XOR that produces a biometric lock. The key is then rejected and the biometric lock and the key hash are saved.

To evaluate a BCK, the accuracy (False Acceptance and Rejection Rates) and security (guessing difficulty of a client's key by an adversary) must be materialized. The BCK binding/generation is an extraction algorithm that yields real biometric traits followed by a quantization algorithm to give a biometric binary form of traits. The entropy of the extracted traits before binary conversion is checked out if client's and impostor's samples have nearly Gaussian distributions. The security of BCKs is affected if the information of a sub-module is guessed. An error correction scheme can be used to decrease the biometric traits' entropy. User Based Transformations, UBTs, use passwords/PINs generated keys, without them, the biometric templates cannot be annulled. Unsecured cryptographic key will permit eavesdroppers to guess and employ the binary biometric form to discover any key the individual may think to bind in the future. The main possible attacks against biometric systems are:

- Fake biometric,

- Replay attack,
- Override feature extractor,
- Modify feature representation,
- Override matcher,
- Modify stored template,
- Channel attack between database and the matcher, and
- The decision override.

Among them, the attack against biometric templates causes the greatest damage and is hard to detect. The attackers can modify the enrolled stored biometric templates and replace the genuine template with a fake one to gain unauthorized access. Additionally, templates of the enrolled clients can be illegally utilized for cross-matching across different systems without user knowledge (Stavroulakis & Mark, 2010). A practical biometric system should store the encrypted/transformed version of a template instead of in raw/plaintext format to ensure template security. User privacy can be achieved by using fool-proof techniques on the templates. Standard encryption techniques do not provide good security for biometric templates. There are two better methods for protecting the template: feature transform and bio-cryptography. In the former, a transformation function converts the biometric template into a transformed one. In the matching process, the same transformation function queries the traits so that the transformed query is matched with the transformed template. If the transformed biometric template has been compromised, it cannot be linked to the raw biometrics. In bio-cryptography techniques a secret key is protected using biometric traits. Although the secret key and biometric template are hidden in the public information, it is not possible to extract the key or template from the public information directly. As subdivisions, in key binding bio-cryptography the public information is derived from binding the secret key and biometric template while in key generation bio-cryptography, the public information is obtained from the biometric template only; the secret key comes from the public information and the query biometric traits (Kai & Jiankun, 2010).

Most of the current cryptographic schemes rely on computational hardness that fails to hold in the presence of a quantum computer (Fehr, Mosca, Rötteler, & Dagstuhl, 2011). Thus, a large scale use of quantum computers will have a bad effect on the cryptographic security. However, biometric technologies are emerging as successful security means (Jagadeesan, Thillaikkarasi, & Duraiswamy, 2011) and unlike passwords, they give extremely immune security (Ambalakat, 2005). Different traits can be utilized by an individual system or independent systems which can operate separately and their outcomes may be combined. Multimodal-biometric authentication is characterized by its high security and efficiency in recognition. As mentioned in Section 6, biometric authentication provides very reliable and automated verification due to their unique biological feature that cannot be lost, duplicated or forgotten.

CONCLUSION

In modern information transmission, classical cryptography is not immune against interference by third parties and is therefore, not used. For more secure transmission of information, unbreakable cryptographic means are needed. This necessitates the utilization of advanced schemes such as nanotechnology and biometric systems. A multidisciplinary approach in information security represents an intermixing of security, privacy, safety of information and communication technology. In this field, nanotechnology can improve information processing systems and combine large memory-storage capabilities with very fast access and conservation of data. Cryptography requires a difficult to guess protection key to ensure confidentiality and integrity of information. The big growth in computers will allow one bit of information to be stored in one atom. Tunneling effect, however, could arise at atomic scales which put a problem to standard computation. Classically, a particle moving in a potential well is bouncing between the walls but when the potential is larger than the total energy, the particle cannot go. In quantum mechanics, particles can penetrate these classically forbidden regions and escape from their cage. This is a wave description in impenetrable media where waves are not localized and carry energy. The task of the quantum information theory is to process the information by the wave function of a quantum system. Quantum computers could efficiently perform some tasks which are not feasible on a classical computer and to revolutionize the online security. On the other hand, they could allow the design of exponentially fast quantum algorithms that could threaten the privacy of most of actual business transactions. In this context, the problematic tunneling effect is advantageous for security because it prevents the ultimate miniaturization of computers by not allowing them to have single-atom components. Biometric cryptography and authentication can explore the possibility to use numeric measurements based on biological observations to determine the authenticity of individuals. They provide strong means of protection against biometric system attacks and more reliable and automated verification due to unique measurable biological feature.

REFERENCES

Ahmad, F., Amri, A., Zuriati, A. Z., & Elissa, N. M. (2009). The Simplicity of Developing Chaotic Regime Cryptography. In *Proceedings of the Second International Conference on Computer and ICCEE '09 Proceedings* []. ICCEE.]. *Electrical Engineering, 2,* 227–230.

Al-Assam, H., & Jassim, S. (2012). Security evaluation of biometric keys. *Computers & Security, 31,* 151–163. doi:10.1016/j.cose.2012.01.002

Al-Saidi, N., Said, M. R., & Othman, W. A. (2012). Password Authentication Based on Fractal Coding Scheme. *Journal of Applied Mathematics.*

Ambalakat, P. (2005). Security of Biometric Authentication Systems. In *Proceedings of 21st Computer Science Seminar.* Academic Press.

Artur, K. E. (1991). Quantum cryptography based on bell's theorem. *Physical Review Letters, 67*(6), 661–663. doi:10.1103/PhysRevLett.67.661

Bharat, B. (2007). Introduction to Nanotechnology. In *Springer Handbook of Nanotechnology.* Springer.

Bouwmeester, D., Ekert, A., & Zeilinger, A. (2000). *The Physics of Quantum Information.* Springer. doi:10.1007/978-3-662-04209-0

Calixto, M. (2009). Quantum computation and cryptography: an overview. *Natural Computing, 8*(4), 663–679. doi:10.1007/s11047-008-9094-8

Charles, H. B. (1992). Quantum cryptography using any two non-orthogonal states. *Physical Review Letters, 68*(21), 3121–3124. doi:10.1103/PhysRevLett.68.3121

Charles, H. B., Francois, B., Louis, S., & John, S. (1992). Experimental quantum cryptography. *J. Cryptol., 5*(1), 3–28.

Charles, H. B., & Gilles, B. (1984). Quantum cryptography: public key distribution and coin tossing. In *Proceedings of the International Conference on Computers, Systems and Signal Processing.* Academic Press.

Charles, H. B., Gilles, B., Claude, C., Richard, J., Asher, P., & William, K. W. (1993). Teleporting an unknown quantum state via dual classical and Einstein-Podolsky-Rosen channels. *Physical Review Letters, 70*(13), 1895–1899. doi:10.1103/PhysRevLett.70.1895

Chen, J., Gwu, Xu, L., Gu, X., Ewu, & Zeng, H. (2009). Stable quantum key distribution with active polarization control based on time-division multiplexing. *New Journal of Physics, 11*(6). doi:10.1088/1367-2630/11/6/065004

David, D. (1985). Quantum theory, the Church-Turing principle and the universal quantum computer. *Proceedings of the Royal Society of London. Series A, Mathematical and Physical Sciences, 40,* 97–117.

Deutsch, D. (1985). The foremost paper about the universal theoretical quantum computer. *Proceedings of the Royal Society of London. Series A, 400,* 97–117. doi:10.1098/rspa.1985.0070

Drexler, K. E. (1986). Engines of Creation: The Coming Era of Nanotechnology. Anchor Books.

Ehud, G. (2007). Plenty of room for biology and bottom, an introduction to bio-nano-technology. Imperial College Press.

Falko, D., & Frank, K. (2012). Towards security in nano-communication: Challenges and opportunities. *Nano Communication Networks*, *3*(3), 151–160. doi:10.1016/j.nancom.2012.08.001

Fehr, S., Mosca, M., Rötteler, M., & Dagstuhl, R. S. (2011). Quantum Cryptanalysis. *Dagstuhl Reports. Schloss Dagstuhl*, *1*(9), 58–75.

Feynman, R. P. (1960). There's Plenty of Room at the Bottom. *Engineering and Science*, *23*(5), 22–36.

Fox, R. (2001). *Optical Properties of Solids*. Oxford University Press.

Ganesan, K., Ishan, S., & Mansi, N. (2008). Public Key Encryption of Images and Videos in Real Time Using Chebyshev Maps. In *Proceedings of Fifth International Conference on Computer Graphics, Imaging and Visualisation*. Academic Press.

Gordon, J. P., & Kogelnik, H. (2000). PMD fundamentals: Polarization mode dispersion in optical fibers. *Proceedings of the National Academy of Sciences of the United States of America*, *97*(9), 4541–4550. doi:10.1073/pnas.97.9.4541

Hughes, J. R., Alde, D. M., Dyer, P., Luther, G. G., Morgan, G. L., & Schauer, M. (1995). *Quantum Cryptography, LA-UR-95-806*. University of California.

Jacob, M., Zheshen, Z., Pierre, D., Catherine, L., Jeffrey, H. S., & Dirk, E. (2013). High-dimensional quantum key distribution using dispersive optics. *Physical Review A.*, *87*, 062322. doi:10.1103/PhysRevA.87.062322

Jagadeesan, A., Thillaikkarasi, T., & Duraiswamy, K. (2011). Protected Bio-Cryptography Key invention from Multimodal Modalities: Feature Level Fusion of Fingerprint and Iris. *European Journal of Scientific Research*, *49*(4), 84–502.

James, M. A. (2003). Why We Need a New Definition of Information Security. *Computers & Security*, *22*(4), 308–313. doi:10.1016/S0167-4048(03)00407-3

Kai, X., & Jiankun, H. (2010). Bio-Cryptography. In *Handbook of Information and Communication Security*. Springer.

Loudon, R. (Ed.). (2000). *The Quantum Theory of Light* (3rd ed.). Oxford University Press.

Michler, P., Kiraz, A., Becher, C., Schoenfeld, W. V., Petroff, P. M., & Lidong, Z. et al. (2000). A Quantum Dot Single-Photon Turnstile Device. *Science*, *290*(5500), 2282–2285. doi:10.1126/science.290.5500.2282

Moloktov, S. N., & Nazin, S. S. (1996). Quantum cryptography based on quantum dots. *JETP Letters*, *63*(8), 646–651.

Moreau, T. (2004). *An Information Security Framework Addressing the Initial Cryptographic Key Authentication Challenges*. CONNOTECH Experts-Conseil Inc.

Moreau, T. (2000). *Initial Secret Key Establishment Including Facilities for Verification of Identity*. US patent document 6,061,791. Washington, DC: US Patent Office.

Nicolas, G., Gregoire, R., Wolfgang, T., & Hugo, Z. (2002). Quantum cryptography. *Reviews of Modern Physics*, *74*(1), 145–195. doi:10.1103/RevModPhys.74.145

Nicolas, G., Gregoire, R., Wolfgang, T., & Hugo, Z. (2002). Quantum cryptography. *Reviews of Modern Physics*, *74*(1), 145–195. doi:10.1103/RevModPhys.74.145

Stavroulakis, P., & Mark, S. (2010). *Handbook of Information and Communication Security*. Springer. doi:10.1007/978-3-642-04117-4

Stucki, D., Walenta, N., Vannel, F., Thew, R. T., Gisin, N., Zbinden, H., & Gray, S. C. (2009). High rate, long-distance quantum key distribution over 250 km of ultra-low loss fibers. *New Journal of Physics*, *11*, 075003. doi:10.1088/1367-2630/11/7/075003

Sudbury, T. (1993). Instant Teleportation. *Nature*, *362*, 586–587. doi:10.1038/362586a0

Taniguchi, N. (1974). On the Basic Concept of Nano-Technology. Proc. Intl. Conf. Prod. Eng Tokyo.

Vielhauer, C. (2006). Fundamentals in Biometrics. *Advances in Information Security*, *18*, 11–31. doi:10.1007/0-387-28094-4_2

Vielhauer, C. (2006). Biometric user authentication for IT security From Fundamentals to Handwriting. *Advances in Information Security*, *18*, 1153–4648.

William, E. B., Donna, F. D., Ray, A. P., Polk, W. T., Elaine, M. N., Sabari, G., & Emad, A. N. (2004). *Electronic Authentication Guideline.* National Institute of Standards and Technology, NIST Special Publication 800-63.

KEY TERMS AND DEFINITIONS

Authentication: The first step of information security over insecure communication network which verifies and confirms the user identity before being accessed to data.

Biometrics: A scientific discipline which utilizes biological traits (DNA, speech, face fingerprint, iris signature, ear, etc.) to verify and identify an individual through the analysis and measurement of his biological data.

Confidentiality (Privacy): The protection of all personally identifiable data by maintaining some authorized restrictions on information access and disclosure. It is the main objective of cryptography and the most common factor of information security.

Identification: A psychological process which explains the nature of identification as an imaginary process. It determines the user's identity by making use of his biometric features when compared with references of all registered individuals in the biometric system.

Nanotechnology: A multidisciplinary use of materials and processes that refer to the control, manipulation, and applications of Nano-scale devices. Materials in a scale below 100 nm have different characteristics from their bulk counterpart.

Photon Polarization: The orientation of an electric vector inside a plane perpendicular to the photon direction of propagation. When the electric vector rotates during the propagation, the photon is said to be circularly polarized. Otherwise, when the direction of its electric vector is constant, the photon is linearly polarized.

Quantum Dots: Quasi-zero-dimensional semiconductor Nanocrystals that exhibit quantum mechanical properties; which are intermediate between those of bulk semiconductors and of discrete molecules. Their excitons (electron-hole pairs) are fully quantized in a discrete spectrum of energy levels and confined in all three spatial dimensions.

Quantum Entanglement: Refers to quantum dots that emit two photons travelling in opposite directions with their polarization entangled (connected); i.e. if one is observed "up", the other is observed "down" and vice versa.

Single Photon Laser: A laser of which, the gain medium is an electronic state, a quantum dot that emits a single photon when put through an optical pumping.

Chapter 8
ICA and PCA–Based Cryptology

Sattar B. Sadkhan Al Maliky
University of Babylon, Iraq

Nidaa A. Abbas
University of Babylon, Iraq

ABSTRACT

Blind Source Separation (BSS) represented by Independent Component Analysis (ICA) has been used in many fields such as communications and biomedical engineering. Its application to image and speech encryption, however, has been rare. In this chapter, the authors present ICA and Principal Component Analysis (PCA) as a category of BSS-based method for encrypting images and speech by using Blind Source Separation (BSS) since the security encryption technologies depend on many intractable mathematical problems. Using key signals, they build a suitable BSS underdetermined problem in the encryption and then circumvent this problem with key signals for decoding. The chapter shows that the method based on the BSS can achieve a high level of safety right through building, mixing matrix, and generating key signals.

INTRODUCTION

At first we would like to touch on the subject of Principal Component Analysis (PCA) because it is older scientifically than ICA. Principal Component Analysis (PCA) is a statistical method that consists in reducing the dimensions of the data set through linear combinations. The idea is to search for linear combinations that allow separating at best the possible values of the data. In other words, PCA searches for linear combinations with the largest variances, and when several linear combinations are needed, it considers the variances in decreasing order of importance.

The power of PCA is that it reduces the dimension of the data set in such a way that it conserves the most interesting components of the data set. In the signal processing world the statistical transformation involved in PCA is often called the Karhunen-Loeve transformation, another often used name is the Hotelling transformation. The major disadvantage of this transformation is its huge computation time. As this transformation has no fixed basis vectors, in the case of a Fourier transformation, the basis vectors that we will obtain are linked to the data set. (Lilian Bohy & Jean-Jacques Quisquater, 2003)

DOI: 10.4018/978-1-4666-5808-0.ch008

On the other hand, Independent Component Analysis (ICA) belongs to a class of BSS methods to separate data into underlying informational components, where such data can take the form of images, sounds, telecommunication channels or stock market prices.

ICA defines a generative model for the observed multivariate data, which is typically given as a large database of samples. In the model, the data variables are assumed to be linear or nonlinear mixtures of some unknown latent variables, and the mixing system is also unknown. The latent variables are assumed nonGaussian and mutually independent and they are called the independent components of the observed data. These independent components, also called sources or factors, can be found by ICA.

ICA can be seen as an extension to principal component analysis (PCA) and factor analysis (FA). ICA is much more powerful technique, however, capable of finding the underlying factors or sources when these classic methods fail completely.

The data analysis by ICA could originate from many different kinds of application fields, including digital images and document databases, as well as economic indicators and psychometric measurements. Frequently, the measurements are given as a set of parallel signals or time series; the term BSS is used to characterize this problem. Typical examples are mixtures of simultaneous speech signals that have been picked up by several microphones, brain waves recorded by multiple sensors, interfering radio signals arriving at a mobile phone, or parallel time series obtained from some industrial process.

ICA is subjected to a variety of disciplines, such as statistics, signal processing, neural networks, applied mathematics, neural and cognitive sciences, information theory, artificial intelligence, and engineering. (A. Hyvrinen & E. Oja, 2001)

Blind Source Separation (BSS) is a technique of array signal processing which aims to recover a set of unknown mutually independent source signals from their observed mixtures without knowing the mixing coefficients.

ICA is a special case of BSS with linear and instantaneous mixture. BSS has hopeful applications to communications, biomedical engineering, cocktail party problem, etc. Its applications to signal encryption focused on the speech and image encryption (W. Kasprzak & A. Cichocki, 1996; Qiu-Hua Lin & Hua-Lou Liang, 2004).

With the rapid development of multimedia and networking technologies, the security of multimedia data becomes more and more important in many real applications. To meet such an increasing demand, during the past two decades many encryption schemes have been proposed for protecting multimedia data, including speech signals, images and videos. (Shujun Li & Guanrong Chen, 2008).

This chapter is devoted to study two statistical tools, namely the Principle Component Analysis (PCA) and the Independent Component Analysis (ICA) and their roles in cryptology. The basic features of the ICA and PCA models in many speech and image encryption applications are examine.

BACKGROUND

Cryptology, the study of cryptosystems, can be divided into three disciplines. Cryptography is interested in the design of cryptosystems; cryptanalysis studies the breaking of cryptosystems, while security evaluation is interested in the design of different methods suitable to evaluate the security (complexity) of the crypto system under consideration. These three disciplines are closely related; when setting up a cryptosystem, the analysis of its security plays an important role and evaluation of its strength against analysis is also an important aspect.

Modern communication techniques, using computers connected through networks, make all data even more vulnerable to these threats. Also, new issues have come up that were not relevant before, e.g. how to add a (digital) signature to an electronic document in such a way that the signer cannot deny later he signed that the document. (Henk C.A. Van Tilborg, 1999). Therefore a variety of the encryption techniques has been introduced.

We explore a PCA and ICA (represented by blind source separation) based speech and image using two disciplines from cryptology, noting that the restrictions and evaluation methods are within it.

An application of the ICA is proposed for hidden image transmission by communication channel (W. Kasprzak & A. Cichocki, 1996). The authors also use the compression of PCA and signal quantization. To ease simple power analysis, (Lilian Bohy & Jean-Jacques Quisquater, 2003) applied PCA. Also discussed that PCA and ICA permit improving the signal to noise ratio (SNR) of signals that used the differential side channel analysis, which makes the application of classical methods to recover cryptographic keys easier. We can say that the first use of speech encryption using BSS was by (Qiu-Hua Lin & Hua-Lou Liang, 2004). Their approach integrates a modified time domain scrambling scheme with an amplitude scrambling method which masks the speech signal with a random noise by specific mixing. The resulting system could securely encrypt the speech files for storing speech messages and transmit them over the Internet.

(Qiu-Hua Lin & Hua-Lou Liang, 2005) present a BSS-based method for encrypting images and speeches by using the BSS underdetermined problem. Other works of the same authors (Qiu-Hua Lin & Hua-Lou Liang, 2006) on image encryption based on blind source separation (BSS) takes advantage of the underdetermined BSS problem to encrypt multiple confidential images. Their paper presents a fast decryption algorithm based on adaptive noise cancellation by using the knowledge of the key images, which are used in the BSS-based method and available at the receiving side.

In cryptanalysis (Shujun Li, & Guanrong Chen, 2008) propose underdetermined BSS principle to design image and speech encryption. Their paper, discusses some other security defects of the schemes such as:

1. It has a low sensitivity to part of the key and to the plaintext;
2. It is weak against a ciphertext-only differential attack;
3. A divide-and-conquer (DAC) attack breaks part of the key.

Another application of ICA is for military application presented by (Nikolaos Doukas & Nikolaos v. Karadimas, 2008). Their paper uses the underdetermined source separation problem as a basis for a cryptographic mechanism, also the preliminary of cryptanalysis is presented that verifies the adequacy of the new scheme for use in mobile military communication units and other applications where security is critical. The proposed system was tested using signal to interference ratio (SIR) as an objective measure. (Abedelaziz Mohaisen & Dowon Hong, 2008) introduced a modified multiple rotation based transformation (MRBT) technique for special mining applications mitigating the ICA attack while maintaining the advantages of the rotation based transformation (RBT) as an application for privacy preserving data mining.

(Nikolaos Doukas & Nikolaos V. Karadimas, 2008) designed a BSS scrambler that could not produce any distortions to the data and would be of such computational complexity that it could be embedded in portable secure communications devices. (Xiao Fei, Guisong Liu & Bochuan Zheng, 2008) introduce a chaotic encryption system using "PCA / neural network ". The PCA neural network can produce the chaotic behavior under certain conditions so that it serves as a pseudo-random number generator to generate random private keys. (Sano, Natsuki, Sinohara & Yasusi, 2009) propose the Privacy Preserving Independent Component Analysis (PPICA) to conduct ICA in a privacy preserving manner. (Nidaa A. Abbas, 2009) propos the application of analog speech scrambler using a statistical method based on PCA. This proposal was tested using Linear Predictive Coding (LPC) and Signal-to-Noise Ratio (SNR). In Decryption process (Da-Peng Guo & Qiu-Hua Lin, 2010) analyzed the correlation of speech signals with key signals, and then used the correlation calculation to achieve speech decryption. (Dowon Hong & Abedelaziz Mohaisen, 2010) used the Multiple rotation-based transformation (MRBT) for mitigating a priori knowledge Independent Component Analysis of (AK-ICA) attack on rotation-based transformation (RBT), which is used for privacy-preserving data clustering. To solve the weakness of underdetermined BSS problem. (Atef Mermoul & Adel Belouchrani, 2010) propose an approach based on the subspace concept together with the use of nonlinear functions and key signals. (M. Abdelaziz Elaabid & Sylvain Guilley, 2010) introduce a method based on the threshold of leakage data to accelerate the profiling or the matching stages. Indeed, leveraging on an engineer's common sense, it is possible visually to foresee the shape of some eigenvectors thereby expecting their estimation towards their asymptotic value by authoritatively zeroing weak components containing mainly non-informational noise. These methods empower an attacker, in that it saves the traces when converging towards correct values of the secret. (Jason L. Wright & Milos Manic, 2010) compare the application of three different dimension reduction techniques to the problem of classifying functions in object code form whether being cryptographic in nature or not. A simple classifier is used to compare dimensionality reduction via sorted covariance, principal component analysis, and correlation-based feature subset selection. (Youssef Souissi & Florent Flament, 2010) introduce First Principal Components Analysis (FPCA) which is employed in evaluating the relevance of partitioning and uses

the projection on the first principal directions as a distinguisher. FPCA is considered as a novel application of the PCA. (Jip Hogenboom, 2010) propose the use of PCA to improve the correlation for the correct key guess for Differential Power Analysis attacks on simulated DES traces, software DES traces, hardware DES traces and hardware AES-256 traces. (Atef Mermoul, 2011) propose an approach of iterative encryption algorithm based on the subspace concept together with the use of nonlinear functions and key signals. The proposed technique presents an interesting feature only a part of the secret key parameters used during encryption is necessary for decryption. Furthermore, the iterative encryption algorithm provides no contents if no plain-text are fed into the input. To evaluate the performance of speech scrambling (Sattar B. Sadkhan & Nidaa A. Abbas, 2011) propose some methods based on statistical metrics called ICA and PCA. For ICA method, Approximate Diagonalization of Eigen-matrices (JADE) is carried out while for PCA, the traditional PCA is carried out. (Dimitrios Mavroeidis & Elena Marchiori, 2012) propose the data mining (clustering) formulation of the Differential Power Analysis (DPA) process and provide a theoretical model that justifies and explains the utility of low-order eigenvectors. In their work data mining formulation considers that the key-relevant information is modeled as a "low-signal" pattern that is embedded in a "high-noise" dataset.

INDEPENDENT COMPONENT ANALYSIS (ICA)

ICA is a computational method for separating a multivariate signal into additive subcomponents supposing the mutual statistical independence of the non-Gaussian source signals. It is a special case of blind source separation. The latent variables are assumed nonGaussian and mutually independent and they are called the independent component (IC) of the observed data. These independent components are also called sources or factors that can be found by ICA.

ICA suffers from two ambiguities, they are: -

1. The variances (energies) of the independent components cannot be determined.
2. The order of the independent components cannot be determined.

Various types of mixture can be considered, as:

a. Instantaneous linear mixtures,
b. Convolutive mixtures, or
c. Nonlinear mixtures.

The mixing operation is often assumed to be invertible, but it is not the case for underdetermined mixtures. Such source signals can take their values in the real field or in the complex field, be of constant modulus or belong to a finite alphabet, a priori known or not. When source signals are considered to be random, several assumptions exist. Sources may be:

*   Mutually and statistically independent,
*   Each is identically and independently distributed in time (i.i.d.), or
*   Cyclostationary.

Several statistical methods have been developed to find suitable linear transformation. These include PCA, Factor Analysis (FA), Projection Pursuit (PP), ICA, and many more. The basic linear model relates the unobservable source signal and the observed mixtures:

$$x(t) = As(t) \qquad (1)$$

where $s(t) = [s_1(t), ..., s_m(t)]^T$ is a $m \times 1$ column vector collecting the source signals, similarly vector $x(t)$ collects the n observed signals, A is a $n \times m$ matrix of unknown mixing coefficients, $n \geq m$, and t is the time index. This model is instantaneous (or memoryless) because the mixing matrix contains fixed elements; and is noise-free. If noise is included in the model, it can be treated as an additional source signal or as measurement noise. In the case the model becomes:

$$x(t) = As(t) + n(t) \qquad (2)$$

where the noise vector $n(t)$ is of dimension $n \times 1$. The mixing matrix may be constant, or can be with the time index t. In the time-varying case, A becomes $A(t)$. The above problems are called BSS (Blind Source Separation) or ICA.

To recover the original source signals from the observed mixtures, a simple linear separating system is used:

$$y(t) = Bx(t) \qquad (3)$$

where $y(t) = [y_1(t), ..., y_n(t)]^T$ is an estimate $s(t)$, and B is a $n \times n$ (assume $n = m$) separating matrix, as shown in Figure 1.

ICA ALGORITHMS

There are mainly two distinct approaches towards computing the ICA, they are:

1. Off-line (batch) processing, and
2. On-line (Neural) algorithms.

The batch algorithm employs high order cumulants and is found mainly in the statistical signal processing literature. A standard approach for batch ICA algorithms (like JADE (J. F. Cardoso, 1999)) is the following two stage procedure: -

a. The Decorrelation or whitening. This state seeks to diagonalise the covariance matrix of the input signals. It is carried out by computing the sample covariance matrix, giving the second order statistics of the observed

Figure 1. Mixing and separating. Unobserved signals; observations x(t), estimated source signals y(t)

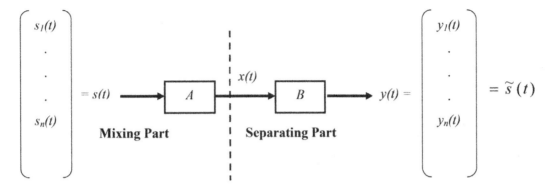

output. From this, a matrix is computed by eigen decomposition which whitens the observed data.

b. Rotation. This stage minimizes the measure of the higher order statistics which will ensure that the nonGaussian output signals are as statistically independent as possible. This stage can be carried out by a unitary rotation matrix, to provide higher order independence. It is carried out by finding a rotation matrix which jointly diagonalizes eigenmatrices formed from the fourth order cumulants of the whitened data. The outputs from this stage are the independent components.

This approach is sometimes called "decorrelation and rotation", and relies on the measured signals being nonGaussian. For Gaussian signals, the higher order statistics are zero already and so no significant separation can be achieved by ICA methods. For nonGaussian random signals the implication is that not only should the signals be uncorrelated, but also that the higher order cross-statistics (e.g., moments or cumulants) are zeros. The JADE algorithm can be summarized as follows:

1. Initialization. Estimate a whitening matrix $\hat{W}$ and set $Z = \hat{W}X$

2. Form statistics. Estimate a maximal set $\{\hat{Q}_i^z\}$ of cumulant matrices.

3. Optimize an orthogonal contrast. Find the rotation matrix $\hat{V}$ such that the cumulant matrices are as diagonal as possible, that is, solve $(\arg\min \sum_i Off(V^+\hat{Q}_i^z V))$

4. Separate. Estimate A as

$$\hat{A} = \hat{V}\hat{W}^{-1} \qquad (4)$$

And/or estimate the components as $\hat{S} = \hat{A}^{-1}X = \hat{V}^+ Z$

On the other hand, neural-based algorithms use the gradient decent of nonlinear activation functions in neuron-like devices and are mainly developed in the neural network community. Algorithms of this approach are on-line algorithms, with real-time applications; the data are available one at the time, meaning that at each time index t we receive an n-dimensional vector of observations $x(t)$. Based on the new received data vector and possibly with a vector of some previously received data, the task is to estimate the initial sources.

PRINCIPAL COMPONENT ANALYSIS (PCA)

Principal component analysis (PCA) and the closely related Karhunen-Lo`eve transform, or the Hotelling transforms, are classic techniques in many applications such as statistical data analysis, feature extraction, and data compression, resulting from the early work of Pearson (K.Pearson,

1901). PCA has been called one of the most valuable results from applied linear algebra and is used mainly in all forms of analysis - from Neuroscience to computer graphics - because it is a simple, non-parametric method of extracting relevant information from confusing data sets. With minimal additional effort, PCA provides a roadmap for how to reduce the complex data set to a lower dimension to reveal the sometimes hidden, simplified structure that often underlies it (Jonathon Shlens, 2009).

In their simplest forms, they assume the observed data can be represented by a linear combination of some unknown hidden factors called sources as described in (1):

PCA exploits the assumption the hidden source signals are not mutually related and reconstructs the source signals *s* by decorrelating observed signals *x*.

PCA is a linear transformation that reduces compresses or simplifies the data set. It does this by transforming the data to a coordinate system so that the greatest variance of the data by a projection of the data ends on the first component (coordinate), the next one in line with the magnitude of variance ends on the second component and so on. In this way one can choose not to use all the components and still capture the most important part of the data.

Under the zero mean assumption, the uncorrelatedness assumption is formerly expressed as:

$$R_s = E\left[SS^T\right] = \Lambda \qquad (5)$$

where R_s represents covariance matrix, Λ is some diagonal matrix and $E[\ ]$ denotes mathematical expectation. The PCA transform W is designed such that the transformed data matrix:

$$Z = WX \qquad (6)$$

has uncorrelated components, i.e., $R_z = \Lambda$. Having this in mind, we derive the PCA transform as follows:

$$R_z = E\left[zz^T\right] = WE\left[XX^T\right]W^T = WR_xW^T = \Lambda \qquad (7)$$

From (7), can be recognized that the PCA transform W is nothing else but a matrix of eigenvectors $\lambda_v[\ ]$ obtained through eigen-decomposition of the data covariance matrix R_x, i.e.,

$$W = \lambda_v^T \qquad (8)$$

A special form of the PCA transform is whitening or sphering transform that makes transforming signals uncorrelated with unit variance. This is formerly expressed as $R_z = I$, where I represent identity matrix. This is equivalent to writing (7) as:

$$R_z = E\left[zz^T\right] = WE\left[XX^T\right]W^T = \Lambda^{-1/2}WR_xW^T\Lambda^{-1/2} = I \qquad (9)$$

Using (9), the whitening transform is obtained as:

$$W = \Lambda^{-1/2}\lambda_v^T \qquad (10)$$

PROPERTIES AND LIMITATIONS OF PCA

PCA is theoretically the best linear scheme, in terms of least mean square error, for compressing a set of high dimensional vectors into a set of lower dimensional vectors and then reconstructing the original set. It is a non-parametric analysis and the answer is unique and independent of any hypothesis about data probability distribution. However, the latter two properties are regarded as weakness as well as strength, in that being non-parametric, no prior knowledge can be incorporated and that PCA compression often results in a loss of information.

The applicability of PCA is limited by the assumptions made in its derivation. These assumptions are (A. Hyvrinen & E. Oja, 2001):

1. **Linearity:** The observed data set is assumed to be linear combinations of certain basis. Non-linear methods such as Kernel PCA have been developed without assuming linearity.
2. **The statistical importance of mean and covariance:** PCA uses the eigenvectors of the covariance matrix and it only finds the independent axes of the data under the Gaussian assumption. For non-Gaussian or multi-modal Gaussian data, PCA simply de-correlates the axes. When a PCA is used for clustering, its main limitation is that it does not account for class separability since it makes no use of the class label of the feature vector. There is no guarantee that the directions of maximum variance will contain good features for discriminating.
3. **The large variances have important dynamics:** PCA simply performs a coordinate rotation that aligns the transformed axes with the directions of maximum variance. It is only believed that the observed data has a high signal-to-noise ratio that the principal components with a larger variance correspond to interesting dynamics and lower ones correspond to noise.

Essentially, PCA involves only rotation and scaling. The above assumptions are made to simplify the algebraic computation on the data set.

INSTANTANEOUS LINEAR MIXTURES

Linear Independent Components Analysis (ICA) has become an important signal processing and data analysis technique, the typical application being blinded source separation in a wide range of signals, such as biomedical, acoustical and cryptology. This section explores two types of linear ICA, underdetermined (the number of sensors is less than that of sources) and instantaneous linear ICA (assumes the sensors and sources are equal).

UNDERDETERMINED BSS

Underdetermined blind source separation (UBSS) is a branch of the problem of blind source separation, which has received much attention especially in Cryptology. The basic idea of UBSS is the number of sensors is less than that of sources. Sparse component analysis (SCA) is the main method to solve the problem of UBSS, which usually consists of two steps: estimate the mixing matrix first and then reconstruct the sources (Tianbao & Jingshu Yang, 2012).

If the number of sources m is larger than the number of sensors n, the mixing is called underdetermined, and is not invertible. Here, the problems of identification of the mixing, mapping A and of source restoration become two distinct problems. For linear memoryless mixtures, even if the mixing matrix is perfectly known, there exists an infinity of solutions. Priors are necessary (for instance sources can be discrete-valued, or sparse, i.e. with a small number of non-zero samples) to restore essential uniqueness of source inputs (P. Comon & C. Jutting, 2010) as shown in Figure 2 the block diagram of underdetermined BSS.

Several methods have been proposed for solving the underdetermined problem, and some of these use the sparseness of speech signals. These methods employ binary masks that extract a signal at time points where the number of active sources is estimated to be only one. However, these methods resulted in an unexpected increase in zero-padding and so the extracted speeches are severely distorted and have loud musical noise.

Figure 2. Block diagram of underdetermined BSS

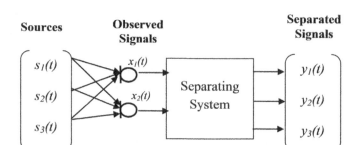

ADVANTAGES OF BSS ENCRYPTION

Traditional BSS applications employ adaptive algorithms possibly in collaboration with the neural network components to converge an approximate solution of the mixing problem that they are faced with. Existing BSS encryption techniques BSS encryption algorithms inherently require the use of some key sequences, i.e. pseudo-data sequences that will be mixed with the useful data in a manner that will render the mixture inseparable.

Encryption keys are generated locally in each of the encoder and decoder, using a pseudo-random number generator. Since these keys ensure the confidentiality of transmission, the choice of the mixing matrix becomes less relevant, provided the necessary conditions for the inseparability are met.

The use of a mixing matrix, that is unknown to both ends of the information transfer and is only about inversion by the decryption stage, becomes redundant. It is therefore proposed that the mixing matrix also be available at the decrypting end of the information transfer. The receiver of the information became significantly less computationally complex, while acquiring the ability to respond to change in the transmitted signal statistics without any transient period or convergence delay. (Nikolaos Doukas & Nikolaos v. Karadimas, 2008)

ENCRYPTION

A block diagram of the BSS based speech (image) encryption system is shown in Figure 3. For encryption, there are two main stages, the segment splitter and the BSS mixing. For image encryption, the *m* input signals of the BSS-based method, can be easily obtained by converting two-dimensional (2-D) images into one-dimensional (1-D) data. After decrypted the 1-D signals then return to 2-D images for presentation (Qiu-Hua Lin, & Hua-Lou Liang, 2004).

SEGMENT SPLITTER

Similar to the time element scrambling,(H. I. Beker & F. C. Piper, 1985) the original speech signal is first divided into equal time periods called the frames. Each frame is then sub-divided into K (K = 2) smaller equal time periods called the segments, which are denoted by $s_1(t), \ldots, s_K(t)$, $t = 1, \ldots, T$, where T is the segment length. Instead of permuting the segments within each of the frames as the time element scrambling does, the proposed system mixes the K speech segments within each frame with K statistically independent key signals (pseudo-random noise) in a specific way.

Figure 3. A block diagram of the BSS based speech/image encryption system

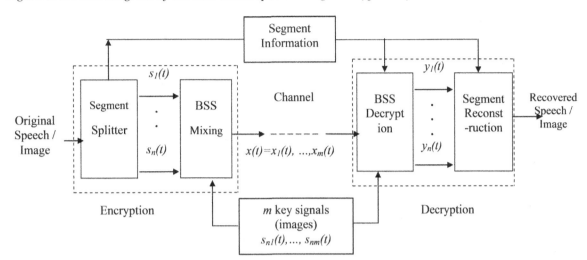

BSS MIXING

In this stage, at first the system generates K statistically independent key Signals $s_{m1}(t), ..., s_{mK}(t)$, $t = 1, ..., T$, with random values uniformly distributed among -1 and 1, and a $K \times 2K$ mixing matrix A, then mixes the K original speech segments $s_1(t), ..., s_K(t)$ and the K key signals $s_{m1}(t), ..., s_{mK}(t)$ by using the BSS mixing $s(t)=[s_1(t), ..., s_K(t), s_{m1}(t), ..., s_{mK}(t)]^T$, $x(t) = As(t) = [x_1(t), ..., x_K(t)]^T$. K mixed speech segments $x_1(t), ..., x_K(t)$, $t = 1, ..., T$, are K encrypted speech segments. Finally, K encrypted speech segments are rejoined together to form one encrypted that frame $x(t) = [x_1(t), ..., x_K(t)]$ for transmission. To achieve the secure goal, the mixing matrix, A_e (underdetermined mixing matrix) is constructed for encryption as follows:

$$A_e = \begin{bmatrix} B & \beta B \end{bmatrix} \tag{11}$$

where ß is a scalar value, usually $1 \leq \beta \leq 3$, B is a $K \times K$ matrix of full rank, which is usually pseudo-randomly generated with values uniformly distributed between -1 and 1.

Using A_e in (11), BSS becomes the difficult case of the underdetermined problem where there are less mixed signals (K) than source signals $(2K)$. As a result, the K original speech segments cannot be separated out from the K encrypted speech segments through BSS without the K key signals.

SEGMENT INFORMATION

To decrypt the encrypted speech received and recover the original speech, some prior knowledge about the segment splitter is needed and the waveform of K original speech segments within each frame is called the segment information. The following information must be recorded: the information about the segment splitter including the number of segments K within each frame and the segment length T; the waveform information including the zero cross count (zcc), the maximum s_{max} and the minimum s_{min} of each original speech segment. For transmission, the segment information may be inserted into the encrypted speech file in a definite format, or transmitted together with the key signals by a secure channel.

DECRYPTION

The decryption part of the system consists of two main stages, the BSS decryption and the segment reconstruction, as shown in Figure 3. The original speech will be recovered frame by frame.

BSS DECRYPTION

At this stage, at first there is a need to retrieve the K encrypted speech segments $x_1(t), ..., x_K(t)$ of each frame from the received encrypted speech by using the segment information K and T. Next, the BSS decryption separates the K original speech segments out of the K encrypted speech segments using K key signals. The K encrypted speech segments are first combined with the K key signals to form $2K$ mixed signals $s(t)=[s_1(t) , ..., s_K(t),_{sm1}(t) , ..., s_{mK}(t)]^T$ in which the BSS algorithm is then performed. In this system the infomax algorithm is used (J. Bell & T. J. Sejnowski, 1995). It is easy to show that the equivalent mixing matrix for the BSS decryption is

$$A_d = \begin{bmatrix} B & \beta B \\ 0 & I \end{bmatrix} \qquad (12)$$

where I is a $K{\times}K$ identity matrix, 0 is a $K{\times}K$ zero matrix. Obviously, this A_d is a $2K{\times}2K$ square matrix of full rank, and the underdetermined problem resulting from the BSS mixing encryption which becomes the simplest BSS case, where the number of the mixed signals is equal to that of the source signals. Therefore, the complete separation of the source signals is available. The K original speech segments and the K key signals can be well recovered through the BSS decryption together, and the K decrypted speech segments, denoted by $u_1(t),..., u_K(t)$, (referring to Figure 3), can be easily obtained by discarding the K key signals using zcc.

$$u(t) = Wx(t) = WAs(t) = PDs(t) \qquad (13)$$

where W is $m{\times}n$ demixing matrix, $u(t)$ m $\times$ 1 output vector, $P \in R^{m{\times}m}$ is a permutation matrix and $D \in R^{m{\times}m}$ is a diagonal scaling matrix. When n < m, i.e., the number of the mixed signals is less than that of the source signals, BSS becomes a difficult case of the underdetermined problem

SEGMENT RECONSTRUCTION

From (13), it be seen that the K decrypted speech segments $u_1(t),..., u_K(t)$ are separated out with permutation and changes of scales and signs, compared with the K original speech segments $s_1(t), ..., s_K(t)$. Therefore, we need to reconstruct the original speech from the decrypted speech segments by using the segment information. First, the order of the K decrypted segments can be correctly rearranged by using the segment information zcc. Then, the waveform of them including the amplitudes and the signs can be readily reconstructed by using the segment information s_{max} and s_{min} of each corresponding original speech segment.

SPEECH SCRAMBLING

Speech scrambling seeks to perform a completely reversible operation on a portion of speech, that is totally unintelligible to unauthorized listener. The most important criteria used to evaluate speech scramblers are (Sattar B. Sadkhan & Nidaa A. Abbas, 2012):

1. The scrambler's ability to produce encrypted speech with low residual intelligibility.
2. The extent to which the encryption and decryption processes effect the quality of the speech recovered by intended reception; and
3. The scrambler's immunity to cryptanalysis attack.

ICA and PCA were implemented in speech scrambling (Sattar B. Sadkhan & Nidaa A. Abbas, 2007; Nidaa A. Abbas, 2009; Sattar B. Sadkhan & Nidaa A. Abbas, 2011). Such implementation uses traditional PCA for scrambling speech, JADE algorithms for ICA as shown in Figure 4.

The steps of the proposed system in Figure 4 (much like those in Figure 3) are: -

- Split the original signal into segments, where each segment has an equal sample, and is independent from each other.
- Choose an interval for the random mixing matrix.
- The result is the scrambled speech, as in (1), where the steps from 1-3 represent the scrambling speech procedure.
- Using JADE or PCA algorithm, the result is the descramble speech as in (4) for JADE algorithm and (10) for PCA algorithm.

PERFORMANCE ANALYSIS

To quantify the performance of the encryption algorithm using ICA, there are many measures to compute the performance of ICA and PCA algorithms.

The signal-to-noise ratio *(SNR)* index is computed. For $s_i(t)$, the ith component of $s(t)$ is the recovered signals by the BSS decryption, which is defined as follows:

$$SNR_i = 10\log_{10}\frac{\sum_{i=1}^{T}\left[(WA)_{ij}s_i(t)\right]^2}{\sum_{j=1}^{M}\sum_{i=1}^{T}\left[(WA)_{ij}s_j\right]^2} \ , \quad i \neq j$$

(14)

where W is the demixing matrix which results from the BSS decryption algorithm used. A is the mixing matrix corresponding to the mixed signals for the BSS decryption, similar to (12). $(WA)_{ij}$, denotes the ith row and the jth column of matrix WA . In (14), the order of the recovered signals is assumed to be the same as that of the source signals, which can be done by permuting the rows of WA.

2. The signal to interference ratio (SIR). If the mixing matrix is A then for the mixed signal transmitted in the channel, the SIR for the ith frame f_i can be measured according to the formula:

$$SIR_i = \frac{A_{ii}\sum_{n=1}^{k}(f_n)^2}{\sum_{\substack{j=1 \\ j\neq i}}^{k}\sum_{m=1}^{k}(A_{ij}f_{jm})^2}$$

(15)

Figure 4. A block diagram of scrambling algorithms (PCA /JADE)

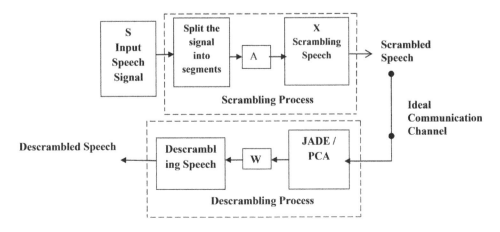

211

The formula of (15) implies that the useful data mixed into the transmit signal are assumed to be additional interference. The validity of this assumption can be appreciated for the case of speech by reference to the cocktail party problem. In this context, competing speech is considered to be the worst case of interference for clear speech.

3. LPC Distance

LPC Distance is used mostly in audio signal processing and speech processing for representing the spectral envelope of a digital signal of speech in compressed form, using the information about a linear predictive model. It is one of the most powerful speech analysis techniques, and one of the most useful methods for encoding good quality speech at a low bit rate and provides extremely accurate estimates of speech parameters.

$$d_{lpc}(c,e) = \ln\left(\frac{a_e R_c a_e^T}{a_c R_c a_c^T}\right) \tag{16}$$

where R_c is the autocorrelation matrix of the clear speech block, vector a_c contains the LPC coefficients for the clear speech block and vector a_ε contains the LPC coefficients for the scrambled speech block.

Figure 5. Plots for two algorithms (JADE and PCA)

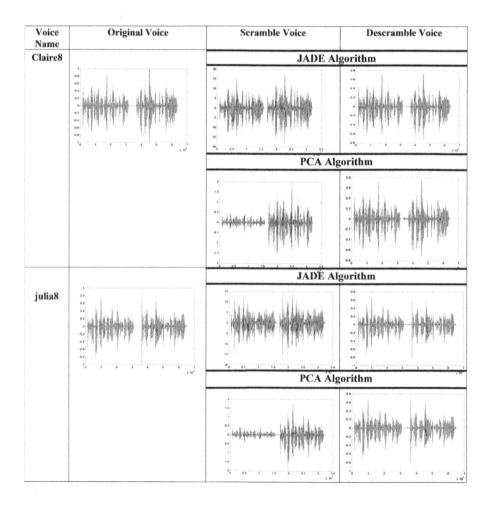

RESULTS AND DISCUSION

To test the validity of the proposed system in Figure 4, the speech was taken from the web page http://www.1speechsoft.com/voices.html, with the variety of samples, and frequency samples. The sentence is "This is an example of the AT&T natural voice speech engine; it is the most human sounding text to speech engine in the world". The results of the two measures (SNR and LPC) are used for the original and scrambled speech as shown in Table 1.

Figure 5 shows the original, scrambled and descrambled forms of the tested signals. It is evident from this table the PCA algorithm is better than JADE algorithm in both SNR and LPC measures

in sampling frequency 8kHz, the difference is very small, while in 16kHz also PCA algorithms is better than JADE algorithms in SNR measure (Sattar B. Sadkhan & Nidaa A. Abbas, 2011).

FUTURE RESEARCH DIRECTIONS

In signal processing, there is a general problem of separating useful signal from noise and interference. The classical approach based on the twentieth century prior assumptions, leading to model probability parameters. Blind source separation (BSS) is trying to reduce these assumptions to the weakest possible. Still many algorithms within the ICA and PCA subject have not been applied

Table 1. Comparison between two algorithms (PCA and JADE)

NO.	Voice Name	Gender	Length Of Voice	Length Of Segment	Type Of Voice	PCA			JADE		
						LPC Distance	SNR	Time in Second	LPC Distance	SNR	Time in Second
1.	Claire8	female	64772	32386	8 bits	7.6392×10^{-4}	12.5689	21.119	7.6296×10^{-4}	13.0003	21.444
2.	julia8	female	65644	32822	8 bits	3.2893×10^{-4}	15.9921	21.412	3.2916×10^{-4}	16.3683	21.469
3.	lauren8	female	64564	32282	8 bits	6.2191×10^{-4}	11.5809	21.085	6.2179×10^{-4}	11.737	21.703
4.	mel8	male	61012	30506	8 bits	8.7876×10^{-4}	10.5325	19.913	8.7828×10^{-4}	10.6681	19.92
5.	Ray8	male	61038	30519	8 bits	1.4×10^{-3}	10.5668	19.863	1.4×10^{-3}	10.7795	19.943
6.	Rich8	male	63630	31815	8 bits	6.1486×10^{-4}	9.2174	20.736	6.1474×10^{-4}	9.2864	20.759
7.	Claire16	female	129546	64773	16 bits	3.0082×10^{-4}	12.5502	21.186	3.005×10^{-4}	12.9872	22.01
8.	Julia16	female	131328	65664	16 bits	1.7166×10^{-4}	15.9727	21.343	1.7167×10^{-4}	16.3278	22.111
9.	Lauren16	female	129128	64564	16 bits	4.6653×10^{-4}	11.5876	21.138	4.6637×10^{-4}	11.7338	21.05
10.	mel16	male	122026	61013	16 bits	4.0124×10^{-4}	10.5363	20.0	4.012×10^{-4}	10.6704	20.377
11.	Ray16	male	122112	61056	16 bits	9.5218×10^{-4}	10.5701	20.039	9.5194×10^{-4}	10.782	20.007
12.	Rich16	male	127296	63648	16 bits	3.5561×10^{-4}	9.2169	20.796	3.5554×10^{-4}	9.2874	20.918

to find out the most efficient algorithm of others. The field is still open for application like stream cipher using binary ICA with XOR mixtures

CONCLUSION

We have described a BSS based speech encryption system. For underdetermined BSS problem, there are two main aspects for the proposed system to ensure its security. *First,* the system encrypts multiple original speech (or multiple images simultaneously) segments within each frame simultaneously instead of treating every segment of speech independently. This makes multiple original speech segments be covered mutually through mixing between them while the key signals cover them. As a result, the encrypted speech sounds like white noise. With the BSS accurate decryption, the proposed system, however, can still achieve excellent audio quality for the recovered speech by separating the key signals out from the encrypted speech segments. *Second*, the system can generate statistically independent key signals for different original speech segments, and does not impose any restriction on the key space. Therefore, the system has a very high level of security, and is suitable for transmitting and storing the secure speech files. From the evaluation tests performed on the scrambled and descrambled speech, we determine that:

- The unintelligibility of the tested scrambled speech.
- The proposed scrambling process is bandwidth preserving operation.
- It is very difficult to decrypt. Hence it is cryptanalytically strong or secure.
- Communication delay caused by scrambling process is small.
- The recovered speech signal at the receiving side is of the good quality and preserves both the intelligibility of the speech and the characteristics of the speaker.

On other hand BSS-based encryption scheme suffers from several security defects, including its vulnerability to a ciphertext-only differential attack, known/chosen-plaintext attack and chosen-ciphertext attack. It remains to see how the BSS-based technique can be further improved for constructing cryptographically strong ciphers.

REFERENCES

Hyvrinen, Karhunen & Oja. (2001). *Independent Component Analysis*. New York: Wiley John and Sons.

Mohaisen & Hong. (2008). Mitigating the ICA Attack against Rotation Based Transformation for Privacy Preserving Clustering. *ETRI Journal, 30*(6), 868–870.

Mermoul & Belouchrani. (2010). A Subspace-based Method for Speech Encryption. In *Proceedings of 10th International Conference on Information Science, Signal Processing and their Applications* (ISSPA 2010), (pp. 538-541). Kuala Lumpur: IEEE.

Mermoul. (2011). An Iterative Speech Encryption Scheme based on Subspace Technique. In *Proceedings of 2011 7th International Workshop on Systems, Signal Processing and their Applications* (WOSSPA), (pp. 361-364). Tipaza, Algeria: IEEE.

Guo & Lin. (2010). Fast Decryption Utilizing Correlation Calculation for BSS-based Speech Encryption System. In *Proceedings of Sixth International Conference on Natural Computation* (ICNC 2010), (pp. 1428- 1432). Yantai, China: IEEE.

Mavroeidis, B. van Laarhoven, & Marchiori. (2012). PCA, Eigenvector Localization and Clustering for Side-Channel Attacks on Cryptographic Hardware Devices. In *Proceedings of the 2012 European Conference on Machine Learning and Knowledge Discovery in Databases* (Vol. 1, pp.253-268). Bristol, UK: Springer-Verlag.

Hong & Mohaisen. (2010). Augmented Rotation-Based Transformation for Privacy-Preserving Data Clustering. *ETRI Journal, 32*(3), 351–361.

Moreau & Comon. (2010). Contrasts. In P. Comon, & C. Jutten (Eds.), *Handbook of Blind Source Separation Independent Component Analysis and Applications* (pp. 65–105). Oxford, UK: Elsevier.

Beker & Piper. (1985). *Secure Speech Communications*. Orlando, FL: Academic Press.

van Tilborg. (1999). *Fundamentals of Cryptology: A Professional Reference and Interactive Tutorial*. London: Kluwer Academic.

Bell & Sejnowski. (1995). An information-maximization approach to blind separation and blind deconvolution. *Neural Computation, 7*(6), 1129–1159.

Cardoso. (1999). High-order contrasts for independent component analysis. *Neural Computation, 11*(1), 157-192.

Wright & Manic. (2010). The Analysis of Dimensionality Reduction Techniques in Cryptographic Object Code Classification. In *Proceedings of 3rd Conference on Human System Interactions* (HSI 2010), (pp. 157 – 162). Rzeszow, Poland: IEEE.

Hogenboom. (2010). *Principal Component Analysis and Side-Channel Attacks*. (Master Thesis). Radboud University Nijmegen.

Shlens. (2009). *A Tutorial on Principal Component Analysis*. Retrieved from http://www.snl.salk.edu/~shlens/pca.pdf

Pearson. (1901). On lines and planes of closest fit to systems of points in space. *Philosophical Magazine, 2*(6), 559–572.

Bohy, N. Samyde, & Quisquater. (2003). Principal and Independent Component Analysis for Cryptographic systems with Hardware Unmasked Units. In *Proceedings of e-Smart 2003*. Retrieved from http://130.203.133.150/viewdoc/download?doi=10.1.1.94.53&rep=rep1&type=pdf

Elaabid & Guilley. (2010). Practical Improvements of Profiled Side-Channel Attacks on a Hardware Crypto-Accelerator –extended version. In *Proceeding AFRICACRYPT'10 Proceedings of the Third international conference on Cryptology in Africa*, (pp. 243-260). Stellenbosch, South Africa: Springer-Verlag.

Abbas. (2009). Speech Scrambling Based on Principal Component Analysis. *MASAUM Journal of Computing, 1*(3), 452-456.

Doukas & Karadimas. (2008a). A Blind Source Separation Based Cryptography Scheme for Mobile Military Communication Applications. *WSEAS Transactions on Communications, 7*(12), 1235–1245.

Doukas & Karadimas. (2008b). Blind Source Separation for digital data protection. In Proceedings of the 10th WSEAS international conference on Mathematical methods, computational techniques and intelligent systems, (pp. 503-508). Corfu, Greece: WSEAS Press.

Comon & Jutten. (2010). Introduction. In P. Comon, & C. Jutten (Eds.), *Handbook of Blind Source Separation Independent Component Analysis and Applications* (pp. 1–22). Oxford, UK: Elsevier.

Lin, Y. Mie & Liang. (2004). A speech encryption algorithm based on blind source separation. In *Proceedings of ICCCAS 2004* (vol. 2, pp. 1013-1017). Chengdu, China: IEEE.

Lin, Y. (2005). Lecture Notes in Computer Science: Vol. 3497. *Liang* (pp. 544–549). Blind Source Separation-Based Encryption of Images and Speeches.

Lin, Y. Mei & Liang. (2006). A Fast Decryption Algorithm for BSS-Based Image Encryption. Lecture Notes in Computer Science, 3973, 318-325.

Sano, N. Sinohara & Yasusi. (2009). Privacy Preserving Independent Component Analysis. In *Proceedings of the 8th Workshop on Stochastic Numerics* (pp. 162-173). Kyoto University Research Institute for Mathematical.

Sadkhan & Abbas. (2011). Performance evaluation of speech scrambling methods based on statistical approach. *Fondazione Giorgio Ronchi, 5*, 601–614.

Sadkhan & Abbas. (2012). Speech Scrambling based on Wavelet Transform. In Baleanu (Ed.), Advances in Wavelet Theory and Their Applications in Engineering, Physics and Technology (pp. 41-58). InTech.

Li, Li, Lo & Chen. (2008). Cryptanalyzing an Encryption Scheme Based on Blind Source Separation. *IEEE Transactions on Circuits and Systems, 55*(4), 1055–1063.

Dong, Lei & Yang. (2013). An Algorithm for Underdetermined Mixing Matrix Estimation. *Neurocomputing, 104*, 26–34.

Kasprzak & Cichocki. (1996). Hidden Image Separation from Incomplete Image Mixtures by Independent Component Analysis. In *Proc. of the 13th Int. ConJ on Pattern Recognition* (Vol. 11, pp. 394–398). Vienna, Austria: IEEE.

Fei, Liu, & Zheng. (2008). A Chaotic Encryption System Using PCA Neural Networks. In *Proceedings of 2008 IEEE Conference on Cybernetics and Intelligent Systems* (pp. 465 – 469). Chengdu, China: IEEE.

Souissi, Nassar, & Guilley, Danger & Flament. (2010). First Principal Components Analysis: A New Side Channel Distinguisher. *Lecture Notes in Computer Science, 6829*, 407–419.

ADDITIONAL READING

Hyvarinen, A., & Oja, E. (2000). Independent Component Analysis: Algorithms and Applications. *Neural Networks, 13*(4-5), 411–430.

Andrzej Cichocki & Shun-ichi Amari. (2002). *Adaptive Blind Signal and Image Processing Learning Algorithms and Applications*. England: Wiley John and Sons.

Cao, X. R., & Liu, R. W. (1996). General Approach to Blind Source Separation. *IEEE Transactions on Signal Processing, 44*(3), 562–571.

Cardoso, J. F., & Souloumiac, A. (1993). Blind Beamforming for Non Gaussian Signals. *IEE Proceedings. Part F. Radar and Signal Processing, 140*(6), 362–370.

Cardoso, J. F. (1998). Blind Signal Separation: Statistical Principles, Proceedings of the SYSID'97, 11th IFAC symposium on system identification, *86(10)*, (pp. 2009–2025), Fukuoka, Japan: IEEE

Fyfe, C. (2005). *Hebbian Learning and Negative Feedback Networks*. London: Springer-Verlag.

Comon, P. (1994). Independent Component Analysis, a New Concept? *Signal Processing, 36*(3), 287–314.

Himberg, J., & Hyvarinen, A. (2001). Independent Component Analysis for Binary Data: An Experimental Study, In Proc. Int. Workshop on Independent Component Analysis and Blind Signal Separation (ICA2001), (pp.552-556), San Diego, California.

Hinton, G. E., Welling, M., The, Y. W., & Osindero, S. K. (2001). A New View of ICA, In Proc. Int. Workshop on Independent Component Analysis and Blind Signal Separation (ICA2001), (pp. 746-751), San Diego, California.

Mackay, D. J. (Ed.). (2003). *Information Theory, Inference, and Learning Algorithms*. New York: Cambridge University Press.

Mansour, A., Jutten, C., & Ohnishi, N. (1998). Kurtosis: Definition and Properties, in The 1998 International Conference on Multisource-Multisensor: Data Fusion (FUSION'98), (pp. 40-46). Las Vegas, USA.

Oja, E., Karhunen, J., & Hyvarinen, A. (1997). From Neural PCA to Neural ICA, In Proc. Int. Conf. on Artificial Neural Networks (ICANN'98), Lausanne, Switzerland, (pp. 1-13). Sweden: Springer

Comon, P., & Jutten, C. (Eds.). (2010). *Handbook of Blind Source Separation Independent Component Analysis and Applications*. Oxford, UK: Elsevier.

Sergios Theodoridis & Konstantinos Koutroumbas. (2003). *Pattern Recognition*. USA: Elsevier.

Sergios Theodoridis & Konstantinos Koutroumbas. (2006). *Pattern Recognition*. USA: Elsevier.

Huang, T.-M., Kecman, V., & Kopriva, I. (2006). *Kernel Based Algorithms for Mining Huge Data Sets Supervised, Semi-supervised, and Unsupervised Learning*. New York: Springer Berlin Heidelberg.

KEY TERMS AND DEFINITIONS

Blind Source Separation (BSS): Is a technique of array signal processing that aims to recover a set of unknown mutually independent source signals from their observed mixtures without knowing the mixing coefficients.

Cryptology: The study of cryptosystems can be divided into two disciplines. Cryptography is interested in the design of cryptosystems, while cryptanalysis studies the breaking of cryptosystems.

Independent Component Analysis (ICA): Is a statistical and computational technique for revealing hidden factors that underlie sets of random variables, measurements, or signals.

Principal Component Analysis (PCA): Is a statistical method that consists in reducing the dimension of a data set through linear combinations.

Speech Scrambling: Seeks to perform a completely reversible operation on a portion of speech, that is totally unintelligible to unauthorized listener.

Underdetermined Source Separation: If the number of sources N is larger than the number of sensors P, the mixing is referred to as underdetermined, and is not invertible.

Chapter 9
An Area–Efficient Composite Field Inverter for Elliptic Curve Cryptosystems

M. M. Wong
Swinburne University of Technology – Sarawak, Malaysia

M. L. D. Wong
Swinburne University of Technology – Sarawak, Malaysia

ABSTRACT

This chapter presents a new area-efficient composite field inverter of the form $GF(q^l)$ with $q=2^{n.m}$ suitable for the hardware realization of an elliptic curve (EC) cryptosystem. Considering both the security aspect and the hardware cost required, the authors propose the utilization of the composite field $GF(((2^2)^2)^{41})$ for EC cryptosystem. For efficient implementation, they have derived a compact inversion circuit over $GF(2^{164})=GF(((2^2)^2)^{41})$ to achieve an optimal saving in the hardware cost required. Furthermore, the authors have also developed a composite field digit serial Sunar-Koc multiplier for the multiplication in the extension field. All of the arithmetic operations in the subfield $GF(2^4)$ are performed in its isomorphic composite field, $GF((2^2)^2)$, leading to a full combinatorial implementation without resorting to the conventional look-up table approach. To summarize the work, the final hardware implementation and the complexity analysis of the inversion is reported towards the end of this chapter.

INTRODUCTION

In recent years, elliptic curve cryptography (ECC) (Koblitz, 1991; Miller, 1986) has attracted an increasing research interest among cryptography researchers. Many researchers have proposed ECC as the means for public key cryptography where two separate keys (credentials) are used for encrypting and decrypting data. The main reason

for the popularity of ECC is owing to the elegance of the mathematics behind ECC and its ability to achieve strong cryptosystems efficiently.

Along with the emergence of ECC in public key cryptography, several EC hardware cryptographic applications have gained their popularity as well. Unlike the software cryptosystems, which are flexible in designs, the hardware cryptosystem realizations are rather constrained in terms

DOI: 10.4018/978-1-4666-5808-0.ch009

of area cost, power consumption and achievable performance.

In the literature, several efficient EC hardware cryptosystems were reported (Chelton & Benaissa, 2008; Sakiyama, Batina, Preneel, & Verbauwhede, 2007; Hein, Wolkerstorfer, & Felber, 2009; Gutub, Tenca, Savas, &Koç, 2003; Goodman & Chandrakasan, 2001; Bednara, Daldrup, Gathen, Shokrollahi, & Teich, 2002; Rodríguez-Henríquez, Morales-Luna, Saqib, & Cruz-Cortés, 2007). Most of these architectures were designed for arbitrary finite fields (either prime fields or binary fields) as opposed to using a specific field. Hence, the efforts were mostly devoted to the issues of reconfigurability and scalability of the ECC processor in achieving high speed or compact cryptosystem. Very few studies were reported on the algorithmic optimization in EC hardware cryptosystem.

As ECC works in the finite field, the complexity of the arithmetic of its underlying field will determine the resources required in the final cryptosystem. Consequently, the first, and the most essential step in constructing a compact and efficient EC hardware cryptosystem is to choose the suitable field for ECC computation. In addition, the scalar multiplication, *kP*, is the most crucial and yet the most complicated operation in any ECC applications. The reason being is that the scalar multiplication in affine space involves a repetition of point additions and point doublings, both requires inversions over the finite field (Hankerson, Menezes, & Vanstone, 2004). Therefore, optimization in the field level is required to search for the potential area minimization of scalar multiplication defined in the affine space. In this work, we present a new efficient inversion circuit through the exploitation of composite field arithmetic for EC hardware cryptosystem.

Overall, our contributions in this work are twofold: First, we introduce an efficient three-level isomorphism composite field, $GF(((2^2)^2)^{41})$, suitable for hardware EC cryptosystems. Second, we propose a new combinatorial inverter using

the Itoh and Tsujii inversion (ITI) algorithm in optimal normal type II basis representation (ON-BII) to eliminate the need for LUTs completely. In addition to that, we present a series of algorithmic optimizations in the subfield $GF((2^2)^2)$ operations, and also a composite field digit serial Sunar-Koc multiplier in the extension field, in order to achieve better area reduction in our design.

BACKGROUND

Composite Binary Field in Elliptic Curve Cryptography

Optimizing an EC cryptosystem at the field level involves three major steps (Kumar,2006):

1. Choose a finite field GF(p) such that the underlying arithmetic is both efficient and intractable.
2. Choose the irreducible polynomial P(x) and the field elements' representations that will simplify the operations' arithmetic.
3. Select an efficient finite field arithmetic algorithm for field addition, multiplication, inversion and reduction.

The first composite field EC cryptosystem was proposed by Harper et. al. (Harper, Menezes, & Vanstone, 1993) using the form $GF((2^n)^m) = GF((2^8)^{13})$ to mitigate the bottleneck caused by the scalar multiplication. Soon after, several works in composite field $GF((2^{16})^{11})$ for EC cryptosystems were also reported independently (Beauregard, 1996; Win, Bosselaers, Vandenberghe, Gersem, & Vandewalle, 1996; Guajardo & Paar, 1997).

However, the work of Frey, Galbraith, Gaudry, Hess and Smart have cast the doubt on the security offered by the composite field as compared to the fields defined in the standards (Gaudry, Hess,

&Smart, 2002; Galbraith & Smart, 1999; Smart, 2001). In this chapter, we argue that ECC defined in composite field is not necessarily weak and this will be discussed in the following section.

Elliptic Curve Discrete Logarithm Problem (ECDLP) in Composite Field

The elliptic curve discrete logarithm problem (ECDLP) is defined as follows. Given an elliptic curve E, defined over a finite field GF(q), a point $P \in E(GF(p))$ of order r, and a second point $Q \in \langle P \rangle$, determine the integer $l \in [0, r-1]$ such that Q = lP. The intractability of the ECDLP will determine the level of security of the EC cryptosystems (Menezes, Teske, &Weng, 2004; Menezes&Teske, 2006).

The best known algorithm for solving the general ECDLP, the Pollard's rho method(Pollard, 1978), which requires an exponential expected running time of $\sqrt{\pi r} / 2$ points additions in solving the ECDLP in ECC (Menezes et al., 2004; Menezes&Teske, 2006). Any field with its instance of the ECDLP that can be solved in a significantly less time than it takes Pollard's rho method to solve the hardest instances is considered weak. In this work, we need to determine a composite field that is not weak for ECC.

In 2000, Gaudry, Hess and Smart (GHS) (Gaudry et al., 2002) showed that the Weil descent attack proposed by Frey (Frey, n.d.) can be used to reduce the ECDLP in the elliptic curves over composite field to an instance of discrete logarithm problem (DLP) in the Jacobian of a hyperelliptic curve over $GF(2^N)$. The study reported only for the case of a prime number $N \in [160, 600]$, $GF(2^N)$ is proven secure from the GHS attack (Menezes&Qu, 2001). In other words, the use of elliptic curves over $GF(2^N)$ where N is a divisible number is not recommended.

For this reason, various investigations had been conducted to confirm the vulnerability caused by using the composite field in ECC (Galbraith & Smart, 1999; Smart, 2001; Maurer,Menezes, &Teske, 2001; Menezes&Teske, 2006; Menezes et al., 2004). The work reported in (Galbraith & Smart, 1999; Smart, 2001; Menezes et al., 2004) provided some evidences that the curves over the fields of composite degree divisible by 3, 4 and 5 should be avoided in cryptographic applications. However, their deductions were proven only for curves of a small range.

Menzes and Teske further explored the cryptographic implications of the generalized GHS attack (see (Hess, 2004)) in binary composite field, $GF(2^N)$ (Menezes&Teske, 2006).In their work, they concluded that the field where N is not divisible by 3, 5, 6,7 or 8 are not(potentially) weak under Hess's generalized GHS attack. Later date, the applicability of the GHS attack on the ECDLP for elliptic curves over $GF(2^N)$ for composite $N \in [160, 600]$ was analyzed by Maurer et al. thoroughly in (Maurer et al., 2001). The elliptic curves over composite field that is susceptible to the GHS attack were identified and listed in their paper. We have adopted this list to select the composite field that is not weak under GHS attack.

OPTIMIZATION FOR ELLIPTIC CURVE HARDWARE CRYPTOSYSTEMS

Proposing a Novel Composite Field Inverter for EC Cryptosystems

Basically, the optimization approach proposed here can be divided into two major parts. First, we select an optimal composite field along with its respective field polynomial and basis representation for EC cryptosystem. While the compact inverter of the general field is commonly reported in the literature, we propose a new area-efficient inverter of specific field such that algorithmic optimization can be employed more effectively to achieve further area reduction. The chosen field has to be both secure and result in compact arithmetic operations which are feasible for small cryptographic applications. We choose composite field here as it provides greater computational efficiency compared to other finite field.

Second, we derive a novel combinatorial inverter for composite field EC hardware cryptosystem. Based on the literature surveys, two main approaches for the inversion over finite field can be found in ECC. These are, namely, the extended Euclidean algorithm (EEA) and the Fermat's Little Theorem (FLT). Win et. al. applied the optimized version of EEA, the Almost Inverse Algorithm (Schroeppel, Orman, O'Malley, &Spats check, 1995) $GF((2^{16})^{11})$ in (Win et al., 1996). On the other hand, the FLT-based inversion, realized as the ITI algorithm (Itoh&Tsujii, 1988; Guajardo &Paar, 2002) for polynomial basis representation over $GF((2^{16})^{11})$ was proposed by Guajardo and Paar (Guajardo &Paar,1997).

However, all of these prior studies were designed with software implementations in mind, where usually look-up tables (LUTs) are utilized in the computation of the subfield arithmetic. Apart from consuming large silicon areas, the use of LUTs in hardware realization will introduce an unbreakable timing delay which in turn will predominate the minimum clock rate attainable by the final cryptosystem. To avoid this delay while saving on silicon areas, one can opt for the combinatorial approach where only combinatorial logic components are used for the final computation. This approach also allows the designer to further improve the clock rate through inserting standard pipeline registers at appropriate points of the system.

To the best of our knowledge, this is the first work that applies the ITI algorithm in ONBII representation for composite field inversion in EC hardware cryptosystems. In addition to that, the inversion involved several multiplications in the extension field and therefore, we proposed a composite field digit serial Sunar-Koc multiplier.

Optimal Normal Basis (ONB) Representation for EC Cryptosystems

The normal basis representation is often a preferred choice over the polynomial basis representation in hardware implementation. The reason is that in normal basis representation, squaring of an element can be performed through a simple cyclic shift. Furthermore, ONB, the special case in normal basis representations, manages to further reduce the complexity of the complicated normal basis multipliers (Savas&Koç, December 1999). Based on these advantages, we choose to work on elliptic curve over composite field of $GF(q^l)$ with $q = 2^{n.m}$ in ONB representation.

For security purposes, the extension field, l, has to be a considerably large prime number and therefore, ONB type II representation is sought here. On the other hand, the subfields n and m, are chosen to be relatively smaller in order to simplify the computation in ECC. Practically, the common choices for the composite binary field $GF(2^N)$ are in the range of $N \in [160, 600]$ (Menezes&Teske, 2006). Our main objective here is to cater the small scale cryptographic applications and ensure that our composite field EC cryptosystem is not vulnerable towards the generalized GHS attack. Hence, we have chosen our field $GF(q^l)$ where the subfield, $q = (2^n)^m = (2^2)^2 \cong 2^4$ and the extension field of prime order, $l = 41$.

In short, we choose $GF(((2^2)^2)^{41})$ for our EC hardware cryptosystem implementation. Next, we perform algorithmic optimization in the multiplicative inversion, the most resource consuming operation, in order to promote further saving in terms of area cost and power consumption. In the next sections, we discuss the derivation of an efficient and yet compact composite field inversion circuit.

Efficient and Compact Inversion over Composite Field $GF(((2^2)^2)^{41})$

In this section, we present the required inversion operation for $GF(((2^2)^2)^{41})$ in ONBII. As the FLT states that, with $A \in GF((2^n)^m)$ and $P(x)$ is an irreducible polynomial defined over $GF((2^n)^m)$ one can obtain $A^{2^{nm}-1} = A.A^{2^{nm}-2} = 1 \bmod P(x)$. Therefore, we can write the inversion of A as;

$$A^{-1} = A^{2^{nm}}$$
$$\equiv (A^{2^{q-1}-1})^2 \tag{1}$$

with q-1 as;

$$q - 1 = \sum_{i=1}^{t} 2^{k_i}, \text{ where } k_1 > k_2 > ... > k_t \tag{2}$$

Using both (1) and (2), A^{-1} can be derived using the chain additions as follows:

$$(A^{2^{q-1}-1})^2 = [(A^{2^{k_t}-1})((A^{2^{2^{k_t-1}}-1})...$$
$$[(A^{2^{2^{k_2}}-1})(A^{2^{2^{k_1}}-1})^{2^{2^{k_2}}}]^{2^{2^{k_3}}}...)2^{2^{k_t}}]^2 \tag{3}$$

Furthermore, the ITI algorithm (Theorem 4.1) that is employed in this work, reduces the inversion over the extension field $GF(q^l)$ to the inversion over its subfield, GF(q). Afterwards, the subfield inversion can be easily performed using the method described in Step 3.

Theorem 1 (Itoh & Tsujii, 1988)

$Let A \in GF((2^n)^m)$, $A \neq 0$ and $r = (n^m - 1) / (n - 1)$. The inverse of an element A can be computed as $A^{-1} = (A^r)^{-1}.A^{r-1}$, with $A \in GF(2^n)$

We shall now present the four major steps required to compute the inversion using the ITI algorithm in the following subsections. Henceforth, we will denote our working field as $GF(q^l)$ with $q = ((2^2)^2)$ and $l = 41$.

Step 1: Exponentiation of $A^{r-1} \in GF(q^l)$

Based on Theorem 1, we need to first determine the computation of A^{r-1} where $A^{r-1} \in GF(q^l)$. Note that the exponent $r-1$ can be expressed as a sum of powers:

$$r - 1 = \frac{ql - 1}{q - 1} - 1$$
$$= q + q^2 + q^3 + ... + q^{l-1} \tag{4}$$

Using (3) and (4), the $A^{r-1} = A^{q^{40}+q^{39}+q^{38}+\cdots+q^2+q}$ can be computed through a series of repeated power raising and multiplications such as follows:

$$A^{q^2} = (A^q)^q$$
$$A^q.A^{q^2} = A^{q^2+q}$$
$$(A^{q^2+q})^{q^2}.(A^{q^2+q}) = A^{q^4+q^3+q^2+q} = A^{\sum_{i=1}^{4} q^i}$$
$$(A^{\sum_{i=1}^{4} q^i})^{q^4}.A^{\sum_{i=1}^{4} q^i} = A^{q^8+q^7+...+q} = A^{\sum_{i=1}^{8} q^i}$$
$$(A^{\sum_{i=1}^{8} q^i})^{q^8}.A^{\sum_{i=1}^{8} q^i} = A^{q^{16}+q^{15}+...+q} = A^{\sum_{i=1}^{16} q^i}$$
$$(A^{\sum_{i=1}^{16} q^i})^{q^{16}}.A^{\sum_{i=1}^{16} q^i} = A^{q^{32}+q^{31}+...+q} = A^{\sum_{i=1}^{32} q^i}$$
$$A^{r-1} = (A^{q^{32}+q^{31}+...+q})^{q^8}.A^{q^8+q^7+...+q} \tag{5}$$

Therefore, the computation of A^{r-1} requires (Itoh&Tsujii, 1988);

$$
\begin{aligned}
\# \, MUL &= \left\lfloor \log_2(l-1) \right\rfloor + HW(l-1) - 1 \\
\# \, EXP &= l - 1
\end{aligned}
$$

(6)

The complexity to compute A^{r-1} using the addition chain (see (5)) is found to be six multiplications in $GF(q^{41})$ and 40 exponentiations to the power of qth, which agrees with (6). The exponentiation to the qth power in normal basis requires only q cyclic shifts. This is significantly more efficient than using the polynomial basis representation which requires modular reduction (Guajardo &Paar, 1997). Meanwhile, the $GF(((2^2)^2)^{41})$ multiplier will be described in the next section.

Step 2: Multiplication of A and A^{r-1} that Yield $A^r \in GF(q)$

In the second step, multiplication of two operands, A, $A^{r-1} \in GF(q^{41})$ will result in $A^r \in GF(q)$. Therefore, we need a specific multiplier which computes only the first coefficient, a_0, of the general multiplication in $GF(q^{41})$.

In this case, we only need to cater the computation for β_1 in C_1, D_1 and D_2 (see Table 2). Similar to the ordinary ONBII multiplication, permutation is first performed on both operands. Next, we will have,

$$
\begin{aligned}
a_0 &= (a_1 b_2 + a_2 b_1) + (a_2 b_3 + a_3 b_2) + \ldots \\
&\quad + (a_{40} b_{41} + a_{41} b_{40}) + (a_{41} b_{41})
\end{aligned}
$$

(7)

which requires a total of 81 multiplications and 81 additions over $GF((2^2)^2)$. While the $GF((2^2)^2)$ multiplication will be described in Step 4, take note that the additions in finite field of character-

istic two are implemented using XOR operation. Last, the resultant a_0 is converted back to its original basis through inverse permutation.

Step 3: Inversion in $GF(q)$ Yields $(A^r)^{-1}$

To avoid the use of LUTs, we design a combinatorial circuit to perform the inversion over the composite field $GF((2^2)^2)$ with respect to normal basis representation. The following irreducible polynomials are required for the computation:

$$
s(z) = z^2 + Tz + 1
$$

(8)

(isomorphism for $GF(2^4)\,/\,GF(2^2)$)

$$
t(w) = w^2 + w + 1
$$

(9)

(isomorphism for $GF(2^2)\,/\,GF(2)$)

Let $\gamma, \delta \in GF(2^4)$, we denote the inverse of $\gamma = (\Gamma_1 Z^4 + \Gamma_0 Z)$ as $\delta = (\Delta_1 Z^4 + \Delta_0 Z)$, which can be computed as stated in (10),

$$
(\Gamma_1 Z^4 + \Gamma_0 Z)^{-1} = [\Gamma_1 \Theta]Z^4 + [\Gamma_0 \Theta]Z
$$

(10)

where $\Theta = [\Gamma_0 \Gamma_1 T^2 + (\Gamma_0^2 + \Gamma_1^2)]^{-1}$. The arithmetic in (10) is further decomposed into arithmetic in the subfield. Therefore, we denote both $g = (g_1 W^2 + g_0 W)$ and $d = (d_1 W^2 + d_0 W)$ as the elements in $GF(2^2)$. Detailed descriptions of the employed architecture can be found in (Wong, Wong, Nandi, &Hijazin, 2011). To summarize, the arithmetic required over the inversion is tabulated in Table 1. The total complexity of our inverter is 9 ANDs and 17 XORs.

Next, we employ an optimization scheme which exploits Algebraic Normal Form (ANF) representation and followed by a sub-structure sharing optimization (Wong &Wong, 2010). This is per-

Table 1. Inversion over $GF((2^2)^2)$ using composite field arithmetic in normal basis representation

Operation	Equation
Inversion in $GF(2^4)$	$\Delta_1 = [\Gamma_1\Gamma_0 T^2 + (\Gamma_1^2 + \Gamma_0^2)]^{-1}\Gamma_0$
	$\Delta_0 = [\Gamma_1\Gamma_0 T^2 + (\Gamma_1^2 + \Gamma_0^2)]^{-1}\Gamma_1$
Inversion in $GF(2^2)$	$d_1 = g_0$
	$d_0 = g_1$
Multiplication in $GF(2^2)$	$[(g_1 + g_0)(d_1 + d_0) + (g_1 d_1)]W^2 + [(g_1 + g_0)(d_1 + d_0) + (g_0 d_0)]W$

formed by converting the subfield $GF((2^2)^2)$ inversion into several logical expressions, which will then be reduced using a common subexpression elimination (CSE) algorithm. As a result from this optimization scheme, the total area of our ANF represented $GF((2^2)^2)$ inversion is now reduced to 8 ANDs and 12 XORs.

Step 4: Multiplication of $(A^r)^{-1}.A^{r-1}$

In the final step, we need to multiply $A^{r-1} \in GF(q^l)$ (from Step 1) and $(A^r)^{-1} \in GF(q)$ (from Step 3) to deduce A^{-1}. This step requires 41 multiplication in GF(q), which will be described in the following.

Table 2. Construction of C_1, D_1 and D_2

	β_1	β_2	β_3	...	β_{39}	β_{40}	β_{41}
C_1	$a_1 b_2 + a_2 b_1$ $a_2 b_3 + a_3 b_2$ $\vdots$ $a_{40} b_{41} + a_{41} b_{40}$	$a_1 b_3 + a_3 b_1$ $a_2 b_4 + a_4 b_2$ $\vdots$ $a_{39} b_{41} + a_{41} b_{39}$	$a_1 b_4 + a_4 b_1$ $a_2 b_5 + a_5 b_2$ $\vdots$ $a_{38} b_{41} + a_{41} b_{38}$	...	$a_1 b_{40} + a_{40} b_1$ $a_2 b_{41} + a_{41} b_2$	$a_1 b_{41} + a_{41} b_1$	
D_1		$a_1 b_1$	$a_1 b_2 + a_2 b_1$	...	$a_1 b_{38} + a_{38} b_1$ $a_2 b_{37} + a_{37} b_2$ $\vdots$ $a_{19} b_{20} + a_{20} b_{19}$	$a_1 b_{39} + a_{39} b_1$ $a_2 b_{38} + a_{38} b_2$ $\vdots$ $a_{20} b_{20}$	$a_1 b_{40} + a_{40} b_1$ $a_2 b_{39} + a_{39} b_2$ $\vdots$ $a_{20} b_{21} + a_{21} b_{20}$
D_2	$a_{41} b_{41}$	$a_{40} b_{41} + a_{41} b_{40}$	$a_{39} b_{40} + a_{40} b_{39}$ $a_{40} b_{40}$	...	$a_3 b_{41} + a_{41} b_3$ $a_4 b_{40} + a_{40} b_4$ $\vdots$ $a_{22} b_{22}$	$a_2 b_{41} + a_{41} b_2$ $a_3 b_{40} + a_{40} b_3$ $\vdots$ $a_{21} b_{22} + a_{22} b_{21}$	$a_1 b_{41} + a_{41} b_1$ $a_2 b_{40} + a_{40} b_2$ $\vdots$ $a_{21} b_{21}$

$GF((2^2)^2)$ General Multiplication: Let $\gamma, \delta \in GF((2^2)^2)$ be $\{\Gamma_1 Z^4 + \Gamma_0 Z\}$ and $\{\Delta_1 Z^4 + \Delta_0 Z\}$ respectively. Multiplication of γ and δ can be derived as,

$$
\begin{aligned}
&(\Gamma_1 Z^4 + \Gamma_0 Z)(\Delta_1 Z^4 + \Delta_0 Z) \\
&= (\Gamma_1 \Delta_1)(Z^4)^2 + (\Gamma_1 \Delta_0 + \Gamma_0 \Delta_1)Z^4 Z + (\Gamma_0 \Delta_0)Z^2 \\
&= [(\Gamma_1 + \Gamma_0)(\Delta_1 + \Delta_0)N + \Gamma_1 \Delta_1]Z^4 + \\
&\quad [(\Gamma_1 + \Gamma_0)(\Delta_1 + \Delta_0)N + \Gamma_0 \Delta_0]Z
\end{aligned}
\tag{11}
$$

with 9 ANDs and 23 XORs. Next, we eliminate the redundant common factors in the $GF((2^2)^2)$ multiplier and followed by merging certain sub-operations within to improve area reduction. Note that in the $GF((2^2)^2)$ multiplier, there are two $T\Gamma$ scalers,

$$
\begin{aligned}
T\Gamma &= W^2(g_1 W^2 + g_0 W) \\
&= g_0 W + (g_1 + g_0)W^2
\end{aligned}
\tag{12}
$$

and a $T^2\Gamma$ scaler,

$$
\begin{aligned}
T^2\Gamma &= W(g_1 W^2 + g_0 W) \\
&= (g_1 + g_0)W + g_1 W^2
\end{aligned}
\tag{13}
$$

Furthermore, there are three $GF(2^2)$ multiplications, of which each is followed by a $T\Gamma$ scaler or $T^2\Gamma$ scaler. Therefore, we can combine the $GF(2^2)$ multiplier (see Table 1) with their respective scaler; (12) or (13) such as follows,

$$
\begin{aligned}
&GF(2^2) \text{ mult with } T\Gamma \\
&= [(g_1 + g_0)(d_1 + d_0) + (g_1 d_1)]W^2 + [(g_1 d_1 + g_0 d_0)]W \\
&GF(2^2) \text{ mult with } T^2\Gamma \\
&= [(g_1 d_1 + g_0 d_0)]W^2 + [(g_1 + g_0)(d_1 + d_0) + (g_1 d_1)]W
\end{aligned}
\tag{14}
$$

Using this approach, we achieve an additional reduction of three XORs. Therefore, the complexity of our $GF((2^2)^2)$ multiplier is reduced to 9 ANDs and 20 XORs only.

Composite Field Digit Serial Sunar-Koc Multiplication

While squaring and exponentiation in normal basis can be easily accomplished by cyclic shift (free operation), it is crucial to derive an area-efficient normal basis multiplier for our composite field inverter in EC cryptosystem. As discussed in previous section an inversion over $GF(((2^2)^2)^{41})$ requires six multiplications in the extension field. In this study, we have chosen to employ the Sunar-Koc multiplication algorithm. The Sunar-Koc multiplier (Koç&Sunar, 2001), requires 25% less XOR gates than the conventional Massey-Omura multipliers (Omura& Massey, May 1986). In a nutshell, the algorithm for deriving a Sunar-Koc multiplier involves the following:

1. Convert the elements represented in the basis M to the basis N (shifted canonical) through permutation.
2. Perform the multiplication in basis N.
3. Convert the result back to the basis M using inverse permutation. Sunar-Koc multiplier is a full parallel multiplier with high performance and consuming large scale of FPGA resource. The complexity and the time delay of this full parallel multiplier is summarized below:

$$
\begin{aligned}
&\# \text{XOR gates} = m^2 \\
&\# \text{AND gates} = m^2 - 1 \\
&Delay = T_A + (\lceil (m-2)/(m-n) \rceil + 1 + \lfloor \log_2(m-1) \rfloor)T_x
\end{aligned}
$$

However, the objective of this study is to design a compact inverter, suitable for smaller scale EC cryptosystem. Therefore, the default structure of Sunar-Koc multiplication is not suitable for our work.

While many works have reported on high performance bit parallel Sunar-Koc multiplier, the first bit serial Sunar-Koc multiplier was reported by Wang et al. in (Wang, Tian, Bi,&Niu, 2006). Unlike bit parallel architecture, bit serial multiplier is area-efficient, resource saving but slow in term of performance, which is only suitable for area-constrained and low-speed applications.

Here, we extend the work in (Wang et al., 2006) to derive a digit serial Sunar-Koc multiplier, that is both area-efficient and having moderate sample rates. In digit serial architecture, data words of length W are partitioned into digits of L bits and are processed at a rate of L bits per clock cycle that yields the output result on every $K = W/L$ clock cycles. Therefore, our multiplier of the field $GF(2^{164} \cong GF(((2^2)^2)^{41}))$ will be partitioned into $K = 41$ digit of $L = 4$ bits, and the arithmetic in the digit level will be performed using composite field arithmetic.

Let $A, B \in GF(q^{41})$, we need first to convert the operands to basis N;

$$A = \sum_{i=1}^{41} a_i\beta_i = \sum_{i=1}^{41} a_i(\gamma^i + \gamma^{-i})$$
$$B = \sum_{i=1}^{41} b_i\beta_i = \sum_{i=1}^{41} b_i(\gamma^i + \gamma^{-i})$$

Next, the product C=AB is computed as follows:

$$C = \left(\sum_{i=1}^{41} a_i(\gamma^i + \gamma^{-i})\right)\left(\sum_{j=1}^{41} b_j(\gamma^j + \gamma^{-j})\right)$$
$$= C_1 + D_1 + D_2 \text{ (see Table 2)}$$

with

$$C_1 = \sum_{1 \leq i,j \leq 41} a_i b_j(\gamma^{i-j} + \gamma^{-(i-j)}) \qquad (15)$$

$$D_1 = \sum_{i=1}^{41}\sum_{j=1}^{41-i} a_i b_j(\gamma^{i-j} + \gamma^{-(i+j)}) \qquad (16)$$

$$D_2 = \sum_{i=1}^{41} \sum_{j=42-i}^{41} a_i b_j(\gamma^{i-j} + \gamma^{-(i+j)}) \qquad (17)$$

The multiplication in basis N constructs C_1, D_1 and D_2 which are listed in Table 2.The sums of the appropriate terms will produce the productoftheoperandsAandB. $C = C_1 + D_1 + D_2$. Last, we need to convert the product C back to its original basis M using the inverse permutation.

Using the formula tabulated in Table 2, the structure of our digit serial multiplier designed in FPGA is as depicted in Figure 1. Based on the digit serial multiplier structure, two type of registers are required, *RegA* and *RegB*, consisting of $K.L$=164 bits long and $L(2 \times K+1)$= 332 bits long respectively. *RegA* is used to store the 41 operand a of order $a_1, a_2, a_3, ..., a_{41}$ of which each operand consists of 4 bits. Meanwhile *RegB* stores83 operands b of order $0, b_1, b_2, b_3, ..., b_{41}, b_{41}, b_{40}, b_{39}, ..., b_3, b_2, b_1$ of which each operation consists of 4 bits. Symbol L and N in the architectures represent 4-bit adder and 4-bitmultiplier. Unlike the previous work on digit serial multiplier, our architecture employed composite field for the arithmetic in the digit level. While the 4-bit adder can be constructed using 4 XOR gates, the 4-bit multiplier will be performed in the field $GF((2^2)^2)$. This $GF((2^2)^2)$ multiplier is as derived in (11).

A complexity comparison of the proposed digit serial multiplier to some popular normal basis (NB) multipliers is given in Table 3. The first row of the table stated the word level Massey-Omura multipliers (Omura& Massey, May 1986), while the improved Massey-Omura (IMO) (L. Gao&Sobelman, 2000) is stated in the second row. The third and fourth rows states the AND-efficient digit serial (AEDS) (Reyhani-Masoleh&Hasan, 2002) and XOR-efficient digit serial (XEDS) (Reyhani-Masoleh&Hasan, 2002) multiplier respectively. Meanwhile, the word level sequential multiplier with parallel output of type 1 and type

Figure 1. Digit Serial Multiplier for $GF(((2^2)^2)^{41})$

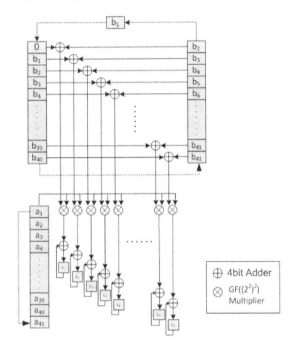

Note that we perform composite field arithmetic for the digit level multiplier, over the field $GF((2^2)^2)$, which has a complexity of 9 ANDs and 20 XORs and critical path of 1 AND and 4 XORs. Therefore, the total complexity of our proposed digit serial multiplier at the field $GF(((2^2)^2)^{41})$ will be 369 ANDs, 1148 XORs and using 496 bits register. Based on the analysis as tabulated in Table 3, it can be seen that our proposed architecture consumes the fewest number of AND gates and XOR gates. The number of registers is also comparable to the lowest number of registers required by previously reported work. It is also worth noting that the critical path of our architecture is 1 ANDs and 8 XORs, which is relatively small compared to the other NB multipliers.

Discussion and Results

2(Reyhani-Masoleh&Hasan, 2005) are stated in row fifth and sixth respectively.

The overview of our proposed $GF(((2^2)^2)^{41})$ inverter is as depicted in Figure 2. To demonstrate the efficacies of our inverter in EC hardware

Table 3. Complexity and performance for the proposed composite field digit serial multiplier versus other NB multipliers. Given W is the length of the data words and L is the length of the digits. Note that M_{AND}, M_{XOR} and Tm represents total AND gates, total XOR gates and the critical path of our digit level multiplier over $GF((2^2)^2)$.

Multiplier	#AND	#XOR	#Reg	Critical Path Delay	#Cycle	Basis
WLMO (Omura& Massey, May 1986)	N(2M-1)	N(2M-2)	2M	$T_A + (1 + \lfloor \log_2 M \rfloor T_x)$	$\lceil M/N \rceil$	NB
IMO (L. Gao&Sobelman, 2000)	NM	N(2M-2)	2M	$T_A + (1 + \lfloor \log_2 M \rfloor T_x)$	$\lceil M/N \rceil$	NB
AEDS (Reyhani-Masoleh&Hasan, 2002)	(N+1)M/2	(N+1)(3M/2-2) +1	2M	$T_A + (1 + \lfloor \log_2 M \rfloor T_x)$	$\lceil M/N \rceil$	NB
XEDS (Reyhani-Masoleh&Hasan, 2002)	N(M-1)+M	(N+1)(M-1)	2M	$T_A + (1 + \lfloor \log_2 M \rfloor T_x)$	$\lceil M/N \rceil$	NB
w-SMPOI (Reyhani-Masoleh&Hasan, 2005)	(NM/2) + M + N+ 1	2NM/2 +M+N-1	3M	$2T_A + (3 + \lceil \log_2 (N-1) \rceil T_x)$	$\lceil M/N \rceil$	NB
w-SMPOII (Reyhani-Masoleh&Hasan, 2005)	NM + M + N + 1	NM + M+N-1	3M	$2T_A + (3 + \lceil \log_2 (N-1) \rceil T_x)$	$\lceil M/N \rceil$	NB
Proposed work	(M/N)M_{AND}	4(2M/N)+(M/N)M_{XOR}	3M+N	$2T_A + T_m$	M/N	NB

cryptosystem, its computational cost is benchmarked with the previous works. From our literature review, the most recent and comparable work that we can find is the work by Guajardo and Paar, reported in 1997 (Guajardo &Paar, 1997).

Guajardo and Paar proposed a conversion scheme that is closely comparable to our work but in software implementation. Similar to our work, they had also employed the ITI algorithm for inversion over composite field elements. However, their arithmetic was performed in two levels composite field of $GF((2^n)^m)$, using the polynomial basis representation where LUTs were utilized for multiplication and inversion over $GF(2^n)$. Similar to the work by Guajardo and Paar, the other previous works of the composite

field EC cryptosystems (Guajardo &Paar, 1997; Beauregard, 1996; Win et al., 1996; Harper et al.,1993) also employed a pre-computed table method in the subfield arithmetic. This method is by the means of performing log and antilog conversion which is explained below.

As all the elements of $GF(2^n)$ form a cyclic group, the element $a_i \in GF(2^n)$ can be expressed as a multiple of a primitive element α, where $a_i = \alpha^i$. Therefore, all of the pair (a_i, i) will be stored in two tables, log-table sorted on the first component (a_i) and antilog-table sorted on the second component (i) (Guajardo &Paar, 1997; Win et al.,1996). Each of the table took up 2^n of n bits, resulting in a total memory requirement of 64bits for field $GF(2^4)$. These tables are used to calculate the multiplication and the inversion of

Figure 2. Overview of our proposed compact and efficient inversion over $GF(((2^2)^2)^{41})$. The $GF(((2^2)^2)^{41})$ multiplier in Step 1 is illustrated in Figure 1.

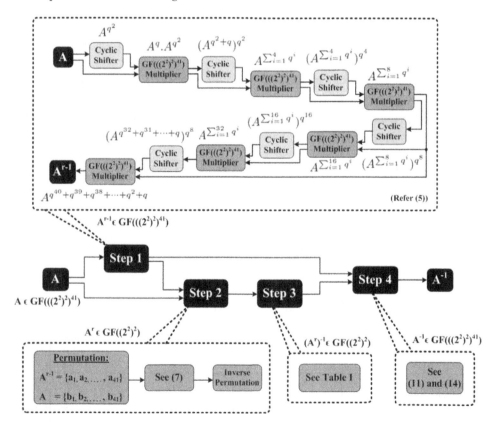

field elements $a_j, a_k \in GF(2^n)$. The product of two field elements can be derived as $a_j a_k = \text{antilog}[\log(a_k) + \log(a_j)] \;(\text{mod }(2^n-1))$. On the other hand, the inversion operation can be expressed as

$$a_j^{-1} = \text{antilog}[-\log(a_j) \;(\text{mod }(2^n-1))].$$

Based on these equations, one multiplication and one inversion over the subfield $GF(2^4)$ would take up three and two LUTs each.

Another pre-computed table method can be seen in the conventional LUT approach. This is done by having all the possible input combinations and their respective multiplication outputs are pre-computed and stored in memory form. In this case, only one LUT is required for each of the multiplication and inversion operation. This results in a total memory requirement of 480 bits for multiplication and 64 bits for inversion.

On the other hand, without using any LUT, our $GF((2^2)^2)$ inverter can be constructed using 8 ANDs and 12 XORs while our $GF((2^2)^2)$ multiplier is built up of 9 ANDs and 20 XORs. An inversion over $GF(((2^2)^2)^{41})$ requires an inversion and several multiplications in the subfield, $GF((2^2)^2)$. Hence, the complexity of the $GF((2^2)^2)$ multiplier serves as the major factor

that would determine the amount of hardware resources required (area and power) and the performance of the overall inverter architecture. In this study, we would like to point out the advantages of using combinatorial finite field inverter in hardware implementation as opposed to the pre-computed table method.

Apart from our combinatorial inverter, we have constructed another two composite field inverters, by having the $GF(2^4)$ multipliers implemented using the log and antilog conversion (see Figure 3) and the conventional LUT method. For verification and validation purposes, we have implemented the three architectures in Cyclone III EP3C120F780I7 FPGA. Having the architectures synthesized using Quartus II 7.2sp3, the summary of the hardware requirements are tabulated in Table 4.

From Table 4, it is evident that our combinatorial approach has outperformed the LUT-based approaches in term of performance and at the same time requiring less amount of hardware resources. In addition to that, such approach enables further optimization in architectural level such as pipelining for speed enhancement. On the contrary, the LUT which is implemented as a single memory block in FPGA, limits the possibility for subpipelining in the architecture and hence constrained the highest achievable processing speed.

Figure 3. Inversion and multiplication in $GF(2^4)$ using log and antilog conversions

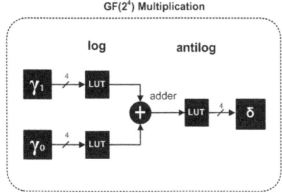
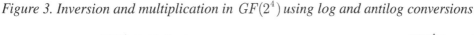
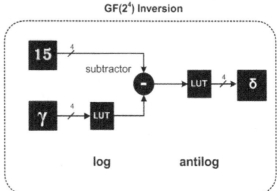

Table 4. Hardware analysis of FPGA implementation for $GF(((2^2)^2)^{41})$ inverter with the $GF(2^4) / GF((2^2)^2)$ multiplier implemented using (i) combinatorial circuitry as proposed in our work (ii) log and antilog conversions and (iii) multiplication LUT. Device used for all of the implementations is EP3C120F780I7 Cyclone III.

	(i) Combinatorial Circuitry	(ii) Log and Antilog Conversions	(iii) Multiplication LUT
Total LE	8,440	53,858	66,103
Total Combinatorial Functions	8,440	52,332	64,584
Dedicated logic register	4,959	4,663	4,663
Total Register	4,959	4,663	4,663
Fmax (MHz)	134.35	111.07	102.10
Total Thermal Power Dissipation (mW)	289.35	939.20	1221.64
Core Dynamic Thermal Power Dissipation (mW)	117.60	703.90	958.76
Core Static Power Dissipation (mW)	99.80	104.17	105.58
I/O Thermal Power Dissipation (mW)	71.95	131.13	157.30

In order to further show the advantages of using composite field arithmetic and combinatorial circuitry, we also include several reported designs for the computation of multiplicative inversion over $GF(2^m)$ in hardware platforms for benchmarking. The computational cost and area of these works and our work are summarized in Table 5. From Table 5, the time complexity of the work by Deng et al. in (Deng, Bai, Guo, & Wang, 2009) is the smallest but it comes with a higher hardware cost. Meanwhile, our architecture is slower in terms of timing performance but it consumes relatively smaller amount of hardware resources, of which would be suitable for medium range or lightweight applications.

Overall, our results in this study have shown that, 1, Our three-level isomorphism composite field inversion for ECC is distinctive from the previous works as the computation can be performed using combinatorial circuitry. 2, The combinatorial inverter is indeed more compact and with better performance compared to the pre-computed table methods suggested in the previous studies. 3, The composite field inverter is highly desirable in the EC hardware cryptosystem as it offers better computational efficiency and effectiveness, in terms of hardware cost and the achievable performance, compared to those that worked in binary finite field $GF(2^m)$.

FUTURE RESEARCH DIRECTIONS

Cryptography plays a vital role in the wide variety of applications that require secure communication mechanisms. Apart from the security requirements, implementation of the cryptographic systems presents specific challenges. The challenges are: First, as many applications require (near) real-time interaction communication, the overheads needed for encrypting and decrypting the data must be minimal. Second, many cryptographic applications are realized on embedded platforms, which are inherently constrained in terms of area and power consumption. However, in most hardware implementations, there exists a definite trade-off between hardware performance and its requirement. As a result, meeting these two challenges at the same time is a difficult task.

In this chapter, we proposed algorithm optimizations, which have successfully lead to the significant area reduction in hardware reduction

Table 5. Computational cost comparison of various multiplicative inverter architectures in hardware platform (CLB = Configurable Logic Block, LE = Logic Element)

	Platform	Finite Field	Cycles	Freq(MHz)	Timing (µS)	Area
Goodman et al. (Goodman &Chandrakasan, 2001)	0.25µCMOS	$GF(2^{256})$	3,712	50	74.24	440,000 Gates
Gutub et al. (Gutub et al., 2003)	0.5µCMOS	$GF(2^{256})$	5,000	50	100	50,000 Gates
Rodríguez-Henríquez et al. (Rodríguez-Henríquez, Saqib, & Cruz-Cortes, 2005)	Xilinx Virtex	$GF(2^{193})$	-	-	1.37	-
Gao et al. (X. Gao, Ou, Dong, & Jin, 2006)	EPIC20FC4000	$GF(2^{193})$	-	-	3.64	-
Rodríguez-Henríquez et al. (Standard) (Rodríguez-Henríquez et al., 2007)	Xilinx VirtexE	$GF(2^{193})$	28	21.2	1.32	10,065 CLBs +12 BRAMs
Rodríguez-Henríquez et al. (Parallel) (Rodríguez-Henríquez et al., 2007)	Xilinx VirtexE	$GF(2^{193})$	20	21.2	0.943	11,131 CLBs + 12 BRAMs
Yang et al. (Yang & Li, 2008)	EP1C20FC400C6	$GF(2^{233})$	-	-	3.11	-
Deng et al. (Deng et al., 2009)	0.35µCMOS	$GF(2^{233})$	26	30	0.867	655,100 Gates
Deng et al. (Deng et al., 2009)	0.18µCMOS	$GF(2^{233})$	26	100	0.26	702,881 Gates
Wei (Wei, 2010)	Xilinx Virtex5	$GF(2^{191})$	25	50	0.5	-
Our work	Cyclone III	$GF(((2^2)^2)^{41})$	247	100	2.47	8,440 LE

in the EC cryptosystem. For the next step, we can further optimize the resultant inversion circuitry in term of its speed performance. As our proposed work is pure combinatorial circuitry, we can efficiently employ architectural optimizations such as the pipelining and the subpipelining. This can be performed by inserting rows of registers in between operations or sub-operations. Consequently, the fastest speed available is bounded by shorter critical path.

Though the area-speed-power trade-off is inevitable in hardware implementations, it would still be worthwhile to investigate and to find the optimum circuitry design that strikes a balance in between the hardware resource consumption and its performance. This study will be reserve as our future work.

CONCLUSION

This work presented a compact combinatorial inverter for EC cryptosystems over $GF(((2^2)^2)^{41})$ in ONBII representation. With this, we substantially reduced the hardware cost of the scalar multiplication in ECC. Unlike the previous reports, we performed further isomorphisms in the subfield, $GF(2^4) \cong GF((2^2)^2)$, such that the need for LUTs was eliminated completely. Our field was selected carefully such that it is secure and at the same time promotes simplicity by using the composite field arithmetic.

While the extension field *l* have to be a prime number, we used the ONBII representation, which enabled the 40 exponentiations be done easily using simple cyclic shifts. In essence, the complexity of the subfield arithmetic will determine the complexity of the composite field arithmetic as a whole. An inversion over $GF(((2^2)^2)^{41})$ would require an inverter and several multipliers in $GF((2^2)^2)$. We have also presented a series of algorithmic optimization that successfully reduced the complexity of the subfield operators. As a result, without the use of LUT, our inverter and multiplier in the subfield consumes 8 ANDs and 12 XORs and 9 ANDs and 20 XORs respectively. We have also proven the advantage of using a combinatorial inverter in EC hardware cryptosystem as opposed to log and antilog conversions and the conventional LUT approaches. The proposed architecture is compact, with the least power consumption and giving the best performance in terms of clock cycles.

REFERENCES

Beauregard, D. (1996). *Efficient Algorithms for Implementing Elliptic Curve Public-key Schemes*. (Master's Thesis). Worcester Polytechnic Institute, Worcester, MA.

Bednara, M., Daldrup, M., von zur Gathen, J., Shokrollahi, J., & Teich, J. (2002). Reconfigurable Implementation of Elliptic Curve Crypto Algorithms. In *Proceedings of International Parallel and Distributed Processing Symposium, IPDPS 2002* (pp. 157-164). Fort Lauderdale, FL: IEEE Computer Society.

Chelton, W., & Benaissa, M. (2008). Fast Elliptic Curve Cryptography on FPGA. *IEEE Transactions on Very Large Scale Integration VLSI Systems*, *16*(2), 198–205. doi:10.1109/TVLSI.2007.912228

Deng, Q., Bai, X., Guo, L., & Wang, Y. (2009). A Fast Hardware Implementation of Multiplicative Inversion in $GF(2^m)$. In *Proceedings of Asia Pacific Conference on Postgraduate Research in Microelectronics & Electronics* (PrimeAsia'2009), (pp. 472-475). Shanghai, China: IEEE.

Frey, G. (1999). Applications of Arithmetical Geometry to Cryptographic Constructions. In *Proceedings of the Fifth International Conference on Finite Fields and Applications* (pp. 128–161). Springer.

Galbraith, S., & Smart, N. (1999). A Cryptographic Application of Weil Descent. In *Proceedings of Cryptography and Coding: 7th IMA International Conference*. Springer.

Gao, L., & Sobelman, G. (2000). Improved VLSI Designs for Multiplication and Inversion in $GF(2^m)$ Over Normal Bases. In *Proceedings of 13th Annual IEEE International ASIC/SOC Conference* (pp. 97-101). Arlington, VA: IEEE Circuit and Systems.

Gao, X., Ou, H., Dong, X., & Jin, J. (2006). *Research on FPGA Implementation of Algorithm for Computing Inversion in*. Computer Engineering and Applications.

Gaudry, P., Hess, F., & Smart, N. (2002). Constructive and Destructive Facets of Weil descent on Elliptic Curves. *Journal of Cryptology*, *15*, 19–46. doi:10.1007/s00145-001-0011-x

Goodman, J., & Chandrakasan, A. (2001). An Energy-efficient Reconfigurable Public-key Cryptography Processor. *Journal of Solid-State Circuits*, *36*(11), 1808–1820. doi:10.1109/4.962304

Guajardo, J., & Paar, C. (1997). Efficient Algorithms for Elliptic Curve Cryptosystems. In *Proceedings of 17th Annual International Cryptology Conference, CRYPTO'97* (pp. 342-356). Springer.

Guajardo, J., & Paar, C. (2002). Itoh-tsujii inversion in Standard Basis and Its Application. *Designs, Codes and Cryptography*, *25*, 207–216. doi:10.1023/A:1013860532636

Gutub, A. A.-A., Tenca, A. F., Savas, E., & Koç, C. K. (2003). Scalable and Unified Hardware to Compute Montgomery Inverse in GF(p) and GF(2). In *Revised papers from the 4th International Workshop on Cryptographic Hardware and Embedded Systems* (pp. 484–499). London, UK: Springer-Verlag.

Hankerson, D., Menezes, A. J., & Vanstone, S. (2004). Elliptic Curve Arithmetic. In *Guide to Elliptic Curve Cryptography* (pp. 75–147). New York: Springer-Verlag.

Harper, G., Menezes, A., & Vanstone, S. (1993). Public-key Cryptosystems With Very Small Key Lengths. In *Proceedings of the 11th Annual International Conference on Theory and Application of Cryptographic Techniques* (pp. 163–173). Berlin: Springer-Verlag.

Hein, D., Wolkerstorfer, J., & Felber, N. (2009). *ECC is Ready for RFID — A Proof in Silicon*. Berlin: Springer-Verlag. doi:10.1007/978-3-642-04159-4_26

Hess. (2004). Generalising the GHS attack on the Elliptic Curve Discrete Logarithm Problem. *LMS Journal of Computation and Mathematics, 7*, 167-192.

Itoh, T., & Tsujii, S. (1988). A Fast Algorithm for Computing Multiplicative Inverses in $GF(2^m)$ Using Normal Bases. *Information and Computation Elsevier, 78*, 171–177. doi:10.1016/0890-5401(88)90024-7

Koblitz, N. (1991). Constructing Elliptic Curve Cryptosystems in Characteristic 2. In *Proceedings of Advances in Cryptology - CRYPTO '90, 10th Annual International Cryptology Conference* (pp. 156-167). Santa Barbara, CA: Springer.

Koç, C. K., & Sunar, B. (2001). An Efficient Optimal Normal Basis Type II Multiplier. *IEEE Transactions on Computers, 50*, 83–87. doi:10.1109/12.902754

Kumar, S. S. (2006). *Elliptic Curve Cryptography for Constrained Devices*. (PhD Dissertation). Faculty of Electrical Engineering and Information Technology, Ruhr University Bochum, Germany.

Maurer, M., Menezes, A., & Teske, E. (2001). Analysis of the GHS Weil Descent Attack on the ECDLP Over Characteristic Two Finite Fields of Composite Degree. In *Proceedings of the Second International Conference on Cryptology: Progress in Cryptology* (pp. 195–213). London, UK: Springer-Verlag.

Menezes, A., & Qu, M. (2001). Analysis of the Weil Descent Attack of Gaudry, Hess and Smart. In *Proceedings of the 2001 Conference on Topics in Cryptology: The Cryptographer's Track at RSA* (pp. 308–318). London, UK: Springer-Verlag.

Menezes, A., & Teske, E. (2006). Cryptographic Implications of Hess' Generalized GHS Attack. *Applicable Algebra in Engineering. Communication and Computing, 16*, 439–460.

Menezes, A., Teske, E., & Weng, A. (2004). Weak Fields for ECC. In *Proceedings of the 2004 Conference on Topics in Cryptology – CT-RSA 2004, The Cryptographers' Track at the RSA* (pp. 1997-1997). San Francisco, CA: Springer.

Miller, V. S. (1986). Use of Elliptic Curves in cryptography. *Lecture Notes in Computer Science, 85*, 417–426. doi:10.1007/3-540-39799-X_31

Omura, J., & Massey, J. (1986). *Computational Method and Apparatus for Finite Field Arithmetic* (Patent US4587627).

Pollard, J. M. (1978). Monte Carlo Methods for Index Computation Mod P. *Mathematics of Computation, 32*, 918–924.

Reyhani-Masoleh, A., & Hasan, M. (2002). Efficient Digit-Serial Normal Basis Multipliers over $GF(2^m)$. In *Proceedings of IEEE International Symposium on Circuits and Systems, ISCAS 2002* (pp. 781-784). Scottsdale, AZ: IEEE Circuits and Systems.

Reyhani-Masoleh, A., & Hasan, M. (2005). Low Complexity Word-level Sequential Normal Basis Multipliers. *IEEE Transactions on Computers*, *54*(2), 98–110. doi:10.1109/TC.2005.29

Rodríguez-Henríquez, F., Morales-Luna, G., Saqib, N. A., & Cruz-Cortés, N. (2007). Parallel Itoh—Tsujii Multiplicative Inversion Algorithm for a Special Class of Trinomials. *Designs, Codes and Cryptography*, *45*, 19–37. doi:10.1007/s10623-007-9073-6

Rodríguez-Henríquez, F., Saqib, N. A., & Cruz-Cortes, N. (2005). A Fast Implementation of Multiplicative Inversion Over $GF(2^m)$. In *Proceedings of the International Conference on Information Technology: Coding and Computing*, ITCC'05 (pp. 574–579). Washington, DC: IEEE Computer Society.

Sakiyama, K., Batina, L., Preneel, B., & Verbauwhede, I. (2007). Multicore Curve-Based Cryptoprocessor with Reconfigurable Modular Arithmetic Logic Units over $GF(2^n)$. *IEEE Transactions on Computers*, *56*(9), 1269–1282.

Savas, E., & Koç, C. K. (1999). *Efficient Methods for Composite Field Arithmetic (Technical Report)*. *Electrical & Computing Engineering*. Oregon State University.

Schroeppel, R., Orman, H., O'Malley, S. W., & Spatscheck, O. (1995). Fast Key Exchange with Elliptic Curve Systems. In *Proceedings of the 15th Annual International Cryptology Conference on Advances in Cryptology* (pp. 43–56). London, UK: Springer-Verlag.

Smart, N. P. (2001). How secure are Elliptic Curves Over Composite Extension Fields? In *Proceedings of Advances in Cryptology - Eurocrypt 2001, International Conference on the Theory and Application of Cryptographic Techniques* (pp. 30-39). Innsbruck, Austria: IACR.

Wang, Y., Tian, Z., Bi, X., & Niu, Z. (2006). Efficient Multiplier Over Finite Field Represented in Type II Optimal Normal Basis. In *Proceedings of Sixth International Conference on Intelligent Systems Design and Applications*, ISDA '06. (pp. 1132 -1128). Jinan, China: IEEE.

Wei, D.-M. (2010). A Fast Implementation of Modular Inversion Over $GF(2^m)$ Based on FPGA. In *Proceedings of the 2nd IEEE International Conference on Information Management and Engineering*, ICIME 2010 (pp. 465 -468). Cape Town, South Africa: IEEE.

Win, E. D., Bosselaers, A., Vandenberghe, S., Gersem, P. D., & Vandewalle, J. (1996). A Fast Software Implementation For Arithmetic Operations in $GF(2^n)$. In *Proceedings of the International Conference on the Theory and Applications of Cryptology and Information Security: Advances in Cryptology* (pp. 65–76). London, UK: Springer-Verlag.

Wong, M. M., & Wong, M. L. D. (2010). A High Throughput Low Power Compact AES S-box Implementation Using Composite Field Arithmetic and Algebraic Normal Form Representation. In *Proceedings of the 2nd Asia Symposium on Quality Electronic Design*, ASQED 2010 (pp. 318-323). Penang, Malaysia: IEEE.

Wong, M. M., Wong, M. L. D., Nandi, A. K., & Hijazin, I. (2011). Construction of Optimum Composite Field Architecture for Compact High-throughput AES S-boxes. *IEEE Transactions on Very Large Scale Integration VLSI Systems*, *20*(6), 1151–1155. doi:10.1109/TVLSI.2011.2141693

Yang, X., & Li, Z. (2008). *Improvement and Implementation of Modular Inversion Algorithm on the Finite Field*. Computer Engineering and Applications.

ADDITIONAL READING

Amara, M., & Siad, A. (2011, May).Elliptic Curve Cryptography and Its Applications. In 7th International Workshop on Systems, Signal Processing and their Applications, WOSSPA 2011 (pp.247-250). Tipaza, Algeria: IEEE.

Batina, L., Örs, S. B., Preneel, B., & Vandewalle, J. (2003, May). Hardware Architectures for Public Key Cryptography. VLSI Journal. *Integration (Tokyo, Japan)*, *34*, 1–64.

Bednara, M., Daldrup, M., Teich, J., von zurGathen, J., & Shokrollahi, J. (2002). Tradeoff Analysis of FPGA Based Elliptic Curve Cryptography. In IEEE International Symposium on Circuits and Systems ISCAS 2002. (pp. 797-800). Arizona, US: IEEE Circuits and Systems.

Caelli, W. J., Dawson, E. P., & Rea, S. A. (1999). In PKI, Elliptic Curve Cryptography, and Digital Sgnatures. *Computers & Security*, *18*, 47–66. doi:10.1016/S0167-4048(99)80008-X

Chelton, W. N., & Benaissa, M. (2008, February). Fast Elliptic Curve Cryptography on FPGA. IEEE Transactions on Very Large Scale Integration (VLSI). *Systems*, *16*(2), 198–205.

Cojocaru, A. C., & Shparlinski, I. E. (2009, June). On the Embedding Degree of Reductions of an Elliptic Curve. *Information Processing Letters*, *109*, 652–654. doi:10.1016/j.ipl.2009.02.018

Dan, Y. P., Zou, X. C., Liu, Z. L., Han, Y., & Yi, L. H. (2009, April). Design of Highly Efficient Elliptic Curve Crypto-processor with Two Multiplications Over GF(2^{163}). *Journal of China Universities of Posts and Telecommunications*, *16*, 72–79. doi:10.1016/S1005-8885(08)60206-X

Deepthi, P. P., & Sathidevi, P. S. (2009, January). New Stream Ciphers Based on Elliptic Curve Point Multiplication. *Computer Communications*, *32*, 25–33. doi:10.1016/j.comcom.2008.09.002

Dormale, G. M., & Quisquater, J. J. (2007, March). High-speed hardware implementations of Elliptic Curve Cryptography: A survey. *Journal of Systems Architecture*, *53*, 72–84. doi:10.1016/j.sysarc.2006.09.002

Ernst, M., Henhapl, B., Klupsch, S., & Huss, S. (2004, March). FPGA Based Hardware Acceleration for Elliptic Curve Public Key Cryptosystems. *Journal of Systems and Software*, *70*, 299–313. doi:10.1016/S0164-1212(03)00075-X

Fournaris, A. P., & Koufopavlou, O. (2008, September). Creating an Elliptic Curve Arithmetic Unit for Use in Elliptic Curve Cryptography. In IEEE International Conference on Emerging Technologies and Factory Automation, ETFA 2008, pp. 1457 - 1464. Hamburg, Germany: IEEE.

Gueron, S., & Kounavis, M. (2008, April).A Technique for Accelerating Characteristic 2 Elliptic Curve Cryptography. In Fifth International Conference on Information Technology: New Generations, ITNG 2008 (pp.265-272). Nevada, US: IEEE.

Järvinen, K. (2011, September). Optimized FPGA-based Elliptic Curve Cryptography Processor for High-Speed Applications. VLSI Journal. *Integration (Tokyo, Japan)*, *44*, 270–279.

LaMacchia, B. A., & Manferdelli, J. L. (2006). New Vistas in Elliptic Curve Cryptography. *Information Security Technical Report*, *11*, 186–192. doi:10.1016/j.istr.2006.09.002

Leinweber, L., Papachristou, C., & Wolff, F. G. (2009, October) Efficient Architectures for Elliptic Curve Cryptography Processors for RFID. In IEEE International Conference on Computer Design, ICCD 2009 (pp.372-377). Lake Tahoe, CA, USA: IEEE.

Morales-Sandoval, M., & Feregrino-Uribe, C. (2005, February).A Hardware Architecture for Elliptic Curve Cryptography and Lossless Data Compression. In 15th International Conference on Electronics, Communications and Computers, CONIELECOMP 2005 (pp. 113- 118). Puebla, Mexico: IEEE.

Morales-Sandoval, M., Feregrino-Uribe, C., Cumplido, R., & Algredo-Badillo, I. (2009, January). An Area/Performance Trade-off Analysis of a $GF(2^m)$ Multiplier Architecture for Elliptic Curve Cryptography. *Computers & Electrical Engineering, 35*, 54–58. doi:10.1016/j.compeleceng.2008.05.008

Peter, S., Langendorfer, P., & Piotrowski, K. (2007, April). Flexible Hardware Reduction for Elliptic Curve Cryptography in $GF(2^m)$. In Europe Conference & Exhibition in Design, Automation & Test 2007, DATE '07 (pp.1-6). France: IEEE.

Rahuman, A. K., & Athisha, G. (2010, December). Reconfigurable Architecture for Elliptic Curve Cryptography. In International Conference on Communication and Computational Intelligence, INCOCCI 2010, (pp.461-466). Erode, India: IEEE.

Rodríguez-Henríquez, F., Saqib, N. A., & Díaz-Pérez, A. (2004, August). A Fast Parallel Implementation of Elliptic Curve Point Multiplication Over $GF(2^m)$. *Microprocessors and Microsystems, 28*, 329–339. doi:10.1016/j.micpro.2004.03.003

Shanmugam, R. (2001, October). Elliptic Curves and Their Applications to Cryptography: An Introduction. *Neurocomputing, 41*, 193. doi:10.1016/S0925-2312(01)00332-0

Smart, N. P. (2001, July). A Comparison of Different Finite Fields for Elliptic Curve Cryptosystems. *Computers & Mathematics with Applications (Oxford, England), 42*, 91–100. doi:10.1016/S0898-1221(01)00133-X

Song Ju. (2012, July).A Lightweight Key Establishment in Wireless Sensor Network Based on Elliptic Curve Cryptography. In 2012 IEEE International Conference on Intelligent Control, Automatic Detection and High-End Equipment, ICADE 2012 (pp.138-141). Beijing, China: IEEE.

Tsaur, W. J., & Chou, C. H. (2005, September). Efficient Algorithms for Speeding Up the Computations of Elliptic Curve Cryptosystems. *Applied Mathematics and Computation, 168*, 1045–1064. doi:10.1016/j.amc.2004.10.010

Vanstone, S. A. (1997). Elliptic curve cryptosystem — The Answer to Strong, Fast Public-key Cryptography for Securing Constrained Environments. *Information Security Technical Report, 2*, 78–87. doi:10.1016/S1363-4127(97)81331-3

Vanstone, S. A. (2003, July). Next Generation Security for Wireless: Elliptic Curve Cryptography. *Computers & Security, 22*, 412–415. doi:10.1016/S0167-4048(03)00507-8

Wang, Y. B., Dong, X. J., & Tian, Z. G. (2007, August). FPGA Based Design of Elliptic Curve Cryptography Coprocessor. In Third International Conference on Natural Computation, ICNC 2007, (pp.185-189). Hainina, China: IEEE.

KEY TERMS AND DEFINITIONS

Composite Field Arithmetic (CFA): A special case of Galois field $GF(2^k)$, where k is a composite integer.

Elliptic Curve Cryptography (ECC): A public-key cryptography based on algebraic structure of elliptic curves over the finite field.

Fermat's Little Theorem (FLT): One of the main approaches to perform the inversion over finite field apart from the extended Euclidean algorithm (EEA). In general, the theorem stated that, in the notation of modular arithmetic, any integer a and prime number p, we can derived an expression as, $a^p \equiv a \pmod{p}$.

Field Programmable Gate Arrays (FPGA): A semiconductor device that can be reconfigured and reprogrammed after manufacturing. It contains reconfigurable block, called the Logic Elements (LE) that can be interwired into many configurations.

Itoh-Tsujii Inversion (ITI) Algorithm: A FLT-based inversion algorithm (refer Theorem 1). It does not perform a complete inversion, but reducing the extension field inversion to inversion in the subfield such that it can be done relatively easier using available inversion algorithm.

Optimal Normal Basis Representation (ONB): A special case of normal basis representation and is classified as optimal normal basis type I and optimal normal basis type II.

Multiplicative Inversion: Reciprocal of number a, such that $aa^{-1} \equiv 1 \pmod{p}$ with $a \in \mathbb{Z}_p$.

Chapter 10
RSA–Public Key Cryptosystems Based on Quadratic Equations in Finite Field

Sattar B. Sadkhan Al Maliky
University of Babylon, Iraq

Luay H. Al-Siwidi
University of Babylon, Iraq

ABSTRACT

The importance of Public Key Cryptosystems (PKCs) in the cryptography field is well known. They represent a great revolution in this field. The PKCs depend mainly on mathematical problems, like factorization problem, and a trapdoor one-way function problem. Rivest, Shamir, and Adleman (RSA) PKC systems are based on factorization mathematical problems. There are many types of RSA cryptosystems. Rabin's Cryptosystem is considered one example of this type, which is based on using the square order (quadratic equation) in encryption function. Many cryptosystems (since 1978) were implemented under such a mathematical approach. This chapter provides an illustration of the variants of RSA-Public Key Cryptosystems based on quadratic equations in Finite Field, describing their key generation, encryption, and decryption processes. In addition, the chapter illustrates a proposed general formula for the equation describing these different types and a proposed generalization for the Chinese Remainder Theorem.

INTRODUCTION

The idea of a *public-key cryptography* was put forward by Diffie and Hellman in 1976. Then, in 1977, Rivest, Shamir, and Adleman invented the well-known RSA Cryptosystem. Several public-key cryptosystems have been proposed, whose security is based on different computational problems. The most important are the RSA

Cryptosystem (and variation of it), in which the security is based on the difficulty of factoring large integers; and the ElGAmal Cryptosystem (and it's variations such as Elliptic Curve Cryptosystems) in which the security is based on the discrete logarithm problem (Diffie & Hellman, 1976).

Prior to Diffie and Hellman, the idea of public-key cryptography was already proposed by James Ellis in January 1970, in a paper entitled " The

DOI: 10.4018/978-1-4666-5808-0.ch010

Possibility of Non-secret Encryption". This paper was not published in the open literature and was one of the five papers released by the GCHQ (British Government Communication Headquarters) officially in December 1997. also among these five papers was a 1973 paper written by Clifford Cocks, entitled " A Note on Non-secret Encryption," in which a public-key cryptosystem is described that is essentially the same as the RSA cryptosystem (Douglas, 2006).

A public-key cryptosystem can never provide unconditional security. This is because an opponent, on observing a ciphertext y, can encrypt each possible plaintext in turn using the public encryption rule (e_k) until he/she finds the unique x such that $y = e_k (x)$. It is helpful to think of a public-key in terms of an abstraction called a *trapdoor one-way function*. This notation can be defined as:

Bob's public encryption function, (e_k), should be easy to compute. We have just noted that computing the inverse function (i.e., decrypting) should be hard (for anyone other than Bob). It is well known that a function that is easy to compute but hard to invert is often called a *one-way function*. In the context of encryption, we desire that (e_k) be an *injective one-way function* so that decryption can be performed. Unfortunately, although there are many *injective functions* * that are believed to be one-way, there currently do not exist such functions that can be proved to be one-way (Nimrod & Christos, 1989).

Example of a function (which is believed) to be one-way:

Suppose n is the product of two large primes p and q, and let b be a positive integer. Then define $f: Zn \rightarrow Zn$ to be

$$f(x) = x^b \bmod n.$$

(if $gcd(b, \phi(n))=1$, then this is in fact an RSA encryption function).

In the classical model of cryptography, Alice and Bob secretly choose the key (K). K then gives

rise to an encryption rule (e_k) and a decryption rule (d_k). In these cryptosystems, (d_k) is either the same as (e_k), or easily derived from it. For example, in DES (Block Cipher Type), the decryption process is identical to encryption process, but the key schedule is reversed. A cryptosystem of this type is known as a symmetric-key cryptosystems, since exposure of either of (e_k) or (d_k) renders the system insecure. Figure 1 shows two-party communication using encryption, with a secure channel for key exchange. The decryption key can be efficiently computed from the encryption key.

One drawback of symmetric-key cryptosystem is that it requires the prior communication of the key (K) between Alice and Bob, using a secure channel before any cipher text is transmitted. In practice, this may be very difficult to achieve. For example, suppose Alice and Bob live far away from each other and they decide that they want to communicate electronically, using email. In a situation such as this, Alice and Bob may not have a reasonably secure channel.

The idea behind a public-key cryptosystem is that it might be possible to find a cryptosystem where it is computationally infeasible to determine (d_k) given (e_k). If so, then the encryption rule (e_k) is a public key which could be published in a directory. The advantage of a public-key cryptosystem is that Alice can send and encrypt message to Bob (without the prior communication of a shared secret key) by using the public encryption rule (e_k). Bob will be the only person that can decrypt the cipher text, using the decryption rule (d_k), which is called private key. Figure 2 shows the block diagram of the two-party communication using encryption, with unsecured channel for key exchange (Richard, 2003).

In mathematics, an injective function is a function that preserves distinctness: it never maps distinct elements of its domain to the same element of its codomain. In other words, every element of the function's codomain is mapped by *at most* one element of its domain.

239

Figure 1. Encryption using secret key technique

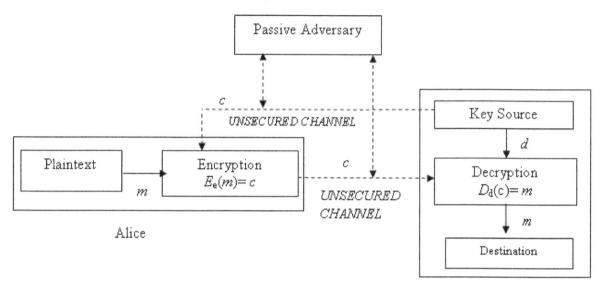

Notice how Figure 2 differs from Figure 1 in a symmetric-key cipher. Here the encryption key is transmitted to Bob over an unsecured channel. This unsecured channel may be the same channel on which the cipher text is being transmitted .Since the encryption key need not be kept secret, it may

be made public. Any entity can subsequently send encrypted messages to Bob which only Bob can decrypt. Figure 3 illustrates this idea.

In constructing a *public-key cryptosystem*, then it is not sufficient to find an *injective one-way function*. We do not want (e_k) to be one-way

Figure 2. Encryption using public-key techniques

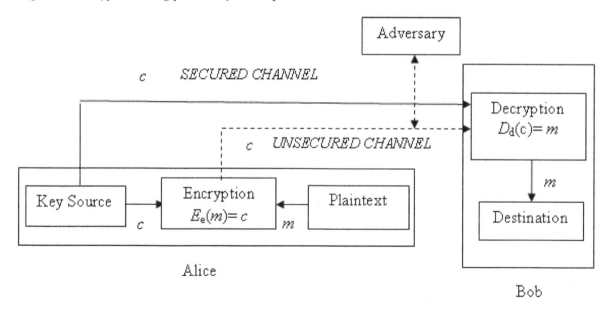

Figure 3. Schematic use of public-key encryption

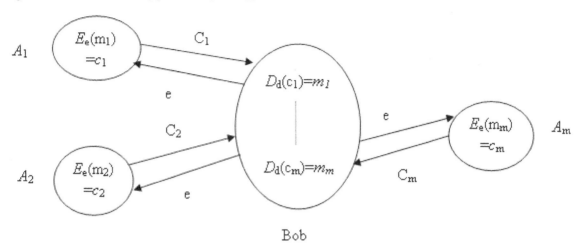

Bob

from Bob's point of view, because he needs to be able to decrypt messages that he receives in an efficient way. Thus, it is necessary that Bob possess a trapdoor, which consists of secret information that permits easy inversion of (e_k). That is Bob can decrypt efficiently because he has more extra secret knowledge, namely, K, which provides him with the decryption function (d_k). So a function is *a trapdoor one-way function* if it is a *one-way function*, but it becomes easy to invert with the knowledge of a certain trapdoor (Kranakis, 1984).

The inverse function (f^{-1}), of the function $f(x) = x^b \bmod n$, has a similar form: $f(x) = x^a \bmod n$ for an appropriate value of a. The trapdoor is an efficient method for computing the correct exponent a (given b), which makes use of the factorization of n. Public-key cryptography has many advantages:

- Only the private key must be kept secret (authenticity of public keys must, however, be guaranteed).
- The administration of keys on a network requires the presence of only a functionally trusted TTP as opposed to an unconditionally trusted TTP. Depending on the mode of usage, the TTP might only be required

in an "off-line" manner, as opposed to in real time.

- Depending on the mode of usage, a private key/public key pair may remain unchanged for considerable periods of time, e.g., many sessions (even several years).
- Many public-key schemes yield relatively efficient digital signature mechanisms. The key used to describe the public verification function is typically much smaller than that for the symmetric-key counterpart.
- In a large network, the number of keys necessary may be considerably smaller than in the symmetric-key scenario.

On the other hands the disadvantages of public-key encryption are:

- Throughput rates for the most popular public-key encryption methods are several orders of magnitude slower than the best known symmetric-key schemes.
- Key sizes are typically much larger than those required for symmetric-key encryption, and the size of public-key signatures is larger than that of tags providing data origin authentication from symmetric-key techniques.

- No public-key scheme has been proven to be secure (the same can be said about block ciphers). The most effective public-key encryption schemes found to date have their security based on the presumed difficulty of a small set of number-theoretic problems.

- Public-key cryptography does not have so extensive a history as symmetric-key encryption, being discovered only in the mid 1970s (Schroeder, 1986).

Security

Some encryption schemes can be proven secure on the basis of the presumed difficulty of a mathematical problem, such as factoring the product of two large primes or computing discrete logarithms. Note that "secure" here has a precise mathematical meaning, and there are multiple different (meaningful) definitions of what it means for an encryption scheme to be "secure". The "right" definition depends on the context in which the scheme will be deployed. The most obvious application of a public key encryption system is confidentiality - a message that a sender encrypts using the recipient's public key can be decrypted only by the recipient's paired private key. This assumes, of course, that no flaw is discovered in the basic algorithm used (Pascal, 1994).

The RSA CRYPTOSYSTEM

The RSA cryptosystem uses computations in Zn, where n is the product of two distinct odd primes p and q. For an integer n, note that $\phi(n) = (p-1)(q-1)$. To verify the encryption and decryption are inverse operations, since

$$ab \equiv 1 \ (mod \ \phi(n))$$

we have

$$ab = t \ \phi(n) + 1$$

For some integers $t \geq 1$. Suppose that $x \in Zn$; then

$$X^{(b)a} \equiv x^{(t\phi(n) + 1)}(mod \ n)$$

$$\equiv ((x^{(t\phi(n) + 1)})^t) \ x \ (mod \ n)$$

$$\equiv 1^{(t)}x \ (mod \ n)$$

$$\equiv x \ (mod \ n)$$

as described.

Example (1): Suppose Bob chooses $p = 2357$ and $q = 2551$. Then $n = p.q = 6012707$ and $\phi(n) = (p-1)(q-1) = 2356*2550 = 6007800$. Choose $e = 3674911$, and using Extended Euclidean algorithm, it is possible to find $d = 422191$, such that $e.d = 1 \ (mod \ \phi(n))$. Now Bob's public Key is the pair ($n = 6012707$, $e = 367491$). Conversely Bob's private key is $d = 422191$.

Encryption: To encrypt a message $m = 5234673$, Alice uses an algorithm for modular exponentiation to compute:

$$c = m^{(e)}mod \ n = 5234673^{\ 367391} mod \ (6012707) = 3650502$$

and sends this ciphered message to Bob.

Decryption: To decrypt (c), Bob computes:

$$m = c^{d}mod \ n = 3650502^{422191} \ mod \ (6012707) = 5234673$$

The security of the RSA Cryptosystem is based on the belief that the encryption function $e_k(x) = x^b$ $mod \ n$ is a *one-way function*, so it will be computationally infeasible for an opponent to decrypt a cipher text. The trapdoor that allows Bob to decrypt cipher text is knowledge of the factorization $n = pq$. Since Bob knows this factorization, he can compute $\phi(n) = (p-1)(q-1)$, and then computes the decryption exponent a using the "Extended Euclidean Algorithm" (Douglas, 2006)

Security of RSA

This subsection discusses various security issues related to RSA encryption.

- **Relation to factoring:** The task faced by a passive adversary is that of recovering plaintext from the corresponding cipher text, given the public information of the intended receiver . This is called the RSA problem (RSAP). There is no efficient algorithm known for this problem.
- **Small encryption exponent:** In order to improve the efficiency of encryption, it is desirable to select a small encryption exponent .
- **Forward search attack:** If the message space is small or predictable, an adversary can decrypt a cipher text by simply encrypting all possible plaintext messages until it is obtained. Salting the message as described above is one simple method of preventing such an attack.
- **Small decryption exponent:** As the case with the encryption exponent, it may seem desirable to select a small decryption exponent in order to improve the efficiency of decryption.
- **Multiplicative properties:** Let m_1 and m_2 be two plaintext messages, and let c_1 and c_2 be their respective RSA encryptions. Observe that

$$(m_1 m_2)^e \equiv m_1^e m_2^e \equiv c_1 c_2 \pmod{n}$$

- **Common modulus attack:** The following discussion demonstrates why it is imperative for each entity to choose its own RSA modulus . It is sometimes suggested that a central trusted authority should select a single RSA modulus, and then distribute a distinct encryption/decryption exponent.

THE SECOND ORDER EQUATION ON RSA-TYPE PUBLIC KEY CRYPTOSYSTEMS

This section will illustrate different RSA-Types of PKC that use (mainly) the second order (quadratic) function in the encryption process. The first example of such type is the Rabin Cryptosystem.

The Rabin Cryptosystem

Rabin cryptosystem is computationally secure against a chosen-plaintext attack provided that the modules $n = pq$ cannot be factored. Therefore, the Rabin Cryptosystem provides an example of a provably secure cryptosystem: assuming that the problem of factoring is computationally infeasible, the Rabin Cryptosystem is secure (Rabin, 1979).

Description of Rabin Cryptosystem:

Let $n = pq$, where p and q are primes and $p, q \equiv 3 \pmod 4$. Let $P = C = Zn$, and define

$$K = \{ (n, p, q) \}$$

For $K = (n, p, q)$, define

$$e_k(x) = x^2 \bmod n$$

and

$$d_k(y) = \sqrt{y} \bmod n$$

The value n is the public key, while p and q are private key.

The requirement that $p, q \equiv 3 \pmod 4$ can be omitted. Moreover, the cryptosystem still "works" if we take $P = C = Zn$ instead of Zn.

One drawback of the Rabin cryptosystem is that the encryption function (e_k) is not an injection, so decryption cannot be done in an unambiguous fashion. This can be proved as follows:

Suppose that y is a valid cipher text; this means that $y = x^2 \bmod n$ for some $x \in Zn$.

There are four square roots of y *modulo n*, which are the four possible plaintext positions that are encrypted to y. In general, there will be no way for Bob to distinguish which of these four possible plaintexts is the "right" plaintext, unless the plaintext contains sufficient redundancy to eliminate three of these four possible values .

The Decryption problem from Bob's point of view can be described as follows:

Bob is given a cipher text y and wants to determine x such that:

$x^2 \equiv y \ (mod \ n)$

This is a quadratic equation in Zn in the unknown x, and decryption requires extracting square roots *modulo n*. This is equivalent to solving the two congruencies

$z^2 \equiv y \ (mod \ p)$

and

$z^2 \equiv y \ (mod \ q)$

Euler's criterion can be used to determine if y is a quadratic residue *modulo p* (and *modulo q*). In fact, y will be a quadratic residue *modulo p* and *modulo q* if encryption is performed correctly. Unfortunately, Euler's criterion does not help us find the square roots of y; it yields only an answer "yes" or "no".

When $p \equiv 3 \ (mod \ 4)$, there is a simple formula to compute square roots of quadratic residues *modulo p*. Suppose y is quadratic residue *modulo p*, where $p \equiv 3 \ (mod \ 4)$. Then

$(\pm y^{((p+1)/4)})^2 \equiv y^{((p+1)/2)} \ (mod \ p),$

$\equiv y^{((p-1)/2)} \ (mod \ p),$

$\equiv y \ (mod \ p)$

And, here, again we have made use of Euler's criterion, which says that if y is a quadratic residue *modulo p*, then $y^{((p-1)/2)} \equiv 1 \ (mod \ p)$. Hence, the two square roots of y *modulo p* are $\pm \ y^{((p+1)/4 \ ))2}$ *mod p* . In a similar fashion, the two square roots of y *modulo q* are: $\pm \ y^{((p+1)/4 \ ))2}$ *mod q*. It is then straightforward to obtain the four square roots of y *modulo n* using the Chinese Remainder Theorem.

Example (2): Suppose $n = 77 = 7 \times 11$. Then the encryption function is:

$e_k(x) = x^2 mod \ 77$

The decryption function is:

$d_k(y) = \sqrt{y} \ mod \ 77$

Suppose Bob wants to decrypt the cipher text $y = 23$. It is first necessary to find the square roots modulo 7 and modulo 11. Since 7 and 11 are both congruent 3 modulo 4, we use the formula:

$23^{((7+1)/4)} \equiv 2^2 \equiv 4 \ (mod \ 7)$

and

$23^{((11+1)/4)} \equiv 1^3 \equiv 1 \ (mod \ 11)$

Using the Chinese Remainder Theorem, we compute the four square roots of 23 modulo 77 to be $\pm 10, \pm 32$ mod 77. Therefore, the four possible plaintexts are $x = 10, 32, 45,$ and 67. It can be verified that each of these plaintexts yields the value 23 when squared and reduced to modulo 77. This proves that 23 is indeed a valid cipher text.

Security of Rabin Public-Key Encryption

- The task faced by a passive adversary is to recover plaintext from the corresponding cipher text. This is precisely the SQROOT problem (that the problems of factoring and computing square roots modulo are computationally equivalent). Hence, if it is assumed that factoring is computationally intractable, the Rabin public-key encryption scheme is provably secure against a passive adversary.

- While provably secure against a passive adversary, the Rabin public-key encryption scheme succumbs to a chosen-cipher text attack. Such an attack can be mounted as follows.

Note: A drawback of Rabin's public-key scheme is that the receiver is faced with the task of selecting the correct plaintext from among four possibilities. This ambiguity in decryption can easily be overcome in practice by adding prespecified redundancy to the original plaintext prior to encryption.

William's Cryptosystem

William in 1980 presented a modified version of the RSA public key cryptosystem. This modification relates to the preprocessing of the message before being transformed by a trapdoor one way function of the kind given by (William, 1985):

Let $n = pq$ where p and q are two (large) primes of the form $p \equiv 3 \pmod 8$ and $q \equiv 7 \pmod 8$. Define $\mu(n)$ as $\mu(n) = lcm\ [p\text{-}1, q\text{-}1]$ where lcm is the least common multiple. For the above choice of p and q, clearly $\mu(n)$ is an even integer. Select an (odd) integer e to be relatively prime to $\mu(n)$.

Also William's cryptosystem can be described as a system based on Rabin's cryptosystem, but with using two keys (c_1, c_2), which can be considered as public keys. We can recover the plain text (M) using these keys. There are conditions for choosing the prime numbers $(p$ and $q)$ as (Muller, 2001):

$p \equiv$ -1 mod, and $q \equiv$ -1 mod 4

Key Generation

- Randomly generation of two large prime numbers p and q, such that:

$p \equiv$ -1 mod, and $q \equiv$ -1 mod 4

- Calculation of $n = p \cdot q$ and k, such that: $k = (0.5 \cdot (1/4\ (p\text{-}1).(q\text{-}1)+1))$
- Random generation of small integer number S such that J$[S, n] = 1$.
- Public key is $< S, n >$, while secret key is $< k, p, q >$.

Encryption Process

The space of plain text messages M will be encrypted, since J$[M, n] = \pm 1$, as follows:

- Calculate the first element of the public key:

$c_1 = 1$ if J$[M, n] =$ -1 $c_1 = 0$ if J$[M, n] = 1$, That means $c_1 \in \{0,1\}$

- Calculate $\acute{N}$, where $\acute{N} \equiv S^{(c1)} \cdot M$ mod n
- Calculate the second element of the public key c_2, where $c_2 \equiv \acute{N}$ mod 2, that means $c_2 \in \{0,1\}$.
- Calculate the cipher text E(M) as:

$E(M) \equiv \acute{N}^2$ mod n.

The transmitted cipher text consists of the following three elements: (E(M), c_1, c_2) (Seberry, & Pieprzyk, 1989), .

Example (3): If $p = 7$, $q = 11$, encipher $M = 54$ using William Cryptosystem with the used keys $< 3, 7, 11, 19, 31, 23 >$

Solution:

- Calculate $n = p.q = 11 \cdot 7 = 77$
- Suppose $S = 4$

$J[S, N] = J[S, p\} * J[S, q]$

$J[4, 7] = 4^3 \bmod 7 = 1$ and $J[4, 11] = 4^5 \bmod 11 = 1$

then $J[S, n] = 1*1 = 1$

- Public Key $= < S, R > = < 4, 77 >$, and Secret Key $= < K, p, q >$

$K = 0.5 [(1/4) (p-1) (q-1) = 1] = 0.5 [0.25 (6) (10) + 1] = 0.5[64/4] = 64/8 = 8$

The Secret Key $= < 8, 7, 11 >$

$J[M, R] = J[M, p]. J[M, q]$

$J[54, 7] = 54^3 \bmod 7 = -1$

$J[54, 11] = 54^5 \bmod 7 = -1$

then $J[54, 77] = (-1). (-1) = 1$, then $c1 = 0$.

$M = S^{(C1)}. M. \bmod N = 4^0 . 54 \bmod 77 = 54$

$c2 = M \bmod 2 = 54 \bmod 2 = 0$

$E(M) = (M)^2 . \bmod n = (54)^2 \bmod 77 = 67$

The Encrypted Message $< 64, c1=0, c2 = 0 >$

Decrypting the Cipher Text Message:

$M_k = [E(M)]^k \bmod n = [67]^8 \bmod 77 = [-10]^8 \bmod 77 = 10^8 \bmod 77 = 23$

$M_1 = S^{c1} . (-1)^{c1}. M_k \bmod n = (4)^0 . (-1)^0 . 23 \bmod 77 = 23$

then $c_2 = 0$

$M = n-M_1 = 77-23 = 54$

Goldwasser's Cryptosystem

The Goldwasser–Micali (GM) cryptosystem is an asymmetric key encryption algorithm developed by Shafi Goldwasser and Silvio Micali in 1982. GM has the distinction of being the first probabilistic public-key encryption scheme which is provably secure under standard cryptographic assumptions. However, it is not an efficient cryptosystem, as cipher texts may be several hundred times larger than the initial plaintext. To prove the security properties of the cryptosystem, Goldwasser and Micali proposed the widely-used definition of semantic security. The GM cryptosystem is semantically secure based on the assumed intractability of the quadratic residuosity problem modulo a composite $n = pq$ where p, q are large primes. This assumption states that given (x, n) it is difficult to determine whether x is a quadratic residue modulo n (i.e., $x = y^2 \bmod n$ for some y), when the *Jacobi symbol* for x is $+1$. The quadratic residue problem is easily solved given the factorization of n, while new quadratic residues may be generated by any party, even without knowledge of this factorization. The GM cryptosystem leverages this asymmetry by encrypting individual plaintext bits as either random quadratic residues or non-residues (modulo n), all with quadratic residue symbol $+1$. Recipients use the factorization of n as a secret key, and decrypt the message by testing the quadratic residuosity of the received ciphertext values. Because GM produces a value of size approximately $|n|$ to encrypt every single bit of a plaintext, GM encryption results in substantial ciphertext expansion. To prevent factorization attacks, it is recommended that $|n|$ be several hundred bits or more (Goldwasser & Micali, 1982)

Scheme Definition

GM consists of three algorithms: a probabilistic key generation algorithm which produces a public and a private keys, a probabilistic encryption algorithm, and a deterministic decryption algorithm. The scheme relies on deciding whether a given value x is a square mod n, given the factorization (p, q) of n. This can be accomplished using the following procedure (Blum & Goldwasser, 1985):

1. Compute $x_p = x \bmod p$, $x_q = x \bmod q$.
2. If $x_p^{(p-1)/2} \equiv 1 \pmod{p}$ and $x_q^{(q-1)/2} \equiv 1 \pmod{q}$, then x is a quadratic residue mod n.

Key Generation

- Generate randomly two Large Prime numbers (p, q), such that $n = p.q$
- Generate randomly real number y such that $J[y, p] = -1$, and $J[y,q] = -1$.
- The public key is $< y, n >$, and the private key is $< p.q >$.

Encryption Process

To encrypt the plain text message M, such that $0 \le M < n$, the following steps must be followed:

- Transform the plain text into binary representation $M = (m_1, \ldots\ldots, m_k)$.
- Generate randomly integers $x_i \in Ź_n$ for all $1 \le i \le k$.
- Calculate the values of Z_i for all $1 \le i \le k$ from the formula:

$z_i = x_i^2 \bmod n$

- Calculate the values of c_i for all $1 \le i \le k$ such that:

$c_i = z_i$ if $m_i = 0$, or $c_i = y.z_i$ if $m_i = 0$

The encrypted message will be: $c = (c_1, \ldots.., c_n)$.

Decryption Process

To recover the plain text M from the cipher text c, we follow:

$m_i = 0$ if $J[c_i, p] = 1$ and $J[c_i, q] = 1$, or $m_i = 1$ others.

The plain text M will be: $M = (m_1, m_2, \ldots., m_k)$.

Complexity

The Blum-Goldwasser cryptosystem is efficient system both for encryption and decryption, comparable to the current standard, RSA encryption. During encryption, the GM cryptosystem actually performs faster than the standard in all but a few special cases. In decryption, the initial calculations have a fixed number of steps, with additional steps based on message size. This makes it less efficient than RSA for short messages, but a quicker decryption for long messages. Decryption is also accomplished in linear time (Menezes & Oorschot, 1996)

Security

The GM cryptosystem is susceptible to a chosen-cipher text attack. This attack is based on an attacker finding a cipher text and its decryption without knowing the key. With this knowledge, the attacker may be able to determine the initial seed x_0, thus destroying the security of the system. Thus, the probability of having the same seed is extremely low. Another possible way to block this attack is with an authentication challenge. This would require challenging the attacker for the private key, similar to a password to gain network access. This should also work to prevent this attack (Goldwasser & Micali, 1984).

Example (4): *(Blum-Goldwasser probabilistic encryption with artificially small parameters) Key generation.*

Entity A selects the prime $p = 499$, $q = 547$, each congruent to 3 mod 4, and computes $n = pq = 272953$. Using the Extended Euclidean Algorithm, A computes the integers $a = -57$, $b = 52$ satisfying $ap + bq = 1$. A's public key is $n = 272953$, while A's private key is (p,q,a,b). *Encryption:* The parameters k and h have the values 18 and 4, respectively. B represents the message m as a string $m_1 m_2 m_3 m_4 m_5 (t = 5)$ where $m_1 = 1001$, $m_2 = 1100$, $m_3 = 0001$, $m_4 = 000$, $m_5 = 1100$. B the selects a random quadratic residue $x_0 = 159201 (= 399^2 \mod n)$, and computes: as shown in Table 1 and $x_6 = x_5^2 \mod n = 139680$. B sends the ciphertext.

$c = (0010, 0000, 1100, 1110, 0100, 139680)$ to A.

Decryption: To decrypt c, A computes

$d_1 = ((p+1)/4)^6 \mod (p-1) = 463$
$d_2 = ((q+1)/4)^6 \mod (q-1) = 337$

$u = (x_6)^{463} \mod p = 20$

$v = (x_6)^{337} \mod q = 24$

$x_0 = vap + ubq \mod n = 159201$

Finally, A uses x_0 to construct the x_i and p_i just as B did for encryption, and recovers the plaintext m_i, by XORing the p_i with the ciphertext blocks c_i.

Okamoto First Version

Okomatoa offered in (1986) a simple cryptosystem, containing one addition and one multiplication under modulo of large number. The decryption algorithm contains only one module and square root . The size of the encrypted message is three times that of the plain text (Okamoto & Uchiyama, 1998):

Key Generation

- Random generation of two large prime numbers p, q such that $p < q$.
- Calculation the value of modulo n such that $n = p^2 q$.
- Randomly generate two integer numbers a, b such that:

$0 < a < \sqrt{(p.q)/2}$, $a \in (Z_{p.q})^*$

$0 < b < p$

- Calculate the value of u, such that $u = a + b.p.q$
- The public key is $< u, n >$ and the secret key is $< p, q, a, b >$

Table 1.

i	$x_i = x_{i-1}^2 \mod n$	p_i	$p_i \oplus m_i$
1	180539	1011	0010
2	193932	1100	0000
3	245613	1101	1100
4	130286	1110	1110
5	40632	1000	0100

Encryption Process

The space of the plain text M is encrypted such that $0 < M < ((0.5) . n^{(1/3)})$ in the following formula:

$$E(M) \equiv [\, M + u\,]^2 \bmod n$$

Decryption Process

To recover the plain text M from the cipher text $E(M)$, there are two algorithms:

- **The First Algorithm:**
  - Calculate the value of x such that $x \equiv E(M) \bmod p.q$
  - Calculate the plain text from the equation $M = \sqrt{x}$ - a
- **The Second Algorithm:**
  - Calculate the value of y, such that y = $\llcorner (E(M) / pq) \ulcorner$
  - Calculate the plain text M from the $M \equiv (y/2b) - a$

Example (5): Let $p = 23$, $q = 29$ and modulo $n = p^2q = 15341$, and $pq = 667$.

Suppose that $a = 8$, and $b = 5$. Encrypt $M = 12$ using Fist Version of OKAMOTO cryptosystem
Solution:

1. Calculate u, it will be: $u = 3343$, and hence the encrypted message is:

$$E(M) = 1107 \bmod 15341$$

2. To decrypt the enciphered message to get the plaintext (M), we will apply the two algorithms:
   a. **The first algorithm:**
      i. Calculate the value x, such that: $x = 400 \bmod 667$, hence the plaintext message is:

$$M = \sqrt{400} - 8 = 12$$

b. **The second algorithm:**
   i. Calculate the value y, such as: $y = 12$, hence the plaintext message (M) will be:

$$M = (16\text{-}80)/12 \bmod 23 = 12$$

Okamoto Second Version

Okamoto in 1987 modified his first version algorithm such that the Koyama cryptanalysis method cannot be valid on the modified version. And the size of the new cipher text message is (4.5) larger than the size of the plain text message

The Okamoto–Uchiyama cryptosystem was discovered in 1998 by T. Okamoto and S. Uchiyama. The system works in the group $(Z / nZ)^*$, where n is of the form p^2q and p and q are large primes. Like many public key cryptosystems, this scheme works in the group $(Z / nZ)^*$. A fundamental difference of this cryptosystem is that here n is of the form p^2q, where p and q are large primes. This scheme is homomorphic and hence malleable (Okamoto & Uchiyama, 1998).

Key Generation

- Random generation of two different large prime numbers p, q such that $p < q$.
- Calculate the value of the modulo n such that $n = p^2.q$.
- Randomly generate integer numbers a_1, a_2, b_1, b_2 such that:

$$0 < a_i < (0.5) . P^{/3} , i = 1, 2$$

$$0 < b_i < P$$

- Calculate u_1, u_2 such that:

$$u_1 = a_1 + b_1.p.q$$

$$u_2 = a_2 + b_2.p.q$$

- Calculate the value of u such that: $u \equiv u_2 . (u_1)^{-1} \bmod p.q$
- The public key is $< n, u >$ and the private key is $< p, q, a_1, a_2, b_1, b_2 >$

Encryption Process

The space of the plain text message (M) will be enciphered as a pair of values (M_1, M_2) such that it satisfies: $0 < M_i < n^{(1/3)}$ for i = 0, 1 and

$$E(M) \equiv [M_1 + M_2 u]^2 \bmod n$$

Decryption Process

- Calculate the value of x such as: $x \equiv E(M) . (u_1)^2 \bmod p.q$
- Calculate value of y such that: $y = {}^{\llcorner}(E(M) * (u_1)^2 \bmod R) / p.q \ulcorner$
- Calculate the value of z such that: $z = \sqrt{x}$
- Calculate value of w such that : $w \equiv (y / (2z)) \bmod p$
- Calculate the values of M_1, and M_2 from the following two equations:

$$M_1 \equiv (b_2.z - a_2.w) (a_1.b_2 - a_2.b_1)^{-1} \bmod p$$

$$M_2 \equiv (a_1.w - b_1.z) (a_1.b_2 - a_2.b_1)^{-1} \bmod p$$

Security

The security of the *entire* message can be shown to be equivalent to factoring n. The semantic security rests on the p-subgroup assumption, which assumes that it is difficult to determine whether an element x in $(Z / nZ)^*$ is in the subgroup of order p. This is very similar to the quadratic residuosity problem and the higher residuosity problem.

KIT Cryptosystem

At 1987 Kuosawa, Ito and Takeuchi (KIT) proposed public key cryptosystem. It is considered as a sample of Second Order RSA – Type cryptosystem with security equivalent to the problem of factorization of a large number (Kurosawa, Ito & Takeuchi, 1987) .

Key Generation

- Random generation of two different large prime numbers p, q, and $n = p.q$
- Randomly generate real number c such that it satisfies:

$$J[c, q] = -1 \text{ and } J[c, p] = -1$$

- Public key is $< c, n >$ and secret key is $< p, q >$

Encryption Process

To encrypt the plain text space (M) such that $0 < M < n$ and GCD (M, n) = 1

- Encrypt the plain text message M as follows:

$$E(M) \equiv [M^2 + c] . M^{-1} \bmod n$$

- Calculate the values of t, s such that

$s = 0$ if $J[M, n] = 1$, or $s = 1$ if $J[M, n] = -1$

$t = 1$ if $(c . M^{-1}) \bmod n > M$, or $t = 0$ if $(c . M^{-1}) \bmod n < M$

The cipher text consists of three parts t, s, and $E(M)$, that means ($E(M), s, t$).

Decryption Process

To recover the plain text from the cipher text $(E(M), s, t)$ we will follow the following steps:

- Solve the equation of second degree: $M^2 - E(M) \cdot M + c = 0$ under $(\bmod\ p)$ to get the roots s_1 and s_2 and solve the same equation under the $(\bmod\ q)$ to get the roots r_1 and r_2 with the same procedure followed with Rabin's cryptosystem (1979) .
- Use Chinese Remainder Theorem (CRT) to get $M_1, M_2, M_3,$ and M_4.
- The plain text message M will be:
  - If the value of $s = 0$ then plain text M will be:

$M = \text{Min}\ (M_1, M_2)$ if t = 0, or $M = \text{Max}\ (M_3, M_4)$ if t = 1

  - If the value of $s = 1$ then plain text M will be:

$M = \text{Min}\ (M_3, M_4)$ if t = 0, or $M = \text{Max}\ (M_3, M_4)$ if t = 1

Example (6): Let $p = 7$ and $q = 11$, and $n = p.q = 77$. Let $c = 5$. Encrypt the plaintext $M = 03$ using KIT.

Solution: The message encryption will be:
$E(M) = [3 + 5*26] \bmod 77 \equiv 56$
Calculate value S, and t, such that:

$J[\ M, n\ ] = -1$ because $S = 1$

$5*26 \bmod 77 = 53 > M = 3$ Because $t = 0$

Hence the plain text will be $< 56, 1, 0 >$

Decryption Algorithm

To get M from the plaintext $< 56, 1, 0 >$, we need to solve the second order equation:

$M^2 - 56.M + 5 = 0$ to the $(\bmod\ p = 7)$. Hence the roots will be $S_1 = 4$ and $S_2 = 3$, and for the mod $q = 11$, the roots will be $r_1 = 3$ and $r_2 = 8$.

Using CRT we will get: $M_1 = 25, M_2 = 31, M_3 = 53,$ and $M_4 = 3$. And since $S = 1$ and $t = 3$, hence the plain text message M will be:

$M = \min\ (53, 3) = 3$

Shimada Cryptosystem

Key Generation

- Randomly generate two large prime numbers p and q, such that (Shimada, 1992):

$J[-1, p] = -1, J[2, p] = 1$

$J[-1, q] = -1, J[2, p] = -1$

- Calculate the mod n such that $n = p.q$
- The public key is n, and the private key is $< p, q >$

Encryption Process

- Calculate the value of y such that $y \equiv M^2 \bmod n$
- Calculate the cipher text $E(M)$ from the equations

$t_e(M) = 1$ if $0 \leq M \leq (n-1)/2$, or $t_e(M) = -1$ if $(n-1)/2 \leq M \leq n-1$

$u_e(M) = 1$ if $J[M, n] = 1$ or $J[M, n] = 0$, or $u_e(M) = -1$ if $J[M, n] = -1$

The cipher text will be E(*M*).

Decryption Process

Decryption the cipher text message E(*M*) to obtain plain text *M*, as follows:

• Calculate the value of y such that:

$y \equiv$ E(*M*) . [t_d (E(*M*) . u_d (E(*M*))]$^{-1}$ mod *n*, and

$$t_e(E(M)) = \begin{cases} 1 \text{ if } J\big[E(M),n\big] = J\big[E(M),q\big] = 0 \\ J\big[E(M),q\big] \text{ if } J\big[E(M),p\big] = 0 \text{ and} \\ J\big[E(M),q\big] \neq 0 \\ J\big[E(M),p\big] \text{ if } J\big[E(M),p\big] = 0 \end{cases}$$

• Solve the second order equation ($M^2 - y = 0$) mod *p* to get the two roots s_1 and s_2, and the same equation can be solved under (mod *q*) to get the two roots r_1 and r_2 the same manner followed at Rabin's cryptosystem.

• Use the CRT to get M_1, M_2, M_3, and M_4. Then the plain text message will be one of the four values of M_i, $1 \leq i \leq 4$, which satisfy the following two conditions:

$t_e (M_i) = t_d$ (E(*M*))

$u_e (M_i) = u_d$ (E(*M*))

Example (7): Let *p*=7 and *q* =3 and *n* =21. Encipher message (*M* = 05) using Shimada Cryptosystem.
  Solution:

• **Encryption Process:**
  ○ Calculate y: $y = 5^2$ mod 21 = 4
  ○ Calculate $t_e(5) = 1$, and $u_e(5) = 1$
  ○ E(*M*) = 4 mod 21 = 4
• **Decryption Process:**
  ○ Calculate y: y = 4 mod 21 = 4

○ Calculate roots of the equation: $M^2 - 4 = 0$ for modulo *p* =7, then: S_1=2 and S_2= 5
○ Calculate roots of the equation: $M^2 - 4 = 0$ for modulo *q* =3, then: r_1= 2 and r_2 = 1
○ Using CRT, we get M_1=2, and M_2 =19, M_3=16 and M_4=5
○ Calculate values of $t_d(4)$ and $u_d(4)$, hence $t_d(4) = 1$, and $u_d(4)$=1. Since $u_e(5)$=1 and $t_e(5) = 1$, then the plain text message is: $M = M_4 = 05$.

PROPOSED GENERALIZED FORMULA FOR RSA – SECOND ORDER TYPE

It is possible to write the RSA type cryptosystem of the second order in the encryption process (*c* =M^2 mod *n*), and the module n is a multiplication of two different large primes (*p* and *q*), as follows (Al Swidi, 1998):

$$f(M) = (S^{2c1})^\alpha \cdot (U_e \cdot t_e)^\beta \cdot (1/M^2)^\gamma \cdot (M + c / M)^\lambda \cdot (M + b) M \text{ mod } n$$

where *f*(*M*) is the encryption function in term of the variable *M* which represents the plain text, where $0 \leq M < n$, and the values c_1, S, c, b are public keys and $U_e \in \{1,2\}$, $t_e \in \{-1, 1\}$. They are calculated as follows:

1. If J[*M*,*n*] = 1, then $U_e = 1$, $c_1 = 0$

J[*M*,*n*] = 0, then $U_e = 1$

J[*M*,n] = -1, then $U_e = 2$, c_1 =1

2. *b* is Real number (chosen randomly) such that: $0 \leq b < n$.
3. *S* is Real number (chosen randomly) such that: J[*S*, *n*]= -1
4. *c* is Real number (chosen randomly) such that: J[*c*, *p*]= J[*c*, *q*]= -1

5. t_e is a real number taking the value 1 if $0 \le M \le (n-1)/2$, and taking the value (-1) if $(n-1)/2 < M \le (n-1)$. Then the function $f(M)$ represents:

   a. Rabin (1979) Encryption Function if $\alpha = \beta = \gamma = \lambda = 0$.

   b. William (1980) Encryption Function if $\beta = \gamma = \lambda = b = 0, \alpha = 1$.

   c. GoldWasser (1984) Encryption function if $\alpha = \beta = \lambda = b = 0$, $\gamma = 1$

   d. KIT (1987) Encryption Function if $\alpha = \beta = b = 0$, $\gamma = \lambda = 1$

   e. Shimada (1992) Encryption Function if: $\alpha = \gamma = \lambda = b = 0$, $\beta = 1$

Some Conditions are valid to the cryptosystems of the second degree:

- In Rabin, Goldwasser, Okamato and KIT cryptosystems there are no conditions on choosing p and q, just they must be large different numbers.

- In William and Shimada Cryptosystems, there are conditions which must be considered for choosing p and q, as follows:
  - In William's cryptosystem: $p = q = -1 \bmod 4$, while
  - In Shimada cryptosystem: $(p-1)/2$, and $(q-1)/2$ must be odd numbers, and

J[2,q]= -1 and J[2,p]=1

- These Cryptosystems do not use Euler function ϕ (n), because their encryption functions (for each of them) are of second degree, since: $(GCD(\phi$ $(n), 2) = 2)$

While on the other hand, the Decryption Algorithms for the second degree RSA-Type cryptosystems can be considered with the followings:

- Rabin's, Shimada and KIT cryptosystems uses the CRT in the decryption process.

- William's, Goldwasser and Okamoto decryption processes do not use the CRT.

- CRT can be used in the decryption process for the Okamoto (first version), and building the decryption algorithm depends on CRT.

Since $E(M) \equiv (M + u)^2 \bmod n$

$\equiv M^2 + 2uM + u^2 \bmod n$, then

$M^2 + 2uM + (u^2 - E(M)) \equiv 0 \bmod n$

The distinguishing factor of the equation: $M^2 + 2uM + (u^2 - E(M)) \equiv 0$ will be:

$d = (2u)^2 - 4 (u^2 - E(M))$

$d = 4 E(M)$.

and following the same procedure adopted in Rabin's decryption process, and getting (M_1, M_2, M_3, M_4), then testing is made to find out which one satisfies the condition:

$0 \le M_i < 0.5 . (n)^{1/3}$

It will be the correct plain text message.

PROPOSED DEVELOPMENT OF CRT

This section provides the developed formula of the CRT, with examples that verify the proposed concept and a comparison is made with the conventional CRT from the complexity point of view (Salman, 1995).

Theorem (1): Let ($p_1, p_2, \ldots, p_n$) be different prime numbers, such that GCD (p_i, p_j) =1 for each i≠j. Then:

1. For $a_i \in Zp_i$ for the values $1 \leq i \leq n$, there exists one unique element $x \in Zn$, and $x \equiv a_i \bmod p_i$ verify the system of linear congruence: for the values $1 \leq i \leq n$, where $n = \Pi p_i$

2. If $u_i.p_{i+1} \equiv 1 \bmod \Pi p_i$, for all $1 \leq i \leq n-1$, then x will be in this form:

$$X \equiv (...(((a_1-a_2)u_1 \bmod p_1)p_2 +a_2).....)-a_{n-1})u_{n-2}$$
$$\bmod \Pi p_i) \, p_{n-1} + a_{n-1}) -a_n) \, u_{n-1} \bmod \Pi p_i) \, p_n + a_n$$

Example (8): Solve the system of linear congruence using the modified CRT according to theorem (1).

$x \equiv 3 \bmod 2$

$x \equiv 0 \bmod 3$

$x \equiv 4 \bmod 5$

$x \equiv 1 \bmod 7$

Solution: Calculate u_1, u_2, and u_3, then:

$u_1 \equiv 1 \bmod 2$, $u_2 \equiv 5 \bmod 6$, $u_3 \equiv 13 \bmod 30$,

$x \equiv ((.... (3-0).1 \bmod 2).3 +0) -4).5 \bmod 6).5$
$+4)-1).13 \bmod 30).7 +1 \equiv 99 \bmod 210$

$x \equiv 99 \bmod 210$

Result (1): Let $n_1, n_2, .., n_n$ different integers, and $GCD(n_i,n_j)=1$ for each $i \neq j$, then:
  a. For the numbers $a_i \in Z_n$ for all $1 \leq i \leq n$, the unique element $x \in Z_n$, exists and satisfies the linear congruencies $x \equiv a_i \bmod n_i$, to the values $1 \leq i \leq n$, where $n = \Pi n_i$
  b. If $u_i. n_{i+1} \equiv 1 \bmod \Pi n_i$ for all $1 \leq i \leq n$, then x will take this formula:

$$x \equiv ((...(((a_1-a_2)u_1 \bmod n_1) \, n_2 +a_2).....) - a_{n-1}) \, u_{n-2}$$
$$\bmod \Pi n_i) \, n_{n-1} + a_{n-1}) -a_n) \, u_{n-1}$$

$\bmod \Pi n_i) \, n_n + a_n$

Theorem (2): Let $(p_1,p_2, ..., p_n)$ be different prime numbers, such that $GCD(p_i, p_j) =1$ for each $i \neq j$. Then:

  • For each polynomial $f_i(x)$ on the field Zp_i for the $1 \leq i \leq n$, there exists unique polynomial $f(x)$ on the field Z_n, which satisfies the linear congruence:

$f(x) \equiv f_i(x) \bmod p_i$ for the values $1 \leq i \leq n$, and $n = \Pi p_i$

  • If $u_i . p_{i+1} \equiv 1 \bmod \Pi p_i$ for $1 \leq i \leq n$, then $f(x)$ in (a) above will be represented as follows:

$$f(x) \equiv (...(((f_1(x)-f_2(x))u_1 \bmod p_1)p_2 +f_2(x))...) -$$
$$f_{n-1}(x)) \, u_{n-2} \bmod \Pi p_j) \, p_{n-1} +f_{n-1}(x)) -f_n(x))u_{n-1} \bmod$$
$$\Pi p_j) \, p_n +f_n(x)$$

Example (9): Solve the linear congruence using theorem (2):

$f(x) \equiv x^3 + x +1 \bmod 3$

$f(x) \equiv x^2 + 2 \bmod 5$

$f(x) \equiv x +4 \bmod 7$

Solution: Calculate u_1 and u_2, which give: $u_2=13 \bmod 15$, and $u_1=2 \bmod 3$, then:

$f(x) \equiv 70x^3 + 21x^2 + 85x +18 \bmod 105$

Result (2): Let $R_1, ..., R_n$ be different integer numbers, such that $GCD(R_i,R_j) = 1$, for all $i \neq j$.

  • For any polynomial $f_i(x)$ on the ring Z_{Ri} for $1 \leq i \leq n$, there exists unique polynomial $f(x)$ on the ring Z_R, where the congruencies are satisfied:

$f(x) \equiv f_i(x) \bmod R_i$ for all $1 \leq i \leq n$ and $R = \Pi R_j$

- If $u_i . R_{i+1} \equiv 1 \bmod \Pi R_j$ for all $1 \leq i \leq n$, then $f(x)$ in the (a) above will be given as:

$f(x) \equiv (\ldots(((f_1(x) - f_2(x))u_1 \bmod R_1)R_2 + f_2(x))\ldots) - f_{n-1}(x))u_{n-2} \bmod \Pi R_j) R_{n-1}$

$+ f_{n-1}(x)) - f_n(x))u_{n-1} \bmod \Pi R_j) R_n + f_n(x)$

Theorem (3): Let $P_1, \ldots, P_n$ be a different prime numbers, such that GCD $(P_i, P_j) = 1$, for $i \neq j$, and $u_1(x), \ldots, u_n(x)$ will be irreducible polynomials in the fields $Z_{P1}, \ldots, Z_{pn}$ respectively, and gcd $(u_i(x), u_j(x)) = 1$ for all $i \neq j$. Then:

1. For any polynomial $f(x)$ in the fields Zp_i for all $1 \leq i \leq n$, there exists unique polynomial $f(x)$ on the ring Z_R, where the linear congruencies will be satisfied:

$f(x) \equiv f_i(x) \bmod (u_i(x), P_i)$ for the values: $1 \leq i \leq n$ and $R = \Pi P_i$

2. If $h_i(x). u_{i+1}(x) \equiv 1 \bmod (\Pi u_j, \Pi P_j)$ for all $1 \leq i \leq n-1$, then the polynomial $f(x)$ in (1) above will be given as:

$f(x) \equiv (\ldots(((f_1(x) - f_2(x))h_1 \bmod u_1(x)) u_2(x) + f_2(x))\ldots) - f_{n-1}(x)) h_{n-2}(x) \bmod \Pi u_j(x)) u_{n-1}(x) + f_{n-1}(x)) - f_n(x)) h_{n-1}(x) \bmod \Pi u_j(x)) + f_n(x)$

Result (3): Let $R_1, \ldots, R_n$ be different integers, such that gcd $(R_i, R_j) = 1$, for all $i \neq j$, and $u_1(x), \ldots, u_n(x)$ are polynomials on the rings $Z_{R1}, \ldots, Z_{Rn}$ respectively, where gcd $(u_i(x), u_j(x)) = 1$ for all $i \neq j$, then (Al Swidi, 1998):

- For any polynomial $f_i(x)$ on the rings Z_{Ri} for all $1 \leq i \leq n$, there exists a unique polynomial $f(x)$ on the ring Z_R, where the linear congruencies:

$f(x) \cong f_i(x) \bmod (u_i(x), R_i)$ for the values $1 \leq i \leq n$ and $R = \Pi R_i$

- If $h_i(x) . u_{i+1}(x) \equiv 1 \bmod \Pi u_j$ for all $1 \leq i < n$. Then the polynomial in $f(x)$ above will be given as:

$f(x) \equiv (\ldots(((f_1(x) - f_2(x))h_1 \bmod u_1(x)) u_2(x) + f_2(x))\ldots) - f_{n-1}(x)) h_{n-2}(x) \bmod \Pi u_j(x)) u_{n-1}(x) + f_{n-1}(x)) - f_n(x)) h_{n-1}(x) \bmod \Pi u_j(x)) + f_n(x)$

CONCLUSION

1. It is clear that the proposed generalized formula for the RSA- Second Order Types is suitable for all the mentioned types of the previously known RSA –Second Order (like Rabin, William, and others). Such formula will help in unifying the treatment of the 7 mentioned cryptosystems.

2. The modified CRT will reduce the number of calculated elements. This clearly comes from the theorems (1, 2, and 3). The number of likely elements is (n) in the conventional CRT theorems, while in the modified theorems, the number is (n-1). This will result in reduction in speed and storage in computer implementations.

3. When comparing the formulas of the likely element in the conventional CRT method, we will see that N_i is a multiplication of (n-1) of the prime numbers to a modulo which is a prime number. On the other hand in the theorems (1 and 2) we see that u_1 is the likely element of single prime number taking a single modulo which is also a prime number, and u_2 is the likely element of single prime number to a modulo which is a multiplication of (n-1) of prime numbers, i.e., the calculation of likely numbers in the developed formula is faster than in the conventional formula. The same matter is valid to theorem (3).

4. When comparing between the unique solution in the conventional formula and developed formula. When n=3, then the number of multiplication processes is (8) and the number of addition processes (3) in the conventional formula, while in the developed formula, the number of multiplication process is (5) and the number of additions and subtractions is (4). Hence the number of operations in the modified formula is less than that in the conventional formula. This will result in improving the calculation process and reducing the storage capacity by about 18%.

REFERENCES

Al Swidi, L. (1998). *A study of mathematical structure for cryptanalytic methods of public key cryptosystems and proposing a new cipher systems*. (Unpublished doctoral dissertation). Al-Mustansiriya University, Baghdad, Iraq.

Blum, M., & Goldwasser, S. (1985). An Efficient Probabilistic Public Key Encryption Scheme which Hides All Partial Information. In Proceedings of Advances in Cryptology - CRYPTO '84, (pp. 289–299). Springer.

Diffie, W., & Hellman, M. (1976). New Direction in Cryptography. *IEEE Transactions on Information Theory*, 22(11), 644–654. doi:10.1109/TIT.1976.1055638

Douglas, R. (2006). *Cryptography Theory and Practice*. Champan & Hall/CRC.

Goldwasser, S., & Micali, S. (1982). Probabilistic encryption and how to play mental poker keeping secret all partial information. In *Proceedings of the fourteenth annual ACM symposium on Theory of computing* (pp. 365–377). ACM Publisher.

Kranakis, E. (1984). *Primality and Cryptography*. New York: John Wiley & Sons.

Kurosawa, K., Ito, T., & Takeuchi, M. (1987). Public key cryptosystem using a reciprocal number with the same intractability as factoring a large number. *Electronics Letters*, 23(15), 809–810. doi:10.1049/el:19870573

Menezes, A., Oorschot, V., & Paul, C. (1996). *Handbook of Applied Cryptography*. CRC Press. doi:10.1201/9781439821916

Muller, S. (2001). *On the security of a Williams based public key encryption scheme. Report to University of Klagenfurt*. Austria: Springer- Verlag.

Nimrod, M., & Christos, H. P. (1989). *A Note on Total Functions, Existence Theorems, and Computational Complexity*. Retrieved from http://citeseerx.ist.psu.edu/viewdoc/summary?doi=10.1.1.9.5230

Okamoto, T., & Uchiyama, S. (1998). A New Public Key Cryptosystem as secure as factoring. In *Proceedings of Advances in Cryptology* (pp. 308–318). Springer Verlag. doi:10.1007/BFb0054135

Pascal, P. (1999). Public-key cryptosystem based on Composite Degree Residusity Classes. In *Proceedings of Advances in Cryptology- Eurocrypt'99* (Vol. 1592, pp. 223–238). Berlin: Springer.

Rabin, M. (1979). *Digital Signature and Public key functions as intractable as factorization. MIT/LCS/TR-212, January. MIT/LCS/TM-82*. CAMBRIDGE, United State.

Richard, A. (2003). *RSA and Public Key Cryptography*. Chapman & Hall/CRC.

Salman, S. (1995). *Analytical study of some public key cryptosystems depending on some evaluation parameters*. (Unpublished M.Sc. Dissertation). University of Technology, Baghdad, Iraq.

Schroeder, M. R. (1986). *Number theory in science and communication*. Berlin, Germany: Springer Verlag. doi:10.1007/978-3-662-22246-1

Seberry, J., & Pieprzyk, J. (1989). *Cryptography-An Introduction to Computer Security*. Prentice Hall.

Shimada, M. (1992). Another practical public key cryptosystem. *Electronics Letters*, *28*(23), 2146–2147. doi:10.1049/el:19921377

William, H. (1985). Some public Key Crypto Functions as Intractable as Factorization. In *Proceeding of Crypto'84 (LNCS)* (Vol. 196, pp. 66–70). Berlin: Springer.

ADDITIONAL READING

Boris, S. (2008), Cryptosystem Based on Extraction of Square Roots of Complex Integers, Fifth International Conference on Information Technology: New Generations. IEEE Computer Society. (pp: 1190-1191), Washington, DC, USA: IEEE Computer Society

Chang, C., & Hwang, S. (1997). A simple approach for generating RSA keys. *Information Processing Letters*, *63*(1), 19–21.

Chang, C., & Tsu, S. (2000). An Improvement on Shimada's Public-Key Cryptosystem. *Tamkang Journal of Science and Engineering*, *3*(2), 75–79.

Chen, T. (2005). A threshold signature scheme based on the elliptic curve cryptosystem. *Applied Mathematics and Computation*, *162*(1), 1119–1134.

Chien, H. (2013). Combining Rabin cryptosystem and error correction codes to facilitate anonymous authentication with un-traceability for low-end devices. *Computer Networks*, *57*(14), 2705–2717.

Christopher, W. (2005). *Multivariate Quadratic Polynomials in Public Key Cryptography*. Belgium: Katholieke Universiteit Leuven.

Daniel, J. (2008), RSA signatures and Rabin–Williams signatures: the state of the art, Available at: http:// cr.yp.to/sigs/rwsota-20080131.pdf.

Goldwasser, S., & Mihir, B. (2008), Lecture Notes on Cryptography. Available at: http://www-cse.ucsd.edu/users/mihir.

Lu, R., & Zhenfu, C. (2005). Non-interactive deniable authentication protocol based on factoring. *Computer Standards & Interfaces*, *27*(4), 401–405.

Mario, D., & Rosario, G. (2006). Provably secure threshold password- uthenticated key exchange. Science direct. *Journal of Computer and System Sciences*, *72*, 978–1001.

Martínez, S. et al. (2012). Non-Reducible Meyer–Müller's Like Elliptic Curve Cryptosystem, Browse Journals & Magazines. *Latin America Transactions*, *10*(3), 1730–1733.

Mihnea, R. (2008), Public-key Cryptography: The RSA and the Rabin Cryptosystem, BACHELOR OF SCIENCE THESIS, Available at: http://www.google.com/url?sa=t&rct=j&q=&esrc=s&source=web&cd=1&cad=rja&uact=8&ved=0CCYQFjAA&url=http%3A%2F%2Fbiginteger.googlecode.com%2Ffiles%2FPublic-key%2520Cryptography%2520-%2520The%2520RSA%2520and%2520the%2520Rabin%2520Cryptosystems.pdf&ei=IoY2U8-1DYv9ygOHrIDwBA&usg=AFQjCNFca4SuuxmTjNzO0HH8XHpZo_CbTA&sig2=BU0waPP8aXbnRgxFFIUtHQ&bvm=bv.63808443,d.bGQ

Saravana, K., & Vaishnavi, T. (2012), Rabin Public Key Cryptosystem for Mobile Authentication, IEEE-International Conference On Advances In Engineering, Science And Management (ICAESM -2012), (p: 854 - 860), United State, IEEExplore Digital Library: Publisher.

Seung, G., & Hoeteck, W. (2012). Lossy trapdoor functions from homomorphic reproducible encryption. *Information Processing Letters*, *112*(20), 794–798.

Shenghui, S., & Shuwang, L. (2012). A public key cryptosystem based on three new provable problems. *Theoretical Computer Science*, 426–427.

Tai, W., et al. (2012), A Security Enhancement on A Remote User Authentication Scheme Based on the Rabin Cryptosystem with Secure Password Updating, 26th International Conference on Advanced Information Networking and Applications Workshops. (pp: 160-164), Washington, DC, USA, IEEE Computer Society.

KEY TERMS AND DEFINITIONS

Chinese Remainder Theorem (CRT): The Chinese remainder theorem is a result about congruencies in number theory and its generalizations in abstract algebra. It was first published in the 3rd to 5th centuries by Chinese mathematician Sun Tzu. In its basic form, the Chinese remainder theorem will determine a number n that when divided by some given divisors leaves given remainders.

Greatest Common Divisor (GCD): In mathematics, the greatest common divisor (gcd), also known as the greatest common factor (gcf), or highest common factor (hcf), of two or more integers (at least one of which is not zero), is the largest positive integer that divides the numbers without a remainder. For example, the GCD of 8 and 12 is 4. This notion can be extended to polynomials, see Polynomial greatest common divisor, or to rational numbers (with integer quotients).

Key Generation: Is the process of generating keys for cryptography. A key is used to encrypt and decrypt whatever data is being encrypted/decrypted. Modern cryptographic systems include symmetric-key algorithms (such as DES and AES) and public-key algorithms (such as RSA).

Symmetric-key algorithms use a single shared key; keeping data secret requires keeping this key secret. Public-key algorithms use a public key and a private key. The public key is made available to anyone (often by means of a digital certificate). A sender encrypts data with the public key; only the holder of the private key can decrypt this data.

Public Key Cryptography (PKC): Public-key cryptography, also known as asymmetric cryptography, refers to a cryptographic algorithm which requires two separate keys, one of which is secret (or private) and one of which is public. Although different, the two parts of this key pair are mathematically linked. The public key is used to encrypt plaintext or to verify a digital signature; whereas the private key is used to decrypt ciphertext or to create a digital signature.

Rivest-Shamir-Adleman (RSA): RSA is a cryptosystem, which is known as one of the first practicable public-key cryptosystems and is widely used for secure data transmission. In such a cryptosystem, the encryption key is public and differs from the decryption key which is kept secret. In RSA, this asymmetry is based on the practical difficulty of factoring the product of two large prime numbers, the factoring problem. RSA stands for Ron Rivest, Adi Shamir and Leonard Adleman, who first publicly described the algorithm in 1977.

Security: Traditional definitions of encryption security guarantee secrecy for any plaintext that can be computed by an outside adversary. In some settings, such as anonymous credential or disk encryption systems, this is not enough, because these applications encrypt messages that depend on the secret key.

Trapdoor One-Way Function: In computer science, a one-way function is a function that is easy to compute on every input, but hard to invert given the image of a random input. Here, "easy" and "hard" are to be understood in the sense of computational complexity theory, specifically the theory of polynomial time problems. Not being one-to-one is not considered sufficient of a function for it to be called one-way.

Chapter 11
Cryptographic Key Distribution and Management

Martin Rublík
University of Economics, Slovakia

ABSTRACT

Cryptographic key distribution and management is one of the most important steps in the process of securing data by utilizing encryption. Problems related to cryptographic key distribution and management are hard to solve and easy to exploit, and therefore, they are appealing to the attacker. The purpose of this chapter is to introduce the topics of cryptographic key distribution and management, especially with regards to asymmetric keys. The chapter describes how these topics are handled today, what the real-world problems related to cryptographic key distribution and management are, and presents existing solutions as well as future directions in their solving. The authors present the cryptographic key management and distribution problems from a multidisciplinary point of view by looking at its economic, psychological, usability, and technological aspects.

INTRODUCTION

Encryption is especially useful for providing security related services such as protecting data integrity and confidentiality, or supporting authentication processes (ITU-T, 1991). Though encryption is a vital part of a security system, it should be viewed only as one of the countermeasures. Encryption protection can be circumvented or broken at many levels. Encryption systems can be broken at design or implementation level, or can be simply bypassed. There exist several examples and proof-of-concepts of applied cryptography related attacks at design and implementation level, but most of the real-world attacks are simply bypassing the cryptography protection. Cryptographic protecion is circumvented either by attacking at

application layer (Langley, 2013) where the data is unencrypted, or by attacking the key management and distribution infrastructure (Leavitt, 2011).

In this chapter we present why it is appealing for the attackers to take advantage of weak cryptographic key management and distribution. Hence we focus on description of existing approaches to symmetric and public key distribution and management from the user's point of view (usability) and from the security infrastructure provider's point of view (economics).

In the first part of the chapter we present basic topics related to cryptographic key distribution and management. We outline key management life-cycle and describe the dependencies between its phases and security services as defined by (ITU-T, 1991). We also explain important factors

DOI: 10.4018/978-1-4666-5808-0.ch011

that affect the approach to key distribution and management.

In the second part we briefly describe different key distribution and management approaches relevant to symmetric cryptography. We mention especially pre-shared keys and key distribution centers.

Because public key cryptography is commonly used for key distribution of symmetric keys, we focus extensively on public key distribution and management in the third part of the chapter. In particular, we describe centralized, decentralized and hierarchical approaches to public key distribution and management.

In the fourth part we compare particular approaches to public key distribution and management and outline their core characteristics, advantages and issues.

Finally, in the last part of the chapter, we further examine existing and future solutions to the issues of X.509 public key infrastructure. We chose X.509 public key infrastructure because it is most widely deployed Internet cryptographic key infrastructure and provides key management services for common network encryption protocols such as SSL/TLS, IPSec and S/MIME.

GENERAL CONCEPTS IN KEY MANAGEMENT AND DISTRIBUTION

In order to protect data integrity and confidentiality by using encryption the involved parties must share cryptographic keys. Modern encryption systems are designed in a way that protects the data if the encryption algorithm is known and encrypted data is available to the attacker. Many of the systems are designed to further protect the data even if the attacker knows the encryption algorithm, knows the encrypted data, and can decrypt some of the data. It is however impossible to protect the data if the attacker can gain access to the entire set of cryptographic keys. Hence, key management and distribution is crucial for cryptographic protection.

According to (NIST, 2007) cryptographic key management lifecycle consists of several phases. Their simplified illustration is expressed by Figure 1.

Especially hard part of key management lifecycle is trust establishment and key distribution in pre-operational phase. In these processes involved parties need to prove the possession of cryptographic keys, and exchange them in a secure manner.

There are several approaches applicable to distribution of cryptographic keys and trust establishment. Their suitability depends on a number of factors. Factors that are especially important include: type and purpose of performed cryptographic transformation and security service that requires this transformation, overall number of entities that are part of the process, the skills and psychological characteristics of the users and system administrators involved in the process. These factors influence the trade-off between usability, security, and costs of approach to key distribution and management.

Security services as defined by (ITU-T, 1991) include: authentication, data confidentiality, data integrity and non-repudiation. These services affect key management and distribution process in its several phases, especially in: key generation phase, trust establishment phase, revocation phase, escrow and backup phases. For example consider that non-repudiation service should be provided. The cryptographic keys supporting non-repudiation service need to be generated by its owner, or at least the keys need to be generated in a way that provides sufficient assurance that the private key couldn't been used by anyone except its owner. Detailed illustration of dependencies is provided by Table 1.

Core aspect affecting the overall scale of cryptographic key distribution infrastructure is the number of users employing the cryptographic keys. It is evident that it is much easier to deploy and maintain small amount of cryptographic keys, than to operate a large scale Internet wide cryptographic key distribution infrastructure.

Figure 1. Key management phases

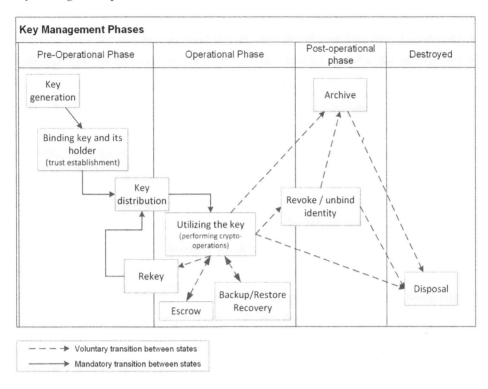

Table 1. Dependencies between key management phases and (chosen) security services

Security Service Key Management Phase Affected	Authentication	Data Confidentiality	Non-Repudiation
Key generation	Sufficient assurance that the private key can be used only by its holder should be provided.	Key generation should be done in a secure way that prevents the attacker from gaining access to private key.	Sufficient assurance that the private key can be used only by its holder must be provided.
Binding key and its holder's identity	The binding should provide a unique link to the holder's identity (with respect to information systems that make use of authentication service). Pseudonyms can be used.	Unique link to holder's identity is not required. Pseudonyms can be used.	Holder's identity and cryptographic keys should be associated in a legally binding way. Pseudonyms should not be used unless clearly marked and traceable.
Escrow / Key Recovery	Key escrow/recovery should not be used.	Key escrow/recovery might be desirable especially in enterprise environments.	Key escrow/recovery must not be used.
Backup and restore	Key backup and restore is not crucial.	Key backup and restore is important especially for protecting data-at-rest.	Key backup and restore is not crucial.
Revocation (Unbinding the holder's identity)	Revocation service or keys with short lifetime might be necessary in order to deal with key compromise (protection against impersonation attacks).	Revocation service or keys with short lifetime are necessary in order to deal with key compromise (protection against man-in-the-middle and impersonation attacks).	Timely revocation service is necessary in order to deal with key lost and compromise situations (protection against impersonation and repudiation attacks).

In several situations (as we describe later) the problem of trust establishment and key distribution is left to the users. The overall security of key distribution is therefore no more secure than the decision made by a specific user. In these cases technical skills and psychological characteristics of involved users and system administrators affect the overall security significantly. Especially psychological characteristics influence how the risk is perceived by the users that are either general users or experts in computer systems (Camp, Asgharpour, & Liu, 2007).

Cryptography and cryptographic key management is even less intuitive to general users than other topics in computer security such as computer viruses and network worms. Unfortunately, survey (Kienzle & Elder, 2003) indicates that the network worms and other types of malicious software do not need to be very innovative in order to be successful. As pointed out by (Furnell, 2005) this is a failure in application user interface design and not a failure on the user's side. The conclusion that usability is challenging in applications that utilize cryptography and perform key distribution is also encouredged by (Whitten & Tygar, 1999) and (Sheng, Broderick, & Koranda, 2006).

Usability and overall number of entities and their skills and psychological characteristics seem to be one of the core aspects that influence the complete security and feasibility of key distribution. For example it is feasible (Kahn, 1996) to use one-time pad encryption in very specific situations (small amount of high-valued data, small amount of involved, highly disciplined entities), despite its high and impractical requirements on key management. For more practical applications we discuss further flat, hierarchical, centralized, and decentralized approaches to trust establishment and key distribution in symmetric and public key cryptographic systems.

SYMMETRIC KEY DISTRIBUTION AND MANAGEMENT

In classical (symmetric) encryption systems involved parties share the same cryptographic key for encryption and decryption. Therefore, in order to apply protection one must establish a secure channel for key distribution. This secure channel needs to maintain *authenticity* and *confidentiality* of transmitted cryptographic keys.

In the real world this is achieved either by utilizing secure out-of-bound channels such as pre-shared keys, quantum key distribution, or by utilizing network security protocols and asymmetric encryption systems or trusted third parties.

Pre-Shared Keys

Pre-shared key is typically agreed upon all involved parties before they need to protect data by encryption. The pre-shared key is often distributed by employing out-of-bound channel, such as personal agreement or sharing a key through a telephone line. After the pre-shared key is distributed, it can be used directly for protecting the data, or it can be used for further key distribution.

Because pre-shared keys are usually exchanged by persons, they are often based on passwords or passphrases. However the passwords are not suitable as cryptographic keys because of their variable length and predictability. Encryption algorithms are designed to be fast, thus using a predictable password as a key would make them more susceptible to dictionary attacks.

In order to slow down the dictionary attacks keys are derived from passwords and passphrases by using a special function called *key stretching* function. The key stretching functions are designed to be slow, so the attacker cannot efficiently mount a dictionary attack.

In practice the pre-shared key distribution is popular in small scale environments. Pre-shared keys are used mostly for protecting network communications in local area networks and in networks with small number of nodes.

Pre-shared key distribution is a supported in many network security standards. Among others it is supported in Wi-Fi network protection standard Wi-Fi Protected Access (WPA) as well as in Internet Protocol Security (IPSec). Additionally, pre-shared keys are also supported in Transport Layer Security (TLS), but this part of TLS is not usually implemented in ordinary applications.

Typically pre-shared key distribution is not used in networks with larger scale because of management and scaling issues. Pre-shared keys are hard to manage, especially in cases when the pre-shared secret was compromised and should be changed. The scaling issues result from the fact that the pre-shared key should be different for every pair of communicating entities. This means that if we have N network nodes we need at least $N*(N-1)/2$ pre-shared keys.

Key Distribution Centers

The scaling and management issues can be more or less solved by involving a trusted third party called *key distribution center* (KDC). KDC first sets up a unique pre-shared key with every entity that is part of the system. These keys are called *master keys*. Afterwards, when two entities want to exchange encrypted data, they use KDC services for secure key distribution. The key that is distributed to these entities by a KDC is called *session key*.

Two advantages follow from this approach. First, only N master keys are required for N communicating entities. This improves the scalability of the solution. Second, if a session key is compromised only data that is protected by that particular key are jeopardized. Because session keys should be used only for limited amount of time, this improves the security and manageability of the solution.

The key distribution center is usually implemented as described by (Needham & Schroeder, 1978) or (Stallings, 2011). We summarize the necessary steps as follows.

1. Alice and Bob set-up master keys with KDC. We denote the keys MK_A and MK_B. This step needs occur only once per life of the master key, which last much longer than the session key.
2. When Alice wants to send encrypted data to Bob she asks KDC for a session key.
3. KDC sends the session key to Alice. This key is encrypted both with MK_A and MK_B
4. Alice sends the encrypted session key to Bob and starts the communication.

The steps involved in secure key distribution of the session key are specified in Needham–Schroeder protocol illustrated by Figure 2.

Though the Needham–Schroeder protocol illustrated by Figure 2 included replay attacks countermeasures, Denning and Sacco found a weakness in the protocol (Denning & Sacco, 1981). The protocol was fixed by introducing time stamps and time checks. With this correction the protocol serves as a basis for popular authentication and key distribution protocol Kerberos.

Kerberos is used especially for authentication in many enterprise environments because of the good support in Windows and UNIX-based operating systems. But Kerberos is supported by many popular network security protocols also for key distribution. Most notable security protocols that support symmetric key distribution by Kerberos are IPSec (Thomas, 2001) and TLS (Medvinsky & Hur, 1999).

Though Kerberos is used in large and medium networks and enterprises, it did not succeed in the Internet infrastructure. Employing a KDC for distributing cryptographic keys implies several

Figure 2. Key distribution center

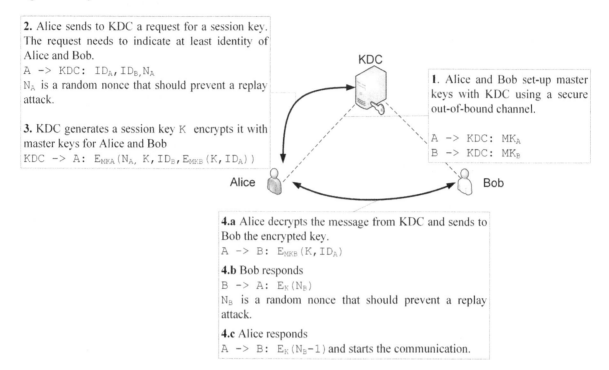

2. Alice sends to KDC a request for a session key. The request needs to indicate at least identity of Alice and Bob.

`A -> KDC: ID_A, ID_B, N_A`

N_A is a random nonce that should prevent a replay attack.

3. KDC generates a session key K encrypts it with master keys for Alice and Bob

`KDC -> A: E_MKA(N_A, K, ID_B, E_MKB(K, ID_A))`

KDC

1. Alice and Bob set-up master keys with KDC using a secure out-of-bound channel.

`A -> KDC: MK_A`
`B -> KDC: MK_B`

Alice

Bob

4.a Alice decrypts the message from KDC and sends to Bob the encrypted key.

`A -> B: E_MKB(K, ID_A)`

4.b Bob responds

`B -> A: E_K(N_B)`

N_B is a random nonce that should prevent a replay attack.

4.c Alice responds

`A -> B: E_K(N_B-1)` and starts the communication.

drawbacks. First, it is necessary to provide an online infrastructure for key distribution by KDC. Second, KDC is a single point of failure, both from security and from performance point of view.

These drawbacks can be partially mitigated by building a hierarchy of KDCs (Stallings, 2011). Unfortunately hierarchical KDCs still suffer from trust issues similar to issues applicable to public key distribution and management. Therefore in Internet scale the symmetric keys are usually distributed by utilizing advantages of public key cryptography.

PUBLIC KEY DISTRIBUTION AND MANAGEMENT

In asymmetric encryption systems involved parties possess a pair of cryptographic keys. One of the keys is used for encryption/verification process (*public key*) and is available to everyone. The other one (*private key*), is used for decryption/authentication process and is available only to its holder.

In order to distribute the public keys one must establish a secure channel that needs to maintain the *authenticity* of transmitted keys. Providing secure channel that maintains authenticity of transmitted keys is difficult, and means that asymmetric key distribution and management needs to take care of establishing the trust between involved parties.

The trust relationship is set up either directly between the involved parties or indirectly through a mediator. Direct trust setup is employed in naïve approaches to key distribution and management such as key continuity.

Indirect trust establishment enables more complex approach to key distribution and management. Later in this chapter we describe how indirect trust establishment makes possible centralized and decentralized key distribution.

Key Continuity

The most simplistic approach to key distribution and trust management is *key continuity*. With key continuity approach a secure channel for key distribution is provided out-of-band by verifying the public key directly by the user. This approach can be compared to pre-shared key distribution in symmetric key encryption. The entities exchange a key in a secure manner through a secure channel before encrypted communication occurs through insecure channel.

The public key is either verified directly, or indirectly by comparing its derivative created in a secure way (such as its hash). The first approach is employed[1] by popular remote access protocol SSHv1 (Ylonen, 1996). The latter is in use by secure VoIP protocol ZRTP for authenticating Diffie Hellman parameters necessary for key exchange (P. Zimmermann, 2011; Martin & Schertler, 2009). After the user confirms authenticity of the public key it is stored locally, so the user does not need to verify it in future. This approach is therefore called also Trust on First Use (*ToFU*).

Besides the mentioned world-wide deployments there exists several proof-of-concepts for incorporating key continuity in order to protect e-mail communications (Garfinkel & Miller, 2005), (Gutmann, 2004). Unfortunatelly though there is security improvement in utilizing ToFU for protecting e-mail communications (Garfinkel & Miller, 2005), even today these implementations haven't been widely deployed.

Key continuity is not deployed widely enough because it is believed that it does not scale well (Zimmermann & Callas, 2009), lacks possibility of key revocation, it is not legally binding to key holder (it does not provide non-repudiation necessary for electronic signatures), and last but not least, it is not implemented in a user friendly way, which makes it susceptible to phishing attacks (Garfinkel & Miller, 2005). The last conclusion is also supported by Peter Gutmann's paper (Gutmann, 2011). Gutmann presumes that the SSH keys are not verified by the users connecting to remote systems. His hypotheses is based on the fact that help-desk supporting personnel in two distinct large organizations were unable to recall a single case of any user ever verifying any SSH server key out-of-band. Both of these organizations were medium sized and engaged several thousand computer-literate users.

Decentralized Key Distribution

Decentralized key distribution is based on key certification. Key distribution is provided in two ways. First, users exchange public keys directly by utilizing secure channel (same way as in key continuity), but afterwards the users can digitally sign/certify other public keys (trust keys indirectly). This way it is possible to build a trust relationship and distribute public keys between users through insecure channel (send signed keys by Internet, publish them in directory/keyserver or on a web page).

Decentralized key distribution is used for example in popular mail encryption standard OpenPGP. OpenPGP designers (Zimmermann & Callas, 2009) define trust as follows: "Trust is the mechanism we use to decide that a key is valid. A key is *valid* if it is actually owned by the person who claims to own it. Validity is a score and can be used only to determine whether the name on a key is accurate. Trust is a relationship that helps us determine validity."

OpenPGP trust model (Web-of-Trust) provides two levels of trust for every entity: fully trusted and partially trusted. Valid keys are keys either: directly trusted (signed by the verifier), or signed by entity that is fully trusted by verifier, or signed by at least two entities that are at least partially trusted by verifier. This concept is illustrated by following example and Figure 3.

In example illustrated by Figure 3 Alice signed three keys: Cecil's, Bob's and Dan's. Each of these keys is directly trusted and therefore valid from Alice's perspective. Moreover Alice fully trusts

Figure 3. OpenPGP trust model (Web-of-trust) illustration

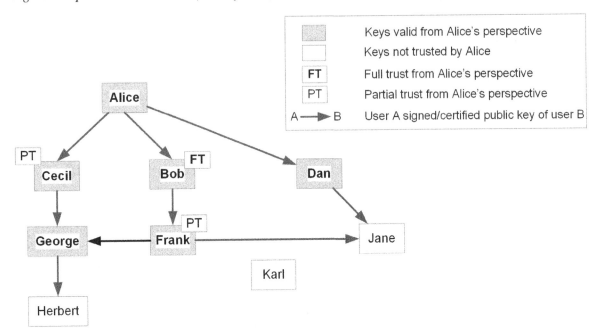

Bob for signing/certifying other public keys and partially trusts Cecil for signing/certifying other public keys.

Frank's key is valid due the fact that it is certified by Bob, furthermore Alice decided she will partially trust Frank as well. Finally George's public key is valid from Alice's perspective as it is signed by two partially trusted entities: Cecil and Frank.

On the other side Karl's key is not valid as there is no connection between Karl and Alice. Also even though George signed Herbert's key, it is not valid from Alice's perspective as Alice does not trust George for key certification. Finally Jane's key is not valid from Alice's perspective because it is signed only by one partially trusted entity (Frank). Dan signed it as well but he is not trusted for key certification by Alice.

In decentralized key distribution infrastructures it is possible to perform trust revocation. For example Web-of-Trust model offers two mechanisms for revocation: key revocation and signature/certification revocation. The first mechanism is useful if Alice lost her keys, or her private key is

compromised. The latter mechanism is used if Alice was tricked into signing for example Dan's key.

Signature/certification revocation is performed in the same way as the signature creation. If Alice decides she was tricked into signing Dan's key, she will sign statement asserting the certification was invalid.

The key revocation in Web-of-Trust model is performed via revocation certificate. Revocation certificate is a statement asserting the key is no longer valid. This certificate should be signed by the key that needs to be revoked. Thus revocation certificate should be generated immediately after generating key pair in pre-operational phase (see Figure 1) and stored in a secure place. If the user's private key is lost or compromised, the user needs to publish this certificate and notify other users in order to revoke key.

Though the possibility of trust revocation in decentralized key distribution infrastructure is a huge improvement, it still suffers from several issues (Zimmermann & Callas, 2009). The most notable drawback is lack of simple mechanism for distribution of revocation information. The revocation information is distributed in decentralized key distribution infrastructure by same means as cryptographic keys. This means that either one needs to distribute the revocation certificate to everyone that could need it, or publish it to a central directory (keyserver).

According to (Zimmermann & Callas, 2009) Web-of-Trust scales at the low end up to few thousand people. Moreover if people share a single community, enterprise or organization, it scales even up tens of thousands of people. This estimate was empirically proven to be correct by a study (Ulrich, Holz, Hauck, & Carle, 2011). The study examined Web-of-trust Internet infrastructure by analysing existing keys and certifications distributed through public keyservers. The study covered almost 3,000,000 keys and found that largest strongly connected component in the Web-of-Trust graph projection consists of about 45,000 nodes. On the other hand, majority of strongly connected components consisted only of about 10-100 nodes. The study concludes that Web-of-Trust is efective public key distribution infrastructure within smaller node neighborhoods, and particularly for those users that frequently sign other keys and are active in the Web-of-Trust.

Unfortunately several downsides remain for decentralized key distribution as well. First, the decentralized key distribution has low support in most of European Union country legislations for legally binding electronic transactions. These are mostly supported by electronic signatures built upon a centralized hierarchical key distribution infrastructure. Second, decentralized key distribution, especially Web-of-Trust, has complicated and hard to understand trust model (Zurko & Simon, 1996), (Abdul-Rahman, 1997). Finally, this also affects the usability of Web-of-Trust, which is in fact in a bad shape (Whitten & Tygar, 1999), (Kapadia, 2007).

Flat Centralized Key Distribution

In flat centralized public key distribution infrastructure significant amount of key management phases is under supervision of a single central authority. This central authority is usually responsible for generating the cryptographic key pairs, binding the public key and its holder's identity, and for the overall key distribution process.

Flat centralized key distribution approach is mostly used in conjunction with identity based encryption[2]. *Identity based encryption* is a public-key encryption technology that allows a user to calculate a public key from an arbitrary string (Martin L., 2008). In identity based encryption the holder's public key can be directly derived from holder's identity (such as e-mail address, personal number, IP address, or DNS name). Consequently, identity based encryption should enable intuitive and user friendly approach to key distribution (Martin L., 2008).

Identity based encryption is built upon a central authority called *private key generator* (Baek, Newmarch, Safavi-Naini, & Susilo, 2004). The private key generator has its own cryptographic key pair. This key pair is used within key distribution infrastructure for generating other participants' key pairs. The public key of a private key generator is used for construction of participant's public keys. Its corresponding private key is used for generating participant's private keys. This principle is demonstrated by Figure 4 which is described below as follows.

Let us assume Alice wants to send encrypted message to Bob. Alice and Bob need to trust joint private key generator (PKG). From Alice's point of view this means that she has obtained PKG's public parameters especially PKG's public key, applicable cryptographic algorithms and other public information (Appenzeller, Martin, & Schertler,

Figure 4. IBE example

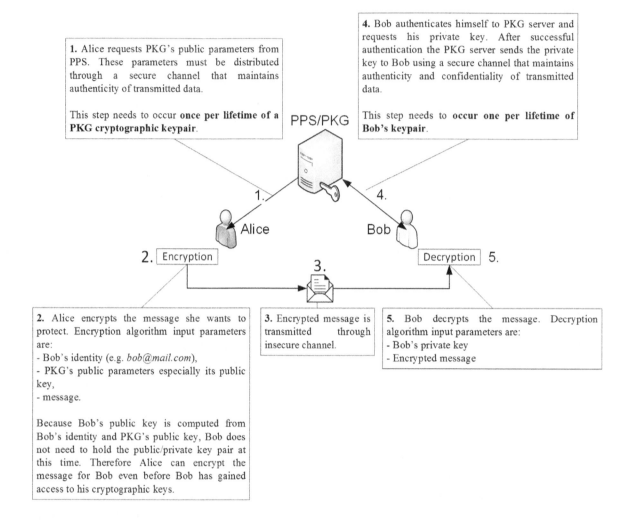

1. Alice requests PKG's public parameters from PPS. These parameters must be distributed through a secure channel that maintains authenticity of transmitted data.

This step needs to occur **once per lifetime of a PKG cryptographic keypair**.

4. Bob authenticates himself to PKG server and requests his private key. After successful authentication the PKG server sends the private key to Bob using a secure channel that maintains authenticity and confidentiality of transmitted data.

This step needs to **occur one per lifetime of Bob's keypair**.

PPS/PKG

Alice   Bob

2. Encryption   Decryption 5.

3.

2. Alice encrypts the message she wants to protect. Encryption algorithm input parameters are:
- Bob's identity (e.g. *bob@mail.com*),
- PKG's public parameters especially its public key,
- message.

Because Bob's public key is computed from Bob's identity and PKG's public key, Bob does not need to hold the public/private key pair at this time. Therefore Alice can encrypt the message for Bob even before Bob has gained access to his cryptographic keys.

3. Encrypted message is transmitted through insecure channel.

5. Bob decrypts the message. Decryption algorithm input parameters are:
- Bob's private key
- Encrypted message

2009). Alice can obtain these parameters either from a dedicated *public parameter server* (PPS) or directly from PKG. After completing the initial trust setup Alice can use PKG's public key and Bob's identity in order to encrypt messages for Bob. To decrypt a message Bob needs to authenticate himself to the PKG and prove his identity. Subsequently, Bob obtains his private key which is used decrypt the message.

Besides more intuitive key and identity binding mechanism, identity based encryption is also attractive because of small communication overhead. Alice needs to obtain PKG's public parameters at least once per its key pair lifetime.

Likewise Bob needs to communicate with PKG only when he needs to obtain his private key. In theory, this could be limited also once per Bob's key pair lifetime.

Identity based encryption provides trust revocation by using short-term cryptographic keys. Bob's key lifetime can be limited by combining Bob's identity and his key pair validity time interval (Martin & Schertler, 2009). In such case Bob's identity in encryption algorithm parameters is modified to *bob@mail.com\|not-before-date*. This way is Bob forced to request new key from PKG each time new *not-before-date* is specified.

This type of revocation mechanism is preventive; revocation occurs regardless of key compromise. Thus this mechanism might be more effective in environments where key compromise is not be detected easily. On the other hand shortening Bob's key pair lifetime increases the communication overhead. Especially the number of times Bob needs to authenticate to PKG are increased. Consequently secure channel that maintains authenticity and confidentiality of transmitted data between PKG and Bob needs to be set-up more frequently.

Another noteworthy feature of identity based encryption is built-in key escrow. Because Bob's private key is generated by PKG and not directly by Bob, PKG can reveal this key to Bob or other (authorized) entity at any time. This significantly simplifies key backup and restore from the user's point of view, but also poses a threat of impersonation. If an attacker is able to authenticate to PKG as Bob, the attacker can obtain any private key issued to Bob up to current date (Martin & Schertler, 2009).

Support for non-repudiation and authentication services in identity based encryption is arguable due to key escrow feature. Though identity based signature schemes exists (Shamir, 1985), (Hess, 2003), (Joye & Neven, 2009), it is believed that identity based encryption should not provide authentication and non-repudiation services (Martin L., 2008). This presumption is also supported by the fact that identity based signatures are not deployed in practice.

In real-world flat centralized key distribution infrastructure and identity based encryption is mostly used in enterprise environments for encryption of data, especially for e-mail protection. Notable implementations include Microsoft Exchange Hosted Protection and implementations by Voltage Security. These implementations combine identity based encryption for end-to-end encryption of data between users and SSL/TLS protocol for protecting communications between users and PKG/PPS.

There were also attempts to implement and standardize the usage of identity based encryption in SSL/TLS protocol (Roschke, Ibraimi, Cheng, & Meinel, 2010), (Huang, 2009). These attempts were unsuccessful, because flat centralized key distribution suffers from similar problems as hierarchical centralized key distribution which is utilized by SSL/TLS protocol (Rescorla, 2008), (Rescorla, 2009).

Hierarchical Centralized Key Distribution

Hierarchical centralized key distribution is based on key certification in a similar way as decentralized key distribution. The main difference resides in responsibility for key certification. In decentralized key distribution the keys can be certificated by anyone, whereas in centralized key distribution the keys are certified by dedicated entities. These authorities are responsible for binding the public key and its holder's identity.

Most known and widespread centralized key distribution infrastructure is X.509 public key infrastructure (PKI). In X.509 PKI the authorities responsible for binding the public key and its holder's identity are called *certification authorities* and the binding is realized through X.509 *certificates* signed by these authorities.

In centralized infrastructures the key distribution is de-facto reduced to key distribution of certification authorities' public keys (trust anchors, for example self-signed certificates). These keys/certificates are distributed mostly with software that is performing the cryptographic operations. These could be either applications (such as Firefox, Opera) or third party services for cryptographic key distribution (such as services provided by operating system, e.g. Microsoft Windows Root Certificate Program or Apple Root Certificate Program). The software that performs the cryptographic operations needs to be trusted and distributed through a secure channel that maintains authenticity of transmitted data. This means that centralized cryptographic key distribution does not introduce new requirements related to providing secure authenticated channel.

Certification authorities (CA) either issue certificates directly to the users (also called end entities) or to other certification authorities. The reason for having a hierarchy of certification authorities is to simplify their key/certificate distribution. This way it is possible to build an infrastructure, where only a small number of *root* certification authorities issue certificates to many subordinate certification authorities, thus many fewer root CA certificates need to be distributed. With multiple subordinate certification authorities every certification authority can have its own scope of issuing certificates. This means an own set of policies that place requirements on operational procedures, security precautions, and procedures to verify the identities of end entities.

In theory multiple subordinate certification authorities should provide a flexible and scalable hierarchical key distribution infrastructure that can be constrained by the scope of the issued certificates. This scope can be defined in several ways. One way to limit the scope is to limit the purpose of the certificate, or more specifically, to limit its usage and application (e.g. secure mail, electronic and qualified electronic signatures, network and transport layer encryption etc.). Another way to limit the scope is policy constraint. Policy constraints incorporate different security and identity verification procedures or reflect different amount of resources invested into private key protection (e.g. private keys are protected by smart cards or hardware security modules). Finally the scope can be controlled by utilizing naming constraints. If a certification authority is limited by name constraints, it can issue certificates only with specific name structure. For example such certification authority might issue only certificates for end entities located in a specific country or certificates for a specific DNS domain.

Theoretically X.509 public key infrastructure provides an elegant solution for trust revocation.

Certification authorities provide revocation service, either by publishing a black-list of untrusted certificates (*certificate revocation lists*), or by providing an online service for determining the validity of issued certificates. The location of files in former case or services in latter case are stored in X.509 certificate. Relying parties that use the certificate use these information to check if the certificate has not been revoked.

X.509 certificates are widely used for many purposes. X.509 public key infrastructure is used for distribution and managing of keys used for network level encryption (SSL/TLS, IPSec) as well as application level encryption, signing and authentication (S/MIME, electronic signatures, code signing, etc.). To explain the basic points of key certification, distribution and revocation in X.509 we choose SSL/TLS example illustrated by Figure 5.

Unfortunately even though X.509 PKI looks appealing at first sight, due to its complexity and flexibility it is hard to implement in real-world in an efficient and secure way (Gutmann, 2002). Especially SSL/TLS PKI is known to be in poor condition due to the prevalence of certificate errors, improper configuration and administrator's mistakes (Holz, Braun, Kammenhuber, & Carle, 2011), and too many certification authorities with poor security practices (Peter & Burns, 2010), (Arnbak & Van Eijk, 2012).

There were several actual attacks against SSL/TLS PKI. In 2011 two widely trusted certification authorities: Comodo CA and DigiNotar, were breached. During the security breach fraudulent certificates were issued to an attacker that did not control the specific DNS domain names (Leavitt, 2011). This way the attacker could mount a successful attack against any web site that used SSL/TLS protocol communications encryption as long as he could control the network on lower layers. There are indications that these fraudulent certificates were used during an Iranian attack on public e-mail services such as Google's Gmail (Arnbak & Van Eijk, 2012).

Figure 5. SSL/TLS example

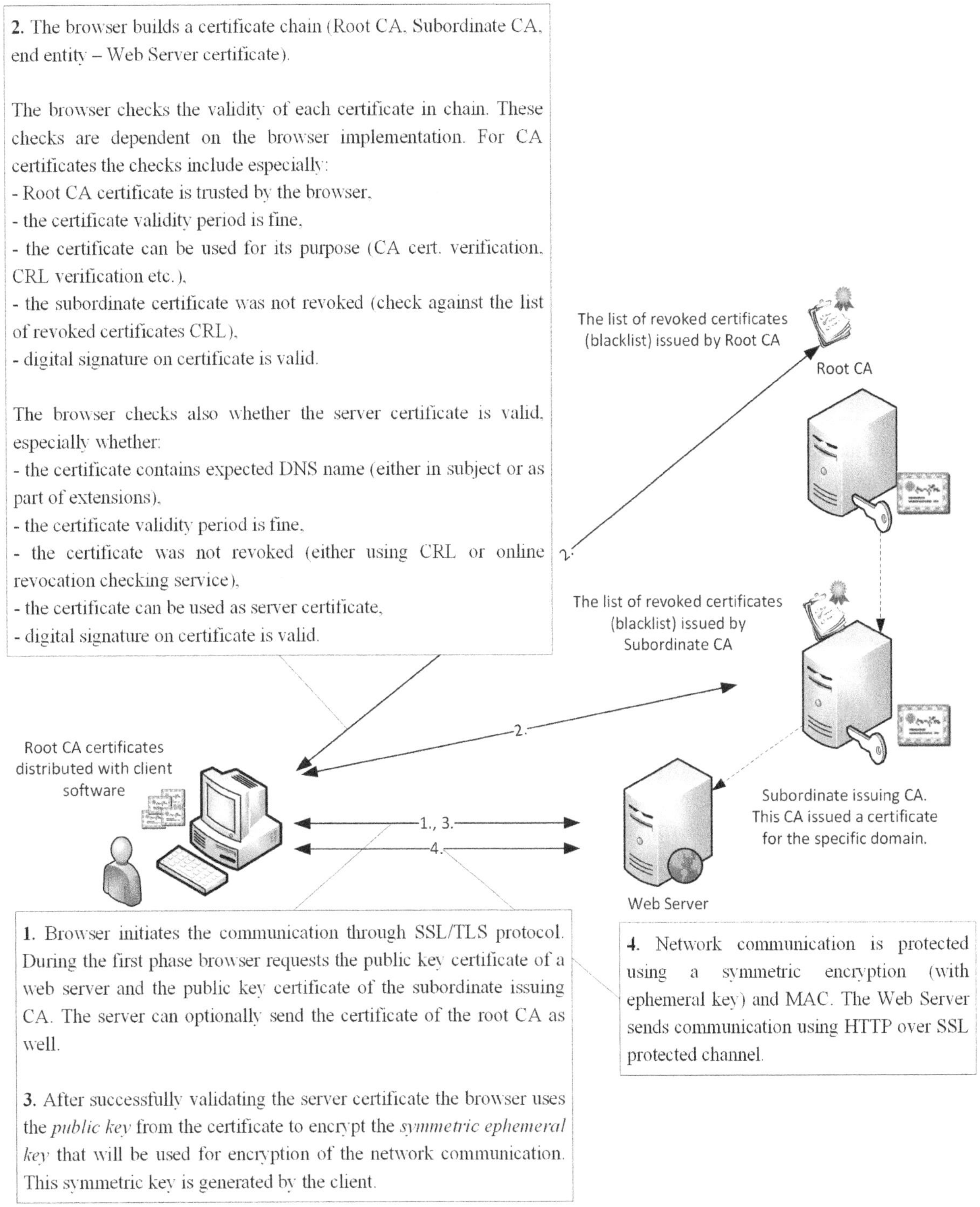

2. The browser builds a certificate chain (Root CA, Subordinate CA, end entity – Web Server certificate).

The browser checks the validity of each certificate in chain. These checks are dependent on the browser implementation. For CA certificates the checks include especially:
- Root CA certificate is trusted by the browser,
- the certificate validity period is fine,
- the certificate can be used for its purpose (CA cert. verification, CRL verification etc.),
- the subordinate certificate was not revoked (check against the list of revoked certificates CRL),
- digital signature on certificate is valid.

The browser checks also whether the server certificate is valid, especially whether:
- the certificate contains expected DNS name (either in subject or as part of extensions),
- the certificate validity period is fine,
- the certificate was not revoked (either using CRL or online revocation checking service),
- the certificate can be used as server certificate,
- digital signature on certificate is valid.

The list of revoked certificates (blacklist) issued by Root CA

Root CA

The list of revoked certificates (blacklist) issued by Subordinate CA

Root CA certificates distributed with client software

Subordinate issuing CA. This CA issued a certificate for the specific domain.

Web Server

1. Browser initiates the communication through SSL/TLS protocol. During the first phase browser requests the public key certificate of a web server and the public key certificate of the subordinate issuing CA. The server can optionally send the certificate of the root CA as well.

3. After successfully validating the server certificate the browser uses the *public key* from the certificate to encrypt the *symmetric ephemeral key* that will be used for encryption of the network communication. This symmetric key is generated by the client.

4. Network communication is protected using a symmetric encryption (with ephemeral key) and MAC. The Web Server sends communication using HTTP over SSL protected channel.

The attack is quite simple. During the first phase of a SSL/TLS protocol handshake, the attacker performs a man in the middle attack by inserting a legitimate certificate from compromised certification authority. If the certification authority is not aware of the compromise, or if the attacker can block CRL/OCSP communication with CA, then the browser cannot determine whether the certificate was fraudulently issued and considers the certificate valid. Following this, the client will encrypt the symmetric key with attacker's public key and attacker can decrypt all the traffic designated for the web server. He can than act as an active proxy server in the communication.

The reasons why this attack is relatively easy can be summarized as follows. Revocation either by certificate revocation lists or online validation services is by default fail-safe; meaning that if the browser is unable to retrieve revocation information the SSL/TLS channel setup proceeds, and sometimes it proceeds even without a warning (TrustWave SpiderLabs, 2011). As mentioned earlier there are many (perhaps too many) certification authorities trusted by the internet browsers. Therefore it is easier for the attacker to find a less secured but equally trusted certification authority. Also with so many certification authorities it is hard for an average user to determine which are trustworthy and which are not (Schultze, 2010).

Furthermore the attack can be even less sophisticated and still successful. The attacker can issue the web server certificate by a self-crafted certification authority that is not trusted by the browser. Most of the internet browsers will show a warning that the certificate is issued by an untrusted certification authority and recommend the user to abandon the page. Unfortunately significant amount users ignore this warning, thus the attack is successful. This suggestion is backed up by a study performed on more than 400 users (Sunshine, Egelman, Almuhimedi, Atri, & Cranor, 2009). This study showed that more than 30% of users ignored warnings related to untrusted certification authorities.

Several attacks of this nature were detected on the Internet. Among others it is worthy to mention that in 2011 Facebook has been targeted by this type of attack (Eckersley, 2011) and in 2013 popular source code repository Github was attacked as well (CloudShark, 2013).

But as we stated earlier, it is hard to blame the users for ignoring browser warnings, when the TLS/SSL PKI is in a bad shape. In a thorough study covering SSL/TLS certificates from Alexa Top 1 Million Hosts (Holz, Braun, Kammenhuber, & Carle, 2011) it has been shown that only around 18% of certificates were valid with regards to checking rules implemented in popular browsers. The remaining certificates could not be used for securing TLS/SSL channel unless user acknowledged a browser warning.

A more recent example of hierarchical key distribution infrastructure is DNSSEC PKI. DNSSEC PKI does not suffer from some problems of traditional X.509 PKI. DNSSEC PKI is focused only on distribution and management of keys relevant for securing the DNS, and constrains certification authorities out-of-box, thus it is more focused and constrained than traditional X.509 PKI.

DNSSEC makes use of two types of keys: zone signing key (ZSK) and key signing key (KSK). ZSK is used for signing actual DNS resource records (RR) and KSK is used for signing ZSK. This way ZSK can be rolled over more often, thus it needs to fulfill less stringent security requirements (such as requirements on key size or operational security) than KSK.

Public key part of ZSK is published along with public key part of KSK in domain. In order to provide chain-of-trust public key part of KSK (its identifier tag- hash) is published as a signed record in the parent DNS domain. The chain of trust is illustrated by Figure 6.

DNSSEC PKI does not suffer from the overflexibility of X.509 PKI. Unfortunately it still too complex, especially with regards to deployment and overall infrastructure operations related to DNS. A study covering aspects of large-scale

Figure 6. DNSSEC chain of trust example

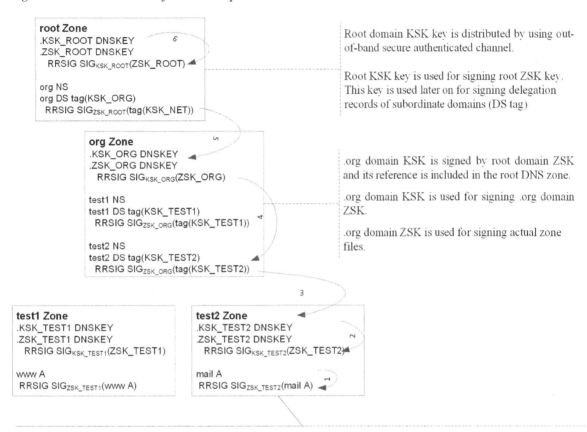

Example: mail.test2.org A DNS record should be verified.

1. mail.test2.org DNS record signature is verified by test2 zone signing key (ZSK_TEST2)

2. ZSK_TEST2 DNS record signature is verified by test2 key signing key (KSK_TEST2)

3. KSK_TEST2 signed tag (key identifier) is published in parent domain (org) and verified by org zone signing key (ZSK_ORG)

4. ZSK_ORG DNS record signature is verified by org key signing key (KSK_ORG)

5. KSK_ORG signed tag (key identifier) is published in root domain and verified by root zone signing key (ZSK_ROOT)

6. ZSK_ROOT DNS record signature is verified by root key signing key (KSK_ROOT) which is distributed by out-of-band secure authenticated channel

Internet deployment of DNSSEC (Yang, 2011) shows that several issues related to X.509 PKI operations apply also to DNSSEC PKI. Moreover new problems arise because of large-scale delegation of certification authorities.

As (Yang, 2011) states the fundamental challenge in operating DNSSEC is that the system spans over tens of millions of independent administrative domains, while the provision of security, as defined in DNSSEC, requires sym-

phonic actions from all of them. As the public keys of different zones are authenticated through a single hierarchical PKI, any local change in a zone's public key may require synchronization across administrative domains, because the new key must be authenticated by the zone's parent and used to authenticate the zone's children. This causes serious scaling issues for the domains that may have millions of children zones underneath them. The coordination process is also lengthy and error prone as it involves human operators, yet any out-of-sync configurations can break the chains of trust and disrupt the DNS service due to authentication failure.

These issues and the fact that DNSSEC does not improve network security significantly unless it is deployed wide enough (Friedman, 2011) lead to slow adoption of DNSSEC. Though the deployment trend is steadily rising over six years (Verisign Labs, 2013), its overall coverage is presumed to be less than 2% of second level DNS domains (Eggert, 2013). To be more specific less than 1% of *.edu* DNS domains are DNSSEC enabled and less than 0.3% of *.net* and *.com* DNS domains are DNSSEC enabled. On the other hand Czech second level domain is a bright example of how DNSSEC penetration can be achieved. Actual DNSSEC penetration in *.cz* DNS domain is about

38% (cz.nic, 2013), and has been achieved by great CZ.NIC effort especially in terms of marketing, smart economic policy, trainings, users and administrators education (Filip, 2011).

COMPARISON OF PUBLIC KEY DISTRIBUTION APPROACHES

We summarize existing approaches and deployed public key distribution and management infrastructures in tables below.

Table 2 illustrates core characteristics of public key distribution approaches, Table 3 compares their practical aspects, and Table 4 outlines overall advantages and disadvantages of a particular key distribution approach.

Table 2. Public key distribution approaches- Core characteristics

Key Distribution Approach Characteristics	Key Continuity	Decentralized Key Distribution
	Flat centralized key distribution	**Hierarchical centralized key distribution*** * specific aspects for particular PKI implementation are amended respectively (e.g. X.509 or DNSSEC)
Secure (Authenticated) Channel Requirements	**K** Each time new public key binding is set up or modified.	**D** Each time when direct binding is setup.
	F Once for distribution of PKG's public parameters. Moreover secure channel that preserves authenticity and **confidentiality** of transmitted data is required every time an entity requests private key.	**H** Theoretically once; during the distribution of trusted third parties certificates/trust anchors.
Trust Options (Direct / Indirect)	**K** Public key bindings must be verified directly.	**D** Public key bindings are verified either directly or indirectly by trusting other participants of the infrastructure.
	F Public key bindings are established through identity directly. Private key is obtained by its holder after successful authentication to PKG.	**H** Public key bindings are established / verified by trusted third party.
Trust Revocation	**K** Impossible without authenticated channel. Everyone (who makes use of the public key) needs to be notified about the trust revocation through an authenticated channel.	**D** Theoretically possible, not much used in practice. Everyone (who makes use of the public key) should check key servers for trust revocation.
	F Possible via short-term keys. Shortening the end entity key validity period increases communication overhead and might introduce administrative and operational issues.	**H-X.509** Everyone (who makes use of the public key) should check certification authority services for trust revocation. **H-DNSSEC** Possible via short-term keys. DNSSEC key revocation needs to consider the DNS caching mechanisms.

Table 3. Public key distribution approaches - practical aspects

Key Distribution Approach Characteristics	Key Continuity	Decentralized Key Distribution
	Flat centralized key distribution	**Hierarchical centralized key distribution*** * specific aspects for particular PKI implementation are amended respectively (e.g. X.509 or DNSSEC)
Practical implementations	**K** SSH, ZRTP	**D** PGP
	F IBE: RFC 5408, RFC 5409	**H** X.509, DNSSEC
Scalability	**K** Low ~ 10-100 keys - parties	**D** Medium ~ 10.000 keys - parties / Enterprise wide
	F Medium ~ Enterprise wide	**H** High ~ Internet wide
Usability in existing applications	**K** Hard to use for common users, Easy to configure for administrators.	**D** Hard to use for common users.
	F Intuitive for common users, easy to configure for administrators.	**H** Hard to use for common users, hard to configure and operate for administrators.
Estimated infrastructure costs[3]	**K** Low Set-up: Up to 15 minutes *per key* ~ 15 USD	**D** Medium Set-up: At least an hour *per key*/user ~ 60 USD
	F Medium Set-up: 30,000 USD Operational: Up to 10 USD per user/month (enterprise environment)	**H** High - Approximately 100,000 USD for enterprise certification authority Operational: Up to 20 USD per user/month (enterprise environment)

REINFORCING THE EXISTING (TLS/SSL) X.509 PUBLIC KEY INFRASTRUCUTRE

As we stated earlier, several incidents indicate that SSL/TLS PKI is prone to mis-issuance of X.509 certificates. According to (Schultze, 2010) the fundamental weaknesses reside in the fact that any CA can issue a certificate vouching that the subscriber controls any domain name, accurate or not. This is due missing/unimplemented constraints in X.509 trust model and unclear/undisclosed delegation of trust to other certification authorities by root certification authorities.

The DNS-Based Authentication of Named Entities (DANE)

Two reinforcement solutions for X.509 SSL/TLS PKI trust model were standardized recently. Both of them make use of DNS infrastructure in order to provide additional binding to the public keys and their holders' identity and provide a way to constrain the trust.

Last year IETF DANE Working Group published RFC 6698. The purpose of this RFC is to introduce a new DNS resource record TLSA, and provide additional security measure for existing SSL/TLS PKI.

TLSA DNS resource record binds TLS port, DNS name and holder's public key association. The public key association can provide either X.509 certificate or raw public key, or its hash. Also the binding can be direct (subject's public key or X.509 certificate) or indirect (issuing certification authority public key or X.509 certificate). An example of such association is provided by Figure 7.

Because DNS is not secure by default, DANE relies on DNSSEC in order to provide authenticated channel for the associations. This way the traditional X.509 public key infrastructure can be combined along with DNSSEC PKI. By combining DNSSEC PKI and X.509 PKI the attacker would need to subvert a regular certification authority in order to issue a false certificate and compromise the target's DNSSEC infrastructure as well.

Table 4. Public key distribution approaches - overall advantages and disadvantages

Key Distribution Approach Characteristics	Key Continuity	Decentralized Key Distribution
	Flat centralized key distribution	**Hierarchical centralized key distribution*** *- specific aspects for particular PKI implementation are amended respectively (e.g. X.509 or DNSSEC)
Advantages	**K** - Simple, inexpensive, and easy to setup and operate	**D** - Scales well for medium size environments - Flexible trust model
	F - Simple and easy to setup - Intuitive public keys - Built-in escrow (from operational and compliance point of view)	**H** - Scales well for internet wide infrastructures. **H-X.509** - Overall flexibility - Possible to use for legally binding operations **H-DNSSEC** - Hierarchy is inherently constrained by DNS namespace
Disadvantages and concerns	**K** - Missing revocation - Low scalability	**D** - Complicated trust model - Complicated revocation
	F - Every time entity requests its private key a secure channel must to be established. - Key holders need to authenticate to PKG by other means than provided by PKG. This means that key holders need shared secret such as password, X.509 certificate, or cryptographic key. - Built-in escrow (from privacy and non-repudiation point of view)	**H** - Costly to set up and operate - Too complicated, hard to implement correctly **H-X.509** - Constraints on the hierarchy are not implemented in practice - Revocation does not work in practice - Mis-issuance of X.509 certificates happens in practice - Though X.509 hierarchy should be used for constraining trust, it is mostly used for profit **H-DNSSEC** - Slow adoption - Error prone certification process, with complicated trust relationships (registry, registrar, registrant, zone operator)

Figure 7. Example of DANE TLSA RR

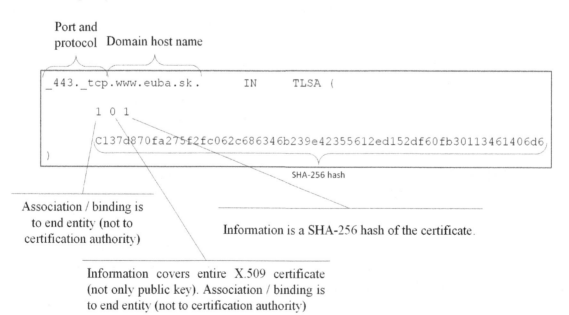

In theory DANE should significantly reduce attack surface for the attacker (Osterweil, Kaliski, Larson, & McPherson, 2012). Without DANE protection the attacker could compromise any certification authority in order to launch a man in the middle attack. If DANE protection is applied the attacker needs to compromise the DNSSEC infrastructure, with much less applicable certification authorities (Osterweil, Kaliski, Larson, & McPherson, 2012).

The attack surface for traditional X.509 SSL/TLS PKI is estimated to at least 150 targets. The DANE reduces this attack surface (Osterweil, Kaliski, Larson, & McPherson, 2012) to the number of authoritative name servers potentially involved in resolving a DNS name. This process involves the name servers from the root DNS zone until the zone that contains the particular DNS name. The precise number of name servers varies depending on a particular domain, but in general it is by order of magnitude smaller than the number of targets in X.509 SSL/TLS PKI. A practical survey (Ramasubramanian & Sirer, 2005) of 593,160 unique webserver names crawled by the Yahoo! and DMOZ.org directories shows, that median number of the names servers in the chain is 26 and the average number of the name servers in the chain is 44.

Moreover as illustrated by Figure 7, TLSA RR can bear all the information necessary for creating a secure SSL/TLS channel. Thus DANE can be used for public key distribution without the necessity for X.509 certification authorities.

Unfortunately, as we stated before, the DNSSEC is not widely deployed and we shall see if DANE could be one of the deployment drivers. Also with DANE deployed, one would need to incorporate the trust and public key distribution changes into user interface and other browsers' components. Finally, as shown by studies (Holz, Braun, Kammenhuber, & Carle, 2011) and (Yang, 2011), it is hard to believe that DNSSEC and DANE could be applied in a large scale in an error proof way.

DNS Certification Authority Authorization

A similar approach to DANE was chosen by the PKIX IETF working group. RFC 6844 describes the Certification Authority Authorization (CAA) DNS resource record. CAA DNS RR allows a DNS domain holder to specify one or more certification authorities that are authorized to issue certificates for the domain.

The resource record could contain information about a certification authority that is allowed to issue a certificate for a specific domain, as well as contact information that could be used by a certification authority in cases, where the CA is unauthorized to issue a certificate (based on CAA RR). In this way the domain owner could be notified when someone is trying to acquire a certificate from another CA than the one that is indicated in CAA RR.

The main difference between CAA and DANE RR is that CAA RR is designated for certification authorities whereas DANE is designated for client processing. Also CAA RR cannot be used for secure key distribution. It is intended only as an additional cross-check condition in certificate vetting and issuance process.

Because the CAA cannot be used for key distribution purposes, the DNSSEC protection of the information in transit is not required. Thus CAA can be deployed without DNSSEC and also without any changes to the client codebase. This means that CAA is ready for deployment de-facto immediately.

Certificate Transparency

Similarly to CAA the Certificate Transparency is a cross-checking, auditing, and monitoring countermeasure. The goal is to make it impossible (or at least very difficult) for a certification authority to issue a certificate for a domain without it being visible to the owner of that domain.

The main idea is to create a distributed logging infrastructure that should log every publicly issued TLS X.509 certificate. This would be achieved by running several servers with cryptographically secured append-only logs. Clients could verify correctness of each log and monitor when new certificates are added. Certificate Transparency clients can be divided by their role into several groups: submitters, TLS clients, monitors and auditors.

Submitters can post a certificate to log servers. Anyone can be a submitter, examples are: certification authorities, holder of public key or a relying party. The only current condition for accepting the submission is that the certificate should be issued by a globally trusted certification authority. This should prevent spamming the log.

TLS clients make use of the log by accepting the proof of submissions of a particular certificate to the log. They validate the proof of submissions by utilizing asymmetric cryptographic protocols. The current proposal of Certificate Transparency Internet-Draft does not deal with public key distribution necessary for validating the proof of submissions.

Monitors and auditors cross-check that the logs are correctly operated. Moreover monitors could check for specific certificates or domain names in interest in order to detect mis-issuance.

The Certificate Transparency is still in experimental stage but if it is approved it should be deployed incrementally. Nonetheless, the final aim is to *require* the proof of submission by the TLS client for every publicly trusted certificate issued after a certain date (Langley, 2012).

Though the direct benefit of the certificate transparency is conditioned by changing the TLS client codebase, the entire Internet TLS infrastructure would benefit if the updated TLS client codebase is deployed widely enough. The benefit is similar to benefit that brings Google Chrome public key pinning. Public key pinning is a term for hardcoded public keys and domain names into the Google Chrome internet browser. This feature helps to detect mis-issued certificates for high valued sites, especially related (but not only) to Google online services. DigiNotar breach (Leavitt, 2011) and Turktrust certificate mis-issuance (Rosa & Schultze, 2013) had been detected thanks to public key pinning. It is straightforward that after the mis-issuance is detected the MITM attack has lower chance to succeed.

Certificate Transparency could be perceived as a scalable certificate pinning solution. The fact that it is driven by Google gives a high chance that it would be implemented at least in Google Chrome when it is finished. If the Certificate Transparency would be deployed as planned in a fail-secure blocking way (Langley, 2012), it would significantly reduce the risk of social engineering, incorrect user decisions and it would also drive usability changes in the browser towards better directions.

CONCLUSION

It is easiest to use pre-shared keys and key continuity distribution approach for smaller scale systems and forget about complexities introduced by more robust key distribution approaches. If the system needs to scale more, or revocation capabilities are needed, it is necessary to pick either a decentralized or centralized public key distribution approach.

Decentralized public key distribution is best suited for small enterprise environments and medium sized closed communities. In these environments decentralized public distribution provides a cost effective, but not very user friendly way to protect data confidentiality, authentication and non-repudiation.

Flat centralized key distribution and identity based encryption is used mostly in enterprise environments, where supervised key escrow is considered desirable feature. Identity based encryption provides user friendly and cost effective way to protect data confidentiality, but lacks support for authentication and non-repudiation in real-world implementations.

Hierarchical key distribution supports wide range of security services including: authentication, data confidentiality and non-repudiation. Hence hierarchical key distribution, especially X.509 PKI, is often implemented in enterprise environment for email protection, encryption of network communications, authentication, and digital and electronic signatures. Hierarchical key distribution is also most deployed solution internet-wide and X.509 hierarchical PKI is defacto the only real-world implemented approach for managing SSL/TLS public keys on the Internet.

Though X.509 PKI approach has severe trust issues, it will probably stay the most widespread Internet public key infrastructure for a while. The solutions for the X.509 PKI trust problems are hard to deploy, especially when it is necessary to update client codebase, or another infrastructure needs to be deployed in a large scale.

Therefore, as short term solution CAA is most appealing, as it needs to be accepted only by certification authorities and certificate holders. In the long run Certificate Transparency is designed to provide the monitoring and detection of fraudulently issued certificates, and DANE with DNSSEC could extend the possibilities of key distribution and provide cross-checks as well.

Most of the key distribution approaches as implemented by software today, suffer from poor usability and the possibility to override security by the user's decision. Until hard fails on key distribution errors are implemented, the users will be bypassing security warnings and putting themselves to risk. But in order to implement hard fails, the infrastructure needs to be fixed first.

REFERENCES

Abdul-Rahman, A. (1997). The pgp trust model. EDI-Forum. *Journal of Electronic Commerce*, *10*(3), 27–31.

Abelson, H., Anderson, R., Bellovin, S. M., Benaloh, J., Blaze, M., & Diffie, W. et al. (1997). The Risks of Key Recovery, Key Escrow, and Trusted Third-Party Encryption. *World Wide Web Journal*, *2*(3), 241–257.

Adida, B., Hohenberger, S., & Rivest, R. L. (2005). Lightweight encryption for email. In *Proceedings of USENIX steps to reducing unwanted traffic on the internet workshop* (SRUTI) (pp. 93-99). Cambridge, UK: USENIX.

Amann, B., Vallentin, M., Hall, S., & Sommer, R. (2012). *Extracting Certificates from Live Traffic: A Near Real-Time SSL Notary Service. TR-12-014*. ICSI.

Appenzeller, G., Martin, L., & Schertler, M. (2009). *Identity-Based Encryption Architecture and Supporting Data Structures* (RFC 5408). Retrieved from http://tools.ietf.org/html/rfc5408

Arnbak, A., & Van Eijk, N. (2012). *Certificate Authority Collapse: Regulating Systemic Vulnerabilities in the HTTPS Value Chain*. TRPC. Retrieved from http://ssrn.com/abstract=2031409

Baek, J., Newmarch, J., Safavi-Naini, R., & Susilo, W. (2004). A Survey of Identity-Based Cryptography. In *Proceedings of Australian Unix Users Group Annual Conference* (pp. 95-102). Melbourne: AUUG.

Boldyreva, A., Vipul, G., & Virendra, K. (2008). Identity-based encryption with efficient revocation. In *Proceedings of the 15th ACM conference on Computer and communications security* (pp. 417-426). Alexandria: ACM.

Callas, J., & Gutmann, P. (2013). *How much does it cost to start a root CA?* Retrieved from http://lists.randombit.net/pipermail/cryptography/2013-January/thread.html#3575

Camp, J., Asgharpour, F., & Liu, D. (2007). Experimental Evaluations of Expert and Non-expert Computer Users' Mental Models of Security Risks. [Pittsburgh, PA: WEIS.]. *Proceedings of WEIS*, *2007*, 1–24.

Chandramouli, R., & Scott, R. (2009). Open issues in secure DNS deployment. *IEEE Security & Privacy*, *7*(5), 29–35. doi:10.1109/MSP.2009.129

Chen, L., Harrison, K., Moss, A., Soldera, D., & Smart, N. P. (2002). Certification of public keys within an identity based system. In *Proceedings of Information Security* (pp. 322–333). Springer. doi:10.1007/3-540-45811-5_25

CloudShark. (2013, January 29). *MITM Attack Capture Shared Through CloudShark*. Retrieved from http://appliance.cloudshark.org/news/cloudshark-in-the-wild/mitm-attack-capture-shared-through-cloudshark/

cz.nic. (2013, February 27). *Statistics*. Retrieved from http://www.dnssec.cz/stats/?stat_type=1&zone=2&time_step=month&from_year=2012&from_month=2&from_day=1&to_year=2013&to_month=2&to_day=26&submit=1

Denning, D. E., & Sacco, G. M. (1981). Timestamps in key distributed protocols. *Communications of the ACM*, *24*(8), 533–535. doi:10.1145/358722.358740

Eckersley, P. (2011, May 5). *A Syrian Man-In-The-Middle Attack against Facebook*. Retrieved from https://www.eff.org/deeplinks/2011/05/syrian-man-middle-against-facebook

Eggert, L. (2013, February 25). *DNSSEC Deployment Trends*. Retrieved from http://eggert.org/meter/dnssec

enisa. (2009). *The costs of DNSSEC deployment*. Heraklion: ENISA.

Ferris. (2006). The Total Cost of Ownership for Voltage Identity-Based Encryption Solutions. *San Francisco: Ferris Research.*

Filip, O. (2011). *DNSSEC.CZ*. Retrieved from http://dakar42.icann.org/bitcache/23b46cc058a604df99944c7080b98194591c8fd5?vid=28941&disposition=attachment&op=download

Friedman, A. (2011). *Economic and Policy Frameworks for Cybersecurity Risks*. Center for Technology Innovation at Brookings.

Furnell, S. (2005). Why users cannot use security. *Computers & Security*, *24*(4), 274–279. doi:10.1016/j.cose.2005.04.003

Garfinkel, S. L. (2003). Email-based identification and authentication: An alternative to PKI? *IEEE Security & Privacy*, *1*(6), 20–26. doi:10.1109/MSECP.2003.1253564

Garfinkel, S. L., & Miller, R. C. (2005). Johnny 2: a user test of key continuity management with S/MIME and Outlook Express. In *Proceedings of the 2005 symposium on Usable privacy and security* (pp. 13-24). Pittsburgh, PA: ACM.

Gentry, C. (2003). Certificate-based encryption and the certificate revocation problem. In Proceedings of Advances in Cryptology - EUROCRYPT 2003 (pp. 272-293). Springer.

Gentry, C., & Silverberg, A. (2002). Hierarchical ID-Based Cryptography. [Springer.]. *Proceedings of ASIACRYPT*, *2002*, 548–566.

Gutmann, P. (2002). PKI: it's not dead, just resting. *Computer*, *35*(8), 41–49. doi:10.1109/MC.2002.1023787

Gutmann, P. (2004). Why isn't the internet secure yet, dammit. In *Proceedings of AusCERT Asia Pacific Information Technology Security Conference*. Royal Pines: AusCERT.

Gutmann, P. (2011). Do Users Verify SSH Keys?. *login, 36*(4), 35-36.

Gutmann, P. (2011, April 20). *The real cost of free certificates*. Retrieved from https://mail1.eff.org/pipermail/observatory/2011-April/000199.html

Herley, C. (2009). So Long, And No Thanks for the Externalities: The Rational Rejection of Security Advice by Users. In *Proceedings of Workshop on New security paradigms* (pp. 133-144). New York: ACM.

Herzberg, A., & Margulies, R. (2012). Training Johnny to Authenticate (Safely). *IEEE Security and Privacy*, *10*(1), 37–45. doi:10.1109/MSP.2011.129

Hess, F. (2003). Efficient identity based signature schemes based on pairings. In *Proceedings of Selected Areas in Cryptography* (pp. 310–324). Springer. doi:10.1007/3-540-36492-7_20

Holz, R., Braun, L., Kammenhuber, N., & Carle, G. (2011). The SSL landscape: a thorough analysis of the x. 509 PKI using active and passive measurements. In *Proceedings of the 2011 ACM SIGCOMM conference on Internet measurement conference* (pp. 427-444). ACM. Retrieved December 2011, from http://www.net.in.tum. de/fileadmin/bibtex/publications/papers/imc-pkicrawl-2.pdf

Holz, R., Riedmaier, T., Kammenhuber, N., & Carle, G. (2012). X. 509 forensics: Detecting and localising the SSL/TLS men-in-the-middle. [Springer.]. *Proceedings of Computer Security–ESORICS*, *2012*, 217–234.

Huang, M. (2009, December). *Identity-Based Encryption (IBE) Cipher Suites for Transport Layer*. Retrieved from http://tools.ietf.org/html/draft-huang-tls-ibe-00

ITU-T. (1991, August 30). *X. 800 Security Architecture for Open Systems Interconnection for CCITT applications*. Retrieved from http://www.itu.int/rec/T-REC-X.800-199103-I/en

Jääskeläinen, K. (2013). *SSH Key Management: A Gaping Hole in Your Encrypted Critical Infrastructure*. Retrieved from http://www.infosecurityproject.com/2013/Download/BO1.1_A%20Gaping%20Hole%20in%20Your%20Encrypted%20Critical%20Infrastructure.pdf

Joye, M., & Neven, G. (2009). *Identity-based cryptography* (Vol. 2). Amsterdam: IOS Press.

Kahn, D. (1996). *The Codebreakers*. New York: Simon & Schuster.

Kapadia, A. (2007). A case (study) for usability in secure email communication. *IEEE Security & Privacy*, *5*(2), 80–84. doi:10.1109/MSP.2007.25

Khurana, H. B. (2006, January). *On the risks of IBE*. Retrieved from http://citeseerx.ist.psu.edu/viewdoc/download?doi=10.1.1.86.9742&rep=rep1&type=pdf

Kienzle, D. M., & Elder, M. C. (2003). Recent Worms: A Survey and Trends. In *Proceedings of the 2003 ACM workshop on Rapid malcode* (pp. 1-10). Washington, DC: ACM.

Langley, A. (2012, November 6). *Certificate Transparency*. Retrieved from http://www.imperialviolet.org/2012/11/06/certtrans.html

Langley, A. (2013, January 13). *Real World Crypto 2013*. Retrieved from http://www.imperialviolet.org/2013/01/13/rwc03.html

Leavitt, N. (2011). Internet Security under Attack: The Undermining of Digital Certificates. *Computer*, *44*(12), 17–20. doi:10.1109/MC.2011.367

Martin, L. (2008). *Introduction to identity-based encryption*. Norwood, MA: Artech House.

Martin, L., & Schertler, M. (2009, January). Using the Boneh-Franklin and Boneh-Boyen Identity-Based Encryption Algorithms with the Cryptographic Message Syntax (CMS) *(RFC 5409)*. *Retrieved from* http://tools.ietf.org/html/rfc5409

Medvinsky, A., & Hur, M. (1999, October). *Addition of Kerberos Cipher Suites to Transport Layer Security (TLS)* (RFC 2712). Retrieved from http://www.ietf.org/rfc/rfc2712.txt

Needham, R. M., & Schroeder, M. D. (1978). Using encryption for authentication in large networks of computers. *Communications of the ACM*, *21*(12), 993–999. doi:10.1145/359657.359659

NIST. (2007). *Recommendation for Key Management*. Retrieved from http://csrc.nist.gov/publications/nistpubs/800-57/sp800-57-Part1-revised2_Mar08-2007.pdf

Osterweil, E., Kaliski, B., & Larson, M., & McPherson. (2012). *Reducing the X. 509 Attack Surface with DNSSEC's DANE*. Securing and Trusting Internet Names. SATIN.

Ozment, A., & Schechter, S. E. (2006). *Bootstrapping the adoption of internet security protocols*. Paper presented at the Fifth Workshop on the Economics of Information Security. Cambridge, UK.

Payne, B. D., & Edwards, W. K. (2008). A brief introduction to usable security. *IEEE Internet Computing, 12*(3), 13–21. doi:10.1109/MIC.2008.50

Peter, E., & Burns, J. (2010). *Defcon 18*. Retrieved December 2011, from http://www.youtube.com/watch?v=gpZ6AbkqBQo

Ramasubramanian, V., & Sirer, E. G. (2005). Perils of Transitive Trust in the Domain Name System. In *Proceedings of the 5th ACM SIGCOMM conference on Internet Measurement*. Berkeley, CA: USENIX Association.

Rescorla, E. (2008, February 27). *Comments on draft-kupwade-sip-iba-00*. Retrieved from http://www.ietf.org/mail-archive/web/sip/current/msg22283.html

Rescorla, E. (2009, July 16). *Review of draft-huang-tls-ibe-00*. Retrieved from http://www.ietf.org/mail-archive/web/tls/current/msg03611.html

Rosa, S., & Schultze, S. (2013). Trust Darknet: Control and Compromise in the Internet's Certificate Authority Model. *IEEE Internet Computing*, 18–25. doi:10.1109/MIC.2013.27

Roschke, S., Ibraimi, L., Cheng, F., & Meinel, C. (2010). Secure Communication using Identity Based Encryption. In *Proceedings of Communications and Multimedia Security* (pp. 256–267). Springer. doi:10.1007/978-3-642-13241-4_23

Schechter, S. (2013). *The User IS the Enemy, and (S)he Keeps Reaching for that Bright Shiny Power Button!* Paper presented at the Workshop on Home Usable Privacy and Security. Newcastle, UK.

Schultze, S. B. (2010). The Certificate Authority Trust Model for SSL: A Defective Foundation for Encrypted Web Traffic and a Legal Quagmire. *Intellectual Property and Technology Law Journal*, 3-8.

Shamir, A. (1985). Identity-based cryptosystems and signature schemes. In *Proceedings of Advances in cryptology* (pp. 47–53). Springer. doi:10.1007/3-540-39568-7_5

Sheng, S., Broderick, L., & Koranda, C. A. (2006). *Why Johnny still can't encrypt: evaluating the usability of email encryption software*. Retrieved from https://cups.cs.cmu.edu/soups/2006/posters/sheng-poster_abstract.pdf

Soghoian, C., & Stamm, S. (2012). Certified lies: Detecting and defeating government interception attacks against ssl (short paper). In *Proceedings of Financial Cryptography and Data Security* (pp. 250–259). Springer. doi:10.1007/978-3-642-27576-0_20

Stallings, W. (2011). Cryptography and Network Security Priniciples and Practice. *New York: Prentice Hall.*

Sunshine, J., Egelman, S., Almuhimedi, H., Atri, N., & Cranor, L. (2009). Crying wolf: An empirical study of SSL warning effectiveness. In *Proceedings of the 18th Usenix Security Symposium* (pp. 339-416). Retrieved from http://www.usenix.org/events/sec09/tech/full_papers/sunshine.pdf

Tanimoto, S., Yokoi, M., Sato, H., & Kanai, A. (2011). Quantifying Cost Structure of Campus PKI. In *Proceedings of 11th International Symposium Applications and the Internet* (SAINT) (pp. 315-320). Munich: IEEE.

Thomas, M. (2001, June). *Requirements for Kerberized Internet Negotiation of Keys* (RFC 3129). Retrieved from http://www.ietf.org/rfc/rfc3129.txt

TrustWave SpiderLabs. (2011, May). Retrieved December 2011, from http://blog.spiderlabs.com/2011/04/certificate-revocation-behavior-in-modern-browsers.html

Tsai, C.-R. (2002). Non-repudiation in practice. In Proceedings of The Second International Workshop for Asian Public Key Infrastructures. *National Taiwan University.*

Ulrich, A., Holz, R., Hauck, P., & Carle, G. (2011). Investigating the OpenPGP Web of Trust. [Berlin: Springer.]. *Proceedings of Computer Security–ESORICS*, *2011*, 489–507.

Verisign Labs. (2013, February 20). *Global DNSSEC deployment tracking*. Retrieved from http://secspider.cs.ucla.edu/growth.html

Vratonjic, N., Freudiger, J., Bindschaedler, V., & Hubaux, J.-P. (2013). The inconvenient truth about web certificates. [Springer.]. *Proceedings of Economics of Information Security and Privacy*, *III*, 79–117. doi:10.1007/978-1-4614-1981-5_5

Whitten, A., & Tygar, J. D. (1999). Why Johnny can't encrypt: A usability evaluation of PGP 5.0. In *Proceedings of the 8th USENIX Security Symposium* (pp. 169-184). Washington, DC: McGraw-Hill.

Yang, H. O. (2011). Deploying cryptography in Internet-scale systems: A case study on DNSSEC. *IEEE Transactions on Dependable and Secure Computing*, 656–669. doi:10.1109/TDSC.2010.10

Yao, D., Fazio, N., Dodis, Y., & Lysyanskaya, A. (2004). ID-based encryption for complex hierarchies with applications to forward security and broadcast encryption. In *Proceedings of the 11th ACM conference on Computer and communications security* (pp. 354-363). Washington, DC: ACM.

Ylonen, T. (1996). SSH - secure login connections over the Internet. In *Proceedings of the 6th USENIX Security Symposium* (pp. 37-42). San Jose, CA: USENIX Association.

Zimmermann, A. J. (2011, April). *ZRTP: Media Path Key Agreement for Unicast Secure RTP* (RFC 6189). Retrieved from http://tools.ietf.org/html/rfc6189

Zimmermann, P., & Callas, J. (2009). The Evolution of PGP's Web of Trust. In Beautiful Security: Leading Security Experts Explain How They Think, (pp. 107-130). Academic Press.

Zurko, M. E., & Simon, R. T. (1996). User-centered security. In *Proceedings of the 1996 workshop on New security paradigms* (pp. 27-33). Lake Arrowhead: ACM.

ADDITIONAL READING

Amann, B., Vallentin, M., Hall, S., & Sommer, R. (2012). *Extracting Certificates from Live Traffic: A Near Real-Time SSL Notary Service. TR-12-014*. ICSI.

Boldyreva, A., Vipul, G., & Virendra, K. (2008). Identity-based encryption with efficient revocation. In Proceedings of the 15th ACM conference on Computer and communications security (pp. 417-426). Alexandria: ACM.

Chandramouli, R., & Scott, R. (2009). Open issues in secure DNS deployment. *IEEE Security & Privacy*, *7*(5), 29–35. doi:10.1109/MSP.2009.129

Chen, L., Harrison, K., Moss, A., Soldera, D., & Smart, N. P. (2002). *Certification of public keys within an identity based system. Information Security* (pp. 322–333). Springer Berlin Heidelberg.

Garfinkel, S. L. (2003). Email-based identification and authentication: An alternative to PKI? *IEEE Security & Privacy*, *1*(6), 20–26. doi:10.1109/MSECP.2003.1253564

Gentry, C. (2003). *Certificate-based encryption and the certificate revocation problem. Advances in Cryptology - EUROCRYPT 2003* (pp. 272–293). Springer Berlin Heidelberg. doi:10.1007/3-540-39200-9_17

Gentry, C., & Silverberg, A. (2002). Hierarchical ID-Based Cryptography. [Springer Berlin Heidelberg.]. *ASIACRYPT, 2002*, 548–566.

Herzberg, A., & Margulies, R. (2012). Training Johnny to Authenticate (Safely). *IEEE Security and Privacy, 10*(1), 37–45. doi:10.1109/MSP.2011.129

Holz, R., Riedmaier, T., Kammenhuber, N., & Carle, G. (2012). X. 509 forensics: Detecting and localising the SSL/TLS men-in-the-middle. [Springer Berlin Heidelberg.]. *Computer Security–ESORICS, 2012*, 217–234.

Payne, B. D., & Edwards, W. K. (2008). A brief introduction to usable security. *IEEE Internet Computing, 12*(3), 13–21. doi:10.1109/MIC.2008.50

Schechter, S. (2013). The User IS the Enemy, and (S)he Keeps Reaching for that Bright Shiny Power Button! Workshop on Home Usable Privacy and Security. Newcastle.

Soghoian, C., & Stamm, S. (2012). *Certified lies: Detecting and defeating government interception attacks against ssl (short paper). Financial Cryptography and Data Security* (pp. 250–259). Springer Berlin Heidelberg.

Tsai, C.-R. (2002). Non-repudiation in practice. The Second International Workshop for Asian Public Key Infrastructures. National Taiwan University.

Vratonjic, N., Freudiger, J., Bindschaedler, V., & Hubaux, J.-P. (2013). The inconvenient truth about web certificates. [Springer New York.]. *Economics of Information Security and Privacy, III*, 79–117.

Yao, D., Fazio, N., Dodis, Y., & Lysyanskaya, A. (2004). ID-based encryption for complex hierarchies with applications to forward security and broadcast encryption. In Proceedings of the 11th ACM conference on Computer and communications security (pp. 354-363). Washington: ACM

KEY TERMS AND DEFINITIONS

Asymmetric Cryptography: Traditional (*symmetric*) encryption and decryption algorithms utilize the same *secret* cryptographic key for protecting the information. Asymmetric encryption and decryption algorithms utilize pair of cryptographic keys (*key pair*): public key and private key. Public key is used for information encryption, but the encrypted information can be decrypted only by private key. This concludes that public key can be known to unauthorized actors as well, without putting the protected information at risk.

Certification Authority (CA): Certification authority is a trusted third party whose main responsibility is to issue and manage public key certificates. Certification authority should attest that identity included in an issued public key certificate was verified in a trustworthy manner. The identity verification process is typically documented in CA policies as well as other CA operational aspects. These policies are made public to relying parties that make use of the certificates issued by particular CA.

Certificate Transparency: The aim of certificate transparency is to provide publicly available audit logs that contain issued public key certificates as well as their issuing certification authority. This way the certificate holders will be able to monitor for certificates issued for them and be able to detect an impersonation attack.

Cryptographic Key: Encryption and decryption algorithms used for protecting a particular piece of information are usually known to authorized as well as unauthorized actors. In order to protect the information from unauthorized access a special parameter is used as an additional input for encryption and decryption process. This parameter is called cryptographic key.

Cryptographic Key Distribution: When there are several authorized actors involved in encryption and decryption of particular information, they need to share their cryptographic keys (either secret cryptographic key or public keys). The process of sharing these keys in a secure manner is called cryptographic key distribution.

DANE: DNS Based Authentication of Named Entities provides alternate public key distribution infrastructure by utilizing DNS and DNSSEC. DANE defines a new DNS resource record that can hold information about public key certificate association with a specified DNS domain or host.

DNSSEC: DNSSEC adds integrity and authenticity service to the DNS by utilizing asymmetric cryptography and digitally signing DNS responses. DNSSEC makes use of strictly hierarchical public key infrastructure that is coincident to the DNS hierarchy (authoritative name server acts as a certification authority for its zone).

Encryption: Is the algorithmic process of transforming information in a way that protects several its security attributes, especially one or more from following set: confidentiality, integrity and authenticity. Only authorized actors can reverse this process - *decrypt* the protected information in order to access or manipulate it.

Public Key Certificate: The certificate is a data structure that binds public cryptography key and information about its holder identity. This entire structure is public and its authenticity/ integrity is protected by cryptographic means.

Most widespread type of public key certificate is a X.509 certificate. X.509 certificates are used for example for protecting HTTP/SSL communications, securing email communications and verifying electronic and digital signatures.

Public Key Infrastructure (PKI): The set of hardware, software, people, policies, and procedures needed to create, manage, store, distribute, and revoke public key certificates.

ENDNOTES

[1] In SSHv2 similar approach to ZRTP can be used.

[2] Identity based encryption might be as well used along with hierarchical based key distribution infrastructures. See for example (Adida, Hohenberger, & Rivest, 2005).

[3] These estimates come mostly from practical experience. According to (Jääskeläinen, 2013) average time to setup SSH key is 15 minutes, and approximate cost per hour of a security administrator is $60 (Jääskeläinen, 2013), (Gutmann, 2011).

The estimate for PGP key set up costs come from (Whitten & Tygar, 1999), where the users have had 90 minutes to sign/encrypt mail using PGP. From our experience it takes approximately an hour to configure PGP and train a user.

Estimates for IBE and PKI originate in a research sponsored by Voltage Security (Ferrris Research, 2006) as well as expert discussions (Gutmann, 2011), (John Callas, 2013) and our practical experience.

Chapter 12
New Developments in Quasigroup–Based Cryptography

Aleksandra Mileva
University "Goce Delčev", Macedonia

ABSTRACT

This chapter offers an overview of new developments in quasigroup-based cryptography, especially of new defined quasigroup-based block ciphers and stream ciphers, hash functions and message authentication codes, PRNGs, public key cryptosystems, etc. Special attention is given to Multivariate Quadratic Quasigroups (MQQs) and MQQ public key schemes, because of their potential to become one of the most efficient pubic key algorithms today. There are also directions of using MQQs for building Zero knowledge ID-based identification schemes. Recent research activities show that some existing non-quasigroup block ciphers or their building blocks can be represented by quasigroup string transformations. There is a method for generating optimal 4x4 S-boxes by quasigroups of order 4, by which a more optimized hardware implementation of the given S-box can be obtained. Even some block ciphers' modes of operations can be represented by quasigroup string transformations, which leads to finding weaknesses in the interchanged use of these modes.

INTRODUCTION

Most of the known constructions of cryptographic primitives use structures from the associative algebra as groups, rings and fields. Two eminent specialists on quasigroups, Dénes and Keedwell, 2001 once proclaimed the advent of a new era in cryptology, consisting in the application of non-associative algebraic systems as quasigroups and neo-fields. Quasigroups and their combinatorial equivalent Latin squares are very suitable for this purpose, because of their structure, their features, their big number and because they lead to particular simple and yet efficient primitives.

In the recent years, the number of researchers in this field has increased, and the effort of the involved researchers is directed, not only to development of new quasigroup based cryptographic primitives, but also, to quasigroup representation of existing cryptographic primitives or their build-

DOI: 10.4018/978-1-4666-5808-0.ch012

ing blocks and modes of operations. A good survey of quasigroup's application in cryptology is given by Shcherbacov (2009) (also in Shcherbacov, 2010 and Shcherbacov, 2012), but you can see also (Glukhov, 2008). The mission of this chapter is to offer a comprehensive and in-depth overview of the recent developments and current state of the art in this field, so, it is not like a repetition of the previous survey, but more like complementary material and extension. However, some results are repeated, because of their importance.

We can justify multidisciplinary prospective of this topic in cryptology and information security by the fact that quasigroups and quasigroup transformations are deployed similarly in coding theory for designing error-detecting and error-correcting codes based on quasigroups (for example, Gligoroski, Markovski & Kocarev, 2007; Bakeva & Ilievska, 2009; Popovska-Mitrovikj, Bakeva & Markovski, 2011; Shcherbakov 2012), check character systems (for example, Verhoeff, 1969; Schulz 1991; Belyavskaya, Izbash & Shcherbacov, 2003; Belyavskaya, Izbash & Mullen, 2005), in cryptanalysis (for example, Bakeva & Dimitrova, 2010; Hu, 2010), etc.

In the earlier designs, security was based on secret quasigroup operations, large number of quasigroups of the same order, large number of isotopies for a given carrier, secret permutation *J* in *CI*-quasigroups, etc. The newer designs base their security mostly on the difficulty to solve systems of quasigroup equations or system of multivariate polynomial equations over finite fields, but also you can find security based on secret order of elements in quasigroup operation, secret leaders and/or order of used elementary quasigroup transformations, secret order of used quasigroups from some predefined set of quasigroups, etc.

Cryptographic community is intrigued with the notation of multivariate quadratic quasigroups (MQQs) and new MQQ-based schemes. MQQs are used for construction of multivariate quadratic polynomials over finite fields as trapdoor functions for public key cryptographic schemes, and they are one of the five classes of the recent multivariate quadratic (MQ) public key schemes. MQ schemes are based on problem of solving a system of multivariate quadratic polynomial equations and this problem is NP-Complete. There is no known polynomial-time quantum algorithm to solve MQ problem, so these schemes offer a post-quantum security. All MQ schemes have superior performances compared to the popular public key cryptosystems, because of their highly parallelizable nature, and in particular, the MQQ scheme has more efficient decryption i.e. signing phase, compared to other MQ schemes.

Organization of the chapter is as follows: in first Section we provide basic definitions for quasigroups and quasigroup string transformations, in second Section we give known quasigroup based hash functions, MACs, stream ciphers, block ciphers, pseudo-random number generators, and some older public key cryptosystems. Because of the significance of multivariate quadratic quasigroups for recent public key cryptography, third Section is entirely dedicated to MQQs and MQQ based public key schemes. Fourth Section gives several novel applications of quasigroups in cryptography, and it is followed by future research directions, open problems and conclusion.

PRELIMINARIES

The term "quasigroup" was introduced by Moufang (1935) and this algebraic structure is natural generalization of the concept of a group. Quasigroups do not have to have identity element and not be associative, so sometimes they are considered as "non-associative groups".

Definition 1: A *quasigroup* $(Q, \bullet)$ is a set Q with a binary operation $\bullet$ (known as multiplication) satisfying the following properties:

1. Q is a groupoid ($\forall a, b \in Q, a \bullet b \in Q$);
2. For all $a, b \in Q$, there exist unique $x, y \in Q$, so that $a \bullet x = b$ and $y \bullet a = b$.

In other words, each of the equations $a \bullet x = b$ and $y \bullet a = b$ has a unique solution, for any elements $a, b \in Q$. The number of elements of Q is its order. To every finite quasigroup $(Q, \bullet)$ of order r, given by its Cayley table, an equivalent combinatorial structure $r \times r$ Latin square can be associated, consisting of the main body of the table. A subset P of a quasigroup $(Q, \bullet)$ is a *subquasigroup* of Q if it is closed under operation $\bullet$.

Given a quasigroup $(Q, \bullet)$, five operations $/, \backslash, \cdot, //, \backslash\backslash$ on the set Q can be derived by:

$x / y = z \Leftrightarrow z \bullet y = x$, right division,

$x \backslash y = z \Leftrightarrow x \bullet z = y$, left division,

$x \cdot y = z \Leftrightarrow y \bullet x = z$, opposite multiplication,

$x // y = z \Leftrightarrow y / x = z \Leftrightarrow z \bullet x = y$, opposite right division,

$x \backslash\backslash y = z \Leftrightarrow y \backslash x = z \Leftrightarrow y \bullet z = x$, opposite left division.

The set $Par(\bullet) = \{\bullet, /, \backslash, \cdot, //, \backslash\backslash\}$ is said to be the set of *parastrophes* of quasigroup operation $\bullet$. $|Par(\bullet)| \leq 6$, i.e., some of the parastrophes may coincide between themselves. For each $g \in Par(\bullet)$, (Q, g) is a quasigroup too, known as the *conjugate* of Q. The quasigroup $(Q, \cdot)$ is called a *transpose* of $(Q, \bullet)$. Quasigroups in which $Par(\bullet)$ has only one element are called *totally-symmetric* or *TS-quasigroups*. TS-quasigroups can also be defined as quasigroups satisfying the identities $x \bullet y = y \bullet x$ (*commutative* quasigroups) and $(x \bullet y) \bullet x = y$ (*semisymmetric* quasigroups). TS-quasigroups satisfying the identity $x \bullet x = x$ (*idempotent* quasigroups) are called *Steiner quasigroups*.

There is also an algebraic definition of quasigroup:

Definition 2: An *algebraic quasigroup* $(Q, \bullet, \backslash, /)$ is an algebra of type $(2, 2, 2)$ satisfying the identities:

$y = x \bullet (x \backslash y)$,

$y = x \backslash (x \bullet y)$,

$y = (y / x) \bullet x$,

$y = (y \bullet x) / x$.

Since there is no difference between quasigroup $(Q, \bullet)$ and algebraic quasigroup $(Q, \bullet, \backslash, /)$ when Q is finite set, we will essentially use the name quasigroups for both of them.

Example 1: Let $Q = \mathbb{Z}_4 = \{0, 1, 2, 3\}$. The quasigroup $(Q, \bullet)$ of order 4 and its conjugates are given on Table 1.

Definition 3: A *left quasigroup* $(Q, \bullet)$ is a groupoid satisfying the law: for all $a, b \in Q$, there exist unique $x \in Q$, so that $a \bullet x = b$.

Definition 4: A *right quasigroup* $(Q, \bullet)$ is a groupoid satisfying the law: for all $a, b \in Q$, there exist unique $x \in Q$, so that $x \bullet a = b$.

Another types of quasigroups, that can be find applied in cryptology are:

- *Stein quasigroups* - $x \bullet (x \bullet y) = y \bullet x$;
- *Schroeder quasigroups* - $(x \bullet y) \bullet (y \bullet x) = x$;
- *Totally anti-symmetric quasigroups* –

$(c \bullet x) \bullet y = (c \bullet y) \bullet x \Rightarrow x = y$ and $x \bullet y = y \bullet x \Rightarrow x = y$;

- *(r, s, t)-inverse quasigroups* – if there exist a permutation J in Q and integers r, s and t

Table 1. The quasigroup (Q, •) and its conjugates

•	0	1	2	3		/	0	1	2	3		\	0	1	2	3
0	2	1	0	3		0	3	2	0	1		0	2	1	0	3
1	1	2	3	0		1	1	0	3	2		1	3	0	1	2
2	3	0	2	1		2	0	1	2	3		2	1	3	2	0
3	0	3	1	2		3	2	3	1	0		3	0	2	3	1

·	0	1	2	3		//	0	1	2	3		\\	0	1	2	3
0	2	1	3	0		0	3	1	0	2		0	2	3	1	0
1	1	2	0	3		1	2	0	1	3		1	1	0	3	2
2	0	3	2	1		2	0	3	2	1		2	0	1	2	3
3	3	0	1	2		3	1	2	3	0		3	3	2	0	1

such that, for all $x, y \in Q$ the equation $J^r(x • y) • J^s x = J^t y$ is true;

- *Crossed inverse* or *CI-quasigroups* - if there exist a permutation J in Q such that, for all $x, y \in Q$ the equation $(x • y) • Jx = y$ is true.

Two quasigroups $(Q, •)$ and $(Q, *)$ are *orthogonal* if for any $u, v \in Q$, there exists a unique pair of elements x and y of Q such that $x • y = u$ and $x * y = v$. Moreover a set $\{(Q, •_i) \mid i=1, …, t, t \leq 2\}$ of quasigroups of order r is said to be a set of *mutually orthogonal quasigroups* if any two distinct quasigroups are orthogonal. When we speak about Latin squares such a set is called a set of *mutually orthogonal Latin squares, MOLS*. The maximal possible number of MOLS of order r is $(r-1)$ and if so, the set is said to be *complete*.

We can define also n-ary quasigroups. For this purpose we are going to use the definition from Belousov (1972).

Definition 5: An n-ary groupoid (Q, f) is an n-ary *quasigroup* (of order $|Q|$) if any n elements of the $a_1, a_2, …, a_{n+1} \in Q$, satisfying the equality

$$f(a_1, a_2, …, a_n) = a_{n+1}$$

uniquely specifies the remaining one.

Previously defined quasigroup is in fact a 2-ary quasigroup or binary quasigroup. To every finite n-ary quasigroup of order r, an equivalent combinatorial structure n-dimensional Latin hypercube of order r can be associated.

Given n-ary quasigroups (Q, f) and (Q, h), we say that (Q, f) *is isotopic to* (Q, h) if there are permutations $\alpha_1, \alpha_2, …, \alpha_{n+1}$ on Q such that

$$\alpha_{n+1} f\left(\alpha_1, \alpha_2, …, \alpha_n\right) = h\left(\alpha_1\left(\alpha_1\right), \alpha_2\left(\alpha_2\right), …, \alpha_n\left(\alpha_n\right)\right)$$

for every $a_j \in Q$. The ordered tuple $(\alpha_1, \alpha_2, …, \alpha_{n+1})$ is called an *isotopism* or *isotopy* of (Q, f) upon (Q, h). The relation "is isotopic to" is an equivalence relation in the set of all n-ary quasigroups of order r. The equivalence classes are called the classes of isotopism or isotopy classes.

We use quasigroups for definition of quasigroup string transformations (or simply quasigroup transformations). Most of the quasigroup string transformations transform a given string in other string with equal length t. Let $(Q, •)$ be a finite quasigroup. Consider the set Q as an alphabet with word set $Q^+ = \{x_1 x_2 … x_t \mid x_i \in Q, t \leq 1\}$. Every quasigroup transformation applied on a given string in one pass is called an *elementary quasigroup transformation*. A composition of elementary quasigroup transformations is called a *composite quasigroup transformation*.

For fixed letter $l \in Q$ (called a *leader*) elementary quasigroup transformations e_l, d_l: $Q^+ \to Q$ are defined in (Markovski, Gligoroski & Andova, 1997), as follows:

$$e_l(x_1x_2 \ldots x_t) = (z_1z_2 \ldots z_t) \Leftrightarrow z_j = z_{j-1} \bullet x_j, \; 1 \le j \le t,$$

$$d_l(z_1z_2 \ldots z_t) = (x_1x_2 \ldots x_t) \Leftrightarrow x_j = z_{j-1} \backslash z_j, \; 1 \le j \le t,$$

where $z_0 = l$. e_l and d_l are permutations, and $e_l \circ d_l = d_l \circ e_l = I$, where I is identity permutation on Q. For this two transformations, we will use also the representations e and d, or $e_{l,\bullet}$ and $d_{l,\backslash}$. In 1999, Markovski, Gligoroski & Bakeva define another two elementary quasigroup transformations e'_l, d'_l: $Q^+ \to Q^+$ (or only e' and d') as follows:

$$e'_l(x_1x_2 \ldots x_t) = (z_1z_2 \ldots z_t) \Leftrightarrow z_j = x_j \bullet z_{j-1}, \; 1 \le j \le t,$$

$$d'_l(z_1z_2 \ldots z_t) = (x_1x_2 \ldots x_t) \Leftrightarrow x_j = z_j / z_{j-1}, \; 1 \le j \le t,$$

where $z_0 = l$. e'_l and d'_l are permutations, and $e'_l \circ d'_l = d'_l \circ e'_l = I$. This is true also if, instead of quasigroup, we use left quasigroups for e and d transformations, and right quasigroups for e' and d' transformations. Let $\bullet_1, \bullet_2, \ldots, \bullet_s$ be quasigroup operations defined on Q, $l_1, l_2, \ldots l_s$ be fixed elements from Q and $t_{l_i} \in \{e_{l_i}, d_{l_i}, e'_{l_i}, d'_{l_i}\}$, where $1 \le i \le s$. The following composite quasigroup transformations E, D, E', D' and T are defined in (Markovski, Gligoroski & Bakeva, 1999) and it is shown that they are permutations:

$$E = E^{(s)}_{l_s, \, l_{s-1}, \ldots, l_1} = e_{l_s} e_{l_{s-1}} \ldots e_{l_1}$$

$$D = D^{(s)}_{l_s, \, l_{s-1}, \ldots, l_1} = d_{l_s} d_{l_{s-1}} \ldots d_{l_1}$$

$$E' = E'^{(s)}_{l_s, \, l_{s-1}, \ldots, l_1} = e'_{l_s} e'_{l_{s-1}} \ldots e'_{l_1}$$

$$D' = D'^{(s)}_{l_s, \, l_{s-1}, \ldots, l_1} = d'_{l_s} d'_{l_{s-1}} \ldots d'_{l_1}$$

$$T = T^{(s)}_{l_s, \, l_{s-1}, \ldots, l_1} = t_{l_s} t_{l_{s-1}} \ldots t_{l_1}$$

Special kind of E transformation is the *quasigroup reverse string transformation* $\mathcal{R}$, first introduced by Gligoroski (2005), where the leaders are the elements of the string, taken in reverse order. There are extensive theoretical studies and numerical experiments of the sequences produced by quasigroup transformations E, D, E' and D' (Markovski, Gligoroski & Bakeva, 1999; Markovski & Kusakatov, 2000; Markovski & Kusakatov, 2002-2003). If we allow different (not necessarily) quasigroup operations $\bullet_1, \bullet_2, \ldots, \bullet_t$ and $\backslash_1, \backslash_2, \ldots, \backslash_t$ to be used in every step of e_l and d_l transformations, respectfully, we are talking about generalized e_l and d_l transformations (Mileva & Markovski, 2012).

Let $(Q, \bullet_1)$ and $(Q, \bullet_2)$ be two orthogonal quasigroups. Mileva & Markovski (2010) defined an orthogonal quasigroup string transformation OT: $Q^+ \to Q^+$ by the following iterative procedure:

$OT(x_1) = x_1$, $OT(x_1, x_2) = (x_1 \bullet_1 x_2, x_1 \bullet_2 x_2)$ and

if $OT(x_1, x_2, \ldots, x_{t-1}) = (z_1, z_2, \ldots, z_{t-1})$ is defined for $t > 2$, then

$OT(x_1, x_2, \ldots, x_{t-1}, x_{t-1}) = (z_1, z_2, \ldots, z_{t-2}, z_{t-1} \bullet_1 x_t, z_{t-1} \bullet_2 x_t)$.

If we allow $Q = \mathbb{Z}_{2^n}$ to be with group operation $+$ addition modulo 2^n, we can define several others quasigroup transformations. Elementary quasigroup additive and reverse additive string transformations A_l, RA_l: $Q^+ \to Q^+$ are defined in (Markovski & Mileva, 2008), as follows:

$A_l(x_1 x_2 \ldots x_t) = (z_1 z_2 \ldots z_t) \Leftrightarrow z_j = (z_{j-1} + x_j) \bullet x_j, \ 1 \leq j \leq t$, where $z_0 = l$

$RA_l(x_1 x_2 \ldots x_t) = (z_1 z_2 \ldots z_t) \Leftrightarrow z_j = x_j \bullet (x_j + z_{j+1}), \ 1 \leq j \leq t$, where $z_{t+1} = l$.

These transformations are not bijective mappings. We can create composite quasigroup transformations M by composition of different A and/or RA transformations with different leaders.

Petrescu (2010) gives several quasigroup string transformations, defined by 3-ary quasigroup (Q, α), suggesting that similarly generalized transformations can be defined with n-ary quasigroups (this like an idea can be found in Shcherbakov, 2003). Every ternary quasigroup (Q, α) forms an algebra $(Q, \alpha, \alpha_1, \alpha_2, \alpha_3)$ with 4 ternary operation, satisfying the following identities

$\alpha(\alpha_1(x_1, x_2, x_3), x_2, x_3) = x_1, \ \alpha_1(\alpha(x_1, x_2, x_3), x_2, x_3) = x_1$

$\alpha(x_1, \alpha_2(x_1, x_2, x_3), x_3) = x_2, \ \alpha_2(x_1, \alpha(x_1, x_2, x_3), x_3) = x_2$

$\alpha(x_1, x_2, \alpha_3(x_1, x_2, x_3)) = x_3, \ \alpha_3(x_1, x_2, \alpha(x_1, x_2, x_3)) = x_3.$

For fixed leaders $a_1, a_2, a_3, a_4 \in Q$, the following six quasigroup transformations $F_i, G_i : Q^+ \to Q^+, 1 \leq i \leq 3$, are given:

$$F_1(x_1 x_2 \ldots x_t) = (z_1 z_2 \ldots z_t) \Leftrightarrow$$
$$z_j = \begin{cases} \alpha(x_1, \alpha_1, \alpha_2), & j = 1 \\ \alpha(x_1, \alpha_3, \alpha_4), & j = 2 \\ \alpha(x_j, z_{j-2}, z_{j-1}), & j > 2 \end{cases}$$

$$G_1(x_1 x_2 \ldots x_t) = (z_1 z_2 \ldots z_t) \Leftrightarrow$$
$$z_j = \begin{cases} \alpha_1(x_1, \alpha_1, \alpha_2), & j = 1 \\ \alpha_1(x_1, \alpha_3, \alpha_4), & j = 2 \\ \alpha_1(x_j, x_{j-2}, x_{j-1}), & j > 2 \end{cases}$$

$$F_2(x_1 x_2 \ldots x_t) = (z_1 z_2 \ldots z_t) \Leftrightarrow$$
$$z_j = \begin{cases} \alpha(\alpha_1, x_1, \alpha_2), & j = 1 \\ \alpha(\alpha_3, x_1, \alpha_4), & j = 2 \\ \alpha(z_{j-2}, x_j, z_{j-1}), & j > 2 \end{cases}$$

$$G_2(x_1 x_2 \ldots x_t) = (z_1 z_2 \ldots z_t) \Leftrightarrow$$
$$z_j = \begin{cases} \alpha_2(\alpha_1, x_1, \alpha_2), & j = 1 \\ \alpha_2(\alpha_3, x_1, \alpha_4), & j = 2 \\ \alpha_2(x_{j-2}, x_j, x_{j-1}), & j > 2 \end{cases}$$

$$F_3(x_1 x_2 \ldots x_t) = (z_1 z_2 \ldots z_t) \Leftrightarrow$$
$$z_j = \begin{cases} \alpha(\alpha_1, \alpha_2, x_1), & j = 1 \\ \alpha(\alpha_3, \alpha_4, x_1), & j = 2 \\ \alpha(z_{j-2}, z_{j-1}, x_j), & j > 2 \end{cases}$$

$$G_3(x_1 x_2 \ldots x_t) = (z_1 z_2 \ldots z_t) \Leftrightarrow$$
$$z_j = \begin{cases} \alpha_3(\alpha_1, \alpha_2, x_1), & j = 1 \\ \alpha_3(\alpha_3, \alpha_4, x_1), & j = 2 \\ \alpha_3(x_{j-2}, x_{j-1}, x_j), & j > 2 \end{cases}$$

It is easy to check that F_i and G_i are permutations, and $F_i \circ G_i = G_i \circ F_i = I$.

One interest of people working on quasigroup based cryptography is to find what properties should have a quasigroup, so that it can be used as non-linear building block in cryptographic primitives and it can contribute to the defense against linear and differential attacks. First, we will give Boolean representation of quasigroups. Every quasigroup $(Q, \bullet)$ of order 2^b can be represented as vector valued Boolean function $B: \{0,1\}^{2b} \to \{0,1\}^b$ as follows:

$x \bullet y = (x_1, x_2, \ldots, x_b) \bullet (y_1, y_2, \ldots, y_b) = B(x_1, x_2, \ldots, x_b, y_1, y_2, \ldots, y_b) =$

$(p_1(x_1, x_2, \ldots, x_b, y_1, y_2, \ldots, y_b), p_2(x_1, x_2, \ldots, x_b, y_1, y_2, \ldots, y_b), \ldots, p_b(x_1, x_2, \ldots, x_b, y_1, y_2, \ldots, y_b))$

where p_i are $2b$-ary Boolean functions of B and $(x_1, x_2, \ldots, x_b)$ is binary representation of x. We can represent B by ANF and in that case, we say that B is represented by b-tuple of polynomials $(p_1, p_2,\ldots,p_b)$ and algebraic degree of B is the maximum of the degrees of its component polynomials. This representation helps to classify the quasigroups into linear and non-linear (Gligoroski, Dimitrova & Markovski, 2009). Linear quasigroups have all component polynomials of the degree 1. Mileva & Markovski (2008) examined the correlation matrices and prop ration tables, two tools defined in (Daemen, 1995) which are important for linear and differential cryptanalysis, for quasigroups of order 4. There is one interesting paper (Drapal, 2001) about Hamming distance of quasigroups.

The quasigroup transformations can also be represented as vector valued Boolean functions, and they can be classified also as linear and non-linear. Mileva (in press) analyses E, D, A_l, and RA_l quasigroup string transformations as Boolean functions, examining their correlation matrices and prop ration tables. Linear quasigroups produce linear E and D transformations. Experimental results showed that non-linear E transformations have better propagation characteristics (smaller maximal prop ratio), with less correlation between their input and output, than D transformations produced by the same quasigroups. Also nonlinear quasigroups can produce linear E transformations in some cases, but not linear D transformations.

The notation of shapeless quasigroup (Gligoroski, Markovski & Kocarev, 2006) is important when we search for quasigroups suitable for cryptography, because used quasigroups need to have as less structure as possible. One way to generate a shapeless quasigroups is given in (Mileva & Markovski, 2012).

Definition 6: A quasigroup $(Q, \bullet)$ of order r is said to be *shapeless* iff it is non-idempotent, non-commutative, non-associative, it does not have neither left nor right unit, it does

not contain proper sub-quasigroups, and there is no $k < 2r$ for which identities of this kinds are satisfied:

$$\underbrace{x \bullet (\ldots \bullet (x \bullet y))}_{k} = y, \text{ and } y = ((y \bullet x) \bullet \underbrace{\ldots \bullet x)}_{k}.$$

Another quasigroups can be expressed by bivariate polynomial over a ring $\left(\mathbb{Z}_{2^n}, +, \cdot\right)$, as $x * y = P(x, y)$, and they are known as *polynomial quasigroups*. The following theorem is given by Rivest (2001).

Theorem 1: A bivariate polynomial $P(x, y)$ over a ring $\left(\mathbb{Z}_{2^n}, +, \cdot\right)$ is a quasigroup, if and only if the four univariate polynomials $P(x, 0)$, $P(x, 1)$, $P(0,y)$ and $P(1,y)$ are all permutations.

If only first two univariate polynomials are permutations, $P(x, y)$ is right quasigroup, and vice versa. If only last two univariate polynomials are permutation, $P(x, y)$ is left quasigroup, and vice versa.

QUASIGROUP BASED CRYPTOGRAPHIC ALGORITHMS

If we want to use a quasigroup in a cryptographic primitive, there are two possibilities: to represent the quasigroup by its Cayley table or by some transformations. In the first case, quasigroup operation is obtained by look-up table and a lots of memory is needed. For example, if you want to represent a quasigroup of order 2^8, you need at least $(2^8)^2$ 1B=64KB, but for bigger orders this becomes even impossible. If the quasigroup is of order 2^{256} the only way to represent it, is with some transformations, for example, by isotopies. Earlier designs have used small quasigroups represented by Cayley tables, but novel designs are using large quasigroups of orders 2^{32}, 2^{64}, 2^{256} and 2^{512}, represented by isotopies, Diagonal method and orthomorphisms, Feistel networks, T-functions, permutation polynomials, etc.

In the sequel, we present several types of quasigroup based cryptographic algorithms.

Hash Functions

Hash functions are functions that take a variable-size input messages and map them into fixed-size output, known as hash result, message digest, hash-code etc. They are considered as "Swiss army knife" because of their versatile application in checking data integrity, digital signature schemes, commitment schemes, password based identification systems, digital timestamping schemes, pseudo-random string generation, key derivation, one-time passwords etc.

First attempts for using quasigroups and quasigroup transformations for creating cryptographic hash functions do not have actual implementations, such as (Markovski, Gligoroski & Bakeva, 2001; Dvorsky, Ochodkova & Snašel, 2001; Dvorsky, Ochodkova & Snašel, 2002, Gligoroski, Markovski, & Bakeva, 2003).

Snášel, Abraham, Dvorsky, Krömer, & Platoš (2009) continue to develop the hash function proposed in the second and third paper. They define their hash function only as one elementary e_a transformation of the message X= $x_1 x_2 \ldots x_t$:

$$H_\alpha (x_1 x_2 \ldots x_t) = (\ldots((a \bullet x_1) \bullet x_2) \ldots \bullet x_t = e_a (x_1 x_2 \ldots x_t)$$

The leader *a* here plays the role of an initialization vector. Also, they proposed to use huge quasigroups obtained by isotopies from the quasigroup $(Q, *)$ of modular subtraction, which is defined as $x * y = x + (r - y) \bmod r$, where $|Q| = r$. The isotopy (w, ρ, π) (w, ρ and π are permuta-

tions on Q) defines a new quasigroup operation by

$$x \bullet y = \pi^{-1} \left(w(x) + (r - \rho(y)) \bmod r \right).$$

The quasigroup of modular subtraction has a right unit 0 and is isotopic to the group $(\mathbb{Z}_r, +)$. If r is an even number, $(\mathbb{Z}_r, +)$ has a proper subgroup, the subset of even numbers. Arguments why to use quasigroup of modular subtraction as a carrier is given in (Dvorsky, Ochodkova & Snašel, 2002), and its isotopies can be evolved even with genetic algorithm (Snášel, Dvorsky, Ochodkova, Krömer, Platoš, & Abraham, 2010). Vojvoda (2004) shows how easily can be constructed second preimages and collisions based on the insertions of arbitrary number of right unit anywhere in the given message, if the quasigroup of modular subtraction is used. A preimage, second preimage and collision attacks against the hash function created with quasigroups isotopic to the quasigroup of modular subtraction, are based on inverting the mappings defining the isotopy (Slaminková & Vojvoda, 2010). It still remains an open question whether such a construction of a hash function is secure if "hard-to-invert" mappings are used for the isotopy.

A generic hash function with quasigroup reverse string transformation $\mathcal{R}$ has been described in (Gligoroski, Markovski, & Kocarev, 2006), with first implementation with name Edon-$\mathcal{R}$ (256, 384, 512) described in (Gligoroski, & Knapskog, 2008). We are going to explain here Edon-$\mathcal{R}$, the most famous its implementation and the fastest First round candidate of NIST SHA-3 competition, designed by Gligorovski, Ødegård, Mihova, Knapskog, Kocarev, Drapal & Klima (2008).

Edon-$\mathcal{R}$ is wide-pipe iterative hash function with standard MD-straitening. The chaining value H_i and the message input M_i for the ith round are composed of two q-bits blocks, $q = 256, 512,$

i.e. $H_i = \left(H_i^1, H_i^2\right)$ and $M_i = \left(M_i^1, M_i^2\right)$, and the new chaining value H_{i+1} is produced as follows

$$H_{i+1} = \left(H_{i+1}^1, H_{i+1}^2\right) = \mathcal{R}\left(H_i^1, H_i^2, M_i^1, M_i^2\right),$$

$\mathcal{R}$ is little bit modified reverse string transformation, in a sense that two parts from the message are taken reversed when are used like a leaders, and the order of leaders is $\bar{M}_i^2, H_i^1, H_i^2,$ $\bar{M}_i^1$. The compression function $\mathcal{R}$ uses two huge quasigroups of order 2^{256} and 2^{512} (the biggest so far) and their operations are defined by isotopies of Abelian group $\left(\left(\mathbb{Z}_2^w\right)^8, +_8\right)$, $w = 32$ and 64, respectfully ($+_8$ is component wise addition on two 8-dimensional vectors in $\left(\mathbb{Z}_2^w\right)^8$) as

$$X*Y = \pi_1\left(\pi_2\left(X\right) +_8 \pi_3\left(Y\right)\right)$$

where $X = (X_0, X_1,..., X_7)$, $Y = (Y_0, Y_1, ..., Y_7) \in \left(\mathbb{Z}_2^w\right)^8$ and $\pi_i : \mathbb{Z}_2^q \to \mathbb{Z}_2^q$, $1 \le i \le 3$, are permutations. Used quasigroups are non-associative, non-commutative and without identity, and for their definition authors use only bitwise xoring, left rotations and addition modulo 2^{32} and 2^{64}.

First cryptanalysis on Edon-$\mathcal{R}$ was given by Khovratovich, Nikolic & Weinmann (2008), but Gligorovski & Ødegård (2009) disputed the validity of the model in which this attack is compared to generic attacks. Klima (2008) showed that Edon-$\mathcal{R}$ is vulnerable to generic multicollisions and multipreimages attacks, with small additional work factor. The complexity of obtaining 2^K multicollisions is $K*2^{n/2}$ (hash) computations and $2^{n/2}$ memory. Novotney & Ferguson (2009) gived a distinguishing attack for Edon-$\mathcal{R}$-512 that requires around 2^{54} compression function evaluations, and this can be extended to recover the intermediate hash state just before the last

block, which breaks a number of common usage patterns for hash functions such as some KDF and MAC constructions. Leurent (2009) showed practical key-recovery attack against secret-prefix on Edon-$\mathcal{R}$.

There is another First round candidate to the NIST SHA-3 competition based on quasigroups – NaSHA, designed by Markovski & Mileva (2008). It is also wide-pipe iterative hash function with standard MD-straitening. NaSHA-$(m, 2, 6)$, m=224, 256, 384, 512, is one implementation of the family of hash functions NaSHA-(m, k, r), where m is the length of message digest, k is the number of elementary quasigroup string transformations A_l and RA_l, and r is from the order 2^{2^r} of used quasigroups. Every round consists of one linear transformation, followed by the $\mathcal{MT}$ quasigroup string transformation, which is a composition of k alternate quasigroup string transformations A_l and RA_l. NaSHA use novel design principle: the quasigroups used in every iteration in compression function are different, and depend on the processed message block. Even in one iteration, different quasigroups are used for two quasigroup transformations. Quasigroups in NaSHA are of order 2^{64} and they are produced from known starting bijection from order 2^8, only by using xoring, addition modulo 2^{64} and table lookups. Quasigroups are obtained by Sade's diagonal method (Sade, 1957) using Extended Feistel Networks as orthomorphisms and complete mappings on the groups $(\mathbb{Z}_2^{16}, \oplus)$, $(\mathbb{Z}_2^{32}, \oplus)$ and $(\mathbb{Z}_2^{64}, \oplus)$.

Nikolić & Khovratovich (2008) presented free-start collision attack, which requires 2^{32} computations for all digests, and free-start preimage attack, which requires around 2^{128} computations for NaSHA-224/256 and 2^{256} computations for NaSHA-384/512. Ji, Liangyu, & Xu (2008) gave a collision attack on NASHA-512, but Markovski, Mileva, Dimitrova, & Gligoroski (2009) disputed this attack, because his probabilistic nature. Li & Li (2009) gave truncated differential collision attack on NaSHA-384/512 with claimed complexity 2^{192} and free start collisions for all versions of NaSHA with examples.

Another interesting application of quasigroups is the quasigroup folding, a 2 time slower security fix of the MD4 family of hash functions (Gligoroski, Markovski, & Knapskog, 2005), with shapeless randomly generated quasigroup $(Q, *)$ of order 16. This technique is applied at the end of every iterative step of hash function. Every 32-bit register is seen as a concatenation of 8, 4-bit variables $a_1, a_2,..., a_8$. Variables a_1, a_2, a_3, a_4 are replaced with b_1, b_2, b_3, b_4, where $b_1 = a_1 * a_5$, $b_2 = a_6 * a_2$, $b_3 = a_3 * a_7$, and $b_4 = a_8 * a_4$. The similar technique has been used in (Gligoroski, Markovski, & Knapskog, 2006), where new hash function SHA-1Q2 has been constructed from SHA-1. The new hash function uses the message expansion part with similar quasigroup folding and has only 8 internal iterative steps (it is 3% faster that SHA-1).

Message Authentication Codes

Message Authentication Codes (MACs) take a message and a secret key as an input, and output authentication tag or MAC value, which protects data integrity and authenticity of the message.

First authentication scheme based on quasigroups was given by Denes & Keedwell (1992). Let $(Q, \bullet)$ be a quasigroup and let $M = m_1 ... m_n$, $m_i \in Q$, $1 \leq i \leq n$, be a message that need to be signed with authentication tag $b_0 ... b_{s-1}$, $bj \in Q$, $0 \leq j < s$. After signing, authentication tag is concatenated to the message and $m_1 ... m_n b_0 ... b_{s-1}$ is send to the receiver. First, the message M is divided into s blocks B_j, $0 \leq j < s$, where $|B_j| = t = \left\lceil \dfrac{n}{s} \right\rceil$ and $B_j = \{ m_{j_1},..., m_{j_t} \}$. The last block B_{s-1} can contain $l \leq t$ elements. Then b_j can be calculate by

$$b_j = \left(... \left(\left(m_{j_1} \bullet m_{j_2} \right) \bullet m_{j_2} \right) \bullet ... \right) \bullet m_{j_t}$$

with exception of the last value b_{s-1} for which only l elements are used for calculating. After that, the message and signature are concatenated and sent. The security of this authentication scheme lies in how the blocks B_j are created, and for that aim authors suggest the use of the Latin square L with elements $\{0, 1, ..., s-1\}$ as a secret key. Positions in L are numbered from 1 to s for the first row, $s+1$ to $2s$ for the second row and so on, $(s-1)s+1$ to s^2 for the last row. During block B_j formation, positions of j in L are read as $j_1, ..., j_t$ and proper elements $m_{j_1},..., m_{j_t}$ from the message M are chosen. The authors also suggest the use of the same structure for quasigroup and Latin square, for saving memory. The process can be made faster by precomputing of the blocks B_j.

Security of this scheme is analyzed by Dawson, Donowan & Offer (1996). One problem with this scheme is that it does not have an output with fixed sizes, it is not really a MAC. Also, properties of the quasigroup $(Q, \bullet)$ are not being utilized and it will work even in the case of a group instead of quasigroup.

A proper quasigroup based MAC algorithm, known as QMAC was described by Meyer (2006). In QMAC, $(Q, \bullet)$ is public and the secret key is the order in which the message elements are multiplied together to create the MAC-value, i.e. the parentheses scheme. Also one fixed element c is incorporated in key which serves to hide the innermost multiplications. Without c, one can start an adaptive chosen-text attack, described by the author. The authentication tag for a message $M = m_1 ... m_t$ is computed by multiplying the message elements together in the order specified by the key K, except that every innermost multiplication $(m_i \bullet m_{i+1})$ is replaced by $((m_i \bullet c) \bullet m_{i+1})$. This can be represented as $h_K(m_1, ..., m_t)$. Security of this scheme relies on the structure of used quasigroup. Huge "highly non-associative" quasigroup without any structure are preferable. The author gives 3 different methods for constructing MAC value for large messages and we are going to explain here only one. Let every message block consists of t elements over Q and let $|M| = Nt$, with padding.

$$H_0 = \text{IV} \in Q$$

$$H_{i+1} = H_i \bullet h_K(m_{it+1}, \ldots, m_{(i+1)t}), \ 0 \le i \le N\text{-}1$$

$$\text{QMAK}_K(M) = H_N$$

The author also gives nice representation of the key and show that the size of the keyspace increases exponentially in the length of the key.

Another quasigroup based MAC is defined by Bakhtiari, Safavi-Naini & Pieprzyk (1997). Let $(Q, \bullet)$ be a quasigroup of order $q = 2^t$ and let $b = q/2$ isotopies of $(Q, \bullet)$ are given as $(Q, \bullet_1)$, ..., $(Q, \bullet_b)$. Authors first define the family of hash functions $H = \left\{ h : Q^{q^2} \to Q^q \right\}$ and then they use the Wegman-Carter universal-hash construction (Carter & Wegman, 1979). Let M be a message of the length q^2 with its letters arranged in $q \times q$ matrix. Following sets are defined $S_{r,c} = \{ r \bullet_1 c, \ldots, r \bullet_b c \}$, $1 \le r, c \le q$. Hash result D is represented as q-tuple $(d_1, \ldots, d_q)$ and at the beginning all $d_k = 1$. The final output is calculated by

$$d_{i \bullet_k j} = m_{i,j} \bullet d_{i \bullet_k j}, 1 \le k \le b, 1 \le i, j \le q.$$

Secret key is quasigroup $(Q, \bullet)$ and its b isotopies. Authors suggest the key to be represented as (K_1, K_2), where K_1 is critical set of the correspondent Latin square to $(Q, \bullet)$ and K_2 is information about the used permutations for obtaining the isotopies. The authors suggest that it is enough for security to take $q = 16$ and $b = 8$. One problem with this MAC is that the authors did not give any discussion about key space, and its relation regarding the order of the chosen quasigroup.

Stream and Block Ciphers

Stream cipher is a symmetric key algorithm, which encrypt plaintext bits, usually individual bytes (or bits), one at a time, using an encryption transformation which varies with time. Usually stream cipher generates so called keystream which is combined with plaintext stream by some combiner-type algorithms, which in most cases is simple bitwise xoring operation (*binary additive stream cipher*). Stream ciphers can be divided as synchronous and self-synchronous or asynchronous. *Synchronous stream ciphers* generate the keystream independently of the plaintext and ciphertext. *Self-synchronous* or *asynchronous stream ciphers* use n bits of ciphertext to generate the keystream so it has limited error propagation - the one-bit error may produce incorrect decryption of the following n bits.

A block cipher is a type of symmetric-key cryptographic system that consists of two algorithms: one for encryption and the other for decryption. Encryption algorithm takes two inputs: a fixed-length block of plaintext data and a secret key, and produces a block of ciphertext data of the same length. Decryption algorithm is performed by applying the reverse transformation to the ciphertext block using the same secret key.

One of the earliest quasigroup based encryption method is given in (Sarvate & Seberry, 1986), where a set of $\{L_1, \ldots, L_k\}$ MOLS of order n is used. The secret key is pair of different squares (L_c, L_d) and if the message is encoded as a pair (i, j), it can be encrypted in the pair (α, β), that occur at the intersection of row i and column j of the Latin squares L_c and L_d. Decryption is done by simple scanning of L_c and L_d and because of the orthogonality, unique pair of coordinates (i, j) will be obtained.

An early attempt to use quasigroups for constructing synchronous stream cipher is made by Kościelny (1996). For that purpose, he suggests to use quasigroup $(Q, \bullet)$ obtained by isotopies from group, isomorphic to the additive group of GF(q) or cyclic group of order q or Abelian loop of even order q. Several Maple 7 routines for generating quasigroups isomorphic to the interior of: cyclic group of order q, multiplicative group and additive group of a finite field GF(p^m) and their isotopies can be found in (Kościelny, 2002). For creating the stream cipher, he uses the two conjugates of the given quasigroup, $(Q, \backslash)$ and $(Q, /)$. Let $m_1 m_2 m_3 \ldots$ denote the stream of characters of the plaintext, $c_1 c_2 c_3 \ldots$ denote the stream of characters of the ciphertext and $k_1 k_2 k_3 \ldots$ denote the keystream. The author suggests 6 ways for enciphering and deciphering:

$$c_i = m_i \bullet k_i, \, m_i = c_i / k_i$$

$$c_i = k_i \bullet m_i, \, m_i = k_i \backslash c_i$$

$$c_i = k_i / m_i, \, m_i = c_i \backslash k_i$$

$$c_i = m_i / k_i, \, m_i = c_i \bullet k_i$$

$$c_i = m_i \backslash k_i, \, m_i = k_i / c_i$$

$$c_i = k_i \backslash m_i, \, m_i = k_i \bullet c_i$$

If $(Q, \bullet)$ is not associative, than m_i can be mapped into 6 different characters, which is a progress in comparison with binary additive stream ciphers. The secret key may have five components: the sequence of characters interacting with the stream of the characters of a plaintext, the quasigroup $(Q, \bullet)$ and three permutations needed to form the conjugate quasigroups. One security argument is that the set of all isotopies of a quasigroup of order q forms a group of order $(q!)^3$.

Markovski, Gligoroski & Andova (1997) try to create a quasigroup based asynchronous stream cipher. They use a quasigroup $(Q, \bullet)$ as a secret key, and its conjugate $(Q, \backslash)$. The cipher stream is obtained by simple e_l transformation with fixed leader on the characters of the plaintext and the decryption is done by d_l transformation with the same leader. Several years letter, Ochodkova & Snášel (2001) use exactly the same method for encoding the file.

In (Markovski, Gligoroski & Stojčevska, 2000) is presented a quasigroup based enciphering

method, where encryption is done by $\mathrm{T}^{(s)}_{l_s, \, l_{s-1}, \ldots, l_1}$ transformation and decryption with the opposite transformation. This in fact is an asynchronous stream cipher. Used quasigroup is publicly known, and the secret key are the leaders $l_1, \ldots, l_s$ and the order of e_l or d_l transformations in encryption transformation. Interesting is that the authors implemented this in the Ytalk 3.0.2 software for on-line chat over Internet and for that aim they used quasigroup of order 128 with alphabet first 128 characters of ASCII table.

Satti (2007) gives a quasigroup based crypto-system Multi-Level Indexed Quasigroup Encryption (MLQE) system, which can be used as stream or block cipher that involves the Trusted Authority. This cryptosystem is not elaborated enough. The encryption use several e transformations (6 for its implementation) with different leaders. The main difference from the previous designs is that it uses different quasigroup operation for every transformation. First half of e transformations are made by different isotopies of one quasigroup of a smaller order, and the second half by different isotopies of one quasigroup of a bigger order. He also suggests one not very practical manner of implementing this cipher. He suggests sender and receiver to have stored two quasigroups and their isotopies as an arrays. Even more, quasigroups and their isotopies must be changed in regular intervals. The choice of the quasigroups and isotopies indexing is issued by the Trusted Authority in regular intervals. The Trusted Authority use some algorithm for generating order of quasigroups and indexes of isotopies, and they, together with a nonce, are the secret key. There is also a so called hidden key, which consists of the leaders and, it is produced by some algorithm in both communication parties. Satti, & Kak (2009) describe one application of MIQE to speech scrambling.

The most famous quasigroup based stream cipher, which has been intrigue the cryptography community for a several years is Edon80, designed by Gligoroski, Markovski & Knapskog (2008). It is one of the few left unbroken eSTREAM final-ists. Especially interesting about this crypto-graphic primitive is that it uses 4 quasigroups of very small order, 4 actually, and it is still resisting to all attacks. The authors claimed that 64 out of 576 quasigroups of order 4 are very suitable for using in Edon80, and they have chosen the qua-sigroups with the lexicographic order 61, 241, 350 and 564. Only quasigroup 350 is shapeless, 61 is commutative, 241 has left unit 1 and satisfy the identity $x \bullet_{241} (x \bullet_{241} (x \bullet_{241} (x \bullet_{241} y))) = y$ and 564 satisfy the identity $x \bullet_{564} (x \bullet_{564} y) = y$. Inter-esting remark is that all 64 quasigroups, suitable for Edon80, are isotopic to the quasigroup of modular subtraction and the group $\left(\mathbb{Z}_4, +\right)$ (Vo-jvoda, Sýs & Jókay, 2007).

Edon80 is a binary additive stream cipher, with average period of 2^{91} and with three modes of operation: KeySetup, IVSetup and Keystream mode. First two modes serve for initialization of the key and the initial vector IV. The secret key is 80 bits long, and it is divided in 40 2-bits values, each of them selects one of four quasigroup opera-tions. Obtained IV consists also of 40 2-bits values $v_0 v_1 \ldots v_{31} 32100123$ and it has the initial values of the internal states $a_0 \ldots a_{79}$. Encryption is done in Keystream mode and it starts with periodic string that has shape: 01230123…0123….Encryption consists of 80 e_l transformations, with initialized internal states $a_0 \ldots a_{79}$ as leaders. The output of the stream cipher is every second value of the last e_l transformation. In (Gligoroski & Knapskog, 2007) one can find a proposal of adding MAC function-ality to Edon80. A related key attack on Edon80 is suggested by Hell & Johansson, 2007 with the complexity of 2^{69}, although this complexity has been disputed by the Edon80 authors.

Another eSTREAM unbroken phase 3 candi-date that uses quasigroups is CryptMT v3 (Cryp-tographic Mersenne Twister), designed by Mat-sumoto, Saito, Nishimura & Hagita (2007). It is a binary additive stream cipher over the set $B = \mathbb{F}_2^8$, with period multiply of $2^{19937} - 1$. It uses combined generator, consisting of two parts. The first part is so called SFMT (SIMD-oriented Fast Mersenne Twister) generator, which generate 128-bit pseudo-number integer in one step, and the second part is a uniform quasigroup filter with memory of one wordsize. We are interesting in used qua-sigroup. Let Q be the ring $\mathbb{Z}/2^{32}$ of integers modulo 2^{32} and every $x \in Q$ corresponds to a 33-bit odd integer $2x + 1 \mod 2^{33}$. Quasigroup op-eration $\bullet$ is defined as

$$x \bullet y = 2xy + x + y \mod 2^{32}$$

what is essentially the multiplication of 33-bit odd integers. This quasigroup is associative, commutative, with unit 0 and has several proper subquasigroups.

Petrescu (2010) gives an enciphering method using 3-ary quasigroups, which can be used as a self-synchronous stream cipher (little bit different from the first version in Petrescu, 2007). Let $(Q, \alpha, \alpha_1, \alpha_2, \alpha_3)$ be publicly known 3-ary quasigroup, which will be used as a seed and as an isotope carrier. The secret key is represented by eight values $a_1, a_2, \ldots a_8 \in Q$, and the number i, $1 \leq i \leq 3$, which choose one of the three F_i quasigroup string transformations, with leaders a_5, a_6, a_7, a_8. The values a_1, a_2, a_3, a_4 define the quasigroup $(Q, \beta, \beta_1, \beta_2, \beta_3)$, isotopic to $(Q, \alpha, \alpha_1, \alpha_2, \alpha_3)$, which will be used in quasigroup string transformations, in the following way:

$$\beta(x_1, x_2, x_3) = f_4(\alpha(f_1^{-1}(x_1), f_2^{-1}(x_2), f_3^{-1}(x_3))),$$

where $f_j = f_{a_j}$, $1 \leq j \leq 4$, are publicly known permutations on Q. The author gave one imple-mentation with seed quasigroup $(\mathbb{Z}_{256}, \alpha, \alpha_1, \alpha_2, \alpha_3)$, $\alpha(x_1, x_2, x_3) = (x_1 - x_2 - x_3) \mod 256$. Chakrab-arti, Pal & Gangopadhyay, 2012 give a new version of this encryption scheme, in which publicly known 3-quasigroup (for seed) is replaced with the 3-quasigroup generated from binary quasig-roup derived from the key. Csörgö & Shcherbacov,

2011 showed that Petrescu method and its generalization with n-ary quasigroups are vulnerable relative to chosen ciphertext attack and chosen plaintext attack. Other ideas how to create stream cipher from n-ary quasigroups one can find in (Shcherbacov, 2012).

Conjugate quasigroups are used in another cipher also, designed from Xu (2010). He uses n different quasigroups $(Q, \bullet_i)$ of order n, with their conjugate quasigroups $(Q, //_i)$ and $(Q, \backslash\backslash_i)$. For every quasigroup, he defines an $E^{(i)}$ quasigroup transformation, as a composition of three e transformations with different quasigroup conjugates and leaders l_j, $1 \leq j \leq 3$, as

$$E^{(i)} = e^{(i)}_{l_{i1}, //_i} \equiv e^{(i)}_{l_{i2}, \backslash\backslash_i} \equiv e^{(i)}_{l_{i3}, i},$$

and encryption is the composition of all n $E^{(i)}$ transformations, or

$$Encrypt = E^{(1)} \circ E^{(2)} \circ \ldots \circ E^{(n)}.$$

Dimitrova, Bakeva, Popovska-Mitrovikj & Krapež (2013), based on the Krapež (2010) idea, suggest so called *parastrophic quasigroup transformation* $PE_{l,p}$, in which the input string is divided into n blocks with different lengths (some lengths my coincide) and starting with some leader l and value p, every block is transformed by e_{l_i} transformation ($1 \leq i \leq n$), but with one of the 6 conjugates of a given quasigroup. The leader l_i, and the conjugates for every block are calculated by the formula, and $l_1 = l$.

Two papers independently (Bakeva & Dimitrova, 2010; Hu, 2010), find the distribution of m-tuples in an arbitrary string processed by application of quasigroup $E^{(n)}$ transformation ($m > n$), which can be used for the statistical chosen plaintext attack on the given cryptosystem.

Marnas, Angelis & Bleris (2004) have been suggested a new quasigroup based transformation

scheme for All-Or-Nothing (AON) transformation, introduced by Rivest, 1997. AON transformation is used for pre-processing of the message into pseudo-message, before the encryption, that it is computationally infeasible for the attacker to decrypt the message if any of the pseudo-message block is missing. Quasigroup modification uses a quasigroup $(Q, \bullet)$ of order 256 represented as a permutation in the set of $Q = \mathbb{Z}^*_{257}$, with one difference, 256 stands for 0. The message is transformed into pseudo-message by one e transformation using fixed leader l. The message is constructed as message to encrypt = leader l + first row of the quasigroup + pseudo-message and it is only 257B longer than original message. First row of the quasigroup is needed, because the other elements of its Cayley table are defined as $a_{i,j} = i * j = i \cdot a_{1,j} \bmod 257$. Then the actual encryption takes place with any known algorithm. On the other side, by the actual decryption, the pseudo-message is obtained first. After that, the quasigroup $(Q, \backslash)$ is formed first, and then decryption is done by using d_l transformation. The authors did not mention one thing, that with their modification, the basic idea of AONT is violated. The attacker can start with decrypting without knowing all pseudo-message blocks. For example, if he knows only those blocks that contains the quasigroup and the leader, he can starts decrypting character by character only if he obtains characters in right order.

Pseudo-Random Number Generators

A *random number generator (RNG)* is a device or algorithm which outputs a sequence of statistically independent and unbiased binary digits. It can be hardware-based or software-based. A *pseudo-random number generator (PRNG)* is an deterministic algorithm for generating a pseudo-random sequence of numbers that approximates the properties of random numbers. They are necessary for generation of keys, nonces, challenges etc. Pseudo-randomness comes from the fact that the sequence is completely determined by a relatively small set of initial values, called the PRNG's state, which is initialized by random seed. Random seeds are often generated from the state of the computer system (such as the time), a cryptographically secure pseudo-random number generator (CSPRNG) or from a hardware random number generator. PRNGs need to have very long periods and simple and fast software implementation. Common classes of these algorithms are the linear congruence functions and the linear feedback shift registers, which have relatively small periods and are highly predictable. Many problems of the earlier generators are avoided by the newer PRNGs, like Mersenne Twister, which has a large period of $2^{19937}-1$. PRNG can be made also from other cryptographic primitives as stream and block ciphers and hash functions.

A PRNG passes all polynomial-time statistical tests if no poly algorithm can distinguish between output sequence and truly random sequence of the same length with probability significantly greater that ½. An PRNG is *cryptographically secure pseudo-random number generator (CSPRNG)* iff it passes the *next-bit test* (or right-unpredictable or forward unpredictable), i.e. given first k bits in input, no polynomial-time algorithm can predict the $(k + 1)^{st}$ bit with probability significantly greater than ½. similarly holds for *previous-bit test* (or left-unpredictable or backward-unpredictable).

Sittuation with quasigroup based PRNG is not promising. there are three quasigroup based PRNGs, and all are broken. Dimitrova & Markovski (2004) have been proposed one quasigroup based PRNG - QPRSG with arbitrary large period, based on E transformation, which was attacked by Battey & Parakh (2012). Battey & Parakh (2012) showed that QPRSG gives very bad statistical test results, and that the QPRSG output can be compressed by a factor of about 1000, which means there is very little (pseudo) entropy in produced sequences. In the same paper, Battey & Parakh gave a new quasigroup based PRNG – LOQG

PRNG 256, but for this PRNG there is an attack from Dichtl & Böffgen (2012). They found out how many output bytes of LOQG PRNG 256 are needed in order to predict all future output bytes, so this algorithm do not pass next-bit-test, and showed two others attacks, and one undesirible property. Markovski, Gligoroski & Kocarev (2005) have been proposed a new method for simulating unbiased physical sources of randomness and improving the properties of existing PRNGs, which is based on the E and E' quasigroup string transformations. The authors stated that their method is flexible, highly parallel, with linear complexity and is capable of producing a random number sequence from a very biased stationary source. Dichtl (2007) showed that this PRNG is ineffective, because of the use of bijective post-processing function (E and E' transformation), and it is very easy to attack.

Public Key Cryptosystems: Older Attempts

Public key algorithms encrypt messages using a non-secret key. They are much slower than symmetric key algorithms, so they are usually used for key agreement and key management between two communication parties, and then, the actual communication is continued by some symmetric fast block or stream cipher algorithm.

In a public key encryption scheme a pair of encryption key and decryption key (public and private key) is generated for each user, and all the encryption keys are made public (decryption key is private key for the user). When sending a secret message to a receiver, the sender encrypts the message with the receiver's public key. Receiver decrypt the message with his private key. So, a public key encryption scheme is comprised of three algorithms: a key generation algorithm, an encryption algorithm and a decryption algorithm. The design of a public key cryptosystem can be based on a trapdoor one-way function. A *trapdoor one-way function* is a function f onto a set X that anyone can compute efficiently; however inverting f is hard unless one is also given some "trapdoor" information.

In 1999 Keedwell made an attempt to design a quasigroup based public-key algorithm. For that aim, CI-quasigroup $(Q, \bullet)$ with long inverse cycle $(c, c', c'', \ldots, c^{(t-1)})$, of length t, is used. $(c, c', c'', \ldots)$ is called the inverse cycle, associated with the element c, if c' is the right crossed-inverse of c, c'' is that of c', and so on. The author use the following theorem for constructing wanted quasigroup.

Theorem 2: Let $(Q, \cdot)$ be an Abelian group of order n such that $n + 1$ is composite. Define a binary operation $\bullet$ on the elements of Q by the relation $a \bullet b = a^r b^s$, where $rs = n + 1$. Then $(Q, \bullet)$ is a CI-quasigroup and the right crossed inverse of the element a is a^u, where $u = (-r)^3$.

A key distributing center would be established as the only entity with knowledge of the long inverse cycle. This center will distribute a public key $c_i^u \in Q$ and a private key $c_i^{u+1} \in Q$ to each user U_i, where $Jc_i^u = c_i^{u+1}$. Every user can perform the quasigroup operation $\bullet$. When user U_i wish to send a message m to user U_j, he would send $c_j^u \bullet m$, and U_j with his private key c_j^{u+1} will decipher as $(c_j^u \bullet m) \bullet c_j^{u+1} = m$. The key exchange can be done without the key distributing center also, if the sender and the receiver have knowledge of J. Then the sender will choose randomly $c^u \in Q$ and he will send it together with the ciphertext $c^u \bullet m$ to the receiver. The receiver will use J to obtain the value c^{u+1} and to decrypt the message by $(c^u \bullet m) \bullet c^{u+1} = m$. Big drawback of this method is that if the attacker knows the permutation J, he can decipher any encrypted message.

Another public-key algorithm based on CI-quasigroups is given by Golomb, Welch, & Dénes (2001).

Kościelny & Mullen (1999) tried to build a quasigroup-based public key cryptosystem with the help of previous defined Kościelny's stream-cipher, but this is not a public-key cryptosystem in a real sense. There is no public and private keys, but only encryption and decryption procedure in which random k_x bytes, as public portion of the key, are used for initial condition of used PRNG, for obtaining the keystream K. Used quasigroup is also part of the secret key. Everybody with knowledge of used quasigroup and k_x can obtain the secret key K and can do decryption or encryption. At the end, security of this cryptosystem reduces to secret quasigroup.

The public key stream cipher based on quasigroups is given by Gligoroski (2004). It uses the ElGamal algorithm in the initialization phase and E transformations for encryption, with appropriate D transformation for decryption. The cryptographic strength of the proposed stream cipher is based on the fact that breaking it would be at least as hard as solving systems of multivariate polynomial equations modulo big prime number p which is NP-hard problem and there aren't any fast randomized or deterministic algorithms for solving it.

MULTIVARIATE QUADRATIC QUASIGROUPS AND PUBLIC KEY CRYPTOSYSTEMS

Perhaps the most important application of quasigroups in cryptography, especially in public-key cryptography, comes from the notation of Multivariate Quadratic Quasigroups (MQQ), first defined in (Gligorovski, Markovski & Knapskog, Multivariate quadratic trapdoor functions based on multivariate quadratic quasigroups, 2008). They are used for construction of multivariate quadratic polynomials over finite fields as trapdoor functions for public key cryptographic schemes.

Definition 7: A quasigroup $(Q, \bullet)$ of order 2^n is called *Multivariate Quadratic Quasigroup (MQQ) of type $Quad_{n-k}Lin_k$* if exactly $(n - k)$ of the polynomials p_i are of degree 2 (i.e., are quadratic) and k of them are of degree 1 (i.e., are linear), where $0 \leq k < n$.

The MQQ's inventors give also the following theorem for sufficient conditions some quasigroup $(Q, \bullet)$ to be MQQ.

Theorem 3: Let $A_1 = \left[f_{ij} \right]_{d \times d}$ and $A_2 = \left[g_{ij} \right]_{d \times d}$ be two $d \times d$ matrices of linear Boolean expressions, and let $b_1 = \left[u_i \right]_{d \times 1}$ and $b_2 = \left[v_i \right]_{d \times 1}$ be two $d \times 1$ vectors of linear or quadratic Boolean expressions. Let the functions f_{ij} and u_i depend only on variables $x_1, \ldots, x_d$, and let the functions g_{ij} and v_i depend only on variables $x_{d+1}, \ldots, x_{2d}$. If

$$\text{Det}\left(A_1\right) = \text{Det}\left(A_2\right) = 1$$

in $GF(2)$ and if

$$A_1 \times \left(x_{d+1}, \ldots, x_{2d}\right)^T + b_1 \equiv$$
$$A_2 \times \left(x_1, \ldots, x_d\right)^T + b_2$$

then the vector valued operation

$$\left(x_1, \ldots, x_{2d}\right) = A_1 \times \left(x_{d+1}, \ldots, x_{2d}\right)^T + b_1$$

defines a quasigroup $(Q, \bullet)$ of order 2^d that is MQQ.

For a randomly generated quasigroup of order 2^d, $d \geq 4$, the algebraic degrees are higher than 2, so MQQs need to be constructed someway. One method that randomly generates vector valued Boolean function of algebraic degree 2, and then

check if it is a MQQ or not, is given in (Ahlavat, Gupta & Pal, 2009).

The first trapdoor one-way function that use quasigroup string transformations with multivariate quadratic quasigroups (MQQ) is given in (Gligoroski, Markovski, & Knapskog, Multivariate quadratic trapdoor functions based on multivariate quadratic quasigroups, 2008). Obtained public key algorithm is a bijective mapping, it does not perform message expansions, can be used for encryption and signatures, and its speed is 500–1000 times faster than the most popular public key schemes. The modification of the algorithm is given in (Gligoroski, Markovski, & Knapskog, A public Key Block Cipher based on Multivariate Quadratic Quasigrops, 2008). The authors give heuristic algorithm for finding MQQ of type $Quad_{d-k}Lin_k$ of order at most 2^5. With it, they generate two large sets of MQQ of type $Quad_4Lin_1$ and $Quad_5Lin_0$ (with more than 2^{20} elements each) in preprocessing phase, and they pick randomly 2 quasigroups from the first set, and 6 from the second set. Then, they generate n multivariate quadratic polynomials with n variables $P' = \{P'_i (x_1, \ldots, x_n) \mid i = 1, \ldots, n\}$, where $n = 140, 160, \ldots$ is the size of the block, using generalized d transformation with chosen quasigroups and bijection of Dobbertin, with requirement - minimal rank of quadratic polynomials when represented in matrix form to be at least 8.

The public key is formed by the n multivariate quadratic polynomials with n variables $\mathbf{P} = \{P_i (x_1, \ldots, x_n) \mid i = 1, \ldots, n\}$ using transformations $T \circ P' \circ S: \{0, 1\}^n \rightarrow \{0, 1\}^n$ where T and S are two nonsingular linear transformations, and P' is a bijective multivariate quadratic mapping on $\{0, 1\}^n$ obtained previous.. The size of the public key is $n \times \left(1 + \dfrac{n \times (n + 1)}{2}\right)$ bits. T and S together with 8 chosen MQQs $\bullet_1, \ldots, \bullet_8$ form the private key. The size of the private key expressed in Kb is $\dfrac{1}{2^{13}}\left(2n^2 + 40960\right)$.

Encryption is done by direct applying of multivariate quadratic polynomials over a vector $x = (x_1, \ldots, x_n)$, i.e. $y = \mathbf{P}(x)$. Decryption/signing is done by using of T^{-1}, S^{-1}, Dobbertin inverse and left divisions $\backslash_i$ of the quasigroup operations $\bullet_i$, $i = 1, \ldots, 8$. In fact, the owner of the private key needs to store conjugates with left divisions (left parastrophes) of key's quasigroup operations. This algorithm has one implementatition for wireless sensor networks on platform TelosB and MICAz, given by Maia, Barreto & de Oliveira (2010). Unfortunately, the encryption/decryption part was successfully broken up to $n = 300$, by Mohamed, Ding, Buchmann & Werner (2009) by both the MutantXL algorithm and the F_4 algorithm. By removing 1/4 of the public key equations this scheme can still be used for digital signatures. Cryptanalysis given in (Faugère, Ødegård, Perret & Gligoroski, 2010) explained exactly why the MQQ systems are so easy to solve in practice. They conclude that if a suitable replacement for the Dobbertin transformation is found, MQQ can possibly be made strong enough to resist pure Gröbner attacks for adequate choices of quasigroup size and number of variables.

Markovski, Samardziska, Gligoroski & Knapskog (2010) proposed a new algorithm, called LQLP-s, that is aimed to overwhelm the weaknesses of the previous scheme and to prevent Gröbner basis attacks. s is the length of the message. For that reason, they produce a hybrid type of polynomials for trapdoor functions: over the field $GF(2)$, and over the ring $\mathbb{Z}_{256}$ with the same set of Boolean variables, using multivariate quadratic left quasigroups (MQLQ – left quasigroups that have Boolean functions of degree 2) and left polynomial quasigroups (LPQ).

The authors give a construction of MQLQs, using the following theorem:

Theorem 4: Let $\mathrm{A}_1 = \left[f_{ij}\right]_{d \times d}$ and $\mathrm{A}_2 = \left[g_{ij}\right]_{d \times d}$ be two $d \times d$ nonsingular matrices of linear Boolean expressions, such that the functions

f_{ij} and g_{ij} depend only on variables $\mathrm{x}_1, \ldots, \mathrm{x}_\mathrm{d}$. Let $\mathrm{D} = \left[d_{ij}\right]_{d \times d}$ be nonsingular Boolean matrix, $\mathrm{c} = \left[c_i\right]_{d \times 1}$ be a Boolean vector, and let $Q = \{0, 1, \ldots 2^d\text{-}1\}$. The vector valued operation

$$_{vv}\left(\mathrm{x}_1, \ldots, \mathrm{x}_{2d}\right) = \mathrm{D} \times (\mathrm{A}_1 \mathrm{n}\left(\mathrm{x}_{d+1}, \ldots, \mathrm{x}_{2d}\right)^{\mathrm{T}} + \mathrm{A}_2 \times \left(\mathrm{x}_1, \ldots, \mathrm{x}_\mathrm{d}\right)^{\mathrm{T}} + \mathrm{c}^{\mathrm{T}})$$

defines a left quasigroup $(Q, \bullet)$ of order 2^d that is MQLQ, where $Q = \{0, 1, \ldots 2^d\text{-}1\}$. The parastrophe $\backslash_\bullet$ of $\bullet$ is defined by

$$\backslash_{vv}\left(x_1, \ldots, x_{2d}\right) = \mathrm{A}_1^{-1} \times \left(\mathrm{D}^{-1} \times \left(x_{d+1}, \ldots, x_{2d}\right)^{T} \text{-} \mathrm{A}_2 \times \left(x_1, \ldots, x_\mathrm{d}\right)^{T} \text{-} \mathrm{c}^{T}\right).$$

For LQLP-160, first by the *MQLQequations* algorithm, using 16 random left quasigroups of order 2^5, d transformation with random leader L and random 80×80 Boolean matrix S_{80}, 80 *MQ* polynomials $p_i(x_1, x_2, \ldots, x_{160})$ over the field $GF(2)$ are generated. By the algorithm *LPolyQequations*, from 4 randomly chosen nonsingular 10×10 matrices S_{10}, S'_{10}, S''_{10}, S'''_{10} over the ring $\mathbb{Z}_{256}$, one randomly chosen constant vector *const*, 10 randomly chosen left polynomial quasigroups, 10 multivariate polynomials $q_i(C_1, \ldots, C_{10}, D_1, \ldots, D_{10})$ over $\mathbb{Z}_{256}$ are generated ($C_1, \ldots, C_{10}, D_1, \ldots, D_{10}$ is 20B input). There are also two auxiliary algorithms *InverseMQLQ* and *InverseLPolyQ* for the decryption phase. The algorithm *MLQLPolyQ* from 160 Boolean variables using random a nonsingular 160×160 Boolean matrix S and two nonsingular 80×80 Boolean matrices S_L and S_R, we generate 80 *MQ* polynomials $p_i(x_1, x_2, \ldots, x_{160})$ over the field $GF(2)$ and 10 multivariate polynomials $q_i(C_1, \ldots, C_{10}, D_1, \ldots, D_{10})$ over $\mathbb{Z}_{256}$, which form 90 equations with 160 Boolean unknowns. These polynomials, together with 160×160 matrix $A=S'S$, where $S' = \begin{bmatrix} S_L & 0 \\ 0 & S_R \end{bmatrix}$, are the public key, and it can be stored in 143KB. The private key consists of the following tuple (S, S_{80}, S_L, S_R, S_{10}, S_{10}', S_{10}'', S_{10}''', *const*, L, 16 random left quasigroups, 10 polynomial quasigroups), and it can be stored in 6KB.

Samardziska, Markovski & Gligoroski (2010) presented an effective general and straightforward polynomial time construction of MQQ of arbitrary order and degree using T-functions (see the Theorem below), but also they gave the lower bound on the number of MQQs. The authors give sufficient and necessary conditions for a T-function to be a permutation or a quasigroup, and make a complete characterization of the T-functions that define permutations and quasigroups.

Gligorovski, Ødegård, Jensen, Perret, Faugère, Knapskog & Markovski (2011) describe a digital signature variant of the original MQQ public key algorithm, called MQQ-SIG, which is 300-3500 times faster than RSA or ECDSA in software, and 10,000 times in hardware. They use a method known as *minus modifier* - by removing half of the equations in the public key, they believe that Gröbner basis and MutantXL attacks cannot be launched on the remaining known equations. Under the assumption that solving $n/2$ quadratic MQQ's equations with n variables is as hard as solving systems of random quadratic equations, they show that in the random oracle model their signature scheme is provably CMA resistant.

The length of the signatures is $2n$ bits where $n = 160, 192, 224$ or 256, and its conjectured security level is at least $2^{\frac{n}{2}}$. MQQ-SIG uses MQQs of order 2^d, presented as

$$x*y = B \times U(x) \times A_2 \times y + B \times A_1 \times x + c)$$

where A_1, A_2 and B are nonsingular $d \times d$ matrices in $GF(2)$, c is a random d dimensional vector in $GF(2)$ and $U(x)$ is an upper triangular matrix with all diagonal elements equal to 1, and the elements above the main diagonal are linear expressions of the variables of $x = (x_1, \ldots, x_d)$. These quasigroups satisfy two additional condition. The multivariate quadratic system is presented with $S \circ P' \circ S'$ where S' is affine bijective transformation, S is a nonsingular linear transformation, and P is a central bijective multivariate quadratic mapping, for which a nonstandard quasigroup transformation is used.

The authors have had two possibilities how to build MQQ of order 2^8, MQQ from T-functions (Samardziska, Markovski & Gligoroski, 2010), which can be encoded in 256B, and bi-linear MQQ (Chen, Knapskog & Gligoroski, 2010) with 81B, and because the experiments did not show any differences in security, they chose the second type. Both technics for MQQ's construction produce operations over $GF(2)$.

One disadvantage of this algorithm, common to all other MQ schemes, is the large size of the public key (from 125 to 512 Kb), and a typical technique to reduce the public key in MQ schemes is to use polynomials over bigger fields $GF(p^k)$, where p is prime and $k > 1$. Samardziska, Chen & Gligoroski (2012) extended the previously two known constructions of MQQ for operations over the prime field of characteristic 2 (T-functions and bilinear), to construction in Galois fields of any characteristic and order. If the construction of MQQs over $GF(2)$ in MQQ-SIG is replaced with construction of MQQs over $GF(2^k)$, the size of the public key will be reduced up to 58 times. The authors provided a new algorithm for the decryption process in MQQ based cryptosystems that improves the performance of the previously known approach and that decreases the size of the private key.

Another MQQ-based public key encryption scheme, known as MQQ-ENC is given by Gligoroski & Samardjiska (2012). This scheme is probabilistic with negligible probability of decryption errors, by using a universal hash function for elimination of the possibly wrong plaintext candidates. It has similarity with MQQ-SIG, because it uses quasigroup string transformations for internal mapping P', and specially constructed affine mappings S and T from two circulant matrices There are some difference also – it uses left MQQs, instead of bilinear MQQs (but with the same order), it is defined over the field $\mathbb{F}_{2^k}$ for any $k \geq 1$, and can be easily extended to any $\mathbb{F}_{p^k}$, for p prime number. The trapdoor is constructed using a minus modifier with fixed small number of removed equations. MQQ-ENC still need to be implemented.

Samardziska & Gligoroski (2011) gave two proposals for identity (ID) based identification schemes, and proved them as Zero Knowledge. The first scheme is IP2S-ID is an ID version of the Patarin's IP with two secrets (Patarin, 1996). The second scheme is LMQQ-ID, which combines two problems: the problem of Isotopy of Left Multivariate Quasigroups (LMQIsot) and the MQ problem. This scheme can be seen as generalization of the Wolf & Preneel, 2010 scheme.

NEW APPLICATIONS OF QUASIGROUPS

There are research activities for representing some existing cryptographic primitives, or their building blocks and modes of operations by quasigroups and quasigroup string transformations, which lead to finding weaknesses in their deployment or to improving their hardware implementations.

Gligoroski, Andova & Knapskog (2008) proved that CBC and OFB modes of operation (for block ciphers) can be represented as e_{IV} transformations with the initial vector IV as a leader, and that OFB is a special case of the more general CBC mode

where the encryption of a string of all zeros is performed. For that purpose, the authors first showed that the operation defined on $Q = \{0, 1\}^b$ (b is the length of one block in bits) as

$$X *_K Y = CIPH_K (X \oplus Y)$$

where $X, Y \in Q$, and $CIPH_K$ is underlined block cipher's encryption function for a given key $K \in \{0,1\}^k$, is a commutative quasigroup operation for any key K. So we can use $*$ instead of $*_K$. The left division for this quasigroup operation is defined as $X \backslash_* Y = CIPH_K^{-1} (Y) \oplus X$. Let the plaintext P be divided in n blocks P_i, $1 \leq i \leq n$ of length b bits, and let $C = (C_1, C_2, ..., C_n)$ be the obtained ciphertext. The two modes are given as follows:

- CBC Encryption $C = e_{IV, *} (P_1, P_2, ..., P_n)$
- CBC Decryption $P = d_{IV, \backslash_*} (C_1, C_2, ..., C_n)$
- OFB Encryption $C = e_{IV, *} (\mathbf{0}) \oplus P$
- OFB Decryption $P = e_{IV, *} (\mathbf{0}) \oplus C$

More important, the authors showed that in a case of interchanged use of CBC and OFB modes, the plaintext can be obtained from the c iphertext, without the knowledge of the secret key. An attack on the CTR mode is described also, when it is used together with CBC mode, if they both use the same secret key. For this attack, the found autotopism between the quasigroups $(Q, \oplus)$ ($\oplus$ is XOR operation) and $(Q, *)$ is used, which includes the CTR encryption of the string of all zeros.

Another interesting and novel application of a quasigroups is (Mihajloska & Gligoroski, 2012) awarded paper for generating an optimal 4×4 S-boxes (usually the only non-linear building block of most of today lightweight block ciphers) by non-linear quasigroups $(Q, \bullet)$ of order 4, $Q=\{0, 1, 2, 3\}$ and e transformations. They obtain the permutation $f: Q^2 \Rightarrow Q^2$, which maps 4 bits in 4 bits, as in the following Algorithm 1 given in pseudo-language.

The authors made an exhaustive search for $k = 2$ (or 4 e transformations and 4 leaders), and they found 1024 optimal 4×4 S-boxes, with all of the output bits to have algebraic degree 3. They made also an exhaustive search for $k = 4$ (or 8 e transformations and 8 leaders), and they found 331, 264 optimal 4×4 S-boxes, with all of the output bits to have algebraic degree 3.

Using this algorithm, Mihajloska, Yalcin & Gligoroski (2013) offer a methodology for more optimized hardware implementation of cryptographically strong 4×4 S-boxes, which not only iteratively reuse the same circuit to implement several different S-boxes, but it leads to bit level serialization and S-box implementation below 10 GEs.

Mileva & Markovski (2013) examine several block ciphers that use Feistel networks or their generalizations, and rewrite their rounds by quasigroup operations, using ideas from (Mileva & Markovski, 2012). Special attention is given to the block ciphers Misty1, Camellia, Four-Cell, Four-Cell⁺ and SMS4. For all of them, one feature is the same - they use bijections as round functions in their Feistel networks. The authors represent them by generalized e transformations, by applying different quasigroups of orders 2^b, where b is the length of the block in bits.

Example 2: SMS4 (translated from Chinese by Diffie & Ledin, 2008) is a Chinese Generalized Feistel cipher with block and key size of 128 bits. It uses 32 rounds which are *type-4* Parameterized Extended Feistel Networks (PEFNs - Mileva & Markovski, 2013). The output of i-th round is represented by

$$X_i = \left(x_i, x_{i+1}, x_{i+2}, x_{i+3} \right) = \left(x_i, x_{i+1}, x_{i+2}, x_{i-1} \oplus f_{sk_i} \left(x_i \oplus x_{i+1} \oplus x_{i+2} \right) \right)$$

where

$$X_0 = \left(x_0, x_1, x_2, x_3 \right) \in \left(\{0,1\}^{32} \right)^4$$

is the plaintext and

$$X_{i-1} = \left(x_{i-1}, x_i, x_{i+1}, x_{i+2} \right)$$

is the input i-th round, $1 \leq i \leq 32$. The ciphertext is

$$C = \left(x_{35}, x_{34}, x_{33}, x_{32} \right).$$

We are not interested in the structure of f_{sk_i}, the only important thing is that f_{sk_i} is a permutation for fixed sk_i. So, the type 4 PEFN $F_{0,0,0,0,sk_i}$ is an orthomorphism in a group

$$\left(\left(\{0,1\}^{32} \right)^4, \oplus \right),$$

and the corresponding quasigroups

Algorithm 1.

> **Input:** Starting string (x_1, x_2), where $(x_1, x_2) \in Q^2$
> **Output:** The permutation f
> For $x_1 = 0$ to 3
> For $x_2 = 0$ to 3
> pos = 0;
> For $i = 1$ to k
>
> $(y_1, y_2) = e_{l_{2i-1}} (x_1, x_2)$;
>
> $(x_2, x_1) = e_{l_{2i}} (y_2, y_1)$;
>
> end
> $f(pos) = (x_1, x_2)$;
> end
> end

$$\left(\left(\left\{ 0,1 \right\}^{32} \right)^{4}, \ast_{i} \right)$$

are defined as

$$X \ast_{i} Y = F_{0,0,0,0,sk_{i}} \left(X \oplus Y \right) \oplus Y$$

SMS4 can be written as generalized $e_{l, \ast_{1}, \ast_{2}, \ldots, \ast_{32}}$ transformation of string that consists of 32 zeros **0** and $l = X_{0}$, with 32 different quasigroups of order 2^{128} as:

$$C = e_{X_{0}, \ast_{1}, \ast_{2}, \ldots, \ast_{32}} \left(\underbrace{0,0,\ldots 0}_{32} \right)$$

As last remark, used quasigroups are diagonally cyclic, non-associative, anti-commutative, and Shroeder quasigroups.

FUTURE RESEARCH DIRECTIONS

There are continuous research activities in MQQ-based public key cryptography. Some of the suggested algorithms need to be implemented, and additional research should be done on reducing the size of the public key. These schemes are relatively new, so a thorough cryptanalysis is needed. There are also novel research activities in zero knowledge ID-based identification schemes, which need to go further, till implementation and cryptanalysis.

Quasigroup representation of some block ciphers can be used to analyze the block ciphers from a totally new perspective. Instead of analyzing the strength of the block ciphers via different number of rounds, the described block ciphers can be instantiated with smaller quasigroups and then those miniature block ciphers that have the same structure as the original ones can be ana-

lyzed (idea from D. Gligoroski). Additionally, the possibility to construct distinguishers for block ciphers with quasigroup representation need to be explored. One need to examine does the structure of the quasigroups in quasigroup representation of block ciphers, somehow influences the block cipher's security.

In investigating of the connections between cryptographic primitives and quasigroups, one can try to find quasigroup representations of MDS matrices (which are equivalent with linear multipermutations) and in this way, we can obtain a truly quasigroup based block cipher build as a S-P network, which can compete with the most famous ciphers today. Neither of the 4×4 S-boxes used in today lightweight cryptography is not yet represented by the suggested quasigroup methodology, so if someone do that, maybe will obtain a more optimized hardware representation of the existing lightweight block ciphers.

One can try to obtain an optimal 8×8 S-box using quasigroups from smaller order 4 or 16. Finding hidden quasigroups in other block ciphers is also a challenge. So, the story of quasigroup based cryptography is far from its end, there is space for versatile future research.

CONCLUSION

This chapter give a short overview of the recent developments in quasigroup based cryptographic primitives, like hash functions, MACs, stream and block ciphers, public key algorithms, etc. Special attention is given to MQQ public key schemes. New applications of quasigroups in cryptology are given through representation of some existing cryptographic primitives, or their building blocks and modes of operations by quasigroups and quasigroup string transformations.

REFERENCES

Ahlavat, R., Gupta, K., & Pal, S. K. (2009). *Fast Generation of Multivariate Quadratic Quasigroups for Cryptographic Applications*. IMA Conference on Mathematics in Defence. Retrieved January 15, 2013 from http://www.ima.org.uk/_db/_documents/defence09_ahlawat_v2.pdf

Bakeva, V., & Dimitrova, V. (2010). Some Probabilistic Properties of Quasigroup Processed Strings useful for Cryptanalysis. In M. Gušev & P. Mitrevski (Eds.), *Proceedings of ICT Innovation 2010* (pp. 61-70). Berlin: Springer.

Bakeva, V., & Ilievska, N. (2009). A probabilistic model of error-detecting codes based on quasigroups. *Quasigroups and Related Systems, 17*(2), 151–164.

Bakhtiari, S., Safavi-Naini, R., & Pieprzyk, J. (1997). A Message Authentication Code based on Latin Square. In V. Varadharajan, J. Pieprzyk, & Y. Mu (Eds.), *Proceedings of ACISP'97*, (LNCS), (vol. 1270, pp. 194-203). Berlin: Springer.

Battey, M., & Parakh, A. (2012). A Quasigroup Based Random Number Generator for Resource Constrained Environments. *IACR Cryptology ePrint Archive. Report, 2012*, 471.

Belousov, V. D. (1972). n-ary quasigroups. Kishinev, Moldova: Ştiinţa.

Belyavskaya, G. B., Izbash, V. I., & Mullen, G. L. (2005). Check character systems using quasigroups: II. *Designs, Codes and Cryptography, 37*(3), 405–419. doi:10.1007/s10623-004-4033-x

Belyavskaya, G. B., Izbash, V. I., & Shcherbacov, V. A. (2003). Check character systems over quasigroups and loops. *Quasigroups and Related Systems, 10*, 1–28.

Carter, J. L., & Wegman, M. N. (1979). Universal Class of Hash Functions. *Journal of Computer and System Sciences, 18*(2), 143–154. doi:10.1016/0022-0000(79)90044-8

Chakrabarti, S. Pal1, S. K., & Gangopadhyay, G. (2012). An Improved 3-Quasigroup based Encrytion Scheme. In S. Markovski, & M. Gušev (Eds.), *Web Proceedings of ICT Innovations 2012* (pp. 173-184). ICT. Retrieved January 15, 2013 from http://ictinnovations.org/2012/htmls/papers/WebProceedings2012.pdf

Chen, Y., Knapskog, S. J., & Gligoroski, D. (2010). Multivariate quadratic quasigroups (MQQs), Construction, bounds and complexity. In *Proceedings of Inscrypt, 6th International Conference on Information Security and Cryptology*. Science Press of China.

Csörgö, P., & Shcherbacov, V. (2011). *On some quasigroup cryptographical primitives*. arXiv: 1110.6591v1.

Daemen, J. (1995). *Cipher and Hash Function Design. Strategies based on Linear and Differential Cryptanalysis*. (Doctoral dissertation). Katholieke Universiteit Leuven.

Dawson, E., Donowan, D., & Offer, A. (1996). Ouasigroups, isotopisms and authentication schemes. *Australasian Journal of Combinatorics, 13*, 75–88.

Dénes, J., & Keedwell, A. D. (1992). A new authentication scheme based on Latin squares. *Discrete Mathematics, 106/107*, 157–161. doi:10.1016/0012-365X(92)90543-O

Dénes, J., & Keedwell, A. D. (2001). Some applications of non-associative algebraic systems in cryptology. *Pure Mathematics and Applications, 12*(2), 147–195.

Dichtl, M. (2007). Bad and Good Ways of Postprocessing Biased Physical Random Numbers. In A. Biryukov (Ed.), *FSE 2007, (LNCS)* (Vol. 4593, pp. 137–152). Berlin: Springer-Verlag. doi:10.1007/978-3-540-74619-5_9

Dichtl, M., & Böffgen, P. (2012). Breaking Another Quasigroup-Based Cryptographic Scheme. *Cryptology ePrint Archive. Report, 2012*, 661.

Diffie, W., & Ledin, G. (Eds.). (2008). SMS4 encryption algorithm for wireless networks *IACR Cryptology ePrint Archive. Report, 2005*, 329.

Dimitrova, V., Bakeva, V., Popovska-Mitrovikj, A., & Krapež, A. (2013). Cryptographic Properties of Parastrophic Quasigroup Transformation. In S. Markovski, & M. Gušev (Eds.), *Advances in Intelligent Systems and Computing - ICT Innovations 2012* (Vol. 207, pp. 235–243). Berlin, Germany: Springer-Verlag. doi:10.1007/978-3-642-37169-1_23

Dimitrova, V., & Markovski, J. (2004). On Quasigroup Pseudo Random Sequence Generators. In *Proceedings of the 1ˢᵗ Balkan Conference in Informatics* (pp. 393-401). Thessaloniki, Greece: Academic Press.

Drapal, A. (2001). Hamming distances of groups and quasi-groups. *Discrete Mathematics, 235*(1-3), 189–197. doi:10.1016/S0012-365X(00)00272-7

Dvorsky, J., Ochodkova, E., & Snašel, V. (2001). Hash function based on quasigroups. In V. Matyáš (Ed.), *Proceedings of Mikulášska kryptobesídká* (pp. 27–36). Praha, Czech Republic: Academic Press.

Dvorsky, J., Ochodkova, E., & Snašel, V. (2002). Hash function based on large quasigroups. In V. Matyáš (Ed.), *Proceedings of Velikonocní kriptologie* (pp. 1–8). Brno, Czech Republic: Academic Press.

Dvorsky, J., Ochodkova, E., & Snašel, V. (2002). Generation of large quasigroups: an application in cryptography. In *Procedings of AAA (Arbeitstagung Allgemeine Algebra-Workshop on General Algebra)*. Palacky Univ.

Faugère, J.-C., Ødegård, R. S., Perret, L., & Gligoroski, D. (2010). Analysis of the MQQ Public Key Cryptosystem. In S.-H., Heng, R.N., Wright, & B.-M. Goi, (Eds.), CANS 2010, (LNCS), (vol. 6467, pp. 169–183). Berlin: Springer.

Gligoroski, D. (2004). *Stream cipher based on quasigroup string transformations in . Contributions, Sec. Math. Tech. Sci.* MANU.

Gligoroski, D. (2005). Candidate one-way functions and one-way permutations based on quasigroup string transformations. *IACR Cryptology ePrint Archive. Report, 2005*, 352.

Gligoroski, D., Andova, S., & Knapskog, S. J. (2008). On the Importance of the Key Separation Principle for Different Modes of Operation. In L. Chen, Y. Mu, & W. Susilo (Eds.) *Proceedings of ISPEC 2008*, (LNCS), (vol. 4991, pp. 404-418). Berlin: Springer.

Gligoroski, D., Dimitrova, V., & Markovski, S. (2009). Quasigroups as Boolean functions, their equation systems and Groebner bases. In M. Sala, T. Mora, L. Perret, S. Sakata, & C. Traverso (Eds.), *Groebner Bases, Coding, and Cryptography*. Berlin, Germany: Springer. doi:10.1007/978-3-540-93806-4_31

Gligoroski, D., & Knapskog, S. J. (2007). Adding MAC Functionality to Edon80. *International Journal of Computer Science and Network Security, 7*(1), 194–204.

Gligoroski, D., Markovski, S., & Bakeva, V. (2003). On infinite class of strongly collision resistant hash functions Edon-F with variable length of output. In *Proceedings of 1st International Conference on Mathematics and Informatics for Industry* (pp. 302-308). Thessaloniki, Greece: Academic Press.

Gligoroski, D., Markovski, S., & Knapskog, S. J. (2005). A Fix of the MD4 Family of Hash Functions - Quasigroup Fold. In *Proceedings of NIST Cryptographic Hash Workshop*. Gaithersburg, MD: NIST. Retrieved January 15, 2013 from http://csrc.nist.gov/groups/ST/hash/documents/Gligoroski_MD4Fix.pdf

Gligoroski, D., Markovski, S., & Knapskog, S. J. (2006). A Secure Hash Algorithm with only 8 Folded SHA-1 Steps. *International Journal of Computer Science and Network*, 6(10), 194–205.

Gligoroski, D., Markovski, S., & Knapskog, S. J. (2008). Multivariate quadratic trapdoor functions based on multivariate quadratic quasigroups. In *Proceedings of the American Conference on Applied Mathematics* (pp. 44-49). Harvard.

Gligoroski, D., Markovski, S., & Knapskog, S. J. (2008). A Public Key Block Cipher based on Multivariate Quadratic Quasigrops. *IACR Cryptology ePrint Archive. Report, 2008*, 320.

Gligoroski, D., Markovski, S., & Knapskog, S. J. (2008). The Stream Cipher Edon80. In *New Stream Cipher Designs: The eSTREAM Finalists, (LNCS)* (Vol. 4986, pp. 152–169). Berlin: Springer. doi:10.1007/978-3-540-68351-3_12

Gligoroski, D., Markovski, S., & Kocarev, L. (2006). Edon-, an Infinite Family of Cryptographic Hash Functions. In *Proceedings of The Second NIST Cryptographic Hash Workshop*. UCSB. Retrieved January 15, 2013 from http://csrc.nist.gov/groups/ST/hash/documents/GLIGOROSKI_EdonR-ver06.pdf

Gligoroski, D., Markovski, S., & Kocarev, L. (2007). Error-Correcting Codes Based on Quasigroups. In *Proceedings of 16th International Conference on Computer Communications and Networks - ICCCN 2007* (pp. 165-172). Honolulu, HI: ICCCN.

Gligoroski, D., & Samardjiska, S. (2012). The Multivariate Probabilistic Encryption Scheme MQQ-ENC. *IACR Cryptology ePrint Archive. Report, 2012*, 328.

Gligoroski, G., & Knapskog, S. (2008). Edon-(256, 384, 512)-an Efficient Implementation of Edon- Family of Cryptographic Hash Functions. *Commentationes Mathematicae Universitatis Carolinae*, 49(2), 219–239.

Gligorovski, D., & Ødegård, R. S. (2009). On the Complexity of Khovratovich et al's Preimage Attack on EDON-R. *IACR Cryptology ePrint Archive. Report, 2009*, 120.

Gligorovski, D., Ødegård, R. S., Jensen, R. E., Perret, L., Faugère, J.-C., Knapskog, S. J., & Markovski, S. (2011). MQQ-SIG: An Ultra-Fast and Provably CMA Resistant Digital Signature Scheme. In L. Chen, M. Yung, & L. Zhu (Eds.), *INTRUST 2011, (LNCS)* (Vol. 7222, pp. 184–203). Berlin, Germany: Springer.

Gligorovski, D., Ødegård, R. S., Mihova, M., Knapskog, S. J., Kocarev, L., Drapal, A., & Klima, V. (2008). Cryptographic Hash Function EDON-. *Submission to NIST, First Round SHA-3 Candidate*. Retrieved January 15, 2013 from http://csrc.nist.gov/groups/ST/hash/sha-3/Round1/documents/Edon-RUpdate.zip

Glukhov, M. M. (2008). On application of quasigroups in cryptology. *Applied Discrete Mathematics*, 2, 28–32.

Golomb, S., Welch, L., & Dénes, J. (2001). Encryption system based on crossed inverse quasigroups. *US Patent, WO0191368*.

Hell, M., & Johansson, T. (2007). A Key Recovery Attack on Edon80. In K. Kaoru (Ed.), *Proceedings of ASIACRYPT 2007*, (LNCS), (vol. 4833, pp. 568-581). Berlin, Germany: Springer.

Hu, Y. (2010). Security analysis of cryptosystem based on quasigroups. In *Proceedings of IEEE International Conference on Progress in Informatics and Computing* (pp. 431-435). IEEE.

Ji, L., Liangyu, X., & Xu, G. (2008). Collision attack on NaSHA-512. *IACR Cryptology ePrint Archive. Report, 2008,* 519.

Keedwell, A. D. (1999). Crossed inverse quasigroups with long inverse cycles and applications to cryptography. *Australasian Journal of Combinatorics, 20,* 241–250.

Khovratovich, D., Nikolic, I., & Weinmann, R. P. (2008). *Cryptanalysis of Edon-R.* Retrieved January 15, 2013 from http://ehash.iaik.tugraz.at/uploads/7/74/Edon.pdf

Klima, V. (2008). *Multicollisions of EDON-R hash function and other observations.* Retrieved January 15, 2013 from http://cryptography.hyperlink.cz/BMW/EDONR_analysis_vk.pdf

Kościelny, C. (1996). A method of constructing quasigroup-based stream-ciphers. *Applied Mathematics and Computer Science, 6,* 109–121.

Kościelny, C. (2002). Generating quasigroups for cryptographic applications. *International Journal of Applied Mathematics and Computer Science, 12*(4), 559–569.

Kościelny, C., & Mullen, G. L. (1999). A quasigroup-based public-key cryptosystem. *International Journal of Applied Mathematics and Computer Science, 9*(4), 955–963.

Krapež, A. (2010). An application of quasigroup in cryptology. *Mathematica Macedonica, 8,* 47–52.

Leurent, G. (2009). Key Recovery Attack against Secret-prefix Edon-. *IACR Cryptology ePrint Archive. Report, 2009,* 135.

Li, Z., & Li, D. (2009). Collision Attack on NaSHA-384/512. *IACR Cryptology ePrint Archive, Report 2009: 026.*

Maia, R. J. M., Barreto, P. S. L. M., & de Oliveira, B. T. (2010). Implementation of Multivariate Quadratic Quasigroup for Wireless Sensor Network. In M. L. Gavrilova, C. J. K. Tan, & E. D. Moreno (Eds.), *Transactions on Computational Science XI, (LNCS)* (Vol. 6480, pp. 64–78). Berlin, Germany: Springer. doi:10.1007/978-3-642-17697-5_4

Markovski, S., Gligoroski, D., & Andova, S. (1997). Using quasigroups for one-one secure encoding. In *Proceedings of VIII Conf. Logic and Computer Science LIRA97* (pp. 157-162). Novi Sad, Serbia: LIRA.

Markovski, S., Gligoroski, D., & Bakeva, V. (1999). Quasigroup String Processing - Part 1. *Contributions, Sec. Math. Tech. Sci. MANU XX, 1-2,* 13–28.

Markovski, S., Gligoroski, D., & Bakeva, V. (2001). Quasigroups and Hash Functions. In *Proceedings of VI International Conference on Discrete Mathematics and Applications.* Bansko, Bulgaria: Academic Press.

Markovski, S., Gligoroski, D., & Kocarev, L. (2005). Unbiased Random Sequences from Quasigroup String Transformations. In H. Gilbert, & H. Handschuh (Eds.), *FSE 2005, (LNCS)* (Vol. 3557, pp. 163–180). Berlin, Germany: Springer. doi:10.1007/11502760_11

Markovski, S., Gligoroski, D., & Stojčevska, B. (2000). Secure two-way on-line communications by using quasigroup enciphering with almost public key. *Novi Sad Journal of Mathematics, 30*(2), 43–49.

Markovski, S., & Kusakatov, V. (2000). Quasigroup String Processing - Part 2. *Contributions, Sec. Math. Tech. Sci. MANU XXI, 1-2,* 15–32.

Markovski, S., & Kusakatov, V. (2002-2003). Quasigroup String Processing – Part 3. *Contributions, Sec. Math. Tech. Sci. MANU XXIII-XXIV, 1-2,* 7–27.

Markovski, S., & Mileva, A. (2008). NaSHA. *Submission to NIST, First Round SHA-3 Candidate*. Retrieved January 15, 2013 from http://csrc.nist.gov/groups/ST/hash/sha-3/Round1/documents/NaSHAUpdate.zip

Markovski, S., Mileva A., Dimitrova, V., & Gligoroski, D. (2009). On a Conditional Collision Attack on NaSHA-512. *IACR Cryptology ePrint Archive, Report 2009: 034*.

Markovski, S., Samardziska, S., Gligoroski, D., & Knapskog, S. J. (2010). Multivariate Trapdoor Functions Based on Multivariate Left Quasigroups and Left Polynomial Quasigroups. In C. Cid & J. C. Faugère (Eds.), *Proceedings of the Second International Conference on Symbolic Computation and Cryptography* (pp. 237-251). Royal Holloway, University of London.

Marnas, S. I., Angelis, L., & Bleris, G. L. (2004). All-Or-Nothing Transform Using Quasigroups. In *Proceedings of 1ˢᵗ Balkan Conference in Informatics* (pp. 183-191). Thessaloniki, Greece: Academic Press.

Matsumoto, M., Saito, M., Nishimura, T., & Hagita, M. (2007). CryptMT3 Stream Cipher. In *New Stream Cipher Designs: The eSTREAM Finalists, (LNCS)* (Vol. 4986, pp. 7–19). Berlin, Germany: Springer. doi:10.1007/978-3-540-68351-3_2

Matsumoto, M., Saito, M., Nishimura, T., & Hagita, M. (2007). A Fast Stream Cipher with Huge State Space and Quasigroup Filter for Software. In C. Adams, A. Miri, & M. Weiner (Eds.), *Proceedings of Selected Area in Cryptography, (LNCS)* (Vol. 4876, pp. 246–263). Berlin, Germany: Springer. doi:10.1007/978-3-540-77360-3_16

Meyer, K. A. (2006). *A new message authentication code based on the non-associativity of quasigroups*. (Doctoral Dissertation). Iowa State University.

Mihajloska, H., & Gligoroski, D. (2012). Construction of Optimal 4-bit S-boxes by Quasigroups of Order 4. [Rome, Italy: SECURWARE.]. *Proceedings of SECURWARE, 2012*, 163–168.

Mihajloska, H., Yalcin, T., & Gligoroski, D. (2013). How lightweight is the Hardware Implementation of Quasigroup S-boxes. In S. Markovski, & M. Gušev (Eds.), *Advances in Intelligent Systems and Computing - ICT Innovations 2012* (pp. 121–127). Springer. doi:10.1007/978-3-642-37169-1_12

Mileva, A. (2012). Analysis of some quasigroup transformations as Boolean functions. *MASSIE 2009, Mathematica Balkanica, Fasc 3-4*.

Mileva, A., & Markovski, S. (2008). Correlation Matrices and Prop Ratio Tables for Quasigroups of order 4. In *Proceedings of the 6ᵗʰ International Conference for Informatics and Information Technology* (pp. 17-22). Ohrid, Macedonia: Academic Press.

Mileva, A., & Markovski, S. (2010). Quasigroups String Transformations and Hash Function Design. In D. Davcev, & J. M. Gómez (Eds.), *ICT Innovations 2009* (pp. 367–376). Berlin, Germany: Springer. doi:10.1007/978-3-642-10781-8_38

Mileva, A., & Markovski, S. (2012). Shapeless quasigroups derived by Feistel orthomorphisms. *Glasnik Matematicki, 47*(2), 333–349. doi:10.3336/gm.47.2.09

Mileva, A., & Markovski, S. (2013). Quasigroup Representation of some Feistel and Generalized Feistel Ciphers. In S. Markovski, & M. Gušev (Eds.), *Advances in Intelligent Systems and Computing - ICT Innovations 2012 207* (pp. 161–171). Berlin, Germany: Springer. doi:10.1007/978-3-642-37169-1_16

Mohamed, M. S., Ding, J., Buchmann, J., & Werner, F. (2009). Algebraic Attack on the MQQ Public Key Cryptosystem. In *Proceedings of 8th International Conference on Cryptology and Network Security* (pp. 391-401). Berlin, Germany: Springer.

Moufang, R. (1935). Zur Struktur von Alternativkörpern. *Mathematische Annalen, 110*, 416–430. doi:10.1007/BF01448037

Nikolić, I., & Khovratovich, D. (2008). *Free-start attacks on NaSHA*. Retrieved January 15, 2013 from http://ehash.iaik.tugraz.at/uploads/3/33/Free-start_attacks_on_Nasha.pdf

Novotney, P., & Ferguson, N. (2009). Detectable correlation in Edon-. *IACR Cryptology ePrint Archive 2009: 378.*

Ochodkova, E., & Snášel, V. (2001). Using quasigroups for secure encoding of file system. Abstract of Talk on Conference Security and Protection of information. Brno, Czech Republic.

Patarin, J. (1996). Hidden Fields Equations (HFE) and Isomorphisms of Polynomials (IP), two new Families of asymmetric Algorithms. In U. Maurer (Ed.), *Proceedings of EUROCRYPT '96, (LNCS)*, (vol. 1440, pp. 33–48). Berlin, Germany: Springer.

Petrescu, A. (2007). Applications of quasigroups in cryptography. In *Proceedings of Interdisciplinarity in Engineering. TG-Mures*. Romania: Academic Press.

Petrescu, A. (2010). *n*-quasigroup Cryptographic Primitives: Stream Ciphers. *Studia Univ. Babes Bolyai. Informatica, 60*(2), 27–34.

Popovska-Mitrovikj, A., Bakeva, V., & Markovski, S. (2011). On random error correcting codes based on quasigroups. *Quasigroups and Related Systems, 19*(2), 301–316.

Rivest, R. L. (1997). All-or-nothing Encryption and the Package Transform. In E. Biham (Ed.), *Proceedings of Fast Software Encryption '97, (LNCS)* (Vol. 1267, pp. 210–218). Berlin, Germany: Springer. doi:10.1007/BFb0052348

Rivest, R. L. (2001). Permutation polynomials modulo 2^w. *Finite Fields and Their Applications, 7*, 287–292. doi:10.1006/ffta.2000.0282

Sade, A. (1957). Quasigroups automorphes par le groupe cyclique. *Canadian Journal of Mathematics, 9*, 321–335. doi:10.4153/CJM-1957-039-3

Samardziska, S., Chen, Y., & Gligoroski, D. (2012). Algorithms for Construction of Multivariate Quadratic Quasigroups (MQQs) and Their Parastrophe Operations in Arbitrary Galois Fields. *Journal of Information Assurance and Security, 7*(3), 164–172.

Samardziska, S., & Gligoroski, D. (2011). Identity-Based Identification Schemes Using Left Multivariate Quasigroups. [Tapir Akad, Forlag: NIK.]. *Proceedings of, NIK-2011*, 19–30.

Samardziska, S., Markovski, S., & Gligoroski, D. (2010). Multivariate Quasigroups Defined by T-functions. In C. Cid & J. C. Faugère (Eds.), *Proceedings of the Second International Conference on Symbolic Computation and Cryptography* (pp. 117-127). Royal Holloway, University of London.

Sarvate, D. G., & Seberry, J. (1986). Encryption methods based on combinatorial designs. *Ars Combinatoria, 21A*, 237–246.

Satti, M., & Kak, S. (2009). Multilevel Indexed Quasigroup Encryption for Data and Speech. *IEEE Transactions on Broadcasting, 55*(2), 270–281. doi:10.1109/TBC.2009.2014993

Satti, M. V. K. (2007). *Quasi-Group Based Crypto-System*. (Master thesis). Louisiana State University.

Schulz, R.-H. (1991). A note on check character systems using latin squares. *Discrete Mathematics, 97*(1-3), 371–375. doi:10.1016/0012-365X(91)90451-7

Shcherbacov, V. A. (2003). *On some known possible applications of quasigroups in cryptology.* Retrieved January 15, 2013 from http://www.karlin.mff.cuni.cz/~drapal/krypto.pdf

Shcherbacov, V. A. (2009). Quasigroups in cryptology. *Computer Science Journal of Moldova, 17*(2), 193–228.

Shcherbacov, V. A. (2010). *Quasigroups in cryptology.* arXiv:1007.3572.

Shcherbacov, V. A. (2012). *Quasigroup based crypto-algorithms.* arXiv:1201.3016v1.

Slaminková, I., & Vojvoda, M. (2010). Cryptanalysis of a hash function based on isotopy of quasigroups. *Tatra Mountains Mathematical Publications, 45,* 137–149. doi:10.2478/v10127-010-0010-0

Snášel, V., Abraham, A., Dvorsky, J., Krömer, P., & Platoš, J. (2009). Hash function based on large quasigroups. In G. Allen et al. (Eds.), *ICCS 2009, Part I, (LNCS)* (Vol. 5544, pp. 521–529). Berlin, Germany: Springer. doi:10.1007/978-3-642-01970-8_51

Snášel, V., Dvorsky, J., Ochodkova, E., Krömer, P., Platoš, J., & Abraham, A. (2010). Evolving Quasigroups by Genetic Algorithms. In J. Pokorny, V. Snášel & K. Richta (Eds.) *Proceedings of DATESO 2010* (pp. 108-117). Stedronin-Plazy, Czech Republic: DATESO.

Verhoeff, J. (1969). Error detecting decimal codes. *Mathematical Centre Tracts, 29.*

Vojvoda, M. (2004). Cryptanalysis of one hash function based on quasigroup. *Tatra Mountains Mathematical Publications, 29,* 173–181.

Vojvoda, M., Sýs, M., & Jókay, M. (2007). A Note on Algebraic Properties of Quasigroups in Edon80. In *Proceedings of SASC 2007.* Bochum, Germany: SASC.

Wolf,, C., & Preneel. (2010). MQ*-IP: An Identity-based Identification Scheme without Number-theoretic Assumptions. *ICAR Cryptology ePrint Archive, Report 2010/087.*

Xu, Y. (2010). A Cryptography Application of Conjugate Quasigroups. In *Proceedings of the International Conference on Web Information Systems and Mining 2010,* (vol. 2, pp. 63-65). Sanya, China: Academic Press.

ADDITIONAL READING

Ars, G., Faugère, J.-C., Imai, H., Kawazoe, M., & Sugita, M. (2004). Comparison Between XL and Gröbner basis Algorithms. In P. J. Lee (Ed.), *Advances in Cryptology, ASIACRYPT 2004, LNCS 3329* (pp. 338–353). Berlin, Heidelberg, New York: Springer-Verlag. doi:10.1007/978-3-540-30539-2_24

Belousov, V. D. (1967). *Foundations of the theory of quasigroups and loops.* Moscow, Russia: Nauka. (In Russian)

Belyavskaya, G. B. (2012). Recursively r-differentiable quasigroups within S-systems and MDS-codes. *Quasigroups and Related Systems, 20*(2), 157–168.

Carter, G., Dawson, E., & Nielsen, L. (1995). DESV: A Latin Square variation of DES. In Proceedings of the *Workshop on Selected Areas in Cryptography* (pp. 144-158), Ottawa, Canada.

Chen, Y., Gligoroski, D., & Knapskog, S. J. (2013). On a special class of multivariate quadratic quasigroups (MQQs). *Journal of Mathematical Cryptology, 7*(2), 111–142.

Courtois, N., Klimov, A., Patarin, J., & Shamir, A. (2000). Efficient Algorithms for Solving Overdefined Systems of Multivariate Polynomial Equations. In B. Preneel (Ed.), *Advances in Cryptology, EUROCRYPT 2000, LNCS 1807* (pp. 392–407). Berlin, Heidelberg, New York: Springer-Verlag. doi:10.1007/3-540-45539-6_27

Damm, H. M. (2007). Totally anti-symmetric quasigroups for all orders n ≠ 2, 6. *Discrete Mathematics, 307*(6), 715–729. doi:10.1016/j.disc.2006.05.033

Damm, H. M. (2011). Half quasigroups and generalized quasigroup orthogonality. *Discrete Mathematics, 311*(2-3), 145–153. doi:10.1016/j.disc.2010.10.004

Dénes, J., & Keedwell, A. D. (1974). *Latin squares and their applications*. New York, NY: Academic Press.

Dénes, J., & Keedwell, A. D. (Eds.). (1991). *Latin squares: New developments in the theory and applications. Annals of Discrete Mathematics, 46*. Amsterdam, NL: Elsevier Science Publishers.

Dimitrova, V. (2010). *Quasigroup processed strings, their Boolean presentation and application in cryptography and coding theory*. Doctoral dissertation. University Sts. Cyril and Methodius, Skopje.

Dobbertin, H. (1998). One-to-one highly nonlinear power functions on $GF(2^n)$. *Applicable Algebra in Engineering. Communication and Computing, 9*(2), 139–152.

Evans, A. B. (2002). On orthogonal orthomorphisms of cyclic and non-abelian groups. *Discrete Mathematics, 243*, 229–233. doi:10.1016/S0012-365X(01)00211-4

Faugère, J.-C. (1999). A new efficient algorithm for computing Gröbner basis (F4). *Journal of Pure and Applied Algebra, 139*(1-3), 61–88. doi:10.1016/S0022-4049(99)00005-5

Faugère, J.-C., & Joux, A. (2003). Algebraic Cryptanalysis of Hidden Field Equation (HFE) Cryptosystems Using Gröbner Bases. In D. Boneh (Ed.), *Advances in Cryptology CRYPTO 2003, LNCS 2729* (pp. 44–60). Heidelberg, Germany: Springer. doi:10.1007/978-3-540-45146-4_3

Fiat, A., & Shamir, A. (1986). How to prove yourself: Practical solutions to identification and signature problems. In A. M. Odlyzko (Ed.), *Proceedings of CRYPTO '86, LNCS 263* (pp. 186–194). Berlin, Heidelberg, Germany: Springer.

Goldwasser, S., Micali, S., & Rackoff, C. (1989). The knowledge complexity of interactive proof-systems. *SIAM Journal on Computing, 18*(1), 186–208. doi:10.1137/0218012

Imai, H., & Matsumoto, T. (1986). Algebraic Methods for Constructing Asymmetric Cryptosystems. In J. Calmet (Ed.), *AAECC-3. LNCS 229* (pp. 108–119). Heidelberg, Germany: Springer.

Johnson, D. M., Dulmage, A. L., & Mendelsohn, N. S. (1961). Orthomorphisms of groups and orthogonal latin squares I. *Canadian Journal of Mathemtics, 13*, 356–372. doi:10.4153/CJM-1961-031-7

Kaltofen, E. (1985). Sparse Hensel Lifting. In Proceedings of *EUROCAL'85, European Conf. Comput. Algebra 2* (pp. 4–17).

Keedwell, A. D., & Shcherbacov, V. A. (2003). Construction and properties of (r,s,t)-inverse quasigroups. I. *Discrete Mathematics, 266*(1-3), 275–291. doi:10.1016/S0012-365X(02)00814-2

Krapež, A. (2013). Cryptographically suitable quasigroups via functional equations. In S. Markovski, & M. Gušev (Eds.), *Advances in Intelligent Systems and Computing - ICT Innovations 2012 207* (pp. 265–273). Berlin, Heidelberg, Germany: Springer. doi:10.1007/978-3-642-37169-1_26

Laywine, C. F., & Mullen, G. L. (1998). *Discrete Mathematics Using Latin Squares*. New York, NY: John Wiley & Sons, Inc.

Leander, G., & Poschmann, V. (2007). On the Classification of 4 Bit S-Boxes. In Proceedings of the *1ˢᵗ International Workshop on Arithmetic of Finite Field, LNCS 4547* (pp. 159–176). Berlin Heidelberg, Germany: Springer-Verlag.

Markovski, S., Dimitrova, V., & Samardziska, S. (2010). Identities Sieves for Quasigroups. *Quasigroups and Related Systems, 18*(2), 149–164.

Matsumoto, T., & Imai, H. (1988). Public Quadratic Polynomial-Tuples for Efficient Signature-Verification and Message-Encryption. In C. G. Günther (Ed.), *EUROCRYPT 1988. LNCS 330* (pp. 419–453). Heidelberg, Germany: Springer. doi:10.1007/3-540-45961-8_39

McKay, B. D., Meynert, A., & Myrvold, W. (2007). Small Latin squares, quasigroups and loops. *Journal of Combinatorial Designs, 15*, 98–119. doi:10.1002/jcd.20105

Menezes, A. J., van Oorschot, P. C., & Vanstone, S. A. (2001). *Handbook of Applied Cryptography*. Boca Raton, FL: CRC Press.

Mileva, A. (2010). *Cryptographic primitives with quasigroup transformations*. Doctoral dissertation. University Sts. Cyril and Methodius, Skopje.

Pflugfelder, H. O. (1991). *Quasigroups and Loops: Introduction*. Berlin: Heldermann Verlag.

Samardziska, S. (2009). *Polynomial n-ary quasigroups of order p^w*. Master thesis. University Sts. Cyril and Methodius, Skopje.

Samardziska, S., & Gligoroski, D. (2012). Left MQQs whose left parastrophe is also quadratic. *Commentationes Mathematicae Universitatis Carolinae, 53*, 397–421.

Shcherbacov, V. A. (2012). Quasigroup based hybrid of a code and a cipher. In S. Markovski, & M. Gušev (Eds.) Web Proceedings of *ICT Innovations 2012* (pp. 411-417). Retrieved January 15, 2013 from http://ictinnovations.org/2012/htmls/papers/WebProceedings2012.pdf.

Smith, J. D. H. (2006). *An introduction to quasigroups and their representations*. Boca Raton, FL: CRC Press, Taylor & Francis Group. doi:10.1201/9781420010633

Stinson, D. R. (2005). *Cryptography: Theory and Practice* (3rd ed.). Boca Raton, FL: CRC Press, Taylor & Francis Group.

Vaudenay, S. (1995). On the need for multipermutations: Cryptanalysis of MD4 and SAFER. In B. Preneel (Ed.), *FSE 94, LNCS 1008* (pp. 286–297). Berlin, Heidelberg, New York: Springer Verlag. doi:10.1007/3-540-60590-8_22

Wolf, C., & Preneel, B. (2005). Taxonomy of public key schemes based on the problem of multivariate quadratic equations. *IACR Cryptology ePrint Archive, Report 2005/077*.

KEY TERMS AND DEFINITIONS

Complete Mapping: Permutation ϕ: $G \to G$, where $(G, +)$ is a group, such that the mapping θ: $G \to G$ defined by $\theta(x) = x + \phi(x)$ ($\theta = I + \phi$, where I is the identity mapping) is again a permutation of G. The mapping θ is the *orthomorphism* associated to the complete mapping ϕ.

Feistel Transformation: Transformation that takes any function f (known as round function) and produces a permutation. First, the input is split into two halves. The one half swaps with the result obtained from XOR-ing the output of the function f applied to this half, and the other half.

Feistel Cipher: Block cipher with Feistel structure, in which every round is a Feistel transformation.

Latin Square: $n \times n$ array, filled with n distinct elements, each of them appears exactly once in each row and exactly once in each column.

MQ-Problem: NP-Complete problem of finding the solution of a system of multivariate quadratic polynomial equations.

(r, n) Multipermutation: A function $f: Q^r \rightarrow Q^n$ over an alphabet Q, such that two different $(r+n)$-tuples of the form $(x, f(x))$ cannot collide in any r positions.

Quasigroup: A groupoid $(Q, \bullet)$ in which there exist unique $x, y \in Q$, so that $a \bullet x = b$ and $y \bullet a = b$, for all $a, b \in Q$.

Quasigroup String Transformation: Application of at least one quasigroup operation on a given string.

S-Box (Substitution Box): A non-linear part of most of the block ciphers, which performs substitution.

Chapter 13
Influence of the Intra–Modal Facial Information for an Identification Approach

Carlos M. Travieso
University of Las Palmas de Gran Canaria, Spain

Marcos del Pozo-Baños
University of Las Palmas de Gran Canaria, Spain

Jaime R. Ticay-Rivas
University of Las Palmas de Gran Canaria, Spain

Jesús B. Alonso
University of Las Palmas de Gran Canaria, Spain

ABSTRACT

This chapter presents a comprehensive study on the influence of the intra-modal facial information for an identification approach. It was developed and implemented a biometric identification system by merging different intra-multimodal facial features: mouth, eyes, and nose. The Principal Component Analysis, Independent Component Analysis, and Discrete Cosine Transform were used as feature extractors. Support Vector Machines were implemented as classifier systems. The recognition rates obtained by multimodal fusion of three facial features has reached values above 97% in each of the databases used, confirming that the system is adaptive to images from different sources, sizes, lighting conditions, etc. Even though a good response has been shown when the three facial traits were merged, an acceptable performance has been shown when merging only two facial features. Therefore, the system is robust against problems in one isolate sensor or occlusion in any biometric trait. In this case, the success rate achieved was over 92%.

DOI: 10.4018/978-1-4666-5808-0.ch013

INTRODUCTION

In this chapter, we develop a new theory in which the features individually and separate human beings can provide at least the same information embedded in the face. In other words, the whole is not greater than the sum of the parts.

In this chapter, we explore the possibility of applying the model introduced in this new psychological theory, in order to improve the performance of traditional face recognition systems. This theory highlights the importance of face recognition based on the analysis of the features and adding the results of the analysis of the whole face. That is, to build a facial identification system based on the model of the human recognition according to the latest findings.

The objective of this chapter is to develop and implement a biometric identification system by merging different intra-multimodal facial features, such as the mouth, eyes and nose. Thereby, the main aim is to improve the efficiency of identification systems based on a single feature for the identification and provide alternatives to the existing fusion methods.

Furthermore, this chapter try to reinforce the hypothesis relate to the face recognition process from the physiological human point of view. Therefore, it will be proven that the sum of the analysis of each trait separately and subsequently, the merge the data obtained, provides at least the same information as the whole face when the system is configured in identification mode for identify subjects Additionally, the isolated traits and the whole face biometric were combined in order to analyze if this combination improve the performance of the system. Finally, it was intended to test the efficacy of multimodal systems against possible occlusions or problems in any uni-modal sensor, highlighting the advantages of the multi-biometric systems.

In order to develop a robust and reliable system, has been found the best combination and configuration of pre-processing tools, which require less computation time and offer the highest success rate. The Independent Component Analysis (ICA), Principal Component Analysis (PCA) and Discrete Cosine Transform (DCT) were used as parameterization techniques. It was established a comparison that allow select the one that best suits to each trait. The classification system is implemented by using Support Vector Machines (SVM).

The following figure shows the general scheme of the system implementation.

The identification and verification of people has been a goal to accomplish by humans throughout history. In fact, in most processes involving people, his identity is almost as important as the actions carried out. For example, in the communication process, the sender, the receiver or the transmitter of the message are, in most cases, as important as the message.

Figure 1. Different facial features

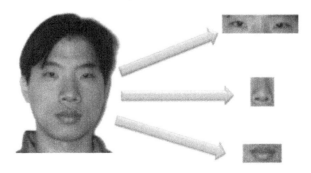

Furthermore, the identification of people is especially critical in security restricted or forensic identifications, in which an identification error can have serious consequences to property or persons. Therefore, techniques have been developed that allow the recognition from differentiated characteristics of each person such as voice, face, fingerprint, iris, signature verification, hand geometry, etc. These characteristics are called biometric modalities (Bolle et al., 2003).

From these technologies can derive various applications. For example, in the areas of physical and logical access control to keep information or properties, in airports, healthcare system, financial system, vehicle environment, working desk, personal computer and also in the area of control for the presence attendance tracking and work timetable. They can also be useful in the field of justice and public order to facilitate administration and revenue in prisons, identification at crime scenes and other forensic applications.

The goal of the developers of facial identification systems is to find the system that matches or even improve the ability of humans to recognize faces. Therefore, it is interesting to ask how the system identification of human faces and if possible or beneficial resemble the systems developed human model. This is an issue that has been carried out a long time and, although there are several theories, has not reached a conclusion that allows say categorically how to identify human faces.

The main theories of face processing (Blair & Homa, 2003; (Tanaka & Farah, 1993), suggest that they are not perceived as a collection of individual features, but as an integrated whole, where different features relate to each other, creating a particular impression of a person. Also, there is some studies, which show differences between processing of facial features and identification of a person (Moscovitch et al., 1997). In fact, clinical case studies of patients suffering prosopagnosia (also called face blindness, is a disorder that prevents some people identify familiar faces), would show dissociation between the two types of pro-

cessing (Damasio et al., 1982). While the theory is based on considering that people recognize the face holistically is widespread, there are recent studies that seem to contradict this hypothesis (Goldstein et al., 1971).

During the last decade the multimodal biometric approach for user identification has shown a clear trend. For instance, recent works such as (Monwar, Gavrilova & Wang, 2011; Tharwat, Ibrahim and Ali, 2012; Hariprasath & Prabakar, 2012; Dinakardas, Sankar & George, 2013) have implemented this idea. Monwar et. al has used both, physiological biometric characteristics as well as soft biometric information. The face, ear and iris were used in the first group while the gender, ethnicity and eye colour in the second. In the work presented by Tharwat et. al. the ear and finger knuckle were used as biometric traits. Hariprasath and Prabakar selected the iris and the palm print as characteristics in their multimodal system. In the last multimodal system presented, Monwar et. al. used the face, fingerprint and the iris as the biometrics features.

Although the reliability of the multimodal biometric system is higher than uni-modal systems, the security is an important concern. Thus, has been proposed new methods to evaluate the robustness of such systems against spoofing attacks (Akhtar, Fumera, Marcialis, & Roli, 2012; Biggio, Akhtar, Fumera, Marcialis, & Roli, 2012).

SOLUTIONS AND RECOMMENDATIONS

The main focus of this chapter relies on the optimal design of the intra-modal biometric systems proposed in Figure 2.

Database: The databases used in this work are those available in cvc.ya.edu/projects/ yalefacesB/ yalefacesB.html, www.cl.cam.ac.uk, www.nist. gov/itl/iad/ig/colorferet corresponding to Yale face database, ORL face database, FEREST face database respectively. The facial traits were extracted

Figure 2. General schedule of our proposal

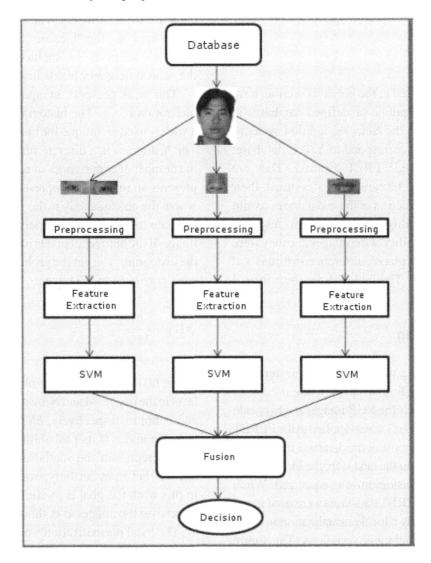

from each image, building in this way the final database used to develop the systems proposed.

Preprocessing: Since each database has its own characteristic regarding to the format, illumination, number of channels, etc., it was necessary to apply an image preprocessing in order to normalize and analyze all the images under the same parameters. Afterward, it was developed a specific preprocessing for each trait due it was needed adjust the normalization sizes.

Feature Extractor: In this phase, the discriminant features were extracted. The feature extraction

was applied by using three transforms domains: Principal Component Analysis (PCA), Independent Component Analysis (ICA) and Discrete Cosine Transform (DCT).

Classifier: The Support Vector Machines were used as classifier system. The classifier is the responsible to assign certain of facial traits to the corresponding classes. The recognition rate is obtained as output of the classifier.

Fusion: In this phase were applied various fusion techniques. The user's identification was reached by merging the scores given by each expert system.

Database

As was commented in the previous section, have been used three public predefined databases in order to evaluate the facial recognition systems. These databases correspond to YALE database, ORL database and FERET database. They are widely used by researchers to contrast their methods. The selection of these databases assure the system reliability since allow test its response against the variability of the images due they were taken in different places, different conditions and different cameras. The Table 1 shows the principal characteristics.

Preprocessing

The preprocessing was built by several steps and will differ depending of the database used. The first stage converts the RGB images to gray scale format. This conversion was applied to the FERET database due the most of the database images use the RGB model. In the next step, the images were resized and the histogram was equalized. When the YALE and FERET databases were used it was necessary to apply a local normalization in order to reduce the brightness variations. The figure 3 shows the resulting of the RGB to gray scale conversion applied in the first step.

Since the traits images extracted have different sizes, it is necessary to normalize them to a fixed size. For example, the eyes images from the YALE database were fixed to 4x12 pixels, from the ORL database to 6x27 pixels and from the FERET database to 4x13 pixels. The resize was carried out by applying the "bicubic" method where the value of each pixel is computed depending from the nearest neighbor pixels inside a 4x4 square.

This work presents an equalization and normalization block. The histogram equalization is a widely used technique for image enhancement. The histogram is a discrete function that counts the number of occurrences of each gray level that presents an image. It is represented in a diagram where the abscissa axis is the gray level and the ordinate the frequency of each gray level in the image. If the number of pixels in the image divides the histogram, you get the probability function of each gray level in the image:

$$p(i) = \frac{h(i)}{M \times N} \tag{1}$$

where h(i) is the number of observation of gray level in the image. M and N are the number of rows and columns respectively, $h(i)$ is the histogram function and $p(i)$ its probability. The histogram doesn't represent the spatial distribution of the intensity but represent the type of acquisition made. In this work the goal is to eliminate the lighting effect over the images as is shown in the Figure 3:

The local normalization was applied over the databases where lighting is not uniform such the FERET and YALE database. The local normalization was implemented as:

$$g(x,y) = \frac{f(x,y) - m_f(x,y)}{\sigma_f(x,y)} \tag{2}$$

Table 1. Principal characteristics from the YALE, ORL and FERET databases

Database	Users	Nº Images Per User	Illumination	Color Model	Resolution (Pixels)
Yale	15	11	Variable	Gray scale	243 x 320
ORL	40	10	Fixed	Gray scale	92 x 112
FERET	75	6-12	Variable	Gray scale and RGB	256 x 384

Figure 3. (a) Original image (b) Gray scale image

Where the *f(x,y)* is the original image and $m_f(x,y)$ its local average. $\sigma_f(x,y)$ is a *f(x,y)* local variance estimation and *g(x,y)* is the resulting image. In the Figure 4 it can be observed the effect of applying local normalization.

Figure 4. a) Original image. (b) Image with the equalization of its histogram

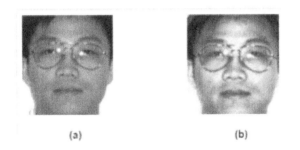

(a)   (b)

Figure 5. a) Original image b) Image after local normalization

FEATURE EXTRACTION

Discrete Cosine Transform

The DCT is similar to the Discrete Fourier Transform (DFT) (Oppenheim et al., 1998) but using only the real numbers. It takes a set of points in a spatial domain and transformed them into an equivalent representation in the frequency domain. Furthermore, the DCT minimizes some of the problems arising with the application of the DFT to data series. A DCT transform produces many useful coefficients as input samples (Pan et .al, 2000).

The following equations provide the mathematical definitions of the DCT (analysis) and IDCT (synthesis) of an picture *I(x,y)* with size *HxW* respectively to two dimensions.

$$C(u,v) = \frac{2}{\sqrt{WH}} a(v)a(u) \sum_{x=0}^{W-1}\sum_{y=0}^{H-1} I(x,y)$$

$$\cos\left[\frac{(2x+1)u\pi}{2W}\right]\cos\left[\frac{(2y-1)v\pi}{2H}\right]$$

(3)

$$I(x,y) = \frac{2}{\sqrt{WH}} \sum_{u=0}^{W-1}\sum_{v=0}^{H-1} a(v)a(u)C(x,y)$$

$$\cos\left[\frac{(2x+1)u\pi}{2W}\right]\cos\left[\frac{(2y-1)v\pi}{2H}\right]$$

(4)

The main purpose of the DCT is the preprocessing of the original samples treating the spatial. These spatial frequencies are relative to the level of detail present in an image. Most existing information on the DCT coefficients of a face is contained in the low frequency coefficients, gathering information about the hair, the eyes, the contour of the mouth and the location (Pan et .al, 2000). Therefore, when extracting the characteristics of different images, the parameters are selected from the upper left of the coefficient matrix obtained after the transformation (see Figure 6 b).

Principal Component Analysis (PCA)

PCA is a method that performs a linear dimension reduction while maintaining the inherent information of the input data. Ideally, are searched $m < n$ variables that are n linear combinations of the original variables and not correlated among them, collecting most of the information or data variability. That is, given an n-dimensional input (feature space), it is desirable to find new m characteristics (feature vectors of m components) that allow to represent the original space, *where m < n*. The feature vectors are orthogonal to each other, so the problem is the projection of an n-dimensional space into another of m dimension.

The projection from one space to a smaller space dimension is carry out by performing a change of coordinates (see Figure 7), so that the new orthogonal axes are equivalent to those where the input data have a higher variance. The principal components (PCs) will correspond to the projections of the input data on the axes of the new coordinate system. The first PC is chosen along the maximum variance direction. The second PC is chosen along the second maximum variance direction. This process is repeated with the other PCs (Turk and Pentland,1991).

The goal of PCA is to find the basis that expresses the distribution of the face images within the entire space, called space images. These vectors describe the subspace basis of images of

faces, the "space of faces". Each vector with size $d=N^2$ describe an image with size *NxN*, and they represent a linear combination of the basis vector from the subspace. As these vectors are eigenvectors of the covariance matrix corresponding to the original image space and as they are similar to a face, they are called eigenfaces.

Independent Component Analysis (PCA)

ICA is an analysis tool aimed at decomposing an observed signal (image of a face) in a linear combination of independent sources. It arises from the technique known by its acronym BSS or Sepparation Blind Source (Hesse and James, 2005). which tries to separate sources from its combinations.

While PCA decorrelate the input signals using a second order statistics (minimizing the mean square error of the projection), ICA minimizes dependence higher orders, in particular with order equal 4.

There are many algorithms to apply this parameterization technique. Perhaps the most widely used in the field of face recognition is the called FastICA (Hesse and James, 2005). However, the first tests with the algorithm in this project have not been successful. That is why another algorithm to implement ICA has been chosen, the called JADE-ICA (Joint Approximate Diagonalization of Eigenmatrices). This algorithm is based on calculation of higher order statistics and the diagonalization of the eigenvalue decomposition of the signal mixtures (Cardoso and Souloumiac, 1993).

Classification

In this module have been used pattern recognition techniques in order to obtain an answer for the person identification. It was implemented an algorithm called Vector Support Machines which is a biclase system, that is, only able to discrimi-

Figure 6. a) Original image, b) DCT coefficients

nate between two different classes. The SVMs are based on the concept of decision planes, which are defined by the decision limits. A decision plane is that which is defined as the separation plane of between a set of object samples composed by samples from different classes. From a series of geometric properties, the model calculates a decision plane among those classes for discrimination. In the Figure 8 an example of decision plane is illustrated which shows how the decision plane is capable of separating red samples from green samples.

This is achieved by a mathematical function called kernels, mapping the different samples so that they can be separated linearly, as seen in the simple case. That is, the SVM transforms the data to a higher dimensional space via a kernel function, i.e, the data are mapped implicitly to that higher space as shows the Figure 9.

Since in this work there are *M* classes depending of the database used, the biclase classifier is extended to a *M* classes classifier. To achieve this aim have been implemented the one vs all technique (Platt et al., 2000), (Hsu and Lin, 2002), (Rifkin and Klautau, 2004). In this technique *M* binary classifiers were implemented where each classifier is trained to discriminate one class. One class is defined as positive class and the remaining as negative classes. When the result is a positive class in more than one classifier, the class will be assigned to the class with the largest margin.

The classifier system was configured in training mode and test mode. In training mode the system built a model that it will use in the test mode. When the model is built, the classifier can determine, by using labels, the class where a given sample belongs. In test mode or classification, when an unknown sample is introduced to the system, the

Figure 7. Axes change after apply PCA

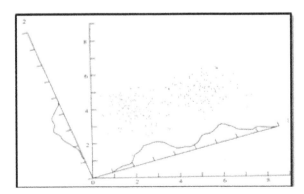

Figure 8. Decision plane between two classes

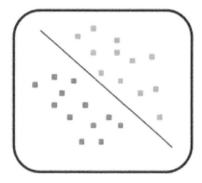

classifier system decides to which class this new sample belong by using the model built in the test mode.

Fusion

This process is called multimodal fusion. The aim is to get an identification result from the uni-modal results. It is possible to perform the multimodal fusion in four levels: 1) Sensor, where are combined the signals from the different biometrics. 2) Feature of each biometric trait. 3) Success rate provided by each system of each trait (Scores). 4) Decision made by each system (Whytock, 1998), (Daugman, 2000).

In this work the multimodal fusion was carried out in the level 3, i.e, multimodal score fusion. In this approach each biometric system provides a success rate that was obtained by comparing the biometric features and the models built for each person. This process gives a multimodal score and a decision from the biometric scores.

EXPERIMENTAL RESULTS

Four main experiments have been carried out: First, the systems were configured in order obtain the success rate of each uni-modal system while in the second experiment were configured as bi-modal systems and in the third experiment, were configured as three-modal system. Finally, in the fourth experiment, the systems were configured in order to perform the multimodal fusion using the three biometrics traits and the whole face. All the experiments were performed using the dataset described in Introduction section and it was applied the pre-processing described in Solutions and Recommendations section.

Since it was need it four expert systems, (three for the facial biometric traits and one for the whole face) and there were used three feature extractors (PCA, ICA, DCT), there were designed twelve systems. For all the experiments, the systems were designed by applying a supervised learning strategy and using the first M features obtained from the PCA, ICA, DCT projections as inputs for a RBF-kernel LS-SVM with regularization and kernel parameters. The former parameter (the number of features) was varied during experimentation, while the two parameters (the regularization

Figure 9. Mapping de samples to a higher dimensional space

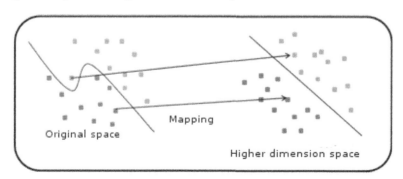

and the kernel parameters) were automatically optimized by iteration using validation results.

To obtain more reliable performance, the available samples were divided into training and test sets by using the K-Folds cross-validation technique (Kuncheva, 2007), so that the system was trained and tested with totally different samples. In particular for the final results, experiments with K equal 10 were run. It is worth it to mention that the training and testing sets were computed for each class individually, having into account that each class has different number of samples. In this work was used a multimodal fusion of the systems by using the sum, product, weighted sum and maximum of the scores (Kuncheva, 2007), (Ma et al., 2005).

The following sections are dedicated to present the experimentation and results of the described techniques, applied into the system configured in identification mode. The results are presented for each database according to the experiment carried out.

YALE Database

This database has 15 user and 11 images per user. Since was applied the k-fold cross-validation with k = 10 there were used 10 images for the training and 1 for the test in each of the 10 iterations.

Uni-Modals Systems

The first biometric trait used was the mouth. As can be observed in Table 2 the success rate are between 66,87% and 73,79% depending which feature extractor was used. In this case DCT and

PCA are more adaptive. The standard deviation was high for all the feature extractors, reaching up 10,11 points. The best behavior was presented by using ICA obtaining 3,21 points.

The following table shows the results using the nose as biometric trait. It can be observed that the results obtained by using ICA and PCA are similar, around 75%, while when was used DCT the success rate was 70%. The standard deviation was high, between 7,87 and 12,07 points.

The third expert system developed has used the eyes as biometric trait. This system has presented a better behavior, where the success rate by using ICA and PCA was around 80% and DCT 74,2%. The standard deviation is more stable points than the previous biometric traits. The Table 4 shows the results reached.

The following table shows the results using the whole face in order to have a reference to compare the preliminary results and to obtain stronger conclusions. Moreover, this biometric was merged with the three biometric traits in the multimodal fusion phase. In the case where the whole face was used, it can be observed that PCA and ICA present the highest success rate, reaching up 99% with a small standard deviation comparing with the previous systems.

Bi-Modals Systems

In this case was carried out all the possible combination between traits, features extractors and fusion technique. Therefore, by combining two from three available traits and three feature extractors, there were made 27 combinations. Moreover, the multimodal fusion has been carried out by apply-

Table 2. Expert system results for nose identification as biometric trait using the YALE database

Feature Extractor	Training Samples	Test Samples	Success Rate	Standard Deviation
DCT	150	10	71,21%	10,11
ICA	150	10	66,87%	3,21
PCA	150	10	73,79%	5,71

Table 3. Expert system results for eyes identification as biometric trait using the YALE database

Feature Extractor	Training Samples	Test Samples	Success Rate	Standard Deviation
DCT	150	10	70,25%	12,07
ICA	150	10	75,50%	10,88
PCA	150	10	75,16%	7,87

Table 4. Expert system results for eyes identification as biometric trait using the YALE database

Feature Extractor	Training Samples	Test Samples	Success Rate	Standard Deviation
DCT	150	10	74,20%	7,97
ICA	150	10	79,75%	7,85
PCA	150	10	80,08%	6,38

ing the 4 multimodal fusion techniques described in section 6. The Table 6 shows the results of the biometric traits fusion of the mouth and nose. It can be observed that one bi-modal system present better results, between 91% and 92% of success rate. The standard deviation is more stable but high, around 5 and 7 points.

The Table 7 shows the results obtained when the mouth and eyes were merged. The best result was 92,12%, quite similar to the best result of the previous bi-modal fusion. The standard deviation depends of the feature extractor used for each biometric trait. When it was used DCT for the mouth and PCA for the eyes, it was obtained the lowest standard deviation, around 3,5 points. The highest standard deviation was reached when was used ICA for the mouth and PCA for the eyes, reaching up 9,6 points.

The last combination of traits corresponds to the nose and eyes. In this case is achieved a better result reaching up 94% in the best case and 89,33% in the worse. The Table 8 shows the results and it can be observed that the best combination of feature extractor was ICA-ICA.

Three-Modals System

After complete the fusion of the two traits, the three biometrics systems for the three facial traits were merged: mouth, nose and eyes. As is shown in the Table 9, the highest success rate was 98.66% and has presented the lowest standard deviation, 2,81 points.

Fusion of the Three Modals System and Whole Face System

The last fusion was carried out by merging the three-modal system and the whole face system. This fusion attempt to provide more information relate to the influence of the each trait to a whole face recognition system. In the Table 10 are presented the highest results, achieving up 100% of success rate.

ORL Database

The ORL database is formed by 40 users and 10 images per user. In this case, there were used 9 images for training and 1 for test. In the following sections the results of each multimodal fusion are presented.

Table 5. Expert system results for face identification using the YALE database

Feature Extractor	Training Samples	Test Samples	Success Rate	Standard Deviation
DCT	150	10	90,70%	5,64
ICA	150	10	99,66%	1,05
PCA	150	10	99,01%	3,16

Table 6. Fusion results of the mouth-nose bimodal system using the YALE database

Feature extractor		Average of the success rate			
Mouth	**Nose**	**Sum**	**Product**	**Weighted Sum**	**Maximum**
DCT	DCT	90,04% ± 7,22	90,04% ± 7,22	89,37% ± 7,19	87,08% ± 9,22
DCT	ICA	**92,14%± 4,88**	**92,14% ± 4,88**	91,14% ± 6,26	89,45% ± 7,66
DCT	PCA	91,41% ± 5,41	91,41% ± 5,41	90,75% ± 5,56	88,45% ± 8,07
ICA	DCT	84,75% ± 7,75	84,75% ± 7,75	86,12% ± 8,48	81,79% ± 6,50
ICA	ICA	88,12% ± 5,95	88,12% ± 5,95	90,75% ± 7,78	83,45% ± 5,59
ICA	PCA	86,75% ± 7,03	86,75% ± 7,03	88,08% ± 6,11	81,79% ± 6,50
PCA	DCT	89,79% ± 7,60	90,41% ± 7,06	88,45% ± 7,43	86,45% ± 6,24
PCA	ICA	92,12% ± 7,99	91,45% ± 8,16	90,79% ± 7,64	89,12% ± 6,86
PCA	PCA	91,12% ± 6,06	91,75% ± 5,18	90,45% ± 5,29	88,79% ± 6,90

Table 7. Fusion results of the mouth-eyes bimodal system using the YALE database

Feature Extractor		Average of the Success Rate			
Mouth	**Nose**	**Sum**	**Product**	**Weighted Sum**	**Maximum**
DCT	DCT	86,45% ± 5,39	85,79% ± 5,76	87,12% ± 5,82	82,50% ± 7,50
DCT	ICA	88,37%± 4,82	88,37% ± 4,82	87,75% ± 7,02	87,04% ± 7,48
DCT	PCA	90,37% ± 3,35	90,04% ± 3,55	88,70% ± 3,28	86,37% ± 4,64
ICA	DCT	83,41% ± 7,24	83,41% ± 7,24	85,41% ± 6,90	79,75% ± 4,71
ICA	ICA	90,70% ± 6,46	90,70% ± 6,46	90,41% ± 6,32	86,37% ± 8,98
ICA	PCA	87,04% ± 9,25	87,04% ± 9,25	89,66% ± 8,67	83,37% ± 9,60
PCA	DCT	91,37% ± 6,34	91,37% ± 6,34	90,04% ± 5,69	87,70% ± 7,41
PCA	ICA	**92,12% ± 7,99**	91,45% ± 8,16	90,79% ± 7,64	89,12% ± 6,86
PCA	PCA	91,04% ± 5,47	90,37% ± 5,57	92,04% ± 5,27	87,37% ± 6,67

Uni-Modals Systems

As the results have shown in the previous database, the results from the uni-modal system are worse than the provided by combined systems. The Table 11 shows the results when was used the mouth as biometric trait. The highest success rate achieved was 74,5% and the lowest 67,5%. The standard deviation has varied from 3,21 to 6,32.

The following table shows the results using the nose as biometric trait. It can be observed that the

Table 8. Fusion results of the nose-eyes bimodal system using the YALE database

Feature Extractor		Average of the Success Rate			
Mouth	Nose	Sum	Product	Weighted Sum	Maximum
DCT	DCT	91,66% ± 6,89	91,66% ± 6,89	91,00% ± 7,03	91,66% ± 6,89
DCT	ICA	92,33% ± 4,98	92,33% ± 4,98	90,37% ± 6,39	89,33% ± 6,44
DCT	PCA	92,00% ± 6,88	92,00% ± 6,88	90,00% ± 7,85	91,66% ± 6,89
ICA	DCT	92,33% ± 5,88	92,33% ± 5,88	90,33% ± 5,54	93,66% ± 5,07
ICA	ICA	**94,00% ± 3,78**	93,33% ± 4,44	93,04% ± 3,32	91,00% ± 6,67
ICA	PCA	91,66% ± 5,27	92,00% ± 5,25	93,00% ± 5,54	91,33% ± 6,32
PCA	DCT	92,00% ± 6,88	92,00% ± 6,88	91,66% ± 6,13	90,66% ± 5,62
PCA	ICA	93,00% ± 4,56	93,00% ± 4,56	92,37% ± 3,87	89,33% ± 6,44
PCA	PCA	92,00% ± 6,12	92,66% ± 4,91	92,00% ± 6,88	90,33% ± 6,74

Table 9. Fusion results of three-bimodal system using the YALE database

Feature extractor			Average of the success rate			
Mouth	Nose	Sum	Product	Weighted Sum	Maximum	Mouth
DCT	ICA	DCT	97,66% ± 4.45	97,66% ± 4.45	97,00% ± 4,56	95,41% ± 5,34
DCT	DCT	PCA	97,33% ± 3,44	97,66% ± 3,16	95,33% ± 4,49	95,33% ± 4,49
ICA	ICA	ICA	97,66% ± 4,45	97,66% ± 4,45	96,33% ± 4,56	92,04% ± 5,27
ICA	PCA	ICA	97,66% ± 4,45	97,66% ± 4,45	97,00% ± 4,56	92,04% ± 5,27
PCA	DCT	DCT	**98,66% ± 2,81**	**98,66% ± 2,81**	96,70% ± 3,47	93,70% ± 4,56
PCA	PCA	PCA	97,66% ± 3,16	97,66% ± 3,16	97,00% ± 4,56	94,37% ± 5,44
PCA	PCA	DCT	98,04% ± 3,15	98,66% ± 2,81	96,70% ± 3,47	93,70% ± 5,07
PCA	ICA	DCT	97,37% ± 3,39	97,37% ± 3,39	96,04% ± 4,63	96,70% ± 4,68
PCA	PCA	ICA	98,33% ± 2,83	98,33% ± 2,83	96,33% ± 4,56	94,70% ± 4,20
PCA	DCT	PCA	98,34% ± 4,23	98,34% ± 4,23	96,74% ± 4,13	93,37% ± 5,44

Table 10. Fusion results of the three-bimodal system and the whole face system using the YALE database

Feature Extractor				Average of the Success Rate			
Mouth	Nose	Sum	Product	Weighted Sum	Maximum	Mouth	Nose
DCT	DCT	DCT	ICA	100%	100%	99,66% ± 1,05	98,70% ± 2,72
PCA	ICA	PCA	ICA	100%	100%	100%	99,04% ± 2,13
DCT	DCT	PCA	ICA	100%	100%	99,67% ± 1,05	98,33% ± 2,83
PCA	ICA	DCT	PCA	100%	100%	99,17% ± 1,87	98,70% ± 2,70
PCA	DCT	DCT	PCA	100%	100%	99,04% ± 2,13	97,08% ± 3,10

Table 11. Expert system results for mouth identification as biometric trait using the ORL database

Feature extractor	Training samples	Test samples	Success rate	Standard deviation
DCT	360	40	69,75%	3,21
ICA	360	40	67,50%	6,45
PCA	360	40	74,50%	6,32

Table 12. Expert system results for nose identification as biometric trait using the ORL database

Feature Extractor	Training Samples	Test Samples	Success Rate	Standard Deviation
DCT	360	40	81,50%	5,02
ICA	360	40	78,25%	6,24
PCA	360	40	80,50%	7,14

Table 13. Expert system results for eyes identification as biometric trait using the ORL database

Feature extractor	Training samples	Test samples	Success rate	Standard deviation
DCT	360	40	66,50%	5,91
ICA	360	40	65,00%	4,71
PCA	360	40	74,25%	7,99

Table 14. Expert system results for face identification using the ORL database

Feature extractor	Training samples	Test samples	Success rate	Standard deviation
DCT	360	40	94,50%	4,21
ICA	360	40	92,50%	2,65
PCA	60	40	94,25%	3,12

results are very similar. The standard deviation is large and has varied from 5,02 to 7,14 points.

The third expert system has used the eyes as biometric trait. The Table 13 shows that the best result was achieved when was applied PCA, reaching up 74,25% while ICA and DCT have obtained 65% and 66,5 respectively. The deviation standard was also large, varying from 4,71 to 7,99 points.

As in the previous database, it was implemented a system for the whole face. In this case the success rate has varied from 92,5% to 94,5%. The deviation standard show a better behavior compared to the isolates traits and has varied from 2,65 to 4,21 points.

Bi-Modals System

The first bi-modal system developed has used the mouth and nose as biometric traits. In the Table 15 it can be observed that the highest success rate correspond to 93%. The deviation standard has ranged from 3,49 to 7,78 points.

The Table 16 shows the results obtained from the second bi-modal system, that is, using the mouth and the eyes as biometric traits. The highest

Table 15. Fusion results of the mouth-nose bimodal system using the ORL database

Feature extractor		Average of the success rate			
Mouth	Nose	Sum	Product	Weighted Sum	Maximum
DCT	DCT	90,75% ± 5,00	90,75% ± 5,06	89,50% ± 6,21	85,25% ± 6,21
DCT	ICA	86,75% ± 6,01	87,00% ± 5,52	85,25% ± 4,77	82,25% ± 7,58
DCT	PCA	88,12% ± 5,95	88,12% ± 5,95	90,75% ± 7,78	83,45% ± 5,59
ICA	DCT	88,25% ± 4,57	88,25% ± 4,57	91,25% ± 3,77	80,50% ± 4,97
ICA	ICA	88,25% ± 3,54	88,00% ± 3,49	88,00% ± 3,68	85,00% ± 4,56
ICA	PCA	87,75% ± 6,91	87,75% ± 6,91	89,50% ± 5,74	82,00% ± 6,21
PCA	DCT	92,75% ± 4,32	92,75% ± 4,32	**93,00% ± 4,21**	89,25% ± 5,14
PCA	ICA	88,25% ± 6,01	88,25% ± 5,40	88,50% ± 5,29	84,25% ± 7,55
PCA	PCA	92,25% ± 4,47	92,25% ± 4,47	92,50% ± 5,00	87,50% ± 4,85

Table 16. Fusion results of the mouth-eyes bimodal system using the ORL database

Feature extractor		Average of the success rate			
Mouth	Nose	Sum	Product	Weighted Sum	Maximum
DCT	DCT	86,75% ± 6,56	86,75% ± 6,56	87,25% ± 6,58	79,25% ± 4,41
DCT	ICA	80,00% ± 5,13	80,25% ± 5,45	81,00% ± 5,29	76,25% ± 7,37
DCT	PCA	83,41% ± 7,24	83,41% ± 7,24	85,41% ± 6,90	79,75% ± 4,71
ICA	DCT	81,75% ± 6,77	82,00% ± 6,54	82,25% ± 5,58	74,75% ± 8,37
ICA	ICA	85,25% ± 3,21	85,25% ± 3,21	85,25% ± 2,99	79,00% ± 5,67
ICA	PCA	85,15% ± 6,45	85,25% ± 6,71	88,25% ± 6,01	79,50% ± 6,54
PCA	DCT	88,50% ± 6,36	88,75% ± 6,37	88,75% ± 6,37	84,00% ± 6,99
PCA	ICA	86,50% ± 5,79	86,50% ± 5,79	88,25% ± 6,01	80,25% ± 6,39
PCA	PCA	**92,25% ± 5,06**	**92,25% ± 5,06**	91,25% ± 5,80	87,50% ± 5,52

Table 17. Fusion results of the nose-eyes bimodal system using the ORL database

Feature extractor		Average of the success rate			
Mouth	Nose	Sum	Product	Weighted Sum	Maximum
DCT	DCT	90,00% ± 4,56	90,25% ± 4,47	88,50% ± 2,93	86,00% ± 4,59
DCT	ICA	87,50% ± 3,80	87,50% ± 3,80	91,25% ± 4,12	79,75% ± 6,71
DCT	PCA	85,25% ± 3,21	85,25% ± 3,21	85,25% ± 2,99	79,00% ± 5,67
ICA	DCT	88,00% ± 4,21	88,25% ± 3,73	86,25% ± 3,38	82,50% ± 5,13
ICA	ICA	89,25% ± 5,00	89,00% ± 4,44	89,50% ± 4,53	83,50% ± 5,02
ICA	PCA	89,75% ± 2,99	89,75% ± 2,99	89,75% ± 2,48	85,50% ± 3.29
PCA	DCT	89,25% ± 5,14	89,50% ± 5,10	88,75% ± 4,28	85,00% ± 6,45
PCA	ICA	86,75% ± 5,24	87,00% ± 5,31	88,50% ± 4,11	79,00% ± 4,59
PCA	PCA	**91,50% ± 3,16**	**91,50% ± 3,16**	91,25% ± 3,17	86,75% ± 4,57

success rate achieved was 92,25% and the lowest was 74,75%. The standard deviation has varied from 2,99 to 8,37 and has depended of the feature extractor used.

The third bi-modal system has used the nose and the eyes as biometric traits. The Table 17 show the results achieved where the maximum success rate was 91,5%. The standard deviation was lower than the previous bi-modal systems and has varied from 2,48 to 6,71 points.

Three-Modals System

In the Table 18 are shown the best results when was merged the three traits to built the multimodal system. As with the previous database, this system provide better results achieving up 97,25% in the best case and 87,25% in the worse. The standard deviation has presented a better behavior with 2,75 points with the highest success rate.

Table 18. Fusion results of three-bimodal system using the ORL database

Feature Extractor			Average of the Success Rate			
Mouth	Nose	Sum	Product	Weighted Sum	Maximum	Mouth
DCT	DCT	DCT	96,00% ± 2,93	96,00% ± 2,93	94,75% ± 2,99	89,00% ± 3,16
DCT	DCT	PCA	**97,25 ± 2,75**	**97,25% ± 2,75**	95,50% ± 3,29	90,75% ± 4,25
DCT	ICA	PCA	95,00% ± 3,33	95,00% ± 3,72	93,75% ± 3,58	88,25% ± 4,41
DCT	PCA	PCA	95,50% ± 3,07	95,75% ± 3,12	95,25% ± 2,93	89,75% ± 5,06
PCA	DCT	DCT	96,00% ± 2,93	96,00% ± 2,93	96,00% ± 2,68	91,75% ± 3.34
PCA	DCT	ICA	94,75% ± 3,42	94,75% ± 3,42	96,00% ± 2,68	87,25% ± 6,50
PCA	PCA	DCT	94,75% ± 3,21	94,75% ± 3,21	95,75% ± 2,89	91,25% ± 3,77
PCA	ICA	DCT	94,75% ± 2,99	94,75% ± 2,99	93,25% ± 4,25	87,50% ± 5,65
PCA	ICA	PCA	95,50% ± 3,07	95,50% ± 3,07	94,50% ± 3,68	89,25% ± 4,25
PCA	DCT	PCA	97,00% ± 2,58	97,00% ± 2,58	97,25% ± 1,84	93,25% ± 3,12

Table 19. Fusion results of the three-bimodal system and the whole face system using the ORL database

Feature extractor				Average of the success rate			
Mouth	Nose	Sum	Product	Weighted Sum	Maximum	Mouth	Nose
PCA	PCA	PCA	DCT	100%	100%	99,50% ± 1,05	95,75%± 3,54
PCA	PCA	PCA	ICA	100%	100%	98,25% ± 1,68	98,00%± 1,97
PCA	PCA	DCT	DCT	99,75%± 0,79	99,75%± 0,79	99,50% ± 1,05	96,25%± 2,42
PCA	ICA	PCA	DCT	99,75%± 0,79	99,75%± 0,79	99,00% ± 1,29	93,75%± 3,58
PCA	DCT	PCA	DCT	99,75%± 0,79	99,75%± 0,79	99,75% ± 0,79	95,50%± 3,68

Fusion of the Three Modals System and Whole Face System

Finally all the expert systems were merged achieving up 100% of success rate. The Table 19 shows the highest results in this experimentation. When the success rate was less than 100% the standard deviation was less than 1 point.

FERET Database

This database has formed by 75 users and a total of 600 images. The methodology was the same applied in the previous databases. First are presented the uni-modal systems, then the bi-modal systems, the three biometric traits are merged in the third system and finally are combined with the expert system of the whole face.

Uni-Modals System

The Table 20 present the results obtained from the first uni-modal system, i.e., using the mouth as biometric trait. The best result was achieved when was applied PCA, reaching up 77,23%. The standard deviation has varied from 5,98 to 7,97 points.\

The next uni-modal system has used the nose as biometric trait. In this system the maximum success rate achieved was 88,10% and the lowest 85,18%. The Table 21 shows the results obtained when was used each feature extractor. The standard deviation has presented a better behaviour and has varied from 4,74 to 5,25 points.

The third uni-modal system has used the eyes as biometric system. The table 22 shows that the highest success rate 89,37% and it is the highest of all the uni-modal systems. The standard present a similar behavior and has varied from 3,59 to 4,77 points.

Table 20. Expert system results for mouth identification as biometric trait using the FERET database

Feature Extractor	Training Samples	Test Samples	Success Rate	Standard Deviation
DCT	600	75	74,26%	5,98%
ICA	600	75	66,03%	7,41%
PCA	600	75	77,23%	7,97%

Table 21. Expert system results for nose identification as biometric trait using the FERET database

Feature Extractor	Training Samples	Test samples	Success Rate	Standard deviation
DCT	600	75	85,18%	4,74
ICA	600	75	86,28%	4,67
PCA	600	75	88,10%	5,25

Table 22. Expert system results for eyes identification as biometric trait using the FERET database

Feature Extractor	Training Samples	Test Samples	Success Rate	Standard Deviation
DCT	600	75	89,37%	3,59
ICA	600	75	87,80%	5,09
PCA	600	75	89,09%	4,77

The last uni-modal system developed has used the whole face as biometric input. As in the previous experiments, this system present the best results achieving up 91,29% of success rate. The standard deviation also has presented a similar behavior and has varied from 4,06 to 6,36 points.

Bi-Modals System

The first bi-modal system merged the mouth and nose as biometric traits. The highest success rate achieved was 96,27% using PCA for the mouth and DCT for the nose. The standard deviation was 2,29 points for the maximum success rate.

The second bi-modal system has used the mouth and eyes as biometric trait. In the Table 24 it can be observed that the maximum success rate was 97,63% and the lowest 88,05%. The

standard deviation was less than 1.5 points when the maximum of success rates was achieved.

The third bi-modal system has combined the nose and eyes as biometric traits. In this case the maximum success rate achieved was 98.15% with a standard deviation equal to 1,73 points.

THREE-MODALS SYSTEM

The Table 27 shows the 10 highest results achieved with the three-modal system. As can be observed the best combination has provide a 99,46% of success rate and was the best result of the three databases when was carried out the same experiment.

Table 23. Expert system results for face identification using the FERET database

Feature Extractor	Training Samples	Test Samples	Success Rate	Standard Deviation
DCT	600	75	87,05%	6,36
ICA	600	75	90,75%	4,06
PCA	600	75	91,29%	4,82

Table 24. Fusion results of the mouth-nose bimodal system using the FERET database

Feature Extractor		Average of the Success Rate			
Mouth	**Nose**	**Sum**	**Product**	**Weighted Sum**	**Maximum**
DCT	DCT	93,39% ± 3,31	93,39% ± 3,31	92,59% ± 2,97	91,26% ± 3,26
DCT	ICA	93,65% ± 3,56	93,89% ± 3,36	92,59% ± 3,47	89,20% ± 3,04
DCT	PCA	94,45% ± 3,15	94,45% ± 3,15	93,92% ± 3,31	90,19% ± 4,87
ICA	DCT	90,98% ± 3,11	90,71% ± 3,14	**96,27% ± 2,29**	88,05% ± 1,41
ICA	ICA	89,40% ± 5,16	89,40% ± 5,16	92,32% ± 4,05	85,40% ± 5,73
ICA	PCA	87,83% ± 5,40	87,83% ± 5,40	93,14% ± 2,97	83,30% ± 5,07
PCA	DCT	93,91% ± 3,32	94,18% ± 3,71	93,39% ± 4,06	92,31% ± 4,06
PCA	ICA	95,22% ± 3,74	95,22% ± 3,74	94,41% ± 4,29	91,48% ± 4,19
PCA	PCA	93,70% ± 4,00	93,70% ± 4,01	93,12% ± 3,55	91,56% ± 4,67

Table 25. Fusion results of the mouth-eyes bimodal system using the FERET database

Feature Extractor		Average of the Success Rate			
Mouth	Nose	Sum	Product	Weighted Sum	Maximum
DCT	DCT	97,12% ± 2,55	97,12% ± 2,55	95,48% ± 2,56	93,36% ± 3,80
DCT	ICA	94,43% ± 4,76	94,43% ± 4,76	93,87% ± 4,03	92,66% ± 5,18
DCT	PCA	97,10% ± 3,61	97,37% ± 3,00	96,57% ± 2,76	94,71% ± 4,13
ICA	DCT	90,98% ± 3,11	90,71% ± 3,14	96,27% ± 2,29	88,05% ± 1,41
ICA	ICA	94,70% ± 3,07	94,70% ± 3,07	95,49% ± 3,08	90,45% ± 4,75
ICA	PCA	94,18% ± 3,21	93,91% ± 2,75	97,63% ± 2,30	88,80% ± 4,03
PCA	DCT	97,40% ± 2,88	97,40% ± 2,88	**97,63% ± 1,44**	95,02% ± 4,36
PCA	ICA	96,57% ± 3,30	96,57% ± 3,30	95,24% ± 4,08	93,12% ± 5,01
PCA	PCA	97,11% ± 2,56	97,11% ± 2,56	96,82% ± 2,45	93,91% ± 5,13

Table 26. Fusion results of the nose-eyes bimodal system using the FERET database

Feature Extractor		Average of the Success Rate			
Mouth	Nose	Sum	Product	Weighted Sum	Maximum
DCT	DCT	96,08% ± 3,24	96,33% ± 3,02	96,56% ± 2,49	94,98% ± 2,88
DCT	ICA	96,83% ± 1,94	97,08% ± 1,94	96,81% ± 2,76	95,50% ± 2,46
DCT	PCA	97,65% ± 2,54	97,65% ± 2,54	97,62% ± 1,49	94,98% ± 3,86
ICA	DCT	95,77% ± 2,54	95,77% ± 2,54	96,81% ± 2,44	92,91% ± 3,97
ICA	ICA	97,06% ± 2,64	97,06% ± 2,64	93,46% ± 4,82	93,46% ± 4,82
ICA	PCA	96,31% ± 2,47	96,31% ± 2,47	96,02% ± 2.24	92,68% ± 4,97
PCA	DCT	**98,15% ± 1,73**	**98,15% ± 1,73**	97,08% ± 1,98	97,10% ± 2,63
PCA	ICA	98,13% ± 1,81	98,13% ± 1,81	97,34% ± 3,12	94,20% ± 4,36
PCA	PCA	97,65% ± 1,86	97,65% ± 1,86	97,64% ± 1,90	95,77% ± 2,84

Table 27. Fusion results of three-bimodal system using the FERET database

Feature Extractor			Average of the Success Rate			
Mouth	Nose	Sum	Product	Weighted Sum	Maximum	Mouth
DCT	DCT	PCA	98,68% ± 1,81	98,68% ± 1,81	96,83% ± 1,61	96,83% ± 3,00
DCT	ICA	PCA	98,96% ± 1,33	98,96% ± 1,33	97,89% ± 1,66	95,03% ± 3,85
DCT	PCA	ICA	98,65% ± 1,41	98,65% ± 1,41	98,13% ± 2,55	95,81% ± 3,60
DCT	PCA	PCA	98,72% ± 2,13	98,72% ± 2,13	98,17% ± 1,72	96,86% ± 2,64
PCA	ICA	ICA	**99,46% ± 1,12**	**99,46% ± 1,12**	98,96% ± 1,33	96,09% ± 3,59
PCA	PCA	PCA	99,21% ± 1,26	99,21% ± 1,26	98,69% ± 1,37	96,60% ± 3,18
PCA	PCA	DCT	98,39% ± 2,25	98,39% ± 2,25	98,65% ± 1,90	96,62% ± 3,76
PCA	ICA	DCT	98,69% ± 1,37	98,69% ± 1,37	98,65% ± 1,90	95,53% ± 2,66
PCA	ICA	PCA	98,96% ± 1,33	98,96% ± 1,33	98,96% ± 1,33	95,55% ± 3,57
PCA	PCA	ICA	98,92% ± 1,38	98,92% ± 1,38	98,40% ± 1,87	96,08% ± 3,82

Table 28. Fusion results of the three-bimodal system and the whole face system using the FERET database

Feature Extractor				Average of the Success Rate			
Mouth	Nose	Sum	Product	Weighted Sum	Maximum	Mouth	Nose
DCT	DCT	PCA	ICA	100%	100%	100%	99,47% ± 1,09
DCT	ICA	ICA	ICA	100%	100%	100%	98,98% ± 1,76
ICA	DCT	ICA	ICA	100%	100%	100%	96,83% ± 3,50
ICA	ICA	ICA	ICA	100%	100%	100%	96,60% ± 3,26
PCA	ICA	ICA	ICA	100%	100%	100%	98,98% ± 1.76

Fusion of the Three Modals System and Whole Face System

The last system includes the whole face system. In the Table 28 are shown the 5 highest results. As in the YALE and ORL was achieved 100% with the best combination of feature extractors.

CONCLUSION AND FUTURE RESEARCH DIRECTIONS

This work has studied the influence of the intra-modal facial information for an identification approach. The systems developed were divided in three phases. The first phase has covered the pre-processing of the images, where the effects of the background and noise were removed. In this phase was extracted and normalized the biometric traits used: mouth, nose and eyes. The whole face was also used in order to have a reference point which compare. In the second phase the resulting images were then transformed by using PCA, ICA and DCT. The optimal number of PCA, ICA and DCT coefficients M was found by heuristics and the resulting characteristics were classified using an LS-SVM. The regularization and kernel parameters were automatically optimized by the system dividing the training samples in training and validation sets and retraining the system with the optimal configuration using all available training data. The combination of these features extractor to the biometric traits chosen

was proposed in order to analysis the influence of intra-modal facial information.

As can be observed in the tables from 1 to 28 the adaptation of the PCA, ICA and DCT to different databases and their respective changes of illumination, was satisfactory. While it is true that PCA showed slightly higher results, we can conclude that the three techniques are perfectly valid and with a correct combination, bring improvements in the outcomes. The recognition rates obtained by multimodal fusion of three facial features has reached values above 97% in each of the databases used, confirming that the system is adaptive to images from different sources, sizes, lighting conditions, etc. Besides has been proven the good response when the three facial traits were merged, it has been shown an acceptable performance merging only two facial features. Therefore, the system is robust against problems in one isolate sensor or occlusion in any biometric trait. In this case the success rate achieved was over 92% for each database.

On the other hand, has been reinforced the hypothesis on how is the recognition process for humans. A separated analysis of the facial traits shows promising results and invites further research along these lines. It can be highlighted the success rates achieved by including the whole face. With the three databases was achieved 100% of success rate in certain combinations. This is consistent with the theory that multi-algorithms systems are able to improve success rates of identification systems.

Finally, it can be conclude that it has been designed a reliable system, with a good response to different databases, which simulate different conditions that could occur in reality. Also important, has been shown the importance of using multimodal systems since the system can identify with acceptable success rate against problems in the sensor or biometric occlusion.

There are interesting research direction to fallow. Firstly, include soft biometrics information since it would be interesting to use other characteristics such as age or race.

Improve the pre-processing modules. It can carry out a study of pre-processing techniques for homogeneity of different databases, both standard databases as well as those developed for a specific application. This is an area that can provide improvements not only for face recognition but also extrapolated to many existing recognition systems.

Study new methods of parameterization. In this work have been used three widespread methods on the face recognition field. However, it could be tested new improvement of these methods or use new techniques.

The development of a specific kernel for SVM classifiers, it has been an alternative for improving the results is to develop a custom kernel able to adapt itself to the needs of the problem analysed. This option involves a higher degree of complexity, which leads to make a preliminary assessment to consider whether it worth this complexity increase depending of the results expected.

Implement system using compiled languages. Since this work has been developed in MATLAB language, the implementation of the system using compiled languages will provide a significant improvement concerning computing time in all the phases of the system.

ACKNOWLEDGMENT

This chapter is partially supported by funds from "Cátedra Telefónica 2009/10 – ULPGC" and by the Spanish Government, under Grant MCINN TEC2009-14123-C04-01.

REFERENCES

Akhtar, Z., Fumera, G., Marcialis, G. L., & Roli, F. (2012). Evaluation of multimodal biometric score fusion rules under spoof attacks. In *Proceedings of 5th IAPR International Conference on Biometrics* (pp. 402-407). New Delhi, India: IEEE.

Arlot, S., & Celisse, A. (2010). A survey of cross-validation procedures for model selection. *Statistics Surveys, 4*, 40–79. doi:10.1214/09-SS054

Biggio, B., Akhtar, Z., Fumera, G., Marcialis, G. L., & Roli, F. (2012). Security evaluation of biometric authentication systems under real spoofing attacks. *IET Biometrics, 1*(1), 11–24. doi:10.1049/iet-bmt.2011.0012

Blair, M., & Homa, D. (2003). As easy to memorize as they are to classify: The 5–4 categories and the category advantage. *Memory & Cognition, 31*(8), 1293–1301. doi:10.3758/BF03195812 PMID:15058690

Bolle, R. M., Connell, J. H., Pankanti, S., Ratha, N. K., & Senior, A. W. (2003). *Guide to biometrics*. Springer.

Cardoso, J. F., & Souloumiac, A. (1993). Blind beamforming for non-Gaussian signals. In *Radar and Signal Processing* []. IET.]. *IEE Proceedings. Part F. Communications, Radar and Signal Processing, 140*(6), 362–370. doi:10.1049/ip-f-2.1993.0054

Damasio, A. R., Damasio, H., & Van Hoesen, G. W. (1982). Prosopagnosia Anatomic basis and behavioral mechanisms. *Neurology, 32*(4), 331–331. doi:10.1212/WNL.32.4.331 PMID:7199655

Daugman, J. (2000). *Biometric decision landscapes*. Technical Report-University of Cambridge Computer Laboratory.

Dinakardas, C. N., Sankar, S. P., & George, N. (2013). A multimodal performance evaluation on two different models based on face, fingerprint and iris templates. In *Proceedings of 2013 International Conference on Emerging Trends in VLSI, Embedded System, Nano Electronics and Telecommunication System (ICEVENT)* (pp. 1-6). Tiruvannamalai, India: IEEE.

FERET Database. (n.d.). Retrieved from www.nist.gov/itl/iad/ig/colorferet

Goldstein, A. J., Harmon, L. D., & Lesk, A. B. (1971). Identification of human faces. *Proceedings of the IEEE*, *59*(5), 748–760. doi:10.1109/PROC.1971.8254

Hariprasath, S., & Prabakar, T. N. (2012). Multimodal biometric recognition using iris feature extraction and palmprint features. In *Proceedings of 2012 International Conference on Advances in Engineering, Science and Management (ICAESM)* (pp. 174-179). Tamil Nadu, India: IEEE.

Hesse, C. W., & James, C. J. (2005). The FastICA algorithm with spatial constraints. *IEEE Signal Processing Letters*, *12*(11), 792–795. doi:10.1109/LSP.2005.856867

Hsu, C. W., & Lin, C. J. (2002). A comparison of methods for multiclass support vector machines. *IEEE Transactions on Neural Networks*, *13*(2), 415–425. doi:10.1109/72.991427 PMID:18244442

Kuncheva, L. I. (2007). Combining Pattern Classifiers: Methods and Algorithms. *IEEE Transactions on Neural Networks*, *18*(3), 964–964. doi:10.1109/TNN.2007.897478

Ma, Y., Cukic, B., & Singh, H. (2005). A classification approach to multi-biometric score fusion. In *Audio-and Video-Based Biometric Person Authentication* (pp. 65–83). Springer. doi:10.1007/11527923_50

Monwar, M. M., Gavrilova, M., & Wang, Y. (2011). A novel fuzzy multimodal information fusion technology for human biometric traits identification. In *Proceedings of 2011 10th IEEE International Conference on Cognitive Informatics & Cognitive Computing (ICCI* CC)* (pp. 112-119). IEEE.

Moscovitch, M., Winocur, G., & Behrmann, M. (1997). What is special about face recognition? Nineteen experiments on a person with visual object agnosia and dyslexia but normal face recognition. *Journal of Cognitive Neuroscience*, *9*(5), 555–604. doi:10.1162/jocn.1997.9.5.555 PMID:23965118

Oppenheim, A. V. A., Willsky, A. S. A., Nawab, S. H., & Hernández, G. M. (1998). *Señales y sistemas 2ED*. Prentice Hall.

ORL Database. (n.d.). Retrieved from www.cl.cam.ac.uk

Pan, Z., Rust, A. G., & Bolouri, H. (2000). Image redundancy reduction for neural network classification using discrete cosine transforms. In *Proceedings of the IEEE-INNS-ENNS International Joint Conference on Neural Networks* (Vol. 3, pp. 149-154). IEEE.

PGM Format Especification. (n.d.). Retrieved from netpbm.sourceforge.net/doc/pgm.html

Platt, J. C., Cristianini, N., & Shawe-Taylor, J. (2000). Large margin DAGs for multiclass classification. *Advances in Neural Information Processing Systems*, *12*(3), 547–553.

Rifkin, R., & Klautau, A. (2004). In defense of one-vs-all classification. *Journal of Machine Learning Research*, *5*, 101–141.

Tanaka, J. W., & Farah, M. J. (1993). Parts and wholes in face recognition. *The Quarterly Journal of Experimental Psychology*, *46*(2), 225–245. doi:10.1080/14640749308401045 PMID:8316637

Tharwat, A., Ibrahim, A. F., & Ali, H. A. (2012). Multimodal biometric authentication algorithm using ear and finger knuckle images. In *Proceedings of 2012 Seventh International Conference on Computer Engineering & Systems (ICCES)* (pp. 176-179). IEEE.

Turk, M., & Pentland, A. (1991). Eigenfaces for recognition. *Journal of Cognitive Neuroscience*, *3*(1), 71–86. doi:10.1162/jocn.1991.3.1.71 PMID:23964806

Whytock, A. W. (1998). *European Patent No. EP 0878780*. Munich, Germany: European Patent Office.

YALE Database. (n.d.). Retrieved from cvc.ya.edu/projects/yalefacesB/yalefacesB.html

ADDITIONAL READING

Ben-Yacoub, S., Abdeljaoued, Y., & Mayoraz, E. (1999). Fusion of face and speech data for person identity verification. *Neural Networks*. *IEEE Transactions on*, *10*(5), 1065–1074.

Blair, M., & Homa, D. (2003). As easy to memorize as they are to classify: The 5–4 categories and the category advantage. *Memory & Cognition*, *31*(8), 1293–1301. doi:10.3758/BF03195812 PMID:15058690

Brunelli, R., & Falavigna, D. (1995). Person identification using multiple cues. *Pattern Analysis and Machine Intelligence. IEEE Transactions on*, *17*(10), 955–966.

Burges, C. J. (1998). A tutorial on support vector machines for pattern recognition. *Data Mining and Knowledge Discovery*, *2*(2), 121–167. doi:10.1023/A:1009715923555

Burges, C. J. (1998). A tutorial on support vector machines for pattern recognition. *Data Mining and Knowledge Discovery*, *2*(2), 121–167. doi:10.1023/A:1009715923555

Campbell, J. P. Jr. (1997). Speaker recognition: A tutorial. *Proceedings of the IEEE*, *85*(9), 1437–1462. doi:10.1109/5.628714

Cevikalp, H., Neamtu, M., Wilkes, M., & Barkana, A. (2005). Discriminative common vectors for face recognition. *Pattern Analysis and Machine Intelligence. IEEE Transactions on*, *27*(1), 4–13.

Deniz, O., Castrillón, M., & Hernández, M. (2003). Face recognition using independent component analysis and support vector machines. *Pattern Recognition Letters*, *24*(13), 2153–2157. doi:10.1016/S0167-8655(03)00081-3

Dezhong, Z., & Fayi, C. (2008, October). Face recognition based on wavelet transform and image comparison. In *Computational Intelligence and Design, 2008. ISCID '08. International Symposium on* (Vol. 2, pp. 24-29). IEEE.

Duin, R. P. (2002). The combining classifier: to train or not to train? In *Pattern Recognition, 2002. Proceedings. 16th International Conference on* (Vol. 2, pp. 765-770). IEEE.

Fox, N. A., Gross, R., de Chazal, P., Cohn, J. F., & Reilly, R. B. (2003, November). Person identification using automatic integration of speech, lip, and face experts. In *Proceedings of the 2003 ACM SIGMM workshop on Biometrics methods and applications* (pp. 25-32). ACM.

Gargouri Ben Ayed, N., Masmoudi, A. D., & Masmoudi, D. S. (2011, March). A new human identification based on fusion fingerprints and faces biometrics using lbp and gwn descriptors. In Systems, Signals and Devices (SSD), 2011 8th International Multi-Conference on (pp. 1-7). IEEE.

Gross, R., & Brajovic, V. (2003). An image preprocessing algorithm for illumination invariant face recognition. In Audio-and Video-Based Biometric Person Authentication (pp. 1055-1055). Springer Berlin/Heidelberg.

Gutta, S., Huang, J. R., Jonathon, P., & Wechsler, H. (2000). Mixture of experts for classification of gender, ethnic origin, and pose of human faces. *Neural Networks. IEEE Transactions on, 11*(4), 948–960.

Heusch, G., Rodriguez, Y., & Marcel, S. (2006, April). Local binary patterns as an image preprocessing for face authentication. In *Automatic Face and Gesture Recognition, 2006. FGR 2006. 7th International Conference on* (pp. 6-pp). IEEE.

Hong, L., & Jain, A. (1998). Integrating faces and fingerprints for personal identification. *Pattern Analysis and Machine Intelligence. IEEE Transactions on, 20*(12), 1295–1307.

Indovina, M., Uludag, U., Snelick, R., Mink, A., & Jain, A. (2003). Multimodal biometric authentication methods: a COTS approach. *Proc. MMUA*, 99-106.

Jain, A. K., Dass, S. C., & Nandakumar, K. (2004). Can soft biometric traits assist user recognition? *age, 20*, 39.

Jain, A. K., Prabhakar, S., & Chen, S. (1999). Combining multiple matchers for a high security fingerprint verification system. *Pattern Recognition Letters, 20*(11), 1371–1379. doi:10.1016/S0167-8655(99)00108-7

Jain, A. K., & Ross, A. (2004). Multibiometric systems. *Communications of the ACM, 47*(1), 34–40. doi:10.1145/962081.962102

Khan, M. M., Javed, M. Y., & Anjum, M. A. (2005, August). Face recognition using sub-holistic PCA. In *Information and Communication Technologies, 2005. ICICT 2005. First International Conference on* (pp. 152-157). IEEE.

Kittler, J., & Alkoot, F. M. (2003). Sum versus vote fusion in multiple classifier systems. *Pattern Analysis and Machine Intelligence. IEEE Transactions on, 25*(1), 110–115.

Kittler, J., & Messer, K. (2002). Fusion of multiple experts in multimodal biometric personal identity verification systems. In *Neural Networks for Signal Processing, 2002. Proceedings of the 2002 12th IEEE Workshop on* (pp. 3-12). IEEE.

Liu, S. B., Yuan, Z. Y., Zhao, J. H., & Wang, X. L. (2009, July). An approach to face recognition based on wavelet decomposition, SPCA and SVM. In *Machine Learning and Cybernetics, 2009 International Conference on* (Vol. 2, pp. 989-993). IEEE.

Mu-chun, Z. O. U. (2008, December). Face Recognition Based on FastICA and RBF Neural Networks. In *Information Science and Engineering, 2008. ISISE'08. International Symposium on* (Vol. 1, pp. 588-592). IEEE.

Oja, E., Hyvarinen, A., & Karhunen, J. (2001). Independent component analysis.

Sabareeswari, T. C., & Stuwart, S. L. (2010). Identification of a Person Using Multimodal Biometric System. *International Journal of Computer Applications IJCA, 3*(9), 12–16. doi:10.5120/769-1077

Shu, C., & Ding, X. (2006, August). Multi-biometrics fusion for identity verification. In *Pattern Recognition, 2006. ICPR 2006. 18th International Conference on* (Vol. 4, pp. 493-496). IEEE.

Sirovich, L., & Kirby, M. (1987). Low-dimensional procedure for the characterization of human faces. *JOSA A, 4*(3), 519–524. doi:10.1364/JOSAA.4.000519 PMID:3572578

Travieso, C. M., Alonso, J. B., & Ferrer, M. A. (2004, October). Facial identification using transformed domain by svm. In *Security Technology, 2004. 38th Annual 2004 International Carnahan Conference on* (pp. 321-324). IEEE.

Xiang, Y., & Su, G. (2008, June). Multi-parts and multi-feature fusion in face verification. In *Computer Vision and Pattern Recognition Workshops, 2008. CVPRW'08. IEEE Computer Society Conference on* (pp. 1-6). IEEE.

Xie, X., & Lam, K. M. (2006). An efficient illumination normalization method for face recognition. *Pattern Recognition Letters*, *27*(6), 609–617. doi:10.1016/j.patrec.2005.09.026

Yang, X., Zhang, T., Zhou, Y., & Yang, J. (2008, July). Gabor phase embedding of gait energy image for identity recognition. In *Computer and Information Technology, 2008. CIT 2008. 8th IEEE International Conference on* (pp. 361-366). IEEE.

KEY TERMS AND DEFINITIONS

Artificial Intelligence: Is the study and design of intelligent agents.

Biometric Analysis: Refers to the analysis of the distinctive, measurable characteristics used to label and describe individuals.

Expert System: Artificial intelligent system that try to imitate the decision-making skill of a human expert.

Feature Extractor: Is the method used to extract the discriminative information of the source analyzed.

Machine Learning: Is the branch of the artificial intelligence that builds and study systems in order to carry out a defined task based on the experience.

Multimodal Fusion: Technique based on combine inputs of different in order to obtain a more robust system.

Patter Recognition: In machine learning, is the process where labels are assigned to a given value that belong to a certain class.

Chapter 14
Biometrics:
Identification and Security

Muzhir Shaban Al-Ani
Anbar University, Iraq

ABSTRACT

It is important to know that absolute security does not exist, and the main goal of the security system is to reach an optimal approach that satisfies the customer requirements. Biometrics is a small part of the security system that aims to replace a traditional password or a key. Biometrics offer higher security levels by simply ensuring that only the authorized people have access to sensitive data. It is easy to copy or get a traditional password using different methods (legal or illegal), but it is difficult to copy a key of biometric pattern such as iris or fingerprint or other patterns. Recent years have seen a boom in the use of biometric techniques in the design of modern equipment to maintain the information and personal identification. This chapter focuses on biometrics (types and technologies), personal identification, and specifications, and then how to implement these performances in security. Finally, a future aspect of merging technologies and disciplines is a good issue to treat via a specific concentration of information technology. In this chapter, two approaches are proposed: a novel thinning algorithm for fingerprint recognition and a novel e-passport based on personal identification.

INTRODUCTION

The traditional security approach is so like the waterfall approach in software engineering. First identifying all the requirements via a systematic risk assessment, then design your security and decide which controls you are going to use to reduce the identified risk. Then after implementation phase, in which you create your security policy and/or implement your controls, you start testing phase. What we do have is a security audit, but the traditional security audit really only tests whether the implementation is still done. An audit does

in general not try to test the effectiveness of your security (Ratha, Connell & Bolle 2001).

The term "biometrics" is derived from the Greek words "bio" (means life) and "metrics" (means measure). Automated biometric systems have only become available over the last few decades, due to significant advances in the field of computer processing. Many of these new automated techniques are based on ideas that were originally thousands of years ago. Biometrics is a multidisciplinary fields that composedofseveralusuallyseparatebranchesoflearningfieldsofexpertise. Many researches are published in this

DOI: 10.4018/978-1-4666-5808-0.ch014

field that focuses on multidisciplinary subjects and applications, these subjects serving in many fields (Anil & Ross, 2002).

Biometrics includes physical and behavioral characteristics that is an academic discipline, or field of study, it is a branch of knowledge that is taught and researched at the college or university level. The University of Paris consisted of four faculties: Theology, Medicine, Canon Law and Arts. Most academic disciplines have their roots in the mid-to-late-19th century secularization of universities, when the traditional curricula were supplemented with non-classical languages and literatures, social sciences such as political science, economics, sociology and public administration, and natural science and technology disciplines such as physics, chemistry, biology, and engineering (Oleson, & Voss, 1979).

BACKGROUND OF BIOMETRIC

Traditional Security

Traditional security system may face with many problems:

- Based on passwords, or identification cards
- Can be lost easily.
- Can be forgotten easily.
- Can be stolen easily.
- Can be used by a thief or intruder to access data.

Problems may appear with current security systems (Jain, Patrick & Arun, 2007):

- Increasing use of IT technology that need more effort to protect data.
- Each person may have multiple accounts/passwords.
- It is difficult to remember so many passwords, so we need to create simple passwords using such as birthdays, wife, friends name, dog, cat … etc.
- It is easy to crack passwords, because most passwords are simple and weak.
- For strong passwords, it is difficult to remember multiple such passwords and it is easy to forget them.

Biometric technology can provide a higher degree of security compared to traditional authentication technologies. Biometrics is preferred over traditional methods for many reasons which include the fact that the physical presence of the authorized person is required at the point of identification. This means that only the authorized person has access to the resources.

Effort by people to manage several passwords has left many choosing easy or general words, with considerable number writing them in known places. This idea leads to passwords easily guessed and compromised. Also, tokens can be easily stolen as that is you have. By contrast, it is impossible for biometrics data to be guessed or even stolen in the same manner as token or passwords.

Biometric characteristics have identified many factors that determine the suitability of a physical biometric characteristic or behavioral biometric characteristic to be used in a biometric application (Jain, Bolle, & Pankanti, 1999).

- **Universality:** In which everyone should have it.
- **Uniqueness:** Small probability that two persons are the same with this characteristic.
- **Permanence:** In which invariance with time.
- **Collectability:** That can be measured quantitatively.
- **Performance:** That high identification accuracy.
- **Acceptability:** That acceptance by people.
- **Circumvention:** How easy to fool the system by fraudulent techniques.

Levels of Authentication

Biometric authentication deals with the technologies that measure and analyzes human physical and behavioral characteristics for authentication.

The aim of authentication is to reach an optimal criteria's is the design of the proposed system, these levels are categorized into the following as shown in Figure 1 (Kumar, Wong, Shen, & Jain, 2003) (Wayman, 2001):

- Something you have as token that can be key, card and badge.
- Something you know as password, PIN and memory.
- Something you are such as biometric that can be physiological and behavioral.

Activities in the Federal Government of America

Biometrics.gov is an association that provides basic information and links to specific biometric activities in the Federal Government of America. The site includes four main parts (Ratha, Connell, & Bolle, 2001). (Jain & Ross, 2002).

Figure 1. Levels of authentication

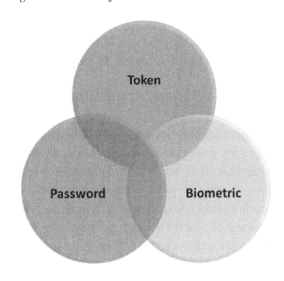

- **Biometrics Reference:** This provides general information about biometric technologies, government programs and privacy planning.
- **Presidential Directives:** This provides text of Presidential Directives that touch on biometrics or federal biometric activities.
- **NSTC Subcommittee on Biometrics and Identity Management Room:** This provides information on the National Science & Technology Council's Subcommittee on Biometrics and Identity Management.
- **Standards:** This provides information on federal biometric standards policy, and a registry of recommended standards.

Biometric Adaptation

Many factors are considered in biometric adaptation, in addition, potential and challenges faced by biometric technologies. In selecting a specific biometric technology and solution to clients the following criteria's must be considered as shown in Figure 2:

- Size and type of user group that.
- The state of the user.
- Simplicity and Ease to use.
- User training are required.
- Transfer of knowledge is required.
- Error incidence such as due to age.
- Security and accuracy requirement needed.
- User acceptance level, privacy and anonymity.
- Standardization and technical support.
- Cost required for overall system.
- Accuracy required for the system.

There are numerous of applications that perform biometric systems. Most applications currently concentrate on security, physical and logical access control and many more enhancements are underway. These applications include

Figure 2. Criteria's that must be considered in biometric adaptation

the following areas (O'Gorman, 2003). (Huang, Malka, Evans, & Katz, 2011):

- Immigration such as border control, frequent travelers, air ports,
- Banking/Financial Services such as ATMs, Payment Terminals, Cashless Payment, Automated Checked Cashing, etc.
- Computer & information technology security such as Internet Transactions, PC login etc.
- Healthcare such as privacy concern, patient information control, drug control etc.
- Law and order such as public ID card, voting, gun control, prison, parole etc.
- Gatekeeper/ door access control as secure installations, military, hotel building management etc.

- Telecommunication such as telephony, mobile phone, subscription fraud, call center, games etc.
- Time and attendance such as schools, universities and companies.
- Welfare, including health care services.
- Consumer products such as automated service machines, lock-set, PDA, … etc.

Biometric Pattern Acquisition

The most suitable definition of biometrics is the automated use of physiological characteristics or behavioral characteristics to determine or verify identity. Physiological biometrics is based on measurements and data derived from direct measurement of a part of the human body. Fingerprint pattern, iris pattern, retina pattern, hand geometry, and face pattern are leading physiological biometrics. Behavioral characteristics are based on an action taken by a person. Behavioral biometrics are based on measurements and data derived from an action, and indirectly measure characteristics of the human body. Voice, keystroke, and signature are leading behavioral biometric technologies in their applications.

Traditional pattern acquisition of biometric data is so difficult to apply and implement. Introducing of technologies via biometric recognition devices is very important issue. Many electronic hardware devices are designed and manufactured and each devices is concerned with each biometric technology as shown in Figure 3 (Benson Edwin Raj. & Thomson Santhosh, 2009). (Prabhakar, Pankant, & Jain, (2003).:

- **Finger-Scan:** Desktop peripheral, mouse, keyboard, screen, image scanner, camera.
- **Face-Scan:** Digital image camera.
- **Voice-Scan:** Microphone, telephone, mobile.
- **Iris-Scan:** Infrared camera, PC camera.
- **Retina-Scan:** Proprietary desktop or wall-mounted device.
- **Hand-Scan:** Proprietary desktop or wall-mounted device.
- **Signature-Scan:** Digital signature capture, digital scanner.
- **Gait-Scan:** Digital video camera.

Biometric System Structure

Many biometric systems are implemented to perform various applications and most of them are concerned on biometric security. A biometric system is a pattern recognition system that operates by acquiring biometric data (physical biometric and behavioral biometric) from an individual, extracting a feature set from the acquired data, and comparing this feature set against the template set in the database. Depending on the application

Figure 3. Biometric technology devices

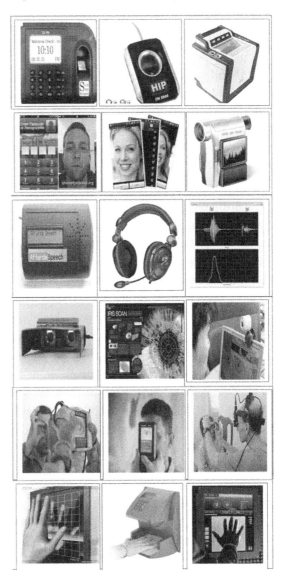

context, a biometric system may operate either in verification level or identification level.

In the verification level, the system validates a person's identity by comparing the captured biometric data with the own biometric templates that stored in system database. In such a system, an individual who desires to be recognized claims an identity, usually via a PIN (Personal Identification Number), a user name, a smart card, etc., and the system conducts a one-to-one comparison to determine whether the claim is true or not. Identity verification is typically used for positive recognition, where the aim is to prevent multiple people from using the same identity.

In the identification level, the system recognizes an individual by searching the templates of all the users in the database for a match. Therefore, the system conducts a one-to-many comparison to establish an individual's identity (or fails if the subject is not enrolled in the system database) without the subject having to claim an identity.

Identification is a critical component in negative recognition applications where the system establishes whether the person is who denies being. The purpose of negative recognition is to prevent a single person from using multiple identities. Identification may also be used in positive recognition for convenience (the user is not required to claim an identity). While traditional methods of personal recognition such as passwords, PINs, keys, and tokens may work for positive recognition, negative recognition can only be established through biometrics. The block diagrams of a verification system and an identification system are depicted in Figure 4 (Vijay, Amarpreet, Rakesh, & Gurpreet, 2010). (Bubeck & Sanchez, 2003).

Biometric System Operation

There are different types of biometric systems that deal with the implemented application. The operation of these biometric systems depends on the following steps:

- Person registers by providing the system with human physical biometric and behavioral biometric characteristics.
- This information is processed by a designed algorithm and then saved into a certain database.
- The implemented algorithm creates a digital representation of the obtained biometric characteristics.

- Each subsequent attempt to use the system requires the biometric to be captured again and processed into a digital template.
- The constructed template then compared to those existing in the database to determine a matching process.

Testing and Statistics Metrics

Biometric systems are subject to several kinds of errors. Many matrices are used for biometric testing and statistics and below some of metrics (Mansfield & Wayman, 2002). (Mordini & Petrini, 2007). (Cappelli, Maio, Maltoni, Wayman, & Jain, 2006). (Yang, Xie, 2012):

- Fundamental performance metrics includes:
  - **Failure-To-Enroll Rate (FTE):** Proportion of the user population for whom the biometric system fails to capture or extract usable information from the biometric sample.
  - **Failure-To-Acquire Rate (FTA):** Proportion of verification or identification attempts for which a biometric system is unable to capture a sample or locate an image or signal of sufficient quality.
  - **False-Match-Rate (FMR):** The rate for incorrect positive matches by the matching algorithm for single template comparison attempts.
  - **False-Non-Match Rate (FNMR):** The rate for incorrect negative matches by the matching algorithm for single template comparison attempts.
- Verification system performance metrics includes,
  - **False Rejection Rate (FRR):** Proportion of authentic users that are incorrectly denied.

Figure 4. Block diagram of biometric system

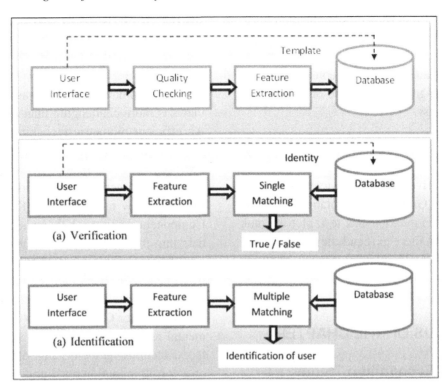

If a verification transaction consists of a single attempt, the false reject rate would be given by:

$$FRR(t) = FTA + FNMR(t) \_ (1 - FTA) \qquad (1)$$

- **False Acceptation Rate (FAR):** Proportion of impostors that are accepted by the biometric system. If a verification transaction consists of a single attempt, the false accept rate would be given by:

$$FAR(t) = FMR(t) \_ (1 - FTA) \qquad (2)$$

- **Receiver Operating Characteristic Curve (ROC):** Plot of the rate of FMR as well as FAR.
- **Equal Error Rate (EER):** This error rate corresponds to the point at which the FAR and
- **FRR Cross (Compromise between FAR and FRR):** It is widely used to evaluate

and to compare biometric authentication systems. More the EER is near to 0%, better is the performance of the target system.

- ○ Identification system performance metrics includes:
- **Identification Rate (IR):** The identification rate at rate r is defined as the proportion of identification transactions by users enrolled in the system in which the user's correct identifier is among those returned.
- **False-Negative Identification-Error Rate (FNIR):** Proportion of identification transactions by users enrolled in the system in which the user's correct identifier is not among those returned. For an identification transaction consisting of one attempt against a database of size N, it is defined as:

$$FNIR(t) = FTA + (1 - FTA) \_ FNMR(t) \qquad (3)$$

- **False-Positive Identification-Error Rate (FPIR):** Proportion of identification transactions by users not enrolled in the system, where an identifier is returned. For an identification transaction consisting of one attempt against a database of size N, it is defined as:

$$FPIR = (1 - FTA) \_ (1 - (1 - FMR)N) \quad (4)$$

- **Cumulative Match Characteristic Curve (CMC):** Graphical presentation of results of an identification task test, plotting rank values on the x-axis and the probability of correct identification at or below that rank on the y-axis.

MAIN FOCUS OF THE CHAPTER

Biometric Recognition Trends

Biometric recognition trends and their applications play an important part in our life. This section presents some biometric recognition techniques that are published by the author in the last two years.

Multi-View Face Detection Based on Kernel Principal Component Analysis and Kernel Support Vector Techniques (2011)

Detecting biometric faces patterns across multiple views is more challenging than in a front view. An efficient biometric recognition approach is presented here using a kernel machine based approach for learning such nonlinear mappings to provide effective view-based representation for multi-view face detection. Kernel Principal Component Analysis (KPCA) is used to project data into the view-subspaces then computed as view-based features. Multi-view face detection is performed by classifying each input image into face or non-face class via two classes of Kernel Support Vector Classifier (KSVC). The Experimental results is demonstrated successfully via face detection over a wide range of facial variation of color, illumination condition, position, scale, orientation, 3D pose, and expression in images from several collection data. The proposed system is subdivided into four steps as shown in the Figure 5. Image size normalization, Median filtering, Feature extraction algorithm by using the KPCA and Classification algorithm based on the KSVC.

The experimental result is implemented via constructing multi-view face of biometric data. This database is contained of colored face im-

Figure 5. Proposed face detection system

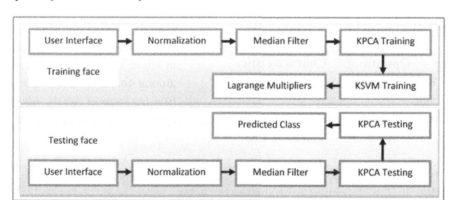

ages of 50 individual persons. Each person is photographed against a uniform white background using a single camera and identical settings (10 photographs for each person). Each photograph has a different combination of viewpoint such as (front 0°, right 45°, right 90°, left 45° and left 90°) and facial expression such as (smiling, laughing, neutral and closed eyes) (Al-Ani & Al-Waisy, 2011).

Gait Recognition Based Improved Histogram (2011)

Biometrics is an important and automated approach of recognizing and identification persons based on a physiological or behavioral characteristic. Gait recognition is a biometric recognition technology that becoming an important and highly used in secure identification and personal verification solutions. The proposed gait recognition system is shown in Figure 6. In biometric system and especially in gait recognition, one of the challenges that use object extraction is to create silhouette image. This work presents an interested method of gait recognition based on histogram of colored image to create silhouette image. The histogram of each color is implemented to decide the range of intensities that represented the background, and then these three silhouettes are intersected to get the final silhouette.

After the proposed algorithm is implemented, different types of videos as biometric data (physical biometric and behavioral biometric) are used to verify the implemented system. Some of these videos are collected from the Internet and other videos are done using an experimental lab. The

obtained extracted object in three colors and their histograms are illustrated in Figure 7 (Al-Ani & Al-Ani, 2011).

An Improved Proposed Approach for Handwritten Arabic Signature Recognition (2011)

Handwritten signature recognition plays an important part in our life and especially in biometric recognition systems including biometric security applications. The proposed handwritten signature recognition system is implemented via many steps such as Discrete Wavelet Transform (DWT), feature vector generation, fusion between feature vectors, then applying Support Vector Machine (SVM). These steps are applied for identification and verification of signatures. The results obtained from the verification process are better than the results obtained from the identification under the same circumstances.

A signature database of biometric data is constructed through the collection of signatures from 100 individuals, with 10 uniform signatures of each individual. The obtained signatures are passed through an optical scanner, then these signatures are stored as digital indexed forms into database. The proposed approach can be divided into three stages: preprocessing, feature extraction and signature verification as shown in Figure 8.

A database of 1000 Arabic signatures is constructed via the signature collection from 100 persons, where each person signs 10 times. 10 signatures for each person as genuine signatures are obtained; in another side obtaining actual forgeries is difficult, two forgery types have been

Figure 6. The proposed gait recognition system

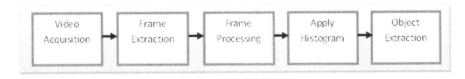

Figure 7. The result of gait recognition system

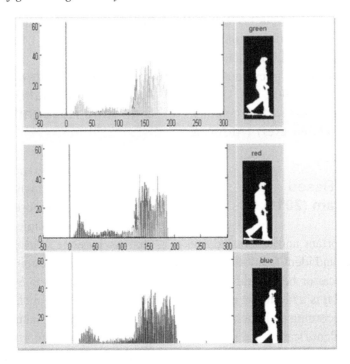

defined in signature verification papers: a skilled forgery is signed by a person who has had access to a genuine signature of practice. A random forgery is signed without having any information about signature, or even the name, of the person whose signature is forged.

Table 1 shows the performance of proposed system, where the results of 4, 5 and 6 signatures are compared via fusion process (Al-Ani & Al-Saidi, 2011).

An Efficient Steganographic Algorithm Using Circular Hiding (2012)

Steganography is the art of hiding information in different cover media, then the hidden information are sending & displaying especially in public places. Different methods have been proposed so far for hiding information. The circular path was used for mapping the pixel which will be usefor embedding data. Compared with the serial embedding the circular path is more difficult to detection. Another algorithm was combined with this method to increase the performance and capacity of information hiding in LSB's method as mentioned here. The structure of the proposed stenographic algorithm**of** LSB using circular hiding is shown in Figure 9 (Al-Ani, Mansor & Kalid 2012).

Table 2 shows a comparison of the results of the metrics of distortion (retrieval percentage error, Mean Squared Error, Signal to Noise Ratio, Peak Signal to Noise Ratio). In any table there are four different places (xc, yc) to hide the data. For any place retrieval percentage error represent is the different between the original message and retrieval message. MSE, SNR, and PSNR will be computing to the same place. Same metrics will be computing again to another place in same image.

Face Recognition Approach Based on Wavelet – Curvelet Technique (2012)

An efficient face biometric recognition approach based on wavelet-curvelet technique is presented in this work. This algorithm based on the similarities embedded in the acquired images, which utilize the wavelet-curvelet technique to extract facial features. The implemented technique can overcome on the other mathematical image analysis approaches. This approach may suffer from the potential for a high dimensional feature space, so it aims to reduce the dimensionality that reduces the required computational power and memory size. Then the Nearest Mean Classifier (NMC) is adopted to recognize different faces. In this work, three major experiments were done and two face databases MAFD & ORL are used. The obtained results indicate a higher recognition rate by the implementation of these techniques. The implemented approach can be summarized into three steps: Wavelet transform, Curvelet transform and Nearest Mean Classifier (NMC) as shown in the Figure 10 (Al-Ani & Al-Waisy, 2012).

The outputs of the high-pass filters, and are three sub-images with the same size as low-pass sub-image, which can presents the details of different images in different directions. In the implemented recognition schema only the approximation sub-band is used as input to the next step, which believe encodes the holistic facial information such as eyes, mouth and the whole facial contour. Figure 11(a) demonstrates the decomposition process by applying (2-DWT) of a face image in level1 and Figure 11(b) depicts two levels wavelet decomposition by applying wavelet transform on the low-frequency band sequentially (Yang, Xie, 2012).

Figure 8. The proposed handwritten Arabic signature recognition

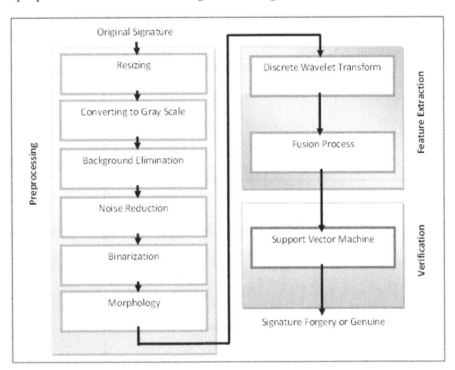

Table 1. The results obtained from the proposed handwritten Arabic signature recognition

	FAR	FRR	% Verification	% Identification
4 fusion	40%	22.7%	92.17%	66.80%
5 fusion	40%	18.8%	93.46%	70.40%
6 fusion	55%	14%	94.96%	71.70%

New Biometric Trends

This section presents two biometric recognition techniques that will proposed by the author in this year.

A Novel Thinning Algorithm for Fingerprint Recognition (2013)

This approach is proposed by the author via implementing a novel thinning algorithm for fingerprint recognition. Thinning process is very important process in all of the biometric recognition systems and especially in fingerprint recognition, so this proposed approach will concentrate on this process and how to improve it.

In a fingerprint, the dark lines of the image are called the ridges and the white area between the ridges is called valleys. This approach is done applying several steps to achieve the goals:

- Collect several biometric data of fingerprint images for the same person.
- Construct a specific fingerprint database.
- Classify the fingerprint according to their characteristics.
- Construct the algorithm to recognize the pattern.
- Test the implemented algorithm to check its accuracy.

The construction of the implemented system is done via several components as shown in Figure 12.

In this system various fingerprint data are collected from selective persons, also these data are collected using various types of data entry

Figure 9. The structure of the proposed steganographic algorithm

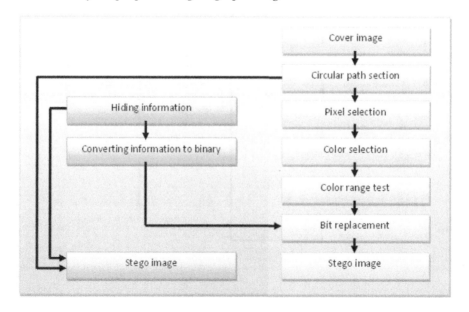

such as traditionally and electronically. Some of these data are regenerated because these data are not adequate for processing, then these data are enhanced via special operations to be adapted to the overall data. Figure 13 shows the steps of undefined fingerprint image procedure done for the original Image to get, gray scale image, enhanced image, thinning image, morphological image and perimeter image. In which the last two images (e) and (f) indicated a specific indication of the pattern. A criteria depends on both false acceptance ratio (FAR) and false rejection ratio (FRR) in addition to Real Acceptance rate (RAR) is used to evaluate the system performance. A set of random group male and female are used for testing the proposed system. Results of admitting the members of this set to a secure system were computed and presented. The evaluation criteria parameters are obtained such as: Real Acceptance rate (RAR) = 0.88, False Acceptance Rate (FAR) = 0.02 and False Rejection Rate (FRR) = 0.10.

A Novel E-Passport Based on Personal Identification (2013)

The forged passports become one of the important challenges facing the world, because each coun-try has its own specifications of their passport. The proposed biometric security system deals with the integrating many factors to develop an efficient e-passport system. The main objective of this system is to compare, update the data con-tinuously and to predict accurate new features for future. The proposed e-passport system is flexible, easy to use, updating and person identification tracking; in addition it is difficult to copy. The proposed e-passport based on the generation of an encrypted key depending on the combination of passport number, birth date and country code. This generated key is watermarked via the human person image posed at the passport.

The infrastructure of the e-passport system is concerned of many data acquisition devices, computers and networks and their supported devices as shown in Figure 14. Considering that these devices are labeled and updated to avoid the damage that may be occurred during the heavy duty working.

The system operations can be performed in the following two steps:

First Step: Starts when the passenger stand in front of the first gate which do many functions:

Figure 10. The implemented face recognition approach

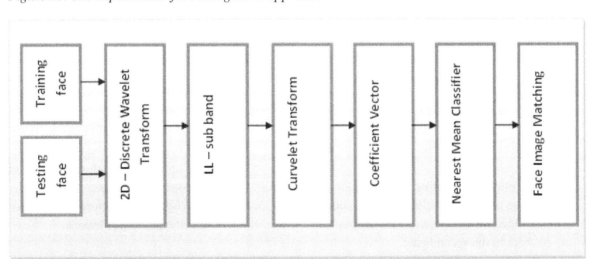

Table 2. Results obtained from the steganographic system

Picture -1- (512 x 384)				
(x, y)	retrieval percentage error	MSE	SNR	PSNR
(30,30)	4%	0.4278407668371	48.406017458756	79.621555679616
(50,50)	4%	2.1027984855375	41.490564514707	69.019222403735
(100,90)	4%	4.7365376852840	38.038270593461	65.492588989062
(200,200)	15%	1.0574361437410	38.038270593461	72.004657451917

Figure 11. Face image in wavelet subbands

a) 1–level wavelet decomposition   b) 2–level wavelet decomposition

Figure 12. Components of fingerprint system

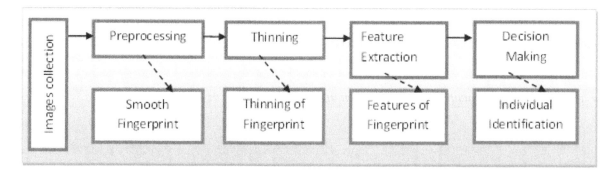

- ◦ A sensor located in front of the first gate activates a camera.
- ◦ Compare the taken picture to the stored one.
- ◦ Compare the stored information of the passport to validate the passport.
- ◦ Open the first gate to pass the passenger to the second gate.

Second Step: Starts when the passenger pass the first gate toward the second gate (all documents are OK) which do many functions:

- ◦ Mark up the entry information when the passenger arrives.
- ◦ Mark up the departure information when the passenger leaves.

Figure 13. Undefined fingerprint image procedure

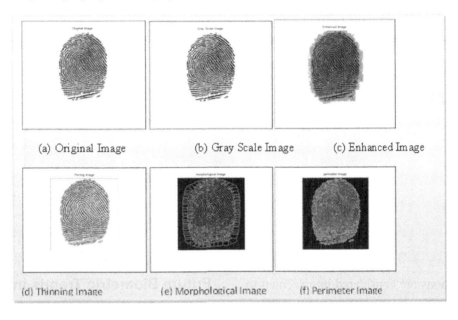

Figure 14. E-passport system infrastructure

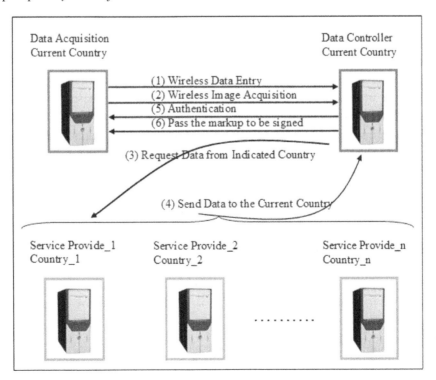

Figure 15. The proposed solution if biometric identification

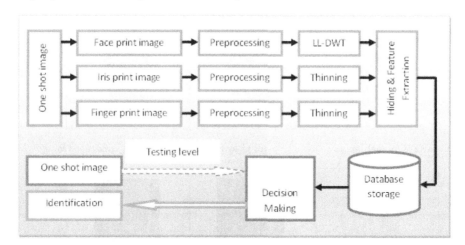

Many actions are considered into account to validate a simple and powerful secure method, these security points are introduced as the following:

- First, RFID tag start working when the passenger is about 10 meters away from the first gate, and the process starts as the passenger stand in front of the first gate, in which the camera starts working.
- Second, we generate a secure encrypted number from a combination of passport number, country number and birth date.
- Third, hide the encrypted number using watermarking operation via the stored image.
- Forth, applying a comparison process between the real face image recognition with that one stored in the passport.
- Fifth, apply a comparison process between the real iris image recognition with that one stored in the passport.

In addition, when there is any mismatching of the information or any doubt, an interrupt stop the procedure and then the passenger is out of permission to pass.

Future Biometric Trends in Security

Fingerprint, Palm, Signature, Keystroke, Voice, Iris, retina, Face, facial, head, specific elements of head, lip, Gait, Odor, DNA, ECG, EEG are biometric characteristics can be resolved from persons that can be used for identification. Biometrics, identification and security may form the future trends of the IT technology over the world. The traditional and famous biometric security systems are concentrated on fingerprint, signature and iris recognition. These systems are in some cases simple and ease to apply, so many companies are adapted these systems in their works.

The future trends of biometric identification tasks may include various fields and applications some of these trends may be concentrated on:

- Analysis of internal structure of body parts.
- Analysis of Body shape recognition.
- Analysis of face vibrations during speaking.
- Analysis of other electrical and magnetic fields created by human body.
- Movement of hands, eyes, lips or any part of the body.
- Recognizing expressions of the person.
- Recognizing additional actions.

- Personal identification using odor.
- Personal identification using electromagnetic emission.

Using biometric technology to recognize citizens and customers, coupled with streamlined processes and effective organizational design, will not only deliver strong identify management capabilities but also lead to better business outcomes and, ultimately, high performance. The application of biometrics in daily activities are expected to deeply transform our life: examples include the services offered in e-commerce, e-banking, registered travelers schemes, smart environments and ambient intelligence.

Solutions and Recommendations

The extended use of Internet and wireless communications in worldwide leads to rise a huge amount of problems and challenges, most of these problems are concentrated on the security of this huge environment. The merging of biometric and security leads to many advanced techniques in wide applications. This section will focus on a new biometric approach that serves for human identification and security, this approach based on hybrid combination of many existing biometric techniques.

The hybrid solution intend to mixing features from one shot of human image, in which we can separate three main parts: face, iris and finger, converting these parts into features serving for personal identification.

The proposed approach as shown in Figure 15 is constructed from the following components:

- One shot image acquisition camera.
- Object separation process, in which the original image is divided into three parts, face print that considered as a cover image, iris print and fingerprint that considered as hiding image features.

- Preprocessing each part of the image.
- Feature extraction fusion from the hiding image features.
- Hiding image features into the face print cover image.
- Database construction corresponding for each individual.
- Decision making to identify the individual.

The powerful of this approach is coming from:

- Mixing may features means more secure system.
- Hiding some of the obtained features into other features leading to efficient system.
- A variable robust key is selected from the cover image.

FUTURE RESEARCH DIRECTIONS

Recently, biometrics introduced in huge amount of applications that's open new fields and research directions. Some of these trends may concerned with:

- Multi-dispensary fields of biometric applications.
- Introduced biometrics in mobile identification and security.
- Fusion of many biometric data obtained from human body.
- Applying Advanced Technologies in biometrics.
- Introduced biometrics in sensitive applications.
- Applying Body emission in personal identification.
- Applying cloud computing biometric authentication.

CONCLUSION

There is no perfect solution in personal identification and security; also we can say that biometric security systems can offer a high degree of personal identification and security. The principles of system design are still required to ensure a high level of security this may coming from the introducing of biometrics features in some form of identification.

Using of distributed database of biometrics in security applications leads many potential risks such as big gathering data, individual refuse and individual privacy, including some problem may be found data entry, in addition many problems may arises in biometric data collection.

Biometric systems need both new technologies and improvements in current technologies to support the advanced in information technologies.

The combination of biometric and security leads to powerful future trend approach, in which focusing on a new biometric approach that serve for human identification and security, this approach obtained of feature extraction that hiding robustly into the face cover image based a certain key obtained from the cover image.

REFERENCES

Al-Ani, M. S., & Al-Ani, I. H. (2011). Gait Recognition Based Improved Histogram. *Journal of Emerging Trends in Computing and Information Sciences*, 2(12).

Al-Ani, M. S., & Al-Saidi, M. M. (2011). An Improved Proposed Approach for handwritten Arabic Signature Recognition. *Advances in Computer Science and Engineering*, 7(1), 25–35.

Al-Ani, M. S., & Al-Waisy, A. S. (2011). Multi-View Face Detection Based on Kernel Principal Component Analysis and Kernel Support Vector Techniques. [IJSC]. *International Journal on Soft Computing*, 2(2). doi:10.5121/ijsc.2011.2201

Al-Ani, M. S., & Al-Waisy, A. S. (2012). Face Recognition Approach Based on Wavelet-Curvelet Technique. *Signal & Image Processing* [SIPIJ]. *International Journal (Toronto, Ont.)*, 3(2).

Al-Ani, M. S., Mansor, F., & Kalid, W. (2012). *An Efficient Steganographic Algorithm Using Circular Hiding*. Iraqi Association of Information Technology.

Anil, K. J., & Ross, A. (2002). Learning User-Specific Parameters in a Multibiometric System. In *Proc. International Conference on Image Processing (ICIP)*. Rochester, NY: ICIP.

Benson Edwin Raj, S., & Thomson Santhosh, A. (2009). A Behavioral Biometric Approach Based on Standardized Resolution in Mouse Dynamics. *International Journal of Computer Science and Network Security*, 9(4).

Bubeck, U., & Sanchez, D. (2003). *Biometric Authentication* (Term Project CS574 Spring 2003). San Diego State University. Retrieved from http://www.ub-net.de/cms/fileadmin/uwe/doc/bubeck-biometrics.pdf

Cappelli, R., Maio, D., Maltoni, D., Wayman, J. L., & Jain, A. K. (2006). Performance Evaluation of Fingerprint Verification Systems. *IEEE Transactions on Pattern Analysis and Machine Intelligence*, 28(1). doi:10.1109/TPAMI.2006.20 PMID:16402615

Huang, Y., Malka, L., Evans, D., & Katz, J. (2011). Efficient Privacy-Preserving Biometric Identification. In *Proceedings of 18th Network and Distributed System Security Conference (NDSS 2011)*. NDSS.

Jain, A. K., Bolle, R., & Pankanti, S. (1999). *Biometrics: Personal Identification in Networked Society*. Kluwer Academic Publishers. doi:10.1007/b117227

Jain, A. K., Patrick, F., & Arun, A. R. (2008). *Handbook of Biometrics*. Springer. doi:10.1007/978-0-387-71041-9

Jain, A. K., & Ross, A. (2002). Learning User-Specific Parameters in a Multibiometric System. In *Proc. International Conference on Image Processing (ICIP)*. Rochester, NY: ICIP.

Kumar, A., Wong, D. C., Shen, H. C., & Jain, A. K. (2003). Personal Verification using Palmprint and Hand Geometry Biometric. In *Proceedings of 4th International Conference on Audio- and Video-based Biometric Person Authentication*. Guildford, UK: Academic Press.

Mansfield, A. J., & Wayman, J. L. (2002). Best Practices in Testing and Reporting Performance of Biometric Devices. Version 2.01, NPL Report CMSC 14/02, National Physical Laboratory, August 2002.

Mordini, E., & Petrini, C. (2007). Ethical and social implications of biometric identification technology. *Annali dell'Istituto Superiore di Sanita*, *43*(1), 5–11. PMID:17536148

O'Gorman, L. (2003). Comparing Passwords, Tokens, and Biometrics for User Authentication. *Proceedings of the IEEE*, *91*(12).

Oleson, A., & Voss, J. (1979). *The Organization of Knowledge in Modern America, 1860-1920*. The Johns Hopkins University Press.

Prabhakar, S., Pankant, S., & Jain, A. K. (2003). Biometric Recognition: Security and Privacy Concerns. *IEEE Security and Privacy Magazine*, *1*(2), 33–42. doi:10.1109/MSECP.2003.1193209

Ratha, N., Connell, J., & Bolle, R. (2001). Enhancing security and privacy in biometrics-based authentication systems. *IBM Systems Journal*, *40*(3), 614–634. doi:10.1147/sj.403.0614

Vijay, D., Amarpreet, S., Rakesh, K., & Gurpreet, S. (2010). Biometric Recognition: A Modern Era for Security. *International Journal of Engineering Science and Technology*, *2*(8), 3364–3380.

Wayman, J. L. (2001). Fundamentals of Biometric Authentication Technologies. *International Journal of Image and Graphics*, *1*(1), 93–113. doi:10.1142/S0219467801000086

Yang, J., & Xie, S. J. (2012). *New Trends and Developments in Biometrics*. InTech. doi:10.5772/3420

ADDITIONAL READING

Alterman, A. (2003). *A piece of yourself: Ethical issues in biometric identification, Ethics and Information Technology* (pp. 139–150). Netherlands: Kluwer Academic Publishers.

Ang, R., Safavi-Naini, R., & McAven, L. (2005). *Cancelable key-based fingerprint templates*. Lecture Notes in Computer Science LNCS.

Anil, K. (2003, November). Jain, & Uludag, U. (2003). Hiding Biometric Data. *IEEE Transactions on Pattern Analysis and Machine Intelligence*, *25*(11)

Anil, K. Jain, Sarat, C. D., & Nandakumar, K. (2004). Soft Biometric Traits for Personal Recognition Systems. *Proceedings of International Conference on Biometric Authentication*, LNCS 3072, pp. 731-738, Hong Kong, July 2004.

Ballard, L., Kamara, S., & Reiter, M. K. (2008). The Practical Subtleties of Biometric Key Generation. *In Proceedings of the 17th Annual USENIX Security Symposium*, pages 61–74, San Jose, CA, USA, 2008.

Bhattacharyya, D., & Ranjan, R. FarkhodAlisherov, A., & Choi M. (2009). Biometric Authentication: A Review. International Journal of u- and e- Service, Science and Technology, Vol. 2, No. 3, September, 2009.

Boyen, X. (2004). Reusable cryptographic fuzzy extractors. *Proceedings of the 11th ACM conference on Computer and Communications Security*, pp. 82–91, ACM Press, New York, USA, 2004.

Boyen, X., Dodis, Y., Katz, J., Ostrovsky, R., & Smith, A. (2005). Secure remote authentication using biometric data. *Advances in Cryptology (EUROCRYPT 2005)*, volume 3494, pp. 147-163, Denmark, May 22-26, 2005.

Cheng, Y. Q. (1991), Human face recognition method based on the statistical model of small sample size. *SPIE Proceedings of the Intelligent Robots and Computer Vision*, vol.1607, Boston, United States, pp. 85–95, 1991.

Clancy, T. C., Kiyavash, N., & Lin, D. J. (2003). Secure Smartcard-Based Fingerprint Authentication. *Proc. ACMSIGMM 2003 Multimedia, Biometrics Methods and Applications Workshop (WBMA'03)*, November 8, 2003, Berkeley, California, USA. pp. 45-52. 2003.

Connie, T., Teoh, A., Goh, M., & Ngo, D. (2005). Palm hashing: a novel approach for cancelable biometrics. *Information Processing Letters*, *93*, 614–634. doi:10.1016/j.ipl.2004.09.014

David, G., Frankel, Y., & Matt, B. (1998). On enabling secure applications through off-line biometric identification. *Proc. IEEE Symp.on Security and Privacy*, Springer-Verlag Berlin Heidelberg, pp. 148–157, 1998.

Hao, F., Anderson, R., & Daugman, J. (2005). Combining cryptography with biometrics effectively. *Tech. Rep. UCAM-CL-TR-640, University of Cambridge*, 2005.

Hong, W. Y., Niu, T. T., & Yong, Z. (2000). Face identification based on singular value decomposition and data fusion. [in Chinese]. *Chinese J. Computer.*, *23*, 2000.

Hong, Z. (1991). Algebraic feature extraction of image for recognition. *Pattern Recognition*, *24*(3), 211–219. doi:10.1016/0031-3203(91)90063-B

Indovina, M., Uludag, U., Snelick, R., Mink, A., & Jain, A. (2003). Multimodal Biometric Authentication Methods: A COTS Approach. *Proc. MMUA 2003, Workshop on Multimodal User Authentication*, pp. 99-106, Santa Barbara, CA, USA, December 11-12, 2003.

Jain, A. K., Nandakumar, K., & Nagar, A. (2008). Biometric Template Security. *EURASIP Journal on Advances in Signal Processing*, 2008. *Article ID, 579416*, 1–17.

Jain, A. K., Nandakumar, K., & Ross, A. (2005, December). Score normalization in multimodal biometric systems. *Pattern Recognition*, *38*(12), 2270–2285. doi:10.1016/j.patcog.2005.01.012

Jain, A. K., Ross, A., & Pankanti, S. (2006, June). Biometrics: A Tool for Information Security. *IEEE Transactions on Information Forensics and Security*, *1*(2), 125–143. doi:10.1109/TIFS.2006.873653

Jain, A. K., & Uludag, U. (2003, November). Hiding biometric data. *IEEE Transactions on Pattern Analysis and Machine Intelligence*, *25*(11), 1494–1498. doi:10.1109/TPAMI.2003.1240122

Kevenaar, T., Schrijen, G., der Veen, M. V., Akkermans, A., & Zuo, F. (2005). Face recognition with renewable and privacy preserving binary templates. *Fourth IEEE Workshop on Automatic Identification Advanced Technologies*, new York, USA, pp. 21–26, 2005.

Kevenaar, T., Schrijen, G. J., Akkermans, A., Damstra, M., Tuyls, P., & Van, der Veen, M. (2006). Robust and Secure Biometrics: Some Application Examples. *Information Security Solutions Europe (ISSE) Conference*, Rome, 10 -12 October, 2006.

Linnartz, J. P. M. G., & Tuyls, P. (2003), New shielding functions to enhance privacy and prevent misuse of biometric templates. AVBPA 2003, vol. 2688, pp. 393–402, 2003.

Nagar, A., & Chaudhury, S. (2006). Biometrics based Asymmetric Cryptosystem Design Using Modified Fuzzy Vault Scheme. *18th International Conference on Pattern Recognition (ICPR'06)*, 2006. ICPR (4), Hong Kong, pp. 537-540. 2006.

Palaniappan, R. (2007, April). Biometrics from Brain Electrical Activity: A Machine Learning Approach. *IEEE Transactions on Pattern Analysis and Machine Intelligence, 29*(4) doi:10.1109/TPAMI.2007.1013 PMID:17299228

Putte, T., & Keuning, J. (2000), Biometrical fingerprint recognition: don't get your fingers burned. *Proc. IFIPTC8/WG8.8, Fourth Working Conf. Smart Card Research and Adv. App.*, pp. 289-303, 2000.

Ratha, N., Connell, J., & Bolle, R. (2006). Cancelable biometrics: A case study in fingerprints. *18th International Conference on Pattern Recognition (ICPR 2006)*, Hong Kong 2006.

Sarat, C. D., Nandakumar, K., & Jain, A. K. (2005). A Principled Approach to Score Level Fusion in Multimodal Biometric Systems. *Proceedings of AVBPA* 2005. NY, USA.

Sarat, C. D., Zhu, Y., & Jain, A. K. (2006, December). Validating a Biometric Authentication System: Sample Size Requirements. *IEEE Transactions on Pattern Analysis and Machine Intelligence, 28*(12).

Soutar, R. D., Stojanov, S., Gilroy, R., & Kumar, B. V. (1998). Biometric encryption using image processing. SPIE, Optical Security and Counterfeit Deterrence Techniques II, 3314, CA, USA, 1998.

Stén, A., Kaseva, A., & Virtanen, T. (2003). Fooling Fingerprint Scanners - Biometric Vulnerabilities of the Precise Biometrics 100 SC Scanner. *4th Australian Information Warfare and IT Security Conference Published by InTech, Croatia, 2003.*

Sutcu, Y., Li, Q., & Memon, N. (2007). How to Protect Biometric Templates. *SPIE Conf. on Security, Steganography and Watermarking of Multimedia Contents IX*, San Jose, CA, USA, January 2007.

Sutcu, Y., Sencar, T., & Memon, N. (2005). *A secure biometric authentication scheme based on robust hashing.* New York, USA: ACM MM-SEC Workshop. doi:10.1145/1073170.1073191

Tuyls, P., Akkermans, A., Kevenaar, T., Schrijen, G., Bazen, A., & Veldhuis, R. (2005). *Practical biometric authentication with template protection* (pp. 436–446). new York, USA: AVBPA.

Tuyls, P., & Goseling, J. (2004). Capacity and examples of template-protecting biometric authentication systems. *ECCV Workshop BioAW*, Volume 3087, pp. 158–170, Prague, Czech Republic, 2004.

Uludag, U., Pankanti, S., & Jain, A. K. (2005). Fuzzy Vault for Fingerprints. AVBPA 2005: audio- and video-based biometric person authentication, Hilton Rye Town NY, 20-22 July (2005), Springer, 20051973, vol. 3546, p.p. 310-319.

Uludag, U., Pankanti, S., Prabhakar, S., & Jain, A. K. (2004, June). Biometric Cryptosystems: Issues and Challenges. *Proceedings of the IEEE, 92*(6), 948–960. doi:10.1109/JPROC.2004.827372

Wang, L., Ning, H., Tan, T., & Hu, W. (2003). Fusion of Static and Dynamic Body Biometrics for Gait Recognition. *Proceedings of the Ninth IEEE International Conference on Computer Vision (ICCV 2003)* Volume 2, Nice, France, 2003.

Yampolskiy, R. V., & Govindaraju, V. (2007). Direct and Indirect Human Computer Interaction Based Biometrics, *Journal of Computers*, Vol. 2, No. 10, December 2007.

KEY TERMS AND DEFINITIONS

Authentication: Biometric authentication verifies user's claimed identity by comparing an encoded value with a stored value of the concerned biometric characteristic.

Behavioral Biometric: A biometric that is based on a behavioral trait of an individual, such behavioral biometrics include speech patterns, signatures and keystrokes.

Biometrics: Biometrics is the science of establishing human identity based on the physical and behavioral characteristics of an individual.

Biometric Data: Refers to any computer data that is created during a biometric process, includes samples, models, fingerprints, similarity scores and all verification or identification data.

Biometric Recognition: Involves the personal recognition based on who you are? That can be described as automated methods to recognize individuals based on physiological and/or behavioral traits.

Biometric Security: Refers to the science of using biometric characteristics to identify a person and some of the products used in this system include fingerprint readers and retinal scanners.

Biometric System: A biometric system is a technological system that uses information about a person (or other biological organism) to identify that person. Biometric systems rely on specific data about unique biological traits in order to work effectively.

Identification: Biometric identification involves the automatic identification of living individuals by using their physiological and behavioral characteristics.

Physical Biometric: A biometric that is based on a physical trait of an individual, such physical biometrics include fingerprints, hand geometry, retinal scans, and DNA.

Verification: Biometric verification is any means by which a person can be uniquely identified by evaluating one or more distinguishing biological traits.

Chapter 15
Routing Based on Security

I. A. Almerhag
University of Tripoli, Libya

ABSTRACT

Even though it is an essential requirement of any computer system, there is not yet a standard method to measure data security, especially when sending information over a network. However, the most common technique used to achieve the three goals of security is encryption. Three security metrics are derived from important issues of network security in this chapter. Each metric demonstrates the level of achievement in preserving one of the security goals. Routing algorithms based on these metrics are implemented to test the proposed solution. Computational effort and blocking probability are used to assess the behavior and the performance of these routing algorithms. Results show that the algorithms are able to find feasible paths between communicating parties and make reasonable savings in the computational effort needed to find an acceptable path. Consequently, higher blocking probabilities are encountered, which is the price to be paid for such savings.

INTRODUCTION

Since the Internet has been publicized there has been a significant, and rapidly growing, interest in being part of this society. According to the Internet World Stats (Miniwatts, 2013) the number of users exceeded 2.5billion in June 2012. By connecting to the Internet one may gain access to a massive amount of data and be able to share, exchange and/or publish information. Securing data while travelling over the network becomes a great concern to network professionals especially following the growth in use of the web in businesses.

Data security has many aspects (authentication, encryption, integrity, etc) and it is highly affected by many factors (computing power, investment, types of attacks, etc). So, defining a security metric under such conditions is absolutely difficult. That involves taking hard decisions regarding: how to measure security, which security feature should be selected and why, how to enumerate that feature, and how it could be used in routing.

Available routing algorithms use conventional metrics like delay, bandwidth, cost and, packet loss. Surprisingly network security has not been used as a Quality of Service (QoS) routing criterion. In addition, researchers in the fields of computer communication and data security have not agreed on a definition of a security metric(s) that could be used for finding the most secure path across an interconnected network.

DOI: 10.4018/978-1-4666-5808-0.ch015

So to demonstrate the level of achievement in preserving each one of the three security goals; three security metrics have been proposed, these metrics have been derived from three important issues of network security, namely: authentication, encryption and traffic filtration techniques (firewalls and intrusion detection systems).

The ultimate goal of this chapter is to describe three security metrics based on different aspects of network security. Then demonstrate how these metrics could be used in quality of service routing to find the most secure path connecting two distant nodes (source and destination) across an interconnected network.

ROUTING METRICS

A routing algorithm and a metric are the basic building blocks for packets routing in WANs. Existing routing protocols are using either a single metric, or multiple metrics. Generally speaking, there is a direct relationship between the number of metrics in use and both the performance and complexity of the routing algorithm. Examples of conventional metrics in use are: hop count, cost, delay, jitter, bandwidth and reliability.

Quality of service routing is a well-known problem and much research has been done in this area. It is concerned with finding a path across a network for a message to follow starting at a source node till it reaches its final destination. This process relies on a routing algorithm that uses topological data, also called metrics or weights, collected in the initial phase. In the case of routing, each forwarding decision is associated with a particular service response, so that a "best-effort" path to a particular destination address may differ from a "low-latency" path, which in turn may differ from a "high-bandwidth" path, and so on.

Basically, QoS is a collection of technologies that allow applications to request and receive predictable service levels in terms of data throughput capacity (bandwidth), latency variations (jitter),

cost, reliability and delay (Cisco Systems, 2001). The main goal of QoS is to provide different services to different network traffic over various technologies. Emerging networks, such as Asynchronous Transfer Mode (ATM), can provide QoS guarantees on bandwidth and delay for the transfer of continuous media data (Eberle & Oertli, 1998).

Using bandwidth is the simplest way to describe QoS. However, it is not good enough to define QoS using a single metric only. Practically, a number of metrics are used to express the concept of QoS. The computation of path metric value depends on the individual metric performance. Three main types of metrics were defined; these are: additive, concave and multiplicative. Typical examples of these metric types are delay, bandwidth and packet loss respectively (Kenyon, 2002).

To deal with a multi-metrics situation routing algorithms usually use one or the other of two approaches; either combining them into a single compound metric or leave them as separate metrics. While the compound metric represents the whole situation using a single value, which eases the process of path computation. The latter choice is preferable since this preserves the details of every measured network characteristic.

Security Goals

Typically, the need for information security and trust in computer systems is described in terms of three fundamental goals namely: Confidentiality, Integrity and Availability (or Access) (CIA) as illustrated in Figure 1.

Confidentiality involves control over who has access to information. Integrity assures that information and programs are changed only in a specified and authorized manner, so that computer resources operate correctly and that the data in them is not subject to unauthorized changes. Availability refers to the readiness of a system to use. That is, making information available to users needing them at the time they acquire them (University of Purdue, 2004).

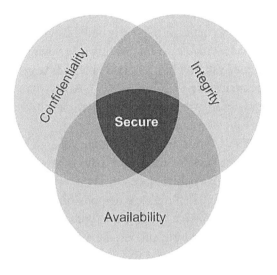

Figure 1. The three security goals

The data sent across the network should be guaranteed to reach the destination unchanged and complete (nothing is missed or added). Doing so requires ensuring that all parts of the network are functioning properly and they are accessible only to authorized personnel.

Authentication, Authorization and Accountability are used as a yardstick for measuring the security of an information system that are known as the three A's of privacy. In an attempt to assure the 3A's of privacy one has to maintain and preserve the CIA of the information at all system levels. That is, securing the hardware (physical level), how people do their jobs(procedural level) and the security software(logical level) (Stamp, 2011).

Preserving data security is essential especially when sending information over a network. Clearly, it has many important aspects like authentication, encryption, firewalls, etc. The sections below will emphasize three important issues of security: access control, device authentication and encryption. And then show how the selected aspects of security can be integrated to define security metrics for quality of service routing purposes.

Access Control

This includes the use of Access Control Lists (ACL), Intrusion Detection/Prevention Systems (IDS/IPS) and firewalls to enhance the overall level of network security. This is achieved by examining every single packet of the incoming and outgoing traffic against a predefined criteria that will result in either forwarding that packet or dropping it.

Usually access control lists are configured on perimeter routers also known as "firewall" routers, which are often situated at the edges of an enterprise network. Routers installed between two LANs also use access lists to control how traffic flows to and from specific parts of the internal network. Lists can control inbound traffic, outbound traffic or both on an interface, therefore to benefit from traffic filtration techniques at least border routers should be configured to use access lists. Basically an access list must be configured for each enabled network protocol on the router interface (Cisco Systems, 2002).

Routers are configurable to behave as a firewall and/or as an IDS, either configuration can prevent a subset of the whole set of known attacks against computer networks. For example firewalls can protect the network from routing based attacks, like source routing and path redirecting to malicious sites using Internet Control Message Protocol (ICMP) redirects (Goncalves, 2002). Intrusion detection systems, on the other hand, detect with high accuracy those attacks with known patterns only, like denial of service attack and then inform administrators of the incidents (Biermann, Cloete & Venter, 2001).

Encryption

Encryption is that technique mostly used on data communication systems to enhance the security and privacy of information. It is (encryption) the process of transforming the original message, known as plain-text, to a scrambled data format, called cipher-text, so that authorized people only can have access to the information.

Certainly encryption is the most important and widely used technique to guarantee secure data transmission. Every cryptosystem consists of two major parts: the algorithm and the key. Moreover, they determine how strong the cryptosystem would be. The algorithm is considered to be perfect, in other words it has no known weaknesses of its own. Then key size became the only factor affecting the strength of the encryption process. Perfect algorithms are vulnerable to brute-force attacks only; where the attacker should try all possible keys to find the correct bit combination (key) necessary to restore the original information. On average, the key is discovered after trying half of the total number of possible keys.

All known cryptographic systems fall into one of the following two categories: symmetrical (secret) key system or asymmetrical (public) key system. Data Encryption Standard (DES) and Rivest Shamir Adleman (RSA) respectively are the best examples of these types. Figure 2 shows how the encryption/decryption processes take place in each system.

The symmetric key system uses the same key both to encrypt the original message and to decrypt the scrambled text; therefore both sender and receiver must own the same key. This implies that: the key should be kept secret, interchanged securely, changed frequently and never sent over the same channel as the message. In other words such a system relies on good and firm key management policies (Stamp, 2011). Any symmetric key is shorter in size than any asymmetric key for the same level of security.

The asymmetric key system generates two different keys for each user. One is available to all users or "public" key, while the other is "private" and it is the user's responsibility to keep it secret. In asymmetric key cryptosystems, two different operating modes are possible: public key cryptography and the digital signature. The first uses the recipient public key to encrypt the message; the second uses the sender's private key instead. In Either mode if one key is used to encrypt or sign a message the other key is used to decrypt it or verify the sender's identity. These systems resolved the key management problem, but run longer and consequently require more processing power.

Each time data (even a single packet) is sent over a communication network it takes different paths to reach its destination, usually this path consists of a number of nodes connected via communication links. During such a trip from source to destination each node will temporarily store, encrypt/decrypt or might process, in one way or

Figure 2. Encryption/decryption processes in(a) symmetrical and (b) asymmetrical key system

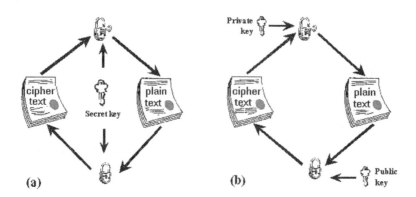

another, that data. The data basically consists of the actual message and a header that specifies the destination's address. All available approaches rely on encryption techniques to transmit data across a network securely both in a node and over a link; two of the most common solutions in use nowadays are briefed below:

- **Link Encryption:** Encrypts data before sending it over the communication link, the next node on the route decrypt the data in order to access the header and decide which route to follow then encrypt it again before sending it out and so on. At each stage the node uses its own key for encryption and decryption.
- **End-to-End Encryption:** Deals with the message and the header differently, while encrypting the first leaves the second as plain text. Consequently, the message is deciphered only at the final destination as the header is available as plain text to intermediate nodes.

Basically, the encryption/decryption operations require a lot of computing power the end-to-end mode is considered to be faster because it applies these operations only twice (at source and destination), whilst the link encryption method applies it at all nodes along the path and is also more secure than the end-to-end encryption method, as nodes temporarily store the data as plain text, which is a great risk. The main disadvantage of this approach is somebody can perform a "traffic flow analysis" as the header is always in plain text format. In other words, one may monitor when and how information is exchanged on the network (Lubbe, 1998).

Key Size and Computing Power

A key of n bits long will generate 2^n different keys. So, it is worth noting that, adding an extra bit to the key doubles the number of possible keys, which

slightly increases the processing time required for encrypting/decrypting data. But, attackers using exhaustive key search will need to spend double the effort (time or investment) required to crack a code, which is one bit shorter (Stamp, 2011). Two factors affect the speed of a brute-force attack: the number of keys to be tried and how long each trial takes. Williams showed that the time needed for such an attack to decrypt a code grows exponentially in relation with the key length (Williams, 2001). The trend in key size growth is demonstrated in Figure 3; it shows the minimum key size needed to secure communication in both asymmetrical and symmetrical cryptosystems (Lenstra & Verheul, 1999).

According to Moor's law the computing power is doubled every 18 months (Wikipedia, 2004); Schneier (1994) also claimed that the ratio of computing power efficiency to price grows ten times each five years. Results obtained by applying both rules are marginally different. So, to maintain today's data security levels the key length must be increased by a single bit at-least every doubling period.

Router Authentication

Neighbor router authentication, or simply "router authentication", is a mechanism used to guarantee that all topology change updates are received from a trusted party. It plays a very important role in enhancing the overall security of an organization's network. If a fabricated route update, for example, has been forwarded to the targeted router deliberately, to force it to redirect all the traffic going out of that router to a malicious destination. That traffic probably contains important and/or confidential information. Such an attack is avoidable if all the involved routers were configured to use neighbor authentication as router authentication can stop spoofing and routing attacks (Deal, 2005). Several routing protocols are capable of benefiting from router authentication, examples of such protocols are: IGRP, IS-IS, OSPF and RIP-V2.

Figure 3. Minimum key size required for secure communication

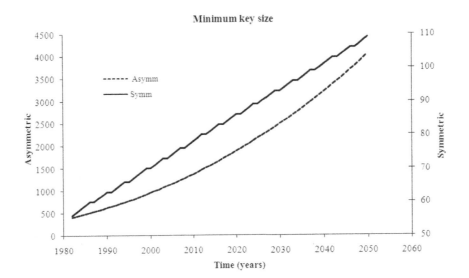

Routers configured to use neighbor authentication, agree on a secret (symmetric) key before any authentication process may take place. Whenever a participating router receives a route update it authenticates the source of every packet using the authentication key. Then the router decides either to accept that packet or to reject it.

Two authentication scenarios are possible; plain text authentication and Message Digest version5 authentication (MD5). Although the former technique is simple and easy to configure it is weak and vulnerable to common attacks. However, the latter is more sophisticated and recommended. Both algorithms are identical in the way they work; still each of them is using a different method to exchange the secret key. Basically, the first method transmits the actual key in a plain text format over the same channel that carries the data. On the other hand, the second approach sends a message digest generated using the key but never communicates the key itself (Cisco Systems, 2005). The MD5 algorithm is based on a one way hash function which produces a 128 bit hash from the original message. Clearly routers using plain text authentication are vulnerable to

update attacks as those routers that are not configured for router authentication. In contrast it is well known that MD5 is vulnerable to exhaustive key search attack only (Stamp, 2011).

SECURITY METRICS

A routing metric is a number associated with a route indicating the goodness of that route. If more than one route are available to a destination then the route with the lowest metric is considered the best. In the above context "goodness" is defined in terms of the level of security the chosen path can maintain; basically the metric value of the selected route has to be the best (i.e. having the minimum degree of vulnerability or the maximum level of security) amongst the available routes. But what makes good security metrics.

Precisely, useful security metrics are those who could show the degree to which goals, like data confidentiality, are being achieved and hence drive the process of the whole security program perfection. However, the means of indicating to which extent some security attributes are in existence defines security metrics specifically (Payne, 2001). Jelen (2000) also stated that good metrics are those known to be Specific, Measurable, Attainable, Repeatable, and Time-dependent.

In previous studies (Alghannam, Woodward & Melor, 2001; Alkahtani, Woodward & Al-Begain, 2003; Alfawaz & Woodward, 2002; Baltatu, Lioy, Maino & Mazzocchi, 2000; Smith & Garcia-Luna-Aceves, 1998) the notion of a security metric was mentioned for the sake of developing multi-metric routing algorithms. Since it was beyond the scope of their work and because the problem was poorly researched, the metric they used was oversimplified and imprecisely defined it had been represented using a single valued metric. While Alghannam and Alkahtani proposed a value between 0 and 1, Alfawaz used a binary value. Moreover, different authors apply different composition rules, Alkahtani claimed that security is an additive metric but Alfawaz dealt with it as a binary metric and Alghannam as a bottleneck (concave) metric.

Lowans (2000) talked about a network security cycle where he suggested ten metrics; few of them are: number of unsuccessful logons, number of guessed passwords, number of security policy violations. In the light of the definition of network security and the three goals of network security; most if not all of these metrics are designed for management purposes with risk assessment in mind. They are applicable at application level only and they do not reflect on the state of network security at a lower level like: the level of security of a communication link and do not show how secure a certain node could be.

Almerhag and Woodward (2005c) have proposed a single security metric based on encryption, namely the key size. Unlike bandwidth or cost the metric value is allocated to nodes rather than links as it is a characteristic of nodes not links. Each node (or all links leaving that node) is assigned a metric value that falls in the range between zero and one inclusive. On one extreme a node is considered to be secure if it uses a key

that can maintain the required security level for the next thirty years. On the other extreme it is vulnerable when the key used is below the recommended size. And between the two margins, there exists a linear relationship between time in years and the metric value.

The security metric was called "Degree of Vulnerability" (DoV), where a metric value of zero is assigned to a secure node or value of one to a vulnerable one. For other nodes the metric value is following the linear scale shown in Figure 4. In mathematical terms the metric value is given by Equation (3).

From the point of view of a routing algorithm, a good metric should represent the value of a network security parameter; this is analogous to a typical routing metric which corresponds to a physical network parameter like bandwidth, delay or packet loss. Therefore, three metrics are proposed in the following sections to show to what extent the goals of network security have been maintained by the system under consideration, followed by a detailed explanation of how these metrics could be used in QoS routing.

THE PROPOSED SECURITY METRICS

Since the status of network security is quite complicated, it cannot be verified using a single feature. So, any effective security metric should integrate a number of important aspects of security to form either: a single compound metric or a collection of metrics each measuring a specific aspect of network security. In this study, the second approach has been adopted for the proposed security metrics; since a compound metric tends to lose the details as a result of the aggregation whereas the multi-metric approach will preserve the detailed state of the network as measured by each metric.

Almerhag and Woodward (2005a) have selected three important issues of network security

Figure 4. The relationship between growth of key size and the metric value

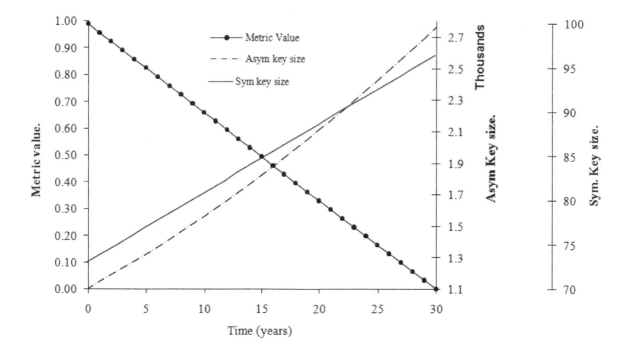

among different security aspects to define the new metrics. The features been used are: router authentication, the key size and access control techniques. The most important issues of network security have been incorporated in the new metrics. The selected features are those that can demonstrate to what extent the three goals of data security could be maintained by a specific information system.

The three metrics are defined based on three important aspects of security; as encryption guarantees the confidentiality of data during transmission, router authentication ensures and validates the identity of the communicating party and traffic filtration and control techniques maintain the availability of information or service. The three sections below explain how to calculate every single metric and the composition rule(s) each metric follows. Where W_p is the metric value of the entire path and W_i is the weight of link i.

Access Control

This is achievable by the use of traffic filtration techniques like: access control lists, intrusion detection/prevention systems and firewalls. Such devices examine every single packet of the incoming and outgoing traffic against predefined criteria that will result in either forwarding that packet or dropping it. Firewalls can protect the network from routing based attacks (Goncalves, 2002) on the other hand; an IDS system assesses any abnormal activity based on a predefined patterns, also called signature, or using statistical data related to the attack then informs the system administrator about the suspected intrusion (Biermann, Cloete & Venter, 2001).

Basically, each node along the path may enclose a firewall and/or an IDS. So, the metric value (W_i) of all links leaving that node is given by Equation (1); where P_{fw} and P_{ids} respectively are the probability that the firewall will prevent an attack and the IDS will detect an attack and react accordingly.

$$W_i = 1 - \left[P_{fw} + P_{ids} - \left(P_{fw} \times P_{ids} \right) \right] \qquad (1)$$

Assume that a properly configured firewall router will eliminate 84% of common breaches and an IDS will protect the system from 79% of known attacks as shown in Figure 5. Clearly, there will be a significant number of attacks that are preventable by both techniques; this leads to the conclusion that this network is vulnerable to 3% only of the total number of known attacks. For the sake of this study, it is assumed that this data is available to system administrators and it is believed that such information may be calculated based on historical data collected over a specified period of time. Furthermore, a routing algorithm may be designed to do that automatically and dynamically during the normal operation of the network.

This security metric follows a multiplicative composition rule and the path's metric value is given by Equation (2).

$$W_p = 1 - \left[W_1 \times W_2 \times W_3 \times \ldots \ldots \times W_n \right] \qquad (2)$$

Figure 5. The percentage of known attacks that firewall/IDS can prevent/detect

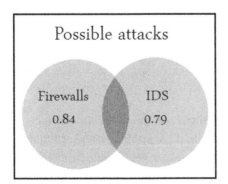

Key Length

Any cryptographic system consists of an encryption algorithm and a secret (or secret and public) key(s). These elements determine the strength of that system also. However, for the sake of this study the algorithm is assumed not to have any built-in weaknesses. This makes the key size as the only factor that influences the strength of any cryptographic system. As a result of the rapid technological advancement in electronics, especially in information technology; more and more sophisticated tools have become available to hackers and crackers, like powerful computers at affordable price, even parallel computing facilities and electronic devices specially designed to break codes.

According to Moor's law, the computing power is doubled every 18 months (Wikipedia, 2004). And clearly adding an extra bit to the key-size doubles the number of possible keys. Therefore, to maintain today's data security levels, the key size used for encryption should also grow in response to that achievement.

So, the key length must be increased by a single bit at-least every doubling period. All links leaving a node are assigned a metric value that falls in the range between zero and one, inclusive. Where zero denotes a secure link and vice versa. At one extreme, a node is considered to be secure if it uses a key that can maintain the required security level for the next thirty years. At the other extreme, it is vulnerable when the key used is below the recommended key size today. Between the two margins, there exists a linear relationship between the metric value and time in years that a key could maintain an acceptable level of security, as shown in Figure (4). Such a value could be calculated using Equation (3) (Almerhag & Woodward, 2005b).

$$W_i = \begin{cases} 1 & \textit{if the size of key used} > \textit{the recommended size} \\ 0.99 - 0.033\ y & \textit{otherwise} \end{cases} \tag{3}$$

where Y is the time span in years the key used guarantees acceptable level of data security.

Figure (4) demonstrates also the growth of key size over the next thirty years for symmetrical and asymmetrical key systems; it also shows the relationship between time and the metric value. The idea behind assigning a metric value of zero to a secure node or value of one to a vulnerable one, is to be able to use the shortest path algorithm to find the least vulnerable (clearly the most secure) path across a network.

Usually every routing metric follows one of the three composition rules. In contrast this security metric is the exception since it may be treated as additive or concave metric; to the best of author's knowledge no other metric has this feature.

It is concave when treated as a bottleneck characteristic. In other words, the path is considered to be as secure as the weakest link. Now the routing algorithm selects links (path) having metric value greater than or equal to the value specified by the QoS requirements. Alternatively, consider it as an additive metric here the path metric value is equal to the summation (average) of all metric values of those links forming that path. Then a shortest path algorithm could be used to find the best path. Given that this path satisfies the QoS requirements.

Key size can be either as additive metric or as a bottleneck characteristic. So, the additive or the concave composition rule could be applied to this metric. If a path is considered to be as secure as the weakest link amongst those links forming that path then the concave composition rule is applicable, so the path will have a metric value given by Equation(4).

$$W_p = Min\left[W_1, W_2, W_3, \ldots\ldots, W_n\right] \tag{4}$$

Clearly when comparing different paths, the path with the smallest number of hops is preferable to others if all links have equal metric values, because the smaller the number of hops is the lower is the chance that a breach could take place. This implies that the metric value of a path could be calculated using Equation (5).

$$W_p = \sum_{i=1}^{n} W_i \ldots \tag{5}$$

Router Authentication

It is an important issue in network security because routers exchange routing updates regularly. Therefore, device authentication is used to guarantee that routers receive reliable routing information. Otherwise, the security of the whole network could be compromised. If for example, an unauthorized or deliberately malicious data fabricated by an unfriendly party were used to update the routing tables. The network traffic then could be diverted to a cruel destination, where confidential information may be revealed or simply the updates are used to prevent the network from functioning effectively.

This metric will have a binary value, that is the metric value is true (or 1) if the authentication protocol is using MD5 to exchange information between neighbor routers and the metric value is false (or 0) otherwise, as described in Equation (6).

$$W_i = \begin{cases} 1\ \textit{if MD5 is used} \\ 0 \qquad \textit{otherwise} \end{cases} \tag{6}$$

Neighbor router authentication is a binary metric. So, if the application/user requires a path that uses a secure router authentication protocol, then this metric value should be true for all links forming that path. In other words, the path metric value could be computed using the logical AND operation given by Equation (7).

$$W_p = W_1 \otimes W_2 \otimes W_3 \otimes \ldots\ldots \otimes W_n \qquad (7)$$

The proposed metrics have implemented and sustained the five features (SMART) that a good metric should have.

THE ROUTING ALGORITHMS

Most available routing protocols use a shortest path algorithm like Dijkstra or Bellman-Ford to solve the routing problem. These algorithms need to know about the complete structure of the network to be able to find the best path. As the problem of QoS routing based on network security has not been studied (or poorly researched) in this context. Therefore, three different solutions have been proposed and implemented based on the metrics defined earlier in a specific order to minimize the complexity of the path computation phase.

EXPERIMENTAL SETUP

Selecting a model for a particular study depends basically on several factors including the nature of the study to be performed, the size of the required generated topology, the weight certain characteristics of the generated topologies may have (Zegura, 2001).

To represent real interconnected networks, the simulation has been designed to generate networks having a number of nodes ranging from 10 to 100. These nodes are randomly distributed on a plane. Then the process of assigning a link between each pair of nodes is governed by Doar's model (Doar, 1996). The goal is to generate a network that is very close to a real wide area network. The simulation operates only on connected networks that have at least a single path between any pair

of nodes and that network should have an average node degree of 4, which equals the node degree of the Internet. Then the routing algorithm is applied to the randomly generated network, and statistics concerning computational effort and blocking probability are collected.

The process of network generation and data collection is repeated 100,000 times for each network size and for each algorithm. Specifically, each run is divided into ten samples where a hundred random networks are generated per sample. Then ten different source/destination combinations are selected per topology and the weights are also changed ten times for each network. Finally, the average values of the computational effort and the blocking probabilities that have been collected throughout the running period of the simulation are calculated and then in a data file.

Three versions of this algorithm have been designed; depending on the way the key size security metric is treated and the way the other two metrics have been ordered. While the first considers key size as a bottleneck parameter the other two consider it as an additive metric. All versions of this algorithm consist of three steps; in the first phase, all links that do not use MD5 to exchange routing updates are removed if the application specifically requires that. These solutions facilitate the process of testing, comparing and benchmarking the solutions and ultimately draw conclusions.

Binary-Concave-Multiplicative (BCM) Algorithm

When the key size metric is dealt with as a bottleneck characteristic, all the links that do not satisfy the application's requirement (having key size smaller than the required value) are also removed. Finally, Dijkstra's algorithm is applied to the simplified network to compute the shortest path between the source and the destination nodes within the remaining network based on the third multiplicative metric (traffic filtration technique).

Binary-Additive-Multiplicative (BAM) Algorithm

Here the key size is treated as an additive metric. Therefore, if a path metric value exceeds the QoS metric value specified by an application that path is dropped. Otherwise, the path's third metric value is checked for the satisfaction of the QoS requirements as before. If that is the case, then a suitable path has been found, if not this process should start over again.

Binary-Multiplicative-Additive (BMA) Algorithm

This version works the same way as the previous one with the exception that the second and third metrics are evaluated in the reverse order. So if a path that satisfies the multiplicative metric has been found the algorithm examines the value of the additive metric to ensure that that value fulfils the application's needs.

RESULTS

Researchers have developed a number of measures to evaluate the performance of routing algorithms. Among those measures the most frequently used two are: the computational effort and the blocking probability. First, the computational effort is the number of operations needed to find a satisfactory path between a source and a destination(s), which in distributed algorithms is also known as the message passing overhead. The second is the blocking probability which is the probability that a connection request has been unsuccessful; that is to say that the routing algorithm was not able to find a path that satisfies the QoS requirements.

During the simulation the values of the previously mentioned performance measures are collected and then the average values of the computational effort and the blocking probability are computed for that run. Finally, the 95% confidence levels for those measures, per network size, have been calculated using the ten different samples.

Computational Effort

The results obtained from both BAM and BMA algorithms are quite close to each other (see Figure 6), since the effort needed to find a path in both cases is almost the same as the only difference between them is the order in which the metrics are satisfied. However, BCM has better performance in terms of the computational effort needed to find a feasible path which is because the latter algorithm takes advantage of the concave metric to reduce the size of network before it starts looking for a satisfactory path within a simplified network. The other two algorithms have to search the full network before any feasible path could be found.

Blocking Probability

The value of the blocking probability for a given network is expected to increase as a result of reducing the size of the network. Because the total number of routes available for choosing by the routing algorithm decreases, hence the probability of finding an acceptable path decreases consequently.

As the criteria for satisfying the key-size and traffic filtration techniques requirements become tighter. In both cases, the simulation randomly generates the QoS requirement values. In the first case "loose", the values generated are not restricted at all under these conditions each metric value can be between zero and one. However, under the "tight" arrangement the metrics values assigned can have a random value within the range $(0, 0.5)$.

Figure 7 below shows the behavior of the three algorithms. The results show that by tightening the QoS requirements the blocking probability increases as this would limit the choices available

Figure 6. Computational effort of the three algorithms

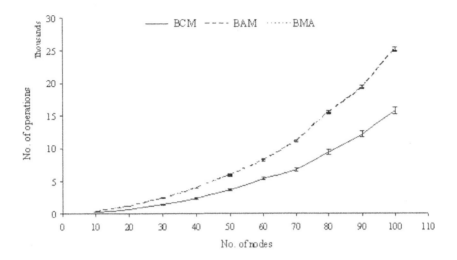

to the routing algorithm because all the links that do not satisfy the requirements are eliminated by the path computation process.

Because satisfying the concave metric has an effect on the network topology. The BCM algo-

rithm has been outperformed by the other two algorithms in terms of this performance measure that could be considered as the price been paid for having reduced the computational effort. Consequently, a balance between the number of

Figure 7. Blocking probability of the three algorithms

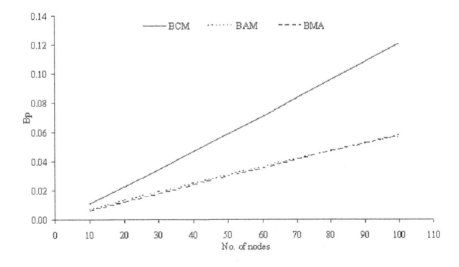

failed connection attempts and the computational effort gained should be maintained.

CONCLUSION

The computer society has not yet agreed on a standard method to measure data security and consequently no specific security metrics have been defined so they could be used by routing algorithms. Security is a complicated feature of computer networks; it cannot be characterized using a single metric. A set of three security metrics has been defined based on selected network security features, so that they are used to find a secure path between source and destination across a network and that path satisfies the QoS constraints specified by the application.

Available and running network security technologies namely: access control, encryption and authentication are used to define the routing metrics. These metrics are believed to be good, reasonable and practical. Because authentication is regarded as the first line of defense against intrusion, cryptography is the key tool that ensures secure transmission of data while traversing the network and access control systems help in guaranteeing the availability of services been delivered by the information system. Each metric thus represents one of the three goals of security (integrity, confidentiality and availability) and demonstrates the level of achievement in preserving that goal.

Measuring the level of security of a certain path is a complicated problem, because of the nature of the problem. This work suggests how the selected aspects have been used to define the security metrics that can be used by routing algorithms to find the most secure path within interconnected networks. Each metric follows a different composition rule: the first is binary, the second is concave and the last is multiplicative.

Results show that BCM has out-performed BAM and BMA in terms of computational effort but at the price of higher blocking probabilities.

That is because of the nature of the concave metric. Furthermore, the results show that the performance of BAM and BMA are almost the same since they only differ in the order of satisfying the last two metrics.

REFERENCES

Alfawaz, M. M., & Woodward, M. E. (2002). *QoS routing with multiple-constraints.* Delson Group Inc. World Wireless Congress.

Alghannam, A., Woodward, M. E., & Melor, J. (2001). Security as a QoS routing issue. In *Proceedings of the 2nd Annual Postgraduate Symposium* (PGNet'01). Liverpool John Moores University.

Alkahtani, A. M., Woodward, M. E., & Al-Begain, K. (2003). The analytic hierarchy process applied to best effort QoS routing with multiple metrics: a comparative evaluation. *Personal Mobile Communications Conference 5th European. Conf. Publ., 492*, 539-544.

Almerhag, I. A., & Woodward, M. E. (2005a). Security as a Quality of Service Routing Problem. In *Proceedings of the 2005 ACM conference on Emerging network experiment and technology.* ACM.

Almerhag, I. A., & Woodward, M. E. (2005b). *Quality of service routing metrics based on selected aspects of network security.* Paper presented at Fourth HET-NET's05. Ilkley, UK.

Almerhag, I. A., & Woodward, M. E. (2005c). *Key-size as a QoS routing metric.* Paper presented at Sixth Informatics Workshop. Bradford, UK.

Baltatu, M., Lioy, A., Maino, F., & Mazzocchi, D. (2000). Security issues in management, control and routing protocols. *Computer Networks, 34*, 881–894. doi:10.1016/S1389-1286(00)00159-6

Biermann, E., Cloete, E., & Venter, L. M. (2001). A Comparison of Intrusion Detection Systems. *Computers & Security*, 20(8), 676–683. doi:10.1016/S0167-4048(01)00806-9

Cisco Systems Inc. (2001). *Network security: An executive overview*. Retrieved from http://www.managednetworks.com/docs/networksecurity-overview.pdf

Cisco Systems Inc. (2002). *Internetworking technologies handbook*. Retrieved from http://www.cisco.com/univercd/cc/td/doc/cisintwk/ito doc/

Cisco Systems Inc. (2005). *Cisco IOS Security Configuration Guide*, Release 12.2.

Deal, R. A. (2005). *Cisco Router Firewall Security*. Indianapolis, IN: Cisco Press.

Doar, J. M. (1996). A Better Model for Generating Test Networks. In *Proceedings of Globecom96*. Academic Press. doi:10.1109/GLOCOM.1996.586131

Eberle, H., & Oertli, E. (1998). Switcherland: a QoS communication architecture for workstation clusters, Computer Architecture. In *Proceedings. The 25th Annual International Symposium on Computer Architecture*, (pp. 98-108). Academic Press.

Goncalves, M. (2002). *Firewalls Complete*. McGraw-Hill. Retrieved from http://www.secinf.net/firewalls_and_VPN/Firewalls_Complete/

Jelen, G. (2000). *SSE-CMM Security Metrics*. Washington, DC: NIST and CSSPAB.

Kenyon, T. (2002). *High Performance Data Network Design: Designer Techniques and Tools*. Elsevier Inc. Press.

Lenstra, A., & Verheul, E. (1999). *Selecting cryptographic key sizes*. Retrieved from http://security.ece.orst.edu/koc/ece575/papers/cryptosizes.pdf

Lowans, P. (2000). *Implementing a network security metrics program*. Retrieved from http://www.giac.org/practical/PaulLowansGSEC.doc

Lubbe, J. (1998). *Basic Methods of Cryptography*. Cambridge, UK: Cambridge University Press.

Miniwatts International Ltd. (2013). *World Internet Usage And Population Statistics* (tech. rep.). Retrieved from http://www.internetworldstats.com/stats.htm

Payne, S. (2001). *A Guide to Security Metrics*. Retrieved from http://rr.sans.org/audit/metrics.php

Schneier, B. (1994). *Applied Cryptography: Protocols, Algorithms and Source Code in C*. John Wiley & Sons.

Smith, B. R., & Garcia-Luna-Aceves, J. J. (1998). Efficient security mechanisms for the border gateway routing protocol. *Computer Communications*, 21(3), 203–210. doi:10.1016/S0140-3664(97)00186-2

Stamp, M. (2011). *Information Security: Principles and Practice* (2nd ed.). Wiley. doi:10.1002/9781118027974

University of Purdue. (2004). *RASC: Confidentiality, Integrity and Availability (CIA)*. Retrieved from http://www.itap.purdue.edu/security/files/documents/RASCCIAv13.pdf

Wikipedia. The Free Encyclopedia. (2008). *Moore's Law*. Retrieved from http://en.wikipedia.org/wiki/Moore's_Law

Williams, L. (2001). *A discussion of The Importance of Key Length in Symmetric and Asymmetric Cryptography*. Retrieved from http://rr.sans.org/encryption/key_length.php

Zegura, E. (2001). *Thoughts on router-level topology modelling*. Retrieved from http://www.postel.org/pipermail/end2end-interest/2001-January/000033.html

KEY TERMS AND DEFINITIONS

Authentication: Is the process of confirming a user or computer's identity. It determines whether someone or something is who or what it is declared to be.

Encryption: Scrambling sensitive information so that it becomes unreadable to everyone except the intended recipient. It is the process of encoding messages (or information) in such a way that eavesdroppers or hackers cannot read it, but that authorized parties can.

Firewall: It controls the incoming and outgoing network traffic by analyzing the data packets and determining whether it should be allowed through or not, based on a predetermined rule set. It can either be software-based or hardware-based.

Intrusion Detection Systems: Is a software application installed on various computers or hardware sensors located at various points along the network. It analyzes data packets both inbound and outbound for malicious activities or policy violations and forwards a report to the management.

Routing: Is the process of moving packets across a network from one host to another.

Routing Metric: A number associated with a route indicating the goodness of that route.

Routing Protocols: A set of rules or standard that determines how routers on a network communicate and exchange information with each other, enabling them to select best routes to a remote network.

Quality of Service: A broad collection of networking technologies and techniques aiming at providing guarantees on the ability of a network to deliver predictable results.

Chapter 16

Forensic Analysis, Cryptosystem Implementation, and Cryptology:
Methods and Techniques for Extracting Encryption Keys from Volatile Memory

Štefan Balogh
Slovak University of Technology, Slovakia

ABSTRACT

The increasing portability of computing devices combined with frequent reports of privacy breaches and identity theft has thrust data encryption into the public attention. While encryption can help mitigate the threat of unintentional data exposure, it is equally capable of hiding evidence of criminal malfeasance. The increasing accessibility and usability of strong encryption solutions present new challenges for digital forensic investigators. Understanding forensic analysis as a multidisciplinary field that searches evidence of crime, the authors focus their topic on particularity of cross-disciplinary issues arising in this area: Forensic analysis uses cryptology, information technology and mathematics in extracting encryption keys from memory. The chapter highlights the virtues of volatile memory analysis by demonstrating how key material and passphrases can be extracted from memory and reconstructed to facilitate the analysis of encrypted data. The authors show current methods for identifying encryption keys in memory and discuss possible defeating techniques and cryptosystem implementation strategies that could be used to avoid the key extraction.

INTRODUCTION

Currently, many organizations and government institutions have some experience, may be major or minor, of losing sensitive data. In May 2007, the Transportation Security Administration (TSA) lost a hard drive containing approximately 100,000 employee bank account details, while in October 2007 two laptops containing names and social security numbers of almost 4,000 employees were stolen.

DOI: 10.4018/978-1-4666-5808-0.ch016

In the same year, the government in the United Kingdom reported that two disks with personal information details of 25 million citizens had been lost.2 This forced many institutions to improve their data security procedures by implementing encryption mechanisms to protect their sensitive data.

Nonetheless, encryption is a double-edged sword. On one hand, it protects our sensitive data, on the other it allows criminals to hide data that would convict them of a crime.

Encryption has been used in relation to pedophilia, terrorism, organized crime and espionage (Denning, 1997).

In 2007, an incident happened when US Customs found child pornography on a Canadian citizen and legal US resident Sebastian Boucher's laptop. The laptop was seized as the evidence and he was charged with transporting the pornography across borders. The problem appeared when examiners tried to open the incriminating drive Z and found out that it was a Pretty Good Privacy encrypted container. Although a forensic duplicate of hard drive was created after the shutdown of the notebook, the examiner could not open the encrypted container. Boucher refused to give the password on the grounds that it violated the Fifth Amendment right against self-incrimination.3

The cooperation between the fields of cryptology, information technology, and forensic analysis is necessary in order to be able to obtain the encrypted evidence. In this chapter, we summarize possibilities, which individual fields of the forensic analysis offer to detect relevant information (evidence), and identify encryption keys, respectively. Moreover, we discuss the current state of and future trends in these areas.

FORENSIC ANALYSIS

Forensic Investigation Possibilities

Today, the forensic investigators cannot use the traditional, widely accepted computer forensic methodology of unplugging the power to a computer and then acquiring a bit-stream image of the system hard drive anymore. Investigators and incident responders are often seeing instances in which the questions they asked cannot be answered using the contents of an imaged hard drive alone. In many cases, the best source of information or evidence is available in computer memory. While the computer operates, RAM stores all the accumulated data for running applications and network communications. There is a great amount of information in RAM that exists only when applications are running. Most of this information cannot be easily obtained from a hard drive (Carvey, 2009).

Information that can be obtained from RAM includes:

network connections, contents of the Instant Messenger client window, memory used by the Instant Messenger client process, decrypted versions of otherwise encrypted data, cryptographic key material, hard drive encryption keys, wireless keys, usernames and passwords, etc. (see short paper titled "The Value of Physical Memory Analysis for Incident Response" written by Hoglund (2008) (Hoglund, Greg is a Chief executive officer (CEO) of HBGary, Inc). Carvey (2009) also described more reasons, why the forensic investigator should collect the contents of RAM.

Volatile memory forensics has become increasingly prominent in the area of forensic analysis and incident response. Live forensics (on-line analysis) involves performing analysis at the same time the evidence is collected. And live systems also allow us to collect much more robust data. Another method used to analyze memory is off-line analysis. When forensic investigator performs the off-line analysis, they first collect digital evidence in live environment (usually a dump of all memory is created), and then that evidence is analyzed on another computer. Evidence must be analyzed on another computer because forensic analysis fights with similar limitations as rootkit detection: live detection can almost always be defeated by resident rootkits (Davis, 2009). On the other hand off-line analysis of the memory allows the investigator to see the state of the operating system without the operating system acting as a filter. Unlike the attempts of finding a rootkit on a live system, the rootkit is unable to take any action to hide itself in the memory image. Therefore, investigators can see the data without the operating system or the rootkit interpreting or blocking the data for them (Kornblum, 2006). Volatile memory forensics can ensure that during incident response or in the first investigation phase we can get the dump of the memory. But, memory forensics is still facing far too many challenges.

Memory Dump

Current methods of capturing memory fall into two basic categories: software and hardware methods.

Software Methods

Software oriented tools use the fact that many operating systems allow reading the contents of memory: virtual devices /dev/mem and /dev/kmem in UNIX, and \Device\PhysicalMemory in Windows. A lot of software tools for obtaining a memory image used these devices. The problem of using these devices is that the image is created in the user mode. But objects in physical memory are (from versions of Windows Server 2003 SP1 and later versions including Vista) unavailable from the user mode. However, they continue to be accessible from kernel mode. For this reason, new methods have been developed that use a custom driver, which enables access to the memory via kernel mode.

Unfortunately, despite the act of running a memory dumping tool itself changes a portion of RAM. When the program is loaded into memory, it can (due to memory paging) move useful information to the page file. Also the result seen by the tools can be modified with resident rootkits. One common characteristic for all of software tools is the need to be loaded into memory in order

to run. Tools alter the digital environment of the original system and cause an adverse impact on the preserved memory data. Law et al. (2009) studied the effect of running different memory acquisition tools on the computer memory content. They observed that some memory acquisition tools are more invasive than others and their general alterations to the memory image content collected at various time intervals were over 35% on average. A useful reference for software oriented tools is in/ can be found in work by Carvey (2009).

Another problem with this method is that memory capture takes a significant amount of time. Current workstations or servers may have 4GB, 8GB or even higher amount of physical memory. This causes the captured data to be inconsistent, since other processes are modifying memory as the capture is proceeding (Libster, 2008).

Wang et al. (2011) present two ways to make the dump of all memory:

- Record the whole memory in one operation which guarantees the memory content to be consistent. This involves freezing the OS during the process;
- Recording only a portion of the memory, resume the OS, and then repeat the process until all the memory is recorded.

However, the OS may hang if it is frozen for a relatively long time, because too many hardware interruptions are lost when frozen. The second method does not interfere too much to the OS, but the memory dump acquired during a relatively long period may not be consistent.

Hardware Methods

The main idea of hardware oriented approaches is to bypass the operating system using a physical device. The device creates a memory access through a single channel, which is independent of the operating system. Very often DMA (Direct Memory Access) feature is used for direct access.

This allows us to obtain a memory image without launching another process or having to use potentially contested features of local system. A concept of special hardware PCI card was introduced by (Carrier et al., 2004). The card can be used to save the contents of memory to the external medium. It must, however, be already present in the system at the time, when we need to access the memory contents. Another possibility of hardware memory access is provided by the FireWire interface. In 2006 Adam Boileau created a program capable of using a Linux machine to copy the contents of memory from another computer (Boileau, 2006). However the disadvantage of this method is that in some configurations, the system Firewire bus has a problem with the upper memory area (UMA Upper Memory Area) (Garcia, 2007). Moreover, FireWire access is often disabled for the security reasons. The FireWire based attack inspired research of using similar alternative interfaces that use DMA. Several attacks, which can gain control of the DMA and read the contents of RAM, were presented. Almost exclusively to these attacks was the fact attacks were based on network cards. More on this can be found in works by Duflot (2010) and Delugré (2010) and Wang et al. (2011).

Live Acquisition

One way for dealing with encryption is to obtain a disk image when the encrypted disks or containers are mounted and computer system is still powered on and running, we perform a so-called "live acquisition" in which the investigator creates a bit-for-bit image of the logical device while the system is still running.

In live acquisition, the investigator reads every block of data on the logical device, each of which is transparently decrypted by the encryption software, resulting in a decrypted representation of the suspect's disk. However, there are some problems in using this approach. They are described in work by Hargreaves (2008) e.g., violation principles of forensic computing like repeatability and verifi-

ability. There are also some cases when it may be impossible or impractical to create a full image of the decrypted data. Furthermore, this approach relies on an operating system which is not credible presenting what is actually on the disk and could be subverted by anti-forensic techniques (Darren, 2006). There are also some cases when it may be impossible or impractical to create a full image of the decrypted data (full volume encryption can now be approximately 1 Terabyte). These problems can be addressed by the recovery of the keys used for encryption, using the recovered keys we can decrypt offline, encrypted container or volume obtained with a traditional, accepted disk image computer forensic methodology. In this case, there will be no dependency on a live acquired disk image that cannot be verified against no longer accessible original (Hargreaves, 2008).

TECHNIQUES FOR OBTAINING ENCRYPTION KEYS

Encrypted evidence is one of the major challenges of current digital investigations and the trends suggest that its use is increasing.

Some authors discuss various approaches to solving the problems with encrypted evidence and describe why it may not be successful (Hargreaves, 2008). They describe different ways to get access to encrypted disks:

- Persuading the suspect to provide the key.
- Locating unencrypted data copies.
- Locating keys or passphrases.
- Intelligent password attacks.
- Exhaustive key search.
- Exploiting implementation vulnerabilities.
- Hardware or software surveillance.

Still they also say that "most of these techniques can be countered by good product design and disciplined use" (p.1370). Therefore, we must look for other solutions. One way is to obtain a disk image when the encrypted disks or containers are mounted and computer system is still powered on and running.

Some tools for encryption like BitLocker have a built-in functionality to decrypt a protected disk by connecting the drive read-only to a forensic examination system (Casey, 2008). However, generally it is not supported in encryption tools. Other way is to recover the keys used for encryption.

Encryption Keys Recovery from Memory

Many disk encryption software can encrypt the data in real time, which means that the data is decrypted at the moment they are stored or recorded (OTFE - On-the-fly encryption). Encryption and decryption is done automatically after a user successfully authenticates to the cryptosystem and symmetric encryption key is unlocked and passed to the cryptographic filter. If the filter receives the key, it can begin transparently decrypting and encrypting all data without any user intervention "on the fly" and any data stored on an encrypted volume can be read (decrypted) without using the correct password. The disc contains only encrypted data and decryption/encryption is going directly in memory, so without the correctly keyed filter layer, all data read from the disk is encrypted.

So, the on-the-fly encryption system, by its nature, decrypts content only when it is being required. Therefore the keys needed for decryption have to be continuously accessible and should always be recoverable from memory. However, this does not only apply to on-the-fly encryption system, but any encryption program must first be loaded into physical or main memory before being run by the processor. Therefore any software that performs encryption must, at some point, have the key material loaded into the system's main memory. If one has access to that memory, he also has access to the key material.

The trick, of course, is being able to identify uniquely the key among the hundreds of megabytes or even gigabytes of other data.

Recently were published some works that describe the possibility of obtaining encryption keys from the system memory or from live image of the system's volatile memory. Already in 1998 Adi Shamir and Nicko van Someren claimed that keys have higher entropy than the other contents of memory and this feature can be used for searching the keys. They focused on locating asymmetric RSA keys on a disk (Shamir, 1999). Nevertheless, the method may have false positive results due to the existence of other random data in memory (e.g., compressed files) Halderman et al. (2008).

There are two major approaches how the encryption keys can be located in memory or memory image:

- **By Looking for the Keys at a Fixed Address in Memory**: It uses the fact that all installations of an application usually contain the password/key in the same fixed location in the memory.
- **By Locating a Particular Pattern:** In the memory, this pattern is always located at a constant distance from the encryption keys, so by searching this pattern, the encryption keys can be found.

We are currently using both approaches in our work (Balogh, 2011), where we demonstrate a new way of recovering the encryption keys using the recent version of Truecrypt (ver. 7.0a).

Technique for Extracting Symmetric and Asymmetric Keys

In well known asymmetric or symmetric cryptosystem brute force attack on the entire keyspace is computationally infeasible. However, using brute force approach on a limited search space on volatile memory would be an attractive option for extracting keys. To search for 128- bit symmetric key aligned to 4-byte machine word in just 4 GB memory dump implies at most 2^{30} possible key values.

The inherent differences between asymmetric and symmetric keys lie in the key generation. Asymmetric key pairs are related to each other and also have measurable mathematical properties unto themselves. Symmetric keys, however, are relatively small pseudorandom numbers, typically just 128 or 256 bits. So they do not have, at least ostensibly, any measurable mathematical properties other than being cryptographically random. For this reason, only the entropy analysis techniques outlined by Shamir and van Someren (mentioned earlier) for testing the mathematical properties of candidate asymmetric keys can be applied to the symmetric space (Shamir, 1999). Moreover, testing symmetric keys for their entropy or randomness usually falls short because it is much more difficult to get a meaningful entropy value for a typical 128 or 256 bit symmetric key block than it is for a common 1,024 or 2,048 bit asymmetric key block.

The other technique for an asymmetric key identification is by exploiting the opportunity of being able to generate a known plaintext/cipher text pair using the public key and an arbitrary block of plaintext. Although, each trial decryption is relatively expensive, this known plaintext can be used to check each candidate private key in the brute force attack. This technique is usually not possible to employ for symmetric keys identification. However, if the target cipher text is a disk, it is often possible to use known plaintext placed in a standard location for the boot loader. Also file system structures and zero-filled sectors can serve as useful known plaintext values.

But asymmetric algorithms are on the order of 1,000 times slower than symmetric algorithms to use and therefore are unacceptably slow for the frequent cryptographic operations required for high-throughput encrypted disk access.[4]

ROLE OF CRYPTOLOGY

The key search in memory requires a mechanism for locating the target keys. The easiest way to do this is by testing each sequence of bytes while having a pair of known plaintext and cipher text available to see whether it decrypts the cipher text correctly.

In practice, however, it is not as straightforward as it may seem. Although, Kerckhoffs' principle states, that cryptosystem should be secure even if every detail about the system, except the key, is public knowledge, it cannot be applicable in this case. Without fully understanding the cryptosystem details, the challenge of brute forcing the keys in memory is compounded by effectively needing to brute force the encryption implementation at the same time. For example, understanding the details of the mode of operation or details about how initialization vectors (IV) are calculated can be a crucial detail (Kaplan, 2007).

Disk encryption tools have been developed by the cryptographic community and they are specifically designed to block stronger modes of operation. (e.g. XTS mode). It should be also mentioned, that knowing all details of the cryptosystem will not always be needed for identifying the key in a brute force attack. For example, in modes such as cipher block chaining (CBC), the initialization vector only affects a single block of plaintext during decryption, but understanding all details of a cryptosystem is necessary for making practical use of the key for full cipher text decryption.

Some cryptosystem vendors do expose this level of detail about their cryptosystems, but in general, it is not usual. Some vendors appear to be moving toward standards and use well known block modes and cryptographic primitives while others implement their own solutions (discussing the security of own solutions is out the scope of this chapter). But even the obscuring details of a cryptosystem do present real challenge. If we deal with implementation using current information technologies all of the cryptographically important data and instructions must be loaded into memory before they are used. Having enough time available, both the secret key and the exact details of each cryptosystem's operation can be discovered even in the case of the most proprietary and closed implementations (Kaplan, 2007).

Key Schedule Technique

The previous assertion that symmetric keys do not have any measurable mathematical properties other than being cryptographically random is only partially true.

Most modern symmetric key cryptosystems are implemented as product ciphers where several iterations or "rounds," each consisting of a series of transformations are done to achieve the desired properties of confusion and diffusion. Each round uses a different subkey derived from the master key using key schedule algorithm. This is useful for identifying keys in volatile memory for two main reasons:

- The key schedule is in a mathematic relationship between the master key and the subkeys, and
- The key schedule is very often, for performance reasons, used pre-computed and is stored in memory.

Halderman (2008) developed an algorithm (Princeton Key Schedule Technique) which takes advantage of the structure of the key schedule. The algorithm targets the key schedule instead of the key itself, searching for blocks of memory that satisfy (or are close to satisfying) the combinatorial properties of a valid key schedule. They presented the algorithm, for locating encryption keys in memory images, which finds the key even in the presence of decay and they also used their own algorithm for reconstruction of corrupted keys.

Their approach to key reconstruction recovered the key without a need to test the decryption of cipher text. The expanded key schedule forms can be understood as a sort of error correcting code for the key, and the problem of reconstructing a (decayed) key from memory may be recast as the problem of finding the closest code word (valid key schedule) to the data once it has been passed through a channel that has introduced bit errors.

They describe successful key recovery for various disk encryption systems. They have applied some of the tools developed in this paper to attack popular on-the-fly disk encryption systems such BitLocker, FileVault, TrueCrypt, Dm-Crypt, Loop-AES. They tested the TrueCrypt versions 4.3a and 5.0a running on Linux system. We make own research using current version of Truecrypt (TrueCrypt 7.0a) which uses XTS encryption mode. The XTS mode uses two encryption keys - the primary key and the secondary key. We were able to successfully recover primary and secondary encryption key using AESKeyFinder tool developed at the Princeton University (Halderman, 2008) and also our own approach. Through our analysis we have found out that encryption keys on Linux base systems are in the HEAP of the last process created by TrueCrypt (Windows systems stores the keys in Non-paged pool). This fact enables us to reduce the size of the image from several GB (in case of listing the entire contents of the memory dump) to only about 1 or 2 megabytes. And it also reduces the time requirements for obtaining the copy of memory and capturing keys (Balogh, 2011).

Defeating Technique for Key Identification

All of the techniques used for the key identification mentioned above have practical drawbacks that limit their usefulness. In our approach the location of the encryption keys can be changed with a new version of an encryption system, so each new version must be the location tested. The limitations of the Princeton Key Schedule Technique are discussed in work by Halderman, et.al. (2008)

for example, finding the encryption keys where the key schedule must be present in memory. So, the technique will not work if the key schedule subkeys will be stored separately from each other or from the master key. It is possible for example to store them in a complicated structure that breaks up their assumed contiguity in memory like an array of pointers to scheduled keys.

Another defense against key identification but as well for key reconstruction is to transform in some way the key stored in memory. One way is to allocate a buffer with same size as the key K is, fill the buffer with random data R, then store K $\oplus$ R or in even more secures application we can store K $\oplus$ H(R) where H is a hash function such as SHA-256 (Halderman,et.al.,2008).

ROLE OF INFORMATION TECHNOLOGY (CRYPTOSYSTEM IMPLEMENTATION)

As we have mentioned in the section speaking about Role of Cryptology, knowing all details of the cryptosystem will not always be needed for identifying the key in a brute force attack, but understanding all details of a cryptosystem is necessary in order to make practical use of the key for full cipher text decryption.

So, if we already know the cryptosystem-specific details it is a good idea to search for specific details about individual cryptosystem implementation that could potentially be exploited to locate a key in memory more efficiently.

Use of Volatile Memory Structure

Key extraction techniques, discussed up to now, treat memory as a blob of unstructured data. But memory is highly structured. Ignoring this structure is similar to the traditional forensics treating a disk image as an unstructured mass of data and performing data identification or string searches, rather than first making use of all of the

existing file system structures (Kaplan, 2007). By understanding the structure of memory and how encryption packages use it, we can better understand where the keys might be stored.

Some authors propose to parse a number of the operating system's data structures to recover the master key from a variable in a clearly identifiable data structure. (Walters, 2007) They demonstrate the feasibility of extracting keying material using structure of memory. They explore Truecrypt version 4.2a, a popular open source file system encryption utility. Because, on Linux, Truecrypt is implemented as a DeviceMapper target they search in memory image for pointers to mapped_device objects. Each mapped_device object in turn maintains a pointer to a dm_table object that also contains a targets member, which points to the Device Mapper target. Device Mapper targets are instantiated in memory as dm_target objects (each Device Mapper target is in memory represented by dm_target object) that stores the TrueCrypt targets local context information – target_ctx object. After using the *ci* member of this object they have found the *master_key* member of the CRYPTO_INFO object and extracted it (Walters, 2007).

This approach requires a detailed understanding of underlying operating system and access to the source code of the application and kernel (Hargreaves, 2008).

Tobias Klein (2006) used user mode process memory dumps as opposed to full memory dumps to extract digital certificates and RSA keys. He search just the memory owned by the process exploiting the standard storage formats for private keys and SSL certificates (described in PKCS #8 and x509 v3) as opposed to the mathematical properties of the keys. With an understanding that standard storage formats a signature for locating them in memory could be created. Using this signature, he extracted the candidate asymmetric keys in their plaintext form by a simple pattern match.

So, along with understanding of how sensitive data is allocated in drivers, it is possible to develop the techniques that may lead to keys more directly.[5] PKCS #1 specified the widely used format for an RSA private key[6] as an ASN.1 object of type RSAPrivateKey with the following fields: version, modulus n, public exponent e, private exponent d, prime1 p, prime2 q, exponent1 d

mod $(p - 1)$, exponent2 d mod $(q-1)$, coefficient q^{-1} mod p, and optional other information. This object is the standard format for storage and interchange of private keys. The object is packaged using DER encoding, and this suggests two techniques for identifying RSA keys in memory: searching for known contents of the fields, or looking for memory that matches the structure of the DER encoding.

Halderman et al. (2008) tried a new method of searching for identifying features of the DER-encoding. They looked for the sequence identifier (0x30) followed a few bytes later by the DER encoding of the RSA version number and then by the beginning of the DER encoding of the next field (02 01 00 02). With this their method found several copies of the server's private key, and no false positives.

The other approach was used in Hargreaves research (2008) where the linear scan method for key recovery was presented. The authors found that the block where the main and the auxiliary keys are located have a recognizable structure. They developed software which gradually passes the entire image of memory byte by byte and considers each block sized 64 bytes a possible area where the main and the auxiliary encryption keys could occur. They use these potential keys to decrypt the first encrypted block volume. If the decrypted value of the first block is consistent with values which refer to file system FAT16, the system was successfully decrypted and the encryption keys have been found. This work deals only with TrueCrypt version 4.1, while the approach described in work by Walters (2007) dealt with TrueCrypt 4.2a designed for Windows XP. Those Truecrypt versions support only CBC (Cipher Block Chaining) encryption mode and

LWR (Liskov, Rivest and Wagner) mode, unlike the current version of TrueCrypt 7.0a, which uses XTS encryption mode. We have to note that the encryption mode is important due to the number of used encryption keys. The XTS mode uses two encryption keys the primary key and the secondary key. And as noted in Walters' work (2007) the linear scan and the memory data structure parsing technique are susceptible to a malicious adversary. Using some very simple techniques, it is possible to hide from both list-walking and linear scanning techniques. Other limitation for linear scan method is that it relies on keys being stored in consistent patterns in memory.

Reducing the Virtual Address Search Space

Very often, the encryption software vendors implement all of the encryption and decryption operations as kernel component (takes the form of a device driver) so keys reside in kernel memory. As the driver is the component that typically handles the cryptographic operations, (driver essentially intercepts *read* and *write* requests made to a particular device and decrypts or encrypts the requested data on the fly) the first assumption that could be made about the location of the key is that it probably resides in kernel memory. A driver can allocate kernel mode memory in a lot of different ways. This means that on a 32 bit machine, the lower two gigabytes of virtual address space (or three gigabytes if the /3GB switch is applied in the boot.ini) can be eliminated because these memory locations are reserved for user mode memory. The higher two gigabytes of virtual address space (or only one if the /3GB switch is applied) is usually used by kernel. This reduction of at least 50 percent of the search space is certainly a good start.

A brute force attack on the reduced search space represented by kernel memory, while being feasible, still can be very time consuming. As we mentioned before Adi Shamir and Nicko van Someren claimed that keys have higher entropy than the other contents of memory. Although the method may have false positive results due to the existence of other random data in memory we try to use this feature for searching the keys. To achieve a significant reduction in the search time, we can add a lower-bound entropy constraint. To do this we compute a test statistic (using NIST Test Suite) for binary sequences in memory, and compare it with experimentally found threshold value. We got usable value by chaining together results from different entropy tests. In practice, it makes sense only if the entropy calculation is less computationally expensive (per byte) than one decryption cycle and plaintext comparison operations, but that should typically be the case.

The overall reduction in extraction of fake keys in a typical situation as high as 98.56% (example memory analysis is depicted in Figure 1). This enables us to reduce the space for key search considerably.

USE OF MEMORY POOL

Any on-the-fly encryption system decrypts content always when it is being required. As encryption codes and keys are used very frequently, they have to be continuously accessible and should always be present in the memory.

To avoid the keys being paged out to disk cryptosystems vendors, it is wise to allocate memory from the non-paged pool. The pool is a kernel mode equivalent of the user mode heap.

Using pools for discrete, long-term storage allocations, such as relatively static encryption keys, is also Microsoft recommendation.[7]

So, if anybody can figure out the unique pool tag used for the key allocation code path in an encryption driver, it can significantly narrow the search space for keys. They can extract that memory, and hence the key, from the pool. For example we found out that Truecrypt driver stores

Figure 1. Example of test statistic result (Monobit test). Thresholds are used to localize areas that contain encryption keys with high probability.

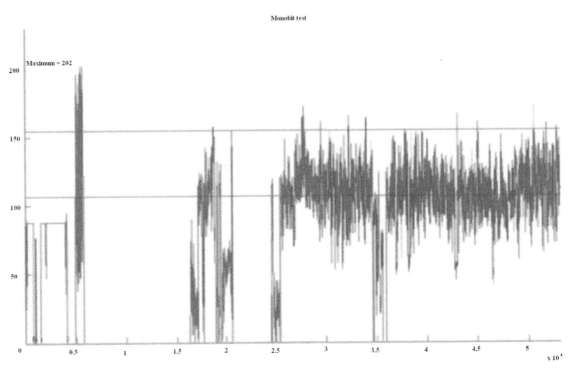

the keys in Non-paged pool. The pool has the tag name "TCMM" (Balogh, 2011).

But authors of the Truecrypt know about this problem with security implementation. In Truecrypt documentation we can read the following:

"TrueCrypt cannot prevent cached passwords, encryption keys, and the contents of sensitive files opened in RAM from being saved unencrypted to memory dump files. Note that when you open a file stored on a TrueCrypt volume, for example, in a text editor, then the content of the file is stored unencrypted in RAM (and it may remain unencrypted in RAM until the computer is turned off). Also note that when a TrueCrypt volume is mounted, its master key is stored unencrypted in RAM"[8].

FUTURE RESEARCH DIRECTIONS

This work is focused on the possibilities of detecting the encryption keys in any abusive attempts as well as in work of forensic analysis. In case of obtaining evidence it is sometimes necessary to have tools that can recognize encrypted evidence. Because encryption is a double-edged sword it is difficult to find appropriate solutions. On one hand, the cipher algorithms makers are trying to achieve the ever greater security, as well as to implementation of those algorithms on the other hand (and again for safety) or rather for the possibility of its abuse to irregular practices we need the safety circumvent (bypasses). The current situation in this area seems like every field to solve tasks in isolation. Cryptology is trying to establish, together with Applied Informatics, the safest solution on the other hand, forensic analysis is looking for ways how it can work around and find the weak spots, which help to break the encryption solution (to use the capability of cryptanalysis and Applied Informatics).

As we can see, although significant progress was made in this area, and many techniques have

been found to detect the encryption key it is always a possibility for slightly independent knowledgeable person to create measures that prevent successful identification of the encryption keys.

Without directly extracted encryption key an investigator's only real option is to recover the suspect's authentication credentials in order to proceed with analysis the encrypted disk image.

These credentials are depending on what methods of authentication are in use. Typically it's in the form of a passphrase but can also include USB tokens, smartcards, and even biometrics. Because the computationally expensive and time-consuming brute force or dictionary attack due to usually strong passphrases (many encryption software now warn or even not allow its users to create weak passphrases) is becoming much less practical, another option, maybe less time-consuming, is applying laws permitting to force the suspect to give the credentials up.

Key disclosure laws already exist in jurisdictions such as the UK,[9] Australia and South Africa which compel individuals to surrender cryptographic keys to law enforcement without regard for the usual common law protection against self-incrimination. These laws have impact not only on public safety posed by terrorist use of encryption technology as claim the law creators or to money laundering prosecution but also to almost any asset protection strategy that attempts to maintain an element of financial privacy such as private banking or family trusts.[10]

The argument does not change as to where the fine line falls between being proactive in regards to terrorism and protecting civil privacy rights. But the choice of using encryption is not always indicative of having something to hide. More often, it involves protection of sensitive data, as in confidential personal information or intellectual business property.

The effectiveness of this option - employing the law in practice - is also in question.

For example terrorists can use master keys on a one-to-one basis, rather than using them to generate pass keys for a series of communications. With a one-to-one key, the authorities could force the terrorist suspect to decrypt only that communication.[11]

Also, as a countermeasure to key disclosure laws, the encryption software vendors have responded by providing their users with deniable encryption technology, which enable a single piece of encrypted data to be decrypted in two or more different ways, creating "plausible deniability"[12]. Some disk encryption software such as BestCrypt, FreeOTFE, and TrueCrypt have begun incorporating the ability to create hidden volumes[13] within an encrypted outer volume or also the Drive Crypt Plus Pack enable users to hide an entire operating system within the free space of another innocuous operating system. If a user is ever forced to divulge the credential, the user can only give the passphrase that unlocks the outer volume or operation system. The authorities would have no way to observe whether another hidden volume or system exists or not. Clearly recognition of encrypted evidence cannot depend on forcing the suspect to give the credentials permitted by law (Kaplan, 2007).

To solve the issues mentioned above, we need to cooperate in multidisciplinary research within many areas. Hypothetically, depending on the implementation, the encryption key could be read directly from memory, and it would be encrypted by a special key depending on actual software installation to provide security. Vendors would provide this specific encryption key for encryption of regular encryption key stored in memory only when required by a Court order or by investigators Of course, there are a lot of technical and legal issues that need to be solved, this is just an example of possible way. Nevertheless, in general, we need to find this kind of solution or a similar resolution.

CONCLUSION

Forensic science is the application of scientific knowledge and uses science & technology to enforce civil and criminal law. It is somewhat difficult to pin down exactly what kind of work a forensic scientist carries out because it includes so many other areas of science. In order to succeed in forensics it is required to apply knowledge from range of fields, topics and methodologies. In this piece of work we mainly focused on digital forensic science. The importance of the interdisciplinary approach in forensic sciences was presented. The typical digital forensic process encompasses the seizure, forensic acquisition and analysis of digital media and the production of a report into collected evidence. The areas that form the digital forensic basis are Computer Science and Criminal Justice. To deal with encrypted evidence knowledge from cryptology and cryptanalysis area is also needed. We proposed the current possibilities of forensic digital analysis as well as a part of cryptanalysis, and methods used for encryption. During the short excursion through known possibilities of how we can capture the encryption keys for decryption the encrypted digital evidence we tried to show how can be the knowledge and awareness of Information technology and Cryptology helpful in this process. To solve the incurred paradox with private security and requirements for forensic digital evidence strong interdisciplinary research, sophisticated key disclosure laws are necessary. Only when meeting these assumptions, it can lead us to right solution that ensures balance between confidentiality and security of information and requirements for a decent non-criminal society.

REFERENCES

Balogh, Š., & Pondelík, M. (2011). Capturing encryption keys for digital analysis. In *Proceedings of The 6th IEEE International Conference on Intelligent Data Acquisition and Advanced Computing Systems*. Prague, Czech Republic: IEEE.

Boileau, A. (2006). *Hit By A Bus: Physical Access Attacks with Firewire Security*. Retrieved from assessment.com

Carrier, B. D., & Grand, J. (2004). A Hardware - Based Memory Acquisition Procedure for Digital Investigations. *The International Journal of Digital Forensics & Incident Response, 1*(1), 50–60.

Carvey, H. (2009). *Windows Forensic Analysis DVD Toolkit* (2nd ed.). Burlington, MA: Syngress.

Casey, E., & Stellatos, G. J. (2008). The Impact of Full Disk Encryption on Digital Forensics. *ACM SIGOPS Operating Systems Review, 42*(3), 93-98. http://doi.acm.org/10.1145/1368506.1368519

Darren, B. (2006). *Low Down and Dirty: Anti-Forensic Rootkits*. Paper presented at Ruxcon 2006. Sydney, Australia.

Davis, M. (2009). *Hacking Exposed Malware & Rootkits*. McGraw-Hill.

Delugré, G. (2010). *Closer to metal: Reverse engineering the Broadcom NetEx-treme's firmware*. Luxembourg: Grand Duchy of Luxembourg.

Denning, D., & Baugh, W. E. (1997). *Cases Involving Encryption in Crime and Terrorism*. Retrieved from http://www.cs.georgetown.edu/~denning/crypto/cases.html

Duflot, L., Perez, Y., Valadon, G., & Levillain, O. (2010). *Can you still trust your network card?* Paper presented at CanSecWest International Conference. Vancouver, Canada.

Garcia, G. (2007). *Forensic physical memory analysis: Overview of tools and techniques*. Helsinki: Telecommunications Software and Multimedia Laboratory.

Halderman, J. A. et al. (2008). Lest we remember: Cold-boot attacks on encryption keys. *Communications of the ACM, 52*(5), 91–98. doi:10.1145/1506409.1506429

Hargreaves, C. H., & Chivers, H. (2008). Recovery of encryption keys from memory using a linear scan. In *Proceedings of Third International Conference on Availability, Reliability and Security*, (pp. 1369-1376). Conference Publishing Services (CPS). http://doi.ieeecomputersociety.org/10.1109/ARES.2008.109

Hoglund, G. (2008). *The Value of Physical Memory for Incident Response*. Retrieved from http://www.hbgary.com/attachments/the-value-of-physical-memory-for-incident-response.pdf

Kaplan, B. (2007). *RAM is Key, Extracting Disk Encryption Keys From Volatile Memory Advisor: Matthew Geiger*. Carnegie Mellon University. Retrieved from http://citeseerx.ist.psu.edu/viewdoc/summary?doi=10.1.1.211.4095

Kornblum, J. D. (2006). Exploiting the Rootkit Paradox with Windows Memory Analysis. *International Journal of Digital Evidence, 5*(1).

Law, F. Y. W., Lai, P. K. Y., Chow, K. P., & Ieong, R. S. C. (2009). *Memory Acquisition: A 2-Take Approach, Computer Science and its Applications, 2009*. Paper presented at CSA '09, the 2nd International Conference. Jeju Island, Korea.

Libster, E., & Kornblum Jesse, D. (2008). A Proposal for an Integrated Memory Acquisition Mechanism. *ACM SIGOPS Operating Systems Review, 42*(3), 14–20. doi:10.1145/1368506.1368510

Shamir, A., & Someren, N. (1999). Playing «hideandseek» with stored keys. *Lecture Notes in Computer Science, 1648,* 118–124. doi:10.1007/3-540-48390-X_9

Walters, A., & Petroni, N. (2007). *Volatools: Integrating volatile memory forensics into the digital investigation process.* Paper presented at Blackhat DC 2007. Arlington, VA. Retrieved from https://www.blackhat.com/presentations/bh-dc-07/Walters/Presentation/bh-dc-07-Walters-up.pdf

Wang, J., Zhang, F., Sun, K., & Stavrou, A. (2011). Firmware-assisted Memory Acquisition and Analysis tools for Digital Forensics. In *Proceedings of IEEE Sixth International Workshop on Systematic Approaches to Digital Forensic Engineering* (SADFE 2011). Oakland, CA: IEEE.

ADDITIONAL READING

Gubanov, Y. (2012). Retrieving Digital Evidence: Methods, Techniques and Issues, www.forensicfocus.com. from http://articles.forensicfocus.com/2012/07/11/retrieving-digital-evidence-methods-techniques-and-issues/

Casey, E. Stellatos, G. J. (2008). The Impact of Full Disk Encryption on Digital Forensics, ACM SIGOPS Operating Systems Review, Volume 42 3, (April 2008), 93-98. DOI= http://doi.acm.org/10.1145/1368506.1368519

Petroni, N. L., Jr., & Walters, A. FATKit: A framework for the extraction and analysis of digital forensic data from volatile system memory, www.sciencedirect.com, from http://dx.doi.org/10.1016/j.diin.2006.10.001

Brian D. Carrier. Risks of live digital forensic analysis, Communications of the ACM - Nextgeneration cyber forensics, Volume 49 Issue 2, February 2006 Pages 56 – 61 from http://dx.doi.org/10.1145/1113034.1113069

Schatz, B. (2007). BodySnatcher: Towards reliable volatile memory acquisition by software. *Digital Investigation, 4S,* S126–S134.

Ring, S., & Cole, E. (2004) Volatile memory computer forensics to detect kernel level compromise. In Lecture notes in Computer Science, 158–170.

Maartmann-Moe, C., Thorkildsen, S. E., & A°rnesc, A. (2009). The persistence of memory: Forensic identification and extraction of cryptographic keys. *Digital Investigation, 6,* S132–S140.

Cohen, F. (2010).Digital Forensic Evidence Examination (2nd ed.). Livermore,CA:ASP Press.452 pages, 504 pages, Publisher: Fred Cohen & Associates, Livermore, CA

Casey, E. (2011) Digital Evidence and Computer Crime, Third Ed.: Forensic Science, Computers, and the Internet, 840 pages, Publisher: Academic Press, 3 Ed. (May 4, 2011), Baltimore, Maryland,USA. ISBN-13: 978-0123742681

Kumar, A. (2003) Discovering passwords in the memory. Online: http://www.infosecwriters.com/text_resources/pdf/Discovering_Passwords_In_Memory.pdf

Pettersson, T. (2007) Cryptographic key recovery from Linux memory dumps. Chaos Communication Camp – Citeseer. http://citeseerx.ist.psu.edu/viewdoc/download?doi=10.1.1.87.7761&rep=rep1&type=pdf

Davidoff, S. (2008) Cleartext Passwords in Linux Memory. Online: http://citeseerx.ist.psu.edu/viewdoc/summary?doi=10.1.1.173.6405

Abbas, A. (2012) Dictionary Attack on TrueCrypt with RIVYERA S3-5000, Parallel and Distributed Systems (ICPADS), 2012 IEEE 18th International Conference. Singapore, IEEE. Online:http://dx.doi.org/10.1109/ICPADS.2012.23

Lowman, S. (2010) The Effect of File and Disk Encryption on Computer Forensics. Online: http://lowmanio.co.uk/share/The Effect of File and Disk Encryption on Computer Forensics.pdf

Lim, S. (2010). Forensic Artifacts Left by Virtual Disk Encryption Tools, Human-Centric Computing (HumanCom), 2010 3rd International Conference, Cebu, Philippines, IEEE

Rutlowska, J. (2007) Beyond the CPU: cheating hardware based RAM forensics. Online: http://invisiblethings.org/papers/cheating-hardware-memoryacquisition-updated.ppt

KEY TERMS AND DEFINITIONS

Digital Evidence: Digital evidence or electronic evidence is any probative information stored or transmitted in digital form that a party to a court case may use at trial. Before accepting digital evidence a court will determine if the evidence is relevant, whether it is authentic and hearsay and whether a copy is acceptable or the original is required.

Digital Forensic: It is a branch of forensic science encompassing the recovery and investigation of material found in digital devices, often in relation to computer crime. The term digital forensics was originally used as a synonym for computer forensics but has expanded to cover investigation of all devices capable of storing digital data.

Disk Encryption: This is a technology which protects information by converting it into unreadable code that cannot be deciphered easily by anyone who is not authorized. Disk encryption uses disk encryption software or hardware to encrypt every bit of data that goes on a disk or disk volume. Disk encryption prevents unauthorized access to data storage.

Key Disclosure Law: A key disclosure law, also known as mandatory key disclosure, is legislation that requires individuals to surrender cryptographic keys to law enforcement. The purpose is to allow access to material for confiscation or digital forensics purposes and use it either as evidence in a court of law or to enforce national security interests.

Memory Acquisition: This is obtaining a verifiably clean snapshot of memory.

Memory Analysis: This is the science of using a memory image to determine information about running programs, the operating system, and the overall state of a computer.

On the Fly Encryption: Also known as Real-time Encryption is a method used by some encryption programs, for example, disk encryption software. "On-the-fly" refers to the fact that the files are accessible immediately after the key is provided, and the entire volume is typically mounted as if it were a physical drive, making the files just as accessible as any unencrypted ones.

Plausible Deniability: A condition in which a subject can safely and credibly deny knowledge of any particular truth that may exist because the subject is deliberately made unaware of existing truth so as to benefit or shield the subject from any responsibility associated through the knowledge of such truth. Plausible deniability actually is a legal concept. It refers to lack of evidence proving an allegation. Standards of proof vary in civil and criminal cases. In civil cases, the standard of proof is "more likely so than not" whereas in a criminal matter, the standard is "beyond a reasonable doubt" If your opponent lacks incontrovertible proof (evidence) of their allegation, you can "plausibly deny" the allegation even though it may be true.

ENDNOTES

[1] PRIVACY RIGHTS CLEARINGHOUSE 2007: A Chronology of Data Breaches, Updated December 31, 2007. DOI= http://www.privacyrights.org/ar/ChronDataBreaches.htm

[2]   BBC 2007: UK's families put on fraud alert. November 20, 2007. DOI=http://www.privacyrights.org/ar/ChronDataBreaches.htm.

[3]   UNITED STATES DISTRICT COURT FOR THE DISTRICT OF VERMONT: Case No. 2:06-mj-91, In Re Boucher 2007 35 (2007), DOI= https://ecf.vtd.uscourts.gov/doc1/1851273316

[4]   Workman, Sean. "Selecting Appropriate Cryptographic Keys." (2005). http://www.primefactors.com/resources/index.cfm?fuseaction=article&rowid=41

[5]   Klein, Tobias. All Your Private Keys are Belong to Us. 2006. <http://www.trapkit.de/research/sslkeyfinder/keyfinder_v1.0_20060205.pdf

[6]   RSA LABORATORIES. PKCS #1 v2.1: RSA cryptography standard. ftp://ftp.rsasecurity.com/pub/pkcs/pkcs-1/pkcs-1v2-1.pdf.

[7]   Memory Management: What Every Driver Writer Needs to Know. Microsoft. 2005. from http://www.microsoft.com/whdc/driver/kernel/mem-mgmt.mspx

[8]   Truecrypt documentation, http://www.truecrypt.org/docs/

[9]   http://www.pcworld.com/article/152221/article.html

[10]   http://www.forbes.com/sites/jonmatonis/2012/09/12/key-disclosure-laws-can-be-used-to-confiscate-bitcoin-assets/

[11]   http://news.cnet.com/2100-7348_3-6073654.html

[12]   http://en.wikipedia.org/wiki/Plausible_deniability

[13]   http://www.truecrypt.org/docs/?s=plausible-deniability

About the Contributors

Sattar B. Sadkhan Al Maliky (S'80, M'06, SM'11) is a professor at the College of Information Technology of the University of Babylon, Hilla, Iraq. He received a PhD degree in Wireless Communication Engineering in 1984, and MSc degree from the VAAZ Academy in Brno, Czech Republic in 1981. His BSc degree in Electrical and Electronic Engineering from Military Engineering College (MTC) in Baghdad, Iraq in 1978. He received a Diploma in Radar Repairing (4 years in 1974) in Iraq, and another Diploma in Cryptography from Switzerland in 1988. His main research interests include wireless digital communication, cryptography, cryptanalysis, security evaluation, information hiding, digital watermarking, ICA, and soft computing techniques. He was the leader of many scientific research groups in different research institutes in Iraq from 1986 – 2003. He is the creator and the chair of IEEE Iraq Section since Sept. 2008. He is the creator and chair of IEEE ComSoc Iraq Chapter since 2011. He is the Editor-in-Chief of 8 international scientific journals, and he is the Associate Editor-in-Chief of 6 international journals, and a member of 20 international scientific journals. He has served as honorable chair, general chair, member of scientific committee, technical program committee chair, and symposium chair for many international conferences. He participated in many international TPCs and several editorial review boards. He has authored or coauthored over 230 papers in refereed international journals and conferences. He has translated 3 books into Arabic. He is the creator and chair of URSI Iraq Committee since 2012. He is the Chair of Iraq Group in BRCORP Institute in 2014.

Nidaa A. Abbas received the M.Sc. degree in "Homogenous Image Compression Using Quadtree" from Computer Science Dept. of the University of Babylon, Iraq in 1999, and the Doctor degree from Computer Science Dept. of the University of Technology, Iraq in 2006, with a thesis titled "A Comparison among Adaptive ICA Algorithms for Blind Speech Signals Separation: Cocktail Party Problem." She has been Vice Chair of IEEE IRAQ Section, Vice Chair of Workshop (ATS-WiMob2009) in Morocco, Editorial Board in IJACT Journal, Member of ICEBE 2009 Program Committee, Member of ICNS 2010 Technical Program Committee, Technical Committee of International Arab Conference of e-Technology, Technical Committee of IAJeT, Editorial Board in *AICIT: The International Association for Information, Culture, Human, and Industry Technology Journal*, and other journals and conferences. Her current research interests include statistical signal processing and neural networks, wavelet, and steganalysis.

* * *

Muzhir Shaban Al-Ani received Ph. D. in Computer and Communication Engineering Technology, ETSII, Valladolid University, Spain, 1994 and is Assistant of Dean at Al-Anbar Technical Institute (1985), Head of Electrical Department at Al-Anbar Technical Institute, Iraq (1985-1988), Head of Computer and Software Engineering Department at Al-Mustansyria University, Iraq (1997-2001), Dean of Computer Science (CS) and Information System (IS) faculty at University of Technology, Iraq (2001-2003). He joined the Electrical and Computer Engineering Department, College of Engineering, Applied Science University, Amman, Jordan, as Associated Professor in 2003. He joined Management Information System Department, Amman Arab University, Amman, Jordan, as Associated Professor, in 2005, and then he joined Computer Science Department at the same university in 2008. He joined the Computer Sciences Department, Anbar University, Anbar, Iraq, as Professor in 2009. His research interests include digital signal processing, parallel processing, digital filters, digital image processing, image compression, computer vision, information hiding, steganography, computer networks, wireless networks, next generation cellular mobile communications, management information systems, management information technology, electronic activities, mobile activities, and related works.

Sufyan T. Faraj Al-Janabi was born in Haditha, Iraq (1971). He obtained his B.Sc. (1992), M.Sc. (1995), and Ph.D. (1999) in Electronic and Communications Engineering from the College of Engineering, Nahrain University in Baghdad. He started as a faculty member in Computer Engineering Dept., University of Baghdad in 1999. Then he became the Head of that department in 2001. From May 2004 – June 2006, he was the Dean of College of Information Technology, Nahrain University. He became the Dean of College of Computer, University of Anbar, Ramadi, from July 2006 – May 2010. His research interests include Internet protocols, information security, and quantum cryptography. Prof. (Faraj) Al-Janabi is the winner of the 1st Award for the Best Research Paper in Information Security from the Association of Arab Universities (AARU), Jordan, 2003. He is also the winner of the ISEP fellowship 2009 and the Fulbright fellowship 2010, USA. He is a member of ACM, ASEE, IACR, and IEEE.

Nadia M. G. Al-Saidi was born in Iraq, 1967. She completed the Bachelor of Science and Master of Science degrees in Applied Mathematics, Applied Sciences Department, University of Technology, Baghdad, Iraq in 1989 and 1995, respectively. In 2003, she received the Ph.D. degree in fractal geometry from the Department of Mathematics and Computer Application Sciences in Al-Nahrain University, Baghdad, Iraq. In 1989, she joined the Applied Sciences Department, University of Technology, as a staff member, then within 1995-1999 as a lecturer, whereas she is now professor since 2011. From 2008-2010, she joined the Institute for Mathematical Research (INSPEM), University Putra Malaysia (UPM) as a post doctorate follow researcher. Her research interests are cryptographic, fractal theory, number theory, and graph theory. She has published more than 52 journal and conference papers.

Ibrahim Almerhag was born in Libya, in 1963. In 2006, he received his PhD in Computing and a MBA in 2002 from Bradford University. He also holds a M.Sc. degree in Electronics and Computer Engineering from the Technical University of Warsaw (1995). He is a graduate of the Electrical and Electronics Engineering Department, University of Benghazi, Libya in Feb. 1986. Formerly, he worked for the University of Sebha and Azzaytuna University. Currently, he is working for the University of Tripoli, Libya, faculty of information technology as an assistant professor. In addition, he is a visiting professor of networking and security at the Libyan Academy Janzur, Libya. His research interests include networking, information security, databases, and image processing.

Jesús B. Alonso-Hernández received the Telecommunication Engineer degree in 2001 and the Ph.D. degree in 2006 from University of Las Palmas de Gran Canaria (ULPGC-Spain) where he is an Associate Professor in the Department of Signal and Communications from 2002. He has researched in different Research Projects. He has numerous papers published in international journals and international conferences. He has been reviewer in different international journals and conferences since 2003. His research interests include signal processing in biocomputing, biometrics, nonlinear signal processing, recognition systems, audio characterization, and data mining. He was a guest editor of special issues for Springer in *Cognitive Computation* and for *Elsevier Neurocomputing*. He was head of excellent network in biomedical engineering in ULPGC. He is Vice-Dean from 2009 to 2013 in School of Telecommunications Engineering in ULPGC.

Luay H. Alswidi has completed his Ph.D (Applied Mathematics) from Mustansyria University, Iraq. His area of Research are Cryptography (asymmetric key cryptography), Mathematical Modeling. He is involved in research and guiding many M.Sc. postgraduate students at the University of Babylon, Education College. He has published many papers in international journals.

Stefan Balogh has been an assistant professor at the Slovak University of Technology Faculty of Electrical Engineering and Information Technology since 2007. He teaches classes in information security, communication protocols, and computer crime. He is completing his Ph.D. in information studies, where his research interests are in the areas of the forensic memory analysis, cryptology, and behavior-based malware detection.

Pierre-Louis Cayrel, after a bachelor degree in mathematics at the University of Avignon, a master in cryptography in Montpellier, and a research master in Limoges, did his PhD at the University of Limoges under the direction of Philippe Gaborit. He defended his PhD in October 2008. His PhD thesis was titled "Design and Optimization of Cryptosystems Based on Error Correcting Codes." Since September 2011, he has been a lecturer at the University Jean Monnet Saint Etienne where he teaches mathematics, computer science, and electronics.

Walid. K. Hamoudi was born in Baghdad, Iraq in 1954. He received his BS degree in physics from Almustansiriya Univ. Baghdad, Iraq, MS degree in Quantum Electronics in 1982 from Essex University, England, and his PhD degree in Laser from the Essex University, England in 1985. He joined the school of Applied Sciences at the University of Technology, Baghdad, Iraq in 1985 as a full time member of staff. Since 1996, he has held a position as Full Professor. He was involved in the optimization of procedures used in laser applications in dermatology, Canada. He joined the faculty of Science and Arts at the University of Nizwa in Oman (2007-2009). His main interests are laser development, industrial and medical laser applications, and nanoscience and laser detectors. Prof. Dr. Walid has published more than 85 journal and conference papers, in addition to 3 university books. He has been an editor in chief of the *Iraqi Journal of Applied Physics* and member of the editorial board of national and international journals.

Sabiha F. Jawad (M'08) has a diploma computer science and an M. Sc. computer science. From 2002 – 2014, she has been a member of staff in Computer Department at Babylon University, Iraq. She has been a member of the Iraqi Computing Union, since Sep. 1996, and is a member of the IEEE institute.

Clyde Meli is an Assistant Lecturer at the Department of Computer Information Systems at University of Malta, Malta. His interests include genetic algorithms, evolutionary information systems, bioinformatics, object-oriented programming, computer graphics, and Web development, search engines, and usability. He is an author of more than 10 papers in technical journals and proceedings of conferences.

Aleksandra Mileva received a Ph.D. in Computer Science in 2010 from the Ss Cyril and Methodius University, Skopje, Republic of Macedonia. She is a fellow of IEEE, and a member of Macedonian CryptoCode Group. Her current research interests includes cryptography, computer and network security, quasigroup theory, algorithms, etc.

Rana S. Mohammed was born in Baghdad, Iraq in 1984. She received the B.Sc. in computer science from Mustansiriyah University, Iraq in 2006 and M.Sc. in computer science from University of Technology, Iraq in 2008, and now she is Ph.D. student in computer science at the University of Babylon, Iraq. She is currently a lecturer in computer science department at the Education College in University of Mustansiriyah. Her main research interests in stream cipher, block cipher, pseudo-random number generator, voice encryption, and chaos theory.

Zuzana Kominkova Oplatkova is an Associate Professor at the Department of Informatics and Artificial Intelligence at Tomas Bata University in Zlin, Czech Republic. Her interests include artificial intelligence, soft computing, artificial neural networks, and evolutionary algorithms. She is an author of more than 80 papers in technical journals and proceedings of conferences.

Marcos del Pozo-Baños received the M.Sc. degree in 2010 in Telecommunication Engineering at University of LasPalmas de Gran Canaria (ULPGC-Spain). He has obtained a M.Sc. in Intelligent Systems and Numerical Application on Engineer at IUSIANI-ULPGC in 2010. He is currently pursuing his Ph.D. degree on electroencephalogram based subject identification. His research lines are neuroscience, biometrics, signal processing, and pattern recognition.

Marek Repka is interested in Information Security, and focused on cryptography and cryptanalysis. He has been specialized in Side-Channel attacks against cryptographic devices. Recently, he has been investigating Side-Channel vulnerabilities in Post-Quantum Cryptography based on Error-Correcting Linear Codes. Marek works for TEMPEST – a provider of IT products and services in Slovakia, which also develops security solutions for a wide range of institutions. He is a (part-time) PhD student at the Institute of Computer Science and Mathematics, Faculty of Electrical Engineering and Information Technology, Slovak University of Technology. The aim of his PhD thesis is the investigation of Side-Channel vulnerabilities and cost-effective countermeasures designing.

Martin Rublík is a senior security consultant at BSP Consulting and a Lecturer at University of Economics in Bratislava. He received his Master's degree at Faculty of Mathematics, Physics and Informatics, Comenius University in Bratislava 2005, and his Ph.D. degree at Faculty of Economic Informatics, University of Economics in Bratislava in 2010. His main area of expertise includes identity management, public key infrastructure, smart cards, network security, and data loss prevention.

Tomas Sochor has been Assistant Lecturer at the University of Ostrava since 1996. He has lectures and seminars in courses focused to computer networks, operating systems, computer security, and associated courses. He is also the instructor of Cisco academy courses. He is an author of more than 30 papers in technical journals and proceedings of conferences.

Jaime R. Ticay-Rivas is a software developer and laboratory staff in Division of Digital Signal Processing at Institute for Technological Development and Innovation in Communications of University of Las Palmas de Gran Canaria (IDeTIC-ULPGC). He received Degree in Telecommunications Engineering specializing in Telecommunication Systems in 2008 at ULPGC (Spain). His research lines are biometrics, data mining, classification systems, environmental intelligence, and parallel computing.

Carlos M. Travieso received the M.Sc. degree in telecommunications, in 1997, and the Ph.D. degree, in 2002, from Polytechnic University of Catalonya and Universidad de Las Palmas de Gran Canaria (ULPGC), respectively. He is an Associate Professor at Universidad de Las Palmas de Gran Canaria, where he has taught since 2005. His research interests lie in the fields of biometrics, pattern recognition, biodiversity conservation, biomedicine applications, and machine learning. He has managed and participated on different European, international, and national research projects. He is member of Image Processing and Artificial Intelligence IASTED Technical Committees. He is reviewer in JCR-ISI International Journals and has been member of PCs for different international conferences. He is Vice-Dean (Head of Graduate and Postgraduate Studies) in School of Telecommunications Engineering in ULPGC.

Eva Volna is an Associate Professor at the Department of Computer Science at University of Ostrava, Czech Republic. Her interests include artificial intelligence, artificial neural networks, evolutionary algorithms, and cognitive science. She is an author of more than 50 papers in technical journals and proceedings of conferences.

M. L. D. Wong received his BEng(Hons) in Electronics and Communication Engineering from the Department of Electrical Engineering and Electronics, University of Liverpool, Merseyside, UK, in 1999. He received his Ph.D. from the same institution in 2004. Dr. Wong joined the School of Engineering, Swinburne University of Technology (Sarawak Campus) (SUTS) as a Lecturer in the same year. Subsequently, he was appointed a Senior Lecturer in 2007 at the same institution. In 2012, Dr. Wong was appointed as an Associate Professor and Deputy Dean, Faculty of Engineering, Computing and Science at Swinburne Sarawak. He was appointed as the Dean of the same Faculty in August 2013. His research interests include statistical signal processing and pattern classification, machine condition monitoring, and VLSI for digital signal processing.

M. M. Wong received her B.E. degree in Computer Systems Engineering from Curtin University of Technology (Sarawak Campus) in 2008. After her first degree, she joined Faculty of Engineering, Computing and Science (FECS) at Swinburne University of Technology (Sarawak Campus) as a Ph.D. research student. She completed her Ph.D in July 2012 with her thesis titled "VLSI Implementation and its Optimisation for Digital Cryptosystems." She is currently a lecturer in the same faculty. Her research interest includes embedded systems and VLSI circuitry designs, cryptographic engineering, optimisation in FPGA-based digital system designs, applications in Galois field arithmetic, and security protocols.

Compilation of References

Abadi, M., Birrell, A., Burrows, M., Dabek, F., & Wobber, T. (2003). Bankable Postage for Network Services. In V. A. Saraswat (Ed.), *Advances in Computing Science – ASIAN 2003: Progamming Languages and Distributed Computation Programming Languages and Distributed Computation* (pp. 72–90). Springer. Retrieved from February 11, 2013, http://link.springer.com/chapter/10.1007/978-3-540-40965-6_6

Abbas. (2009). Speech Scrambling Based on Principal Component Analysis. *MASAUM Journal of Computing, 1*(3), 452-456.

Abbas, A., Khaleel, A., & Tawfeeq, S. (2011). Detection of the photon number splitting attack by using decoy states QKD system. *International Journal of Research and Reviews in Computer Science, 2*(4), 1010–1013.

Abbas, N. (2009). Speech Scrambling Based on Principal Component Analysis. *MASAUM Journal of Computing, 1*(3), 452–456.

Abdulhussein, A. (2012). *Design and implementation of an active quenching driving circuit for single-photon detection.* (M.Sc. Thesis). Institute of Laser for Postgraduate Studies, University of Baghdad, Baghdad, Iraq.

Abdul-Rahman, A. (1997). The pgp trust model. EDI-Forum. *Journal of Electronic Commerce, 10*(3), 27–31.

Abelson, H., Anderson, R., Bellovin, S. M., Benaloh, J., Blaze, M., & Diffie, W. et al. (1997). The Risks of Key Recovery, Key Escrow, and Trusted Third-Party Encryption. *World Wide Web Journal, 2*(3), 241–257.

Abid, A., Nasir, Q., & Elwakil, A. (2009). Implementation of a Chaotically Encrypted Wireless Communication System. In *Proceedings of IEEE international conference on Communications*. IEEExplore-Digital Library. doi:10.1109/ICC.2009.5199069

Adida, B., Hohenberger, S., & Rivest, R. L. (2005). Lightweight encryption for email. In *Proceedings of USENIX steps to reducing unwanted traffic on the internet workshop* (SRUTI) (pp. 93-99). Cambridge, UK: USENIX.

Agrawal, D., & Zeng, Q. (2005). Introduction to Wireless and Mobile Systems (2nd Ed.). Amazon.com.

Ahlavat, R., Gupta, K., & Pal, S. K. (2009). *Fast Generation of Multivariate Quadratic Quasigroups for Cryptographic Applications*. IMA Conference on Mathematics in Defence. Retrieved January 15, 2013 from http://www.ima.org.uk/_db/_documents/defence09_ahlawat_v2.pdf

Ahmad, F., Amri, A., Zuriati, A. Z., & Elissa, N. M. (2009). The Simplicity of Developing Chaotic Regime Cryptography. In *Proceedings of the Second International Conference on Computer and ICCEE '09 Proceedings*[]. ICCEE.]. *Electrical Engineering, 2*, 227–230.

Ahmad, M., Alam, B., & Farooq, O. (2012). Chaos based mixed keystream generation for speech data encryption. [IJCIS]. *International Journal on Cryptography and Information Security, 2*(1), 36–45. doi:10.5121/ijcis.2012.2104

Akhtar, Z., Fumera, G., Marcialis, G. L., & Roli, F. (2012). Evaluation of multimodal biometric score fusion rules under spoof attacks. In *Proceedings of 5th IAPR International Conference on Biometrics* (pp. 402-407). New Delhi, India: IEEE.

Al Swidi, L. (1998). *A study of mathematical structure for cryptanalytic methods of public key cryptosystems and proposing a new cipher systems.* (Unpublished doctoral dissertation). Al- Mustansiriya University, Baghdad, Iraq.

Al-Ani, M. S., & Al-Ani, I. H. (2011). Gait Recognition Based Improved Histogram. *Journal of Emerging Trends in Computing and Information Sciences, 2*(12).

Al-Ani, M. S., & Al-Saidi, M. M. (2011). An Improved Proposed Approach for handwritten Arabic Signature Recognition. *Advances in Computer Science and Engineering, 7*(1), 25–35.

Al-Ani, M. S., & Al-Waisy, A. S. (2011). Multi-View Face Detection Based on Kernel Principal Component Analysis and Kernel Support Vector Techniques.[IJSC]. *International Journal on Soft Computing, 2*(2). doi:10.5121/ijsc.2011.2201

Al-Ani, M. S., & Al-Waisy, A. S. (2012). Face Recognition Approach Based on Wavelet-Curvelet Technique. *Signal & Image Processing*[SIPIJ]. *International Journal (Toronto, Ont.), 3*(2).

Al-Ani, M. S., Mansor, F., & Kalid, W. (2012). *An Efficient Steganographic Algorithm Using Circular Hiding.* Iraqi Association of Information Technology.

Al-Assam, H., & Jassim, S. (2012). Security evaluation of biometric keys. *Computers & Security, 31*, 151–163. doi:10.1016/j.cose.2012.01.002

Alfawaz, M. M., & Woodward, M. E. (2002). *QoS routing with multiple-constraints.* Delson Group Inc. World Wireless Congress.

Alghannam, A., Woodward, M. E., & Melor, J. (2001). Security as a QoS routing issue. In *Proceedings of the 2nd Annual Postgraduate Symposium* (PGNet'01). Liverpool John Moores University.

Alkahtani, A. M., Woodward, M. E., & Al-Begain, K. (2003). The analytic hierarchy process applied to best effort QoS routing with multiple metrics: a comparative evaluation. *Personal Mobile Communications Conference 5th European. Conf. Publ., 492*, 539-544.

Alleaume, R. (Ed.). (2007). SECOQC white paper on quantum key distribution and cryptography. Secoqc-WP-v5, Version 5.1.

Almerhag, I. A., & Woodward, M. E. (2005a). Security as a Quality of Service Routing Problem. In *Proceedings of the 2005 ACM conference on Emerging network experiment and technology.* ACM.

Almerhag, I. A., & Woodward, M. E. (2005b). *Quality of service routing metrics based on selected aspects of network security.* Paper presented at Fourth HET-NET's05. Ilkley, UK.

Almerhag, I. A., & Woodward, M. E. (2005c). *Key-size as a QoS routing metric.* Paper presented at Sixth Informatics Workshop. Bradford, UK.

Al-Saidi, N., Said, M. R., & Othman, W. A. (2012). Password Authentication Based on Fractal Coding Scheme. *Journal of Applied Mathematic*

Alvarez, G., & Li, S. (2006). Some Basic Cryptographic Requirements for Chaos-Based Cryptosystems. *Bifurcation and Chaos, 16*(8), 2129–2151. doi:10.1142/S0218127406015970

Alves, R. T., Delgado, M., Lopes, H. S., & Freitas, A. A. (2004). An artificial immune system for fuzzy-rule induction in data mining. *Lecture Notes in Computer Science, 3242*, 1011–1020. doi:10.1007/978-3-540-30217-9_102

Amann, B., Vallentin, M., Hall, S., & Sommer, R. (2012). *Extracting Certificates from Live Traffic: A Near Real-Time SSL Notary Service. TR-12-014.* ICSI.

Amari, S., & Cichocki, A. (1998). Adaptive Blind Signal Processing- Neural Network Approaches. *IEEE, 86*(10), 2026-2048.

Ambalakat, P. (2005). Security of Biometric Authentication Systems. In *Proceedings of 21st Computer Science Seminar.* Academic Press.

Amparo, F. (2003). Aspects of Pseudorandomness in Nonlinear Generators of Binary Sequences. *Lecture Notes in Computer Science, 2841*, 329–341. doi:10.1007/978-3-540-45208-9_26

Angel, R., et al. (2010). A Fuzzy Logic-based Information Security Control Assessment for Organization. In *Proceedings of 2012 IEEE Conference on Open Systems* (ICOS). IEEExplore Digital Library.

Anil, K. J., & Ross, A. (2002). Learning User-Specific Parameters in a Multibiometric System. In *Proc. International Conference on Image Processing (ICIP)*. Rochester, NY: ICIP.

Appenzeller, G., Martin, L., & Schertler, M. (2009). *Identity-Based Encryption Architecture and Supporting Data Structures* (RFC 5408). Retrieved from http://tools.ietf.org/html/rfc5408

Ariffin, M., & Abu, N. (2009). Cryptosystem: A Chaos Based Public Key Cryptosystem. *International Journal of Cryptology Research*, *1*(2), 149–163.

Arindam, S., & Mandal, J. (2012). Secured Wireless Communication Using Fuzzy Logic based High speed Public Key cryptography (FLHSPKC).[IJACSA]. *International Journal of Advanced Computer Science and Applications*, *3*(10), 137–145.

Arlot, S., & Celisse, A. (2010). A survey of cross-validation procedures for model selection. *Statistics Surveys*, *4*, 40–79. doi:10.1214/09-SS054

Arnbak, A., & Van Eijk, N. (2012). *Certificate Authority Collapse: Regulating Systemic Vulnerabilities in the HTTPS Value Chain*. TRPC. Retrieved from http://ssrn.com/abstract=2031409

Ashlock, D. (2006). *Evolutionary Computation for Modeling and Optimization*. Berlin: Springer-Verlag.

Ashtiyani, M., Birgani, P., & Madahi, S. (2012). Speech Signal Encryption Using Chaotic Symmetric Cryptography. *J. Basic. Appl. Sci. Res.*, *2*(2), 1678–1684.

Asim, M., & Jeoti, V. (2008). Efficient and Simple Method for Designing Chaotic S-Boxes. *ETRI Journal*, *30*(1), 170–172. doi:10.4218/etrij.08.0207.0188

Atici, M., & Stinson, D. (1996). Universal hashing and multiple authentication. *Lecture Notes in Computer Science*, *1109*, 16–30. doi:10.1007/3-540-68697-5_2

Avanzi, R., Hoerder, S., Page, D., & Tunstall, M. (2011). Side-channel attacks on the McEliece and Niederreiter public-key cryptosystems. *Journal of Cryptographic Engineering*, *1*(4), 271–281. doi:10.1007/s13389-011-0024-9

Back, A. (1997). *Hashcash postage implementation announcement*. Retrieved February 14, 2013, from http://www.hashcash.org/papers/announce.txt

Bäck, T., Fogel, D., & Michalewicz, Z. (Eds.). (1997). *Handbook of Evolutionary Computation*. Oxford, UK: Oxford Univ. Press. doi:10.1887/0750308958

Baek, J., Newmarch, J., Safavi-Naini, R., & Susilo, W. (2004). A Survey of Identity-Based Cryptography. In *Proceedings of Australian Unix Users Group Annual Conference* (pp. 95-102). Melbourne: AUUG.

Bakeva, V., & Dimitrova, V. (2010). Some Probabilistic Properties of Quasigroup Processed Strings useful for Cryptanalysis. In M. Gušev & P. Mitrevski (Eds.), *Proceedings of ICT Innovation 2010* (pp. 61-70). Berlin: Springer.

Bakeva, V., & Ilievska, N. (2009). A probabilistic model of error-detecting codes based on quasigroups. *Quasigroups and Related Systems*, *17*(2), 151–164.

Bakhtiari, S., Safavi-Naini, R., & Pieprzyk, J. (1997). A Message Authentication Code based on Latin Square. In V. Varadharajan, J. Pieprzyk, & Y. Mu (Eds.), *Proceedings of ACISP'97*, (LNCS), (vol. 1270, pp. 194-203). Berlin: Springer.

Baldi, M., Bianchi, M., Chiaraluce, F., Rosenthal, J., & Schipani, D. (2011). A variant of the McEliece cryptosystem with increased public key security. In *Proceedings of WCC 2011 - Workshop on coding and cryptography* (pp. 173-182). Paris, France: Inria.

Baldi, M., Bianchi, M., Chiaraluce, F., Rosenthal, J., & Schipani, D. (2011). Enhanced public key security for the McEliece cryptosystem. *CoRR*. Retrieved August 11, 2011, from http://arxiv.org/abs/1108.2462

Baldi, M., Bodrato, M., & Chiaraluce, F. (2008). A New Analysis of the McEliece Cryptosystem Based on QC-LDPC Codes. In *Proceedings of 6th International Conference, SCN 2008* (LNCS), (pp. 246-262). Amalfi, Italy: Springer.

Bal, H. (2005). *Bioinformatics: Principles and Applications*. New Delhi: Tata McGraw-Hill.

Balogh, Š., & Pondelík, M. (2011). Capturing encryption keys for digital analysis. In *Proceedings of The 6th IEEE International Conference on Intelligent Data Acquisition and Advanced Computing Systems*. Prague, Czech Republic: IEEE.

Baltatu, M., Lioy, A., Maino, F., & Mazzocchi, D. (2000). Security issues in management, control and routing protocols. *Computer Networks*, *34*, 881–894. doi:10.1016/S1389-1286(00)00159-6

Bardis, N., Markovsky, A., & Andrikou, D. (2004). *Method for designing pseudorandom binary sequences generators on Nonlinear Feedback Shift Register (NFSR)*. Retrieved August 8, 2013 from http://www.wseas.us/e-library/conferences/athens2004/papers/487-804.pdf

Barker, E., Barker, W., Burr, W., Polk, W., & Smid, M. (2007). *Recommendation for Key Management-Part 1: General (Revised) (Special Publication 800-57 Part 1 Rev. 3). National Institute of Standards and Technology*. NIST.

Barreto, P. S. L. M., Misoczki, R., & Simplício, M. A. Jr. (2011). One-Time Signature Scheme from Syndrome Decoding over Generic Error-Correcting Codes. *Journal of Systems and Software*, *84*(2), 198–204. doi:10.1016/j.jss.2010.09.016

Battey, M., & Parakh, A. (2012). A Quasigroup Based Random Number Generator for Resource Constrained Environments. *IACR Cryptology ePrint Archive. Report*, *2012*, 471.

Bayler, G. (2008). *Penetrating Bayesian Spam Filters*. Saarbrucken: VDM Verlag.

Beauregard, D. (1996). *Efficient Algorithms for Implementing Elliptic Curve Public-key Schemes*. (Master's Thesis). Worcester Polytechnic Institute, Worcester, MA.

Bechman-Pasquinucci, H., & Pasquinucci, A. (2005). Quantum key distribution with trusted quantum relay. *arXiv:* quant-ph/0505089v1.

Becker, A., Joux, A., May, A., & Meurer, A. (2012). Decoding random binary linear codes in 2n/20: How 1+1=0 improves information set decoding. In *Proceedings of Advances in Cryptology - EUROCRYPT (LNCS)* (Vol. 7237, pp. 520–536). Cambridge, UK: Springer.

Bednara, M., Daldrup, M., von zur Gathen, J., Shokrollahi, J., & Teich, J. (2002). Reconfigurable Implementation of Elliptic Curve Crypto Algorithms. In *Proceedings of International Parallel and Distributed Processing Symposium, IPDPS 2002* (pp. 157 -164). Fort Lauderdale, FL: IEEE Computer Society.

Beker, H., & Piper, F. (1985). *Secure Speech Communications*. Elsevier Science & Technology Books.

Beker, H., & Piper, F. (1982). *Cipher System: The Protection of Communications*. Northwood Publication.

Bell & Sejnowski. (1995). An information- maximization approach to blind separation and blind deconvolution. *Neural Computation*, *7*(6), 1129–1159.

Belousov, V. D. (1972). n-ary quasigroups. Kishinev, Moldova: Ştiinţa.

Belyavskaya, G. B., Izbash, V. I., & Mullen, G. L. (2005). Check character systems using quasigroups: II. *Designs, Codes and Cryptography*, *37*(3), 405–419. doi:10.1007/s10623-004-4033-x

Belyavskaya, G. B., Izbash, V. I., & Shcherbacov, V. A. (2003). Check character systems over quasigroups and loops. *Quasigroups and Related Systems*, *10*, 1–28.

Bennett, C. H. (1994), Interferometric quantum cryptographic key distribution system. *US Patent* No. 5,307,410.

Bennett, C. H., & Brassard, G. (1984). Quantum cryptography: public key distribution and coin tossing. In *Proceedings of International Conference on Computers, Systems and Signal Processing*. Academic Press.

Bennett, C. H., Bessette, F., Brassard, G., Salvail, L., & Smolin, J. (1992). Experimental quantum cryptography. *Journal of Cryptology*, *5*(3), 3–28.

Bennett, C. H., Brassard, G., Crepeau, C., & Maurer, U. (1995). Generalized privacy amplification. *IEEE Transactions on Information Theory*, *41*, 1915–1923. doi:10.1109/18.476316

Bennett, C. H., Brassard, G., & Roberts, J.-M. (1988). Privacy amplification by public discussion. *SIAM Journal on Computing*, *17*(2), 210–229. doi:10.1137/0217014

Benson Edwin Raj, S., & Thomson Santhosh, A. (2009). A Behavioral Biometric Approach Based on Standardized Resolution in Mouse Dynamics. *International Journal of Computer Science and Network Security*, *9*(4).

Berlekamp, E. R. (1971). Factoring polynomials over large finite fields. In *Proceedings of the second ACM symposium on Symbolic and algebraic manipulation (SYMSAC '71)*. New York: ACM.

Berlekamp, E., McEliece, R., & van Tilborg, H. (1978). On the inherent intractability of certain coding problems. *IEEE Transactions on Information Theory*, *24*(3), 384–386. doi:10.1109/TIT.1978.1055873

Berndt, M., & Rainer, G. (1986). *Linear Filtering of Nonlinear Shift-Register Sequences*. Retrieved August 8, 2013 from http://citeseerx.ist.psu.edu/viewdoc/download?doi=10.1.1.86.7961&rep=rep1&type=pdf

Bernstein, D. J. (2010). Grover vs. McEliece. In *Proceedings of Post-Quantum Cryptography, Third International Workshop, PQCrypto 2010,* (pp. 73-80). Darmstadt, Germany: Springer.

Bernstein, D. J. (2011a). List decoding for binary Goppa codes. In *Proceedings of Coding and cryptology-third international workshop, IWCC 2011,* (LNCS), (vol. 6639, pp. 62-80). Qingdao, China: Springer.

Bernstein, D. J. (2011b). Simplified high-speed high-distance list decoding for alternant codes. In *Proceedings of the 4th international conference on Post-Quantum Cryptography. PQCrypto'11* (pp. 200-216). Taipei, Taiwan: Springer.

Bernstein, D. J., Lange, T., & Peters, C. (2008). Attacking and Defending the McEliece Cryptosystem. In *Proceedings of the 2nd International Workshop on Post-Quantum Cryptography PQCrypto '08* (pp. 31-46). Cincinnati, OH: Springer Berlin Heidelberg.

Bernstein, D. J., Lange, T., & Peters, C. (2010). Wild McEliece. *Cryptology ePrint Archive: Report 2010/410*. Retrieved Jul 22, 2010, from http://eprint.iacr.org/2010/410

Bernstein, D. J., Lange, T., & Peters, C. (2011a). Wild McEliece Incognito. In *Proceedings of Post-Quantum Cryptography - 4th International Workshop, PQCrypto 2011* (pp. 244-254). Taipei, Taiwan: Springer.

Bernstein, D. J., Lange, T., & Peters, C. (2011b). Smaller decoding exponents: ball-collision decoding. In *Proceedings of 31st Annual Cryptology Conference,* (pp. 743-760). Santa Barbara, CA: Springer.

Bernstein, D. J., Lange, T., Peters, C., & Schwabe, P. (2011). Faster 2-regular Information-Set Decoding. In *Proceedings of the Third international conference on Coding and cryptology (IWCC'11)* (pp. 81-98). Qingdao, China: Springer.

Bernstein, D. J., Lange, T., Peters, C., & Schwabe, P. (2011). Really Fast Syndrome-Based Hashing. *Cryptology ePrint Archive: Report 2011/074*. Retrieved February 14, 2011, from http://eprint.iacr.org/2011/074

Bernstein, D. J., Buchmann, J., & Dahmen, E. (Eds.). (2008). *Post-Quantum Cryptography*. Springer.

Berry, M., & Mainieri, R. (1996). A brief history of chaos. Chaos with us. *cns.physics.gatech.edu*. Retrieved from http://www.cns.gatech.edu/~predrag/courses/PHYS-7224-07/appendHist.pdf

Beuchat, J.-L., Sendrier, N., Tisserand, A., & Villard, G. (2004). FPGA Implementation of a Recently Published Signature Scheme. *Research Report INRIA*. Retrieved 2004, from http://hal.inria.fr/docs/00/07/70/45/PDF/RR-5158.pdf

Bharat, B. (2007). Introduction to Nanotechnology. In *Springer Handbook of Nanotechnology*. Springer.

Biasi, F. P., Barreto, P. S. L. M., Misoczki, R., & Ruggiero, W. V. (2012). Scaling efficient code-based for embedded platforms. *CoRR*. Retrieved December 18, 2012, from http://arxiv.org/abs/1212.4317

Biermann, E., Cloete, E., & Venter, L. M. (2001). A Comparison of Intrusion Detection Systems. *Computers & Security*, *20*(8), 676–683. doi:10.1016/S0167-4048(01)00806-9

Biggio, B., Akhtar, Z., Fumera, G., Marcialis, G. L., & Roli, F. (2012). Security evaluation of biometric authentication systems under real spoofing attacks. *IET Biometrics*, *1*(1), 11–24. doi:10.1049/iet-bmt.2011.0012

Biswas, B., & Sendrier, N. (2008). McEliece Cryptosystem Implementation: Theory and Practice. In *Proceedings of Post-Quantum Cryptography Second International Workshop, PQCrypto 2008* (pp. 47-62). Cincinnati, OH: Springer.

Blackledge, J. (2010). *Cryptography using chaos*. Warson University. Retrieved from http://www.konwersatorium.pw.edu.pl/wyklady/2010_VLZ7_02_wyklad.pdf

Blackledge, J. (2008). Multi-algorithmic Cryptography using Deterministic Chaos with Applications to Mobile Communications. *ISAST Transactions on Electronics and Signal Processing*, *2*(1), 23–64.

Blair, M., & Homa, D. (2003). As easy to memorize as they are to classify: The 5–4 categories and the category advantage. *Memory & Cognition*, *31*(8), 1293–1301. doi:10.3758/BF03195812 PMID:15058690

Blank, N. (2008). *Fighting SPAM: SMTP auth attacks from spammers on the rise*. Retrieved October 10, 2012, from http://www.allspammedup.com/2008/05/fighting-spam-smtp-auth-attacks-from-spammers-on-the-rise/

Blum, M., & Goldwasser, S. (1985). An Efficient Probabilistic Public Key Encryption Scheme which Hides All Partial Information. In Proceedings of Advances in Cryptology - CRYPTO '84, (pp. 289–299). Springer.

Bohy, N. Samyde, & Quisquater. (2003). Principal and Independent Component Analysis for Cryptographic systems with Hardware Unmasked Units. In *Proceedings of e-Smart 2003*. Retrieved from http://130.203.133.150/viewdoc/download?doi=10.1.1.94.53&rep=rep1&type=pdf

Boileau, A. (2006). *Hit By A Bus: Physical Access Attacks with Firewire Security*. Retrieved from assessment.com

Boldyreva, A., Vipul, G., & Virendra, K. (2008). Identity-based encryption with efficient revocation. In *Proceedings of the 15th ACM conference on Computer and communications security* (pp. 417-426). Alexandria: ACM.

Bolle, R. M., Connell, J. H., Pankanti, S., Ratha, N. K., & Senior, A. W. (2003). *Guide to biometrics*. Springer.

Bonissone, P. P. (2002). Hybrid Soft Computing for Classification and Prediction Applications. In *Proceedings of the First International Conference on Computing in an Imperfect World* (pp. 352-353). Berlin: Springer-Verlag.

Bopardikar, A. (1995). *Speech Encryption Using Wavelet Packets*. (Master thesis). department of electrical communication engineering, Indian Institute of Science, India.

Bouwmeester, D., Ekert, A., & Zeilinger, A. (2000). *The Physics of Quantum Information*. Springer. doi:10.1007/978-3-662-04209-0

Brandau, M. (2008). *Implementation of a real-time voice encryption system*. (Master Thesis). University of Applied Sciences Cologne.

Brassard, G., & Salvail, L. (1994). Secret-key reconciliation by public discussion. *Lecture Notes in Computer Science*, *765*, 410–423. doi:10.1007/3-540-48285-7_35

Briegel, H.-J., Dur, W., Cirac, J. I., & Zoller, P. (1998). Quantum repeaters: The role of imperfect local operations in quantum communication. *Physical Review Letters*, *81*, 5932–5935. doi:10.1103/PhysRevLett.81.5932

Bubeck, U., & Sanchez, D. (2003). *Biometric Authentication* (Term Project CS574 Spring 2003). San Diego State University. Retrieved from http://www.ub-net.de/cms/fileadmin/uwe/doc/bubeck-biometrics.pdf

Burton Computer Corporation. (n.d.). *SpamProbe - A Fast Bayesian Spam Filter*. Retrieved February 14, 2013, from http://spamprobe.sourceforge.net/

Buttler, W., Lamoreaux, S., Torgerson, J., Nickel, G., Donahue, C., & Peterson, C. (2005). *Fast, efficient error reconciliation for quantum cryptography*. Univ. of California, Los Alamos National Lab., *arXiv:* quant-ph/0203096.

Calixto, M. (2009). Quantum computation and cryptography: an overview. *Natural Computing*, *8*(4), 663–679. doi:10.1007/s11047-008-9094-8

Callas, J., & Gutmann, P. (2013). *How much does it cost to start a root CA?* Retrieved from http://lists.randombit.net/pipermail/cryptography/2013-January/thread.html#3575

Camp, L. J., & Liu, D. (2006). *Proof of Work (Cannot, Can, Does Currently) Work*. Retrieved February 11, 2013, from http://papers.ssrn.com/abstract=2118235

Camp, J., Asgharpour, F., & Liu, D. (2007). Experimental Evaluations of Expert and Non-expert Computer Users' Mental Models of Security Risks.[Pittsburgh, PA: WEIS.]. *Proceedings of WEIS*, *2007*, 1–24.

Camram Antispam System. (2009). *SourceForge*. Retrieved February 14, 2013, from http://sourceforge.net/projects/camram/

Canetti, R. (2001). Universally composable security: A new paradigm for cryptography protocols. In *Proceeding of FOCS'01*, (pp. 136-145). FOCS.

Cappelli, R., Maio, D., Maltoni, D., Wayman, J. L., & Jain, A. K. (2006). Performance Evaluation of Fingerprint Verification Systems. *IEEE Transactions on Pattern Analysis and Machine Intelligence, 28*(1). doi:10.1109/TPAMI.2006.20 PMID:16402615

Cardoso. (1999). High-order contrasts for independent component analysis. *Neural Computation, 11*(1), 157-192.

Cardoso, J. (1998). Blind Signal Separation: Statistical Principles. *Proceedings of the IEEE, 86*(10), 2009–2025. doi:10.1109/5.720250

Cardoso, J. F., & Souloumiac, A. (1993). Blind beamforming for non-Gaussian signals. In *Radar and Signal Processing*[). IET.]. *IEE Proceedings. Part F. Communications, Radar and Signal Processing, 140*(6), 362–370. doi:10.1049/ip-f-2.1993.0054

Carlos, A., Gaborit, P., & Schrek, J. (2011). A new zero-knowledge code based identification scheme with reduced communication. *CoRR*. Retrieved November 7, 2011, from http://arxiv.org/abs/1111.1644

Carrier, B. D., & Grand, J. (2004). A Hardware - Based Memory Acquisition Procedure for Digital Investigations. *The International Journal of Digital Forensics & Incident Response, 1*(1), 50–60.

Carter, J., & Wegman, M. (1979). Universal classes of hash functions. *Journal of Computer and System Sciences, 18*, 143–154. doi:10.1016/0022-0000(79)90044-8

Carvey, H. (2009). *Windows Forensic Analysis DVD Toolkit* (2nd ed.). Burlington, MA: Syngress.

Casey, E., & Stellatos, G. J. (2008). The Impact of Full Disk Encryption on Digital Forensics. *ACM SIGOPS Operating Systems Review, 42*(3), 93-98. http://doi.acm.org/10.1145/1368506.1368519

Cayrel, P.-L. (2012). Code-based cryptosystems: implementations. *cayrel.net: Code based cryptography*. Retrieved 2012, from http://cayrel.net/research/code-based-cryptography/code-based-cryptosystems/

Cayrel, P.-L., & Dusart, P. (2010). McEliece/Niederreiter PKC: Sensitivity to Fault Injection. In *Proceedings of FEAS, 2010 5th International Conference on Future Information Technology* (pp. 1-6). Busan, Korea: IEEE.

Cayrel, P.-L., Alaoui, S. M. E. Y., Hoffmann, G., & Véron, P. (2012). An improved threshold ring signature scheme based on error correcting codes. In *Proceedings of Arithmetic of Finite Fields - 4th International Workshop, WAIFI 2012,* (pp. 45-63). Bochum, Germany: Springer.

Cayrel, P.-L., El Yousfi, M., Hoffmann, G., Meziani, M., & Niebuhr, R. (2011). Recent progress in code-based cryptography. In *Proceedings of Information Security and Assurance - International Conference,* (pp. 21-32). Brno, Czech Republic: Springer.

Cayrel, P.-L., Gaborit, P., & Prouff, E. (2008). Secure Implementation of the Stern Authentication and Signature Schemes for Low-Resource Devices. In *Proceedings of 8th IFIP WG 8.8/11.2 International Conference, CARDIS 2008,* (pp. 191-205). London, UK: Springer.

Cayrel, P.-L., Hoffmann, G., & Persichetti, E. (2012). Efficient Implementation of a CCA2-Secure Variant of McEliece Using Generalized Srivastava Codes. In *Proceedings of 15th International Conference on Practice and Theory in Public Key Cryptography,* (pp. 138-155). Darmstadt, Germany: Springer.

Cayrel, P.-L., Véron, P., & Alaoui, S. M. E. Y. (2011). A zero-knowledge identification scheme based on the q-ary syndrome decoding problem. In *Proceedings of the 17th international conference on Selected areas in cryptography SAC'10* (171-186). Waterloo, Canada: Springer.

Cecilia, B. (Ed.). (2009). Security: A Multidisciplinary Normative Approach. BrillOnline.com Publishers.

Cederlof, J. (2005). *Authentication in quantum key growing*. (M. Sc. Thesis). Department of Applied Mathematics, Linkopings University, Sweden.

Chakrabarti, S. Pal1, S. K., & Gangopadhyay, G. (2012). An Improved 3-Quasigroup based Encrytion Scheme. In S. Markovski, & M. Gušev (Eds.), *Web Proceedings of ICT Innovations 2012* (pp. 173-184). ICT. Retrieved January 15, 2013 from http://ictinnovations.org/2012/htmls/papers/WebProceedings2012.pdf

Chandramouli, R., & Scott, R. (2009). Open issues in secure DNS deployment. *IEEE Security & Privacy, 7*(5), 29–35. doi:10.1109/MSP.2009.129

Charles, H. B., & Gilles, B. (1984). Quantum cryptography: public key distribution and coin tossing. In *Proceedings of the International Conference on Computers, Systems and Signal Processing*. Academic Press.

Charles, H. B. (1992). Quantum cryptography using any two non-orthogonal states. *Physical Review Letters*, *68*(21), 3121–3124. doi:10.1103/PhysRevLett.68.3121

Charles, H. B., Francois, B., Louis, S., & John, S. (1992). Experimental quantum cryptography. *J. Cryptol.*, *5*(1), 3–28.

Charles, H. B., Gilles, B., Claude, C., Richard, J., Asher, P., & William, K. W. (1993). Teleporting an unknown quantum state via dual classical and Einstein-Podolsky-Rosen channels. *Physical Review Letters*, *70*(13), 1895–1899. doi:10.1103/PhysRevLett.70.1895

Charles, P., & Shari, L. (2003). *Security in Computing*. Prentice Hall Professional.

Chelton, W., & Benaissa, M. (2008). Fast Elliptic Curve Cryptography on FPGA. *IEEE Transactions on Very Large Scale Integration VLSI Systems*, *16*(2), 198–205. doi:10.1109/TVLSI.2007.912228

Chen, Y., Knapskog, S. J., & Gligoroski, D. (2010). Multivariate quadratic quasigroups (MQQs), Construction, bounds and complexity. In *Proceedings of Inscrypt, 6th International Conference on Information Security and Cryptology*. Science Press of China.

Chen, G., Mao, Y., & Chui, C. (2004). A symmetric image encryption scheme based on 3D chaotic cat maps. *Chaos, Solitons, and Fractals*, *21*, 749–761. doi:10.1016/j.chaos.2003.12.022

Chen, J., Gwu, Xu, L., Gu, X., Ewu, & Zeng, H. (2009). Stable quantum key distribution with active polarization control based on time-division multiplexing. *New Journal of Physics*, *11*(6). doi:10.1088/1367-2630/11/6/065004

Chen, L., Harrison, K., Moss, A., Soldera, D., & Smart, N. P. (2002). Certification of public keys within an identity based system. In *Proceedings of Information Security* (pp. 322–333). Springer. doi:10.1007/3-540-45811-5_25

Chesnes, M. (2011). *Dynamical Systems and Chaos: Mathematics and Economic Applications. Mathematics Senior Exercise*. Kenyon College.

Chien, R. (1964). Cyclic decoding procedures for Bose-Chaudhuri-Hocquenghem codes. *IEEE Transactions on Information Theory*, *10*(4), 357–363. doi:10.1109/TIT.1964.1053699

Chizhov, I. V., & Borodin, M. A. (2013). The failure of McEliece PKC based on Reed-Muller codes. *Cryptology ePrint Archive: Report 2013/287*. Retrieved May 15, 2013, from http://eprint.iacr.org/2013/287

Choi, B., & Pak, A. (2008). Multidisciplinarity, inter-disciplinarity and transdisciplinarity in health research, services, education and policy: Discipline, inter-discipline distance, and selection of discipline. *Clinical and Investigative Medicine. Medecine Clinique et Experimentale*, (31): 41–48. PMID:18312747

Cisco Systems Inc. (2001). *Network security: An executive overview*. Retrieved from http://www.managednetworks.com/docs/networksecurityoverview.pdf

Cisco Systems Inc. (2002). *Internetworking technologies handbook*. Retrieved from http://www.cisco.com/univercd/cc/td/doc/cisintwk/ito doc/

Cisco Systems Inc. (2005). *Cisco IOS Security Configuration Guide*, Release 12.2.

Clark, A. (1998). *Optimization Heuristics for Cryptology*. (PhD thesis). Queensland University of Technology.

Clausen, C., Usmani, I., Bussieres, F., Sangouard, N., Afzelius, M., & de Riedmatten, H. et al. (2011). Quantum storage of photonic entanglement in a crystal. *Nature*, *496*, 508–512. doi:10.1038/nature09662 PMID:21228774

Clinton, G. (2009). *Integrating the disciplines: Successful interdisciplinary subjects*. Austria Centre for the Study of Higher Education publication.

CloudShark. (2013, January 29). *MITM Attack Capture Shared Through CloudShark*. Retrieved from http://appliance.cloudshark.org/news/cloudshark-in-the-wild/mitm-attack-capture-shared-through-cloudshark/

Collins, D., Gisin, N., & de Riedmatten, H. (2003). Quantum relays for long distance quantum cryptography. *arXiv: quant-ph/0311101*.

Comon & Jutten. (2010). Introduction. In P. Comon, & C. Jutten (Eds.), *Handbook of Blind Source Separation Independent Component Analysis and Applications* (pp. 1–22). Oxford, UK: Elsevier.

Cormack, G. V., & Lynam, T. R. (2005). *TREC 2005 Spam Track Overview*. Retrieved January, 10, 2013, from http://plg.uwaterloo.ca/~gvcormac/trecspmtrack05

Cormack, G. V., María, J., Sánz, E. P., & Hidalgo, G. (2007). Spam filtering for short messages. In *Proceedings of the 16th ACM conference on Conference on Information and Knowledge Management* (pp. 313-320). New York: ACM.

Cormack, G. V. (2007). Email spam filtering: A systematic review. *Foundations and Trends in Information Retrieval*, *1*(4), 335–455. doi:10.1561/1500000006

Couvreur, A., Gaborit, P., Gauthier, V., Otmani, A., & Tillich, J. P. (2013). Distinguisher-based attacks on public-key cryptosystems using Reed-Solomon codes. *CoRR*. Retrieved Jul 24, 2013, from http://arxiv.org/abs/1307.6458

Cox, R., Bock, D., Bauer, K., Johnston, J., & Snyder, J. (1987). The analog speech privacy system. *AT & T Tech. Journal*, *66*, 119–131.

Csörgö, P., & Shcherbacov, V. (2011). *On some quasigroup cryptographical primitives*. arXiv: 1110.6591v1.

cz.nic. (2013, February 27). *Statistics*. Retrieved from http://www.dnssec.cz/stats/?stat_type=1&zone=2&time_step=month&from_year=2012&from_month=2&from_day=1&to_year=2013&to_month=2&to_day=26&submit=1

Daemen, J. (1995). *Cipher and Hash Function Design. Strategies based on Linear and Differential Cryptanalysis.* (Doctoral dissertation). Katholieke Universiteit Leuven.

Damasio, A. R., Damasio, H., & Van Hoesen, G. W. (1982). Prosopagnosia Anatomic basis and behavioral mechanisms. *Neurology*, *32*(4), 331–331. doi:10.1212/WNL.32.4.331 PMID:7199655

Dantu, R., & Kolan, P. (2005). Detecting spam in VoIP networks. In *Proceedings of the Steps to Reducing Unwanted Traffic on the Internet on Steps to Reducing Unwanted Traffic on the Internet*. Berkeley, CA: USENIX Association.

Darren, B. (2006). *Low Down and Dirty: Anti-Forensic Rootkits*. Paper presented at Ruxcon 2006. Sydney, Australia.

Daugman, J. (2000). *Biometric decision landscapes*. Technical Report-University of Cambridge Computer Laboratory.

David, K., Qi, O., & Sudeshna, S. (2012). Chaos an inter-displinary. *Journal of nonlinear sciences*. Retrieved from http://chaos.aip.org/about/about-the-journal

David, A. (2011). Multidisciplinarity, Interdisciplinarity, Transdisciplinarity, and the Sciences. *International Studies in the Philosophy of Science*, *25*(4), 387–403.

David, D. (1985). Quantum theory, the Church-Turing principle and the universal quantum computer. *Proceedings of the Royal Society of London. Series A, Mathematical and Physical Sciences*, *40*, 97–117.

Davies, D., & Pria, W. (1984). *Security for Computer Network, An Introduction to Data Security in teleprocessing and Electronic funds transfer*. Wiley and Sons.

Davis, M. (2009). *Hacking Exposed Malware & Rootkits*. McGraw-Hill.

Dawson, E. (1996). Cryptanalysis of Summation Generator. In *Proceeding of Auscrypt*. Auscrypt.

Dawson, E., Donowan, D., & Offer, A. (1996). Ouasigroups, isotopisms and authentication schemes. *Australasian Journal of Combinatorics*, *13*, 75–88.

De Greve, K., Yu, L., McMahon, P., Pelc, J., Natarajan, C., & Kim, N. et al. (2012). Quantum-dot spin–photon entanglement via frequency downconversion to telecom wavelength. *Nature*, *491*, 421–426. doi:10.1038/nature11577 PMID:23151585

Deal, R. A. (2005). *Cisco Router Firewall Security*. Indianapolis, IN: Cisco Press.

Delugré, G. (2010). *Closer to metal: Reverse engineering the Broadcom NetEx-treme's firmware*. Luxembourg: Grand Duchy of Luxembourg.

Dénes, J., & Keedwell, A. D. (1992). A new authentication scheme based on Latin squares. *Discrete Mathematics*, *106/107*, 157–161. doi:10.1016/0012-365X(92)90543-O

Dénes, J., & Keedwell, A. D. (2001). Some applications of non-associative algebraic systems in cryptology. *Pure Mathematics and Applications*, *12*(2), 147–195.

Deng, Q., Bai, X., Guo, L., & Wang, Y. (2009). A Fast Hardware Implementation of Multiplicative Inversion in $aa^{-1} \equiv 1 \pmod p$. In *Proceedings of Asia Pacific Conference on Postgraduate Research in Microelectronics & Electronics* (PrimeAsia'2009), (pp. 472 -475). Shanghai, China: IEEE.

Denning, D., & Baugh, W. E. (1997). *Cases Involving Encryption in Crime and Terrorism.* Retrieved from http://www.cs.georgetown.edu/~denning/crypto/cases.html

Denning, D. E., & Sacco, G. M. (1981). Timestamps in key distributed protocols. *Communications of the ACM, 24*(8), 533–535. doi:10.1145/358722.358740

Deutsch, D. (1985). The foremost paper about the universal theoretical quantum computer. *Proceedings of the Royal Society of London. Series A, 400,* 97–117. doi:10.1098/rspa.1985.0070

Dharmapalan, B. (2012). *Scientific Research Methodology.* Amazon.com Publisher.

Dianati, M., & Alleaume, R. (2006). *Architecture of the Secoqc quantum key distribution network.* GET-ENST, France, *arXiv:* quant-ph/0610202v2.

Dichtl, M. (2007). Bad and Good Ways of Post-processing Biased Physical Random Numbers. In A. Biryukov (Ed.), *FSE 2007, (LNCS)* (Vol. 4593, pp. 137–152). Berlin: Springer-Verlag. doi:10.1007/978-3-540-74619-5_9

Dichtl, M., & Böffgen, P. (2012). Breaking Another Quasigroup-Based Cryptographic Scheme. *Cryptology ePrint Archive. Report, 2012,* 661.

Dierks, T., & Allen, C. (1999). The TLS protocol version 1.0. *RFC 2246.*

Dierks, T., & Rescorla, E. (2006). The TLS protocol version 1.1. *RFC 4346.*

Diffie, W., & Hellman, M. (1976). New Direction in Cryptography. *IEEE Transactions on Information Theory, 22*(11), 644–654. doi:10.1109/TIT.1976.1055638

Diffie, W., & Ledin, G. (Eds.). (2008). SMS4 encryption algorithm for wireless networks *IACR Cryptology ePrint Archive. Report, 2005,* 329.

Dimitrova, V., & Markovski, J. (2004). On Quasigroup Pseudo Random Sequence Generators. In *Proceedings of the 1st Balkan Conference in Informatics* (pp. 393-401). Thessaloniki, Greece: Academic Press.

Dimitrova, V., Bakeva, V., Popovska-Mitrovikj, A., & Krapež, A. (2013). Cryptographic Properties of Parastrophic Quasigroup Transformation. In S. Markovski, & M. Gušev (Eds.), *Advances in Intelligent Systems and Computing - ICT Innovations 2012* (Vol. 207, pp. 235–243). Berlin, Germany: Springer-Verlag. doi:10.1007/978-3-642-37169-1_23

Dinakardas, C. N., Sankar, S. P., & George, N. (2013). A multimodal performance evaluation on two different models based on face, fingerprint and iris templates. In *Proceedings of 2013 International Conference on Emerging Trends in VLSI, Embedded System, Nano Electronics and Telecommunication System (ICEVENT)* (pp. 1-6). Tiruvannamalai, India: IEEE.

Doar, J. M. (1996). A Better Model for Generating Test Networks. In *Proceedings of Globecom96.* Academic Press. doi:10.1109/GLOCOM.1996.586131

Dong, Lei & Yang. (2013). An Algorithm for Underdetermined Mixing Matrix Estimation. *Neurocomputing, 104,* 26–34.

Dottling, N., Dowsley, R., Muller-Quade, J., & Nascimento, A. C. A. (2012). A CCA2 Secure Variant of the McEliece Cryptosystem. *IEEE Transactions on Information Theory, 58*(10), 6672–6680. doi:10.1109/TIT.2012.2203582

Douglas, R. (2006). *Cryptography Theory and Practice.* Champan & Hall/CRC.

Doukas & Karadimas. (2008a). A Blind Source Separation Based Cryptography Scheme for Mobile Military Communication Applications. *WSEAS Transactions on Communications, 7*(12), 1235–1245.

Doukas & Karadimas. (2008b). Blind Source Separation for digital data protection. In Proceedings of the 10th WSEAS international conference on Mathematical methods, computational techniques and intelligent systems, (pp. 503-508). Corfu, Greece: WSEAS Press.

Dowsley, R., Müller-Quade, J., & Nascimento, A. C. A. (2009). A CCA2 Secure Public Key Encryption Scheme Based on the McEliece Assumptions in the Standard Model. *Lecture Notes in Computer Science, 5473,* 240–251. doi:10.1007/978-3-642-00862-7_16

Drapal, A. (2001). Hamming distances of groups and quasi-groups. *Discrete Mathematics, 235*(1-3), 189–197. doi:10.1016/S0012-365X(00)00272-7

Drexler, K. E. (1986). Engines of Creation: The Coming Era of Nanotechnology. Anchor Books.

Duan, L.-M., Lukin, M. D., Cirac, J. I., & Zoller, P. (2001). Long-distance quantum communication with atomic ensembles and linear optics. *Nature, 414,* 413–418. doi:10.1038/35106500 PMID:11719796

Duflot, L., Perez, Y., Valadon, G., & Levillain, O. (2010). *Can you still trust your network card?* Paper presented at CanSecWest International Conference. Vancouver, Canada.

Dvorak, A., Habiballa, H., Novak, V., & Pavliska, V. (2003). The concept of LFLC 2000 - Its specificity, realization and power of applications. *Computers in Industry, 51*(3), 269–280. doi:10.1016/S0166-3615(03)00060-5

Dvorsky, J., Ochodkova, E., & Snašel, V. (2001). Hash function based on quasigroups. In V. Matyáš (Ed.), *Proceedings of Mikulášska kryptobesídká* (pp. 27–36). Praha, Czech Republic: Academic Press.

Dvorsky, J., Ochodkova, E., & Snašel, V. (2002). Generation of large quasigroups: an application in cryptography. In *Procedings of AAA (Arbeitstagung Allgemeine Algebra-Workshop on General Algebra).* Palacky Univ.

Dvorsky, J., Ochodkova, E., & Snašel, V. (2002). Hash function based on large quasigroups. In V. Matyáš (Ed.), *Proceedings of Velikonocní kriptologie* (pp. 1–8). Brno, Czech Republic: Academic Press.

Dwork, C. (2002). Fighting spam may be easier than you think. *Microsoft Research SVC.* Retrieved February 14, 2013, from www.cis.upenn.edu/spyce/presentations/Cynthia-Sep-02.pdf

Dwork, C., & Naor, M. (1993). Pricing via processing or combatting junk mail. In *Proceedings of Advances in Cryptology—CRYPTO'92* (pp. 139–147). Berlin: Springer-Verlag. doi:10.1007/3-540-48071-4_10

Earle, A. (2005). *Wireless Security Handbook.* CRC Press.

Eberle, H., & Oertli, E. (1998). Switcherland: a QoS communication architecture for workstation clusters, Computer Architecture. In *Proceedings. The 25th Annual International Symposium on Computer Architecture,* (pp. 98-108). Academic Press.

Eckersley, P. (2011, May 5). *A Syrian Man-In-The-Middle Attack against Facebook.* Retrieved from https://www.eff.org/deeplinks/2011/05/syrian-man-middle-against-facebook

Eggert, L. (2013, February 25). *DNSSEC Deployment Trends.* Retrieved from http://eggert.org/meter/dnssec

Ehud, G. (2007). Plenty of room for biology and bottom, an introduction to bio-nano-technology. Imperial College Press.

Eisenbarth, T., Güneysu, T., Heyse, S., & Paar, C. (2009). MicroEliece: McEliece for Embedded Devices. In *Proceedings of Cryptographic Hardware and Embedded Systems - CHES 2009, 11th International Workshop,* (pp. 49-64). Lausanne, Switzerland: Springer.

Ekert, A. (1991). Quantum cryptography based on Bell's theorem. *Physical Review Letters, 67,* 661–663. doi:10.1103/PhysRevLett.67.661 PMID:10044956

Elaabid & Guilley. (2010). Practical Improvements of Profiled Side-Channel Attacks on a Hardware Crypto-Accelerator –extended version. In *Proceeding AFRICACRYPT'10 Proceedings of the Third international conference on Cryptology in Africa,* (pp. 243-260). Stellenbosch, South Africa: Springer-Verlag.

Elliott, C. (2002). Building the quantum network. *New Journal of Physics, 4,* 46.1-46.12.

Elliott, C. (2004). *The DARPA quantum network.* BBN Technologies, *arXiv:* quant-ph/0412029.

Elliott, C., et al. (2005). *Current status of the DARPA quantum network.* BBN Technologies, *arXiv:* quant-ph/0503058.

Elliott, C., Pearson, D., & Troxel, G. (2003). Quantum cryptography in practice. In *Proceedings of ACM SIGCOMM'03 Conference.* ACM.

enisa. (2009). *The costs of DNSSEC deployment.* Heraklion: ENISA.

Epstein, J. (2011). *Onward to the Digital Revolution: Merchants of Culture.* New York: Scribner Books Publisher.

Eric, A., Michael, C., & Kenneth, W. (1998). Complexity Classes. In *Handbook on Algorithms and Theory of Computation.* CRC Press, Inc.

Erin, C. (2000). *Berlekamp-Massey Algorithm.* University of Minnesota REU. Retrieved July 5, 2013 from www.math.umn.edu/~garrett/students/reu/MB_algorithm.pdf

Essam, M., & Tarek, S. (2004). A Flexible Fuzzy Threat Evaluation Computer System. In *Proceedings of 2004 International Conference on Electrical, Electronic and Computer Engineering.* Cairo, Egypt: IEEExplore Digital Library.

eTesting Labs Conducts Performance Test of Anti-Spam Software. (2001). *PRNewswire.* Retrieved October 6, 2012, from http://www.prnewswire.com/news-releases/etesting-labs-conducts-performance-test-of-anti-spam-software-82337887.html

Exempt IP ranges from RBL lookup? (SpamCop and GMAIL issue). (2011). *SmarterTools.* Retrieved Mar 28, 2014, from http://forums.smartertools.com/threads/exempt-ip-ranges-from-rbl-lookup-spamcop-and-gmail-issue.24180/

Falko, D., & Frank, K. (2012). Towards security in nanocommunication: Challenges and opportunities. *Nano Communication Networks, 3*(3), 151–160. doi:10.1016/j.nancom.2012.08.001

Faraj (Al-Janabi), S. T. (2007). Unconditionally secure authentication in quantum key distribution. *i-Manager's Journal on Software Engineering, 1*(3), 31-42.

Faraj (Al-Janabi), S. T. (2010). Integrating quantum cryptography into SSL. *Ubiquitous Computing and Communication Journal, 5,* 1778–1788.

Faraj (Al-Janabi). S. T. (1999a). Development of new secure optical network models based on quantum cryptography. In *Proceedings of the Federation of Arab Scientific Research Councils Conference on Super-Highway Networks.* Academic Press.

Faraj (Al-Janabi). S. T. (1999b). *Quantum cryptographic key distribution in optical communication networks.* (Ph.D. Thesis). College of Engineering, Al-Nahrain University, Iraq.

Faraj (Al-Janabi). S. T. (2005). A novel quantum cryptographic error elimination technique using simple hamming codes. In *Proceedings of the International Conference on Advanced Remote Sensing for Earth Observation Systems.* KACST and ISPRS.

Faraj (Al-Janabi). S. T. (2008). A novel extension of SSL/TLS based on quantum key distribution. In *Proceedings of the International Conference on Computer and Communication Engineering* (ICCCE08), (Vol. 1, pp. 919-922). ICCCE.

Faraj (Al-Janabi). S. T., Al-Naima, F., & Ameen, S. (2000). Quantum cryptographic key distribution in multiple-access networks. In *Proceeding of 16th IFIP World Computer Congress,* (pp. 42-49). IFIP.

Faraj (Al-Janabi). S. T., Al-Naima, F., & Ameen, S. (2002). Optical network models for quantum cryptography. In *Proceeding of 17th IFIP/Sec2002 Conference.* IFIP.

Faugère, J.-C., Ødegård, R. S., Perret, L., & Gligoroski, D. (2010). Analysis of the MQQ Public Key Cryptosystem. In S.-H., Heng, R.N., Wright, & B.-M. Goi, (Eds.), CANS 2010, (LNCS), (vol. 6467, pp. 169–183). Berlin: Springer.

Faugère, J.-C., Otmani, A., Perret, L., & Tillich, J.-P. (2010). Algebraic Cryptanalysis of McEliece Variants with Compact Keys. In *Proceedings of the 29th Annual international conference on Theory and Applications of Cryptographic Techniques EUROCRYPT'10* (pp. 279-298). Springer.

Faugère, J.-C., Gauthier-Umaña, V., Otmani, A., Perret, L., & Tillich, J.-P. (2013). A Distinguisher for High Rate McEliece Cryptosystems. *IEEE Transactions on Information Theory, 59*(10), 6830–6844. doi:10.1109/TIT.2013.2272036

Faure, C., & Minder, L. (2008). Cryptanalysis of the McEliece cryptosystem over hyperelliptic curves. In *Proceedings of the eleventh International Workshop on Algebraic and Combinatorial Coding Theory* (pp. 99-107). Pamporovo, Bulgaria: ACCT.

Fausett, L. V. (1994). *Fundamentals of Neural Networks.* Prentice-Hall, Inc.

Fehr, S., Mosca, M., Rötteler, M., & Dagstuhl, R. S. (2011). Quantum Cryptanalysis. *Dagstuhl Reports. Schloss Dagstuhl, 1*(9), 58–75.

Fei, Liu, & Zheng. (2008). A Chaotic Encryption System Using PCA Neural Networks. In *Proceedings of 2008 IEEE Conference on Cybernetics and Intelligent Systems* (pp. 465 – 469). Chengdu, China: IEEE.

Feng, Y., et al. (2009). On the Computational Complexity of Parameter Estimation in Adaptive Testing Strategies. In *Proceedings of 15th IEEE Pacific Rim International symposium on Dependable Computing.* IEEExplore Digital Library.

FERET Database. (n.d.). Retrieved from www.nist.gov/itl/iad/ig/colorferet

Ferguson, N., Schneier, B., & Kohno, T. (2012). *Cryptography engineering: design principles and practical applications.* Oxford, UK: John Wiley & Sons.

Fernandez, V. et al. (2007). Passive optical network approach to gigahertz-clocked multiuser quantum key distribution. *IEEE Journal of Quantum Electronics, 43*(2). doi:10.1109/JQE.2006.887175

Ferris . (2006). The Total Cost of Ownership for Voltage Identity-Based Encryption Solutions. *San Francisco: Ferris Research.*

Feynman, R. P. (1960). There's Plenty of Room at the Bottom. *Engineering and Science, 23*(5), 22–36.

Filip, O. (2011). *DNSSEC.CZ.* Retrieved from http://dakar42.icann.org/bitcache/23b46cc058a604df99944c7080b98194591c8fd5?vid=28941&disposition=attachment&op=download

Finiasz, M. (2010). Parallel-CFS: Strengthening the CFS Mc-Eliece-Based Signature Scheme. In *Proceedings of Selected Areas in Cryptography - 17th International Workshop,* (pp. 159-170). Waterloo, Canada: Springer Berlin Heidelberg.

Finiasz, M., & Sendrier, N. (2009). Security Bounds for the Design of Code-based Cryptosystems. In *Proceedings of Advances in Cryptology - ASIACRYPT 2009, 15th International Conference on the Theory and Application of Cryptology and Information Security,* (pp. 88-105). Tokyo, Japan: Springer.

Fischer, J.-B., & Stern, J. (1996). An efficient pseudo-random generator provably as secure as syndrome decoding. In *Proceedings of the 15th annual international conference on Theory and application of cryptographic techniques EUROCRYPT'96* (pp. 245-255). Saragossa, Spain: Springer.

Fox, R. (2001). *Optical Properties of Solids.* Oxford University Press.

Frey, G. (1999). Applications of Arithmetical Geometry to Cryptographic Constructions. In *Proceedings of the Fifth International Conference on Finite Fields and Applications* (pp. 128–161). Springer.

Friedman, A. (2011). *Economic and Policy Frameworks for Cybersecurity Risks.* Center for Technology Innovation at Brookings.

Furnell, S. (2005). Why users cannot use security. *Computers & Security, 24*(4), 274–279. doi:10.1016/j.cose.2005.04.003

Gaborit, P., & Schrek, J. (2012). Efficient code-based one-time signature from automorphism groups with syndrome compatibility. In *Proceedings of IEEE International Symposium on Information Theory, ISIT 2012* (pp. 1982-1986). Cambridge, MA: IEEE.

Gaborit, P., Ruatta, O., & Schrek, J. (2013). On the complexity of the Rank Syndrome Decoding problem. *CoRR.* Retrieved January 6, 2013, from http://arxiv.org/abs/1301.1026

Galbraith, S., & Smart, N. (1999). A Cryptographic Application of Weil Descent. In *Proceedings of Cryptography and Coding: 7th IMA International Conference.* Springer.

Ganesan, K., Ishan, S., & Mansi, N. (2008). Public Key Encryption of Images and Videos in Real Time Using Chebyshev Maps. In *Proceedings of Fifth International Conference on Computer Graphics, Imaging and Visualisation.* Academic Press.

Ganesan, K., Muthukumar, R., & Murali, K. (2006). Look-up table based chaotic encryption of audio files. In *Proceedings of IEEE Asia Pacific Conference on Circuits and Systems* (APCCAS), (pp. 1951 – 1954). IEEE.

Gao, L., & Sobelman, G. (2000). Improved VLSI Designs for Multiplication and Inversion in $a \in \mathbb{Z}$ Over Normal Bases. In *Proceedings of 13th Annual IEEE International ASIC/SOC Conference* (pp. 97 -101). Arlington, VA: IEEE Circuit and Systems.

Gao, X., Ou, H., Dong, X., & Jin, J. (2006). *Research on FPGA Implementation of Algorithm for Computing Inversion in*. Computer Engineering and Applications.

Garcia, G. (2007). *Forensic physical memory analysis: Overview of tools and techniques*. Helsinki: Telecommunications Software and Multimedia Laboratory.

Garfinger, S. (1995). *PGP: Pretty Good Privacy*. O'Reilly & Associates.

Garfinkel, S. L., & Miller, R. C. (2005). Johnny 2: a user test of key continuity management with S/MIME and Outlook Express. In *Proceedings of the 2005 symposium on Usable privacy and security* (pp. 13-24). Pittsburgh, PA: ACM.

Garfinkel, S. L. (2003). Email-based identification and authentication: An alternative to PKI? *IEEE Security & Privacy, 1*(6), 20–26. doi:10.1109/MSECP.2003.1253564

Gaudry, P., Hess, F., & Smart, N. (2002). Constructive and Destructive Facets of Weil descent on Elliptic Curves. *Journal of Cryptology, 15*, 19–46. doi:10.1007/s00145-001-0011-x

Gauthier, V., & Leander, G. (2009). Practical Key Recovery Attacks on Two McEliece Variants. *Cryptology ePrint Archive: Report 2009/509*. Retrieved October 21, 2009, from eprint.iacr.org/2009/509.pdf

Gauthier, V., Otmani, A., & Tillich, J.-P. (2012). A Distinguisher-Based Attack of a Homomorphic Encryption Scheme Relying on Reed-Solomon Codes. *Cryptology ePrint Archive: Report 2012/168*. Retrieved March 29, 2012, from http://eprint.iacr.org/2012/168

Gauthier, V., Otmani, A., & Tillich, J.-P. (2012). A distinguisher-based attack on a variant of McEliece's cryptosystem based on Reed-Solomon codes. *CoRR*. Retrieved April 29, 2012, from http://arxiv.org/abs/1204.6459

Gavrilovska, L., Krco, S., Milutinovic, V., Stojmenovic, I., & Trobec, R. (Eds.). (2011). *Application and Multidisciplinary Aspects of Wireless Sensor Networks: Concepts, Integration, and Case Studies*. Springer-Verlag.

Gentry, C. (2003). Certificate-based encryption and the certificate revocation problem. In Proceedings of Advances in Cryptology - EUROCRYPT 2003 (pp. 272-293). Springer.

Gentry, C., & Silverberg, A. (2002). Hierarchical ID-Based Cryptography.[Springer.]. *Proceedings of ASIACRYPT, 2002*, 548–566.

George, B., & Maria, B. (1995). *Fuzzy Sets, Fuzzy Logic, Applications*. World Scientific.

Gilbert, G., & Hamrick, M. (2000). *Practical quantum cryptography: a comprehensive analysis (part one)*. MITRE Technical Report.

Gilbert, E. N. (1952). A comparison of signaling alphabets. *The Bell System Technical Journal, 31*(3), 504–522. doi:10.1002/j.1538-7305.1952.tb01393.x

Gisin, N., Iblisdir, S., Tittel, W., & Zbinden, H. (2006). Quantum communications with optical fibers. In A. V. Sergienko (Ed.), *Quantum communications and cryptography* (pp. 17–43). Taylor & Francis Group.

Gligoroski, D., Andova, S., & Knapskog, S. J. (2008). On the Importance of the Key Separation Principle for Different Modes of Operation. In L. Chen, Y. Mu, & W. Susilo (Eds.) *Proceedings of ISPEC 2008,* (LNCS), (vol. 4991, pp. 404-418). Berlin: Springer.

Gligoroski, D., Markovski, S., & Bakeva, V. (2003). On infinite class of strongly collision resistant hash functions Edon-F with variable length of output. In *Proceedings of 1st International Conference on Mathematics and Informatics for Industry* (pp. 302-308). Thessaloniki, Greece: Academic Press.

Gligoroski, D., Markovski, S., & Knapskog, S. J. (2005). A Fix of the MD4 Family of Hash Functions - Quasigroup Fold. In *Proceedings of NIST Cryptographic Hash Workshop*. Gaithersburg, MD: NIST. Retrieved January 15, 2013 from http://csrc.nist.gov/groups/ST/hash/documents/Gligoroski_MD4Fix.pdf

Gligoroski, D., Markovski, S., & Knapskog, S. J. (2008). Multivariate quadratic trapdoor functions based on multivariate quadratic quasigroups. In *Proceedings of the American Conference on Applied Mathematics* (pp. 44-49). Harvard.

Gligoroski, D., Markovski, S., & Kocarev, L. (2006). Edon-, an Infinite Family of Cryptographic Hash Functions. In *Proceedings of The Second NIST Cryptographic Hash Workshop*. UCSB. Retrieved January 15, 2013 from http://csrc.nist.gov/groups/ST/hash/documents/GLIGOROSKI_EdonR-ver06.pdf

Gligoroski, D., Markovski, S., & Kocarev, L. (2007). Error-Correcting Codes Based on Quasigroups. In *Proceedings of 16th International Conference on Computer Communications and Networks - ICCCN 2007* (pp. 165-172). Honolulu, HI: ICCCN.

Gligoroski, D. (2004). *Stream cipher based on quasigroup string transformations in . Contributions, Sec. Math. Tech. Sci*. MANU.

Gligoroski, D. (2005). Candidate one-way functions and one-way permutations based on quasigroup string transformations. *IACR Cryptology ePrint Archive. Report, 2005*, 352.

Gligoroski, D., Dimitrova, V., & Markovski, S. (2009). Quasigroups as Boolean functions, their equation systems and Groebner bases. In M. Sala, T. Mora, L. Perret, S. Sakata, & C. Traverso (Eds.), *Groebner Bases, Coding, and Cryptography*. Berlin, Germany: Springer. doi:10.1007/978-3-540-93806-4_31

Gligoroski, D., & Knapskog, S. J. (2007). Adding MAC Functionality to Edon80. *International Journal of Computer Science and Network Security, 7*(1), 194–204.

Gligoroski, D., Markovski, S., & Knapskog, S. J. (2006). A Secure Hash Algorithm with only 8 Folded SHA-1 Steps. *International Journal of Computer Science and Network, 6*(10), 194–205.

Gligoroski, D., Markovski, S., & Knapskog, S. J. (2008). A Public Key Block Cipher based on Multivariate Quadratic Quasigrops. *IACR Cryptology ePrint Archive. Report, 2008*, 320.

Gligoroski, D., Markovski, S., & Knapskog, S. J. (2008). The Stream Cipher Edon80. In *New Stream Cipher Designs: The eSTREAM Finalists, (LNCS)* (Vol. 4986, pp. 152–169). Berlin: Springer. doi:10.1007/978-3-540-68351-3_12

Gligoroski, D., & Samardjiska, S. (2012). The Multivariate Probabilistic Encryption Scheme MQQ-ENC. *IACR Cryptology ePrint Archive. Report, 2012*, 328.

Gligoroski, G., & Knapskog, S. (2008). Edon-(256, 384, 512)-an Efficient Implementation of Edon- Family of Cryptographic Hash Functions. *Commentationes Mathematicae Universitatis Carolinae, 49*(2), 219–239.

Gligorovski, D., Ødegård, R. S., Mihova, M., Knapskog, S. J., Kocarev, L., Drapal, A., & Klima, V. (2008). Cryptographic Hash Function EDON-. *Submission to NIST, First Round SHA-3 Candidate*. Retrieved January 15, 2013 from http://csrc.nist.gov/groups/ST/hash/sha-3/Round1/documents/Edon-RUpdate.zip

Gligorovski, D., & Ødegård, R. S. (2009). On the Complexity of Khovratovich et al's Preimage Attack on EDON-R. *IACR Cryptology ePrint Archive. Report, 2009*, 120.

Gligorovski, D., Ødegård, R. S., Jensen, R. E., Perret, L., Faugère, J.-C., Knapskog, S. J., & Markovski, S. (2011). MQQ-SIG: An Ultra-Fast and Provably CMA Resistant Digital Signature Scheme. In L. Chen, M. Yung, & L. Zhu (Eds.), *INTRUST 2011, (LNCS)* (Vol. 7222, pp. 184–203). Berlin, Germany: Springer.

Glukhov, M. M. (2008). On application of quasigroups in cryptology. *Applied Discrete Mathematics, 2*, 28–32.

Gmail Listed in the RBL dnsbl.njabl.org. (2009). *Google*. Retrieved Mar 6, 2014, from http://productforums.google.com/forum/#!topic/gmail/fXdzg9vfzO4

Gnanajeyaraman, R., Prasadh, K., & Ramar, D. (2009). Audio encryption using higher dimensional chaotic map. *International Journal of Recent Trends in Engineering, 1*(2).

Goldreich, O. (2004). *Foundations of Cryptography: Basic Applications*. Cambridge, UK: Cambridge University Press. doi:10.1017/CBO9780511721656

Goldstein, A. J., Harmon, L. D., & Lesk, A. B. (1971). Identification of human faces. *Proceedings of the IEEE*, *59*(5), 748–760. doi:10.1109/PROC.1971.8254

Goldwasser, S., & Micali, S. (1982). Probabilistic encryption and how to play mental poker keeping secret all partial information. In *Proceedings of the fourteenth annual ACM symposium on Theory of computing* (pp. 365–377). ACM Publisher.

Golomb, S., Welch, L., & Dénes, J. (2001). Encryption system based on crossed inverse quasigroups. *US Patent, WO0191368*.

Goncalves, M. (2002). *Firewalls Complete*. McGraw-Hill. Retrieved from http://www.secinf.net/firewalls_and_VPN/Firewalls_Complete/

Gong, G. (1990). *Nonlinear Generators of Binary Sequences with Controllable Complexity and Double Key*. In *Proceedings of the International Conference on Cryptology: Advances in Cryptology*. London, UK: Springer-Verlag.

Goodman, J., & Chandrakasan, A. (2001). An Energy-efficient Reconfigurable Public-key Cryptography Processor. *Journal of Solid-State Circuits*, *36*(11), 1808–1820. doi:10.1109/4.962304

Goppa, V. D. (1970). A new class of linear error-correcting codes. *Probl. Peredach. Inform.*, *6*(3), 24–30.

Gordon, J. P., & Kogelnik, H. (2000). PMD fundamentals: Polarization mode dispersion in optical fibers. *Proceedings of the National Academy of Sciences of the United States of America*, *97*(9), 4541–4550. doi:10.1073/pnas.97.9.4541

Gottesman, D., & Lo, H.-K. (2005). Proof of security of quantum key distribution with two-way classical communications. *arXiv:* quant-ph/0105121.

Gottesman, D., Lo, H.-K., Lutkenhaus, N., & Preskill, J. (2002). Security of quantum key distribution with imperfect devices. *arXiv:* quant-ph/0212066.

Graham, P. (2002). A Plan for Spam. *Paul Graham*. Retrieved August 26, 2013, from http://www.paulgraham.com/spam.html

Graham, P. (2003). Better Bayesian Filtering. *Paul Graham*. Retrieved March 26, 2014, from http://www.paulgraham.com/better.html

Graham-Cumming, J. (2004), How to beat an adaptive spam filter. In *Proc. of MIT Spam Conference*. Retrieved February 11, 2013, from http://jgc.org/pdf/spamconf2004.pdf

Graham-Cumming, J. (2005). People and Spam. In *Proceedings of MIT Spam Conference 2005*. Retrieved February 14, 2013, from http://jgc.org/pdf/spamconf2005.pdf

Guajardo, J., & Paar, C. (1997). Efficient Algorithms for Elliptic Curve Cryptosystems. In *Proceedings of 17th Annual International Cryptology Conference, CRYPTO'97* (pp. 342-356). Springer.

Guajardo, J., & Paar, C. (2002). Itoh-tsujii inversion in Standard Basis and Its Application. *Designs, Codes and Cryptography*, *25*, 207–216. doi:10.1023/A:1013860532636

Gueye, C. T., & Mboup, E. H. M. (2013). Secure Cryptographic Scheme based on Modified Reed Muller Codes. *International Journal of Security and Its Applications*, *7*(3), 5.

Guo & Lin. (2010). Fast Decryption Utilizing Correlation Calculation for BSS-based Speech Encryption System. In *Proceedings of Sixth International Conference on Natural Computation* (ICNC 2010), (pp. 1428- 1432). Yantai, China: IEEE.

Gutmann, P. (2004). Why isn't the internet secure yet, dammit. In *Proceedings of AusCERT Asia Pacific Information Technology Security Conference*. Royal Pines: AusCERT.

Gutmann, P. (2011). Do Users Verify SSH Keys?. *login*, *36*(4), 35-36.

Gutmann, P. (2011, April 20). *The real cost of free certificates*. Retrieved from https://mail1.eff.org/pipermail/observatory/2011-April/000199.html

Gutmann, P. (2002). PKI: it's not dead, just resting. *Computer*, *35*(8), 41–49. doi:10.1109/MC.2002.1023787

Gutub, A. A.-A., Tenca, A. F., Savas, E., & Koç, C. K. (2003). Scalable and Unified Hardware to Compute Montgomery Inverse in GF(p) and GF(2). In *Revised papers from the 4th International Workshop on Cryptographic Hardware and Embedded Systems* (pp. 484–499). London, UK: Springer-Verlag.

Halderman, J. A. et al. (2008). Lest we remember: Coldboot attacks on encryption keys. *Communications of the ACM*, *52*(5), 91–98. doi:10.1145/1506409.1506429

Hankerson, D., Hoffman, G., Leonard, D., Lindner, C., Phelps, K., Rodger, C., & Wall, J. (2000). *Coding Theory and Cryptography: The Essentials* (2nd ed.). CRC Press.

Hankerson, D., Menezes, A. J., & Vanstone, S. (2004). Elliptic Curve Arithmetic. In *Guide to Elliptic Curve Cryptography* (pp. 75–147). New York: Springer-Verlag.

Hankerson, D., Menezes, A., & Vanstone, S. (2005). *Guide to Elliptic Curve Cryptography*. New York: Springer-Verlag.

Hansell, S. (2004). *TECHNOLOGY, speech by Gates Lends visibility to e-mail stamp in war on spam*. Retrieved February 14, 2013, from http://www.nytimes.com/2004/02/02/business/technology-speech-by-gateslends-visibility-to-e-mail-stamp-in-war-on-spam.html

Hardik, S., & Nidhi, A. (2011). Solving Crypt-Arithmetic problems via genetic algorithm. *International Journal of IT &Management*, *1*(1), 12–17.

Hargreaves, C. H., & Chivers, H. (2008). Recovery of encryption keys from memory using a linear scan. In *Proceedings of Third International Conference on Availability, Reliability and Security*, (pp. 1369-1376). Conference Publishing Services (CPS). http://doi.ieeecomputersociety.org/10.1109/ARES.2008.109

Hariprasath, S., & Prabakar, T. N. (2012). Multimodal biometric recognition using iris feature extraction and palmprint features. In *Proceedings of 2012 International Conference on Advances in Engineering, Science and Management (ICAESM)* (pp. 174-179). Tamil Nadu, India: IEEE.

Harper, G., Menezes, A., & Vanstone, S. (1993). Public-key Cryptosystems With Very Small Key Lengths. In *Proceedings of the 11th Annual International Conference on Theory and Application of Cryptographic Techniques* (pp. 163–173). Berlin: Springer-Verlag.

Harris, E. (2003). *The next step in the spam control war: Greylisting*. Retrieved February 14, 2013, from http://projects.puremagic.com/greylisting/

Haselton, B. (2012). *Zero Errors? Spamhaus Flubs Causing Domain Deletions*. Retrieved October 18, 2012, http://yro-beta.slashdot.org/story/12/10/16/175248/zero-errors-spamhaus-flubs-causing-domain-deletions

Hein, D., Wolkerstorfer, J., & Felber, N. (2009). *ECC is Ready for RFID — A Proof in Silicon*. Berlin: Springer-Verlag. doi:10.1007/978-3-642-04159-4_26

Helen, F. (1989). *Cryptanalysis: A Study of Ciphers and Their Solution*. Amazon.com.

Helgert, H. J. (1974). Alternant Codes. *Information and Control*, *26*(4), 369–380. doi:10.1016/S0019-9958(74)80005-7

Hell, M., & Johansson, T. (2007). A Key Recovery Attack on Edon80. In K. Kaoru (Ed.), *Proceedings of ASIACRYPT 2007*, (LNCS), (vol. 4833, pp. 568-581). Berlin, Germany: Springer.

Herley, C. (2009). So Long, And No Thanks for the Externalities: The Rational Rejection of Security Advice by Users. In *Proceedings of Workshop on New security paradigms* (pp. 133-144). New York: ACM.

Herzberg, A., & Margulies, R. (2012). Training Johnny to Authenticate (Safely). *IEEE Security and Privacy*, *10*(1), 37–45. doi:10.1109/MSP.2011.129

Hess. (2004). Generalising the GHS attack on the Elliptic Curve Discrete Logarithm Problem. *LMS Journal of Computation and Mathematics*, *7*, 167-192.

Hesse, C. W., & James, C. J. (2005). The FastICA algorithm with spatial constraints. *IEEE Signal Processing Letters*, *12*(11), 792–795. doi:10.1109/LSP.2005.856867

Hess, F. (2003). Efficient identity based signature schemes based on pairings. In *Proceedings of Selected Areas in Cryptography* (pp. 310–324). Springer. doi:10.1007/3-540-36492-7_20

Heyse, S. (2010). Low-Reiter: Niederreiter Encryption Scheme for Embedded Microcontrollers. In *Proceedings of Post-Quantum Cryptography, Third International Workshop, PQCrypto 2010,* (pp. 165-181). Darmstadt, Germany: Springer.

Heyse, S., & Güneysu, T. (2012). Towards One Cycle per Bit Asymmetric Encryption: Code-Based Cryptography on Reconfigurable Hardware. In *Proceedings of Cryptographic Hardware and Embedded Systems - CHES 2012 - 14th International Workshop,* (pp. 340-355). Leuven, Belgium: Springer.

Heyse, S., Moradi, A., & Paar, C. (2010). Practical Power Analysis Attacks on Software Implementations of McEliece. In *Proceedings of Post-Quantum Cryptography, Third International Workshop, PQCrypto 2010,* (pp. 108-125). Darmstadt, Germany: Springer.

Heyse, S., von Maurich, I., & Güneysu, T. (2013). Smaller Keys for Code-Based Cryptography: QC-MDPC McEliece Implementations on Embedded Devices. In *Proceedings of Cryptographic Hardware and Embedded Systems - CHES 2013 - 15th International Workshop,* (pp. 273-292). Santa Barbara, CA: Springer.

Heyse, S., & Güneysu, T. (2013). Code-based cryptography on reconfigurable hardware: tweaking Niederreiter encryption for performance. *Journal of Cryptographic Engineering, 3*(1), 29–43. doi:10.1007/s13389-013-0056-4

Hogenboom. (2010). *Principal Component Analysis and Side-Channel Attacks.* (Master Thesis). Radboud University Nijmegen.

Hoglund, G. (2008). *The Value of Physical Memory for Incident Response.* Retrieved from http://www.hbgary.com/attachments/the-value-of-physical-memory-for-incident-response.pdf

Holz, R., Braun, L., Kammenhuber, N., & Carle, G. (2011). The SSL landscape: a thorough analysis of the x. 509 PKI using active and passive measurements. In *Proceedings of the 2011 ACM SIGCOMM conference on Internet measurement conference* (pp. 427-444). ACM. Retrieved December 2011, from http://www.net.in.tum.de/fileadmin/bibtex/publications/papers/imc-pkicrawl-2.pdf

Holz, R., Riedmaier, T., Kammenhuber, N., & Carle, G. (2012). X. 509 forensics: Detecting and localising the SSL/TLS men-in-the-middle.[Springer.]. *Proceedings of Computer Security–ESORICS, 2012,* 217–234.

Hong & Mohaisen. (2010). Augmented Rotation-Based Transformation for Privacy-Preserving Data Clustering. *ETRI Journal, 32*(3), 351–361.

Hsu, C. W., & Lin, C. J. (2002). A comparison of methods for multiclass support vector machines. *IEEE Transactions on Neural Networks, 13*(2), 415–425. doi:10.1109/72.991427 PMID:18244442

Hu, Y. (2010). Security analysis of cryptosystem based on quasigroups. In *Proceedings of IEEE International Conference on Progress in Informatics and Computing* (pp. 431-435). IEEE.

Huang, M. (2009, December). *Identity-Based Encryption (IBE) Cipher Suites for Transport Layer.* Retrieved from http://tools.ietf.org/html/draft-huang-tls-ibe-00

Huang, Y., Malka, L., Evans, D., & Katz, J. (2011). Efficient Privacy-Preserving Biometric Identification. In *Proceedings of 18th Network and Distributed System Security Conference (NDSS 2011).* NDSS.

Huang, F., & Stansfield, E. (1993). Time sample speech scrambler which does not require synchronization. *IEEE Transactions on Communications, 41,* 1715–1722. doi:10.1109/26.241752

Huber, K. (1996). Note on decoding binary Goppa codes. *Electronics Letters, 32*(2), 102–103. doi:10.1049/el:19960072

Hughes, R. (Ed.). (2004). A quantum information science and technology roadmap, part 2: Quantum cryptography. Report of the quantum cryptography technology expert panel, ARDA, LA-UR-04-4085, Version 1.0.

Hughes, J. R., Alde, D. M., Dyer, P., Luther, G. G., Morgan, G. L., & Schauer, M. (1995). *Quantum Cryptography, LA-UR-95-806.* University of California.

Hyvarinen, A. (1999). Survey on Independent Component Analysis. *Neural Computing Surveys, 2*(1), 94–128.

Hyvrinen, Karhunen & Oja. (2001). *Independent Component Analysis.* New York: Wiley John and Sons.

Itoh, T., & Tsujii, S. (1988). A Fast Algorithm for Computing Multiplicative Inverses in $GF(2^m)$ Using Normal Bases. *Information and Computation Elsevier*, *78*, 171–177. doi:10.1016/0890-5401(88)90024-7

ITU-T. (1991, August 30). *X. 800 Security Architecture for Open Systems Interconnection for CCITT applications*. Retrieved from http://www.itu.int/rec/T-REC-X.800-199103-I/en

Jääskeläinen, K. (2013). *SSH Key Management: A Gaping Hole in Your Encrypted Critical Infrastructure*. Retrieved from http://www.infosecurityproject.com/2013/Download/BO1.1_A%20Gaping%20Hole%20in%20Your%20Encrypted%20Critical%20Infrastructure.pdf

Jacob, M., Zheshen, Z., Pierre, D., Catherine, L., Jeffrey, H. S., & Dirk, E. (2013). High-dimensional quantum key distribution using dispersive optics. *Physical Review A.*, *87*, 062322. doi:10.1103/PhysRevA.87.062322

Jagadeesan, A., Thillaikkarasi, T., & Duraiswamy, K. (2011). Protected Bio-Cryptography Key invention from Multimodal Modalities: Feature Level Fusion of Fingerprint and Iris. *European Journal of Scientific Research*, *49*(4), 84–502.

Jain, A. K., & Ross, A. (2002). Learning User-Specific Parameters in a Multibiometric System. In *Proc. International Conference on Image Processing (ICIP)*. Rochester, NY: ICIP.

Jain, A. K., Bolle, R., & Pankanti, S. (1999). *Biometrics: Personal Identification in Networked Society*. Kluwer Academic Publishers. doi:10.1007/b117227

Jain, A. K., Patrick, F., & Arun, A. R. (2008). *Handbook of Biometrics*. Springer. doi:10.1007/978-0-387-71041-9

James, M. A. (2003). Why We Need a New Definition of Information Security. *Computers & Security*, *22*(4), 308–313. doi:10.1016/S0167-4048(03)00407-3

James, P. (2011). *Statistical Mechanics: Entropy, Order parameters, and Complexity*. Oxford, UK: Oxford University Press.

Jayant, N. (1982). Analog scramblers for speech privacy. In *Computers and Security*. North-Holland Publishing Company.

Jayant, N., Cox, R., McDermott, B., & Quinn, A. (1983). Analog scramblers Based on sequential permutations in time and frequency. *The Bell System Technical Journal*, *62*(1), 25–46. doi:10.1002/j.1538-7305.1983.tb04377.x

Jayant, N., McDermott, B., Christensen, S., & Quinn, A. (1981). A comparison of four methods for analog speech scrambling. *IEEE Transactions on Communications*, *29*(1), 38–23. doi:10.1109/TCOM.1981.1094870

Jelen, G. (2000). *SSE-CMM Security Metrics*. Washington, DC: NIST and CSSPAB.

Jerry, M. (2010). *Uncertain Rule-Based Fuzzy Logic Systems: Introduction and New Directions*. University of Southern California, Los Angeles. Retrieved August 8, 2013 from http://sipi.usc.edu/~mendel/book/

Jeyamala, C., Subramanyan, B., & Raman, G. (2011). Ensembles of blowfish with chaos based S-box design for text and image encryption.[IJNSA]. *International Journal of Network Security & Its Applications*, *3*(4), 165. doi:10.5121/ijnsa.2011.3415

Jian, W., Xu, L., & Xiaoyong, J. (2010). A Secure Communication System with Multiple Encryption Algorithms. In *Proceeding of The International Conference on E-Business and E-Government*. Guangzhou, China: IEEExplore- Digital Library.

Ji, L., Liangyu, X., & Xu, G. (2008). Collision attack on NaSHA-512. *IACR Cryptology ePrint Archive. Report*, *2008*, 519.

Jing, N. et al. (2006). An Adaptive fuzzy logic based secure routing protocol in mobile ad hoc networks. *Science Direct –. Fuzzy Sets and Systems*, *157*(12), 1704–1712. doi:10.1016/j.fss.2005.12.007

John, T., & Dominic, W. (2006). *Complexity and Cryptography- an Introduction*. Cambridge University Press.

Jolita, R. (2011). Applying Transdisciplinarity Principles in the Information Services Co-creation Process. In *Proceedings of 2012 Sixth International Conference on Research Challenges in Information Science* (RCIS), (pp. 1 – 11). IEEExplore – Digital Library.

Joye, M., & Neven, G. (2009). *Identity-based cryptography* (Vol. 2). Amsterdam: IOS Press.

Jun, K., Tomohiko, U., & Ryutaroh, M. (2012). *New Parameters of Linear Codes Expressing Security Performance of Universal Secure Network Coding.* Retrieved August 8, 2013 from http://arxiv.org/abs/1207.1936

Kahn, D. (1996). *The Codebreakers.* New York: Simon & Schuster.

Kai, X., & Jiankun, H. (2010). Bio-Cryptography. In *Handbook of Information and Communication Security.* Springer.

Kakavelakis, G., Beverly, R., & Young, J. (2011). Auto-learning of SMTP TCP transport-layer features for spam and abusive message detection. In *Proceedings of USENIX Large Installation System Administration Conference.* Retrieved February 14, 2013, from http://rbeverly.net/research/papers/autolearn-lisa11.pdf

Kak, S., & Jayant, N. (1977). On speech encryption using waveform scrambling. *The Bell System Technical Journal, 56*(5), 781–808. doi:10.1002/j.1538-7305.1977.tb00539.x

Kanso, A. (2010). Self-shrinking chaotic stream ciphers. *Communications in Nonlinear Science and Numerical Simulation, 16*(2), 822–836. doi:10.1016/j.cnsns.2010.04.039

Kanso, A., & Smaoui, N. (2007). Logistic chaotic maps for binary numbers generations. *Chaos, Solitons, and Fractals, 40*(5), 2557–2568. doi:10.1016/j.chaos.2007.10.049

Kapadia, A. (2007). A case (study) for usability in secure email communication. *IEEE Security & Privacy, 5*(2), 80–84. doi:10.1109/MSP.2007.25

Kaplan, B. (2007). *RAM is Key, Extracting Disk Encryption Keys From Volatile Memory Advisor: Matthew Geiger.* Carnegie Mellon University. Retrieved from http://citeseerx.ist.psu.edu/viewdoc/summary?doi=10.1.1.211.4095

Karlberger, C., Bayler, G., Kruegel, C., & Kirda, E. (2007). Exploiting redundancy in natural language to penetrate Bayesian spam filters. In *Proceedings of the first USENIX Workshop on Offensive Technologies.* Retrieved February 11, 2013 from http://dl.acm.org/citation.cfm?id=1323276.1323285

Kasprzak & Cichocki. (1996). Hidden Image Separation from Incomplete Image Mixtures by Independent Component Analysis. In *Proc. of the 13th Int. ConJ on Pattern Recognition* (Vol. 11, pp. 394–398). Vienna, Austria: IEEE.

Katarina, S., Thomas, W., & Santi, R. (2010). *Grid and Cloud Computing: A Business Perspective on Technology and Applications.* Berlin, Germany: Springer-Verlag.

Katz, J., & Lindell, Y. (2007). *Introduction to Modern Cryptography: Principles and Protocols.* Chapman and Hall/CRC.

Keedwell, A. D. (1999). Crossed inverse quasigroups with long inverse cycles and applications to cryptography. *Australasian Journal of Combinatorics, 20,* 241–250.

Keith, J., Richard, B., & Curtis, W. (2009). *Real Digital Forensics: Computer Security and Incident Response.* Amazon.com.

Keith, M. (2012). *Everyday Cryptography: Fundamental Principles and Applications.* Amazon.com.

Kellert, S. (1993). *In the Wake of Chaos: Unpredictable Order in Dynamical Systems.* University of Chicago Press Book. doi:10.7208/chicago/9780226429823.001.0001

Kenyon, T. (2002). *High Performance Data Network Design: Designer Techniques and Tools.* Elsevier Inc. Press.

Key, E. (1976). An analysis of the structure and complexity of nonlinear binary sequence generators. *IEEE Transactions on Information Theory, 22*(6), 732–736. doi:10.1109/TIT.1976.1055626

Khaled, M., Noaman, G., & Jalab, H. A. (2005). Data security based on neural networks. *Task Quarterly, 9*(4), 409–414.

Khan, M. (2009). Anomaly Detection in data streams using fuzzy logic. In *Proceedings of International Conference on Information and Communication Technologies* (pp. 167 – 174). IEEExplore Digital Library.

Khan, M. I., & Sher, M. (2003). Protocols for secure quantum transmission: a review of recent developments. *Pakistan J. of Information and Technology, 2*(3), 265–276. doi:10.3923/itj.2003.265.276

Khovratovich, D., Nikolic, I., & Weinmann, R. P. (2008). *Cryptanalysis of Edon-R.* Retrieved January 15, 2013 from http://ehash.iaik.tugraz.at/uploads/7/74/Edon.pdf

Khurana, H. B. (2006, January). *On the risks of IBE.* Retrieved from http://citeseerx.ist.psu.edu/viewdoc/download?doi=10.1.1.86.9742&rep=rep1&type=pdf

Kienzle, D. M., & Elder, M. C. (2003). Recent Worms: A Survey and Trends. In *Proceedings of the 2003 ACM workshop on Rapid malcode* (pp. 1-10). Washington, DC: ACM.

Kinzel, W. (2006). Theory of interacting neural networks. In Handbook of Graphs and Networks: From the Genome to the Internet. Weinheim, Germany: Wiley-VCH Verlag GmbH & Co. KGaA.

Kinzel, W., & Kanter, I. (2002). *Neural cryptography.* arXiv preprint cond-mat/0208453

Klima, V. (2008). *Multicollisions of EDON-R hash function and other observations.* Retrieved January 15, 2013 from http://cryptography.hyperlink.cz/BMW/EDONR_analysis_vk.pdf

Kobara, K., & Imai, H. (2001). Semantically Secure McEliece Public-Key Cryptosystems-Conversions for McEliece PKC. In *Proceedings of the 4th International Workshop on Practice and Theory in Public Key Cryptography: Public Key Cryptography (PKC '01).* London, UK: Springer.

Koblitz, N. (1991). Constructing Elliptic Curve Cryptosystems in Characteristic 2. In *Proceedings of Advances in Cryptology - CRYPTO '90, 10th Annual International Cryptology Conference* (pp. 156-167). Santa Barbara, CA: Springer.

Kocarev, L., Sterjev, M., Fekete, A., & Vattay, G. (2004). Public-key encryption with chaos. *American Institute of Physics, 14*(3), 1078–1081. PMID:15568922

Koç, C. K., & Sunar, B. (2001). An Efficient Optimal Normal Basis Type II Multiplier. *IEEE Transactions on Computers, 50,* 83–87. doi:10.1109/12.902754

Koetter, P. B. (2004). *Postfix SMTP AUTH (and TLS) HOWTO.* Retrieved October 10, 2012, from http://postfix.state-of-mind.de/patrick.koetter/smtpauth/

Koichiro, D. (2009). Strategy and Methodology of Science Integration in Transdisciplinarity. In *Proceedings of ICROS-SICE International Joint Conference 2009* (pp. 5107 – 5110). IEEExplore Digital Library.

Kornblum, J. D. (2006). Exploiting the Rootkit Paradox with Windows Memory Analysis. *International Journal of Digital Evidence, 5*(1).

Kościelny, C. (1996). A method of constructing quasigroup-based stream-ciphers. *Applied Mathematics and Computer Science, 6,* 109–121.

Kościelny, C. (2002). Generating quasigroups for cryptographic applications. *International Journal of Applied Mathematics and Computer Science, 12*(4), 559–569.

Kościelny, C., & Mullen, G. L. (1999). A quasigroup-based public-key cryptosystem. *International Journal of Applied Mathematics and Computer Science, 9*(4), 955–963.

Kranakis, E. (1984). *Primality and Cryptography.* New York: John Wiley & Sons.

Krapež, A. (2010). An application of quasigroup in cryptology. *Mathematica Macedonica, 8,* 47–52.

Krasimira, K., Sang, H., & Kyoung, D. (2012). Using Fuzzy Logic for robust event detection in wireless sensor networks. *Ad Hoc Networks, 10*(4), 709–722. doi:10.1016/j.adhoc.2011.06.008

Krishan, A. (2009). *What are Academic Disciplines? Some observation on the Disciplinarty vs. Interdisciplinarity debate.* University of Southampton, National Centre for Research Methods.

Kumar, A., Wong, D. C., Shen, H. C., & Jain, A. K. (2003). Personal Verification using Palmprint and Hand Geometry Biometric. In *Proceedings of 4th International Conference on Audio- and Video-based Biometric Person Authentication.* Guildford, UK: Academic Press.

Kumar, S. S. (2006). *Elliptic Curve Cryptography for Constrained Devices.* (PhD Dissertation). Faculty of Electrical Engineering and Information Technology, Ruhr University Bochum, Germany.

Kuncheva, L. I. (2007). Combining Pattern Classifiers: Methods and Algorithms. *IEEE Transactions on Neural Networks, 18*(3), 964–964. doi:10.1109/TNN.2007.897478

Kurosawa, K., Ito, T., & Takeuchi, M. (1987). Public key cryptosystem using a reciprocal number with the same intractability as factoring a large number. *Electronics Letters, 23*(15), 809–810. doi:10.1049/el:19870573

Kurose, J., & Ross, K. (2003). *Computer Networking. A Top-Down Approach Featuring the Internet* (2nd ed.). Addison Wesley.

Kyrtsou, C., & Labys, W. (2006). Evidence for chaotic dependence between US inflation and commodity prices. *Journal of Macroeconomics*, *28*(1), 256–266. doi:10.1016/j.jmacro.2005.10.019

Landais, G., & Tillich, J.-P. (2013). An Efficient Attack of a McEliece Cryptosystem Variant Based on Convolutional Codes. In *Proceedings of 5th International Workshop, PQCrypto 2013*, (pp. 102-117). Limoges, France: Springer.

Lane, T. (2000). *Machine learning techniques for the computer security*. (Doctoral dissertation). Purdue University.

Lane, A., & Mitsunori, O. (2002). *The Complexity Theory Companion*. Springer-Verlag.

Langley, A. (2012, November 6). *Certificate Transparency*. Retrieved from http://www.imperialviolet. org/2012/11/06/certtrans.html

Langley, A. (2013, January 13). *Real World Crypto2013*. Retrieved from http://www.imperialviolet. org/2013/01/13/rwc03.html

Laurie, B., & Clayton, R. (2004). Proof-of-Work proves not to work, version 0.2. In *Proceedings of Workshop on Economics and Information Security*. Cambridge, UK: University of Cambridge.

Law, F. Y. W., Lai, P. K. Y., Chow, K. P., & Ieong, R. S. C. (2009). *Memory Acquisition: A 2-Take Approach, Computer Science and its Applications, 2009*. Paper presented at CSA '09, the 2nd International Conference. Jeju Island, Korea.

Lawande, Q., Ivan, B., & Dhodapkar, S. (2005). Chaos based Cryptography: A New approach to Secure Communication. *BARC Newsletter*, *258*(7), 1–11.

Leavitt, N. (2011). Internet Security under Attack: The Undermining of Digital Certificates. *Computer*, *44*(12), 17–20. doi:10.1109/MC.2011.367

Lee, K. (2005). *The Information Revolution and Ireland: Prospects and Challenges*. Amazon.com.

Lee, P. J., & Brickell, E. F. (1988). An observation on the security of McEliece's public-key cryptosystem. *Lecture Notes in Computer Science*, 275–280. doi:10.1007/3-540-45961-8_25

Lee, W., Stolfo, S. J., & Mok, K. W. (2000). Adaptive intrusion detection: A data mining approach. *Artificial Intelligence Review*, *14*(6), 533–567. doi:10.1023/A:1006624031083

Lenstra, A., & Verheul, E. (1999). *Selecting cryptographic key sizes*. Retrieved from http://security.ece.orst.edu/koc/ece575/papers/cryptosizes.pdf

Leurent, G. (2009). Key Recovery Attack against Secret-prefix Edon-. *IACR Cryptology ePrint Archive. Report*, *2009*, 135.

Levine, J. (2010). *RFC 5782: DNS blacklists and whitelists*. Retrieved February 15, 2013 from http://tools.ietf.org/html/rfc5782

Levine, J. (2012). *IPv6 DNS blacklists reconsidered*. Retrieved February 15, 2013, from http://www.circleid. com/posts/ipv6_dns_blacklists_reconsidered/

Li, J., & Shen, L. (2006). An Improved multilevel fuzzy comprehensive evaluation algorithm for security performance. *The Journal of China Universities of posts and Telecommunication*, *13*(4), 48-53.

Li, S., Mou, X., & Cai, Y. (2003). *Chaotic Cryptography in Digital World: State-of-the-Art, Problems and Solutions*. Retrived Feb. 16, 2014 from citeseerx.ist.psu.edu/viewdoc/download?doi=10.1.1.5.9967

Li, Z., & Li, D. (2009). Collision Attack on Na-SHA-384/512. *IACR Cryptology ePrint Archive, Report 2009: 026*.

Libster, E., & Kornblum Jesse, D. (2008). A Proposal for an Integrated Memory Acquisition Mechanism. *ACM SIGOPS Operating Systems Review*, *42*(3), 14–20. doi:10.1145/1368506.1368510

Lijuan, Z., & Wang, Q. (2010). A network security evaluation method based on fuzzy and RST. In *Proceedings of 2nd International Conference on Education Technology and Computer* (ICETC) (vol. 2, pp. 40-44). IEEExplore Digital Library.

Li, Li, Lo & Chen. (2008). Cryptanalyzing an Encryption Scheme Based on Blind Source Separation. *IEEE Transactions on Circuits and Systems*, *55*(4), 1055–1063.

Lin, Q., Yin, F., Mei, T., & Liang, H. (2004). A speech encryption algorithm based on blind source separation. In *Proceedings of ICCCAS 2004, International Conference on Communications, Circuits and Systems*, (pp. 1013-1017). IEEExplore Digital Library.

Lin, Y. Mei & Liang. (2006). A Fast Decryption Algorithm for BSS-Based Image Encryption. [REMOVED HYPERLINK FIELD]Lecture Notes in Computer Science, 3973, 318-325.

Lin, Y. Mie & Liang. (2004). A speech encryption algorithm based on blind source separation. In *Proceedings of ICCCAS 2004* (vol. 2, pp. 1013-1017). Chengdu, China: IEEE.

Lin, Y. (2005). Lecture Notes in Computer Science: Vol. 3497. *Liang* (pp. 544–549). Blind Source Separation-Based Encryption of Images and Speeches.

Li, S., Mou, X., & Cai, Y. (2001). Pseudo-Random Bit Generator Based on Couple Chaotic Systems and its Applications in Stream-Cipher Cryptography. *Lecture Notes in Computer Science*, 2247, 316–329. doi:10.1007/3-540-45311-3_30

Liu, J., Gao, F., & Ma, H. (2008). A speech chaotic encryption algorithm based on network.[Harbin, China: IEEExplore Digital Librarey.]. *Proceedings of IIHMSP*, 08, 283–286.

Lomonaco, S. J. (1998). *A quick glance at quantum cryptography*. Dept. of Computer Science and Elect. Engineering, Univ. of Maryland Baltimore County. *arXiv:* quant-ph/9811056.

Lotfi, A. (1999). Fuzzy Systems Handbook (2nd ed.). Amazon.com.

Lothian, N. (2005). *Classifier4J*. Retrieved February 14, 2013, from http://classifier4j.sourceforge.net/

Loudon, R. (Ed.). (2000). *The Quantum Theory of Light* (3rd ed.). Oxford University Press.

Lowans, P. (2000). *Implementing a network security metrics program*. Retrieved from http://www.giac.org/practical/PaulLowansGSEC.doc

Lowd, D., & Meek, C. (2005). Good word attacks on statistical spam filters. In *Proceedings of the Second Conference on Email and Anti-Spam* (CEAS). Redmond, WA: Microsoft.

Lubbe, J. (1998). *Basic Methods of Cryptography*. Cambridge, UK: Cambridge University Press.

Lueg, C. (2005). From spam filtering to information retrieval and back: Seeking Conceptual Foundations for Spam Filtering. *Proceedings of the American Society for Information Science and Technology*, 42(1).

Lu, R., Lin, X., Liang, X., & Shen, X. S. (2011). An efficient and provably secure public-key encryption scheme based on coding theory. *Security and Communication Networks*, 4(12), 1440–1447. doi:10.1002/sec.274

Lutkenhaus, N. (1999). Estimates for practical quantum cryptography. *Physical Review A.*, 59, 3301–3319. doi:10.1103/PhysRevA.59.3301

Ma, F., Cheng, J., & Wang, Y. (1996). Wavelet transform-based analogue speech scrambling scheme. *Electronics Letters*, 32(8), 719–720. doi:10.1049/el:19960471

Maia, R. J. M., Barreto, P. S. L. M., & de Oliveira, B. T. (2010). Implementation of Multivariate Quadratic Quasigroup for Wireless Sensor Network. In M. L. Gavrilova, C. J. K. Tan, & E. D. Moreno (Eds.), *Transactions on Computational Science XI, (LNCS)* (Vol. 6480, pp. 64–78). Berlin, Germany: Springer. doi:10.1007/978-3-642-17697-5_4

Maki, A. (2004). *Simulation of quantum key distribution based on polarization entangled pairs of photons using the basic Ekert protocol*. (M.Sc. Thesis). Institute of Laser for postgraduate studies, University of Baghdad, Baghdad, Iraq.

Manjunath, G., & Anand, G. (2002). Speech encryption using circulant transformations. In *Proceedings of IEEE International Conference on Multimedia and Expo* (pp. 553-556). IEEExplore Digital Library. doi: 10.1109/ICME.2002.1035841

Mansfield, A. J., & Wayman, J. L. (2002). Best Practices in Testing and Reporting Performance of Biometric Devices. Version 2.01, NPL Report CMSC 14/02, National Physical Laboratory, August 2002.

Margaret, A., & David, A. (2002). *Transdisciplinarity: recreating Integrated Knowledge*. Amazon.com.

Maria, E., Abbas, M., & Elisabeth, R. (2009). Fuzzy Logic Applications in Wireless Communications.[IFSA.]. *Proceedings of IFSA-EUSFLAT, 2009*, 763–767.

Mark, N., & Gailly, J. (1995). *The Data Compression Book*. IDG Books Worldwide, Inc.

Markovski, S., & Mileva, A. (2008). NaSHA. *Submission to NIST, First Round SHA-3 Candidate*. Retrieved January 15, 2013 from http://csrc.nist.gov/groups/ST/hash/sha-3/Round1/documents/NaSHAUpdate.zip

Markovski, S., Gligoroski, D., & Andova, S. (1997). Using quasigroups for one-one secure encoding. In *Proceedings of VIII Conf. Logic and Computer Science LIRA97* (pp. 157-162). Novi Sad, Serbia: LIRA.

Markovski, S., Gligoroski, D., & Bakeva, V. (2001). Quasigroups and Hash Functions. In *Proceedings of VI International Conference on Discrete Mathematics and Applications*. Bansko, Bulgaria: Academic Press.

Markovski, S., Mileva A., Dimitrova, V., & Gligoroski, D. (2009). On a Conditional Collision Attack on NaSHA-512. *IACR Cryptology ePrint Archive, Report 2009: 034*.

Markovski, S., Samardziska, S., Gligoroski, D., & Knapskog, S. J. (2010). Multivariate Trapdoor Functions Based on Multivariate Left Quasigroups and Left Polynomial Quasigroups. In C. Cid & J. C. Faugère (Eds.), *Proceedings of the Second International Conference on Symbolic Computation and Cryptography* (pp. 237-251). Royal Holloway, University of London.

Markovski, S., Gligoroski, D., & Bakeva, V. (1999). Quasigroup String Processing - Part 1. *Contributions, Sec. Math. Tech. Sci. MANU XX, 1-2*, 13–28.

Markovski, S., Gligoroski, D., & Kocarev, L. (2005). Unbiased Random Sequences from Quasigroup String Transformations. In H. Gilbert, & H. Handschuh (Eds.), *FSE 2005, (LNCS)* (Vol. 3557, pp. 163–180). Berlin, Germany: Springer. doi:10.1007/11502760_11

Markovski, S., Gligoroski, D., & Stojčevska, B. (2000). Secure two-way on-line communications by using quasigroup enciphering with almost public key. *Novi Sad Journal of Mathematics, 30*(2), 43–49.

Markovski, S., & Kusakatov, V. (2000). Quasigroup String Processing - Part 2. *Contributions, Sec. Math. Tech. Sci. MANU XXI, 1-2*, 15–32.

Markovski, S., & Kusakatov, V. (2002-2003). Quasigroup String Processing – Part 3. *Contributions, Sec. Math. Tech. Sci. MANU XXIII-XXIV, 1-2*, 7–27.

Marnas, S. I., Angelis, L., & Bleris, G. L. (2004). All-Or-Nothing Transform Using Quasigroups. In *Proceedings of 1st Balkan Conference in Informatics* (pp. 183-191). Thessaloniki, Greece: Academic Press.

Martin, L., & Schertler, M . (2009 , January). Using the Boneh-Franklin and Boneh-Boyen Identity-Based Encryption Algorithms with the Cryptographic Message Syntax (CMS) *(RFC 5409). Retrieved from*http://tools.ietf.org/html/rfc5409

Martin, L. (2008). *Introduction to identity-based encryption*. Norwood, MA: Artech House.

Marvin, S., Jim, O., Robert, S., & Barry, L. (2004). *Spread Spectrum Communications Handbook*. New York: The McGraw-Hill, Inc.

Masaru, Y., Yoshiyuki, T., & Yuya, K. (2008). Patterns of Collaboration in Emerging Fields of Trans-Disciplinary Science: The Case of Sustainability Science. In *Proceedings of Portland International Conference on Management of Engineering & Technology* (PICMET 2008) (pp. 174 – 180). Cape Town, South Africa: IEEExplore Digital Library.

Massey, J. (1986). Cryptography- a selective survey. In E. Biglieri, & G. Prati (Eds.), *Digital communications* (pp. 3–21). North-Holland.

Massy, J. (1969). Shift-register synthesis and BCH decoding. *IEEE Transactions on Information Theory, 15*(1), 122–127. doi:10.1109/TIT.1969.1054260

Mathew, K. P., Vasant, S., & Rangan, C. P. (2012). On Provably Secure Code-based Signature and Signcryption Scheme. *Cryptology ePrint Archive, Report 2012/585*. Retrieved October 15, 2012, from http://eprint.iacr.org/2012/585

Mathew, K. P., Vasant, S., Venkatesan, S., & Rangan, C. (2012). An Efficient IND-CCA2 Secure Variant of the Niederreiter Encryption Scheme in the Standard Model. In *Proceedings of 17th Australasian Conference, ACISP 2012,* (pp. 166-179). Wollongong, Australia: Springer.

Matsumoto, M., Saito, M., Nishimura, T., & Hagita, M. (2007). A Fast Stream Cipher with Huge State Space and Quasigroup Filter for Software. In C. Adams, A. Miri, & M. Weiner (Eds.), *Proceedings of Selected Area in Cryptography, (LNCS)* (Vol. 4876, pp. 246–263). Berlin, Germany: Springer. doi:10.1007/978-3-540-77360-3_16

Matsumoto, M., Saito, M., Nishimura, T., & Hagita, M. (2007). CryptMT3 Stream Cipher. In *New Stream Cipher Designs: The eSTREAM Finalists, (LNCS)* (Vol. 4986, pp. 7–19). Berlin, Germany: Springer. doi:10.1007/978-3-540-68351-3_2

Matt, C., & Curtin, M. (2005). *Brute Force: Cracking the Data Encryption Standard.* New York: Springer.

Maurer, M., Menezes, A., & Teske, E. (2001). Analysis of the GHS Weil Descent Attack on the ECDLP Over Characteristic Two Finite Fields of Composite Degree. In *Proceedings of the Second International Conference on Cryptology: Progress in Cryptology* (pp. 195–213). London, UK: Springer-Verlag.

Maurer, U. M. (1993). Secret key agreement by public discussion from common information. *IEEE Transactions on Information Theory, 39,* 733–742. doi:10.1109/18.256484

Mavroeidis, B. van Laarhoven, & Marchiori. (2012). PCA, Eigenvector Localization and Clustering for Side-Channel Attacks on Cryptographic Hardware Devices. In *Proceedings of the 2012 European Conference on Machine Learning and Knowledge Discovery in Databases* (Vol. 1, pp.253-268). Bristol, UK: Springer-Verlag.

May, A., Meurer, A., & Thomae, E. (2011). Decoding random linear codes in $O(2^{0.054n})$. In *Proceedings of Advances in Cryptology - ASIACRYPT 2011 - 17th International Conference on the Theory and Application of Cryptology and Information Security,* (pp. 107–124). Seoul, South Korea: Springer.

Ma, Y., Cukic, B., & Singh, H. (2005). A classification approach to multi-biometric score fusion. In *Audio-and Video-Based Biometric Person Authentication* (pp. 65–83). Springer. doi:10.1007/11527923_50

Mayers, D. (2001). Unconditional security in quantum cryptography. *Journal of the ACM, 48*(3), 351–406. doi:10.1145/382780.382781

McEliece, R. (1978). A Public-Key Cryptosystem Based on Algebraic Coding Theory. *Deep Space Network Progress Report, DSN PR 42–44,* NASA Code 310-10-67-11. Retrieved April 15, 1978, from http://ipnpr.jpl.nasa.gov/progress_report2/42-44/44title.htm

Medvinsky, A., & Hur, M. (1999, October). *Addition of Kerberos Cipher Suites to Transport Layer Security (TLS)* (RFC 2712). Retrieved from http://www.ietf.org/rfc/rfc2712.txt

Mehta, B., & Nejdl, W. (2008). Attack resistant collaborative filtering. In *Proceedings of the 31st annual international ACM SIGIR conference on Research and development in information retrieval* (pp. 75–82). New York, NY: ACM. doi:10.1145/1390334.1390350

Mehta, B., Hofmann, T., & Fankhauser, P. (2007). Lies and propaganda: detecting spam users in collaborative filtering. In *Proceedings of the 12th international conference on Intelligent user interfaces* (pp. 14-21). ACM.

Mehta, B., & Hofmann, T. (2008). A Survey of Attack-Resistant Collaborative Filtering Algorithms. *IEEE Data Eng. Bull., 31*(2), 14–22.

Meli, C. (2013a). *Application and improvement of genetic algorithms and genetic programming towards the fight against spam and other internet malware.* (Doctoral dissertation). University of Malta.

Meli, C. (2013). Millipede, an Extended Representation for Genetic Algorithms. *International Journal of Computer Theory & Engineering, 5*(4).

Menezes, A., & Qu, M. (2001). Analysis of the Weil Descent Attack of Gaudry, Hess and Smart. In *Proceedings of the 2001 Conference on Topics in Cryptology: The Cryptographer's Track at RSA* (pp. 308–318). London, UK: Springer-Verlag.

Menezes, A., Teske, E., & Weng, A. (2004). Weak Fields for ECC. In *Proceedings of the 2004 Conference on Topics in Cryptology – CT-RSA 2004, The Cryptographers' Track at the RSA* (pp. 1997-1997). San Francisco, CA: Springer.

Menezes, A., Oorschot, V., & Paul, C. (1996). *Handbook of Applied Cryptography*. CRC Press. doi:10.1201/9781439821916

Menezes, A., & Teske, E. (2006). Cryptographic Implications of Hess' Generalized GHS Attack. *Applicable Algebra in Engineering. Communication and Computing*, *16*, 439–460.

Mermoul & Belouchrani. (2010). A Subspace-based Method for Speech Encryption. In *Proceedings of 10th International Conference on Information Science, Signal Processing and their Applications* (ISSPA 2010), (pp. 538-541). Kuala Lumpur: IEEE.

Mermoul. (2011). An Iterative Speech Encryption Scheme based on Subspace Technique. In *Proceedings of 2011 7th International Workshop on Systems, Signal Processing and their Applications* (WOSSPA), (pp. 361-364). Tipaza, Algeria: IEEE.

Meyer, K. A. (2006). *A new message authentication code based on the non-associativity of quasigroups*. (Doctoral Dissertation). Iowa State University.

Meziani, M., Hoffmann, G., & Cayrel, P.-L. (2012). Improving the Performance of the SYND Stream Cipher. In *Proceedings of Progress in Cryptology - AFRICACRYPT 2012 - 5th International Conference on Cryptology in Africa*, (pp. 99-116). Ifrane, Morocco: Springer.

Michael, A., & Isaac, L. (2010). Quantum Computation and Quantum Information (10th Anniversary Ed.). Cambridge, UK: Cambridge University Press.

Michler, P., Kiraz, A., Becher, C., Schoenfeld, W. V., Petroff, P. M., & Lidong, Z. et al. (2000). A Quantum Dot Single-Photon Turnstile Device. *Science*, *290*(5500), 2282–2285. doi:10.1126/science.290.5500.2282

Mihajloska, H., & Gligoroski, D. (2012). Construction of Optimal 4-bit S-boxes by Quasigroups of Order 4.[Rome, Italy: SECURWARE.]. *Proceedings of SECURWARE*, *2012*, 163–168.

Mihajloska, H., Yalcin, T., & Gligoroski, D. (2013). How lightweight is the Hardware Implementation of Quasigroup S-boxes. In S. Markovski, & M. Gušev (Eds.), *Advances in Intelligent Systems and Computing - ICT Innovations 2012* (pp. 121–127). Springer. doi:10.1007/978-3-642-37169-1_12

Mileva, A. (2012). Analysis of some quasigroup transformations as Boolean functions. *MASSIE 2009, Mathematica Balkanica, Fasc 3-4*.

Mileva, A., & Markovski, S. (2008). Correlation Matrices and Prop Ratio Tables for Quasigroups of order 4. In *Proceedings of the 6th International Conference for Informatics and Information Technology* (pp. 17-22). Ohrid, Macedonia: Academic Press.

Mileva, A., & Markovski, S. (2010). Quasigroups String Transformations and Hash Function Design. In D. Davcev, & J. M. Gómez (Eds.), *ICT Innovations 2009* (pp. 367–376). Berlin, Germany: Springer. doi:10.1007/978-3-642-10781-8_38

Mileva, A., & Markovski, S. (2012). Shapeless quasigroups derived by Feistel orthomorphisms. *Glasnik Matematicki*, *47*(2), 333–349. doi:10.3336/gm.47.2.09

Mileva, A., & Markovski, S. (2013). Quasigroup Representation of some Feistel and Generalized Feistel Ciphers. In S. Markovski, & M. Gušev (Eds.), *Advances in Intelligent Systems and Computing - ICT Innovations 2012 207* (pp. 161–171). Berlin, Germany: Springer. doi:10.1007/978-3-642-37169-1_16

Miller, V. S. (1986). Use of Elliptic Curves in cryptography. *Lecture Notes in Computer Science*, *85*, 417–426. doi:10.1007/3-540-39799-X_31

Miniwatts International Ltd. (2013). *World Internet Usage And Population Statistics* (tech. rep.). Retrieved from http://www.internetworldstats.com/stats.htm

Misoczki, R., Tillich, J.-P., Sendrier, N., & Barreto, P. S. L. M. (2013). MDPC-McEliece: New McEliece Variants from Moderate Density Parity-Check Codes. In *Proceedings of the 2013 IEEE International Symposium on Information Theory*, (pp. 2069-2073). Istanbul, Turkey: IEEE.

Mittelstrass, J. (2000). *Transdisciplinarity - New Structures in Science*. Retrieved from http://xserve02.mpiwg-berlin.mpg.de/ringberg/Talks/mittels%20-%20CHECKOUT/Mittelstrass.html

Mjolsnes, F. (2012). *A Multidisciplinary Introduction to Information Security*. Chapman and Hall/CRC.

Mnet. (2009). *SourceForge*. Retrieved February 15, 2013, from http://sourceforge.net/projects/mnet/

Mohaisen & Hong. (2008). Mitigating the ICA Attack against Rotation Based Transformation for Privacy Preserving Clustering. *ETRI Journal, 30*(6), 868–870.

Mohamed, M. S., Ding, J., Buchmann, J., & Werner, F. (2009). Algebraic Attack on the MQQ Public Key Cryptosystem. In *Proceedings of 8th International Conference on Cryptology and Network Security* (pp. 391-401). Berlin, Germany: Springer.

Mojo Nation. (2009). *SourceForge*. Retrieved February 15, 2013, from http://sourceforge.net/projects/mojonation/

Mokiy, V. (2013). *Methodology of transdisciplinarity-4, (solution of complicated multi-factor problems of nature and society)*. Amazon.com.

Moloktov, S. N., & Nazin, S. S. (1996). Quantum cryptography based on quantum dots. *JETP Letters, 63*(8), 646–651.

Molter, H. G., Stöttinger, M., Shoufan, A., & Strenzke, F. (2011). A simple power analysis attack on a McEliece cryptoprocessor. *Journal of Cryptographic Engineering, 1*(1), 29–36. doi:10.1007/s13389-011-0001-3

Monwar, M. M., Gavrilova, M., & Wang, Y. (2011). A novel fuzzy multimodal information fusion technology for human biometric traits identification. In *Proceedings of 2011 10th IEEE International Conference on Cognitive Informatics & Cognitive Computing (ICCI* CC)* (pp. 112-119). IEEE.

Mordini, E., & Petrini, C. (2007). Ethical and social implications of biometric identification technology. *Annali dell'Istituto Superiore di Sanita, 43*(1), 5–11. PMID:17536148

Moreau & Comon. (2010). Contrasts. In P. Comon, & C. Jutten (Eds.), *Handbook of Blind Source Separation Independent Component Analysis and Applications* (pp. 65–105). Oxford, UK: Elsevier.

Moreau, T. (2000). *Initial Secret Key Establishment Including Facilities for Verification of Identity*. US patent document 6,061,791. Washington, DC: US Patent Office.

Moreau, T. (2004). *An Information Security Framework Addressing the Initial Cryptographic Key Authentication Challenges*. CONNOTECH Experts-Conseil Inc.

Mosa, E., Messiha, N., & Zahran, O. (2009). Chaotic encryption of speech signals in transform domains. In *Proceedings of ICCES*. Cairo: IEEE Press.

Mosa, E., Messiha, N., Zahran, O., & Abd El-Samie, F. (2010). Encryption of speech signal with multiple secret keys in time and transform domains. *Springer, 13*(4), 231-242.

Moscovitch, M., Winocur, G., & Behrmann, M. (1997). What is special about face recognition? Nineteen experiments on a person with visual object agnosia and dyslexia but normal face recognition. *Journal of Cognitive Neuroscience, 9*(5), 555–604. doi:10.1162/jocn.1997.9.5.555 PMID:23965118

Moufang, R. (1935). Zur Struktur von Alternativkörpern. *Mathematische Annalen, 110*, 416–430. doi:10.1007/BF01448037

Moursund, D. (2005). *Introduction to Information and Communication Technology in Education*. Retrieved from http://pages.uoregon.edu/moursund/Books/ICT/ICTBook.html

Muller, S. (2001). *On the security of a Williams based public key encryption scheme. Report to University of Klagenfurt*. Austria: Springer- Verlag.

Muna, M. (1999). *Design of A Prototype for A Fuzzy Data Fusion System for C⁴I System*. (Unpublished doctoral dissertation). University of Technology, Baghdad, Iraq.

Munakata, T. (2008). *Fundamentals of the New Artificial Intelligence, Neural, Evolutionary, Fuzzy and More* (2nd ed.). Springer-Verlag London Limited.

Nambu, Y., Yoshino, K., & Tomita, A. (2006). One-way quantum key distribution system based on planar lightwave circuits. *Japanese Journal of Applied Physics, 45*, 5344. doi:10.1143/JJAP.45.5344

Nankun, M., & Xiaofeng, L. (2013). An Approach for Designing Neural Cryptography. *Lecture Notes in Computer Science, 7951*, 99–108.

Nankun, M., Xiaofeng, L., & Tingwen, H. (2011). Approach to design neural cryptography: A generalized architecture and a heuristic rule. *Physical Review E: Statistical, Nonlinear, and Soft Matter Physics, 87*(6), 99–108.

Naor, M. (1996). *Verification of a human in the loop or Identification via the Turing Test.* Unpublished draft. Retrieved October 5, 2012, from http://www.wisdom. weizmann.ac.il/~naor/PAPERS/humanabs.html

Neal, K. (2011). The Uneasy Relationship Between Mathematics and Cryptography. *Notices of the AMS, 54*(8), 972–979.

Needham, R. M., & Schroeder, M. D. (1978). Using encryption for authentication in large networks of computers. *Communications of the ACM, 21*(12), 993–999. doi:10.1145/359657.359659

Nguyen, T., Sfaxi, M., & Ghernaouti-Helie, S. (2006). 802.11i encryption key distribution using quantum cryptography. *Journal of Networks, 1*(5), 9–20. doi:10.4304/jnw.1.5.9-20

Nicolas, G., Gregoire, R., Wolfgang, T., & Hugo, Z. (2002). Quantum cryptography. *Reviews of Modern Physics, 74*(1), 145–195. doi:10.1103/RevModPhys.74.145

Nicolescu, B. (2002). Manifesto of Transdisciplinarity. New York: Amazon.com Publisher.

Nicolescu, B. (Ed.). (2008). Transdisciplinarity – Theory and Practice. New York: Amazon.com Publisher.

Niederreiter, H. (1986). Knapsack-type Cryptosystems and Algebraic Coding Theory. *Problems of Control and Information Theory, 15*(2), 159–166.

Nikolić, I., & Khovratovich, D. (2008). *Free-start attacks on NaSHA.* Retrieved January 15, 2013 from http://ehash.iaik.tugraz.at/uploads/3/33/Free-start_attacks_on_Nasha.pdf

Nimrod, M., & Christos, H. P. (1989). *A Note on Total Functions, Existence Theorems, and Computational Complexity.* Retrieved from http://citeseerx.ist.psu.edu/viewdoc/summary?doi=10.1.1.9.5230

NIST. (2007). *Recommendation for Key Management.* Retrieved from http://csrc.nist.gov/publications/nistpubs/800-57/sp800-57-Part1-revised2_Mar08-2007.pdf

Norton, G. (2010). *The Berlekamp-Massey Algorithm via Minimal Polynomials.* Retrieved on July 16, 2013 from http://arxiv.org/pdf/1001.1597.pdf

Novotney, P., & Ferguson, N. (2009). Detectable correlation in Edon-. *IACR Cryptology ePrint Archive 2009: 378.*

O'Gorman, L. (2003). Comparing Passwords, Tokens, and Biometrics for User Authentication. *Proceedings of the IEEE, 91*(12).

Ochodkova, E., & Snášel, V. (2001). Using quasigroups for secure encoding of file system. Abstract of Talk on Conference Security and Protection of information. Brno, Czech Republic.

Okamoto, T., & Uchiyama, S. (1998). A New Public Key Cryptosystem as secure as factoring. In *Proceedings of Advances in Cryptology* (pp. 308–318). Springer Verlag. doi:10.1007/BFb0054135

Oleson, A., & Voss, J. (1979). *The Organization of Knowledge in Modern America, 1860-1920.* The Johns Hopkins University Press.

Omura, J., & Massey, J. (1986). *Computational Method and Apparatus for Finite Field Arithmetic* (Patent US4587627).

Oppenheim, A. V. A., Willsky, A. S. A., Nawab, S. H., & Hernández, G. M. (1998). *Señales y sistemas 2ED.* Prentice Hall.

ORL Database. (n.d.). Retrieved from www.cl.cam.ac.uk

Orloff, J. (2011). *5 Criticisms of the challenge-response solution.* Retrieved February 15, 2013, from http://www.allspammedup.com/2011/05/5-criticisms-of-the-challenge-response-solution/

Osterweil, E., Kaliski, B., & Larson, M., & McPherson. (2012). *Reducing the X.509 Attack Surface with DNSSEC's DANE.* Securing and Trusting Internet Names. SATIN.

Overbeck, R. (2008). An Analysis of Side Channels in the McEliece PKC. *Enhancing Crypto-Primitives with Techniques from Coding Theory. NATO OTAN.* Retrieved 2008, from https://www.cosic.esat.kuleuven.be/nato arw/slides participants/Overbeck slides nato08.pdf

Overbeck, R. (2008). Structural Attacks for Public Key Cryptosystems Based on Gabidulin Codes. *J. Cryptology, 21*(2), 280–301. doi:10.1007/s00145-007-9003-9

Overbeck, R., & Sendrier, N. (2008). Code-Based Cryptography. In *Post-Quantum Cryptography* (pp. 95–145). Springer.

Ozment, A., & Schechter, S. E. (2006). *Bootstrapping the adoption of internet security protocols*. Paper presented at the Fifth Workshop on the Economics of Information Security. Cambridge, UK.

Pan, Z., Rust, A. G., & Bolouri, H. (2000). Image redundancy reduction for neural network classification using discrete cosine transforms. In *Proceedings of the IEEE-INNS-ENNS International Joint Conference on Neural Networks* (Vol. 3, pp. 149-154). IEEE.

Pascal, P. (1999). Public-key cryptosystem based on Composite Degree Residusity Classes. In *Proceedings of Advances in Cryptology- Eurocrypt'99* (Vol. 1592, pp. 223–238). Berlin: Springer.

Pasquinucci, A. (2005). Authentication and routing in simple quantum key distribution networks. UCCI.IT, Italy, *arXiv:*cs.NI/0506003v1.

Patarin, J. (1996). Hidden Fields Equations (HFE) and Isomorphisms of Polynomials (IP), two new Families of asymmetric Algorithms. In U. Maurer (Ed.), *Proceedings of EUROCRYPT '96,* (LNCS), (vol. 1440, pp. 33–48). Berlin, Germany: Springer.

Paterson, K. G., Piper, F., & Schack, R. (2005). *Why quantum cryptography*. Department of Mathematics, University of London. *arXiv:* quant-ph/0406147.

Patidar, V., & Sud, K. (2009). A Novel Pseudo Random Bit Generator Based on Chaotic Standard Map and its Testing.[EJTP]. *Electronic Journal of Theoretical Physics*, *6*(20), 327–344.

Patidar, V., Sud, K., & Pareek, N. (2008). A Pseudo Random Bit Generator Based on Chaotic Logistic Map and its Statistical Testing. *Informatica*, *33*, 441–452.

Patterson, N. (1975). The algebraic decoding of Goppa codes. *IEEE Transactions on Information Theory*, *21*(2), 203–207. doi:10.1109/TIT.1975.1055350

Paul, F. & Daniel, M. (1993). *Fuzzy Logic*. Amazon.com.

Payne, S. (2001). *A Guide to Security Metrics*. Retrieved from http://rr.sans.org/audit/metrics.php

Payne, B. D., & Edwards, W. K. (2008). A brief introduction to usable security. *IEEE Internet Computing*, *12*(3), 13–21. doi:10.1109/MIC.2008.50

Pearson. (1901). On lines and planes of closest fit to systems of points in space. *Philosophical Magazine*, *2*(6), 559–572.

Peev, M., Nolle, M., Maurhardt, O., Lorunser, T., Suda, M., Poppe, A., et al. (2005). A novel protocol-authentication algorithm ruling out a man-in-the-middle attack in quantum cryptography. *arXiv:* quant-ph/0407131.

Persichetti, E. (2012). On a CCA2-secure variant of McEliece in the standard model. *IACR Cryptology ePrint Archive*. Retrieved May 11, 2012, from http://eprint.iacr.org/2012/268

Peter, E., & Burns, J. (2010). *Defcon 18*. Retrieved December 2011, from http://www.youtube.com/watch?v=gpZ6AbkqBQo

Peter, A., Anthony, J., & Raja, P. (2000). On the Theory of Fuzzy Signal Detection: Theoretical and Practical Considerations. *Theoretical Issues in Ergonomics Science*, *1*(3), 207–230. doi:10.1080/14639220110038640

Peter, J. (1995). Adaptive Fuzzy Frequency Hopper. *IEEE Transactions on Communications*, *43*(6), 8111–2117.

Peters, C. (2010). Information-Set Decoding for Linear Codes over F_q. In *Proceedings of Post-Quantum Cryptography, Third International Workshop, PQCrypto 2010,* (pp. 81-94). Darmstadt, Germany: Springer.

Peters, T., et al. (n.d.). *SpamBayes*. Retrieved February 14, 2013, from http://spambayes.sourceforge.net/

Petrescu, A. (2007). Applications of quasigroups in cryptography. In *Proceedings of Interdisciplinarity in Engineering. TG-Mures*. Romania: Academic Press.

Petrescu, A. (2010). *n*-quasigroup Cryptographic Primitives: Stream Ciphers. *Studia Univ. Babes Bolyai. Informatica*, *60*(2), 27–34.

PGM Format Especification. (n.d.). Retrieved from netpbm.sourceforge.net/doc/pgm.html

Phillips, V., Lee, M., & Thomas, J. (1971). Speech scrambling by the re-ordering of amplitude samples. *Radio and Electronic Engineer*, *41*(3).

Platt, J. C., Cristianini, N., & Shawe-Taylor, J. (2000). Large margin DAGs for multiclass classification. *Advances in Neural Information Processing Systems*, *12*(3), 547–553.

Pollard, J. M. (1978). Monte Carlo Methods for Index Computation Mod P. *Mathematics of Computation*, *32*, 918–924.

Poonam, G. (2009). Cryptanalysis of SDES via evolutionary computation techniques.[IJCSIS]. *International Journal of Computer Science and Information Security*, *1*(1), 1–7.

Poor, V., & Wang, X. (1997). Code-Aide Interference suppression for DS/CDMA communications: Parallel Blind Adaptive Implementation. *IEEE Transactions on Communications*, *45*(9), 1101–1111. doi:10.1109/26.623075

Popovska-Mitrovikj, A., Bakeva, V., & Markovski, S. (2011). On random error correcting codes based on quasigroups. *Quasigroups and Related Systems*, *19*(2), 301–316.

Prabakaran, N., Loganathan, P., & Vivekanandan, P. (2008). Neural Cryptography with Multiple Transfers Functions and Multiple Learning Rule. *International Journal of Soft Computing*, *3*(3), 177–181.

Prabhakar, S., Pankant, S., & Jain, A. K. (2003). Biometric Recognition: Security and Privacy Concerns. *IEEE Security and Privacy Magazine*, *1*(2), 33–42. doi:10.1109/MSECP.2003.1193209

Prasadh, K., Ramar, K., & Gnanajeyaraman, R. (2009). Public key cryptosystems based on chaotic chebyshev polynomials. In *Proceedings of International Conference on Advances in Recent Technologies in Communication and Computing, ARTCom '09*. IEEExplore-Digital Library. doi: 10.1109/ARTCom.2009.64

Princeton University. (n.d.). *WordNet*. Retrieved February 14, 2013, from http://wordnet.princeton.edu/

Project, S. P. F. (2007). US Financial Services Industry Group Endorses SPF. *SPF*. Retrieved Mar 10, 2014, from http://www.openspf.org/Press_Release/2007-04-21

Project, S. P. F. (n.d). SPF vs Sender ID. *SPF*. Retrieved Mar 10, 2014, from http://www.openspf.org/SPF_vs_Sender_ID

Proos, J., & Zalka, C. (2003). Shor's discrete logarithm quantum algorithm for elliptic curves. *Quantum Info. Comput.*, *3*(4), 317–344.

Rabin, M. (1979). *Digital Signature and Public key functions as intractable as factorization. MIT/LCS/TR-212, January. MIT/LCS/TM-82.* CAMBRIDGE, United State.

Ramasubramanian, V., & Sirer, E. G. (2005). Perils of Transitive Trust in the Domain Name System. In *Proceedings of the 5th ACM SIGCOMM conference on Internet Measurement*. Berkeley, CA: USENIX Association.

Rastaghi, R. (2013). An Efficient CCA2-Secure Variant of the McEliece Cryptosystem n the Standard Model. *CoRR*. Retrieved February 2, 2013, from http://arxiv.org/abs/1302.0347

Ratha, N., Connell, J., & Bolle, R. (2001). Enhancing security and privacy in biometrics-based authentication systems. *IBM Systems Journal*, *40*(3), 614–634. doi:10.1147/sj.403.0614

Reeds, J., & Sloane, J. (1985). Shift-Register Sequences (Modulo m). *SIAM Journal on Computing*, *14*(3), 505–513. doi:10.1137/0214038

Rescorla, E. (2008, February 27). *Comments on draft-kupwade-sip-iba-00*. Retrieved from http://www.ietf.org/mail-archive/web/sip/current/msg22283.html

Rescorla, E. (2009, July 16). *Review of draft-huang-tls-ibe-00*. Retrieved from http://www.ietf.org/mail-archive/web/tls/current/msg03611.html

Reyhani-Masoleh, A., & Hasan, M. (2002). Efficient Digit-Serial Normal Basis Multipliers over $GF(2^m)$. In *Proceedings of IEEE International Symposium on Circuits and Systems*, ISCAS 2002 (pp. 781-784). Scottsdale, AZ: IEEE Circuits and Systems.

Reyhani-Masoleh, A., & Hasan, M. (2005). Low Complexity Word-level Sequential Normal Basis Multipliers. *IEEE Transactions on Computers*, *54*(2), 98–110. doi:10.1109/TC.2005.29

Richard, A. (2003). *RSA and Public Key Cryptography*. Chapman & Hall/CRC.

Rifkin, R., & Klautau, A. (2004). In defense of one-vs-all classification. *Journal of Machine Learning Research*, *5*, 101–141.

Rivest, R. L. (1997). All-or-nothing Encryption and the Package Transform. In E. Biham (Ed.), *Proceedings of Fast Software Encryption '97, (LNCS)* (Vol. 1267, pp. 210–218). Berlin, Germany: Springer. doi:10.1007/BFb0052348

Rivest, R. L. (2001). Permutation polynomials modulo 2^w. *Finite Fields and Their Applications*, 7, 287–292. doi:10.1006/ffta.2000.0282

Robert, M. (2013). *Entropy and Information Theory*. Springer-Verlag.

Rodríguez-Henríquez, F., Saqib, N. A., & Cruz-Cortes, N. (2005). A Fast Implementation of Multiplicative Inversion Over $GF(2^m)$. In *Proceedings of the International Conference on Information Technology: Coding and Computing*, ITCC'05 (pp. 574–579). Washington, DC: IEEE Computer Society.

Rodríguez-Henríquez, F., Morales-Luna, G., Saqib, N. A., & Cruz-Cortés, N. (2007). Parallel Itoh—Tsujii Multiplicative Inversion Algorithm for a Special Class of Trinomials. *Designs, Codes and Cryptography*, 45, 19–37. doi:10.1007/s10623-007-9073-6

Rosa, S., & Schultze, S. (2013). Trust Darknet: Control and Compromise in the Internet's Certificate Authority Model. *IEEE Internet Computing*, 18–25. doi:10.1109/MIC.2013.27

Roschke, S., Ibraimi, L., Cheng, F., & Meinel, C. (2010). Secure Communication using Identity Based Encryption. In *Proceedings of Communications and Multimedia Security* (pp. 256–267). Springer. doi:10.1007/978-3-642-13241-4_23

Ross, G. (2001). *Security Engineering: A Guide to Building Dependable Distributed Systems*. Wiley Publisher.

Ruspini, E. H., Bonissone, P. P., & Pedycz, W. (1998). *Handbook of Fuzzy Computation*. Bristol, UK: Institute of Physics Pub. doi:10.1887/0750304278

Ruttor, A., Kanter, I., & Kinzel, W. (2006). Dynamics of neural cryptography. *Physical Review E: Statistical, Nonlinear, and Soft Matter Physics*, 75(5), 056104. doi:10.1103/PhysRevE.75.056104

Ruttor, A., Reents, G., & Kinzel, W. (2004). Synchronization of random walks with reflecting boundaries. *Journal of Physics. A, Mathematical and General*, 37(36), 8609. doi:10.1088/0305-4470/37/36/003

Sabiha, F. (2004). *Complexity Evaluation of Binary Pseudo random sequences, using Fuzzy Logic*. (Unpublished Master Thesis). Al-Mustanseryah University, Iraq.

Sade, A. (1957). Quasigroups automorphes par le groupe cyclique. *Canadian Journal of Mathematics*, 9, 321–335. doi:10.4153/CJM-1957-039-3

Sadkhan, S., & Abbas, N. (2006). A Proposed Speech Scrambler Based on Independent Component Analysis. *MJC010368*, 1(1), 1- 6. Retrieved Feb. 16, 2014 from https://uobabylon.academia.edu/CscUob/Posts/311799/list_of_some_published_E_Papers_and_Pre_Prints_on_University_of_Babylon_Website

Sadkhan, S., Abdulmuhsen, N., & Al-Tahan, N. (2007). A proposed analog speech scrambler based on parallel structure of wavelet transforms. In *Proceedings of National Radio Science Conference*. IEEEplore - Digital Library.

Sadkhan, S., & Abbas, N. (2011). Performance evaluation of speech scrambling methods based on statistical approach. *Atti della Fondazione Giorgio Ronchi*, 66(5), 601–614.

Sadkhan, S., & Abbas, N. (2012). Speech scrambling based on wavelet transform. In *Advances in wavelet theory and their applications in engineering physics and technology* (pp. 41–58). InTech. doi:10.5772/37350

Said, E., Mona, L., & Adel, H. (2005). *A New Fuzzy Logic Based Pseudo-Random Bit Generator for Secure DS-CDMA System*. IEEEplore Digital Library.

Sakiyama, K., Batina, L., Preneel, B., & Verbauwhede, I. (2007). Multicore Curve-Based Cryptoprocessor with Reconfigurable Modular Arithmetic Logic Units over $GF(2^n)$. *IEEE Transactions on Computers*, 56(9), 1269–1282.

Sakurai, K., Koga, K., & Muratan, T. (1984). A speech scrambler using the fast Fourier transform technique. *IEEE Journal on Selected Areas in Communications*, 2(3), 434–442. doi:10.1109/JSAC.1984.1146074

Salib, M. (2002). Heuristics in the Blender. In *Proceedings of the 2003 Spam Conference*. Boston: MIT.

Salman, S. (1995). *Analytical study of some public key cryptosystems depending on some evaluation parameters*. (Unpublished M.Sc. Dissertation). University of Technology, Baghdad, Iraq.

Samardziska, S., Markovski, S., & Gligoroski, D. (2010). Multivariate Quasigroups Defined by T-functions. In C. Cid & J. C. Faugère (Eds.), *Proceedings of the Second International Conference on Symbolic Computation and Cryptography* (pp. 117-127). Royal Holloway, University of London.

Samardziska, S., Chen, Y., & Gligoroski, D. (2012). Algorithms for Construction of Multivariate Quadratic Quasigroups (MQQs) and Their Parastrophe Operations in Arbitrary Galois Fields. *Journal of Information Assurance and Security*, 7(3), 164–172.

Samardziska, S., & Gligoroski, D. (2011). Identity-Based Identification Schemes Using Left Multivariate Quasigroups.[Tapir Akad, Forlag: NIK.]. *Proceedings of, NIK-2011*, 19–30.

Sangouard, N., Simon, C., de Riedmatten, H., & Gisin, N. (2011). Quantum repeaters based on atomic ensembles and linear optics. *Reviews of Modern Physics*, 83, 33–79. doi:10.1103/RevModPhys.83.33

Sanjeev, A., & Boaz, B. (2009). *Computational Complexity: A Modern Approach*. Cambridge University Press.

Sano, N. Sinohara & Yasusi. (2009). Privacy Preserving Independent Component Analysis. In *Proceedings of the 8th Workshop on Stochastic Numerics* (pp. 162-173). Kyoto University Research Institute for Mathematical.

Sarvate, D. G., & Seberry, J. (1986). Encryption methods based on combinatorial designs. *Ars Combinatoria, 21A*, 237–246.

Sattar, B., & Sabiha, F. (2005). A proposed Method to Evaluate pseudo random of Hadmard generator using Fuzzy Logic. *AL- Mustanseryah University Journal, 20*(3), 17-24.

Sattar, B., Azhar, H., & Sabiha, F. (2011). Complexity Evaluation of Knapsack Crypto System using Fuzzy Set. *Journal of Basrah Researches (Sciences), 37*(4), 473–480.

Sattar, B., Sawsan, K., & Najwan, A. (2013). Fuzzy Based Pseudo Random Number Generator used for Wireless Networks. *Journal of Al-Nahrain University, 16*(2), 210–216.

Satti, M. V. K. (2007). *Quasi-Group Based Crypto-System*. (Master thesis). Louisiana State University.

Satti, M., & Kak, S. (2009). Multilevel Indexed Quasigroup Encryption for Data and Speech. *IEEE Transactions on Broadcasting*, 55(2), 270–281. doi:10.1109/TBC.2009.2014993

Savas, E., & Koç, C. K. (1999). *Efficient Methods for Composite Field Arithmetic (Technical Report). Electrical & Computing Engineering*. Oregon State University.

Schechter, S. (2013). *The User IS the Enemy, and (S)he Keeps Reaching for that Bright Shiny Power Button!* Paper presented at the Workshop on Home Usable Privacy and Security. Newcastle, UK.

Schneider, G., & Gersting, J. (2012). *Invitation to Computer Science*. Amazon.com.

Schneier, B. (1994). *Applied Cryptography: Protocols, Algorithms and Source Code in C*. John Wiley & Sons.

Schroeder, M. R. (1986). *Number theory in science and communication*. Berlin, Germany: Springer Verlag. doi:10.1007/978-3-662-22246-1

Schroeppel, R., Orman, H., O'Malley, S. W., & Spatscheck, O. (1995). Fast Key Exchange with Elliptic Curve Systems. In *Proceedings of the 15th Annual International Cryptology Conference on Advances in Cryptology* (pp. 43–56). London, UK: Springer-Verlag.

Schultze, S. B. (2010). The Certificate Authority Trust Model for SSL: A Defective Foundation for Encrypted Web Traffic and a Legal Quagmire. *Intellectual Property and Technology Law Journal*, 3-8.

Schulz, R.-H. (1991). A note on check character systems using latin squares. *Discrete Mathematics, 97*(1-3), 371–375. doi:10.1016/0012-365X(91)90451-7

Sciberras, N. (2007). *Extending the SMTP protocol's security by allowing authenticated users to use only their email address when sending emails*. (Doctoral dissertation). University of Greenwich.

Seberry, J., & Pieprzyk, J. (1989). *Cryptography- An Introduction to Computer Security*. Prentice Hall.

Sendrier, N. (2000). Finding the permutation between equivalent linear codes: the support splitting algorithm. *IEEE Transactions on Information Theory*, *46*(4), 1193–1203. doi:10.1109/18.850662

Sergienko, A. (2005). *Quantum Communications and Cryptography*. CRC Press.

Seung, S. (2002). *Multilayer perceptrons and backpropagation learning*. Received February 14, 2013, from http://hebb.mit.edu/courses/9.641/2002/lectures/lecture04.pdf

Sfaxi, M., Ghernaouti-Helie, S., & Ribordy, G. (2005). Using quantum key distribution within IPSec to secure MAN communications. In *Proceedings of the IFIP-MAN 2005 Conference on Metropolitan Area Networks*. IFIP.

Shahriar, S. (2011). A long-distance quantum repeater gets one step closer. *Physics*, *4*, 58. doi:10.1103/Physics.4.58

Shamir, A. (1985). Identity-based cryptosystems and signature schemes. In *Proceedings of Advances in cryptology* (pp. 47–53). Springer. doi:10.1007/3-540-39568-7_5

Shamir, A., & Someren, N. (1999). Playing «hideandseek» with stored keys. *Lecture Notes in Computer Science*, *1648*, 118–124. doi:10.1007/3-540-48390-X_9

Shcherbacov, V. A. (2003). *On some known possible applications of quasigroups in cryptology*. Retrieved January 15, 2013 from http://www.karlin.mff.cuni.cz/~drapal/krypto.pdf

Shcherbacov, V. A. (2010). *Quasigroups in cryptology*. arXiv:1007.3572.

Shcherbacov, V. A. (2012). *Quasigroup based cryptoalgorithms*. arXiv:1201.3016v1.

Shcherbacov, V. A. (2009). Quasigroups in cryptology. *Computer Science Journal of Moldova*, *17*(2), 193–228.

Sheng, S., Broderick, L., & Koranda, C. A. (2006). *Why Johnny still can't encrypt: evaluating the usability of email encryption software*. Retrieved from https://cups.cs.cmu.edu/soups/2006/posters/sheng-poster_abstract.pdf

Shier, D., & Wallenius, K. (2000). *Applied Mathematical Modeling: Multidisciplinary Approach*. Chapman and Hall/CRC.

Shimada, M. (1992). Another practical public key cryptosystem. *Electronics Letters*, *28*(23), 2146–2147. doi:10.1049/el:19921377

Shlens. (2009). *A Tutorial on Principal Component Analysis*. Retrieved from http://www.snl.salk.edu/~shlens/pca.pdf

Shor, P. W. (1997). Polynomial-Time Algorithms for Prime Factorization and Discrete Logarithms on a Quantum Computer. *SIAM Journal on Computing*, *26*(5), 1484–1509. doi:10.1137/S0097539795293172

Shoufan, A., Strenzke, F., Molter, H. G., & Stöttinger, M. (2009). A Timing Attack against Patterson Algorithm in the McEliece PKC. In *Proceedings of Information, Security and Cryptology - ICISC 2009, 12th International Conference,* (pp. 161-175). Seoul, Korea: Springer.

Shoufan, A., Wink, T., Molter, G., Huss, S., & Strenzke, F. A. (2009). Novel Processor Architecture for McEliece Cryptosystem and FPGA Platforms. In *Proceedings of Application-specific Systems, Architectures and Processors* (pp. 98–105). Boston, MA: IEEE. doi:10.1109/ASAP.2009.29

Sidelnikov, V. M., & Shestakov, S. (1992). On Cryptosystems based on Generalized Reed-Solomon Codes. *Discrete Mathematics*, *4*(3), 57–63.

Sidelnikov, V. M., & Shestakov, S. O. (1992). On insecurity of cryptosystems based on generalized Reed-Solomon codes. *Discrete Mathematics*, *2*(4), 439–444.

Simon, M., Eimear, B., McDowell, J., & Aideen, R. (2011). *Disciplinary Procedures in the statutory Professions*. Amazon.com.

Siripanwattana, W., & Srinoy, S. (2008). Information Security based on Soft Computing Techniques. In *Proceedings of the International MultiConference of Engineers and Computer Scientists* (Vol. 1). Hong Kong: International Association of Engineers.

Slaminková, I., & Vojvoda, M. (2010). Cryptanalysis of a hash function based on isotopy of quasigroups. *Tatra Mountains Mathematical Publications*, *45*, 137–149. doi:10.2478/v10127-010-0010-0

Smart, N. P. (2001). How secure are Elliptic Curves Over Composite Extension Fields? In *Proceedings of Advances in Cryptology - Eurocrypt 2001, International Conference on the Theory and Application of Cryptographic Techniques* (pp. 30-39). Innsbruck, Austria: IACR.

Smith, B. R., & Garcia-Luna-Aceves, J. J. (1998). Efficient security mechanisms for the border gateway routing protocol. *Computer Communications*, *21*(3), 203–210. doi:10.1016/S0140-3664(97)00186-2

Snášel, V., Dvorsky, J., Ochodkova, E., Krömer, P., Platoš, J., & Abraham, A. (2010). Evolving Quasigroups by Genetic Algorithms. In J. Pokorny, V. Snášel & K. Richta (Eds.) *Proceedings of DATESO 2010* (pp. 108-117). Stedronin-Plazy, Czech Republic: DATESO.

Snášel, V., Abraham, A., Dvorsky, J., Krömer, P., & Platoš, J. (2009). Hash function based on large quasigroups. In G. Allen et al. (Eds.), *ICCS 2009, Part I, (LNCS)* (Vol. 5544, pp. 521–529). Berlin, Germany: Springer. doi:10.1007/978-3-642-01970-8_51

Sochor, T. (2010). Greylisting method analysis in real SMTP server environment: Case-study. In *Innovations and Advances in Computer Sciences and Engineering* (pp. 423–427). Springer Netherlands. doi:10.1007/978-90-481-3658-2_74

Soghoian, C., & Stamm, S. (2012). Certified lies: Detecting and defeating government interception attacks against ssl (short paper). In *Proceedings of Financial Cryptography and Data Security* (pp. 250–259). Springer. doi:10.1007/978-3-642-27576-0_20

Souissi, Nassar, & Guilley, Danger & Flament. (2010). First Principal Components Analysis: A New Side Channel Distinguisher. *Lecture Notes in Computer Science*, *6829*, 407–419.

Spamassassin Tips. DNSBL Safety Report 5/14/2011. (2011). *Spamassassin Tips*. Retrieved March 6, 2014, from http://www.spamtips.org/2011/05/dnsbl-safety-report-5142011.html

Sridharan, S., Dawson, E., & Goldburg, B. (1990). Speech Encryption using discrete orthogonal transforms. In *Proceedings of 1990 International Conference on Acoustics, Speech, and Signal Processing*, (pp.1647 – 1650). Albuquerque, NM: ICASSP.

Sridharan, S., Dawson, E., & Goldburg, B. (1993). Design and Cryptanalysis of transform based analog speech scramblers. *IEEE Journal on Selected Areas in Communications*, *11*(5), 735–744. doi:10.1109/49.223875

Srinivasan, A., & Selvan, P. (2012). A Review of Analog Audio Scrambling Methods for Residual Intelligibility. *Innovative Systems Design and Engineering*, *3*(7), 22–38.

Stallings, W. (2010). Cryptography and network security (5th ed.). Amazon.com.

Stallings, W. (2011). *Cryptography and network security* (5th ed.). Pearson Education International.

Stamp, M. (2011). *Information Security: Principles and Practice* (2nd ed.). Wiley. doi:10.1002/9781118027974

Stavroulakis, P., & Mark, S. (2010). *Handbook of Information and Communication Security*. Springer. doi:10.1007/978-3-642-04117-4

Stefan, S. et al. (2007). Fuzzy trust Evaluation and credibility development in multi-agent systems. *Science Direct: Applied Soft Computing*, *7*(2), 492–505.

Stern, J. (1994a). A New Identification Scheme Based on Syndrome Decoding. In *Proceedings of the 13th Annual International Cryptology Conference on Advances in Cryptology* (pp. 13-21). Santa Barbara, CA: Springer.

Stern, J. (1994b). Designing Identification Schemes with Keys of Short Size. In *Proceedings of Advances in Cryptology – Proceedings of CRYPTO '94,* (vol. 839, pp. 164-173). Santa Barbara, CA: Springer Berlin Heidelberg.

Stinson, D. (1996). On the connections between universal hashing, combinatorial designs and error-correcting codes. *Congressus Numerantium, 114.*

Stinson, D. (1992). Universal hashing and authentication codes. *Lecture Notes in Computer Science*, *576*, 74–85. doi:10.1007/3-540-46766-1_5

Stinson, D. (2005). *Cryptography: Theory and Practice* (3rd ed.). Chapman and Hall/CRC.

Strang, G. (1991). A chaotic search for i. *The College Mathematics Journal*, *22*(1), 3–12. doi:10.2307/2686733

Strenzke, F. (2010). A Smart Card Implementation of the McEliece PKC. In *Proceedings of 4th IFIP WG 11.2 International Workshop, WISTP 2010,* (pp. 47-59). Passau, Germany: Springer.

Strenzke, F. (2010). A Timing Attack against the Secret Permutation in the McEliece PKC. In *Proceedings of Third International Workshop, PQCrypto 2010,* (pp. 95-107). Darmstadt, Germany: Springer.

Strenzke, F. (2011). Fast and Secure Root-Finding for Code-based Cryptosystems. *IACR Cryptology ePrint Archive.* Retrieved December 11, 2011, from http://eprint.iacr.org/2011/672

Strenzke, F. (2012). Solutions for the Storage Problem of McEliece Public and Private Keys on Memory-Constrained Platforms. In *Proceedings of 15th International Conference, ISC 2012,* (pp. 120-135). Passau, Germany: Springer.

Strenzke, F. (2013). Timing Attacks against the Syndrome Inversion in Code-Based Cryptosystems. In *Proceedings of 5th International Workshop, PQCrypto 2013,* (pp. 217-230). Limoges, France: Springer.

Strenzke, F., Tews, E., Molter, H. G., Overbeck, R., & Shoufan, A. (2008). Side Channels in the McEliece PKC. In *Proceedings of the Second international Workshop on Post-Quantum Cryptography PQCRYPTO 2008,* (LNCS), (pp. 216-229). Cincinnati, OH: Springer.

Stucki, D., Walenta, N., Vannel, F., Thew, R. T., Gisin, N., Zbinden, H., & Gray, S. C. (2009). High rate, long-distance quantum key distribution over 250 km of ultra-low loss fibers. *New Journal of Physics, 11,* 075003. doi:10.1088/1367-2630/11/7/075003

Sudbury, T. (1993). Instant Teleportation. *Nature, 362,* 586–587. doi:10.1038/362586a0

Sugiyama, Y., Kasahara, M., Hirasawa, S., & Namekawa, T. (1976). An erasures-and-errors decoding algorithm for Goppa codes. *IEEE Transactions on Information Theory, 22*(2), 238–241. doi:10.1109/TIT.1976.1055517

Sunshine, J., Egelman, S., Almuhimedi, H., Atri, N., & Cranor, L. (2009). Crying wolf: An empirical study of SSL warning effectiveness. In *Proceedings of the 18th Usenix Security Symposium* (pp. 339-416). Retrieved from http://www.usenix.org/events/sec09/tech/full_papers/sunshine.pdf

Su, Z., Zhang, G., & Jiang, J. (2012). Multimedia security: a survey of chaos based encryption technology. In *Multimedia – A multicplinary Approach to Complex Issues* (pp. 99–124). InTech. doi:10.5772/36036

Symantec to Acquire Brightmail. (2004). *Symantec.* Retrieved October 7, 2012, from http://www.symantec.com/press/2004/n040519.html

Symantec. (2012). *Symantec Intelligence Report.* Retrieved December 6, 2012, from http://www.symantec.com/theme.jsp?themeid=state_of_spam

Tanaka, J. W., & Farah, M. J. (1993). Parts and wholes in face recognition. *The Quarterly Journal of Experimental Psychology, 46*(2), 225–245. doi:10.1080/14640749308401045 PMID:8316637

Taniguchi, N. (1974). On the Basic Concept of Nano-Technology. Proc. Intl. Conf. Prod. Eng Tokyo.

Tanimoto, S., Yokoi, M., Sato, H., & Kanai, A. (2011). Quantifying Cost Structure of Campus PKI. In *Proceedings of 11th International Symposium Applications and the Internet* (SAINT) (pp. 315-320). Munich: IEEE.

Tao, S., Ruli, W., & Yixun, Y. (1998). Perturbance-based algorithm to expand cycle length of chaotic key stream. *IEEE Electronics Letters, 34*(9), 873–874. doi:10.1049/el:19980680

Taughannock Networks. (2004). *An Overview of E-Postage.* Retrieved October 7, 2012, from http://taugh.com/epostage.pdf

Tawfeeq, S. (2006). *Experimental realization of quantum cryptography system based on the BB84 protocol.* (Ph.D. Thesis). Institute of Laser for Postgraduate Studies, University of Baghdad, Baghdad, Iraq.

Tawfeeq, S. (2009). A random number generator based on SPAD dark counts. *Journal of Lightwave Technology, 27*(24), 5665–5667. doi:10.1109/JLT.2009.2034119

Taylor, R. (1995). Near optimal unconditionally secure authentication. *Lecture Notes in Computer Science, 950,* 244–253. doi:10.1007/BFb0053440

Tenn, R. (2003). *Symmetric and Asymmetric Secure Communication Schemes using Nonlinear Dynamics.* (PhD Thesis). University of California, San Diego, CA.

Tharwat, A., Ibrahim, A. F., & Ali, H. A. (2012). Multimodal biometric authentication algorithm using ear and finger knuckle images. In *Proceedings of 2012 Seventh International Conference on Computer Engineering & Systems (ICCES)* (pp. 176-179). IEEE.

Theberge, M. (1996). *Security Evaluation of transform domain speech scramblers*. (M. Sc. Thesis). Columbia University.

Thomas, M. (2001, June). *Requirements for Kerberized Internet Negotiation of Keys* (RFC 3129). Retrieved from http://www.ietf.org/rfc/rfc3129.txt

Thomas, J. (1985). *Data Compression: Techniques and Applications*. Lifetime Learning Publications.

Thomas, M., & Joy, A. (1991). *Entropy, Relative Entropy and Mutual Information*. John Wiley & Sons, Inc.

Tornea, O., & Borda, M. (2009). DNA Cryptographic Algorithms. *IFMBE Proceedings*, *26*, 223–226.

Trend Micro Email Reputation Services. (n.d.). *Trend Micro*. Retrieved October 6, 2012, from https://ers.trendmicro.com/

TrustWave SpiderLabs. (2011, May). Retrieved December 2011, from http://blog.spiderlabs.com/2011/04/certificate-revocation-behavior-in-modern-browsers.html

Tsai, C.-R. (2002). Non-repudiation in practice. In Proceedings of The Second International Workshop for Asian Public Key Infrastructures. *National Taiwan University*.

Tseng, D., & Chiu, J. (2007). An OFDM speech scrambler without residual intelligibility. In *Proceedings of IEEE Region 10 Conference TENCON*. Taipei, Taiwan: IEEExplore-Digital Library.

Turk, M., & Pentland, A. (1991). Eigenfaces for recognition. *Journal of Cognitive Neuroscience*, *3*(1), 71–86. doi:10.1162/jocn.1991.3.1.71 PMID:23964806

Ulrich, A., Holz, R., Hauck, P., & Carle, G. (2011). Investigating the OpenPGP Web of Trust.[Berlin: Springer.]. *Proceedings of Computer Security–ESORICS*, *2011*, 489–507.

University of Purdue. (2004). *RASC: Confidentiality, Integrity and Availability (CIA)*. Retrieved from http://www.itap.purdue.edu/security/files/documents/RASC-CIAv13.pdf

Vacca, J. (Ed.). (2013). *Network and System Security*. Elsevier Inc.

Valerie, W., & Anne, P. (2000). Multidisciplinary Teamworking: Indicators of Good Practice. *Spotlight 77*. Retrieved from http://www.moderntimesworkplace.com/good_reading/GRWhole/Multi-Disciplinary.Teamwork.pdf

Van Meter, R., Ladd, T., Munro, W., & Nemoto, K. (2009). System design for a long-line quantum repeater. *IEEE/ACM Transactions on Networking*, *17*(3), 1002–1013. doi:10.1109/TNET.2008.927260

van Tilborg. (1999). *Fundamentals of Cryptology: A Professional Reference and Interactive Tutorial*. London: Kluwer Academic.

Verhoeff, J. (1969). Error detecting decimal codes. *Mathematical Centre Tracts, 29*.

Verisign Labs. (2013, February 20). *Global DNSSEC deployment tracking*. Retrieved from http://secspider.cs.ucla.edu/growth.html

Vielhauer, C. (2006). Biometric user authentication for IT security From Fundamentals to Handwriting. *Advances in Information Security*, *18*, 1153–4648.

Vielhauer, C. (2006). Fundamentals in Biometrics. *Advances in Information Security*, *18*, 11–31. doi:10.1007/0-387-28094-4_2

Vijay, D., Amarpreet, S., Rakesh, K., & Gurpreet, S. (2010). Biometric Recognition: A Modern Era for Security. *International Journal of Engineering Science and Technology*, *2*(8), 3364–3380.

Vojvoda, M., Sýs, M., & Jókay, M. (2007). A Note on Algebraic Properties of Quasigroups in Edon80. In *Proceedings of SASC 2007*. Bochum, Germany: SASC.

Vojvoda, M. (2004). Cryptanalysis of one hash function based on quasigroup. *Tatra Mountains Mathematical Publications*, *29*, 173–181.

Vollbrecht, K., Muschik, C., & Cirac, J. (2011). Entanglement distillation by dissipation and continuous quantum repeaters. *Physical Review Letters*, *107*(120502), 1–5. PMID:22026761

Volna, E., Kotyrba, M., Kocian, V., & Janosek, M. (2012). Cryptography based on neural 1network. In *Proc. 26th European Conference on Modelling and Simulation* (pp. 386-391). Koblenz, Germany: Univ. of Koblenz-Landau.

Volna, E. (2000). Using Neural network in cryptography. In *The State of the Art in Computational Intelligence* (pp. 262–267). New York: Physica-Verlag HD. doi:10.1007/978-3-7908-1844-4_42

von Maurich, I., & Güneysu, T. (2012). Embedded Syndrome-Based Hashing. In *Proceedings of Progress in Cryptology - INDOCRYPT 2012, 13th International Conference on Cryptology in India,* (pp. 339-357). Kolkata, India: Springer.

Vratonjic, N., Freudiger, J., Bindschaedler, V., & Hubaux, J.-P. (2013). The inconvenient truth about web certificates. [Springer.]. *Proceedings of Economics of Information Security and Privacy*, *III*, 79–117. doi:10.1007/978-1-4614-1981-5_5

Walsh, S. (2012). *Facebook to Monetize Spam*. Retrieved February 15, 2013, from http://www.allspammedup.com/2012/12/facebook-to-monetize-spam/

Walters, A., & Petroni, N. (2007). *Volatools: Integrating volatile memory forensics into the digital investigation process*. Paper presented at Blackhat DC 2007. Arlington, VA. Retrieved from https://www.blackhat.com/presentations/bh-dc-07/Walters/Presentation/bh-dc-07-Walters-up.pdf

Wang, D., & Zhang, Y. (2009). Image Encryption Algorithm Based on S-boxes Substitution and Chaos Random Sequence. In *Proceedings of International Conference on Computer Modeling and Simulation ICCMS*, (pp. 110–113). IEEExplore- Digital Library. doi: 10.1109/ICCMS.2009.26

Wang, J., Zhang, F., Sun, K., & Stavrou, A. (2011). Firmware-assisted Memory Acquisition and Analysis tools for Digital Forensics. In *Proceedings of IEEE Sixth International Workshop on Systematic Approaches to Digital Forensic Engineering* (SADFE 2011). Oakland, CA: IEEE.

Wang, Y., Tian, Z., Bi, X., & Niu, Z. (2006). Efficient Multiplier Over Finite Field Represented in Type II Optimal Normal Basis. In *Proceedings of Sixth International Conference on Intelligent Systems Design and Applications*, ISDA '06. (pp. 1132 -1128). Jinan, China: IEEE.

Wang, C., & Wu, M. (2001). A New Narrowband Interference Suppression Scheme for Spread-spectrum CDMA Communications. *IEEE Transactions on Signal Processing*, *49*(11), 2832–2838. doi:10.1109/78.960430

Wang, H., Hempel, M., Peng, D., Wang, W., Sharif, H., & Chen, H. (2010). Index-based selective audio encryption for wireless multimedia sensor networks. *IEEE Transactions on Multimedia*, *12*, 215–223. doi:10.1109/TMM.2010.2041102

Wayman, J. L. (2001). Fundamentals of Biometric Authentication Technologies. *International Journal of Image and Graphics*, *1*(1), 93–113. doi:10.1142/S0219467801000086

Webb, S., Caverloo, J., & Pu, C. (2006). Introducing the webb spam corpus: Using email spam to identify web spam automatically. In *Proceedings of CEAS 2006 — 3rd Conference on Email and Anti-Spam* (CEAS). Redmond, WA: Microsoft.

Wegman, M., & Carter, J. (1981). New hash functions and their use in authentication and set equality. *Journal of Computer and System Sciences*, *22*, 256–279. doi:10.1016/0022-0000(81)90033-7

Wei, D.-M. (2010). A Fast Implementation of Modular Inversion Over $GF(2^m)$ Based on FPGA. In *Proceedings of the 2nd IEEE International Conference on Information Management and Engineering*, ICIME 2010 (pp. 465 -468). Cape Town, South Africa: IEEE.

White, V. (1999). *Chaos Theory Helps To Predict Epileptic Seizures*. Office Of Public Information, University Of Florida Health Science Cente. Retrieved Feb. 16, 2014 from http://news.bio-medicine.org/medicine-news-2/Chaos-theory-empowers-researchers-to-predict-epileptic-seizures-10007-1/.

Whitten, A., & Tygar, J. D. (1999). Why Johnny can't encrypt: A usability evaluation of PGP 5.0. In *Proceedings of the 8th USENIX Security Symposium* (pp. 169-184). Washington, DC: McGraw-Hill.

Whytock, A. W. (1998). *European Patent No. EP 0878780*. Munich, Germany: European Patent Office.

Wikipedia. The Free Encyclopedia. (2008). *Moore's Law*. Retrieved from http://en.wikipedia.org/wiki/Moore's_Law

William, E. B., Donna, F. D., Ray, A. P., Polk, W. T., Elaine, M. N., Sabari, G., & Emad, A. N. (2004). *Electronic Authentication Guideline*. National Institute of Standards and Technology, NIST Special Publication 800-63.

William, L., & Bilal, M. (2012). *Multicriteria Security System Performance Assessment Using Fuzzy Logic*. Retrieved August 8, 2013 from http://www.scs.org/pubs/jdms/vol4num4/McGill.pdf

William, H. (1985). Some public Key Crypto Functions as Intractable as Factorization. In *Proceeding of Crypto'84 (LNCS)* (Vol. 196, pp. 66–70). Berlin: Springer.

Williams, L. (2001). *A discussion of The Importance of Key Length in Symmetric and Asymmetric Cryptography*. Retrieved from http://rr.sans.org/encryption/key_length.php

William, S. (2003). *Cryptography and Network Security Principles and practices*. Prentice- Hall.

Win, E. D., Bosselaers, A., Vandenberghe, S., Gersem, P. D., & Vandewalle, J. (1996). A Fast Software Implementation For Arithmetic Operations in $GF(2^n)$. In *Proceedings of the International Conference on the Theory and Applications of Cryptology and Information Security: Advances in Cryptology* (pp. 65–76). London, UK: Springer-Verlag.

Wittel, G. L., & Wu, S. F. (2004). On Attacking Statistical Spam Filters. In *Proceedings of CEAS 2006 — third conference on email and anti-spam*. Retrieved October 7, 2012, from http://130.203.133.150/viewdoc/summary,jsessionid=D95619A23260FC405817FD63A207B68E?doi=10.1.1.59.8759

Wolf,, C., & Preneel. (2010). MQ*-IP: An Identity-based Identification Scheme without Number-theoretic Assumptions. *ICAR Cryptology ePrint Archive, Report 2010/087*.

Wong, M. M., & Wong, M. L. D. (2010). A High Throughput Low Power Compact AES S-box Implementation Using Composite Field Arithmetic and Algebraic Normal Form Representation. In *Proceedings of the 2nd Asia Symposium on Quality Electronic Design*, ASQED 2010 (pp. 318-323). Penang, Malaysia: IEEE.

Wong, M. M., Wong, M. L. D., Nandi, A. K., & Hijazin, I. (2011). Construction of Optimum Composite Field Architecture for Compact High-throughput AES S-boxes. *IEEE Transactions on Very Large Scale Integration VLSI Systems*, *20*(6), 1151–1155. doi:10.1109/TVLSI.2011.2141693

Wright & Manic. (2010). The Analysis of Dimensionality Reduction Techniques in Cryptographic Object Code Classification. In *Proceedings of 3rd Conference on Human System Interactions* (HSI 2010), (pp. 157 – 162). Rzeszow, Poland: IEEE.

Wright, J., & Manic, M. (2010). Neural Network Architecture Selection Analysis with Application to Cryptography Location. In *Proceedings of IEEE World Congress on Computational Intelligence* (WCCI 2010). Barcelona, Spain: IEEExplore Digital Library:Publisher.

Wyner, A. (1979). An analog scrambling scheme which does not expand bandwidth, part 1: Discrete time. *IEEE Transactions on Information Theory*, *25*, 261–274. doi:10.1109/TIT.1979.1056050

Wyn, G. (2010). *The Development of a Discipline: The History of the Political Studies Association*. Wiley Publisher.

Xiao, J. (2011). Urban Ecological Security Evaluation and analysis based on Fuzzy Mathematics. *Procedia Engineering*, *15*, 4451–4455. doi:10.1016/j.proeng.2011.08.836

Xingyuan, W., Xiaojuan, W., Jianfeng, Z., & Zhenfeng, Z. (2011). Chaotic encryption algorithm based on alternant of stream cipher and block cipher. *Nonlinear Dynamics*, *63*(4), 587–597. doi:10.1007/s11071-010-9821-4

Xu, Y. (2010). A Cryptography Application of Conjugate Quasigroups. In *Proceedings of the International Conference on Web Information Systems and Mining 2010*, (vol. 2, pp. 63-65). Sanya, China: Academic Press.

Xu, F. X., Chen, W., & Wang, S. et al. (2009). Field experiment on a robust hierarchical metropolitan quantum cryptography network. *Chinese Science Bulletin, 54*(17), 2991–2997. doi:10.1007/s11434-009-0526-3

YALE Database. (n.d.). Retrieved from cvc.ya.edu/projects/yalefacesB/yalefacesB.html

Yang, B.-Y. (Ed.). (2011). *Proceedings of 4th International Workshop*. Taipei, Taiwan: Springer.

Yang, H. O. (2011). Deploying cryptography in Internet-scale systems: A case study on DNSSEC. *IEEE Transactions on Dependable and Secure Computing*, 656–669. doi:10.1109/TDSC.2010.10

Yang, J., & Xie, S. J. (2012). *New Trends and Developments in Biometrics*. InTech. doi:10.5772/3420

Yang, T. (2003). A survey of chaotic secure communication systems. *Int. J. Comp. Cognition, 2*, 81–130.

Yang, X., & Li, Z. (2008). *Improvement and Implementation of Modular Inversion Algorithm on the Finite Field*. Computer Engineering and Applications.

Yao, D., Fazio, N., Dodis, Y., & Lysyanskaya, A. (2004). ID-based encryption for complex hierarchies with applications to forward security and broadcast encryption. In *Proceedings of the 11th ACM conference on Computer and communications security* (pp. 354-363). Washington, DC: ACM.

Yerazunis, B. (2002). Better that human. *Paul Graham*. Retrieved Mar 7, 2014, from http://www.paulgraham.com/wsy.html

Ylonen, T. (1996). SSH - secure login connections over the Internet. In *Proceedings of the 6th USENIX Security Symposium* (pp. 37-42). San Jose, CA: USENIX Association.

Yuan, Z., Chen, Y., Zhao, B., Chen, S., Schmiedmayer, J., & Pan, J. (2008). Experimental demonstration of a BDCZ quantum repeater node. *Nature, 454*(28). PMID:18756253

Yuksel, E., Nielson, H., & Nielson, F. (2010). Characteristics of Key Update Strategies for Wireless Sensor Networks. In *Proceedings of the International Conference on Network Communication and Computer* (ICNCC), (pp. 132-136). Technical University Denmark.

Zadeh, L. A. (1994). Soft Computing and Fuzzy Logic. *IEEE Software, 11*(6), 48–56. doi:10.1109/52.329401

Zaibi, G., Peyrard, F., Kachouri, A., Fournier-Prunaret, D., & Samet, M. (2010). *A new design of dynamic S-Box based on two chaotic maps*. Academic Press. doi:10.1109/AICCSA.2010.5586946

Zalka, C. (1998). Fast versions of Shor's quantum factoring algorithm. *Coronell University Library arXiv. org*. Retrieved 24 June 1998, from http://arxiv.org/abs/quant-ph/9806084

Zdziarski., et al. (n.d.). *DSPAM Project Homepage*. Retrieved February 14, 2013, Retrieved October 7, 2012, from http://dspam.nuclearelephant.com/

Zdziarski, J. (2005). *Ending Spam: Bayesian Content Filtering and the Art of Statistical Language Classification*. Sebastopol, CA: No Starch Press.

Zegura, E. (2001). *Thoughts on router-level topology modelling*. Retrieved from http://www.postel.org/pipermail/end2end-interest/2001-January/000033.html

Zimmermann, A. J. (2011, April). *ZRTP: Media Path Key Agreement for Unicast Secure RTP* (RFC 6189). Retrieved from http://tools.ietf.org/html/rfc6189

Zimmermann, P., & Callas, J. (2009). The Evolution of PGP's Web of Trust. In Beautiful Security: Leading Security Experts Explain How They Think, (pp. 107-130). Academic Press.

Zinman, A., & Donath, J. (2007). Is Britney Spears spam&quest. In *Proceedings of the 4th International Conference on Email and Anti-Spam* (CEAS). Redmond, WA: Microsoft.

Zoller, P. (Ed.). (2005). Quantum information processing and communication: Strategic report on the current status, visions, and goals for research in Europe. QIST ERA-Pilot Project, Version 1.1.

Zurko, M. E., & Simon, R. T. (1996). User-centered security. In *Proceedings of the 1996 workshop on New security paradigms* (pp. 27-33). Lake Arrowhead: ACM.

Index

CPSIA information can be obtained at www.ICGtesting.com
Printed in the USA
BVOW10*1729230514

354336BV00008B/119/P